D0196059

lonely planet

Wales

WITHDRAWN FROM COLLECTION

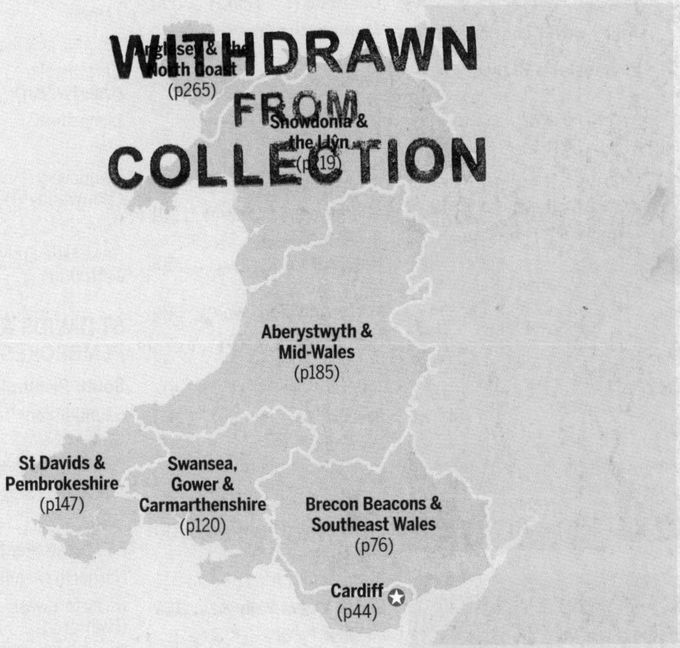

THIS EDITION WRITTEN AND RESEARCHED BY

Peter Dragicevich
Hugh McNaughtan

PLAN YOUR TRIP

JOE DANIEL PRICE / GETTY IMAGES ©

CARDIFF MARKET P68

MARTYN FERRY / GETTY IMAGES ©

WATERFALL, FFOREST FAWR P111

ON THE ROAD

Contents

UNDERSTAND

SURVIVAL GUIDE

SPECIAL FEATURES

Welcome to Wales

The phrase 'good things come in small packages' may be a cliché, but in the case of Wales it's undeniably true.

Wilderness

Compact but geologically diverse, Wales offers myriad opportunities for escaping into nature. It may not be wild in the classic sense – humans have been shaping this land for millennia – but there are plenty of lonely corners to explore, lurking behind mountains, within river valleys and along surf-battered cliffs. An extensive network of paths makes Wales a hiker's paradise – and thousands of people duck across the border from England each year for that reason alone. Things are even more untamed on the islands scattered just off the coast, some of which are important wildlife sanctuaries.

Stones with Stories

Castles are an inescapable part of the Welsh landscape. They're absolutely everywhere. You could visit a different one every day for a year and still not see them all. Some watch over mountain passes, while others keep an eye on the city traffic whizzing by; some lie in enigmatic ruins, while others still have families living in them. There's also an altogether more inscrutable and far older set of stones to discover – the stone circles, dolmens and standing stones erected long before castles were ever dreamt up, before even histories were written.

Beaches

Sure, the climate's not exactly tropical, but regardless of the weather's vagaries, Wales is a superb beach-holiday destination. The beauty of the British coast is cruelly underrated, and Wales has some of the very best bits. When the sun is shining, the beaches fill up with kids building sandcastles and splashing about in the shallows. And when it's not, how about a bracing walk instead? The Wales Coast Path traces the country's entire length, so you're unlikely to run out of track.

Hospitality & Hiraeth

Beyond the scenery, it's the interactions with Welsh people that will remain in your memory the longest. Perhaps you'll recall sitting in a Caernarfon cafe, listening to the locals chatter in the ancient British tongue. Or that time in the pub, screaming along to the rugby with a red-shirted mob. They talk a lot in Wales about 'hiraeth'. A typically Welsh word, it refers to a sense of longing for the green, green grass of home. Even if you're not from Wales, a feeling of hiraeth may well hit you when you leave, only to be sated when you return.

Why I Love Wales

By Peter Dragicevich, Writer

I well remember my first time in Wales – a short trip to Cardiff with a fellow Kiwi living in London. We were so impressed with the castle that we took the train to Caerphilly the following day for an extra serving. I returned shortly afterwards to walk the extraordinarily beautiful Pembrokeshire Coast Path, and I've been back numerous times since and explored most corners of the country. Yet on every visit there's always been another beautiful beach, rugged mountain path or kooky village pub to discover. And, of course, there's always another castle.

For more about our writers, see p352

Above: Mawr Lighthouse, Isle of Angelsey (p286)

Wales

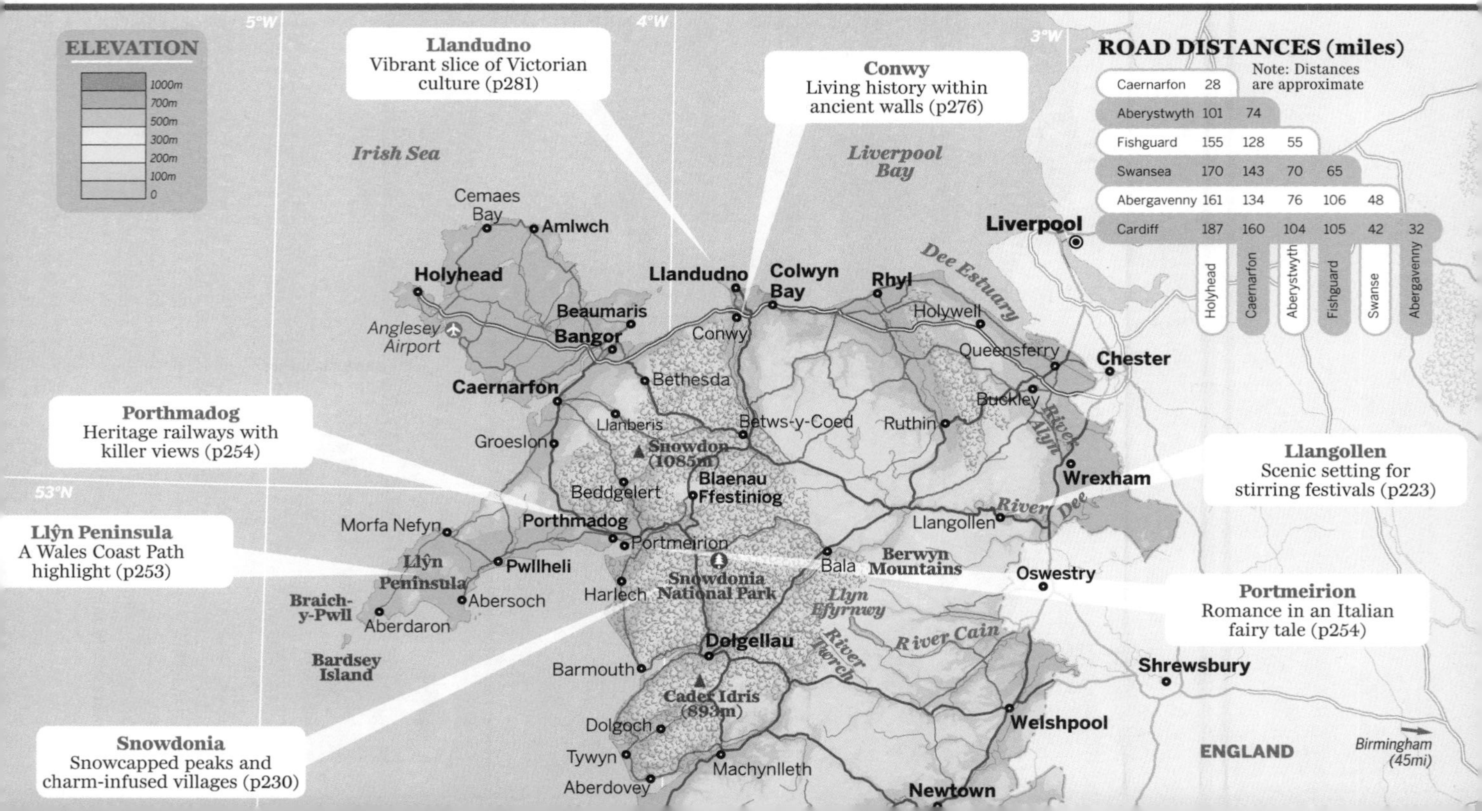

ROAD DISTANCES (miles)

Note: Distances are approximate

	Holyhead	Caernarfon	Aberystwyth	Fishguard	Swanse	Abergavenny
Caernarfon	28					
Aberystwyth	101	74				
Fishguard	155	128	55			
Swansea	170	143	70	65		
Abergavenny	161	134	76	106	48	
Cardiff	187	160	104	105	42	32

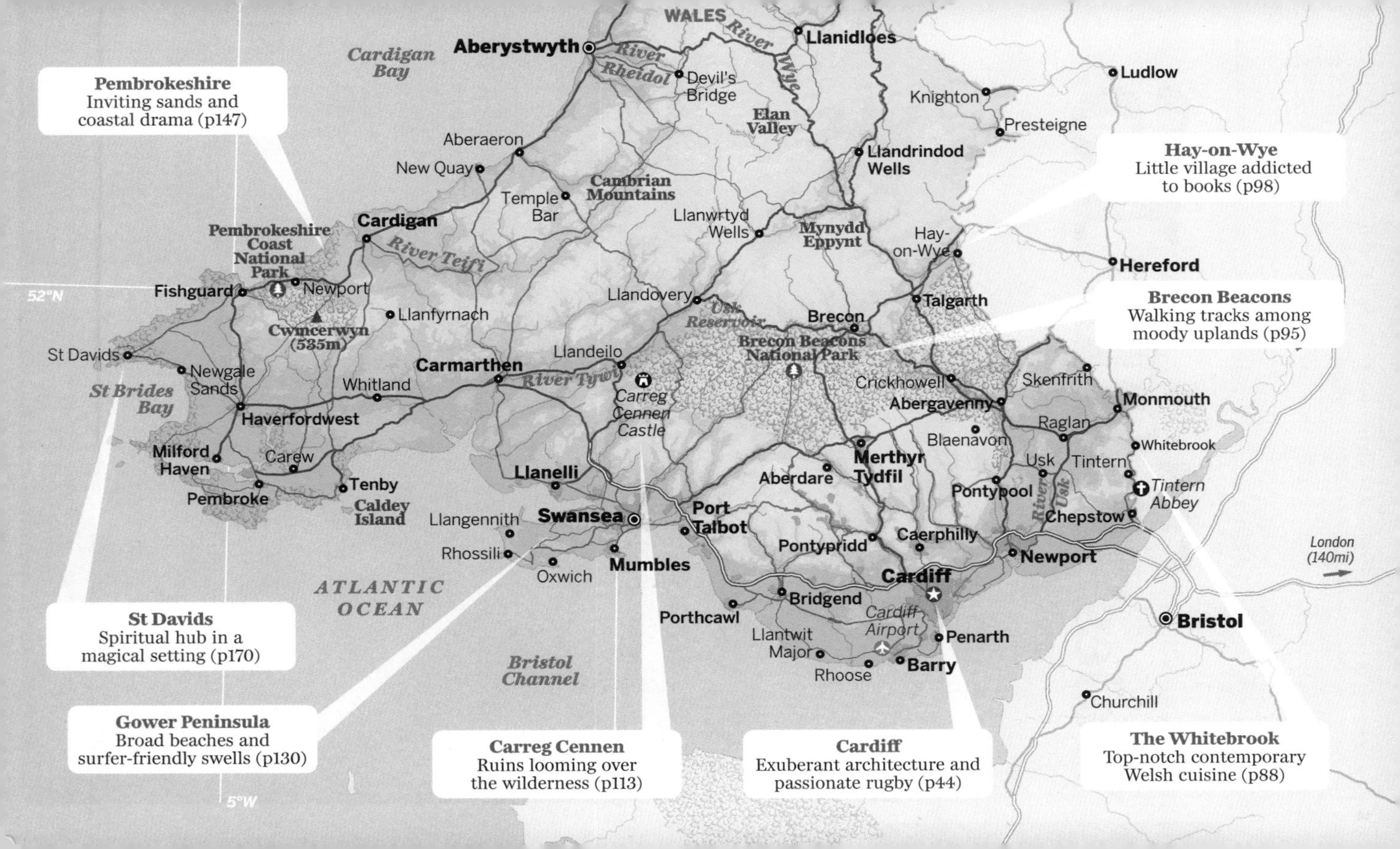
Pembrokeshire
Inviting sands and coastal drama (p147)
Hay-on-Wye
Little village addicted to books (p98)
Brecon Beacons
Walking tracks among moody uplands (p95)
St Davids
Spiritual hub in a magical setting (p170)
Gower Peninsula
Broad beaches and surfer-friendly swells (p130)
Carreg Cennen
Ruins looming over the wilderness (p113)
Cardiff
Exuberant architecture and passionate rugby (p44)
The Whitebrook
Top-notch contemporary Welsh cuisine (p88)
WALES
Cardigan Bay
Aberystwyth
River Rheidol
Devil's Bridge
River Wye
Llanidloes
Ludlow
Knighton
Presteigne
Elan Valley
Llandrindod Wells
Aberaeron
New Quay
Temple Bar
Cambrian Mountains
Llanwrtyd Wells
Mynydd Eppynt
Hay-on-Wye
Hereford
Cardigan
River Teifi
Pembrokeshire Coast National Park
Fishguard
Newport
Cwmcerwyn (535m)
Llanfyrnach
Llandovery
Usk Reservoir
Brecon
Talgarth
Brecon Beacons National Park
52°N
St Davids
Newgale Sands
St Brides Bay
Carmarthen
Whitland
Llandeilo
River Tywi
Carreg Cennen Castle
Crickhowell
Skenfrith
Monmouth
Abergavenny
Raglan
Whitebrook
Blaenavon
Haverfordwest
Milford Haven
Carew
Pembroke
Tenby
Caldey Island
Llanelli
Merthyr Tydfil
Aberdare
Usk
Tintern
Tintern Abbey
Pontypool
River Usk
Chepstow
Swansea
Llangennith
Rhossili
Oxwich
Mumbles
Port Talbot
Pontypridd
Caerphilly
Newport
London (140mi)
ATLANTIC OCEAN
Cardiff
Bridgend
Porthcawl
Cardiff Airport
Llantwit Major
Rhoose
Penarth
Barry
Bristol
Bristol Channel
Churchill
5°W

Wales' Top 16

1

Wales Coast Path

1 Since 2012, all of Wales' famously beautiful coastal paths (p34) have been linked up in one continuous 870-mile route. Walk for two months or for two days – there's no rule that you have to do it all in one go. The best stretches take in the Gower's beautiful beaches, Pembrokeshire's multicoloured cliffs and limestone arches, the remote edges of the Llŷn Peninsula and the ancient vistas of Anglesey. And if you link it up with Offa's Dyke Path, you can circle the entire country! Below: Worms Head (p133), Gower Peninsula

Snowdonia

2 The rugged northwest corner of the country has rocky mountain peaks, glacier-hewn valleys and lakes, sinuous ridges, sparkling rivers and charm-infused villages in abundance. The busiest part is around Snowdon itself, where hordes hike to the summit and many more take the less strenuous cog railway from Llanberis. Elsewhere in Snowdonia's rugged mountains are rarely trodden areas perfect for off-the-beaten-track exploration. Glorious under the summer sun and even better under a blanket of snow, Snowdonia (p230) is one of Wales' absolute treasures.

JOE DANIEL PRICE / GETTY IMAGES ©

CHRIS2766 / GETTY IMAGES ©

St Davids

3 Some places have a presence all of their own, and that's certainly true of precious little St Davids (p170). Officially a city but more like a large village, the peaceful home of Wales' patron saint has attracted the spiritually minded for centuries. Whether you come seeking salvation in the surf, hoping to commune with the whales in the Celtic Deep, or genuinely wishing to embrace the grace of Wales' patron saint, St Davids is a strangely affecting place. Below: St David's Cathedral (p170)

Conwy Castle

4 The golden age of castle building happened to coincide with the golden age of 'let's show the Welsh what's what'. There's barely a town in Wales of any note that doesn't have a castle towering over it. None has a more symbiotic relationship with its settlement than Conwy (p276). The castle still stretches out its enfolding arms to enclose the historic town in a stony embrace, originally designed to keep a tiny English colony safe from the populace they displaced. Even today it's an awe-inspiring sight.

3

RADEK STURGOLEWSKI / SHUTTERSTOCK ©

4

SAMOT / SHUTTERSTOCK ©

BILLY STOCK / SHUTTERSTOCK ©

SERJIO74 / SHUTTERSTOCK ©

Food & Drink

5 It's in the provision of top-notch produce that Wales has found its culinary niche, chanting the mantra 'local, sustainable and organic' all the way. Many fine restaurants have sprung up in the Welsh countryside, such as the Whitebrook (p88) in Monmouthshire, name-dropping their farmers, butchers and other suppliers as if they were rock stars. Local craft breweries supply the better local pubs, while Penderyn Distillery has brought whisky, that nectar of the Celts, back to this once teetotal land. Some classics have never gone away – pass us another Welsh cake, will you? Above: Welsh cakes

Pembrokeshire

6 Whether you come armed with hiking boots, a bucket and spade, or a surfboard, Wales' western extremity won't disappoint. Famous in Britain for its beaches and coastal walks, Pembrokeshire (p147) is a small sampler of all that Wales has to offer. Pembroke has one of Britain's finest Norman castles, and there are smaller versions at nearby Tenby, Manorbier, Carew and Haverfordwest. The Preseli Hills offer upland walking and ancient standing stones. Add to that wildlife reserves, cute villages and an ancient cathedral, and all bases are covered. Above right: St Catherine's Island (p153), Tenby

Ffestiniog & Welsh Highland Railways

7 Once you could only get views this good if you were a hunk of slate on your way to the port. This twin set of narrow-gauge train lines now shuttles rail enthusiasts from Porthmadog up into the mountains of Snowdonia, with the Welsh Highland Railway slicing right past Snowdon to the coast at Caernarfon. The Ffestiniog Railway (p255) heads to the former industrial heartland of Blaenau Ffestiniog, where you can take a whistle stop to delve into the depths of the slate caverns.

VISITBRITAIN/GRANT PRITCHARD ©

Hay-on-Wye

8 When a former US president describes your annual festival as the 'Woodstock of the mind', you know you're doing something right. This unselfconsciously pretty border town has assumed near mythic proportions among both the worldwide literati and lit-loving Brits as the most book-imbued place in the world. Hay (p98) is like a bizarro world version of tabloid culture, where intellectuals are admired, poets are praised and librarians are the new Kardashians. Oh, and there's good beer and food to be had, too.

Gower Peninsula

9 It seems like you're barely out of Swansea when the Gower's beauty starts to assert itself. The roads narrow, the houses fall away and suddenly you're in verdant farmland between windswept hills and the glittering sea. It's this strange combination of accessibility and remoteness that makes the Gower Peninsula (p130) unique, but it's the gorgeous beaches that make it truly special. It comes to a worthy coda with the long sandy miles abutting Rhossili Bay, affording blissful solitude for surfers and beach strollers alike.

Above right: Rhossili Bay (p133)

Brecon Beacons

10 Not as wild as Snowdonia nor as spectacular as the Pembrokeshire Coast, Wales' third national park (p95) manages quite a feat – and that's to be simultaneously bleak and beautiful. Walkers will delight in its unpopulated moors and bald hills, while history buffs can seek out hill forts and barrows, and the enigmatic ruins of abbeys and castles. The towns within the park's confines are some of Wales' most endearingly idiosyncratic, including Hay-on-Wye and Abergavenny – hallowed names for book lovers and food fans respectively.

Rugby

11 Take 30 men with maybe 20 necks between them, divide them into two teams and have them chase an oddly shaped pigskin down a field, and what do you have? A national obsession? A thing of beauty? A good excuse to sing and drink beer? All of the above. That this product of the English public-school system should become such a force of working-class cohesion across the border remains a mystery. For a glimpse into the very soul of Wales, catch a live match at Principality Stadium (p51). Right: Principality Stadium

BECKY STARES / SHUTTERSTOCK ©

ADAM BURTON / ROBERTHARDING / GETTY IMAGES ©

Carreg Cennen Castle

12 Artfully decaying ruins in remote locations have been attracting romantic souls to Wales for hundreds of years, and it's in places like Carreg Cennen (p113) that they reach their apotheosis. The hilltop setting, within the western reaches of Brecon Beacon National Park, is bleak and barren, moody and mysterious. As you edge nearer along country lanes and the castle looms into view in the distance, it's easy to make the mental trade-in of your rental car for a fine steed, galloping bravely towards unknown danger.

Cardiff Bay

13 The transformation of stinky Cardiff Bay (p52) into the shiny architectural showcase of today is a textbook example of urban renewal at its best. Yes, it's cut off from the city centre and there are still abandoned buildings on its fringes, but Cardiff Bay is a worthy testament to the rebirth of an ancient nation as a modern democratic country, increasingly in control of its own destiny. And the transformation is ongoing, with the opening of the Doctor Who Experience, right next to BBC Wales' flash new studio complex.

Eisteddfods

14 More than a mere arts festival or song contest, the eisteddfod is the way in which the nation hooks into its ancient past. Fundamentally, it's a chance for the Welsh people to simply sit *(eistedd)* and be *(bod)*. Sure, the long robes and stone-circle ceremonies can seem a little silly, but if anyone has a claim to the traditions of ancient Britain, it's the Welsh. Both the National Eisteddfod and the youth version ping-pong between North and South Wales annually, but Llangollen's International Musical Eisteddfod (p22) is a permanent fixture.

Llandudno

15 Oh the Victorians, they really did like to be beside the seaside, and Llandudno (p281) is one of the few places where you can still stroll along the prom and have a reasonable chance of hearing a brass band playing 'tiddely-om-pom-pom'. It's not Wales' most beautiful beach but Llandudno has lashings of old-fashioned charm. Where else can you watch Mr Punch squabbling with fellow puppets over sausages and then head into a chintzy hotel for high tea? When it gets too genteel, escape up the Great Orme for a wilderness fix.

Portmeirion

16 One man's devotion to the power of architecture to enhance the environment is encapsulated in Portmeirion (p254), a fanciful slice of baroque Italy clinging to the North Welsh coast. Immerse yourself in the irreality by booking into one of the scaled-down mansions or cutesy cottages facing the piazza. The unreal might shift gears into the surreal if you happen upon a *Prisoner* convention, where fans of the cult television series, filmed here in the 1960s, indulge in dress ups and human chess tournaments.

BRANDON ROSENBLUM / GETTY IMAGES ©

MARSO / SHUTTERSTOCK ©

Need to Know

For more information, see Survival Guide (p325)

Currency
Pound, also called 'pound sterling' (£)

Language
English, Welsh

Visas
Not required for most citizens of Europe, Australia, New Zealand, Canada and the USA.

Money
ATMs are widely available. Major credit cards such as Visa and MasterCard are accepted in most but not all hotels and restaurants.

Mobile Phones
The UK uses the GSM 900/1800 network, which is compatible with most of the world except the Americas. However many new phones have a multiband function that will allow them to work anywhere; check before leaving home.

Time
Greenwich Mean Time (GMT)

When to Go

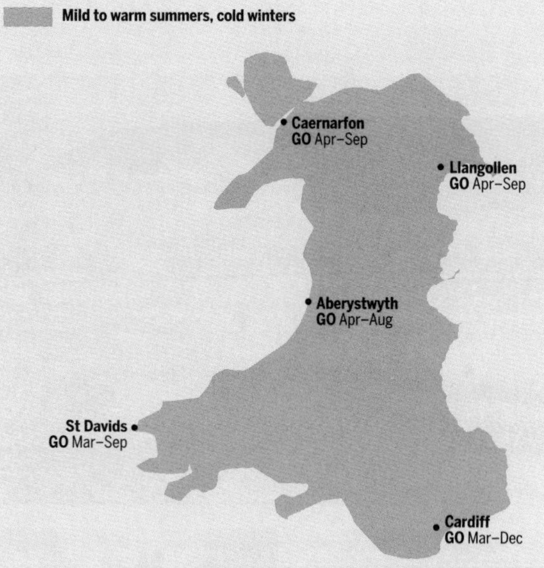

High Season
(Jul–Aug)

- Weather is at its warmest; lots of festivals and events.
- Accommodation prices increase in coastal areas and national parks, but not in cities.
- The absolute peak is the August school holidays.

Shoulder
(Apr–Jun, Sep–Oct)

- The season doesn't kick off until Easter, which can be in March or April.
- Prices rise to peak levels on bank holidays.
- April to June are the driest months; October is one of the wettest.

Low Season
(Nov–Mar)

- Prices rise to peak levels over Christmas and New Year.
- Snow can close roads, particularly in the mountains.
- January and February are the coldest months.

Useful Websites

Visit Wales (www.visitwales.com) Official resource for tourist information.

BBC Wales (www.bbc.co.uk/wales) The national broadcaster's portal on Wales.

WalesOnline (www.walesonline.co.uk) News and views concerning Welsh life.

Traveline Cymru (www.traveline.cymru) Essential public-transport information.

Lonely Planet (www.lonelyplanet.com/wales) Destination information, hotel bookings, traveller forum and more.

Important Numbers

Emergency	☎999
Wales (& UK) country code	☎44
International access code	☎00
Traveline Cymru (public transport)	☎0300 200 22 33
Visit Wales (tourist information)	☎0333 006 3001

Exchange Rates

Australia	A$1	£0.49
Canada	C$1	£0.52
Europe	€1	£0.76
Japan	¥100	£0.62
New Zealand	NZ$1	£0.46
USA	US$1	£0.68

For current exchange rates, see www.xe.com.

Daily Costs

Budget: Less than £50

- Dorm bed: £14–23
- Cheap meal in a cafe or pub: £3–10
- Bus ticket (less than 100 miles): up to £18

Midrange: £50–120

- Double room in a hotel/B&B: £65–130
- Main course in a midrange restaurant: £10–20
- Castle admission: £4–11
- Car rental: per day from £30

Top end: More than £120

- Luxury hotel or boutique B&B room: from £130
- Three-course meal in a top restaurant: £20–50
- Theatre ticket: £10–50

Opening Hours

Opening hours tend to be fairly standard throughout the year, except at venues with an outdoor component (castles, gardens, beach cafes etc), which close earlier in winter.

Banks 9.30am–5pm Monday to Friday, 9.30am–1pm Saturday

Post offices 9am–5pm Monday to Friday, 9am–12.30pm Saturday

Cafes 9am–5pm Monday to Saturday, 11am–4pm Sunday

Restaurants noon–2pm and 6–10pm; often closed Sunday evening and Monday

Pubs 11am–11pm

Shops 9am–6pm Monday to Saturday, 11am–4pm Sunday

Arriving in Wales

London Heathrow Airport Has connecting flights to Cardiff Airport and direct National Express coaches to Chepstow (£40, two hours), Newport (from £25, 2¾ hours), Cardiff (from £25, three hours) and Swansea (from £25, 4¼ hours). For train connections, catch the Heathrow Express to Paddington Station.

Cardiff Airport The T9 Cardiff Airport Express bus heads to central Cardiff (£5, 40 minutes, every 20 minutes). Shuttle buses (£1) head to Rhoose train station, where trains continue to Cardiff Central (£4.40, 33 minutes, hourly). Allow £35 for a shared taxi or £60 for exclusive use.

Holyhead Ferry Terminal Trains head to Rhosneigr (£4.50, 12 minutes), Bangor (£9.40, 30 minutes) and Conwy (£14.70, 1¼ hours).

Fishguard Harbour Trains head to Swansea (£16, two hours) and Cardiff (from £10, three hours).

Getting Around

Car Driving will get you to remote corners of Wales not connected to public transport. Cars can be hired from the main cities and the airports.

Bus The most useful form of public transport, with routes connecting most towns and villages. Many services don't run on Sunday. National Express coaches only stop in major destinations.

Train The network isn't extensive, but it's handy for those towns connected to it. Trains are comfortable and reliable, but more expensive than the buses.

For much more on **getting around**, see p335

If You Like...

Industrial Heritage

Blaenavon A World Heritage Site of well-preserved ironworks and the fascinating Big Pit Coal Mine. (p116)

Pontcysyllte Aqueduct & Canal Another World Heritage Site; this one focuses on Thomas Telford's ingenious canal system. (p224)

National Slate Museum Fascinating complex that's a testimony to the workers who put a roof over most of Britain's heads. (p246)

Rhondda Heritage Park Descend into the Lewis Merthyr coal mine with guides who once worked the black seam. (p118)

Porthgain An exquisite stretch of coast, made arguably more picturesque by the decaying detritus of the slate industry. (p175)

National Waterfront Museum Examine industrial heritage without setting foot anywhere damp, dirty or dark. (p121)

Shopping

The Hayes Cardiff's main shopping strip, flanked by elegant Victorian arcades and a giant mall. (p68)

Hay-on-Wye A nirvana for book lovers but also rich pickings for admirers of antiques, art and antiquarian maps. (p101)

Melin Tregwynt Traditional woollen goods created by a family with 100 years of experience under their belt. (p180)

Craft in the Bay Wales' finest artisans showcase their work in this Cardiff Bay store. (p68)

Narberth If pottering around independent shops in a village-like atmosphere is your thing, Narberth is your place. (p164)

Ruthin Craft Centre Buy directly from the craftspeople at the Centre for the Applied Arts. (p222)

Castles

Caerphilly The most fairy-tale-like of Wales' castles, with a pretty lake serving as its moat. (p118)

Caernarfon Part of an imposing set (including nearby Conwy, Beaumaris and Harlech), which share a World Heritage listing. (p268)

Conwy This one still has its town walls intact, built to protect an exclusive English enclave in the heart of Gwynedd. (p276)

Carreg Cennen The most dramatically positioned fortress in Wales, guarding a lonely stretch of Brecon Beacons National Park. (p113)

Cardiff A decadent layer cake comprising a Roman fort, Norman keep, Plantagenet manor house and Victorian fantasy. (p48)

Chepstow You couldn't design a more threatening 'Keep Out' sign than these battlements on the English–Welsh border. (p84)

Pembroke Walk all along the watchtowers at the birthplace of the Tudor dynasty. (p159)

Beaumaris Symmetry and elegance – a masterclass in castle building. (p291)

Mountains & Moors

Snowdon Wales' loftiest mountain has one of the most visited peaks of any in the world. (p249)

Cader Idris Another of Snowdonia's giants but a much more peaceful one. (p235)

Black Mountains The eastern reaches of Brecon Beacons National Park have a desolateness that's utterly appealing. (p95)

Great Orme A real wild child, looming above the most genteel of seaside resorts. (p282)

Cefn Bryn The windblown spine of the Gower Peninsula is made even more mysterious by its ancient dolmen. (p135)

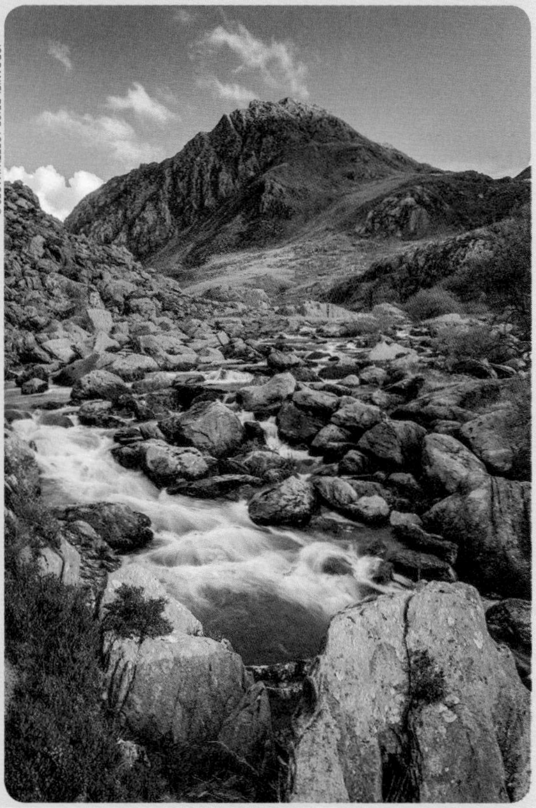

JOE DANIEL PRICE / GETTY IMAGES ©

TINTERN ABBEY / GETTY IMAGES ©

Top: Llyn Ogwen (p246), Snowdonia
Bottom: Tintern Abbey (p87), Lower Wye Valley

Preseli Hills Ponder the improbable in these ancient hills where the bluestones of Stonehenge were sourced. (p181)

Cambrian Mountains Wander the empty expanses that form the 'Green Desert of Wales'. (p203)

Beaches

Rhossili This long stretch of golden sand is so precious it's guarded by a dragon. (p133)

Three Cliffs Bay Another spectacularly beautiful Gower beach, accessible only by foot. (p130)

Barafundle Bay This Pembrokeshire gem hides within the National Trust–managed Stackpole Estate. (p157)

Porth Oer Remote and gorgeous, with 'whispering sands' that squeak as you walk. (p261)

Newport Sands The kind of broad sandy beach where blissful family holiday memories are minted. (p182)

Tenby Beautiful sandy beaches spread out in both directions from the picturesque town centre. (p152)

Ruins

Tintern Abbey Riverside ruins that inspired generations of poets and artists. (p87)

Llanthony Priory Just as picturesque as its much bigger sister at Tintern, and even more isolated. (p96)

Caerleon The Romans came, saw, conquered and bathed – and left behind ruins of barracks, baths and an amphitheatre. (p81)

St Davids Bishop's Palace The wealth and power of the medieval church are on display in this impressive complex. (p171)

Castell Dinas Brân This decaying Welsh castle provides a dramatic backdrop to the already postcard-worthy town of Llangollen. (p225)

Bryn Celli Ddu Burial Chamber For a truly ancient experience, skip the johnny-come-lately castles, abbeys and Roman baths and enter the Neolithic. (p290)

Tre'r Ceiri Hike up the hill for wonderful views and one of the best-preserved Iron Age sites in Europe. (p264)

Parks & Gardens

Bodnant Garden A breathtaking ensemble of formal gardens and woodlands attached to a gracious manor. (p275)

National Botanic Garden of Wales This vast complex is a botanical monument in the making. (p142)

Aberglasney Gardens History is on display in this beautiful set of 400-year-old walled gardens. (p143)

Powis Castle A baroque masterpiece of manicured yews, terraces, formal gardens and orchards. (p217)

Gregynog Hall The exquisite product of considerable time and space – 500 years and 300 hectares, to be exact. (p212)

Roath Park Cardiff's favourite park, with a lake, lighthouse, rose gardens, playgrounds and lots of picnic spots. (p56)

Bute Park Another stunner, bounded by Cardiff Castle and the River Taff, and full of mature trees and daffodils. (p49)

Pubs & Bars

Black Boy Inn Roaring fires, real ales, hearty meals, 500-year-old walls, a resident ghost – what more could you want? (p271)

Tŷ Coch Inn The walk along the sand to this isolated beachfront pub is all part of the package. (p263)

Albion Ale House A rare gem solely devoted to ale, whisky, wine and conversation. (p279)

Old Black Lion Serving thirsty and hungry punters since the 13th century, and still going strong. (p101)

Gwdihŵ Young and hip without being remotely irritating, this is Cardiff's countercultural capital. (p65)

Buffalo Bar Live bands upstairs, cocktails down and great music and people-watching throughout. (p65)

Y Ffarmers A village pub par excellence, tucked away in the undulating hills south of Aberystwyth. (p197)

Neuadd Arms Hotel Beloved of farm dogs, who hog all the best spots by the fire. (p206)

Outdoor Activities

Llangennith Surfers' hub for the Gower Peninsula's Rhossili Bay, and Wales' premier surfing spot. (p134)

Plas Menai The National Watersports Centre offers sailing, powerboating, sea kayaking, windsurfing and stand-up paddleboarding. (p269)

National White Water Centre Near Bala, this is Wales' premier destination for white-water rafting, kayaking and canoeing. (p230)

Plas y Brenin National Mountain Sports Centre Take a course in rock climbing, mountaineering, kayaking or canoeing. (p246)

Celtic Quest Specialists in 'coasteering', invented here on the Pembrokeshire coast. (p175)

Antur Stiniog Serious mountain-biking park in the post-industrial landscape of Blaenau Ffestiniog. (p240)

Month by Month

TOP EVENTS

Hay Festival, May

International Musical Eisteddfod, July

National Eisteddfod of Wales, August

Green Man Festival, August

Abergavenny Food Festival, September

January

Rug up warm for one of Wales' coldest months, with temperatures in single digits (Celsius) throughout the country. Spare a thought for the hardcore surfers braving the swells in Pembrokeshire.

Saturnalia

This Roman-themed beer-drinking, bull-testicle-eating and mountain-bike-chariot-racing festival warms spirits in mid-January in the Welsh home of all things weird and wacky, Llanwrtyd Wells. (p205)

February

The cold doesn't let up in February. In fact, it can even be slightly worse than January. Snowdonia looks glorious in its gleaming white coat.

Six Nations

The highlight of the Welsh rugby calendar, with home matches played at Cardiff's Principality Stadium in February and March, enthusiastically viewed in pubs all over the country. (p57)

March

Temperatures rise slightly, maybe even scraping into double digits in Cardiff, although the Six Nations rugby lads heat things up regardless. Daffodils pop up in time for their namesaint's feast day.

St David's Day Celebrations

Wales honours its patron saint on 1 March, with black-and-gold St David's Cross flags draped throughout the country.

April

Spring finally starts to kick in properly, with temperatures breaking the two-digit mark throughout the country. April's also the driest month in Mid-Wales and much of the north.

Laugharne Weekend

Musicians, comedians and writers take to various small stages in Dylan Thomas' favourite town for the Laugharne Weekend, held over a long weekend in April. (p140)

May

Head to the north coast, where May is both the driest and the sunniest month. There might still be snow on the paths heading up Snowdon though.

Victorian Extravaganza

Hitch up your skirts and stitch up your corset for this dress-up-for-grown-ups festival in Llandudno, held over the early May bank holiday weekend. (p283)

Urdd National Eisteddfod

One of Europe's biggest youth events, this performing arts competition alternates between North and South Wales in May/June.

Hay Festival

Arguably Britain's most important cultural event, this ever-expanding festival of literature and the arts is held over 10 days in late May, bringing an intellectual influx to book-town Hay-on-Wye. (p100)

June

Early summer is the prime time to head out walking, with a winning combination of higher temperatures, lower rainfall and lower winds. Cardiff celebrates its driest month.

Gŵyl Gregynog Festival

This classical music festival brings live music to various historic buildings in northern Powys, with the main action centred on the University of Wales' Gregynog Hall. (p213)

Three Peaks Yacht Race

Departing from Barmouth in late June, this gruelling yachting, cycling and fell running race tackles Snowdon before hitting the highest peaks in Scotland and England. (p237)

July

The best bet for beach weather. July is one of the warmest and driest months for most of the country – although in Wales there are no guarantees.

International Musical Eisteddfod

A week-long festival of music, including big-name evening concerts, held at Llangollen's Royal International Pavilion during the second week of July. (p226)

Royal Welsh Show

Prize bullocks and local produce are proudly displayed at Wales' biggest farm and livestock show at Builth Wells' Royal Welsh Showground. (p206)

August

The good weather continues into August, which is officially the warmest month in Cardiff. It couldn't be described as tropical though; average temperatures only just sneak into the 20s.

National Eisteddfod of Wales

Held alternately in North and South Wales in the first week of August, this is the largest celebration of Welsh culture, music and poetry (https://eisteddfod.wales), steeped in history, pageantry and pomp.

Brecon Fringe Festival

Once a sideline to the sadly defunct Brecon Jazz Festival, the Fringe is now the main event, bringing live music to country pubs scattered all around Brecon. (p106)

Green Man Festival

A firm favourite on the UK's summer music festival circuit, Green Man offers four days of alternative folk and rock music in a verdant Brecon Beacons setting. (p110)

September

Summer comes to an end with more of a fizzle than a jolt, but temperatures start to creep down. Grab your surfboard and head to Pembrokeshire before the chill really sets in.

Brecon Beast

Work up a sweat over a tough 44- or 68-mile mountain-bike course in the Brecon Beacons during this event, held in the middle of the month. (p106)

Abergavenny Food Festival

Held on the third weekend in September, this is the mother of all Welsh food festivals and the champion of the burgeoning local produce scene. (p93)

Festival No 6

The arcane streets of Portmeirion resound with rock music, dance music and comedy over the course of this long weekender. (p256)

Tenby Arts Festival

A week-long festival of autumnal music, literary and theatre events, and sandcastle competitions in the seaside town of Tenby in late September. (p154)

October

Here comes the rain again: October is Aberystwyth's wettest month. The mountains of Snowdonia set about living up to their name, with the earliest falls on the higher peaks.

THOMAS M JACKSON / CONTRIBUTOR / GETTY IMAGES ©

CORNFIELD / SHUTTERSTOCK ©

Top: Welsh band Super Furry Animals performing at the Green Man Festival
Bottom: Hay-on-Wye, home of the Hay Festival

Dylan Thomas Festival

A celebration of the man's work with readings and events in Swansea, kicking off on his birthday on 27 October. (p124)

Gwledd Conwy Feast

Feast on fine food, music and digital art projections at this festival held over a weekend in late October in the historic walled town. (p278)

November

It's the rest of the country's turn to get properly soggy, with the wettest month on both the north and south coasts. It's back to single digits temperature-wise, too.

Mid-Wales Beer Festival

Held in Llanwrtyd Wells (where else), this 10-day festival includes the Real Ale Wobble & Ramble cycling, walking and supping event. (p205)

December

There's no point dreaming of a white Christmas – for many people in Wales it's pretty much a given. Christmas cheer helps combat the gloomiest month, sunshine-wise.

Cardiff's Winter Wonderland

Festive fun for families at the heart of Cardiff's Civic Centre, with an ice-skating rink, fun fair and Santa's grotto. (p58)

LUIS DAVILLA / GETTY IMAGES ©

Plan Your Trip
Itineraries

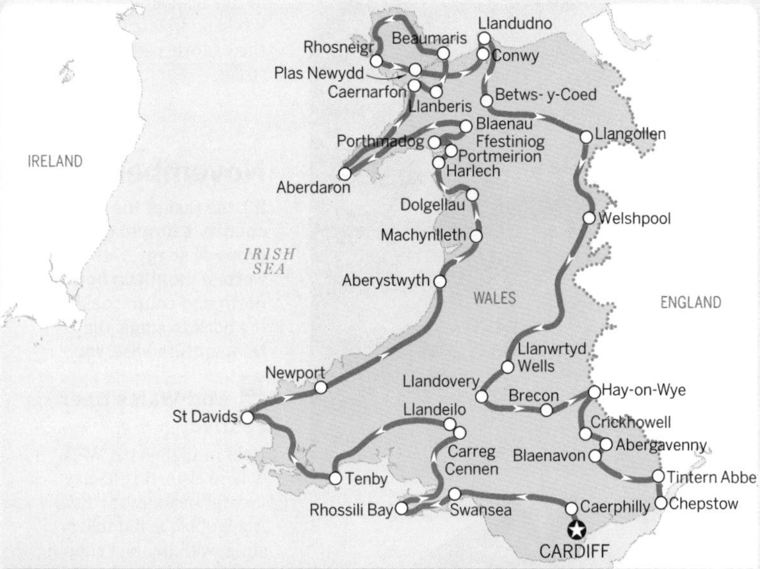

3 WEEKS Full Welsh Circuit

This itinerary has been designed for travellers who have the time and inclination to pack as much of Wales as possible into one big loop.

Start at **Cardiff** and head north to see the fairy-tale castle at **Caerphilly**, before cutting west to **Swansea**. Head out along the Gower Peninsula to spectacular **Rhossili Bay**, and then continue north to remote **Carreg Cennen** in Brecon Beacons National Park. Base yourself in **Llandeilo** for a day of gardens and manor houses.

Head west to the seaside resort town of **Tenby**, within Pembrokeshire Coast National Park, before continuing on to the ancient city of **St Davids**. Head up the coast to **Newport** for a day at the beach and a night of good food. Stop at Pentre Ifan and Castell Henllys on the long, leisurely drive up the coast to studenty **Aberystwyth**.

Continue on through ecofriendly **Machynlleth** and historic **Dolgellau** to **Harlech** and its World Heritage castle. Spend half a day exploring the surreal Italianate village of **Portmeirion** before continuing on to nearby **Porthmadog**. From here you can take a steam train ride on the

Caernarfon Castle (p268)

narrow-gauge Ffestiniog Railway to **Blaenau Ffestiniog** and stop to tour the slate caverns. Head along the Llŷn Peninsula to **Aberdaron** for surf-battered views over Bardsey Island from Braich-y-Pwll.

Follow the coast to **Caernarfon**, and then continue on to **Llanberis**, where you can visit the National Slate Museum and base yourself to tackle Snowdon. Double back to the Menai Strait and cross over to Anglesey to visit **Beaumaris**, **Rhosneigr** and **Plas Newydd**.

Proceed along the north coast to walled **Conwy** and beachy **Llandudno** before turning south to forest-dwelling **Betws-y-Coed**. Head to genteel **Llangollen**, stop at fascinating Powis Castle in **Welshpool**, then continue down through Powys to kooky **Llanwrtyd Wells** and on to the market town of **Llandovery**. Head east to **Brecon**, which is a good base for tackling Pen-y-Fan, and then pop up to famously book-obsessed **Hay-on-Wye**. Cut down through **Crickhowell** to food-focused **Abergavenny**. Visit **Blaenavon**, then skirt Monmouth and follow the peaceful Wye Valley to **Tintern Abbey** and on to the border town of **Chepstow**.

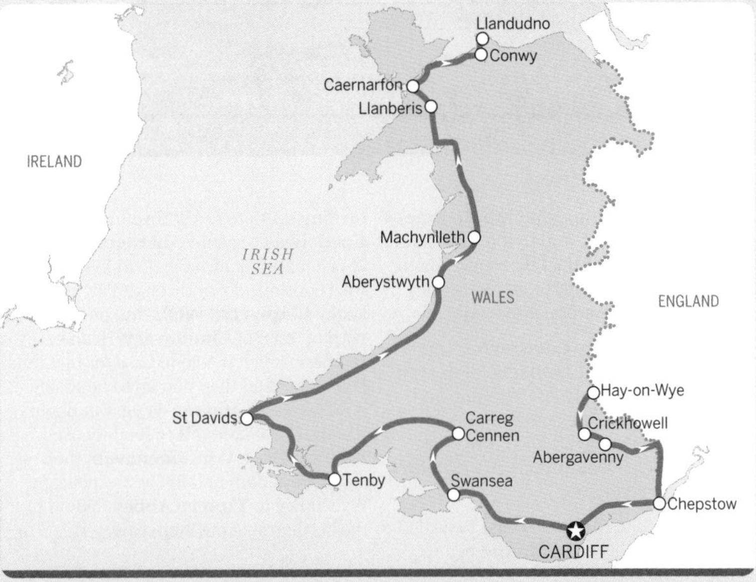
Llandudno
Conwy
Caernarfon
Llanberis
IRELAND
IRISH SEA
Machynlleth
Aberystwyth
WALES
ENGLAND
Hay-on-Wye
St Davids
Carreg Cennen
Crickhowell
Abergavenny
Tenby
Swansea
Chepstow
CARDIFF

JOHNNYGREIG / GETTY IMAGES ©

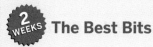

EMMA MANNERS / SHUTTERSTOCK ©

Top: Rhossili Bay (p133)
Bottom: Mad Hatter statue, Llandudno (p281)

2 WEEKS The Best Bits

This short itinerary covers the very best of what Wales has to offer at a breakneck pace. It includes the two major cities, all three of the national parks and some of the best small towns, beaches, mountains and castles.

Start in **Hay-on-Wye**, a pretty little town with a book fetish, and then cut through Brecon Beacons National Park to the pretty village of **Crickhowell** and the neighbouring market town of **Abergavenny**.

The following day head east to Monmouth and trace the Wye Valley down past Tintern Abbey to castle-dominated **Chepstow**, then continue on to **Cardiff**.

Base yourself in the Welsh capital for a couple of days before blasting along the M4 motorway to **Swansea**. Use Wales' second city as a base to explore the Gower Peninsula.

Take a detour to visit the remote ruins of **Carreg Cennen** before continuing on to **Tenby** and **St Davids**.

Continue up the coast to **Aberystwyth** and then inland to **Machynlleth**. Head through the heart of Snowdonia National Park to Dolgellau and onto **Llanberis** to get better acquainted with Snowdon, Wales' highest peak.

Explore the castle towns of **Caernarfon** and **Conwy** before washing up on the Victorian seaside promenade of **Llandudno**.

9 DAYS South Wales Circuit

Taking in the capital, two national parks, numerous castles, many beautiful beaches, industrial sites, and cities associated with Dylan Thomas, St David and Merlin the Magician, this South Welsh circuit ticks off many of the icons of Wales. Make sure you allow time for coastal walks and lazy beach days on the Gower Peninsula and Pembrokeshire (weather dependent, of course), as well as hiking in the Brecon Beacons.

Start by thoroughly exploring **Cardiff** and its surrounds before heading west to **Swansea** for a Dylan Thomas fix. Spend a day on the beach-lined **Gower Peninsula** before proceeding to ancient **Carmarthen**, Merlin's town. Settle in to the seaside vibe at candy-striped **Tenby**, Wales' most appealing resort town and the gateway to Pembrokeshire Coast National Park. Check out the mighty castle at **Pembroke** and head on through **Haverfordwest** and the pretty port of **Solva** to beguiling **St Davids**, a sweet little city in a magical setting. Visit **Fishguard** on your way to food- and beach-loving **Newport**, where neolithic and Iron Age sites await discovery in the surrounding hills.

From **Cardigan**, follow the lush Teifi Valley along the border of Ceredigion, stopping at the cute village of Cenarth and the National Woollen Museum. The Cambrian Mountains stand between here and lovely **Llandeilo**, so cut south towards Carmarthen before heading east. Do your homework first, as there are gardens, manor houses and castles to explore in this part of the Carmarthenshire countryside. Head on to the market town of **Llandovery**, with its fine Georgian buildings, and then skirt the northern edge of Brecon Beacons National Park on your way to **Brecon**. The Beacons spread south from here, offering ample opportunities for walking, horse riding and canal trips. Peaceful **Crickhowell** is another good walking base. Cross the River Usk and cut down towards **Blaenavon**, a small town that wears the legacy of its coal-mining and iron-smelting history on its sleeve, and has been inscribed on the World Heritage list as a result. Backtrack towards **Abergavenny**, home to some of Wales' best country restaurants and gastropubs. Finish with a saunter down the Wye Valley, past romantic Tintern Abbey, to **Chepstow**.

ALBERTPEGO / GETTY IMAGES ©

HUW JONES / GETTY IMAGES ©

Top: Tenby (p152)
Bottom: Fine dining in Abergavenny (p91)

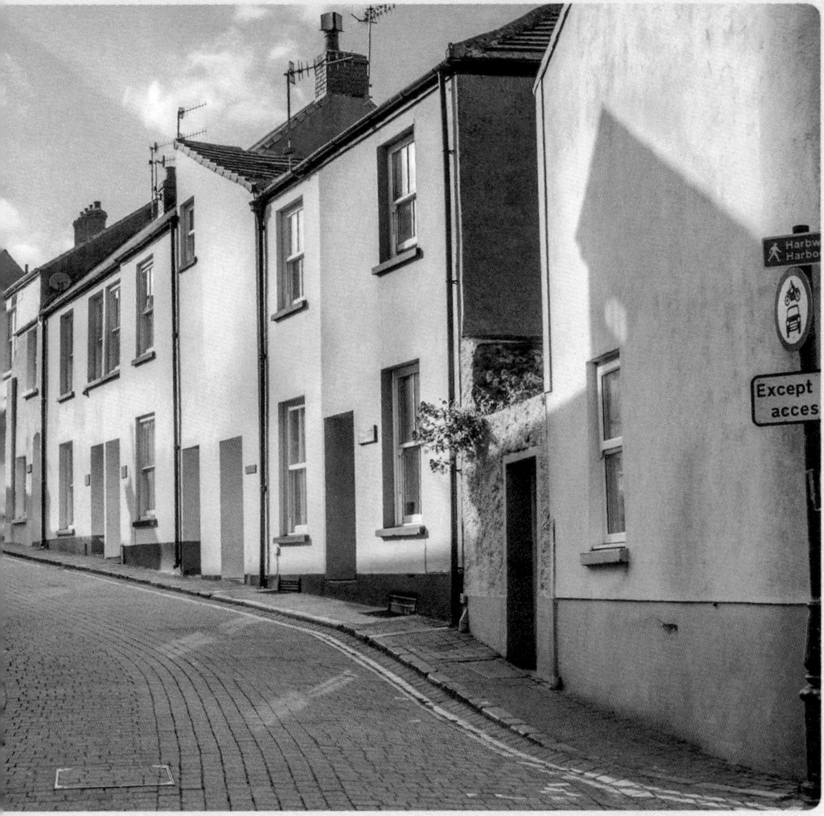
Except

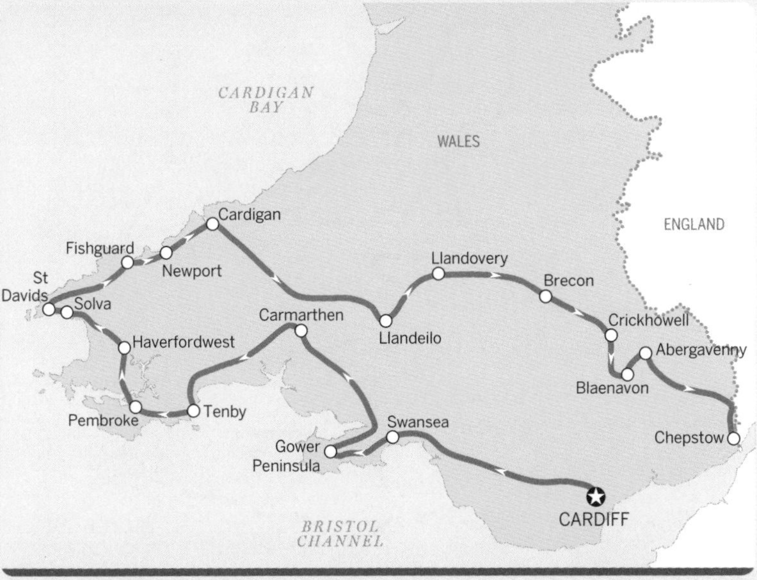
CARDIGAN BAY
WALES
ENGLAND
Cardigan
Fishguard
Newport
St Davids
Solva
Haverfordwest
Pembroke
Tenby
Carmarthen
Llandeilo
Llandovery
Brecon
Crickhowell
Abergavenny
Blaenavon
Chepstow
Swansea
Gower Peninsula
CARDIFF
BRISTOL CHANNEL

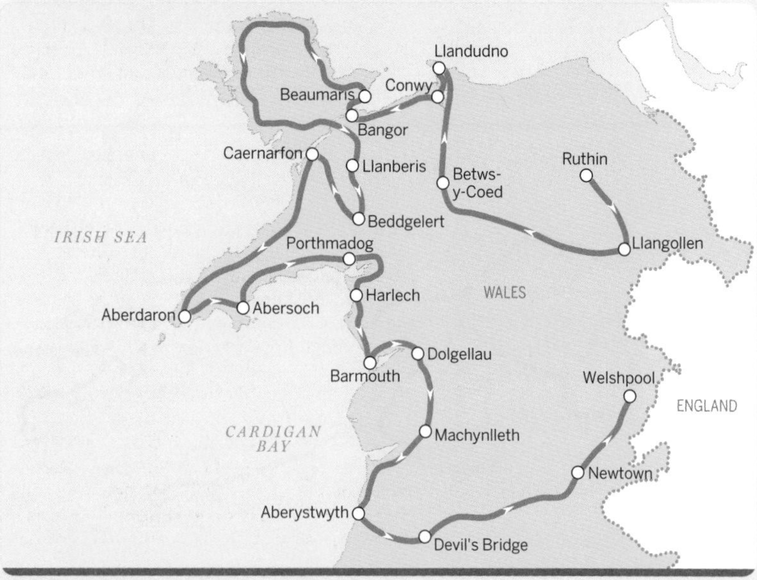
Llandudno
Conwy
Beaumaris
Bangor
Caernarfon
Llanberis
Betws-
y-Coed
Ruthin
IRISH SEA
Beddgelert
Llangollen
Porthmadog
Harlech
WALES
Aberdaron
Abersoch
Dolgellau
Barmouth
Welshpool
ENGLAND
CARDIGAN
BAY
Machynlleth
Newtown
Aberystwyth
Devil's Bridge

JON666 / GETTY IMAGES ©

DAVID WILLIAMS / GETTY IMAGES ©

Top: Beach at Barmouth (p237)
Bottom: Pontcysyllte Aqueduct (p224), Llangollen

10 DAYS North & Mid-Wales

The scenic highlights of North and Mid-Wales include river valleys, spectacular mountains and a widely varied coastline. This itinerary cuts a broad arc through the Welsh-speaking heartland, taking in still more castles, industrial sites and beaches – these things are Welsh clichés for a reason.

Start in historic **Ruthin** and take the beautiful back road that cuts through the bottom of the Clwydian Range to **Llangollen**, a small riverside town famous for outdoor pursuits and its World Heritage–listed canal and aqueduct. From here head west on the A5, swapping Denbighshire for the eastern reaches of Snowdonia National Park. **Betws-y-Coed** makes a pretty base for forest and river walks, and mountain biking.

Put Snowdonia behind you for a few days as you head north on the A470, shadowing the River Conwy. Stop along the way at Bodnant Estate before heading north to the old-fashioned beach resort town of **Llandudno**. Hop down to **Conwy** to immerse yourself in the medieval world between its town walls and tick off castle number one of the 'Castles of Edward I in Gwynedd' World Heritage Site. The A55 hugs the coast as it heads southwest towards **Bangor**. Stop for a quick look at the pier and the cathedral before crossing the Menai Strait to the Isle of Anglesey. Base yourself at **Beaumaris** (where you'll find castle number two) and circle the sacred island of the druids.

Cross the Menai Strait again and head to **Llanberis**, where you can plan your assault on Snowdon, either on foot or by train. Circle the mighty mountain, stopping at **Beddgelert**, before heading back to the coast at **Caernarfon** for castle number three. Circle the remote Llŷn Peninsula, stopping at the beaches and pubs of **Aberdaron** and **Abersoch**. Continue through **Porthmadog**, **Harlech** (castle number four) and beachy **Barmouth** before following the Mawddach Estuary to stony faced, heritage-filled **Dolgellau**. Head south to visit the greenies at **Machynlleth** before rejoining the coast at the buzzy student town of **Aberystwyth**. Stop at the **Devil's Bridge** waterfalls and the gallery at **Newtown**, before finishing at **Welshpool** with a visit to sumptuous Powis Castle.

Hiking in Snowdonia National Park (p230)

Plan Your Trip

Outdoor Activities

Need a dose of the great outdoors? Simple: head to Wales. The terrain lends itself to all manner of activities, from relaxing to rigorous, the landscape is stunning, access is easy and there's always a cosy pub with a warm fire nearby when you need to dry out – which you will.

SEBASTIEN-COELL / GETTY IMAGES ©

Don't Miss Experiences

Birdwatching

Some of the best twitching in Wales can be found around South Stack in Holyhead: expect guillemots, razorbills and even puffins.

Ancient Stones

The most mythology-rich standing stones are in Pembrokeshire's Preseli Hills.

Footsteps of Greatness

Explore the Taf Estuary around Laugharne, the 'heron-priested shore' that inspired Dylan Thomas.

Industrial History

Follow the canal path from Llangollen to Trevor, then take a boat trip over the Pontcysyllte Aqueduct.

Wildlife Encounters

Get close to grey seals, porpoises and dolphins on boat trips in Cardigan Bay.

Walking

Whether you're an ambler or a rambler, Wales is a walker's dream. There are some 25,500 miles of footpaths, bridleways and byways – all public rights of way.

For challenging walks, head for Snowdonia National Park, home to the highest mountain in England and Wales, impressive peaks and dramatic valleys, or for the craggy terrain of the Brecon Beacons, where, in the western end of the park, you can walk in almost total isolation.

And, for the complete experience, connecting the marvellous Wales Coast Path with the inland Offa's Dyke Path lets you circumnavigate the entire country.

One of the growing activities for walkers is geocaching, a kind of treasure hunt with the advantages of satellite navigation GPS units, combined with all the resources of the internet; for more information visit www.geocachingwales.com.

Walking can be enjoyed year-round, but be prepared for crowds in July and August, short days in winter and rain at any time. Guard against the weather with decent, warm clothing, footwear and waterproofs. A map, compass, first-aid kit, food and water are musts for more adventurous hikes. It's advisable to let someone know your intended route and planned return time and to check the weather forecast with the local tourist office before setting off.

For more information, visit www.walking.visitwales.com; the Events section includes details of walking festivals throughout Wales, generally between June and October.

Top Walks

These three national trails are open to walkers and horse riders, and are waymarked with an acorn symbol:

Glyndŵr's Way (http://nationaltrail.co.uk/glyndwrsway; 132 miles) Connecting sites associated with the rebellion led by Owain Glyndŵr in the early 15th century.

Offa's Dyke Path (http://offas-dyke.co.uk; 177 miles) Skirting the Wales–England border through an astonishing range of scenery and vegetation.

Pembrokeshire Coast Path (PCP; http://pembrokeshirecoast.org.uk; 186 miles) Hugging the sea cliffs of the Pembrokeshire Coast National Park, this is one of the UK's most beautiful coastal walks.

National Parks

The wonderfully varied landscapes of Wales' three national parks offer spectacular hikes, from coastal cliffs to jagged peaks.

Snowdonia (www.eryri-npa.gov.uk) Designated in 1951, this North Wales stalwart is also home to the highest mountain in England and Wales and is great for off-season walking.

Pembrokeshire Coast (http://pembrokeshirecoast.org.uk) Coastal walking plus boat trips to a scattering of nearby islands lend an ozone-blown frisson to a walk. Designated in 1952.

Brecon Beacons (http://breconbeacons.org) A rural haven for flora and fauna amid the rugged landscape of the history-carved mountains. Designated in 1957.

Cycling

There are 1197 miles of National Cycle Network, 331 miles of traffic-free rides and 11 cycle-hub destinations around the country, all of them chosen for their access to day-cycling routes and for their cycling infrastructure. Local cycling operators can advise on regional routes, while a handful also offer pan-Wales packages for a countrywide adventure. Look out, too, for local cycling events and festivals.

The traffic-free section of the **National Cycle Network** North Wales Coastal Route, running along the seaside promenade from Colwyn Bay to Prestatyn, is one of the best in the UK for cyclists of all abilities.

Take your own bike or rent one from many outlets across the country. Be aware it's best to stick to tracks marked as bridleways on Ordnance Survey (OS) maps and cycling lanes. Avoid footpaths that haven't been split to incorporate cycling lanes. With the exception of July and August when tourism peaks, the unnumbered roads and lanes are quiet and cyclist friendly.

Mountain biking, South Wales

For mountain biking, Wales offers some of the best facilities in the world – it boasts six purpose-built centres throughout the country. The centres offer a mixture of routes to suit all abilities, and all have one trail designed especially for families. Coed y Brenin Forest near Dolgellau is the premier centre, boasting the rockiest, most technically advanced trails and a dual slalom course.

For more information, check out the cycling pages at www.visitwales.co.uk and www.mbwales.com.

BEST COASTAL PATHS

The 850-mile Wales Coast Path (http://walescoastpath.gov.uk) lets you ramble the country's entire, craggy, glorious coastline. These are our favourite sections:

Carmarthen Bay Coastal & Estuaries Way 55 miles; Amroth to Gower

Ceredigion Coastal Path 63 miles; Ynyslas to Cardigan

Llŷn Coastal Path 95 miles; Caernarfon to Porthmadog

Pembrokeshire Coast Path 186 miles; Poppit Sands to Amroth

Watersports

For canoeing and sea kayaking, head to Pembrokeshire or Anglesey to explore coves and sea caves while paddling the flat waters below the towering cliffs. Inland, Llyn Tegid (Bala Lake) and Llyn Gwynant in North Wales are worth exploring, while slow-moving rivers include River Teifi, near Cardigan, and North Wales' River Dee. Powerful tidal currents create huge standing waves between the Pembrokeshire coast and offshore islands, making

Rafting the River Tryweryn, Bala (p230)

the Pembrokeshire Coast National Park (the only coastal park in Britain) one of the UK's finest sea-kayaking areas. Freshwater and Newgale Sands are favourite kayaking spots. Canoe Wales (www.canoewales.com) lists the waterways that permit kayaking and canoeing.

An incredible variety of sea life and a seabed littered with shipwrecks make diving in Wales an exciting prospect. Pembrokeshire, again, is the diving hot spot, and is the access point for the Smalls, a group of rocks famous for marine life, including a large colony of seals and pods of dolphins. Visibility here can reach up to 25m, although diving is restricted by the weather and tides. In North Wales, plump for Bardsey Island, the Skerries or the Menai Strait. Be aware that tidal currents rage dangerously at many of Wales' best dive sites, so seek advice locally before taking the plunge.

Surrounded by sea on three sides and netting some of the highest tidal ranges in the world – the Severn Estuary has the second-biggest tidal range anywhere – Wales has no shortage of surfing opportunities. Popular beaches can become crowded between April and September but with a little effort, you're sure to find your own space. Sea temperatures are often warmer than you might imagine, thanks to the North Atlantic Drift, but you'll always need a wetsuit, and possibly boots, a hood and gloves in winter.

The Gower Peninsula is home to the Welsh surfing industry, cramming in a wide choice of breaks and plenty of post-surf activity. Hot spots include Caswell Bay, the Mumbles, Langland Bay, Oxwich Bay and Llangennith. The best breaks in Pembrokeshire are to be found at Tenby South Beach, Manorbier, Freshwater West and Westdale Bay. St Davids' immense Whitesands Bay is good for beginners, although it's often busy. You'll find surf schools at most surf beaches. For more information, check the website of the **Welsh Surfing Federation Surf School** (☎01792-386426; www.surfschool.wsf.wales; Llangennith; lessons from £25).

There's great potential for windsurfing all around Wales' coast and on many inland lakes. Many surf beaches are also suitable for windsurfing and have gear hire and lessons available. Rhosneigr, on the Isle of Anglesey, is growing as a centre for windsurfing and other water sports. Check out http://ukwindsurfing.com.

The high-energy sport of coasteering originated in Wales: it involves a combination of wild swimming, climbing, canyoning, jumping and diving to negotiate a rocky coastline. Pembrokeshire, the Gower and Anglesey are particular hot spots.

Opportunities for white-water rafting are limited. One of the few Welsh rivers with big and fairly predictable summertime white water (grades III to IV) is the dam-released Tryweryn near Bala. Moderate rapids (grades II to IV) are found on the River Usk and between Corwen and Llangollen on the River Dee.

For more information about watersports, visit http://watersportswales.co.uk.

Golf

The staging of the prestigious Ryder Cup tournament at the Celtic Manor (http://celtic-manor.com) in Newport in 2010 cemented Wales' reputation as a golfing hub. But there's much beyond the top flight: some 200 well-crafted and scenery-rich golf courses take in everything from snow-coated mountain valleys to wind-swept coastal stretches.

West Monmouthshire Golf Club (☎01495-310233; www.westmongolfclub.co.uk; Golf Rd, Nantyglo, Ebbw Vale; green fees £12-18) The highest golf course in Britain.

Llanymynech Golf Club (☎01691-830983; www.llanymynechgolfclub.co.uk; High Cottage, Pant, Oswestry) Has 15 holes in Wales and three in England. On the fourth, tee off in Wales, putt in England and return to Wales three holes later.

Machynys Peninsula Golf & Country Club (☎01554-744888; http://machynys.com; Nicklaus Ave, Machynys, Llanelli; green fees £20-40) Designed by Gary Nicklaus, son of golf legend Jack; located in Machynys, Llanelli.

Dewstow Golf Club (☎01291-430444; http://dewstow.co.uk; Caerwent; 9/18 holes £12/20) The Park Course has the UK's only par-6 hole – a monster 630m; located in Caerwent, Monmouthshire.

Tenby Golf Club (☎01834-842978; www.tenbygolf.co.uk; The Burrows, Tenby; green fees from £25) Wales' oldest golf club – established in 1888.

Horse Riding

Wales has much to offer the equestrian set, thanks to its mix of sandy beaches, rolling hills and dense forest. Mid-Wales and the Cambrian Mountains, the forests, trails and uplands around Betws-y-Coed, and the gentle Clwydian Range are just some of the prime horsey territory to be explored. Riding schools catering for all levels of proficiency are found throughout the country. You can hire a horse or bring your own steed (guests' horses are offered stabling at some riding centres); check out http://ridingwales.com.

Caving

South Wales harbours a cave area stretching from Crickhowell to Carreg Cennen Castle. Caves are also found in North Wales, on the Gower Peninsula and in Pembrokeshire. Highlights for the more experienced caver include the UK's second-longest cave, **Ogof Draenen**, and the deepest, **Ogof Ffynnon Ddu**. **Porth-yr-Ogof** in the Brecon Beacons and **Paviland Cave** on the Gower Peninsula are better suited to beginners. For more information, contact the British Caving Association (http://british-caving.org.uk).

Climbing

Wales features some of the best climbing sites in the UK: Cader Idris and the slopes between Llanberis and Pen-y-Pass are just two of particular renown. It's hardest to get a foothold during summer when rock faces are particularly crowded. In winter, ice-climbing is popular in Snowdonia. Equip yourself for emergencies, check the Met Office weather forecast and seek advice from local climbing shops, climbers' cafes and tourist-information points before making your ascent.

To get a feel for the rock face, get in touch with Llangollen Outdoors (p226) or take a course at the Plas y Brenin National Mountain Sports Centre (p246) in Capel Curig. For more information, contact the British Mountaineering Council (http://thebmc.co.uk).

Top: The Pyg Track (p249), Snowdonia

Bottom: Horse riding on the Isle of Anglesey (p286)

GROOMEE / GETTY IMAGES ©

LONG-DISTANCE CYCLE RIDES

Two of Wales' most popular long-distance rides come under the auspices of the **National Cycle Network**. End points are linked with the rail network so you can make your way back to the start by train.

Lôn Las Cymru (Greenways of Wales/Welsh National Route; NCN Routes 8 & 42) This 254-mile route runs from Holyhead, through to Hay-on-Wye, then on to Cardiff via Brecon or Chepstow via Abergavenny. Encompassing three mountain ranges – Snowdonia, the Brecon Beacons and the Cambrian Mountains – there's a fair amount of uphill, low-gear huffing and puffing to endure along the way. But each peak promises fantastic views and plenty of downhill, free-wheeling delights.

Lôn Geltaidd (Celtic Trail; NCN Routes 4 & 47) A 337-mile route snaking from Fishguard through the West Wales hills, the Pembrokeshire Coast, the former coalfields of South Wales and ending at Chepstow Castle. The glorious, ever-changing landscape provides a superb backdrop.

Fishing

Wales' abundant rivers and lakes, long and winding coastline, and numerous fisheries offer many opportunities for game, sea and coarse fishing. Many species are found here: brown trout are among the catches on the Rivers Usk, Teifi, Wye, Dee, Seiont and Taff in spring. Reel in Welsh shy *sewin* (wild sea trout) on the banks of the River Towy, Teifi, Rheidol, Dyfi, Mawddach and Conwy in spring and summer. Chances of salmon improve in autumn in the River Usk. During winter catch grayling in the Rivers Wye, Dee and upper Severn.

To angle for sea fish, you don't necessarily need to charter a boat; cast off from any number of spots along the rocky coastline. For advice on likely catches at various locations throughout the year and a comprehensive list of fisheries, see the website of the Environment Agency (www.gov.uk/government/organisations/environment-agency). This is your first port of call for details on how to obtain a fishing licence. For more information on fishing in Wales, visit http://fishing.visitwales.com.

Canyoning

Like white-water rafting without the encumbrance of a raft, canyoning is one for the adrenaline junkies. Having found a suitably terrifying set of rock-bound rapids, you'll climb, slide, shimmy and swim down any way you can, protected only by a helmet, wetsuit and life-vest. The Brecon Beacons and Llangollen are just two of the many areas with companies offering this sport.

Plan Your Trip

Travel with Children

With glorious beaches, monumental castles, thrilling adventure sports, hands-on museums and trails to hike, bike, ride and wander, Wales is a kid's dream destination. The whole country is very family friendly, so roll up and let loose.

Wales for Kids

Wales is well geared towards family travel. Children are generally made to feel welcome, facilities are uniformly good and there are discounts at many attractions for family tickets, plus under-fives often go free. Public transport is easy to negotiate (and free for under-fives) and baby-changing facilities are widespread.

Most hotels and B&Bs can rustle up a cot or heat a bottle, cafes and restaurants usually have high chairs and offer children's menus, and pubs serving food often have gardens with playgrounds. If you're travelling with small children, your biggest difficulty may be finding a family room, as B&Bs and hotels have a limited supply, so it's worth checking self-catering options as well.

Children's Highlights

Beaches

Whitesands Bay, St Davids (p172) A wide, sandy Blue Flag beach with excellent swimming, surfing and rock pooling.

Barafundle Bay, Stackpole (p157) Follow the cliff path over dunes and through stone archways and you'll discover a superb hidden beach.

Best Regions for Kids

Cardiff

The best museums and hands-on exploration in the country.

Southeast Wales

Explore uplifting landscapes in the Black Mountains, Brecon Beacons and along the meandering Wye.

Swansea, Gower & Carmarthenshire

Surf the Gower and explore Wales' most dramatic castle.

Pembrokeshire

Home to fantastic clifftop walking and some of Wales' best beaches.

Mid-Wales

Discover hidden valleys, get back to the land with a farm stay, or ride horses over wild Cambrian uplands.

Snowdonia & the Llŷn

Hike, bike, sail and kayak in the shadow of the country's highest peaks.

Tresaith, near Cardigan (p189) Golden sands, rock pools, a cascading waterfall and, if you're lucky, dolphins visible from the shore.

Oxwich Bay, Gower Peninsula (p131) Miles of golden sand backed by dunes, salt marshes and woodland.

South Beach, Tenby (p193) A velvety-soft beach perfect for sandcastles, ball games and kite flying.

Castles

Beaumaris Castle (p291) The most perfect of Edward I's great castles, with sturdy concentric walls and a wide moat.

Conwy Castle (p276) A stunning fortress looming over the complete medieval walls of Conwy.

Pembroke Castle (p159) A forbidding but family-friendly castle with walks along the walls and passages from tower to tower.

Carreg Cennen (p113) Atmospheric 13th-century ruins with a clifftop passage down to an eerie natural cave.

Caernarfon Castle (p268) A massive, intimidating stronghold with excellent exhibitions pitched at kids and adults alike.

Outdoor Activities

Zip World Blaenau Ffestiniog (p240) Strap the kids in, and watch them sail down zip lines at breathtaking speeds over mountainsides and quarries.

Talyllyn Railway, Tywyn (p236) What kid wouldn't love getting to ride the inspiration behind Thomas the Tank Engine?

Living Room Treehouses, Machynlleth (p201) Sleeping, eating and playing in the canopy is something kids will never tire of.

Gwydyr Stables, Penmachno (p241) Explore Snowdonia's hills and forests on horseback, and at your own pace.

Lôn Las Cymru National Cycle Route 8 lets you take the littlies off-road, all the way from Cardiff to Holyhead.

Thousand Islands Expeditions, St Davids (p173) Head to the edge of the Celtic Deep to spot whales, porpoises and dolphins.

Rainy-day Activities

Techniquest, Cardiff (p53) Whizz-pop science adventures for all.

Centre for Alternative Technology, Machynlleth (p199) Educational, fun and truly green, CAT offers plenty of interactive displays and a great adventure playground for curious kids.

King Arthur's Labyrinth, Corris (p202) Trudge deep into the belly of an old slate mine to see Britain's mythical past resurrected.

National Waterfront Museum, Swansea (p121) For a hands-on family visit, Swansea's landmark museum is hard to beat.

Dan-yr-Ogof, Fforest Fawr (p112) Eerie caves, dinosaurs, shire horses and a petting farm should keep everyone entertained.

Festivals

Urdd National Eisteddfod (p21) One of Europe's largest youth festivals.

Haydays (p100) The part of the famous Hay Festival that's just for kids.

Big Cheese (p119) A fantastic free weekend of historical re-enactments, folk dancing, music and fire-eating.

Victorian Extravaganza (p283) Good old-fashioned family fun with fancy dress, parades and fun fairs.

World Bog Snorkelling Championships (p205) Stand by and watch competitors as they submerge themselves in boggy water for a 110m swim.

Regions at a Glance

Cardiff

Architecture
Sport
Nightlife

Civic Showcases

From the neoclassical glory of the Civic Centre, to dainty Victorian shopping arcades, to Cardiff Bay's cutting-edge modern waterfront, the Welsh capital has plenty to keep building buffs interested.

Rugby & More

Cardiff is the home of Welsh sport, with Principality Stadium completely dominating the city centre and three other major stadiums nearby. The city is never more alive than during a rugby international, when the singing from the stands resonates through the streets. On top of that, the Cardiff City football team and the Glamorgan Cricket Club both have a devoted following.

Cardiff's Bars

An edgy live-music scene, some swish cocktail bars and a swath of old-fashioned pubs attract hordes of revellers every weekend.

p44

Brecon Beacons & Southeast Wales

Walks
Castles
Mines & Forges

Making Tracks

From paths skirting the lush riverside of the Wye Valley to trails through the wild uplands of the Brecon Beacons, there are plenty of excellent walks to tackle in this region.

Fortresses

The southeast has some of Wales' most interesting castles, including Chepstow and remote Carreg Cennen, which is perhaps the most romantically positioned of them all.

Industrial Heritage

Victorian Britain was built on Welsh coal and iron, and the legacy of those industries is preserved in the Blaenavon World Heritage Site and other locations in the industrial heartland of the valleys.

p76

Swansea, Gower & Carmarthenshire

Beaches
Gardens
Market Towns

The Gower

Right on Swansea's doorstep, the Gower Peninsula harbours some of Wales' most beautiful beaches, from family-friendly bays such as Port Eynon to the surfing mecca of Rhossili.

Horticultural Showpieces

Green-fingered travellers will find inspiration in the significant gardens scattered around the green and blissful Carmarthenshire countryside, particularly the National Botanic Garden of Wales.

Rural Centres

The rural towns of Carmarthenshire are full of genteel charm, Georgian architecture and friendly pubs. The market at Carmarthen is a centre for the finest Welsh agricultural products.

p120

St Davids & Pembrokeshire

Coastal Scenery
Castles
Wildlife

Pembrokeshire Coast

One of Britain's most beautiful stretches of coast, Pembrokeshire offers clifftop walks, family-friendly beaches, surfing hot spots and watery adventures galore.

Fortresses

Southern Pembrokeshire is littered with castles, built by the Normans to consolidate their conquests. The kids won't be short on inspiration when they start their own building projects in the sands later.

Island Sanctuaries

Take a boat trip to one of the offshore islands for close encounters with seals, porpoises, dolphins, whales, sharks and sunfish. The cliffs are home to millions of seabirds; you might even spot a puffin.

p147

Aberystwyth & Mid-Wales

Wildlife
Market Towns
Food

Habitats

The once-rare red kite is now the symbol of Powys. Coastal Ceredigion shelters important wetland habitats, while Cardigan Bay is home to bottlenose dolphins, harbour porpoises, Atlantic grey seals, sunfish, basking sharks and leatherback turtles.

Powys

The Powys countryside is scattered with quaint market towns, many of which still serve as farming hubs. The highlight of the annual agricultural calendar is the Royal Welsh Show held in Builth Wells.

Local Produce

The new Welsh gastronomy focuses on the finest fresh, locally grown ingredients. Where better to enjoy them than in the Powys countryside?

p185

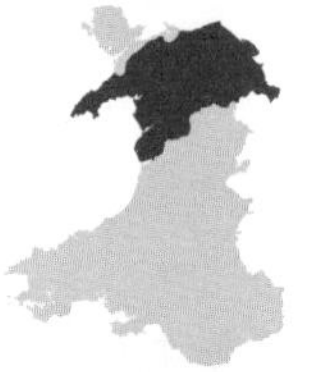

Snowdonia & the Llŷn

Mountains
Quarries
Beaches

Snowdonia

Home to Britain's finest mountain scenery south of the Scottish Highlands, Snowdonia's imposing but accessible peaks provide a scenic backdrop for innumerable outdoor pursuits.

Slate Quarries

Welsh slate once roofed much of the world and Snowdonia's quarries and caverns bear witness to the toil of generations of workers. Some have been converted into museums, while former freight railways now shunt travellers through spectacular terrain.

Surf & Sand

From the family-friendly sands of Barmouth and Tywyn to the surf spots and isolated bays of the Llŷn Peninsula, northwest Wales has plenty of beach to go round.

p219

Anglesey & the North Coast

Castles
Coastal Scenery
Stately Homes

Edward I's Legacy

While there are castles all over Wales, the fortresses created by Edward I in North Wales are the only ones to be recognised as World Heritage Sites. They truly are exemplars of the castle-makers' craft.

Isle of Anglesey

At times wild and rugged, at times gentle and restrained, the Druids' Isle is hugely diverse and rates among the nation's most beautiful stretches of coast.

Menai Mansions

Barons, marquesses and slate magnates all chose to build grand testimonies to their good fortune along the Menai Strait – some of which are now open for the hoi polloi to enjoy.

p265

On the Road

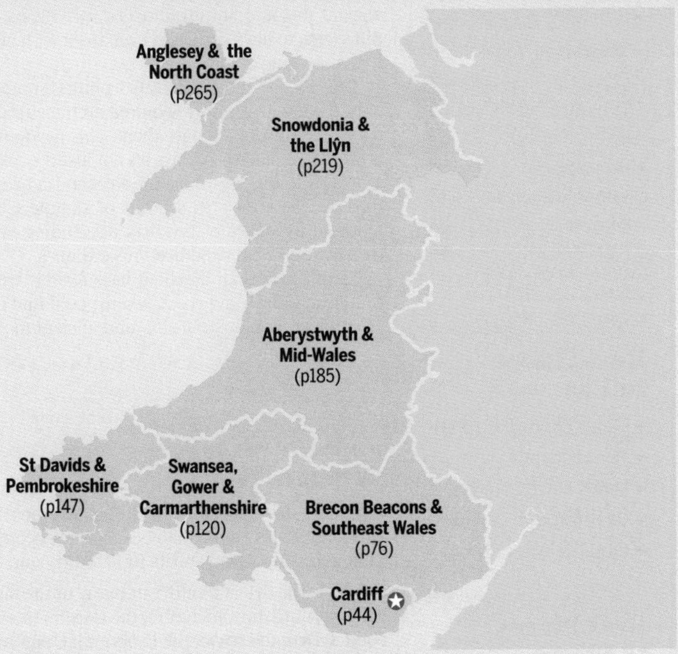
Anglesey & the North Coast (p265)
Snowdonia & the Llŷn (p219)
Aberystwyth & Mid-Wales (p185)
St Davids & Pembrokeshire (p147)
Swansea, Gower & Carmarthenshire (p120)
Brecon Beacons & Southeast Wales (p76)
Cardiff (p44)

Cardiff

POP 346,000

Includes ➡

Best Places to Eat

- Purple Poppadom (p64)
- Fish at 85 (p64)
- Mint & Mustard (p65)
- Oz Urfa (p65)
- Riverside Market (p64)

Best Places to Sleep

- Number 62 (p61)
- Lincoln House (p61)
- Park Plaza (p61)
- River House (p62)
- Safehouse (p60)

Why Go?

The capital of Wales since only 1955, Cardiff has embraced the role with vigour, emerging in the new millennium as one of Britain's leading urban centres. Caught between an ancient fort and an ultramodern waterfront, compact Cardiff seems to have surprised even itself with how interesting it has become.

The city has entered the 21st century pumped up on steroids, flexing its recently acquired architectural muscles as if it's still astonished to have them. This newfound confidence is infectious, and these days it's not just the rugby that draws crowds into the city. Come the weekend, a buzz reverberates through the streets as swarms of shoppers hit the Hayes, followed by waves of revellers descending on the capital's thriving pubs, bars and live-music venues.

Cardiff makes an excellent base for day trips to the surrounding valleys and coast, where you'll find castles, beaches, interesting industrial sites and ancient monuments.

When to Go

- January and February are the coldest months, although Wales' home matches in the Six Nations Rugby Championship warm spirits in February and March.
- June is the driest month but many of the big festivals hold out until July, including the Cardiff International Food & Drink Festival, the Everyman Open Air Theatre Festival and the Welsh Proms. In August, the warmest month, knights storm the castle, classic motor boats converge and gay pride takes over the streets.
- Making the most of the December chill, Cardiff's Winter Wonderland brings ice skating and Santa's grotto to the Civic Centre.

History

In AD 75 the Romans built a fort where Cardiff Castle now stands. The name Cardiff probably derives from Caer Tâf (Fort on the River Taff) or Caer Didi (Didius' Fort), referring to Roman general Aulus Didius. After the Romans left Britain the site remained unoccupied until the Norman Conquest. In 1093 a Norman knight named Robert Fitzhamon (conqueror of Glamorgan and later earl of Gloucester) built himself a castle within the Roman walls and a small town grew up around it. Both were damaged in a Welsh revolt in 1183 and the town was sacked in 1404 by Owain Glyndŵr during his ill-fated rebellion against English domination.

The first of the Tudor Acts of Union in 1536 put the English stamp on Cardiff and brought some stability. But despite its importance as a port, market town and bishopric, only 1000 people were living here in 1801.

The city owes its present stature to iron and coal mining in the valleys to the north. Coal was first exported from Cardiff on a small scale as early as 1600. In 1794 the Bute family,which owned much of the land from which Welsh coal was mined, built the Glamorganshire Canal for shipping iron from Merthyr Tydfil down to Cardiff. In 1840 this was supplanted by the new Taff Vale Railway.

A year earlier the second marquess of Bute had completed the first docks at Butetown, just south of Cardiff, getting the jump on other South Wales ports. By the time it dawned on everyone what immense reserves of coal there were in the valleys – setting off a kind of black gold rush – the Butes were in a position to insist that it be shipped from Butetown. Cardiff was off and running.

The docklands expanded rapidly, the Butes grew staggeringly rich and the city boomed, its population mushrooming to 170,000 by the end of the 19th century and to 227,000 by 1931. A large, multiracial workers' community known as Tiger Bay grew up in the harbourside area of Butetown. In 1905 Cardiff was officially designated a city, and a year later its elegant Civic Centre was inaugurated. In 1913 Cardiff became the world's top coal port, exporting some 13 million tonnes of the stuff.

The post-WWI slump in the coal trade and the Great Depression of the 1930s slowed this expansion. The city was badly damaged by WWII bombing, which claimed over 350 lives. Shortly afterwards the coal industry was nationalised, which led to the Butes packing their bags and leaving town in 1947, donating the castle and a large chunk of land to the city.

Wales had no official capital and the need for one was seen as an important focus for Welsh nationhood. Cardiff had the advantage of being Wales' biggest city and boasting the architectural riches of the Civic Centre. It was proclaimed the first capital of Wales in 1955, chosen via a ballot of the members of the Welsh authorities. Cardiff received 36 votes to Caernarfon's 11 and Aberystwyth's four.

Sights

City Centre

★**National Museum Cardiff** MUSEUM

(Map p50; ☎0300 111 2 333; www.museumwales.ac.uk; Gorsedd Gardens Rd; ⊙10am-4pm Tue-Sun) FREE Devoted mainly to natural history and art, this grand neoclassical building is the centrepiece of the seven institutions dotted around the country that together form the Welsh National Museum. It's one of Britain's best museums; you'll need at least three hours to do it justice, but it could easily consume the best part of a rainy day.

The Evolution of Wales exhibit whizzes onlookers through 4600 million years of geological history, its rollicking multimedia display placing Wales into a global context. Films of volcanic eruptions and aerial footage of the Welsh landscape explain how its scenery was formed, while model dinosaurs and woolly mammoths help keep the kids interested.

The natural-history displays range from brightly coloured insects to the 9m-long skeleton of a humpback whale that washed up near Aberthaw in 1982. The world's largest turtle (2.88m by 2.74m), a leatherback that was found on Harlech beach, is also here, suspended on wires from the ceiling.

The excellent art collection's treasures include a trio of Monet's *Water Lilies,* alongside his scenes of London, Rouen and Venice; Sisley's *The Cliff at Penarth* (the artist was married in Cardiff); Renoir's shimmering *La Parisienne;* a cast of Rodin's *The Kiss;* and Van Gogh's anguished *Rain: Auvers*. Welsh artists such as Gwen and Augustus John, Richard Wilson, Thomas Jones, David Jones and Ceri Richards are well represented, along with famous names from across the border such as Francis Bacon, David Hockney and Rachel Whiteread.

Cardiff Highlights

❶ **Cardiff Castle** (p48) Marvelling at the over-the-top Victorian interiors of the city's ancient citadel.

❷ **Bute Park** (p49) Relaxing on the lawn, against a backdrop of mature trees, flowerbeds, the river and the castle.

❸ **National Museum Cardiff** (p45) Taking an engrossing journey through Wales via the big bang, natural history and fine art.

❹ **St Fagans National History Museum** (p56) Exploring the transplanted historical buildings, Elizabethan manor house and beautiful gardens.

❺ **Cardiff Bay** (p52) Admiring the architectural showpieces that make up this glitzy entertainment, arts and political precinct.

❻ **Live Music** (p67) Checking out the bright young indie acts entertaining the night-time revellers in the various central-city bars and clubs, including prestigious Clwb Ifor Bach.

❼ **Rugby** (p51) Getting swept away by the exhilaration of a fired-up rugby test at Principality Stadium.

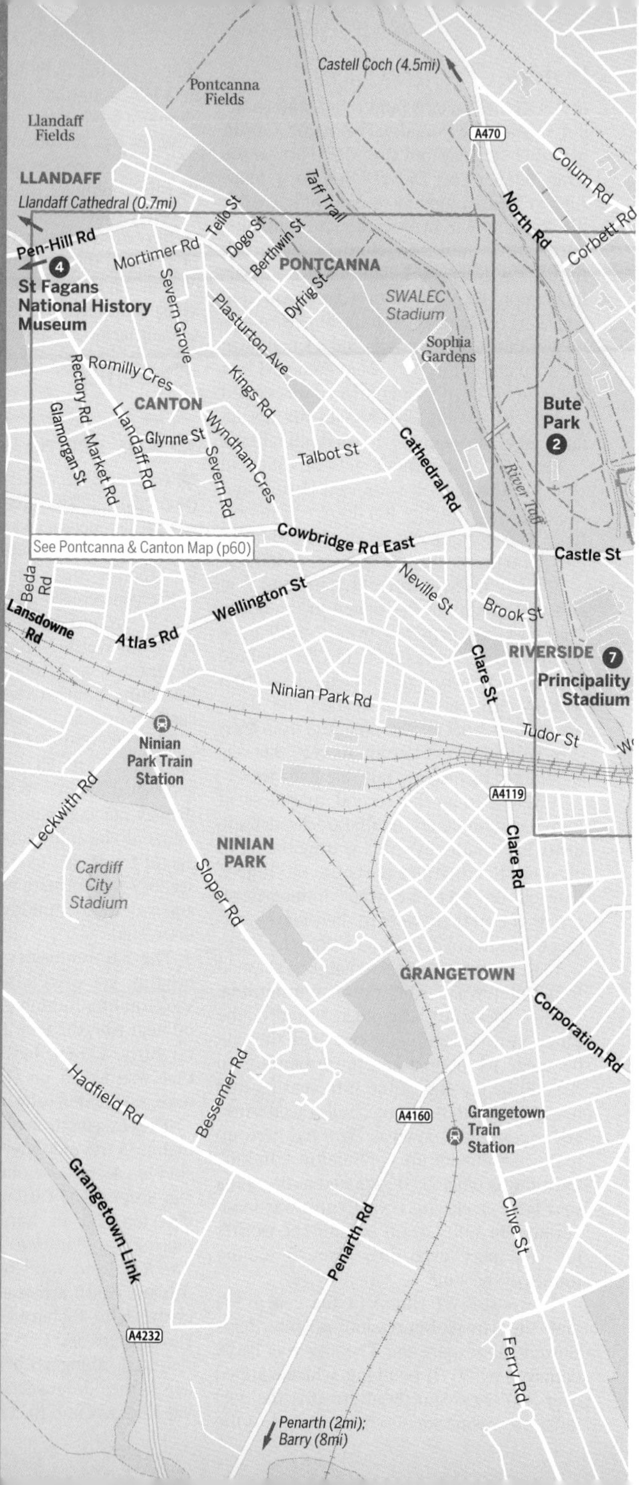

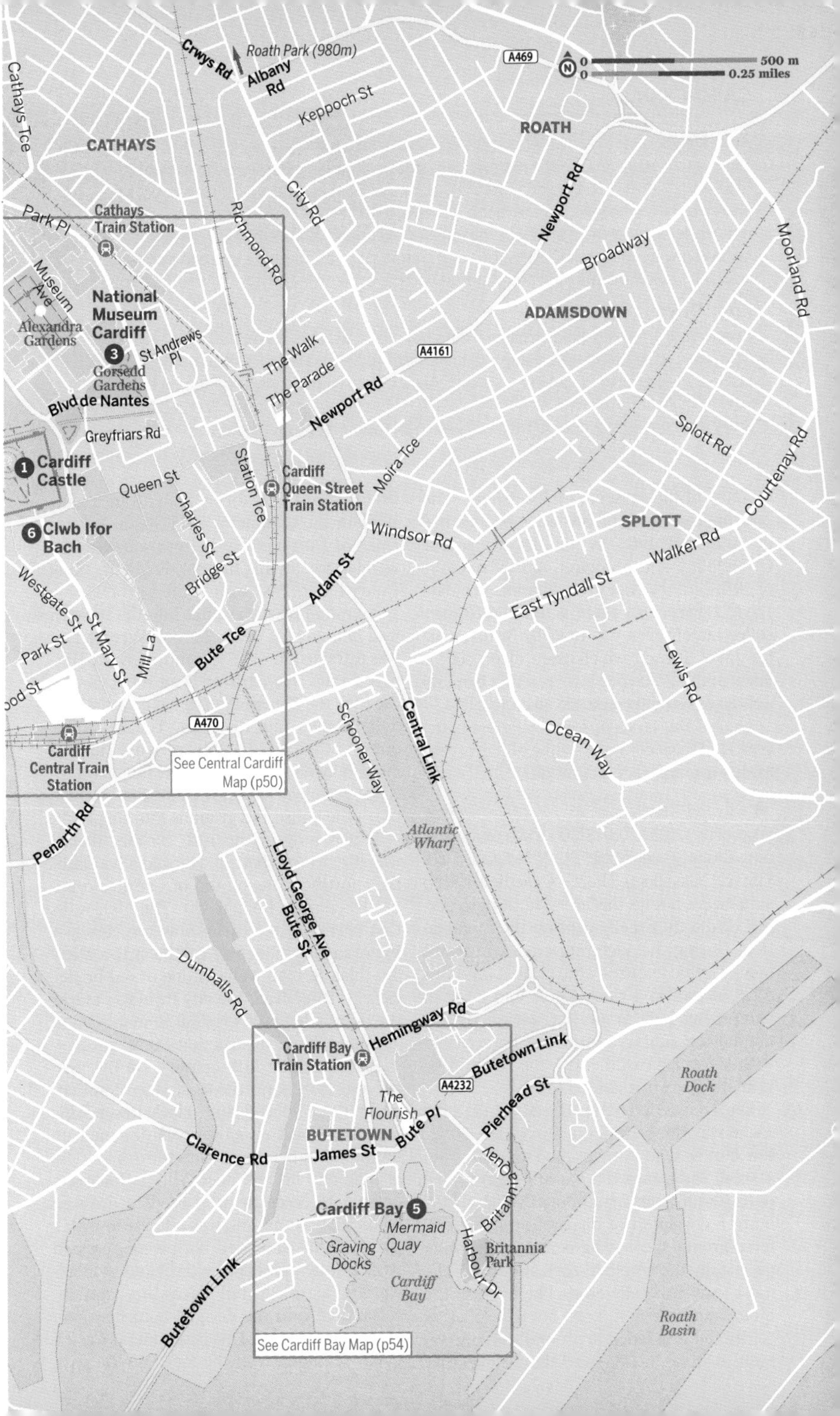

Roath Park (980m)
Crwys Rd
Albany Rd
A469
0 500 m
0 0.25 miles
Cathays Tce
Keppoch St
ROATH
CATHAYS
City Rd
Newport Rd
Park Pl
Cathays Train Station
Richmond Rd
Broadway
Moorland Rd
Museum Ave
National Museum Cardiff
ADAMSDOWN
Alexandra Gardens
3
St Andrews Pl
The Walk
A4161
Gorsedd Gardens
The Parade
Blvd de Nantes
Newport Rd
Greyfriars Rd
Splott Rd
Courtenay Rd
1 Cardiff Castle
Station Tce
Cardiff Queen Street Train Station
Moira Tce
Queen St
Charles St
6 Clwb Ifor Bach
Windsor Rd
SPLOTT
Walker Rd
Bridge St
Adam St
Westgate St
East Tyndall St
St Mary St
Park St
Bute Tce
Lewis Rd
Mill La
Wood St
Schooner Way
Central Link
A470
Ocean Way
Cardiff Central Train Station
See Central Cardiff Map (p50)
Penarth Rd
Atlantic Wharf
Lloyd George Ave
Bute St
Dumballs Rd
Hemingway Rd
Cardiff Bay Train Station
Butetown Link
A4232
Pierhead St
Roath Dock
The Flourish
Bute Pl
BUTETOWN
Clarence Rd
James St
Britannia Quay
Cardiff Bay 5
Mermaid Quay
Graving Docks
Harbour Dr
Britannia Park
Cardiff Bay
Butetown Link
Roath Basin
See Cardiff Bay Map (p54)

CARDIFF IN...

Two Days

Start with a stroll around the historic city centre, stopping to explore the **National Museum Cardiff** (p45) and **Cardiff Castle** (p48) along the way. Lunch could be a picnic in **Bute Park** with treats acquired at **Cardiff Market** (p68) or, if the weather's not cooperating, a meal at any of the reasonably priced central-city eateries. Spend your second day heading back to the future at Cardiff Bay (p52), where you can immerse yourself in forward-thinking architecture and have a **Doctor Who Experience** (p55).

Four Days

Spend your third morning strolling through the past at **St Fagans National History Museum** (p56), then take a day trip to Penarth (p73) and Barry Island (p75). On your last day, head north to explore **Llandaff Cathedral** (p56), then continue on to **Castell Coch** (p52) and **Caerphilly Castle** (p118). For your last night in the Welsh capital, blast away the cobwebs in one of the city's live-music venues (p67).

Many of the museum's impressionist and post-impressionist pieces were bequeathed in 1952 and 1963 by the Davies sisters, Gwendoline and Margaret, granddaughters of 19th-century coal and shipping magnate David Davies. One room is devoted to their collection of seven paintings by British master JMW Turner, which were dismissed as fakes in the 1950s but have recently been reappraised as being genuine all along.

One of the large upstairs galleries is devoted to Welsh ceramics, while others are set aside for temporary exhibitions.

★Cardiff Castle CASTLE

(Map p50; ☎029-2087 8100; www.cardiffcastle.com; Castle St; adult/child £12/9, incl guided tour £15/11; ⏲9am-5pm) There's a medieval keep at its heart, but it's the later additions to Cardiff Castle that really capture the imagination. During the Victorian era, extravagant mock-Gothic features were grafted onto this relic, including a clock tower and a lavish banqueting hall. Some but not all of this flamboyant fantasy world can be accessed with a regular castle entry; the rest can be visited as part of a guided tour.

Until it was donated to the city in 1947, the castle was the private domain of the Butes, the family who transformed Cardiff from a small town into the world's biggest coal port. It's far from a traditional Welsh castle, more a collection of disparate castles scattered around a central green, encompassing practically the whole history of Cardiff. The most conventionally castle-like bits are the motte-and-bailey **Norman shell keep** at its centre (built in wood in around 1081 and rebuilt in stone in 1135) and the 13th-century **Black Tower** that forms the entrance gate. William the Conqueror's eldest son Robert, Duke of Normandy, was imprisoned in the wooden fort by his brother, England's King Henry I, until his death at the age of 83.

A grand house was built into the western wall in the 1420s by the Earl of Warwick and was extended in the 17th century by the Herbert family (the earls of Pembroke), but by the time the Butes acquired it a century later it had fallen into disrepair. The first marquess of Bute hired architect Henry Holland and Holland's father-in-law, the famous landscape architect Lancelot 'Capability' Brown, to get the house and grounds into shape.

It was only in the 19th century that it was discovered that the Normans had built their fortifications on top of Cardiff's original 1st-century Roman fort. The high walls that surround the castle now are largely a Victorian reproduction of the 3rd-century 3m-thick Roman walls. A line of red bricks, clearly visible from the city frontage, marks the point where the original Roman section ends and the reconstruction commences.

Also from the 19th century are the towers and turrets on the west side, dominated by the colourful 40m clock tower. This faux-Gothic extravaganza was dreamed up by the mind-bendingly rich third marquess of Bute and his architect William Burges, a passionate eccentric who used to dress in medieval costume and was often seen with a parrot on his shoulder. Both were obsessed with Gothic architecture, religious symbolism and astrology, influences that were incorporated into the designs both here and at the Butes' second Welsh home at Castell Coch. Yet along with the focus on the past, the plans included all of the mod cons of the Victorian era, such as electric lighting (it was the second house in Wales to feature this newfangled wizardry) and running water in the en suite attached to the upper-floor bedroom.

A 50-minute **guided tour** takes you through the interiors, from the winter smoking room in the clock tower with decor expounding on the theme of time (zodiac symbols grouped into seasons, Norse gods representing the days of the week, and a fright for anyone who dares listen at the door – look up as you pass through the doorway), to the mahogany-and-mirrors narcissism of Lord Bute's bedroom, with a gilded statue of St John the Evangelist (the marquess's name saint) and 189 bevelled mirrors on the ceiling, which reflect the name 'John' in Greek.

The banqueting hall boasts Bute family heraldic shields and a fantastically over-the-top fireplace (look for the image of the imprisoned Duke of Normandy) and is overlooked by that medieval must-have, a minstrels' gallery. Marble, sandalwood, parrots and acres of gold leaf create an elaborate Moorish look in the Arab room. The neighbouring nursery is decorated with fairy-tale and nursery-rhyme characters, while the small dining room has an ingenious table, designed so that a living vine could be slotted through it, allowing diners to pluck fresh grapes as they ate. The Roman-style roof garden seems to underline how much of a fantasy all this really was – designed with southern Italy in mind, rather than Wales.

The regular castle entry allows you access to the banqueting hall and includes an excellent audioguide (available in a children's edition and in a range of languages). Start your visit by viewing the short film, screened in a room above the gift ship, which provides a wordless representation of the castle's journey through history. Leading off from here is a **WWII air raid shelter** preserved in a long cold corridor within the castle walls.

Housed below the ticket office is **Firing Line**, a small but well-organised museum devoted to the Welsh soldier.

★Bute Park — PARK

(Map p50; www.cardiff.gov.uk/parks; ⏲7.30am-sunset) Flanked by the castle and the River Taff, Bute Park was donated to the city along with the castle in 1947. With Sophia Gardens, Pontcanna Fields and Llandaff Fields, it forms a green corridor that stretches north-west for 1½ miles to Llandaff. All were once part of the Bute's vast holdings.

In Cooper's Field, the part of the park just west of the castle, is a stone circle, erected in 1978 when Cardiff hosted the National Eisteddfod. Such so-called **gorsedd stones**

THE BEAUT BUTES

In Cardiff, the Bute name is inescapable. No family has had a bigger impact on the city. An aristocratic Scottish brood related to the Stuart monarchy, the Butes arrived in Cardiff in 1766 in the shape of John, Lord Mount Stuart. He married a local heiress, Charlotte Hickman-Windsor, acquiring vast estates and mineral rights in South Wales in the process. Like his father of the same name (a prime minister under George III), he entered politics and became a Tory MP, privy councillor, ambassador to Spain and, eventually, was awarded the title Marquess of Bute.

Their grandson, the second marquess of Bute, grew fabulously wealthy from coal mining and then in 1839 gambled his fortune to create a large complex of docks in Cardiff. The gamble paid off. The coal-export business boomed, and his son, John Patrick Crichton-Stuart, the third marquess of Bute, became one of the richest people on the planet. He was not your conventional Victorian aristocrat; an intense, scholarly man with a passion for history, architecture, ritual and religion (Catholic), he neither hunted nor fished but instead supported the antivivisection movement and campaigned for a woman's right to a university education. In 1887 he gifted Roath Park to the town. His architectural legacy ranges from the colourful kitsch of Cardiff Castle and Castell Coch, to the neoclassical elegance of the Civic Centre.

The Butes had interests all over Britain and never spent more than about six weeks at a time in Cardiff. By the end of WWII they had sold or given away all their Cardiff assets, the fifth marquess gifting Cardiff Castle and Bute Park to the city in 1947. The present marquess, the seventh, lives in the family seat at Mount Stuart House on the Isle of Bute in Scotland's Firth of Clyde; another maverick, he's better known as Johnny Dumfries, the former Formula One racing driver.

are found all over Wales where eisteddfodau have been held.

Marked out on the lawn nearby are the foundations of the 13th-century **Blackfriars Priory**, which was destroyed in 1404 when Owain Glyndŵr attacked Cardiff and later rebuilt, only to be finally vacated in 1538 when the monastery was dissolved.

Animal Wall SCULPTURE
(Map p50; Castle St) This section of wall on Bute Park's southern edge is topped with stone figures of lions, seals, bears and other

Central Cardiff

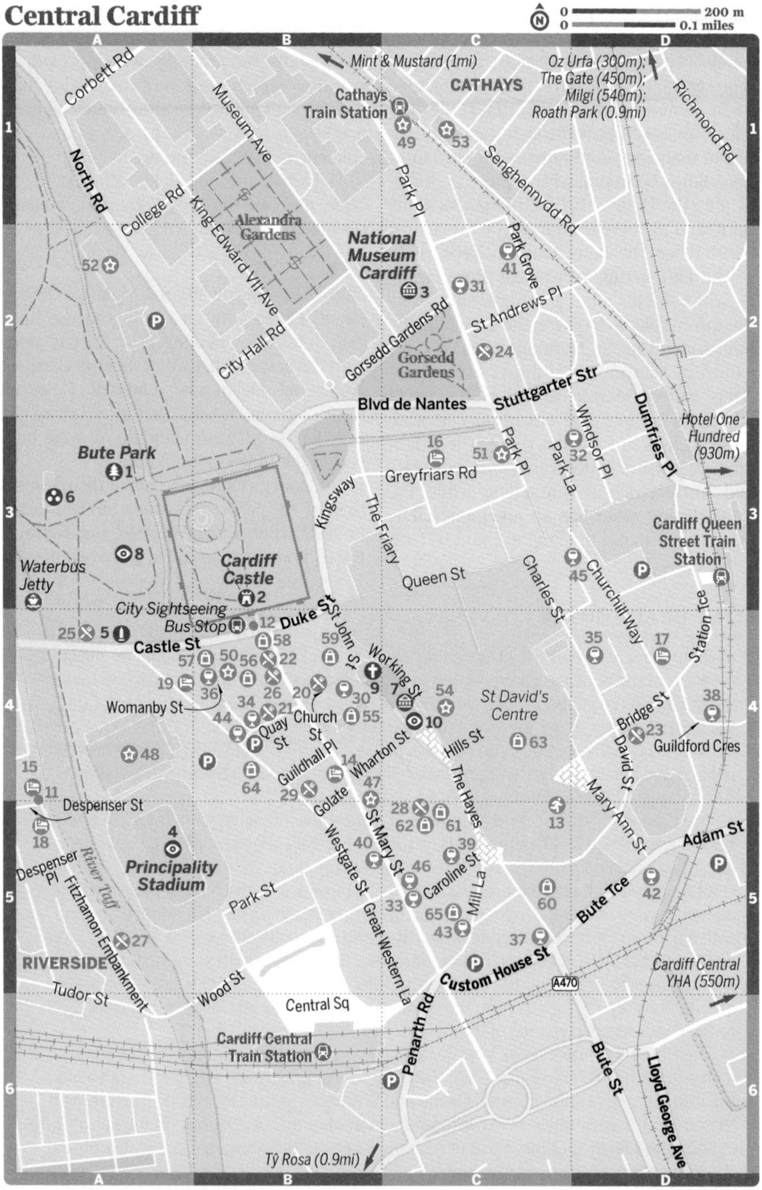

creatures. In the 1930s they were the subject of a newspaper cartoon strip and many Cardiff kids grew up thinking the animals came alive at night.

★ **Principality Stadium** STADIUM

(Millennium Stadium; Map p50; ☎029-2082 2432; www.principalitystadium.wales; Westgate St; tours adult/child £13/9) This spectacular stadium squats like a stranded spaceship on the River Taff's east bank. Originally christened Millennium Stadium (the new name's a nod to sponsors, not the monarchy), this 74,500-seat, £168-million, three-tiered, retractable-roofed arena was completed in time to host the 1999 Rugby World Cup. If you can't get tickets to a match, it's well worth taking a tour. Book online or at the **WRU Store** (Map p50; www.wru.co.uk; 8 Westgate St; 9.30am-5.30pm Mon-Sat, 10am-4pm Sun).

During the tours you get to hang out in the dressing rooms (alas sans players), run through the tunnel to the recorded cheering of a game-day crowd and sit in the VIP box. Tours last about an hour and are held several times a day, except on event days.

Rugby is Wales' national game and when the Principality crowd begins to sing, the whole of Cardiff resonates. To watch a test here is to catch a glimpse of the Welsh

Central Cardiff

Top Sights
1 Bute Park ... A3
2 Cardiff Castle ... B3
3 National Museum Cardiff ... C2
4 Principality Stadium ... A5

Sights
5 Animal Wall ... A4
6 Blackfriars Priory ... A3
7 Cardiff Story ... C4
8 Gorsedd Stones ... A3
9 St John the Baptist Church ... B4
10 Yr Hen Lyfrgell ... C4

Activities, Courses & Tours
11 Cardiff Cycle Tours ... A4
12 City Sightseeing ... B4
13 Treetop Adventure Golf ... C5

Sleeping
14 Mrs Potts ... B4
15 NosDa ... A4
16 Park Plaza ... C3
17 Premier Inn Cardiff City Centre ... D4
18 River House ... A5
19 Safehouse ... A4

Eating
20 Cafe Cittá ... B4
21 Casanova ... B4
Coffee Barker ... (see 56)
22 Goat Major ... B4
23 Little Man Coffee Co. ... D4
Madame Fromage ... (see 56)
24 Park House ... C2
25 Pettigrew Tea Rooms ... A4
26 Potted Pig ... B4
Restaurant Minuet ... (see 56)
27 Riverside Market ... A5
28 The Plan ... C5
29 Zerodegrees ... B4

Drinking & Nightlife
30 10 Feet Tall ... B4
31 29 Park Place ... C2
32 Buffalo Bar ... D3
33 Cambrian Tap ... C5
34 City Arms ... B4
35 Eagle ... D4
36 Full Moon ... B4
37 Golden Cross ... C5
38 Gwdihŵ ... D4
39 Lab 22 ... C5
40 Nine Yards ... B5
41 Pen & Wig ... C2
42 Porter's ... D5
43 Retro ... C5
44 Urban Tap House ... B4
45 WOW ... D3
46 Yard ... C5

Entertainment
47 Cafe Jazz ... B4
48 Cardiff Arms Park ... A4
49 Cardiff University Students' Union ... C1
50 Clwb Ifor Bach ... B4
51 New Theatre ... C3
52 Royal Welsh College of Music & Drama ... A2
53 Sherman Cymru ... C1
54 St David's Hall ... C4

Shopping
Bodlon ... (see 10)
55 Cardiff Market ... B4
56 Castle Arcade ... B4
57 Castle Emporium ... B4
58 Castle Welsh Crafts ... B4
E Ashton's ... (see 55)
59 High St & Duke St Arcades ... B4
60 John Lewis ... C5
61 Morgan Quarter ... C5
62 Spillers Records ... C5
63 St David's ... C4
64 WRU Store ... B4
65 Wyndham Arcade ... C5

WORTH A TRIP

CASTELL COCH

Castell Coch (Cadw; www.cadw.gov.wales; Castle Rd, Tongwynlais; adult/child £6/4.20; 9.30am-5pm Mar-Oct, 10am-4pm Nov-Feb). Cardiff Castle's fanciful little brother, sits perched atop a thickly wooded crag on the northern fringes of the city. It was the summer retreat of the third marquess of Bute and, like Cardiff Castle, was designed by William Burges in gaudy Victorian Gothic style. Raised on the ruins of Gilbert de Clare's 13th-century Castell Coch (Red Castle), the Butes' Disneyesque holiday home is a monument to high camp. An excellent audioguide is included in the admission price.

Lady Bute's huge, circular bedroom is pure fantasy – her bed, with crystal globes on the bedposts, sits in the middle beneath an extravagantly decorated and mirrored cupola, with 28 painted panels around the walls depicting monkeys (fashionable at the time, apparently; just plain weird now). The corbels are carved with images of birds nesting or feeding their young, and the washbasin is framed between two castle towers.

Lord Bute's bedroom is small and plain in comparison, but the octagonal drawing room is another hallucinogenic tour de force, the walls painted with scenes from *Aesop's Fables*, the domed ceiling a flurry of birds and stars, and the fireplace topped with figures depicting the three ages of men and women. The tower to the right of the entrance houses exhibits explaining the castle's history.

Stagecoach buses 26 and 132 (30 minutes) stop at Tongwynlais, which is a 10-minute walk from the castle. Bus 26 continues to Caerphilly Castle, and the two can be combined in a day trip.

psyche, especially when the Six Nations tournament is in full swing. Tickets for international fixtures are difficult to get hold of; other matches are easier. Cardiff Arms Park, Principality's famous predecessor and home to the Cardiff Blues rugby team, lies literally in its shadow. Outside of the rugby season the stadium is used for mammoth events such as Monster Trucks and concerts by the likes of Bruce Springsteen and Beyoncé. The British Speedway Grand Prix is held here in June or July.

St John the Baptist Church CHURCH
(Map p50; 029-2039 5231; www.cardiffstjohncityparish.org.uk; Church St; 10am-3pm Mon-Sat) A graceful Gothic tower rises from this 15th-century church, its delicate stonework looking almost like filigree. Along with the castle keep, this is one of the few remnants of medieval Cardiff. A church has stood on this site since at least 1180. Inside there are regimental flags, elegant pointed arches and a spectacular Elizabethan-era tomb. Free half-hour organ concerts are held here at 1.15pm on the second Friday of each month.

Yr Hen Lyfrgell CULTURAL CENTRE
(The Old Library; Map p50; www.yrhenlyfrgell.wales; The Hayes) *Croeso* (welcome) to a bastion of the Welsh language in the overwhelmingly English-speaking capital. Cardiff's beautiful old library has been converted into a showcase for all things Cymraeg, with an excellent gift shop (p68), a stylish cafe/bar, and rooms where Welsh language lessons are held. Everyone's welcome, even if the only Welsh you can muster is a timid *bore da* (good morning). While you're here, check out the gorgeous Victorian tiles lining the library's original entrance and call into the Cardiff Story museum.

Cardiff Story MUSEUM
(Map p50; 029-2034 6214; www.cardiffstory.com; Yr Hen Lyfrgell, The Hayes; 10am-4pm Mon-Sat) FREE This excellent little museum uses interactive displays, video footage and everyday objects to tell the story of Cardiff's transformation from a small market town into the world's biggest coal port and then into the capital city of today.

Cardiff Bay

Lined with important national institutions, Cardiff Bay is where the modern Welsh nation is put on display in an architect's playground of interesting buildings, large open spaces and public art. The bay's main commercial centre is Mermaid Quay, packed with bars, restaurants and shops.

It wasn't always this way. By 1913 more than 13 million tonnes of coal were being shipped from Cardiff's docks. Following the post-WWII slump the docklands deteriorated into a wasteland of empty basins, cut off from the city by the railway embankment.

The bay outside the docks, which has one of the highest tidal ranges in the world (more than 12m between high and low water), was ringed for up to 14 hours a day by smelly, sewage-contaminated mudflats. The nearby residential area of Butetown became a neglected slum. Since 1987 the area has been radically redeveloped. The turning point came with the completion of a state-of-the-art tidal barrage in 1999.

Butetown History & Arts Centre GALLERY
(Map p54; ☎029-2025 6757; www.bhac.org; Bute St, Butetown; ⏲11am-4pm) FREE Victorian Butetown, immediately north of Mermaid Quay, was the heart of Cardiff's coal trade – a multiethnic community that propelled the city to world fame. This centre is devoted to preserving oral histories, documents and images of the docklands. The displays put the area into both a historical and present-day context, and there's a gallery devoted to temporary exhibitions.

Coal Exchange NOTABLE BUILDING
(Map p54; www.coalexchange.co.uk; Mount Stuart Sq, Butetown) This imposing but semiderelict building was once the nerve centre of the Welsh coal trade, and for a time the place where international coal prices were set. It was here in March 1908 that a coal merchant wrote the world's first-ever £1 million cheque. The building narrowly missed becoming the home of the Welsh government in 1979, and eventually fell into disrepair. In 2016, an ambitious £40 million restoration was announced, with plans to convert it into a luxury hotel.

Techniquest MUSEUM
(Map p54; ☎029-2047 5475; www.techniquest.org; Stuart St, Cardiff Bay; adult/child £6.80/5.40; ⏲9.30am-4.30pm Tue-Sun, daily school holidays) With the aim of introducing kids to science, Techniquest is jam-packed with engrossing, hands-on exhibits that are equally enjoyable for under-fives and inquisitive adults. The digital planetarium stages star tours and science shows.

★**Wales Millennium Centre** ARTS CENTRE
(Map p54; ☎029-2063 6464; www.wmc.org.uk; Bute Pl, Cardiff Bay; tours adult/child £6/free; ⏲9am-7pm) The centrepiece and symbol of Cardiff Bay's regeneration is the superb Wales Millennium Centre, an architectural masterpiece of stacked Welsh slate in shades of purple, green and grey topped with an overarching bronzed steel shell. Designed by Welsh architect Jonathan Adams, it opened in 2004 as Wales' premier arts complex, housing major cultural organisations such as the Welsh National Opera, National Dance Company, BBC National Orchestra of Wales, Literature Wales, HiJinx Theatre and Tŷ Cerdd (Music Centre Wales).

The roof above the main entrance is pierced by 2m-high letter-shaped windows, spectacularly backlit at night, which spell out phrases from Welsh poet Gwyneth Lewis.

You can wander through the large public lobby at will. Guided tours depart at 11am, noon and 2.30pm most days (check online), and lead visitors behind the giant letters, onto the main stage and into the dressing rooms, depending on what shows are on.

Roald Dahl Plass SQUARE
(Map p54; Cardiff Bay) The unusual shape of this large public space is due to its past life as the basin of the West Bute Dock. A large rectangular dock once extended from here all the way up what is now Lloyd George Ave, right to the foot of the city centre, berthing up to 300 ships at a time. Reborn as a square, it was renamed in honour of the Cardiff-born writer. The whole thing is overseen by a soaring, stainless-steel water sculpture, which fans of the *Doctor Who* spin-off series will recognise as the location of the secret entrance to *Torchwood's* underground headquarters. Testimony to the enduring popularity of the show is an impromptu shrine just around the corner, on the waters' edge at Mermaid Quay, where fans leave messages to one of the show's fictional characters, Ianto Jones. Mermaid Quay's management have got into the spirit of things by adding their own plaque.

Pierhead MUSEUM
(Map p54; www.pierhead.org; Cardiff Bay; ⏲10.30am-4.30pm) FREE One of the waterfront's few Victorian remnants, Pierhead is a red-brick and glazed-terracotta French Gothic confection, built in 1897 with Bute family money in order to impress the maritime traffic. Its ornate clock tower earned it the nickname 'Wales' Big Ben'. Inside there's an interesting little display on the history of the bay (including a short film and a slideshow), some important historical documents and a gallery.

★**Senedd** NOTABLE BUILDING
(Map p54; ☎0300 200 6565; www.assembly.wales; Cardiff Bay; ⏲10.30am-4.30pm) FREE Designed by Lord Richard Rogers (the architect behind London's Lloyd's Building

and Millennium Dome and Paris' Pompidou Centre), the home of the National Assembly for Wales is a striking structure of concrete, slate, glass and steel, with an undulating canopy roof lined with red cedar. It has won awards for its environmentally friendly design, which includes a huge rotating cowl on the roof for power-free ventilation and a gutter system that collects rainwater for flushing the toilets.

The lobby and surrounding area is littered with public artworks, including the 'meeting place', a curved bench made of 3-tonne slate blocks from Blaenau Ffestiniog, provided as a place for protesters to rest their legs.

When they're not on recess, the National Assembly meets in a plenary session from 1.30pm on Tuesday and Wednesday. Seats in the public gallery may be prebooked, although there's usually space if you turn up on the day. Free tours take place at 11am, 2pm and 3pm, except for sitting days when only the 11am tour is held.

Norwegian Church Arts Centre ARTS CENTRE (Map p54; ☎029-2087 7959; www.norwegianchurchcardiff.com; Harbour Dr, Cardiff Bay; ⏲10.30am-4.30pm) **FREE** Looking like it's popped out of the pages of a story book, this white-slatted wooden building with a black

Cardiff Bay

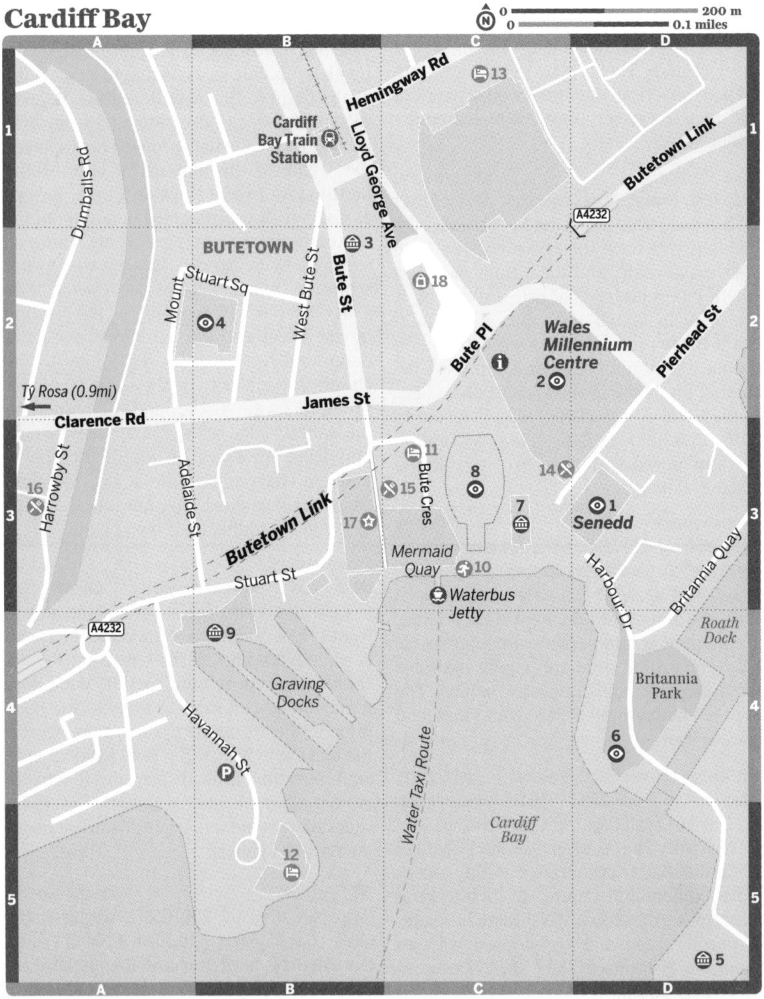

witch's-hat spire was modelled on a traditional Norwegian village church. It was built in 1868 to minister to Norwegian sailors and remained a place of worship until 1974. It has now been reincarnated as an arts centre with a cafe downstairs and a gallery upstairs, hosting exhibitions, concerts, markets and arts courses. Roald Dahl, whose parents were from Norway, was christened here and served as president of the preservation trust that restored and renovated the church.

Cardiff Bay Barrage WATERFRONT

Completed in 1999, this large dam plugged the gap between Penarth and Porth Teigr, containing the waters flowing out from the mouths of the Rivers Taff and Ely, and transforming stinky Cardiff Bay into a freshwater lake. It includes sluice gates to control the water flow, three lock gates to allow passage for boats, and a fish pass that lets migrating salmon and sea trout pass between the rivers and the Bristol Channel.

When it was built, the barrage was a controversial project, as its construction flooded 200 hectares of intertidal mudflats, which, despite their unpleasant aspects, were an important habitat for waterfowl.

A walking and cycling track heads out over the barrage, providing easy access to Penarth (allow 40 minutes if you're walking). This is part of the Bay Trail, a 10km walking and cycling loop that follows the shoreline back to Butetown. Along the way there's a skate park, a playground, some giant boulders of coal, and a series of display boards telling the story of Captain Robert Scott's expedition to the Antarctic, which set sail from Cardiff in 1910. Two years later Scott and his men were dead, having been pipped to the pole by a Norwegian team led by Roald Amundsen.

Doctor Who Experience GALLERY

(Map p54; ☎0844 801 2279; www.doctorwhoexperience.com; Porth Teigr; adult/child £15/11; ⏱10am-5pm (last admission 3.30pm) daily Jul & Aug, Tue-Sun Mar-Jun, Sep & Oct, Wed-Sun Nov-Feb) The huge success of the reinvented classic TV series *Doctor Who,* produced by BBC Wales, has brought Cardiff to the attention of sci-fi fans worldwide. City locations have featured in many episodes; and the first two series of the spin-off *Torchwood* were also set in Cardiff Bay. Capitalising on Timelord tourism, this interactive exhibition is located right next to the BBC studios where the series is filmed – look out for the Tardis hovering outside. Visitors find themselves sucked through a crack in time and thrown into the role of the Doctor's companion. It's great fun – especially when you come face to face with full-size Daleks in full 'ex-ter-min-ate' mode. But don't blink – there are weeping angels about. The 'experience' only takes about 20 minutes but afterwards you're transported into a large two-level warehouse, where you can wander at your leisure around the displays of sets, costumes and props spanning the show's 50-year run.

Cathays & Roath

The bohemian heart of Cardiff lies in the suburbs immediately to the east of the city centre. Proximity to the university makes Cathays' tightly packed Victorian terrace houses popular with students, and while parts of Roath are more well-heeled, the City Rd strip is a little gritty and fabulously multicultural. Few tourists make their way here, but if you want to get a broader taste of Cardiff life, take a stroll along the narrow thoroughfare that starts as City Rd and then morphs into Crwys Rd and then Whitchurch Rd.

Cardiff Bay

Top Sights

1 Senedd D3
2 Wales Millennium Centre C2

Sights

3 Butetown History & Arts Centre B2
4 Coal Exchange B2
5 Doctor Who Experience D5
6 Norwegian Church Arts Centre D4
7 Pierhead C3
8 Roald Dahl Plass C3
9 Techniquest B4

Activities, Courses & Tours

10 Cardiff Sea Safaris C3

Sleeping

11 Jolyons Boutique Hotel C3
12 St David's Hotel & Spa B5
13 Travelodge Cardiff Atlantic Wharf C1

Eating

14 Ffresh C3
15 Moksh C3
16 The Deck A3

Entertainment

17 Glee Club B3

Shopping

18 Craft in the Bay C2

Roath Park PARK

(www.cardiff.gov.uk/parks; Lake Rd, Roath; ⏲7.30am-sunset) Long and narrow Roath Park rivals Bute Park as Cardiff's favourite green space. The third marquess of Bute gifted the land in 1887, and the boggy marsh at its northern end was transformed into a large lake by the erection of a dam. The rest was laid out in the Victorian style, with rose gardens, tree-lined paths, lawns and wild nooks. A cutesy lighthouse was added to the lake in 1915 as a memorial to Captain Robert Falcon Scott.It's a lovely spot for a stroll and a picnic, but if you fancy something a little more diverting, there are cafes, playgrounds, bowling greens, tennis courts and basketball courts, along with boating and fishing opportunities on the lake.

⦿ Llandaff

Llandaff is a peaceful suburb 2 miles northwest of the castle – a former village clustered around a green that has been swallowed up by the expanding city. Buses 25, 62 and 63 run along Cathedral Rd to Llandaff every 10 minutes (twice hourly on Sunday and in the evening).

Llandaff Cathedral CATHEDRAL

(☎029-2056 4554; www.llandaffcathedral.org.uk; Cathedral Green, Llandaff; ⏲7am-6.30pm Sun, 9am-6.30pm Mon-Sat) This venerable cathedral is set in a hollow near the River Taff, on the site of a 6th-century monastery founded by St Teilo. The present building was begun in 1120, but it crumbled throughout the Middle Ages, and during the Reformation and Civil War it was used as an alehouse and then an animal shelter. Derelict by the 18th century, it was largely rebuilt in the 19th, and then repaired again following a German bombing raid in 1941.

The towers at the western end epitomise the cathedral's fragmented history – one was built in the 15th century, the other in the 19th. Inside, a giant arch supports Sir Jacob Epstein's huge aluminium sculpture *Majestas* – its modern style a bold contrast in this gracious, vaulted space. Pre-Raphaelite fans will appreciate the Burne-Jones reredos (screen) in St Dyfrig's chapel and the stained glass by Rossetti and William Morris' company. St Teilo's tomb is located on the south side of the sanctuary.

DON'T MISS

ST FAGANS

Historic buildings from all over the country have been dismantled and re-erected as **St Fagans National History Museum** (☎0300 111 2 333; www.museumwales.ac.uk; St Fagans; parking £5; ⏲10am-5pm) in the semirural surrounds of St Fagans village, five miles west of central Cardiff. More than 40 buildings are on show, including thatched farmhouses, barns, a watermill, a school, an 18th-century Unitarian chapel and shops selling period-appropriate goods. Buses 32, 32A and 320 (£1.80, 26 minutes) head here from Cardiff. By car it's reached from the continuation of Cathedral Rd.

You'll need at least half a day to do the whole complex justice and you could easily spend longer, picnicking in the grounds. It's a great place for kids, with special events in the summer, tractor-and-trailer rides (£1) and an old-time fun fair. Craftspeople are often at hand, demonstrating how blankets, clogs, barrels, tools and cider were once made. In winter, fires are stoked by staff in period costumes.

Highlights include a 16th-century farmhouse imbued with the smell of old timber, beeswax and wood smoke. A row of six miners' cottages from Merthyr Tydfil has been restored and furnished to represent different periods in the town's history, from the austere minimalism of 1805 to all the mod cons of 1985. It took 20 years to move St Teilo's church here (built 1100 to 1520), stone by stone. It's been restored to its original look, before Protestant whitewash covered the vividly painted interior.

St Fagans Castle is no johnny-come-lately to this site. It was originally built by the Normans in 1091 as a motte-and-bailey castle before being rebuilt in stone. The slightly creepy manor house at its heart was grafted on in 1580 and is recognised as one of the finest Elizabethan houses in Wales. The property was donated by the Earl of Plymouth in 1946, along with its lovingly maintained formal gardens and the grounds that encompass the site.

The museum is in the midst of a lengthy multi-million-pound redevelopment, which isn't due to be completed until 2018. Until that time the reproduction Celtic village and indoor galleries are likely to remain closed.

Activities

Cardiff International White Water ADVENTURE SPORTS
(029-2082 9970; www.ciww.com; Watkiss Way; 2hr rafting £40-55; 9am-5pm Thu-Tue, to 8.15pm Wed) This artificial white-water complex offers adrenaline-fuelled rafting, canoeing, kayaking and river-boarding experiences without having to leave the city. There's also indoor surfing, a high-ropes course and a climbing wall, and they run gorge-walking expeditions in the Neath Valley.

Cardiff Sea Safaris CRUISE
(Map p54; 029-2048 7663; www.cardiffseasafaris.co.uk; Mermaid Quay) Offers a 15-minute 'fast blast' within the barrage on a rigid-inflatable boat (£7.50, minimum height 1.2m) along with two-hour 'coastline and island' tours.

Ice Arena Wales ICE SKATING
(029-2078 9630; www.icearenawales.co.uk; Olympian Dr; incl skate hire £7.70-9.70; 10am-3.45pm Mon & Tue, 10am-7pm Wed, 10am-3.45pm & 5.15-8.15pm Thu, 10am-10.30pm Fri, 9.15am-5pm Sat & Sun) This big indoor ice-skating rink offers themed sessions for seniors, tots and students, and roller-disco nights on Thursday and Friday.

Treetop Adventure Golf MINIGOLF
(Map p50; 029-2022 6590; www.adventuregolf.com; L3, St David's; adult/child £7.50/5.50; 11am-10pm) The mega St David's shopping mall (p68) really does have everything – as this jungle-themed minigolf course aptly demonstrates.

Tours

Cardiff History & Hauntings WALKING
(07538 878609; www.cardiffhistory.co.uk) Runs a selection of guided history walks, the most acclaimed of which is the Llandaff Ghost Walk (£10), a two-hour torch-lit stroll through the ruins, lanes and graveyards of old Llandaff. The Margam Ghost Walk (£15) takes in a ruined abbey, Tudor castle and creepy woodland. Private non-ghostly tours include Cardiff's Forgotten Past and Castell Coch (from £30).

Cardiff on Foot WALKING
(07791 803979; www.cardiffwalkingtours.com; adult/child £10/free) Leads guided strolls around the city centre and Cardiff Bay.

Cardiff Cycle Tours CYCLING
(Map p50; 07500 564389; www.cardiffcycletours.com; NosDa, 53-59 Despenser St, Riverside; per person £20) Three-hour guided rides around Cardiff Bay (Docks & The Doctor) or the city centre (Parks & Canals).

See Wales BUS
(029-2022 7227; www.seewales.com; adult/child £48/28) Themed day tours include Mines & Mountains (visiting Big Pit in Blaenavon before heading through Brecon Beacons National Park to the town of Brecon), Romans & Ruins (Caerleon, Tintern Abbey and Raglan Castle) and Golden Gower (Swansea and the Gower Peninsula).

Where When Wales BUS
(07773 786228; www.wherewhenwales.com; adult/child from £48/28) Operates a range of one-day itineraries: South Wales Valleys, Wye Valley, Gower, Wales Borders, West Wales, Mid-Wales. Overnight tours can be customised for groups of eight or more.

City Sightseeing BUS
(Map p50; 07808 713928; www.city-sightseeing.com; adult/child from £13/7.50; 10am-4.30pm) Open-top double-decker tours, departing every 30 minutes from its stop outside Cardiff Castle and making a short circuit of the city. Tickets last 24 hours, and you can hop on and off at any of the stops.

> **OFF THE BEATEN TRACK**
>
> **TAFF TRAIL**
>
> Following canal towpaths, country lanes and disused railway routes, the 55-mile Taff Trail (www.tafftrail.org.uk) walking and cycling route connects Cardiff Bay with Brecon, passing Castell Coch and Merthyr Tydfil on the way. Starting from Brecon will ensure more downhill runs.

Festivals & Events

Six Nations SPORTS
(www.rbs6nations.com; Feb & Mar) The premier European rugby championship, with Wales taking on England, Scotland, Ireland, Italy and France. Cardiff normally hosts two home games – the atmosphere is supercharged. Book accommodation well in advance.

Cardiff Children's Lit Fest LITERATURE
(www.cardiff-events.com; Apr) Nine days of story-telling, reading and activities.

RHS Flower Show Cardiff FAIR
(www.rhs.org.uk; Apr) Three-day flower fest, held in Bute Park.

Festival of Voice MUSIC
(www.festivalofvoice.wales; early Jun) New in 2016, this 10-day festival held in even-numbered years celebrates the human voice across a variety of genres. The stellar starting lineup included gospel choirs, the Welsh National Opera and the likes of Van Morrison, John Cale, Rufus Wainwright, Bryn Terfel, Anna Calvi, Femi Kuti and Ronnie Spector.

Cardiff International Food & Drink Festival FOOD & DRINK
(www.cardiff-events.com; early Jul) Held over a long weekend (Friday to Sunday), this festival sees Roald Dahl Plass filled with producers' stalls, a farmers market, street food and craft stalls.

Welsh Proms MUSIC
(www.stdavidshallcardiff.co.uk; mid-Jul) A week of classical concerts at St David's Hall.

Everyman Open Air Theatre Festival THEATRE
(www.everymanfestival.co.uk; Jul & Aug) Five weeks of theatre, held in Sophia Gardens.

Pride Cymru GAY & LESBIAN
(www.pridecymru.co.uk; mid-Aug) Cardiff's lesbian, gay, bisexual and transgender pride festival includes a street parade and a ticketed day-long celebration in Bute Park.

Grand Medieval Mêlée CARNIVAL
(www.cardiffcastle.com; mid-Aug) A weekend of armoured knights engaging in drills, swordplay, mass battles and general medieval mayhem in Cardiff Castle.

Classic Motor Boat Rally BOATS
(www.cmba-uk.com; mid-Aug) A three-day convergence of racy boats in Cardiff Bay.

Diffusion: Cardiff International Festival of Photography ART
(www.diffusionfestival.org; Oct) A month-long festival of exhibitions, screenings, performance and events, held in various venues.

Cardiff's Winter Wonderland CARNIVAL
(www.cardiff-events.com; mid-Nov–early Jan) Makes the most of the cold weather with an outdoor ice-skating rink and fun fair on the City Hall lawn.

Sleeping

Cardiff has Wales' broadest range of accommodation, including luxury hotels, personable guesthouses and some great hostels.

Most places have higher rates on Friday and Saturday nights. It can be almost impossible to find a bed anywhere near the city on

City Walk
Historic Cardiff

START CARDIFF CROWN COURT
END THE HAYES
LENGTH 1.5 MILES; 90 MINUTES

One of the most elegant administrative quarters in Britain, Cardiff's Civic Centre encompasses formal parks and a grand array of early-20th-century buildings, all dressed in gleaming white Portland stone. Start outside the neoclassical 1 **Cardiff Crown Court**, continue past the baroque-style 2 **City Hall** and turn right and into 3 **Gorsedd Gardens**. Here you'll find a sweet little statue simply titled *Girl* and a gorsedd stone circle, raised for the National Eisteddfod in 1899.

Head towards the classical facade of the 4 **National Museum Cardiff** (p45) and then turn the corner into Park Place. Next is the imposing main building of 5 **Cardiff University**. Head through its black gates and enter via the central door into the short corridor which leads to the foyer (if it's after hours you'll need to circle around the building). In the centre is a white marble statue of John Viriamu Jones, the first principal of the university college.

Head through the door on the other side, curve to the left, cross the road and enter 6 **Alexandra Gardens**. Amid the formal lawns and colourful flowerbeds is an interesting set of war memorials. The standing stone mounted on a pedestal to your left was taken from the battlefield at Mt Harriet in the Falkland Islands, and remembers the Britons killed in the 1982 war. A little further, another standing stone is dedicated to the Welsh volunteers who fought against fascism in the Spanish Civil War. In the centre of the park is the Welsh National War Memorial, erected in 1928 in memory of WWI's dead. A circular colonnade of white Corinthian columns surrounds a statue of a naked angel with a sword, flanked by three servicemen (representing the army, navy and air force) holding aloft wreathes.

Exit the gardens onto King Edward VII Ave. Straight ahead is the old 7 **Glamorgan County Council Building** (now part of Cardiff University), fronted with more Corinthian columns and elaborate statuary (Minerva, to the left, represents min-

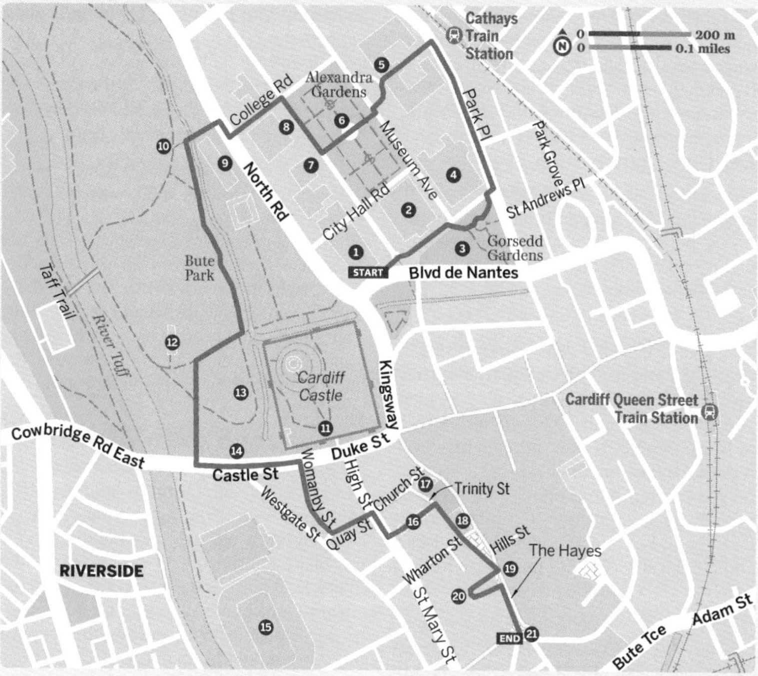

ing; Neptune, on the right, navigation). The 8 **Bute Building**, to the right, also belongs to the university and features Doric columns and a red dragon on its roof.

When you turn left onto College Rd you'll see, straight ahead of you, the very impressive new home of the 9 **Royal Welsh College of Music & Drama** (p67). Cross towards it, turn right and then left past the curved timber-clad end of the building and enter 10 **Bute Park** (p49). Cross the little bridge, turn left and follow the canal towards the rear of 11 **Cardiff Castle** (p48). At the next bridge take the path to the right; you'll shortly come to the remains of 12 **Blackfriars Priory** (p50; on your right) and another circle of 13 **gorsedd stones** (p49; across the lawns to your left).

Veer left and exit through the West Lodge gate. Turn left on Castle St and take a look at the creatures perched on top of the 14 **Animal Wall** (p50). Originally positioned by the castle's main gate, the animals were moved here after WWI. Cross the road and continue until you reach Womanby St, which is lined with warehouses, many of which have been converted into bars. Its unusual name is derived either from Old German meaning 'the strangers' quarter' or a Viking word meaning 'quarter of the houndsman'. As you head down the street you will see 15 **Principality Stadium** (p51) on your right.

Take a left on Quay St; Cardiff's original quay stood here before the River Taff was realigned to make way for the railway in 1860. Turn right on St Mary St and then left to enter 16 **Cardiff Market** (p68). This cast-iron market hall has been selling fresh produce and hardware since 1891. There's an old market office and a clock tower in the centre.

Exit on the far side on Trinity St and stop to admire the tower of 17 **St John the Baptist Church** (p52). Turn right and head towards the beautiful sandstone 18 **Yr Hen Lyfrgell** (p52), which houses the Cardiff Story museum.

Continue down the street and into the heart of the Hayes. The name is derived from a Norman-French word relating to the small garden enclosures that would have once stood here. It's now Cardiff's main shopping strip, and deliciously car-free. 19 **St David's** (p68) mall occupies the entire left-hand flank, but duck into the Victorian-era 20 **Morgan Quarter** (p69) on your right. Finish back on the Hayes under the giant hoop and arrow of the sculpture 21 **Alliance**.

big sporting weekends, especially rugby internationals, so keep an eye on the fixtures and choose another date or book well in advance. It's sometimes so bad that hotels as far away as Swansea get swamped with the overflow.

City Centre

The central city has the best of both the budget and the upmarket accommodation. It's the perfect locale if you're planning a few nights on the tiles, but if you're a light sleeper it can be noisy.

★ Safehouse HOSTEL £
(Map p50; ☎029-2037 2833; www.safehousehostel.com; 3 Westgate St; dm/s/d without bathroom from £14/35/37; 📶) There aren't too many hostels with a grand Victorian sitting room to rival Safehouse's. Built in 1889, this lovely red-brick office building has been thoughtfully converted into a boutique hostel with private rooms and four- to 12-bed dorms. Each bunk bed has its own built-in locker and electrical socket. It's on a busy road, so earplugs are a sensible precaution.

Cardiff Central YHA HOSTEL £
(☎0800 0191 700; www.yha.org.uk; 1 East Tyndall St; dm/r from £15/39; 📶) Until recently this slick establishment was a Mercure hotel, and aside from converting some of the bedrooms into dorms and adding a guest kitchen, the YHA have had the good sense to leave it substantially unchanged. All rooms have modern hotel-style bathrooms and there's plenty of parking. It's flanked by busy roads, but not far from the city centre.

Premier Inn Cardiff City Centre HOTEL £
(Map p50; ☎029-2034 9910; www.premierinn.com; 10 Churchill Way; r from £40; 📶) The Cardiff branch of Britain's biggest chain has 200 beds in a squat mirror-clad former office tower, right in the city centre. It's not flash, but it's comfortable, clean and terrific value – although you'll need to book early and pay in advance to secure the cheapest rates. Request a higher floor for a quieter room.

Mrs Potts HOSTEL £
(Map p50; ☎029-2034 4490; www.mrspottsbackpackers.co.uk; 109 St Mary St; dm from £17; 📶) Despite being on Cardiff's booziest strip, Mrs Potts is far from a party hostel. It occupies a lovely old red-brick building and is full of thoughtful touches such as reading lights, USB ports and privacy curtains in the custom-built bunks. Showers are of the annoying, nonadjustable, push-button variety, but everything is clean and well kept.

Hotel One Hundred HOTEL £
(☎07916 888423; www.hotelonehundred.com; 100 Newport Rd, Adamsdown; s/d from £50/55; P📶)

Pontcanna & Canton

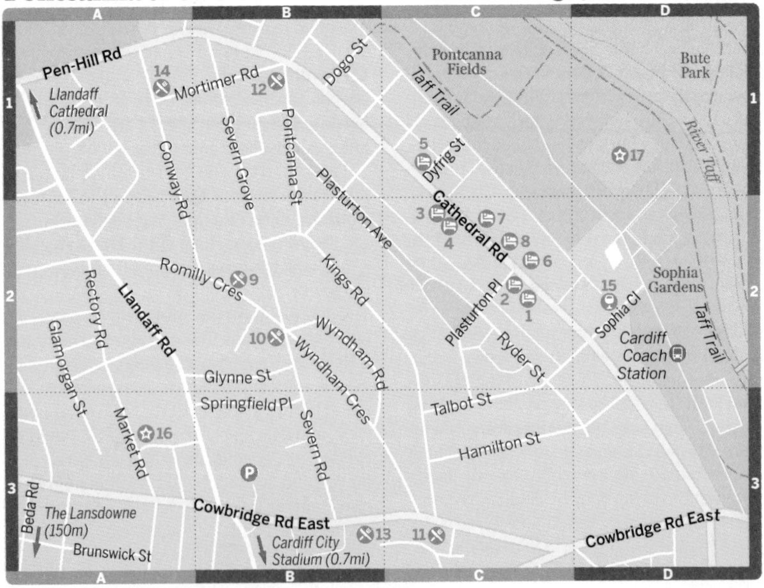

Patterned metallic wallpaper and chandeliers add a touch of glam to the rooms of this small B&B-like hotel. It's on a busy arterial road, so expect some street noise in the front rooms. A continental breakfast is included in the rates. A minimum two-night stay applies, but one-night bookings are accepted for any unsold rooms three days prior to arrival.

★**Park Plaza** HOTEL £££
(Map p50; ☎029-2011 1111; www.parkplazacardiff.com; Greyfriars Rd; r £119-189;) Luxurious without being remotely stuffy, the Plaza has all the five-star facilities you'd expect from an upmarket business-orientated hotel. The snug reception sets the scene, with a gas fire blazing along one wall and comfy wingback chairs. The rear rooms have leafy views over the Civic Centre.

Pontcanna & Canton

Long, leafy Cathedral Rd is lined with B&Bs and small hotels, nearly all of them in restored Victorian town houses. It's only a 15- to 20-minute walk from the city centre, or a £10 taxi ride from the train or bus stations. Street parking is unrestricted but can be tricky to find during working hours.

★**Number 62** GUESTHOUSE ££
(Map p60; ☎07974 571348; www.number62.com; 62 Cathedral Rd, Pontcanna; s/d from £68/77;) The only thing stopping us calling Number 62 a B&B is that breakfast is only offered as an add-on. The cosy, comfortable rooms come with thoughtful extras such as body lotion, make-up wipes and cotton buds. It also has one of the most lovingly tended front gardens of all of the converted town houses on this strip.

★**Lincoln House** HOTEL ££
(Map p60; ☎029-2039 5558; www.lincolnhotel.co.uk; 118 Cathedral Rd, Pontcanna; r £90-150; P) Walking a middle line between a large B&B and a small hotel, Lincoln House is a generously proportioned Victorian property with heraldic emblems in the stained-glass windows of its sitting room, and a separate bar. For added romance, book a four-poster room.

Saco Cardiff APARTMENT ££
(Map p60; ☎0845 122 0405; www.sacoapartments.co.uk; 76 Cathedral Rd, Pontcanna; apt from £117; P) This large town house has been given a contemporary makeover and converted into serviced apartments, complete with comfortable lounges and fitted kitchens. They're set up for longer visits but one-night stays are possible midweek. The two-bedroom apartments are good value for families with kids; there's an extra sofa bed in the lounge.

Beaufort Guest House B&B ££
(Map p60; ☎029-2023 7003; www.beauforthousecardiff.co.uk; 65 Cathedral Rd, Pontcanna; s/d from £57/82; P) Despite a thorough refurbishment, the Beaufort retains an old-fashioned Victorian atmosphere, with period-style furniture, gilt mirrors, heavy drapes and even a portrait of the old Queen herself. The breakfast room is ready for royalty, with candlesticks and blue-and-white china adding a touch of grandeur.

Town House B&B ££
(Map p60; ☎029-2023 9399; www.thetownhousecardiff.co.uk; 70 Cathedral Rd, Pontcanna; s/d £55/73; P) Succinctly named, this elegant Victorian town house on the Cathedral Rd strip has welcoming owners and a relaxed vibe. It retains lots of period features, including original fireplaces, stained-glass windows and a tiled hallway with busy wallpaper. The rooms are more restrained.

Courtfield Hotel B&B ££
(Map p60; ☎029-2022 7701; www.courtfieldhotel.com; 101 Cathedral Rd; s/d from £35/70;) It's the friendliness of hosts, Keith and Norman, and the hearty breakfasts that distinguish this Victorian town house B&B from the Cathedral Rd pack. The decor is suitably

Pontcanna & Canton

Sleeping

1	Beaufort Guest House	C2
2	Cathedral 73	C2
3	Church Guest House	C2
4	Courtfield Hotel	C2
5	Lincoln House	C1
6	Number 62	C2
7	Saco Cardiff	C2
8	Town House	C2

Eating

9	Arbennig	B2
10	Bully's	B2
11	Chai Street	C3
12	Fish at 85	B1
13	Purple Poppadom	B3
14	The Conway	A1

Drinking & Nightlife

15	Y Mochyn Du	D2

Entertainment

16	Chapter	A3
17	SWALEC Stadium	D1

old-fashioned, with moulded cornices, chandeliers and heavy red carpets.

Church Guest House B&B ££
(Map p60; 029-2034 0881; www.churchguesthouse.co.uk; 109 Cathedral Rd; s/d from £45/70) Not as old-fashioned and frilly as many of the grande dames on Cathedral Rd, Church has tidy guest rooms with simple decor and older-style bathrooms. Unlike most of their competitors, they also have single rooms and single rates for double rooms. A continental breakfast is included in the price, but you'll need to pay extra for a cooked option.

Cathedral 73 B&B £££
(Map p60; 029-2023 5005; www.cathedral73.com; 73 Cathedral Rd; r/ste from £150/225; P) This upmarket boutique B&B has nine rooms, suites and apartments in a beautifully restored Victorian town house occupying a prominent corner on the Cathedral Rd strip. Downstairs there's a chichi tea room and piano bar, and there's a pretty garden terrace at the rear.

Riverside & Grangetown

★**River House** HOSTEL £
(Map p50; 029-2039 9810; www.riverhousebackpackers.com; 59 Fitzhamon Embankment, Riverside; dm/s/d incl breakfast from £17/40/42; @) Professionally run by a helpful young brother-and-sister team, the River House has a well-equipped kitchen, small garden and cosy TV lounge. The private rooms are basically small dorm rooms and share the same bathrooms. A free breakfast of cereal, toast, pastries and fruit is provided.

NosDa HOSTEL £
(Map p50; 029-2037 8866; www.nosda.co.uk; 53-59 Despenser St, Riverside; dm from £15, s/d from £45/50, without bathroom £35/44; P@) Directly across the river from Principality Stadium, NosDa ('goodnight' in Welsh) has bright painted rooms above a rocking beer-lovers' bar. Free basic breakfasts and parking make this an appealing budget option.

Tŷ Rosa B&B ££
(0845 643 9962; www.tyrosa.com; 118 Clive St, Grangetown; s/d from £49/59, without bathroom £39/47;) A good 30 minutes' walk from either the bay or central Cardiff (follow the river south, turn right on to Penarth Rd and then left after 650m), this gay-friendly B&B is noted for its sumptuous breakfasts and affable hosts. The thoughtfully equipped rooms are split between the main house and an annexe across the road. Some rooms share bathrooms.

Cardiff Bay

Travelodge Cardiff Atlantic Wharf HOTEL £
(Map p54; 020-3195 4533; www.travelodge.co.uk; Hemingway Rd; r from £60; P) It's the location that makes this the best of the five no-frills Travelodge hotels in Cardiff: it's extremely handy for Cardiff Bay and right by a train station that's only one stop from the city centre. Rooms are clean and comfortable, if predictably generic.

A Space in the City ACCOMMODATION SERVICES ££
(03333 443 606; www.aspaceinthecity.co.uk; apt from £76) This agency lets out luxury, short-stay apartments in the city centre, along the docks and in Cardiff Bay; the best is Quayside in Bute St. Minimum two-night stay.

St David's Hotel & Spa HOTEL ££
(Map p54; 029-2045 4045; www.thestdavidshotel.com; Havannah St, Cardiff Bay; r/ste from £109/166; @) A glittering, glassy tower topped with a sail-like flourish, St David's is already starting to look a little dated. The rooms, however, have been recently renovated and almost all of them have a small private balcony with a bay view. Facilities include a restaurant, bar and day spa.

Jolyons Boutique Hotel HOTEL ££
(Map p54; 029-2048 8775; www.jolyons.co.uk; 5 Bute Cres, Cardiff Bay; r £75-135;) A touch of Georgian elegance in the heart of Cardiff Bay, Jolyons has seven individually designed rooms combining antique furniture with contemporary colours. The front rooms face towards the Millennium Centre, while one of the rear rooms has its own terrace. On the downside, it's not permanently staffed and some guests have reported difficulty getting checked in.

Eating

As Cardiff has become more glossy, cosmopolitan and multicultural, so have its eateries. Perhaps the most dynamic segment of the city's food scene belongs to its Indian community, where a select group of restaurants has been confounding expectations and accumulating plaudits.

City Centre

Pettigrew Tea Rooms CAFE £
(Map p50; 029-2023 5486; www.pettigrew-tearooms.com; West Lodge, Castle St; mains £5-8;

8.30am-5.30pm) Cuppas and cakes are served on delicate china at this perfectly dahling little tea room within the crenellated confines of Bute Park's 1863 gatehouse. Cucumber sandwiches and cream scones are the customary accompaniment to the extensive range of tea on offer – or try the ploughman's platter if you're after something more hearty.

Coffee Barker CAFE £

(Map p50; Castle Arcade; mains £5.50-8.50; 8.30am-5.30pm Mon-Sat, 10.30am-4.30pm Sun;) Slink into an armchair, sip on a silky coffee and snack on salmon scrambled eggs or a sandwich in what is Cardiff's coolest cafe. There are plenty of magazines and toys to keep everyone amused.

Restaurant Minuet ITALIAN £

(Map p50; 029-2034 1794; www.restaurantminuet.co.uk; 42 Castle Arcade; mains £4.50-11; 11am-4.30pm Mon-Sat;) It may look humble, but this little eatery has a reputation for cheap and cheerful, simple Italian food. The menu has a good vegetarian selection, including plenty of meat-free pasta options.

Goat Major PUB FOOD £

(Map p50; 029-2033 7161; www.sabrain.com/goatmajor; 33 High St; pies £7.50; kitchen noon-6pm Mon-Sat, to 4pm Sun;) A solidly traditional wood-lined pub with armchairs, a fireplace and Brains beers on tap. The Goat Major's gastronomic contribution comes in the form of its selection of home-made savoury pot pies served with chips.

Little Man Coffee Co. CAFE £

(Map p50; www.littlemancoffee.co.uk; Bridge St; mains £3-5; 7am-9pm Mon-Sat, 8am-5pm Sun;) With mismatched and recycled furniture, this hipsterish corner cafe serves craft beer into the early evening. Food is limited to the likes of filled croissants, toasted sandwiches, soup and smashed avocado on toast. If you're on a tight budget, the serve-yourself toast and cereal is a good way to start the day.

The Plan CAFE £

(Map p50; 029-2039 8764; www.theplancafe.co.uk; 28 Morgan Arcade; mains £4-9; 8.30am-5pm;) Serving quite possibly Wales' best coffee, this appealing cafe also delivers tasty lunch fare, such as baguettes and salads. Grab a window seat and a newspaper and caffeinate to your racing heart's content.

Cafe Cittá ITALIAN ££

(Map p50; 029-2022 4040; www.cafecitta.com; 4 Church St; mains £7.50-13; noon-9pm Tue-Sat;) Once you're lured through the door by the delicious scents wafting out of the wood-fired oven, you won't want to escape this little slice of *la dolce vita*. The authentic *linguine alla puttanesca* is proof that some traditions shouldn't be messed with. There are only a handful of tables, so book ahead.

Madame Fromage DELI, CAFE ££

(Map p50; 029-2064 4888; www.madamefromage.co.uk; 21-25 Castle Arcade; mains £6-15; 10am-5.30pm Mon-Sat, noon-5pm Sun) One of Cardiff's best delicatessens, with a wide range of charcuterie and French and Welsh cheese, the Madame also has a cafe with tables spilling into the arcade. Here you can read French newspapers and eat a mixture of Breton and Welsh dishes, including rarebit, lamb *cawl* (a stewlike soup) and *bara brith* (fruitcake).

Potted Pig MODERN BRITISH ££

(Map p50; 029-2022 4817; www.thepottedpig.com; 27 High St; mains £18-20; noon-2pm & 7-9pm Tue-Sat, noon-2pm Sun) Located in the vaulted basement of a former bank, the Potted Pig is a thoroughly British bistro, serving the likes of ham hock, quail, Welsh lamb and steak. It's also known for its vast range of gins and speciality tonics.

Zerodegrees ITALIAN ££

(Map p50; 029-2022 9494; www.zerodegrees.co.uk; 27 Westgate St; mains £9-15; noon-midnight;) Within the factory-like setting of an art nouveau garage, this microbrewery and restaurant combines all-day dining with artisan-crafted beers. Excellent food options include a United Nations of pizza toppings (Jamaican, Mexican, Chinese), pasta, salads and kilo pots of mussels (the house specialty).

Casanova ITALIAN £££

(Map p50; 029-2034 4044; www.casanovacardiff.co.uk; 13 Quay St; 2-/3-course lunch £14/18, dinner £25/30, vegetarian £20/25; noon-2.30pm & 5.30-10pm Mon-Sat;) Rather than offering generic Italian dishes or the specialities of just one region, this little charmer offers a selection of authentic regional dishes from all over Italy. The result is a varied menu with half-a-dozen options for each course, including more unusual dishes such as ox-tongue terrine and truffled goats cheese with honey.

Park House MODERN EUROPEAN £££

(Map p50; 029-2022 4343; www.parkhouserestaurant.co.uk; 20 Park Pl; mains £26-28, 2-/3-course lunch £21/26; 11am-4pm & 5.30-10pm

Tue-Sat, noon-4pm Sun;) The ambience is rather stuffy, but the menu at this private members' club is anything but conservative, adding subtle Asian flavours to classic European dishes. Dress up and push the buzzer for admittance.

Pontcanna & Canton

Chai Street INDIAN £

(Map p60; 029-2022 8888; www.chaistreet.com; 153 Cowbridge Rd East, Canton; mains £8-9; noon-11pm;) Colourful glass lamps and Bollywood posters set the scene for this zippy little eatery specialising in Indian street food. It doesn't take bookings and it's insanely popular, but the tasty thali and biryani are well worth waiting for – provided you don't end up seated in the rear corridor by the toilet.

★ Purple Poppadom INDIAN ££

(Map p60; 029-2022 0026; www.purplepoppadom.com; 185a Cowbridge Rd East, Canton; mains £13-18, 2-course lunch £11; noon-2pm & 5.30-11pm Tue-Sat, 1-9pm Sun) Trailblazing a path for 'Nouvelle Indian' cuisine, chef Anand George's kitchen offers its own unique take on regional dishes from all over the subcontinent – from Kashmir to Kerala. Meals are thoughtfully constructed and artfully presented.

Bully's FRENCH ££

(Map p60; 029-2022 1905; www.bullysrestaurant.co.uk; 5 Romilly Cres, Pontcanna; mains £19-22; noon-2pm & 6.30-9pm Mon-Sat, noon-3.30pm Sun;) An assortment of odd things (bank notes, receipts from famous restaurants etc) cover the walls of this cosy neighbourhood bistro, giving little indication of the high-quality French-style dishes served here. The set three-course lunches for two are great value (£35 all up, including half a bottle of wine).

Arbennig EUROPEAN ££

(Map p60; 029-2034 1264; www.arbennig.co.uk; 6-10 Romilly Cres, Pontcanna; mains £14-20, 2-course lunch £13; 11.30am-2.30pm & 6-9.30pm Tue-Sat, 11.30am-4pm Sun;) The bright lighting and cheap napkins take a little of the shine off, but this otherwise smart restaurant (the name means 'Special') does a good line in well-cooked classics. Think light-as-air gnocchi, lamb chops, burgers, steak, grilled fish and a delicious pannacotta to round it off.

The Conway PUB FOOD ££

(Map p60; 029-2022 4373; www.knifeandforkfood.co.uk; 58 Conway Rd, Pontcanna; mains £10-15; noon-11pm;) With a sun-trap front terrace and a pleasantly laid-back vibe, this wonderful corner pub chalks up its delicious seasonal, fresh and local offerings daily. Kids get their own menu, while the grownups can ponder the large selection of wines served by the glass.

★ Fish at 85 SEAFOOD £££

(Map p60; 029-2023 5666; www.fishat85.co.uk; 85 Pontcanna Rd, Pontcanna; mains £19-24; noon-2.30pm & 6-9pm Tue-Sat) By day a fishmongers (hence the lingering smell), by night an elegant restaurant with Cape Cod-ish decor and candles floating in water-filled jars, Fish at 85 is Cardiff's premier spot for a seafood dinner. The menu cherry-picks the best of the day's catch, offering half-a-dozen varieties, exquisitely cooked and in huge portions.

Riverside & Grangetown

★ Riverside Market MARKET £

(Map p50; www.riversidemarket.org.uk; Fitzhamon Embankment, Riverside; 10am-2pm Sun;) What it lacks in size, Riverside Market makes up for in sheer yumminess, its stalls heaving with cooked meals, cakes, cheese, organic meat, charcuterie and bread. There are lots of options for vegetarians and an excellent coffee stall.

Cardiff Bay

The Deck CAFE £

(Map p54; 029-2115 0385; www.thedeckcoffeehouse.co.uk; 20 Harrowby St, Butetown; mains £3-8; 9.30am-4pm Mon, to 5.30pm Tue-Sat) With roses on the wallpaper and pastel bunting strung across the ceiling, this 'coffee house and cakery' has gone for the full nana-chic look in its subterranean dining room (there's no deck, by the way). If you can divert your eyes from the drool-inducing cupcake display, you'll find that they also serve cooked breakfasts, omelettes, sandwiches, salads and hot baguettes.

Moksh INDIAN ££

(Map p54; 029-2049 8120; www.moksh.co.uk; Ocean Bldg, Bute Cres, Cardiff Bay; mains £6-18; noon-2.30pm & 6-11pm;) Moksh's tangerine walls and Buddhist imagery provide ample warning that this is not your typical Indian restaurant. A Goan influence pervades but an adventurous approach incorporates snatches of Chinese, Tibetan, Indonesian and even Moroccan cuisine.

Ffresh
WELSH **££**

(Map p54; ☑029-2063 6465; www.ffresh.org.uk; Wales Millennium Centre, Cardiff Bay; 2-/3-course lunch £17/20, dinner £20/24; ☺noon-9pm Mon-Sat, to 3.30pm Sun; 🅰) Overlooking the Senedd from the glassed-in end of the Millennium Centre, Ffresh has the Welshiest of settings and a menu to match. Local, seasonal produce features heavily in a creative menu that includes some traditional favourites, such as Welsh lamb and cheese.

✕ Cathays & Roath

★ Oz Urfa
MIDDLE EASTERN **£**

(☑029-2048 8739; 156 City Rd, Roath; mains £8-12; ☺10am-11pm) Brightly lit, cheap and exceedingly cheerful, this humble eatery specialises in the food of 'Turkey, Mesopotamia and the Mediterranean'. This translates as delicious mezze, whole roast lamb, fish dishes and shish kebabs cooked over a charcoal grill. Serves are enormous: if you're not too hungry, consider sharing one main between two.

★ Mint & Mustard
INDIAN **££**

(☑029-2062 0333; www.mintandmustard.com; 134 Whitchurch Rd, Cathays; mains £8.25-15; ☺noon-2pm & 5-11pm; 🖉) Specialising in seafood dishes from India's southern state of Kerala, this excellent restaurant combines an upmarket ambience with attentive service and delicious, beautifully presented food. If you're not enticed by the lobster, prawn and fish dishes, there are plenty of vegetarian options and an excellent crusted lamb biryani.

Milgi
VEGETARIAN **££**

(☑029-2047 3150; www.milgilounge.com; 213 City Rd, Roath; mains £10; ☺11am-9.30pm; 🛜🖉) 🍃 A kooky-chic haven for the city's vegerati, Milgi serves a seasonal menu of meat-free salads, pies, burgers and tortilla stacks, including options for the discerning gluten-free vegan. If you're just after a drink, make for the sofa-filled yurt in the back garden.

🍷 Drinking & Nightlife

Cardiff is a prodigiously boozy city. Friday and Saturday nights see the city centre invaded by hordes of generally good-humoured, beered-up lads and ladettes tottering from bar to club to kebab shop, whatever the weather (someone fetch that young woman a coat!). It's not as tacky as it sounds – a lively alternative scene, some swish bars and a swath of old-fashioned pubs keep things interesting.

Try the local Brains SA (meaning Special Ale, Same Again or Skull Attack, depending on how many you've had), brewed by the same family concern since 1882.

🍷 City Centre

Gwdihŵ
BAR

(Map p50; ☑029-2039 7933; www.gwdihw.co.uk; 6 Guildford Cres; ☺3pm-midnight Sun-Wed, noon-2am Thu-Sat) The last word in Cardiff hipsterdom, this cute little bar has an eclectic line-up of entertainment (comedy, DJs and lots of live music, including microfestivals that spill over into the car park) but it's a completely charming place to stop for a drink at any time. If you're wondering about the name, it's the Welsh take on an owl's call.

Buffalo Bar
BAR

(Map p50; ☑029-2031 0312; www.buffalocardiff. co.uk; 11 Windsor Pl; ☺noon-3am) A haven for cool kids about town, the laid-back Buffalo Bar features retro furniture, tasty food, life-affirming cocktails and alternative tunes. There's a small beer garden at the rear, while upstairs a roster of cutting-edge indie bands takes to the stage.

Full Moon
BAR

(Map p50; ☑029-2037 3022; www.thefullmooncardiff.com; 1/3 Womanby St; ☺7pm-midnight Sun-Wed, to 3am Thu, 5pm-4am Fri & Sat) There are no pretences at this friendly, grungy rock bar. Sample from the large selection of rum, whisky and vodka, or try the 'jar of green shit' if you dare. On weekends DJs spin a kooky but highly danceable blend of ska, funk, Motown, soul, punk and indie pop while, upstairs, the Moon Club thrums to live bands.

Pen & Wig
PUB

(Map p50; ☑029-2037 1217; www.penandwigcardiff.co.uk; 1 Park Grove; ☺11.30am-midnight) Latin legal phrases are printed on the walls of this solidly traditional pub, but there's nothing stuffy about the large beer garden or the entertainment roster (open-mic Mondays, quiz Tuesdays, live-music Saturdays). *Caveat emptor:* the impressive range of ales may induce *mens rea* the morning after.

Porter's
BAR

(Map p50; ☑029-2125 0666; www.porterscardiff.com; Bute Tce; ☺5pm-12.30am Mon-Thu, to 3am Fri, noon-3am Sat, to midnight Sun) There's something on most nights at this friendly attitude-free bar, whether it's a quiz, live music, comedy, theatre or a movie screening (there's a little cinema attached). There's a surprisingly wonderful urban beer garden out the back, under the shadow of the railway tracks.

Urban Tap House BAR

(Map p50; ☎029-2039 9557; www.urbantaphouse.co.uk; 25 Westgate St; ⏲noon-2am) A beer-lovers' nirvana, this sprawling grungy-chic corner bar offers a good selection of brews in kegs, casks and bottles. Interesting graffiti-style art covers the walls.

Cambrian Tap PUB

(Map p50; ☎029-2064 4952; www.sabrain.com; St Mary St; ⏲noon-11pm) Cardiff's main brewery's unlikely contribution to the craft-beer revolution, this charming old-style corner pub serves 18 draught taps and a rotating selection of guest ales and local boutique beers. If you're peckish, try one of their gourmet meat pies.

10 Feet Tall BAR

(Map p50; ☎029-2022 8883; www.10feettallcardiff.com; 12 Church St; ⏲3pm-3am Mon-Thu, noon-3am Fri-Sun) This hip three-storey venue merges a cafe, cocktail bar and live-music venue. Good-looking bartenders swish together two-for-£10 cocktails during daily happy hours.

City Arms PUB

(Map p50; www.thecityarmscardiff.com; 10-12 Quay St; ⏲11am-11pm Mon-Wed, to 2am Thu-Sun; 📶) What's affectionately known in these parts as an 'old man's pub' – despite it attracting just as many young geezers – the City Arms is an unpretentious kind of place, its walls lined with rugby memorabilia and beer labels. It gets predictably packed out on rugby weekends, but on weekday afternoons it's a quiet place for a pint.

Lab 22 COCKTAIL BAR

(Map p50; ☎029-2039 9997; www.lab22cardiff.com; 22 Caroline St; ⏲5pm-1am Sun-Fri, to 2.30am Sat) The decor's all over the place (prohibition speakeasy meets Buddha bar meets mad scientist's lair) but the bar staff are slick enough to distract from any design misdemeanours, and the cocktails are excellent. Some nights a live jazz band adds to the ambience.

Nine Yards BAR, CAFE

(Map p50; www.facebook.com/NineYardsCardiff; 94 St Mary St; ⏲8am-late) Billing itself as a Prosecco bar, patisserie and Peroni specialist, Nine Yards serves lip-smacking sweet treats (the cannoli are particularly good) and coffee along with a long list of Italian wines and lagers. Raw pine walls and packing-case shelving lend it a designer-rustic look.

Yard BAR

(Map p50; ☎029-2022 7577; www.yardbarkitchen.co.uk; 42-43 St Mary St; ⏲9am-11pm Sun-Thu, to 2am Fri & Sat; 📶👪) Occupying the site of an 18th-century brewery, Yard sports an industrial-chic decor of stainless steel, polished copper pipes and zinc ducting, with clubby sofas and plenty of tables. Outdoor seating, food and a child-friendly policy pull in families during the day, while live bands entertain on weekends.

29 Park Place BAR

(Map p50; ☎029-2039 7842; www.29parkplace.com; 29 Park Pl; ⏲10am-midnight) We rate the cocktails and ambience much more highly than the food at this hip cafe-bar directly opposite the National Museum. Slink into the comfy chairs, shoot a round of pool or head out to the rear garden for an alfresco beer.

Retro CLUB

(Map p50; ☎029-2034 4688; www.retrocardiff.co.uk; 7 Mill Lane; ⏲5pm-4am Wed, Fri & Sat, to 2am Thu) The 'home of the '90s vibe' is exactly what you'd expect it to be. If you were there in the Britpop heyday, prepare to bop around your handbag all night long.

Pontcanna & Canton

The Lansdowne PUB

(☎029-2022 1312; www.thelansdownecardiff.co.uk; cnr Lansdowne & Beda Rds, Canton; ⏲noon-11pm) With charmingly scruffy rooms sprawling around a central bar, the Lansdowne has an esteemed reputation for its food and for its range of craft beer and cider. They even run their own mini beer festival every June.

Y Mochyn Du PUB

(Map p60; ☎029-2037 1599; www.ymochyndu.com; Sophia Close; ⏲noon-11pm) Right by SWALEC Stadium, the 'Black Pig' is both the de facto cricketer's pub and one of the few places in Cardiff where you might hear Welsh spoken. There's a big variety of beer on tap, including a range of craft ales. Once you've checked out the cricketing memorabilia, head outside to the city's best beer garden.

☆ Entertainment

Pick up a copy of Buzz (www.buzzmag.co.uk), a free monthly magazine with up-to-date entertainment listings, available from the tourist office, bars, theatres and the like. The staff at tourist offices can also help out with recommendations.

Live Music

Massive rock and pop concerts are staged at Principality Stadium (p51). For a more intimate experience, try one of the many bars hosting live bands, such as Gwdihŵ (p65), Buffalo Bar (p65), 10 Feet Tall and Full Moon (p65). Most major arts companies are now based at the Wales Millennium Centre (p53). Regular classical concerts are held in Llandaff Cathedral (p56) and St John the Baptist Church (p52).

★Clwb Ifor Bach LIVE MUSIC
(Map p50; ☎029-2023 2199; www.clwb.net; 11 Womanby St) The legendary Clwb has broken many a Welsh band since it first opened its doors as a Welsh-language social club in 1983, building a reputation as Cardiff's most important indie music venue. It now hosts bands performing in many tongues – from young upstarts to more established acts – along with regular club nights.

Cardiff University Students' Union LIVE MUSIC
(Map p50; ☎029-2078 1400; www.cardiffstudents.com; Park Pl) The students' union hosts regular live gigs by big-name bands, usually of an alternative bent, in its four venues. It also hosts regular comedy, club and quiz nights.

St David's Hall CLASSICAL MUSIC
(Map p50; ☎029-2087 8444; www.stdavidshallcardiff.co.uk; The Hayes) The National Concert Hall of Wales, this is the home of the Welsh Proms in July and a full roster of classical music performances and comedy throughout the year.

Royal Welsh College of Music & Drama MUSIC, THEATRE
(Map p50; ☎029-2039 1391; www.rwcmd.ac.uk; Bute Park) All manner of performances are staged in this impressive building's state-of-the-art venues, including theatre from the college's inhouse Richard Burton Company.

Cafe Jazz JAZZ
(Map p50; ☎029-2038 7026; www.cafejazzcardiff.com; 21 St Mary St; ⊙noon-midnight Tue-Fri, 11am-2am Sat, noon-5pm Sun) It's not exactly your traditional smoky basement, but this cafe-bar is the city's main jazz venue, with live music every night and disco kicking off after the house band on Saturdays.

Theatre, Comedy & Cinema

Other theatre companies are based at the Wales Millennium Centre (p53).

Chapter THEATRE, CINEMA
(Map p60; ☎029-2030 4400; www.chapter.org; Market Rd, Canton) The city's edgiest arts venue, Chapter has a varied rota of contemporary drama, as well as art exhibitions, arthouse cinema, workshops, alternative theatre and dance performances. There's also a very popular cafe-bar, with a big range of European beers and real ale on tap.

Sherman Cymru THEATRE
(Map p50; ☎029-2064 6900; www.shermancymru.co.uk; Senghennydd Rd, Cathays) South

GAY & LESBIAN CARDIFF

Cardiff's small gay and lesbian scene is focused on a cluster of venues on Churchill Way and Charles St. The big event is the annual Pride Cymru (p58), held in mid-August.

Golden Cross (Map p50; 282 Hayes Bridge Rd; ⊙noon-11pm Mon & Tue, to 2am Wed-Sun; 📶) One of the oldest pubs in the city and a long-standing gay venue, this Victorian bar retains its handsome stained glass, polished wood and ceramic tiles. It hosts drag, cabaret, games and karaoke nights, and there's a little dance floor.

Eagle (Map p50; ☎029-2114 0000; www.eaglecardiff.com; 39 Charles St; ⊙5pm-3am Mon-Fri, to 5am Sat, to midnight Sun) A bastion for blokiness, the Eagle has a gay-men-only policy after 9pm on weekends, enabled by a membership system (£3 annually). There's no DJ, drag or back room, just a friendly little basement bar open until the wee smalls. Special events cover the spectrum from kink to karaoke. They also operate the Eagle 50 sauna across the road.

WOW (Map p50; ☎029-2066 6267; www.wow-cardiff.com; 4a Churchill Way; ⊙10am-2.30am Mon-Sat, noon-1.30am Sun; 📶) A strange mix of industrial and camp (exposed ducting, chandeliers and a sequined fireplace), WOW offers 'cheeky hour' drink specials from 4pm to 9pm daily, and there's a busy weekly roster of drag, DJs and karaoke. The WOW Club lurks beneath.

Wales' leading theatre company, Sherman stages a wide range of material, from classics and children's theatre to works by new playwrights.

The Gate PERFORMING ARTS
(☎029-2048 3344; www.thegate.org.uk; Keppoch St, Roath) This big old stone chapel has been converted into an eclectic arts centre, staging everything from theatre and classical music concerts to pop acts and pro wrestling.

New Theatre THEATRE
(Map p50; ☎029-2087 8889; www.newtheatrecardiff.co.uk; Park Pl) This restored Edwardian playhouse hosts various touring productions, including theatre, musicals and pantomime.

Glee Club COMEDY
(Map p54; ☎0871 472 0400; www.glee.co.uk; Mermaid Quay, Cardiff Bay; ⏲Thu-Sat) Hosts touring and local comics.

Sport

Cardiff Arms Park SPECTATOR SPORT
(Map p50; ☎029-2030 2030; www.cardiffrfc.com; Westgate St; tickets £12-24) While the big rugby union test matches held next door at Principality provide a more thrilling spectacle, you're more likely to be able to score tickets to a game here in its historic neighbour. It's home to both the Cardiff Rugby Football Club, aka the Blue & Blacks, founded in 1876, and the Cardiff Blues (www.cardiffblues.com), the professional regional side.

Cardiff City Stadium SPECTATOR SPORT
(☎0845 345 1400; www.cardiffcityfc.co.uk; Leckwith Rd, Canton) This 33,300-seater is home to Cardiff City Football Club, a team that's back in the Championship League after a brief stint in the English Premier League in 2013. Local football fans still hark back to 1927 when the Bluebirds took the English FA Cup out of England for the first (and only) time – Welsh football's equivalent of Owain Glyndŵr's rebellion.

SWALEC Stadium SPECTATOR SPORT
(Map p60; ☎029-2041 9311; www.thesseswalec.com; Sophia Gardens) This is the home of the Glamorgan Cricket Club (www.glamorgancricket.com), the only Welsh club playing in the England and Wales Cricket Board's county championship.

Shopping

If you thought Cardiff's 21st-century makeover was all about political edifices, arts centres and sports stadiums, think again. One of the most dramatic developments in the central city is the transformation of the Hayes shopping strip, with the giant, glitzy extension of the St David's shopping centre now eating up its entire eastern side. Balancing this modern mall is a historic network of Victorian and Edwardian shopping arcades spreading their dainty tentacles either side of St Mary St.

Cardiff Market MARKET
(Map p50; btwn St Mary & Trinity Sts; ⏲8.30am-5.30pm Mon-Sat) For an age-old shopping experience, head to this Victorian covered market, which is packed with stalls selling everything from fresh fish to mobile-phone covers. Stock up here for a picnic in Bute Park with goodies such as fresh bread, cheese, cold meats, barbecued chicken and Welsh cakes. Music fans should head upstairs to Kelly's Records.

Bodlon GIFTS & SOUVENIRS
(Map p50; www.bodlon.com; Yr Hen Lyfrgell, The Hayes; ⏲9am-5pm) If you're after a properly Welshy souvenir that isn't too cheesy (although they do sell cheese), the shop in the Welsh cultural centre is a great option. It stocks locally made art and craft, Welsh-language greeting cards and books, and even a range of kitchen storage containers labelled in Cymraeg. An attached pop-up space showcases Welsh fashion and the like.

Craft in the Bay CRAFTS
(Map p54; ☎029-2048 4611; www.makersguildinwales.org.uk; Lloyd George Ave, Butetown; ⏲10.30am-5.30pm) This retail showcase for the Welsh Makers Guild cooperative sells work by its members, including a wide range of ceramics, textiles, jewellery, glassware and ironwork.

Castle Emporium MARKET
(Map p50; www.facebook.com/TheCastleEmporium; Womanby St; ⏲10am-6pm Tue-Sat) This kooky collection of independent stalls is a great place to rummage for vintage clothes and jewellery.

St David's MALL
(Map p50; www.stdavidscardiff.com; The Hayes; ⏲9.30am-8pm Mon-Sat, 11am-5pm Sun; 📶) Immense is the best way to describe this shiny shopping centre. All of the famous chains you could name have a home here, along with a smorgasbord of eateries, a cinema multiplex and a large branch of the John Lewis department store, which dominates its south end.

Morgan Quarter SHOPPING ARCADE

(Map p50; www.morganquarter.com; btwn St Mary St & The Hayes) Cardiff's oldest arcade (1858), the Royal, connects up with the Morgan Arcade via a series of covered lanes, forming a ritzy shopping precinct called the Morgan Quarter. Along with name-brand fashion, there are shops selling skateboards, vintage books and antiques. Look out for Spillers Records, the excellent Wally's Delicatessen, The Plan cafe and Liam Gallagher's pricey menswear boutique Pretty Green.

Spillers Records MUSIC

(Map p50; ☎029-2022 4905; www.spillersrecords.co.uk; 27 Morgan Arcade; ⏲10am-6pm Mon-Sat) The world's oldest record shop, founded in 1894 (when it sold wax phonograph cylinders), Spillers stocks a large range of CDs and vinyl, and prides itself on catering to the non-mainstream end of the market (it's especially good on punk). In-store gigs promote local talent.

Castle Arcade SHOPPING ARCADE

(Map p50; www.castlequarterarcades.co.uk; btwn Castle & High Sts; ⏲8.30am-6pm Mon-Sat, 10.30am-5pm Sun) The most decorative of the city's arcades, it houses Troutmark Books (mainly secondhand books), Claire Grove Buttons (beads and buttons of every description) and eateries Madame Fromage, Coffee Barker and Cafe Minuet.

Wyndham Arcade SHOPPING ARCADE

(Map p50; btwn St Mary St & Mill Lane) The historic Wyndham arcade (1887) is home to upmarket cafes and the gloriously old-fashioned Havana House, a specialist cigar merchant from a bygone era. It's also known as the 'Bear Shop', thanks to a prominently displayed 200-year-old piece of taxidermy called Bruno.

High St & Duke St Arcades SHOPPING ARCADE

(Map p50; www.castlequarterarcades.co.uk; btwn High & St John Sts; ⏲8.30am-6pm Mon-Fri, 10.30am-5pm Sun) Stop into the New York Deli for a burger or sandwich, then head on to Hobo's for secondhand 1960s and '70s clothing.

Castle Welsh Crafts GIFTS & SOUVENIRS

(Map p50; ☎029-2034 3038; www.castlewelshcrafts.co.uk; 1 Castle St; ⏲9am-5.30pm Mon-Sat, 10.30am-4.30pm Sun) If you're after stuffed dragons, love spoons or Cardiff T-shirts, this is the city's biggest souvenir shop, conveniently located across the street from the castle.

LOVE SPOONS

All over Wales, craft shops turn out wooden spoons with contorted handles in a variety of different designs at a speed that would have left their original makers – village lads with their eyes on a lady – gawking in astonishment. The carving of these spoons seems to date back to the 17th century, when they were made by men to give to women to mark the start of a courtship. If you want to see carving in progress, the St Fagans National History Museum (p56) can usually oblige. Any number of shops will be happy to sell you the finished product. Various symbols are carved into the handles; the meanings of a few of them are as follows:

Anchor I'm home to stay; you can count on me.

Balls in a cage, links in a chain Captured love, together forever; the number of balls or links may correspond to the number of children desired, or the number of years already spent together.

Bell Marriage.

Celtic cross Faith; marriage.

Double spoon Side by side forever.

Flowers Love and affection; courtship.

Horseshoe Good luck; happiness.

Key, lock, little house My house is yours.

One heart My heart is yours.

Two hearts We feel the same way about one another.

Vines, trees, leaves Our love is growing.

Wheel I will work for you.

MATTHEW DIXON / SHUTTERSTOCK ©

1. Cardiff Bay (p52)
Illuminated buildings include the Pierhead museum and the Senned (p53).

2. Animal Wall (p50)
This lioness is just one of the stone animals topping the southern wall of Bute Park (p49).

3. Wales Millennium Centre (p53)
An architectural masterpiece and symbol of Cardiff Bay's regeneration.

4. Castell Coch (p52)
A Victorian Gothic castle on Cardiff's northern edge.

3

DEYMOSHR / SHUTTERSTOCK ©

Information

Tourist Office (Map p54; ☎029-2087 3573; www.visitcardiff.com; Wales Millennium Centre, Bute Pl, Cardiff Bay; ⏰10am-6pm Mon-Sat, to 4pm Sun) Information, advice and souvenirs.

University Hospital of Wales (☎029-2074 7747; www.cardiffandvaleuhb.wales.nhs.uk; The Gateway, Heath Park) Cardiff's main accident and emergency department, located 2 miles north of the Civic Centre.

Getting There & Away

AIR

Cardiff Airport (☎01446-711111; www.cardiff-airport.com) is 12 miles southwest of Cardiff, past Barry. Aside from summer-only services and charters, these are the airlines flying into Cardiff and the destinations they serve:

Aer Lingus (www.aerlingus.com) Dublin.

Citywing (www.citywing.com) Anglesey.

Eastern Airways (www.easternairways.com) Aberdeen, Newcastle.

Flybe (www.flybe.com) London City, Glasgow, Edinburgh, Belfast, Cork, Dublin, Jersey, Paris, Berlin, Munich, Milan, Faro.

KLM (www.klm.com) Amsterdam.

Ryanair (www.ryanair.com) Tenerife-South.

Thomson Airways (www.thomson.co.uk) Málaga, Alicante, Gran Canaria, Tenerife-South, Lanzarote.

Vueling (www.vueling.com) Málaga, Alicante.

BUS

Cardiff's central bus station has closed for a major redevelopment and is due to reopen near the train station in a revitalised Central Square in 2018. In the meantime there are temporary bus stops scattered all around the inner city. See www.traveline.cymru for details.

Bus destinations include Newport (£2.10, 38 minutes, frequent), Abergavenny (£9.10, 2½ hours, 12 daily), Brecon (£8.30, 1¾ hours, eight daily), Swansea (£4.50, 1¼ hours, at least hourly) and Aberystwyth (£17, four hours, two daily).

Megabus (http://uk.megabus.com) offers one-way coach journeys from London to Cardiff (via Newport) from as little as £5.

National Express (www.nationalexpress.com) coaches depart from **Cardiff Coach Station** (Map p60; Sophia Gardens), with destinations including Tenby (£18, 2¾ hours, daily), Swansea (£3.50, one hour, four daily), Chepstow (from £4.80, one hour, four daily), Bristol (£6.10, one hour, four daily) and London (from £5, 3½ hours, four daily).

CAR

Cardiff is easily reached from the M4 (which runs from London to northwest of Swansea). All major car-rental companies have branches in the capital.

TRAIN

Trains from major British cities arrive at Cardiff Central station, on the southern edge of the city centre. Direct services to/from Cardiff include London Paddington (from £40, two hours, two per hour), Abergavenny (£14, 45 minutes, frequent), Swansea (£9.20, one hour, two per hour), Fishguard Harbour (from £10, three hours, two daily) and Holyhead (from £24, five hours, six daily). For the latest timetables and bookings, see www.thetrainline.com.

Getting Around

TO/FROM THE AIRPORT

The T9 Cardiff Airport Express bus (£5, 40 minutes, every 20 minutes) heads between the airport and the city centre via Cardiff Bay.

The 905 shuttle bus (£1, 10 minutes) links the airport terminal to nearby Rhoose Cardiff Airport train station. Trains to Cardiff Central station (£4.40, 33 minutes) run hourly Monday to Saturday and twice-hourly on Sunday.

FlightLink Wales (☎029-2025 3555) has the airport taxi concession, providing minibus shuttles to the city, either on a shared basis (£35) or for exclusive use (£60).

BICYCLE

Cardiff City Council has a dedicated cycling officer and its website (www.keepingcardiffmoving.co.uk) has lots of information including lists of bike shops and route maps.

CAR & MOTORCYCLE

Cardiff doesn't pose many difficulties for drivers, although most of the central city streets between Westgate St, Castle St and St David's are closed to traffic. If you're prepared to walk, it's often possible to find free street parking in the suburbs. Pontcanna's Cathedral Rd has unrestricted parking, but it's difficult to find an empty spot during working hours.

PUBLIC TRANSPORT

Boat

Two boats run alternating waterbus services along the River Taff from Bute Park (Map p50) to Mermaid Quay (Map p54), departing every half-hour from 10.30am to 5pm. The journey takes about 25 minutes and costs £4 each way.

Bus

Local buses are operated by **Cardiff Bus** (☎029-2066 6444; www.cardiffbus.com; trip/day pass £1.80/3.60); buy your ticket from the driver (no change given). Useful routes from stops scattered around the city centre include the Baycar to Cardiff Bay; 13 and 28 to Roath Park; 38 to the City/Crwys/Whitchurch Rd strip through Cathays and Roath; 25, 62 and 63 via Cathedral Rd to Llandaff; and 32 to St Fagans.

Train

Generally the buses are more convenient for short trips than the trains, although there are a handful of stations scattered around the city including Cardiff Central, Cardiff Queen St, Cardiff Bay, Cathays and Grangetown. Expect to pay around £2.

TAXI

Cabs can be hailed in the street, ordered by phone, or picked up at taxi ranks outside the train station, in Duke St opposite the castle, and on the corner of Greyfriars Rd and Park Pl. Reliable companies include **Capital Cabs** (☎ 029-2077 7777; www.capitalcabs.co.uk) and **Dragon Taxis** (☎ 029-2033 3333; www.dragontaxis.com).

VALE OF GLAMORGAN

On the western flank of Cardiff, the largely rural Vale of Glamorgan is a county in its own right but often feels like an extension to the capital. Penarth is literally a stone's throw across the Ely River from Cardiff, and even shares the same telephone code, while Barry Island is more or less Cardiff-by-the-beach.

If you're basing yourself in the city, you'll find a diverting selection of day-trip destinations in the Vale, from the peculiar time-warped traditions of the British seaside, to ancient monuments lurking in lonely fields.

Penarth

POP 22,100

Well-heeled Penarth has transformed from an old-fashioned seaside resort to a virtual suburb of Cardiff, despite it being in the neighbouring county. It's connected to

Around Cardiff

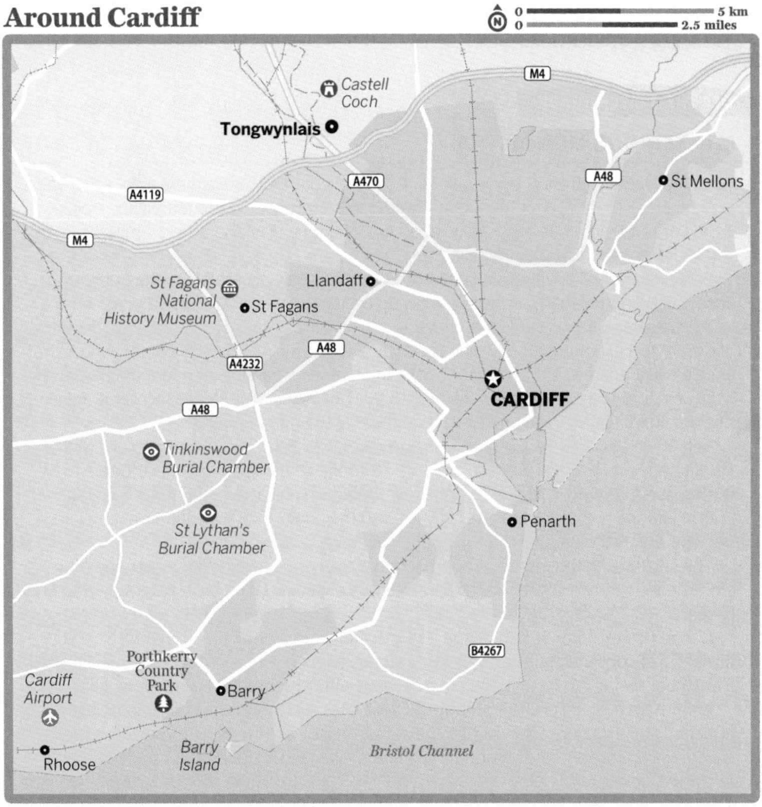

Cardiff Bay by the freshwater lake formed by the construction of the barrage and it now sports a busy marina on the lakefront.

Sights

Ffotogallery GALLERY
(029-2070 8870; www.ffotogallery.org; Plymouth Rd; 11am-5pm Tue-Sat) FREE Also known as the Turner House Gallery, this red-brick building near the train station hosts edgy photographic, video and multimedia exhibitions. It's at its busiest during the month-long Diffusion (p58) international photography festival in October.

Alexandra Gardens PARK
(Beach Rd; 8.20am-dusk) This pretty Edwardian-era park slopes from Penarth's bustling town centre down to the esplanade. Its formal gardens are filled with topiary and colourful flowerbeds.

Penarth Pier Pavilion ARTS CENTRE
(029-2071 2100; www.penarthpavilion.co.uk; The Esplanade; 10am-5pm Sun & Mon, to 7.30pm Tue-Sat) Penarth's rock-strewn shoreline may not be particularly attractive but it is the closest beach to Cardiff. In 1894 it was graced with that icon of the Victorian seaside, a pier. This elegant art deco pavilion followed in 1927, but it went into decline and for decades was left to decay. Following major restorations the pavilion has now reopened, complete with a gallery, cinema and cafe.

Sleeping

Although Penarth has a scattering of hotels and B&Bs, you're much better off staying just over the river in Cardiff.

Eating

Penarth has established itself as an upmarket dining destination for Cardiffians, with a clutch of excellent eateries.

Fig Tree WELSH ££
(029-2070 2512; www.thefigtreepenarth.co.uk; The Esplanade; mains £12-20, 1-/2-/3-course lunch £8.50/11/14; noon-3pm & 6-9pm Tue-Sat, noon-4pm Sun) The name might sound like it has Mediterranean delusions but this Fig Tree is a particularly Welsh affair, with a commitment to sourcing most of its product from

OFF THE BEATEN TRACK

MYSTERIOUS MONOLITHS

Neolithic standing stones, stone circles and burial chambers are a dime a dozen in Wales – so much so that many of them don't even make it into tourist brochures and maps. That's the case with this mysterious duo, each standing in a forlorn field 7 miles west of Cardiff, orientated towards the rising sun.

While located on private farmland, both sites are freely accessible to the public and each has an information post with a wind-up device that plays a recorded commentary.

You'll need your own car to get here and preferably a detailed road map. Head west of Cardiff to Culverhouse Cross and continue west on the A48 to St Nicholas, where the sites are signposted. Turn left at the lights and look for a parking area to the right of the road where you can walk across the field to the Tinkinswood chamber. Continue down this road for a further mile and turn left at the end to find St Lythans.

The 6000-year-old **Tinkinswood chamber** (St Nicholas) FREE consists of a wall of stones supporting a mammoth 7.4m-long, 36-tonne limestone capstone, thought to be the largest of its kind in Britain. It was once covered in an earth mound, but excavations in 1914 left one half of it open after pottery and the bones of 50 people were removed. A brick pillar was then added to prop up the capstone.

The entrance to the mound is approached by a curving avenue of stones, and other stones have been arranged nearby. The site was once known as Castell Carreg – the fairy castle.

Dating from around 4000 BC, the **St Lythans burial chamber (cromlech)** (St Lythans) FREE consists of three supporting stones capped with a large, flat stone, forming a chamber nearly 2m high. It was once covered with a mound that is now long gone.

As with many such pre-Christian/pre-Celtic sites, St Lythans has many local legends attached to it. It was once thought to be a druid's altar and on midsummer's eve the capstone supposedly spins around three times. The field it stands in is known as the Accursed Field.

within 30 miles of the restaurant. It's a great place to tuck into Welsh lamb, mussels and cheese, and the waterfront location and reasonably priced lunch menu gears it perfectly towards day-trippers.

★ Restaurant James Sommerin MODERN BRITISH £££

(☎029-2070 6559; www.jamessommerinrestaurant.co.uk; The Esplanade; mains £20-25, 6/9 courses £60/80; ⊙noon-10.30pm Tue-Sun) The chef with his name on the window earned a Michelin star for his previous Monmouthshire restaurant and is surely on track for another one here. Everything that proceeds from the kitchen is as exquisite looking as it is tasting, incorporating multiple textures and well-balanced flavours as well as tricksy molecular-gastronomy techniques.

Pier 64 STEAK £££

(☎029-2000 0064; www.pier64.co.uk; Penarth Marina, Penarth Portway; mains £15-27; ⊙11.30am-10.30pm Mon-Sat, to 6pm Sun; P 📶) Jutting out over the water in a slick modern building, this upmarket wine bar and steakhouse caters to the boat-shoes brigade with slabs of meat of Flintstones proportions. They also serve plenty of sophisticated bistro-style dishes, including lots of seafood, with a raw bar slicing, dicing and shucking fresh sashimi, ceviche and oysters.

Getting There & Away

Frequent buses head to/from Cardiff (£1.80, 20 minutes) and Barry (£2.50, 30 minutes).

Trains head to/from Cardiff Central (£2.80, 15 minutes) roughly every 15 minutes during the day.

You can walk or cycle along the barrage from Cardiff Bay to Penarth Marina (allow 40 minutes on foot). From here it's a steep but short walk up to the town centre and down again to the pier.

Barry (Y Barri)

POP 51,500

Nowhere have the recent triumphs of the BBC Wales television department been more keenly felt than in Barry, a seaside town 8 miles southwest of Cardiff. If you watch *Doctor Who* or *Being Human*, you'll no doubt be aware that the town is infested with aliens, zombies, ghosts, werewolves and vampires. Yet it's the massive popularity of the altogether more down-to-earth comedy *Gavin & Stacey* that has given the town a new cachet. The staff at Island Leisure (on the Promenade) are used to fans of the show making a pilgrimage to the booth where Nessa (played in the show by co-writer Ruth Jones) worked. Other sites include nearby Marco's Cafe, where Stacey worked, and Trinity St, where Stacey's mum and Uncle Bryn lived.

The big attraction here is the beach at Barry Island, which is well signposted at the south end of the town.

Sights

Barry Island BEACH

Barry Island stopped being a real island in the 1880s when it was joined to the mainland by a causeway. Amusement arcades and fun parks line the waterfront at sandy Whitmore Bay, which is easily the best beach this side of the Gower.

Porthkerry Country Park PARK

(Park Rd; P) Spanning 90 hectares, this vast expanse follows a lush wooded valley terminating at a pebbly beach, overshot by an impressive Victorian railway viaduct. There are plenty of trails, a popular playground for the kids, the remains of a 13th-century mill and the potential to spot buzzards, adders and foxes. The park is well signposted from the road to Barry Island.

Sleeping

Barry has a couple of large, moderately priced chain hotels, one in the town centre and another near the airport. However, we recommend staying in Cardiff and visiting on a day trip.

Eating

There are cafes and pubs scattered around the town centre and oodles of fried-food outlets on Barry Island.

Getting There & Away

Three trains an hour head to Barry and Barry Island stations from Cardiff Central (£3.40, 30 minutes).

Cardiff Bus services depart every 15 minutes during the day (routes 92 to 96, £2.50, one hour), but every 30 minutes in the evening and on Sunday.

Brecon Beacons & Southeast Wales

Includes ➡

Best Places to Eat

- The Whitebrook (p88)
- St John's Place (p101)
- Mango House (p116)
- Walnut Tree (p94)
- Tomatitos Tapas Bar (p101)

Best Places to Sleep

- The Bear (p100)
- Celyn Farm (p96)
- Peterstone Court (p106)
- Coed Owen Bunkhouse (p114)
- Pencelli Castle Caravan & Camping Park (p107)

Why Go?

Wales' southeast corner, where the misty River Wye meanders along the border with England, is the birthplace of British tourism. For over 200 years travellers have visited this tranquil waterway and its winding, wooded vale, where the romantic ruins of Tintern Abbey have inspired poets and artists such as Wordsworth and Turner.

But there's more to the region than the market towns and rural byways of the Lower Wye. To the west, the dramatically serried South Wales valleys tell the story of the Industrial Revolution through heritage sites and still close-knit communities. Move north and the landscape opens out to the magnificent upland scenery of Brecon Beacons National Park, where high mountain roads dip down to remote hamlets and whitewashed ancient churches. The hiking and mountain-biking terrain here is superb.

When to Go

➡ Outdoor types should consider heading to Brecon Beacons National Park in late spring, early summer or early autumn to take advantage of what should be reasonable weather (though there's no guarantee). The narrow country roads may be impassable in winter, and become congested during school summer holidays (mid-July to August). Many hostels and campgrounds don't open till after Easter.

➡ The literary extravaganza of the Hay Festival runs from late May until early June, the Green Man music festival is in August, while foodies should focus a trip around Abergavenny's food festival in September.

NEWPORT (CASNEWYDD)

POP 146,000

Sitting at the muddy mouth of the River Usk and flanked by the detritus of heavy industry, Newport is never going to win any awards for beauty. However, Wales' third-largest city is in the process of smartening itself up, with the shiny new Friars Walk shopping complex opening up the historic city centre to a redeveloped riverside promenade. A handful of interesting sights more than justify a day trip to the city, but you're unlikely to be tempted to stay over.

History

Newport takes its name from the fact that it was built after the 'old port' at Caerleon, further upstream, following the construction of Newport Castle in Norman times. The Welsh name, Casnewydd, actually means 'new castle' for much the same reason. Like many harbour towns in South Wales, it grew rich on the back of the iron and coal industries in the 19th and early 20th centuries. The legacy of these boom times can be glimpsed in the historic facades of Commercial St.

In the second half of the 20th century, Newport's shipbuilding industry disappeared, and the docks declined in importance as coal exports shifted to Barry and iron-ore imports to Port Talbot. In 2001 the huge Llanwern steelworks closed down.

Sights

Tredegar House HISTORIC BUILDING

(NT; ☎01633-815880; www.nationaltrust.org.uk; house adult/child £7.20/3.60, parking £2; ⏲park dawn-dusk year-round, house 11am-5pm Feb-Oct; P) The seat of the Morgan family for more than 500 years, Tredegar House is a stone and red-brick 17th-century building set amid extensive gardens, 2 miles west of Newport city centre. It is one of the finest examples of a Restoration mansion in Britain, the oldest parts dating to the 1670s. The National Trust took over management of the property in late 2011 and has done a great job bringing the fascinating stories of its owners to life.

The Morgans, once one of the richest families in Wales, were an interesting lot. Sir Henry was a 17th-century pirate (Captain Morgan's Rum is named after him); Godfrey, the second Lord Tredegar, survived the Charge of the Light Brigade; and Viscount Evan was an occultist, a Catholic convert and a twice-married homosexual who kept a boxing kangaroo.

On the ground floor, the entrance hall opens into the sumptuous grand dining room. The adjoining 'gilt room' is blanketed in goldleaf and paintings of bare-breasted mythological figures; you're invited to recline on the day bed in order to get a better look. In another parlour there are period costumes to try on and board games to play.

The decor of the upstairs bedrooms jumps forward in time to the 1930s, when Evan Morgan was hosting his fabulous parties at Tredegar. For the full *Downton Abbey* experience, head 'below stairs' to explore the preserve of the Morgan's numerous servants.

St Woolos Cathedral CHURCH

(☎07933 627594; www.newportcathedral.org.uk; Stow Hill; ⏲7.45am-5.30pm Mon-Fri, 10am-6pm Sat, to 8pm Sun) A steep 10-minute walk uphill from the main shopping strip leads to Newport's ancient cathedral. The building provides a fascinating journey through history via a succession of distinct architectural styles.

The main door leads into the oldest part of the building, a 9th-century stone chapel constructed to replace a wooden church built here in 500 on the burial site of Welsh king-turned-monk St Gwynllyw (Woolos is an English corruption of his name). The Normans came next, represented by the magnificent Romanesque arch leading into their grand nave (look up to the curved timbers of the medieval 'wagon roof'). You can see the transition from the Romanesque to the Gothic style in the pointy windows of the outside aisles, which were grafted on later. Newport's prosperous Victorian period is evident in the chancel, while the very end of the building is pure 1960s, including the painted marble effect behind the altar.

Newport Museum & Art Gallery MUSEUM

(☎01633-656656; www.newport.gov.uk/museum; John Frost Sq; ⏲9.30am-5pm Tue-Sat) FREE In the same building as the tourist office and library, Newport Museum covers the town's history from the prehistoric to the 20th century, via the Romans and the Industrial Revolution.

Riverfront ARTS CENTRE

(☎01633-656757; www.newport.gov.uk/riverfront; Kingsway; ⏲10am-6pm Mon-Sat) Opened in 2004, the city's swish cultural centre takes

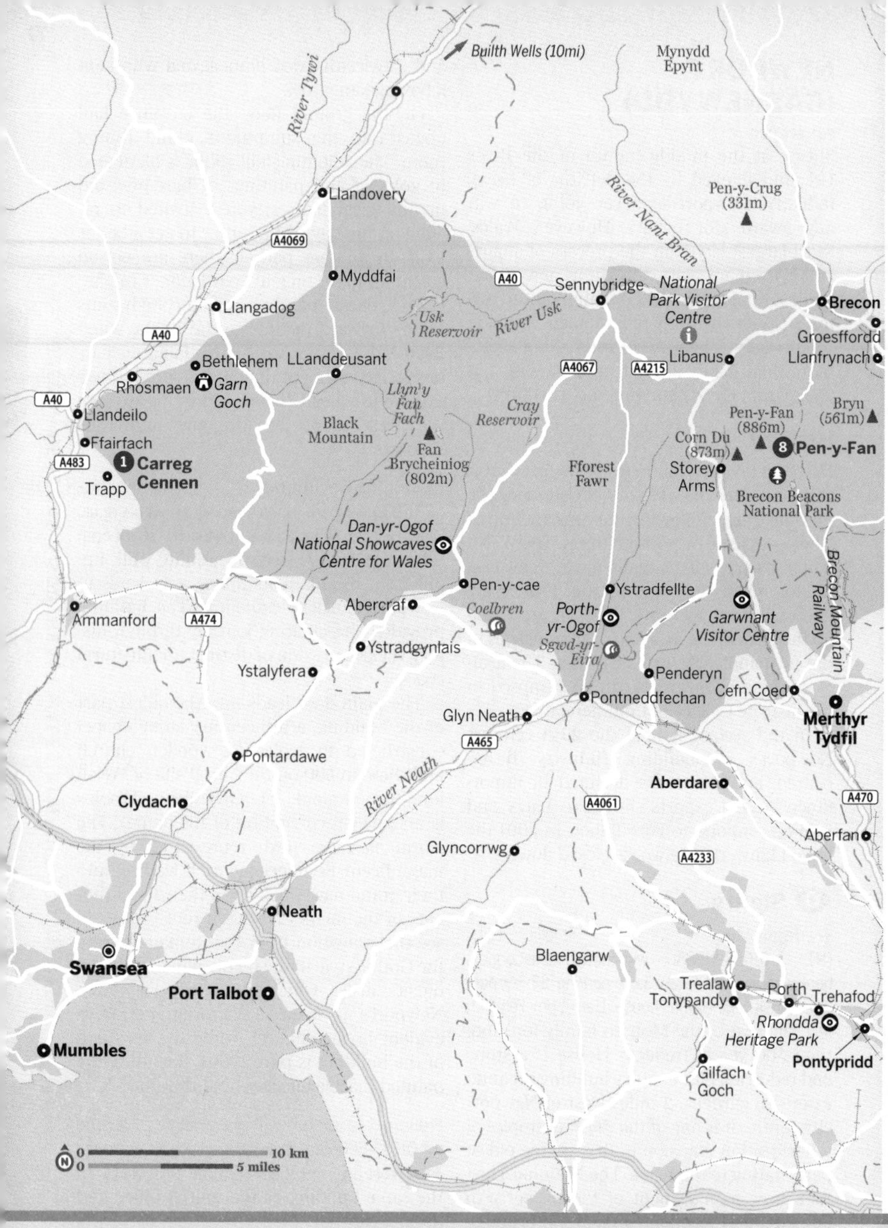

Brecon Beacons & Southeast Wales Highlights

1 Carreg Cennen (p113) Gazing up at Wales' most dramatically positioned ruined fortress.

2 Tintern Abbey (p87) Strolling among romantic riverside ruins in the glorious Wye Valley.

3 Caerphilly Castle (p118) Crossing the moat and wandering into a fairytale.

4 Black Mountains (p95) Taking a spectacular, hair-raising drive through the chapel-dotted Vale of Ewyas.

5 Hay-on-Wye (p98) Soaking up the literary vibe

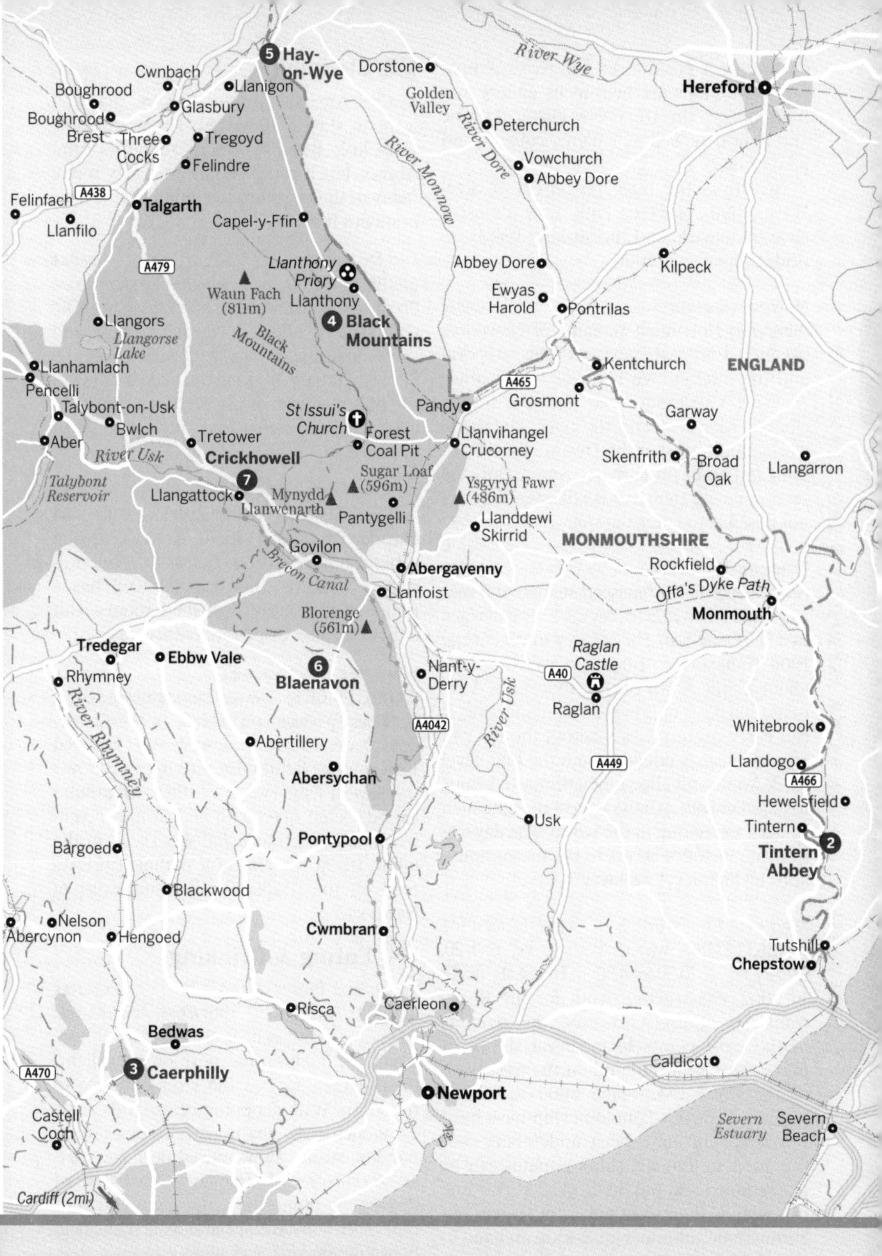

of an elegant rural town absolutely besotted with books.

6 Blaenavon (p116)
Feasting on World Heritage industrial sites and world-class cheese in the South Wales valleys.

7 Crickhowell (p110)
Winding down to a village pace in the heart of Brecon Beacons National Park.

8 Pen-y-Fan (p103)
Avoiding the crowds on the less travelled tracks to the top of the region's highest mountain.

a prominent position by the river. Temporary exhibitions are held in its gallery and it also stages theatre, opera, classical music and dance, as well as cinema, comedy and pantomime.

Nearby is the huge red circle of Steel Wave (1990) by Peter Fink, now almost a civic trademark, and the striking Usk Footbridge (opened in 2006).

Newport Castle CASTLE
(Kingsway) Not much remains of Newport's pre-industrial past apart from the cathedral and the litter-strewn ruins of 14th-century Newport Castle squeezed between traffic-clogged Kingsway and the river. The castle was soundly trashed by Owain Glyndŵr in 1402 and never properly recovered. Only the section facing the river is still standing; it's not possible to enter the site.

Transporter Bridge BRIDGE
(www.newport.gov.uk/transporterbridge; Usk Way; adult/child return £1.50/1, day £3/2; ⏲10am-5pm Wed-Sun Easter-Sep) The spidery towers of the 1906 Transporter Bridge rise over the river, about a mile south of the city centre. A remarkable piece of Edwardian engineering, it can carry up to six cars across the river in a gondola suspended beneath the high-level track, while still allowing high-masted ships to pass beneath. It's the largest of eight such bridges remaining in the world. The day visitor rate includes access to the motor house and the high-level walkway.

Medieval Ship Centre ARCHAEOLOGICAL SITE
(☎01633-274167; www.newportship.org; Unit 20, Estuary Rd; ⏲10.30am-4.30pm Fri & Sat) FREE
In 2002, construction work for the Riverfront Art Centre uncovered the remains of the most complete medieval ship ever found, buried in the mud on the west bank of the River Usk. Some 2000 individual timbers from this 25m-long ship have been recovered and have been undergoing conservation so that the ship's remains can be reassembled and put on display. At the time of research there was not a lot to see, but enthusiastic volunteer guides are on hand to explain the ongoing project.

The ship dates from around 1450 and was built from timber grown in the Basque region between France and Spain.

Sleeping

Really? Are you absolutely sure that you want to stay in Newport? There are some great little B&Bs scattered around its rural fringes, but if you need an inner-city room, many of the big midrange hotel chains have branches here.

Old Rectory B&B ££
(☎01633-430700; www.the-oldrectory.co.uk; Christchurch Rd, Christchurch; r £75; P 📶) The Old Rectory offers a warm welcome and three luxurious rooms with views over the Severn Estuary to England. It's located in the hilltop village of Christchurch, 2.5 miles east of the city centre and only a mile south of Caerleon.

Labuan Guest House B&B ££
(☎01633-664533; www.labuanhouse.co.uk; 464 Chepstow Rd; s/d from £45/70; P 📶) Occupying a handsome Victorian house in Newport's eastern suburbs, this friendly B&B has a range of pleasantly furnished rooms with either en suites or private bathrooms.

West Usk Lighthouse B&B £££
(☎01633-810126; www.westusklighthouse.co.uk; St Brides Wentloog; r £150-160; P 📶) Quirky doesn't even begin to describe this restored 19th-century lighthouse offering views over the Severn Estuary. It's a little worn around the edges but filled with endearingly eccentric details, such as a full-size Dalek in the lobby. It's at the end of a potholed private road off the B4239, 6 miles southwest of Newport.

Eating & Drinking

Le Bistrot Pierre FRENCH ££
(☎01633-744300; http://bistrotpierre.co.uk; Kingsway; mains lunch £9, dinner £14-16; ⏲9am-10pm; 🖉) Taking pole position in a light-filled corner spot at the river entrance to the Friars Walk shopping centre, this snazzy French-style chain eatery serves tasty burgers, steaks, slow-braised beef and *tartes flambées* (Alsatian-style pastry-based pizzas). At dinnertime, the menu expands into more substantial classics such as boeuf bourguignon and cassoulet.

Drago Lounge BAR
(www.thelounges.co.uk; Kingsway; ⏲8am-11pm) Every spare wall of this large hip-looking cafe/bar is covered in vintage mirrors, murals and kooky framed pictures (we particu-

larly like the young Tom Jones on the rear wall). It's an equally good spot for a cuppa, a cocktail, a Corona or a cheeky vino.

Information

Tourist Office (01633-656656; www.newport.gov.uk/tourism; John Frost Sq; 9.30am-5pm Tue-Sat)

Getting There & Around

BUS

Newport's bus station is on Kingsway, adjacent to the Friars Walk shopping centre.

National Express (www.nationalexpress.com) has four coaches a day to/from Swansea (£8.20, 1½ hours), Cardiff (£3.10, 30 minutes), Bristol (£7.30, 35 minutes), London (from £7, three hours) and Birmingham (£23, 2¼ hours).

Newport Bus (www.newportbus.co.uk) covers the local routes, and has services to Cardiff (£2.10, 38 minutes, frequent), Caerleon (£1.70, 11 minutes, frequent), Chepstow (£3.80, 40 minutes, frequent) and Monmouth (£5.45, 57 minutes, nine daily).

TRAIN

Newport train station is on Queensway, immediately north of High St. Direct train destinations include Cardiff (from £5, 16 minutes, frequent), Swansea (£16, 1¼ hours, frequent), Tenby (from £12, 3¼ hours, daily), Holyhead (from £31, 4¾ hours, seven daily) and London Paddington (from £37, two hours, at least hourly).

CAERLEON (CAERLLION)

POP 8070

Hidden in plain view beneath the small, genteel town of Caerleon is one of the largest and most important Roman settlements in Britain. After the Romans invaded in AD 43, they controlled their new territory through a network of forts and military garrisons. The top tier of military organisation was the legionary fort, of which there were only three in Britain – at Eboracum (York), Deva (Chester) and Isca (Caerleon).

Caerleon ('Fort of the Legion') was the headquarters of the elite 2nd Augustan Legion for more than 200 years, from AD 75 until the end of the 3rd century. It wasn't just a military camp but a purpose-built township some 9 miles in circumference, complete with a large amphitheatre and a state-of-the-art Roman baths complex.

Sights

National Roman Legion Museum MUSEUM
(www.museumwales.ac.uk/en/roman; High St; 10am-5pm Mon-Sat, 2-5pm Sun) FREE Put your Caerleon explorations into context at this excellent museum, which paints a vivid picture of what life was like for soldiers in one of the most remote corners of the Empire. It displays a host of intriguing Roman artefacts uncovered locally, from jewellery to armour, including a section of mosaic floor found in the neighbouring churchyard.

Caerleon Roman Fortress Baths RUINS
(Cadw; www.cadw.gov.wales; High St; 9.30am-5pm daily Apr-Oct, 9.30am-5pm Mon-Sat & 11am-4pm Sun Nov-Mar) FREE Like any good Roman town, Caerleon had a grand public bath complex. Parts of the outdoor swimming pool, *apodyterium* (changing room) and *frigidarium* (cold room) remain under a protective roof, and give some idea of the scale of the place. Projections of bathers splashing through shimmering water help bring it to life.

Roman Amphitheatre RUINS
(Cadw; www.cadw.gov.wales; Broadway; 9.30am-5pm daily Apr-Oct, 9.30am-4pm Mon-Sat & 11-4pm Sun Nov-Mar) FREE These turf-covered terraces edged in brick and stone represent the only fully excavated Roman amphitheatre in Britain. It was positioned just outside of the Roman fortress walls and had a capacity of 6000 people. Follow the signs on the other side of the Broadway to see the foundations of the Roman military barracks.

Eating

Stuffed Dormouse BRASSERIE ££
(01633-430142; www.thestuffeddormouse.co.uk; Ponthir Rd; 2-/3-course menu £10/15, exotic meats £15-20; noon-11pm) While its name references a Roman delicacy, you won't find any dormice on the menu – but you will find ostrich, kangaroo, crocodile, llama, snake and zebra in the 'exotic meats' section. It's located about a mile north of the main part of Caerleon.

Getting There & Around

Caerleon is 3 miles northeast of central Newport. Buses head here from Newport (£1.70, 11 minutes, frequent) and Monmouth (£4.35, 45 minutes, eight daily).

ATTILIO PREGNOLATO / SHUTTERSTOCK ©

1. Pen-y-Fan (p105)
One of the most popular hikes in the Brecon Beacons.

2. Monnow Bridge (p88)
The UK's only complete medieval fortified bridge, in Monmouth.

3. Richard Booth's Bookshop (p102)
The most famous of the many specialist bookshops in Hay-on-Wye (p98).

4. Tintern Abbey (p87)
A picturesque riverside abbey built in the late 13th century and left to fall into ruin in 1536.

3

CORNFELD / SHUTTERSTOCK ©

MONMOUTHSHIRE (SIR FYNWY)

You need only ponder the preponderance of castles to realise that this pleasantly rural county was once a wild frontier. The Norman marcher lords kept stonemasons extremely busy, erecting mighty fortifications to keep the unruly Welsh at bay. Despite this stone line marking out a very clear border along the Rivers Monnow and Wye, the 1543 second Act of Union left Monmouthshire in a kind of jurisdictional limbo between England and Wales. This legal ambiguity wasn't put to rest until 1974 when Monmouthshire was definitively confirmed as part of Wales.

The River Wye, Britain's fifth-longest, flows from the mountains of Mid-Wales, tootles its way into England and then returns to the middle ground – forming the border of the two countries – before emptying into the River Severn below Chepstow. Much of it is designated an area of outstanding natural beauty (www.wyevalleyaonb.org.uk), famous for its limestone gorges and dense broadleaved woodland.

Chepstow (Cas-gwent)

POP 14,200

Chepstow is an attractive market town nestled in a great S-bend in the River Wye, with a magnificent Norman castle and one of Britain's best-known racecourses. It was first developed as a base for the Norman conquest of southeast Wales, later prospering as a port for the timber and wine trades. As river-borne commerce gave way to the railways, Chepstow's importance diminished to reflect its name, which means 'market place' in Old English.

OFF THE BEATEN TRACK

WYE VALLEY WALK

The Wye Valley Walk (www.wyevalleywalk.org) is a 136-mile riverside trail running from the river's source on the slopes of Plynlimon Fawr to Chepstow. The section downstream from Monmouth, past Tintern, is particularly beautiful.

Sights

★Chepstow Castle CASTLE

(Cadw; www.cadw.gov.wales; Bridge St; adult/child £4.50/3.40; ⌚9.30am-5pm Mar-Oct, 10am-4pm Nov-Feb) Imposing Chepstow Castle perches atop a limestone cliff overhanging the river, guarding the main river crossing from England into South Wales. It is one of the oldest castles in Britain – building started in 1067, less than a year after William the Conqueror invaded England. The impressive Great Tower dates from this time and includes bricks plundered from the nearby Roman town of Caerwent. It was extended over the centuries, resulting in a long, narrow complex snaking along the hill.

There are plenty of towers, battlements and wall walks to explore and lots of green space in between. Keep an eye out for the primitive latrines extending over the river and for the oldest surviving castle door in Europe, a massive wooden barrier dated to before 1190.

A cave in the cliff below the castle is one of many places where legend says King Arthur and his knights are napping until the day they're needed to save Britain.

Once the entire town was enclosed in fortifications, fastening it to the castle. Parts of the 13th-century **Port Wall** edge the west side of the town centre. You can see it from the Welsh St car park and near the train station. Chepstow's main street, High St, passes through the **Gate House**, the original city gate, which was restored in the 16th century.

Chepstow Museum MUSEUM

(☎01291-625981; Bridge St; ⌚11am-4pm Mon-Sat, 2-4pm Sun) FREE Housed in an 18th-century town house just across the road from the castle, this small, child-friendly museum covers Chepstow's industrial and social history. A collection of 18th- and 19th-century prints and drawings reflects the area's importance to early tourists and students of the picturesque.

St Mary's Priory Church CHURCH

(Upper Church St; ⌚hours vary) Elements of this venerable church, including the wonderful zigzag-patterned arches of its Romanesque doorway, date from the 11th century. It was once part of a Benedictine Abbey established by the Normans at the same time as the castle.

Activities

The Wye Valley Walk has one of its trailheads near the castle in Chepstow, while Offa's Dyke Path (p211) starts just over the river in Sedbury. For a taste of both, you can walk upriver to Tintern on the former, cross the bridge just past the Abbey and take the path to Devil's Pulpit where you can join the latter for the return leg. The total distance is around 13 miles; allow a full day, with lunch at Tintern. Ordnance Survey (OS) *Explorer Map OL14* is recommended. You can cut the walk short at Tintern and return to Chepstow (or continue to Monmouth) by bus.

Festivals & Events

Chepstow Farmers' Market FOOD & DRINK
(High St; ⏲9am-1pm market days) Held on the morning of the second and fourth Saturdays of the month.

Chepstow Festival PERFORMING ARTS
(www.chepstowfestival.co.uk; ⏲Jun & Jul) A four-week-long festival held in even-numbered years, with medieval pageantry, drama and music, outdoor art exhibits, comedy, street entertainment and Shakespeare in the castle.

Chepstow Show FAIR
(www.chepstowshow.co.uk; ⏲Aug) An agricultural one-dayer, with the usual array of livestock, craft and kennel-club competitions.

Chepstow

Top Sights
1 Chepstow Castle B2

Sights
2 Chepstow Museum C2
3 Gate House & Port Wall B3

Sleeping
4 Castle View Hotel C2
5 Three Tuns B2

Eating
6 Boat Inn C1
7 Chepstow Farmers' Market B3
8 Lime Tree B2
9 Mythos! B3
10 Riverside Wine Bar C1

Drinking & Nightlife
11 Coach & Horses Inn A3

Entertainment
12 Chepstow Male Voice Choir A2

Chepstow

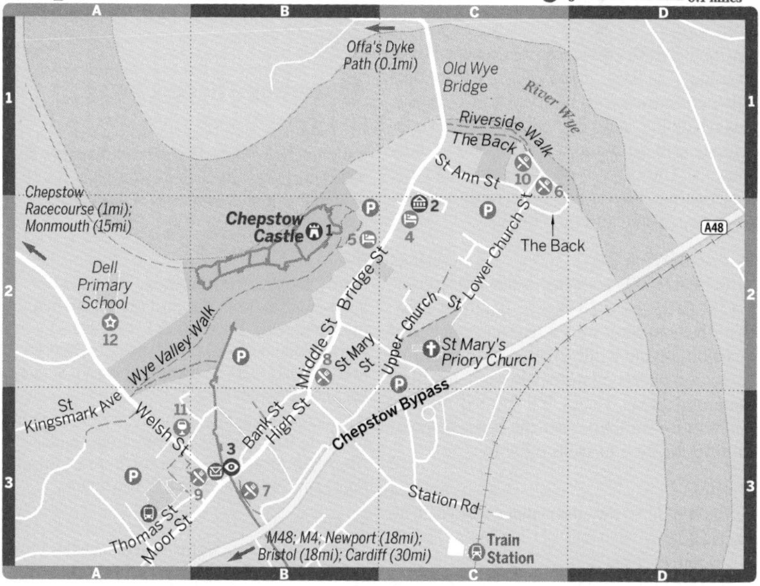

Sleeping

Three Tuns PUB ££

(☎01291-645797; www.threetunschepstow.co.uk; 32 Bridge St; s/d from £50/75) This early 17th-century pub by the castle has had an artful makeover, with rugs and antique furniture complementing the more rugged features of the ancient building. There's often live music downstairs on weekends, but the noise winds down at 11pm.

Castle View Hotel HOTEL ££

(☎01291-620349; www.castleviewhotel.com; 16 Bridge St; s/d from £70/85;) The 300-year-old Castle View has intriguing historic details, including 18th-century wall paintings in two of the bedrooms and hand-painted glass in the back door. Most rooms are small and the floors are creaky, but there's plenty of atmosphere.

Eating & Drinking

Lime Tree CAFE £

(☎01291-620959; www.sabrain.com/limetree; 24 St Mary St; mains £4.50-13; ⏲8.30am-11pm;) The Lime Tree handles the transition from cosy daytime cafe into trendy gastro bar seamlessly. The vastly varied menu stretches from breakfast into sandwiches, burgers and all the traditional tapas favourites. Grab a newspaper and settle into one of the nooks.

Boat Inn PUB FOOD £

(☎01291-628192; www.facebook.com/theboatinnchepstow; The Back; mains £8-10; ⏲10am-11pm Wed-Sun) Strewn with nautical knick-knacks, this riverside pub dishes up better-than-average pub grub and a good menu of daily specials. The three best tables are upstairs, overlooking the river. Entertainment includes open-mic and quiz nights.

Riverside Wine Bar TAPAS ££

(☎01291-628300; www.theriversidewinebar.co.uk; 18a The Back; mains £8-14; ⏲5-11pm Wed, noon-11pm Thu-Sun) Sink into a leather couch and quaff on a wine while grazing through antipasto and cheese platters, skewers, tortillas, pizza and tapas. Heavy gilt-framed mirrors and feature wallpaper set the tone, while in summer the action spills outside.

Mythos! GREEK ££

(☎01291-627222; www.themythos.co.uk; Welsh St; mains £9-18; ⏲noon-midnight Tue-Thu, to 2am Fri & Sat, 5pm-midnight Sun;) Exposed beams, stone walls and dramatic lighting make this lively Greek bar and restaurant memorable, but it's the authentic, delicious food that justifies that exclamation mark in the name: tzatziki, grilled haloumi, spanakopita, lamb and chicken souvlaki, moussaka – served as meze or main-sized portions.

Coach & Horses Inn PUB

(☎01291-622626; Welsh St;) This 16th-century coaching inn gets packed to the rafters during rugby games but it's a great place for a quiet beer or pub meal otherwise. Upstairs there's a handful of en suite rooms.

Entertainment

Chepstow Male Voice Choir LIVE MUSIC

(www.chepstowmvc.co.uk; Dell Primary School, Welsh St; ⏲7-9pm Mon & Thu) Chepstow's equivalent of the cast of *Glee* (albeit a considerably older, exclusively male, much more Welsh version) rehearses twice a week at a local primary school. All fans of booming Welsh manhood are welcome.

Chepstow Racecourse HORSE RACING

(☎01291-622260; www.chepstow-racecourse.co.uk; A466) Set in rolling parkland alongside the River Wye, north of the town centre, Chepstow Racecourse is one of Britain's most famous horse-racing venues. It's home to Wales' most prestigious race meeting, the Welsh Grand National – a roughly 3-mile steeplechase held between Christmas and New Year, which has been run here since 1949.

Getting There & Away

BICYCLE

National Cycle Route 42 starts at Chepstow and heads northwest through Abergavenny. Route 4 (London, Bristol, Swansea, St Davids) also passes through.

BUS

From Chepstow's **bus station** (Thomas St), buses head to/from Newport (£3.80, 40 minutes, frequent), Tintern (£3, 13 minutes, 11 daily), Monmouth (£3.80, 40 minutes, hourly) and Bristol (£5.50, 55 minutes, hourly). Sunday services are limited.

National Express (www.nationalexpress.com) has up to four coaches a day to/from London (from £12, three hours), Cardiff (from £4.80, one hour) and Swansea (from £11, two hours).

TRAIN

There are direct trains to/from Gloucester (£9.80, 30 minutes, frequent), Newport (£7.30, 23 minutes, 14 daily), Cardiff (£9.60, 40 minutes, 16 daily), Swansea (from £11, 1¾ hours, daily) and Fishguard Harbour (from £18, 3¾ hours, daily).

Lower Wye Valley

The A466 road follows the snaking, steep-sided valley of the River Wye from Chepstow to Monmouth, passing through the straggling village of Tintern with its famous abbey. This is a beautiful drive, rendered particularly mysterious when a twilight mist rises from the river and shrouds the illuminated ruins.

Sights

★Tintern Abbey HISTORIC BUILDING
(Cadw; www.cadw.gov.wales; Tintern; adult/child £5.50/4.10; ⏲9am-5pm Mar-Oct, 10am-4pm Nov-Feb; Ⓟ) The haunting riverside ruins of this sprawling monastic complex have inspired poets and artists through the centuries, including William Wordsworth, who penned *Lines Composed a Few Miles Above Tintern Abbey* during a visit in 1798, and JMW Turner, who made many paintings and drawings of the site. It was founded in 1131 by the Cistercian order and left to fall into picturesque ruin after the monks were booted out by Henry VIII in 1536.

The huge abbey church was built between 1269 and 1301, its soaring Gothic arches a testament to the pre-Reformation monastic wealth and power the king so coveted. The finest feature is the ornate tracery that once contained the magnificent west windows. Spreading to the north are the remains of the cloisters, the infirmary, the chapter house, the refectory, the latrines, and a complex system of drains and sewers.

The site is clearly visible from the road, but if you want to explore it properly you'll need a good hour to do it justice. It's best visited either early or towards the end of the day, after the coach-tour crowds have dispersed.

There are plenty of options for riverside walks around Tintern. One of the best begins at the old railway bridge just upstream from the abbey, and leads up to the **Devil's Pulpit**, a limestone crag on the east side of the river with a spectacular view over the abbey (2.5 miles round trip).

Old Station Tintern NOTABLE BUILDING
(☎01291-689566; www.tinternvillage.co.uk/seedo/tintern-old-station; parking per 3/5hr £1/3.50; ⏲10am-5.30pm Apr-Oct; Ⓟ) FREE Just over 1 mile upstream from Tintern Abbey, this Victorian train station has old railway coaches that house a tourist information desk, temporary exhibitions and a cafe. There's a large grassy play area for kids, picnic spots and easy riverside walks.

Sleeping & Eating

Tŷ Bryn B&B ££
(☎01594-531330; www.wyevalleystay.co.uk; Monmouth Rd, Llandogo; r £75-90; Ⓟ📶) Perched on a hillside overlooking a pretty stretch of the river in the village of Llandogo, this old stone house has friendly young owners and

THE WYE TOUR

The Wye Valley has a valid claim to being the birthplace of British tourism. Boat trips along the River Wye began commercially in 1760, but a best-selling book – in fact, one of the first ever travel guidebooks – William Gilpin's *Observations on the River Wye and Several Parts of South Wales* (1771), inspired hundreds of people to take the boat trip down the river from Ross-on-Wye (in England) to Chepstow, visiting the various beauty spots and historical sites en route. Early tourists included many famous figures, such as poets William Wordsworth and Samuel Taylor Coleridge, painter JMW Turner and Admiral Lord Nelson, who made the tour in 1802. Doing the Wye Tour soon became *de rigueur* among English high society.

Local people made good money providing crewed rowing boats for hire, which were equipped with canopies and comfortable chairs and tables where their clients could paint or write, while inns and taverns cashed in on the trade by providing food, drink and accommodation. It was normally a two-day trip, with an overnight stay in Monmouth and stops at Tintern Abbey and Chepstow Castle, among others. In the second half of the 19th century, with the arrival of the railways, the hundreds of tourists increased to thousands, and the tour became so commercialised that it was no longer fashionable.

You can still do the Wye Tour, but these days it's a less glamorous, more DIY affair.

three comfortable en suite rooms, two of which have river views.

Tintern Old Rectory B&B ££

(☎01291-689920; www.tintern-oldrectory.co.uk; Monmouth Rd, Tintern Parva; s/d from £75/83; P 📶 🐾) Dressed in pale pink, blue and cherry-blossom wallpaper, the four sweet rooms in this Tudor-inspired 18th-century house either look over the river or have access to the rear garden. The breakfast menu offers an impressive array of options.

Parva Farmhouse B&B ££

(☎01291-689411; www.parvafarmhouse.co.uk; Monmouth Rd, Tintern Parva; s/d from £65/80) This cosy 17th-century farmhouse has low oak-beamed ceilings, leather Chesterfield sofas, a bar and a wood-burning stove in the lounge, and a garden with beautiful views across the valley. The eight bedrooms are chintzy and appealingly old-fashioned; one has a four-poster.

★ The Whitebrook MODERN BRITISH £££

(☎01600-860254; www.thewhitebrook.co.uk; Whitebrook; 2-/3-/7-course lunch £25/29/47, 3-/7-course dinner £54/67, r incl dinner from £214; ⏲noon-2pm Wed-Sun, 7-9pm Tue-Sun; P 📶) Hidden down narrow country lanes in a remote part of the Wye Valley, this wonderful Michelin-starred restaurant-with-rooms is well worth the effort it takes to reach it. Every plate that proceeds from the kitchen is a little work of art, packed with interesting flavours. If a sober driver is an unlikely prospect, book one of the eight elegant rooms upstairs.

Getting There & Away

Eleven buses a day (fewer on Saturday, none on Sunday) stop here on their journey between Chepstow (13 minutes) and Monmouth (30 minutes).

Monmouth (Trefynwy)

POP 10,500

Against a background of pastel-painted Georgian prosperity, the compact market town of Monmouth bustles and thrives. It sits at the confluence of the Rivers Wye and Monnow, and has hopped in and out of Wales over the centuries as the border shifted back and forth. Today it feels more English than Welsh.

One of Monmouth's claims to fame is Rockfield Studios, a few miles to the northwest. Established in the 1960s, the studio has produced a string of hit albums, including Queen's *A Night at the Opera,* Oasis' *(What's the Story) Morning Glory?* and Super Furry Animals' *Rings Around the World,* and has been used by artists from Iggy Pop to Coldplay. It's not unknown for rock stars to be spotted in Monmouth's pubs and restaurants.

History

The town is famous as the birthplace of King Henry V, victor at the Battle of Agincourt in 1415 and immortalised by Shakespeare. Other locals who have passed into history include the 12th-century historian Geoffrey of Monmouth and Charles Stewart Rolls, co-founder of Rolls-Royce.

When Catholicism was banned in Britain, Monmouthshire was a notable pocket of resistance. In 1679 a Catholic priest, Fr (later St) David Lewis, was discovered, tried in Monmouth and hung, drawn and quartered in nearby Usk.

Sights & Activities

St Thomas the Martyr's Church CHURCH

(www.monmouthparishes.org.uk; St Thomas' Sq; ⏲hours vary) Positioned by the Monnow Bridge, sweet little St Thomas still retains some original features from its founding in around 1180. Inside there's a distinctive Norman Romanesque arch, and pews and a gallery fashioned out of dark wood.

Monnow Bridge BRIDGE

Monmouth's main drag, such that it is, starts at car-free Monnow Bridge, the UK's only complete example of a medieval fortified bridge. It was built in 1272 to protect the English town from the Welsh, but it was later used to extract tolls from people entering the town. Much of what you see now dates from a 1705 restoration.

Monmouth Castle CASTLE

(www.monmouthcastlemuseum.org.uk; Castle Hill) All that remains of Monmouth Castle is a scant section of wall that once enclosed the great hall and the adjoining tower. Despite being the birthplace of a king (Henry V was born here in 1397), it was largely dismantled in the 17th century and the stone used to build Great Castle House next door.

Castle & Regimental Museum MUSEUM

(☎01600-772175; www.monmouthcastlemuseum.org.uk; Castle Hill; ⏲2-5pm Apr-Oct) FREE Inside

Great Castle House, this volunteer-run regimental museum is a labour of love squeezed into a cupboard-sized space. It traces the history of the Royal Monmouthshire Royal Engineers (doubly royal!) from its origins as a 16th-century militia to its current role as the senior regiment of the reserve army.

Shire Hall HISTORIC BUILDING

(☎01600-775257; www.shirehallmonmouth.org.uk; Agincourt Sq; ⌚10am-4pm) **FREE** Fronting Agincourt Sq at the north end of Monnow St, this handsome Georgian building was built in 1724 to house sittings of the assizes court. It was here that three of the leaders of the pro-democracy Chartist movement were sentenced to death for their part in the Newport Rising (p307). You can visit the historic courtroom upstairs and then head down to the holding cells below. There's also a small archaeological display on the ground floor, behind the tourist information desk.

In front of the building is a statue of former Monmouth resident Charles Stewart Rolls (1877–1910), one half of the team that founded Rolls-Royce. Not only a pioneering motorist and aviator, he was the first British citizen to die in an air accident. He's depicted clutching a model of the Wright biplane in which he died.

St Mary's Catholic Church CHURCH

(☎01600-712029; www.monmouth-catholic.org; St Mary St) In 1793, after the official suppression of the faith was relaxed, St Mary's was the first new Catholic church to be opened in Wales. Even then it needed to be discreet and was hidden behind a line of cottages. They've since been removed, explaining why it's set back from the road.

Monmouth

Sights

1 Castle & Regimental Museum B1
2 Monmouth Castle B1
3 Monnow Bridge A3
4 Nelson Museum & Local History Centre B1
5 Shire Hall B1
6 St Mary's Catholic Church C1
7 St Thomas the Martyr's Church A3

Activities, Courses & Tours

8 Monmouth Canoe & Activity Centre D1

Sleeping

9 Monnow Bridge Caravan & Camping Site A2

Eating

10 Bistro Prego C1
11 Misbah Tandoori C1

Monmouth

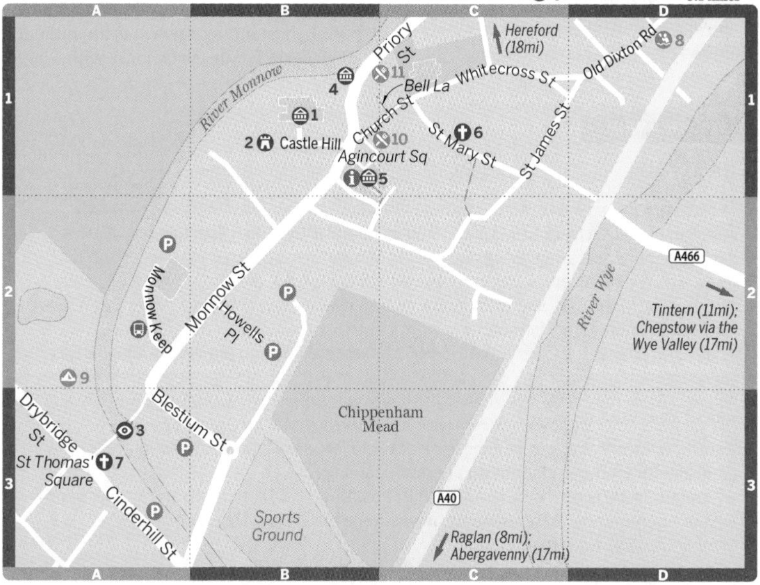

Nelson Museum & Local History Centre MUSEUM
(☎01600-710630; Priory St; ⏰11am-4pm Mon-Sat, 2-4pm Sun) FREE Admiral Horatio Nelson visited Monmouth twice in 1802, officially en route to inspect Pembrokeshire forests for ship timber, though it may have had more to do with his affair with local heiress Lady Emma Hamilton. Despite this tenuous connection, Lady Llangattock, mother of Charles Stewart Rolls (of Rolls-Royce fame), became an obsessive collector of 'Nelsoniana', and the results of her obsession can be seen in this endearing museum. Monmouth history is also covered, including a display on Rolls and some interesting old photographs.

It's fascinating to see how fanatical the Nelson-worship was in 19th-century Britain, with forged items, such as locks of his hair, displayed alongside banal relics of the great man himself.

Monmouth Canoe & Activity Centre CANOEING
(☎01600-716083; www.monmouthcanoe.co.uk; Old Dixton Rd; guided paddles from £40) Rents two-person Canadian canoes (half/full day £35/45), single kayaks (£25/30) and double kayaks (£35/45); prices include return transport. Heading downstream from Monmouth you can reach Whitebrook in half a day, or Chepstow in a day. However, you'll need a guide to navigate the tidal section of the river downstream from Bigsweir Bridge, near Tintern.

Sleeping & Eating

Monnow Bridge Caravan & Camping Site CAMPSITE £
(☎01600-714004; Drybridge St; sites from £7; P) Just across Monnow Bridge from central Monmouth, this tiny campground has a quiet riverside location, despite being only a short stroll from the town centre.

Bistro Prego MODERN BRITISH ££
(☎01600-712600; www.pregomonmouth.co.uk; 7 Church St; mains £13-17, s/d from £45/65; ⏰noon-10pm; 📶) Set on a cobbled lane in the heart of the town, this little bistro serves very good bistro fare which, despite the name, isn't particularly Italian. Upstairs there are eight comfortable, clean, good-value rooms, each with its own bathroom.

The Stonemill MODERN EUROPEAN ££
(☎01600-716273; www.thestonemill.co.uk; B4233, Rockfield; mains lunch £14-17, dinner £17-24; ⏰10am-2pm & 6-9pm Tue-Sat, noon-2.30pm Sun) Housed in a 16th-century barn, 2.5 miles northwest of Monmouth, this upmarket restaurant showcases Welsh produce in Italian- and French-influenced dishes. They pride themselves on making all of their own bread, pasta, pastries, jam, chutneys, ice cream and sorbets. The complex also has six stone and oak-beamed cottages for hire.

Misbah Tandoori BANGLADESHI ££
(☎01600-714940; http://themisbah.com; 9 Priory St; mains £8-15; ⏰noon-2.30pm & 5.30-11pm; 📶✎) Longstanding Misbah is an authentic Bangladeshi family curry house with a large,

WORTH A TRIP

RAGLAN

The last great medieval castle to be built in Wales, **Raglan Castle** (Cadw; www.cadw.wales.gov.uk; adult/child £4.50/3.40; ⏰9.30am-5pm Mar-Oct, 10am-4pm Nov-Feb; P) was designed more as a swaggering declaration of wealth and power than a defensive fortress. A magnificent, sprawling complex built of dusky pink and grey sandstone, it was constructed in the 15th and 16th centuries by Sir William ap Thomas and his son William Herbert, the first earl of Pembroke.

Its centrepiece, the lavish Great Tower, a hexagonal keep ringed by a moat, bears a savage wound from the civil wars of the 1640s, when it was besieged by Cromwell's soldiers. After the castle's surrender the tower was undermined, until eventually two of the six walls collapsed. The impressive courtyards beyond the Great Tower display the transition from fortress to grandiose palace, with ornate windows and fireplaces, gargoyle-studded crenelations and heraldic carvings.

Raglan Castle is on the busy A40, 8 miles southwest of Monmouth and 9 miles southeast of Abergavenny. Buses heading between the two stop at Raglan village, which is a five-minute walk from the castle.

loyal and sometimes famous following. Paul Weller, REM, Oasis and Arthur Scargill have all dined here. Vegetarians are well looked after.

Information

Tourist Office (01600-775257; www.shirehallmonmouth.org.uk; Shire Hall, Agincourt Sq; 10am-4pm)

Getting There & Away

From the central **bus station** (Monnow Keep), buses head to/from Chepstow (£3.80, 40 minutes, hourly), Caerleon (£4.35, 45 minutes, eight daily), Newport (£5.45, 57 minutes, nine daily), Abergavenny (£3.40, 45 minutes, seven daily) and Hereford (£5.50, 50 minutes, six daily). Sunday services are limited.

National Express (www.nationalexpress.com) has a daily coach to/from Birmingham (£20, 1¾ hours), Ross-on-Wye (£4.80, 20 minutes), Newport (£9, 35 minutes) and Cardiff (£11, one hour).

There's free parking on Cinderhill St, near St Thomas the Martyr's Church.

Skenfrith (Ynysgynwraidd)

A chocolate-box village of stone buildings set around a hefty castle and ancient church and skirted by the River Monnow, Skenfrith encapsulates the essence of the Monmouthshire countryside.

The local pub produces its own walk pamphlets (50p) – one route leads over the English border to Garway Church, which is adorned with swastikas and mason's marks from its Knights Templar past.

Sights

Skenfrith Castle CASTLE

(Cadw; www.cadw.gov.wales; 10am-4pm) FREE Skenfrith Castle was built around 1228 by Hubert de Burgh on the site of earlier Norman fortifications. Its keep and walls remain reasonably intact and there are no barriers to prevent you entering and picnicking on the central lawn.

St Bridget's Church CHURCH

(hours vary) Crowned with a squat tower, this 750-year-old red-sandstone church is accessed via a low wooden door with a foot-high step.

Sleeping

Bell at Skenfrith HOTEL £££

(01600-750235; www.skenfrith.co.uk; r £150-230; P) A picturesque village pub, the Bell has a popular restaurant and elegant rooms, all named after fishing flies. Some have four-posters but all marry an antique feel with contemporary comfort. The restaurant serves upmarket country fare, with lots of the produce coming from its kitchen garden.

Getting There & Away

Skenfrith is 8 miles northwest of Monmouth via the B4233, B4347 and B4521. There's no public transport to these parts.

Abergavenny (Y Fenni)

POP 10,100

Bustling, workaday Abergavenny has played many roles on history's stage: Roman fort, Norman stronghold, tanning and weaving centre, and prison for Hitler's deputy. Its enviable location between three shapely hills – the Blorenge, Ysgyryd Fawr (Skirrid), and Sugar Loaf – makes it a superb base for walkers, while its annual food festival and its acclaimed restaurants (the best of which are actually just out of town) attract lovers of fresh, organic, seasonal Welsh cuisine.

Its ancient name, Y Fenni (Welsh for 'place of the smiths'), was given to a stream that empties into the River Usk here, and later anglicised to Gavenny (Abergavenny means 'mouth of the Gavenny'). The Romans established Gobannium Fort here, exactly a day's march from their garrison at Caerleon, which they maintained from AD 57 to 400. Not long after the Norman conquest, a marcher lord, Hamelin de Ballon, built the castle and the town's regional importance grew.

Sights

★ **St Mary's Priory Church** CHURCH

(01873-858787; www.stmarys-priory.org; Monk St; 9am-4pm Mon-Sat) Although you wouldn't guess it from the outside, this large stone church has been described as the 'Westminster Abbey of South Wales' because of the remarkable treasury of aristocratic tombs that lies within. It was founded at the same time as the castle (1087) as part of a Benedictine priory, but the present building dates mainly from the 14th century, with 15th- and 19th-century additions and alterations.

St Mary's survived Henry VIII's dissolution of the monasteries by being converted into a parish church, making it an interesting counterpoint to the ruins of nearby Tintern and Llanthony abbeys. In the northern transept is one of the most important medieval carvings in Europe – a monumental 15th-century wooden representation of the biblical figure of Jesse. It was the base of what must have been a mighty altarpiece showing the lineage of Jesus. It's the only such figure to survive the Reformation. Nearby, a graceful, worn, carved-oak effigy (1325) commemorates Sir John de Hastings, who was responsible for the church's 14th-century transformation.

The church's oldest memorial (1256) is the stone figure near the sanctuary of Eva de Braose, Lady Abergavenny, portrayed holding a shield. Her husband William was hanged after being found in the bedchamber of Prince Llywelyn the Great's wife, daughter of England's King John. The family tradition of royal adultery and execution continued with their direct descendant, Anne Boleyn.

The Herbert Chapel is packed with recumbent effigies. Most depict members of the Herbert family, starting with Sir William ap Thomas, founder of Raglan Castle, and his wife Gwladys – Sir William's feet rest on a lion that looks like it was modelled on a sheep. The oak choir stalls were carved in the 15th century (note the lively misericords and the little dragons at the ends).

Tithe Barn HISTORIC BUILDING
(☎ 01873-858787; www.stmarys-priory.org; Monk St; ⏰ 9am-4pm Mon-Sat) FREE The large blocky building next to the church is the former abbey's 12th-century tithe barn, the place where people brought their obligatory contributions to the church, usually 10% of whatever they produced. This particular one has had a chequered history (it was a 17th-century theatre and a 20th-century disco, among other things) but it has now been fully restored and converted into a heritage centre and a **food hall** focusing on locally sourced Welsh products.

Pride of place goes to the Abergavenny Tapestry, produced by over 60 local volunteers over six years to mark the new millennium. Within its 8m width it depicts the history of the town; look for faint messages from the stitchers in the borders. Elsewhere on this floor a combination of artefacts and touch-screen monitors tells the story of the town and the abbey in an excellent interactive display.

Abergavenny

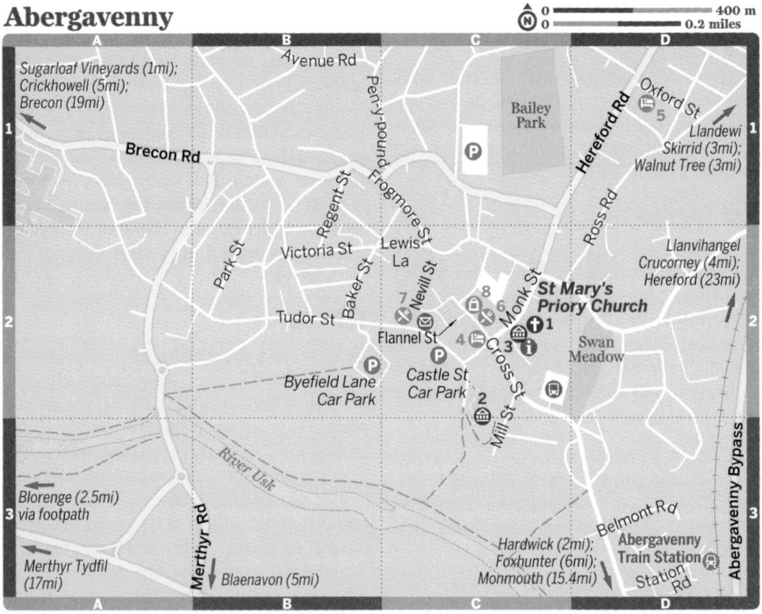

Abergavenny Museum & Castle MUSEUM
(☎01873-854282; www.abergavennymuseum.co.uk; Castle St; ⊙11am-1pm & 2-5pm Mon-Sat, 2-5pm Sun) FREE Abergavenny castle's keep was converted into a hunting lodge during the Victorian era and now houses a small museum. It tells the history of the castle and the town, and includes re-creations of a 19th-century Welsh farmhouse kitchen, a saddlery workshop and Basil Jones' grocery shop. The shop was transferred when it closed in the 1980s and makes a fascinating display, with many items dating back to the 1930s and '40s.

Not much remains of the castle itself except for an impressive stretch of curtain wall on either side of the gatehouse on the northwest side. It was the site of a notorious event in 1175 when the Norman lord William de Braose invited his Welsh rivals for a Christmas dinner and had them massacred. Frequently besieged but never taken, the castle was wrecked by royalist forces in 1645 during the Civil War in order to keep it out of parliamentary hands.

Sugarloaf Vineyards WINERY
(☎01873-853066; www.sugarloafvineyard.co.uk; off Pentre Lane; tastings £3-6; ⊙10.30am-5pm Tue-Sat, noon-5pm Sun Easter-Oct; P) Established in 1992, this vineyard on the northwestern edge of town produces a variety of white and red wines, including an award-winning sparkling. You can take a self-guided tour before sampling the goods at the cafe and store.

Abergavenny

Top Sights
1 St Mary's Priory Church.......................C2

Sights
2 Abergavenny Museum & Castle C2
3 Tithe Barn C2

Sleeping
4 Angel Hotel C2
5 Guest House D1

Eating
Angel Hotel ....(see 4)
6 Cwtch Cafe C2
7 King's Arms C2

Shopping
8 Abergavenny Market...........................C2

Blorenge MOUNTAIN
Of the three mountains encircling Abergavenny, Blorenge (561m) is the closest to town – the round trip is only 5 miles – but it is a steep and strenuous outing, and good walking boots are recommended. This is one of Britain's finest paragliding and hang-gliding sites. In fact, it's so good that the South East Wales Hang Gliding and Paragliding Club (www.sewhgpgc.co.uk) purchased the mountain in 1998 and holds regular competition events here.

From Abergavenny, cross the bridge over the River Usk on Merthyr Rd and immediately turn right and follow the lane past the cemetery and under the main road. Cross the B4246 road in Llanfoist and follow the lane beside the church until it bends left; continue through a tunnel under the canal and then follow a steep path straight uphill (a former tram road that carried coal down to the canal). When you emerge from the woods, there is a final steep climb up an obvious path to the summit.

Activities

If hiking up the three peaks surrounding Abergavenny sounds too strenuous, you can follow easy paths along the banks of the River Usk or explore the towpath of the Monmouthshire and Brecon Canal, which passes 1 mile southwest of the town.

Festivals & Events

South Wales Three Peaks Trial SPORTS
(www.threepeakstrial.co.uk; ⊙Mar) An annual walking challenge held in March to test your endurance and map-reading skills.

Abergavenny Festival of Cycling SPORTS
(www.abergavennyfestivalofcycling.co.uk; ⊙Jul) A mid-July lycra-enthusiasts' meet incorporating the Iron Mountain Sportives, participatory events with 20-mile, 40-mile, 70-mile and 100-mile courses.

Abergavenny Food Festival FOOD & DRINK
(www.abergavennyfoodfestival.co.uk; ⊙Sep) The most important gastronomic event in Wales, held on the third weekend in September, with demonstrations, debates, competitions, courses, stalls and the odd celebrity. But the real drawcard is that this is an enthusiastically local festival, run by volunteers, and not some big-budget food producer's showcase. Kooky things can and do happen.

Sleeping

Angel Hotel HOTEL ££
(☎01873-857121; www.angelabergavenny.com; 15 Cross St; r/cottage from £89/177; P 📶) Abergavenny's top hotel is a fine Georgian building that was once a famous coaching inn. Choose between sleek, sophisticated rooms in the hotel itself, in an adjoining mews, in a Victorian lodge near the castle or in the 17th-century Castle Cottage (sleeping four). There's also a good **restaurant** (mains £14-18, bar £6-14; ⏲noon-11pm) and bar.

Guest House B&B ££
(☎01873-854823; www.theguesthouseabergavenny.co.uk; 2 Oxford St; s/d from £45/80; P 📶 🐾) This family-friendly B&B has six cheerful, flouncy, en suite rooms with mountain views and a mini-menagerie of pigs, rabbits, chickens and parrots. The gregarious owners slap up fantastic breakfasts, including good veggie options.

Eating

While there are some good places to eat in the town centre, Abergavenny's most acclaimed restaurants occupy country pubs in the surrounding farmland.

Town Centre

Cwtch Cafe CAFE £
(☎01873-855466; 58 Cross St; mains £4-6; ⏲9am-5pm Mon-Sat; 📶) Stylish and wonderfully friendly, Cwtch (Welsh for 'hug') entices a scrum of regulars through the doors with its home-made cakes, coffee and lunchtime dishes such as rarebit, pancakes with crispy bacon, quiche and veggie lasagne.

King's Arms PUB FOOD ££
(☎01873-855074; www.kingsarmsabergavenny.co.uk; 29 Nevill St; mains £10-16; ⏲noon-3pm & 6-9pm; 📶 🐾) Abergavenny's most appealing pub dates from the 16th century and has a cosy bar area with low ceilings and a fabulously incongruous oil painting of Martin Scorsese. The neighbouring dining room takes pub food to the next level of sophistication, while still keeping a rustic edge. Upstairs there are 11 comfortable en suite rooms.

Around Abergavenny

The Hardwick MODERN BRITISH ££
(☎01873-854220; www.thehardwick.co.uk; Old Raglan Rd; mains £15-23, s/d from £115/135; ⏲noon-3pm & 6.30-10pm; P) This traditional inn with an old stone fireplace and low ceiling beams has become, under the direction of chef Stephen Terry, a showcase for the best of unpretentious country cooking. Save room for the home-made ice cream. The Hardwick is 2 miles south of Abergavenny on the B4598. Attached are eight elegant rooms.

★**Walnut Tree** MODERN BRITISH £££
(☎01873-852797; www.thewalnuttreeinn.com; Old Ross Rd, Llanddewi Skirrid; mains £21-29, 2-/3-course lunch £25/30; ⏲noon-2.30pm & 6.30-10pm Tue-Sat) Established in 1963, the Michelin-starred Walnut Tree serves the cuisine-hopping meat and seafood creations of chef Shaun Hill, with a focus on fresh, local produce. If you're too full to move far after dinner, elegant cottage accommodation is available. The Walnut Tree is 3 miles northeast of Abergavenny on the B4521.

Shopping

Abergavenny Market MARKET
(☎01873-735811; Cross St; ⏲6am-5pm market days) The 19th-century Market Hall is a lively place, hosting a general market (food, drink, clothes, household goods) on Tuesday, Friday and Saturday, a flea market (bric-a-brac, collectables, secondhand goods) on Wednesday, regular weekend craft and antiques fairs, and a farmers market on the fourth Thursday of each month. Stalls spill out onto the square behind.

Information

Nevill Hall Hospital (☎01873-732732; www.wales.nhs.uk; Brecon Rd; ⏲24hr) Emergency service.

Police Station (☎01633-838111; www.gwent.police.uk; Tudor St)

Tourist Office (☎01873-853254; www.visitabergavenny.co.uk; Tithe Barn, Monk St; ⏲10am-2pm Tue-Sat)

Getting There & Away

BICYCLE

National Cycle Route 42 passes through Abergavenny, heading south to Chepstow and north to Glasbury, where it connects with National Cycle Route 8 (Lôn Las Cymru).

BUS

Direct bus services to/from Abergavenny's station include Cardiff (£9.10, 2½ hours, 12 daily), Merthyr Tydfil (£6.40, 1½ hours, 13 daily),

Monmouth (£3.40, 45 minutes, seven daily), Brecon (£3.40, 45 minutes, 12 daily) and Hereford (£5.30, 50 minutes, six daily).

TRAIN

There are direct trains to/from Cardiff (£14, 45 minutes, frequent), Swansea (£25, 1½ hours, 15 daily), Tenby (from £18, 3¾ hours, daily), Holyhead (from £30, four hours, seven daily) and Manchester (from £25, three hours, 15 daily).

BRECON BEACONS NATIONAL PARK

Rippling dramatically for 45 miles from near Llandeilo in the west all the way to the English border, Brecon Beacons National Park (Parc Cenedlaethol Bannau Brycheiniog) encompasses some of the finest scenery in southern Wales. High mountain plateaus of grass and heather, their northern rims scalloped with glacier-scoured hollows, rise above wooded, waterfall-splashed valleys and green, rural landscapes.

There are four distinct regions within the park: the wild, lonely **Black Mountain** (Mynydd Du) in the west, with its high moors and glacial lakes; **Fforest Fawr** (Great Forest), whose rushing streams and spectacular waterfalls form the headwaters of the Rivers Tawe and Neath; the **Brecon Beacons** (Bannau Brycheiniog) proper, a group of very distinctive, flat-topped hills that includes Pen-y-Fan (886m), the park's highest peak; and the rolling heathland ridges of the **Black Mountains** (Y Mynyddoedd Duon) – not to be confused with the Black Mountain (singular) in the west.

Black Mountains (Y Mynyddoedd Duon)

The hills that stretch northward from Abergavenny to Hay-on-Wye are untamed and largely uninhabited, reaching a height of 811m at windswept Waun Fach.

The scenic and secluded Vale of Ewyas traces the path of the River Honddu through the heart of the Black Mountains, from the village of **Llanvihangel Crucorney** to the exposed Gospel Pass (542m), where a single-track road winds its way through a magically bleak landscape down to Hay-on-Wye. Along the way it passes the picturesque ruins of Llanthony Priory and the hamlet of **Capel-y-Ffin**, where there are more monastic ruins and the 18th-century Church of St Mary the Virgin.

Sights

Ysgyryd Fawr MOUNTAIN

(Skirrid) Of the glacially sculpted hills that surround Abergavenny, Skirrid (486m) is the most dramatic looking and has a history to match. A cleft in the rock near the top was once believed to have split open at the exact time of Christ's death and a chapel was built here on what was considered a particularly holy place (a couple of upright stones remain). During the Reformation, as many as 100 people would attend illegal Catholic Masses at this remote spot.

You can trek here from Llanvihangel Crucorney (5.5 miles) or take the B4521 from Abergavenny to the lay-by at the base of the hill (4 miles). It's a steep climb from here through the woods on a track that can be muddy; wear sensible shoes. Once you clear the tree line the walk is less steep, with a

BRECON BEACONS HIKING & BIKING

There are hundreds of walking routes in the park, ranging from gentle strolls to strenuous climbs. A set of five Walk Cards (£1 each) is available from the town tourist offices in and around the park, as well as the national park visitor centre near Libanus.

Likewise, there are many excellent off-road mountain-biking routes, including a series of 14 graded and waymarked trails detailed in a map and guidebook pack (£7.50).

Ordnance Survey (OS) Landranger maps 160 and 161 cover most of the park, as do Outdoor Leisure maps 12 and 13. These detailed maps include walking and cycling trails.

The **National Park Visitor Centre** (01874-623366; www.breconbeacons.org; Libanus; 9.30am-5pm Easter-Sep) information kiosk has details of walks, hiking and biking trails, outdoor activities, wildlife and geology. There's also a cafe. It's located off the A470, 4 miles southwest of Brecon and 15 miles north of Merthyr Tydfil. Any of the buses on the Merthyr Tydfil–Brecon route stop at Libanus village, a 1.25-mile walk away.

STARGAZING

In 2013 the Brecon Beacons became only the fifth place in the world to be awarded 'dark-sky' status. Light pollution is now closely monitored in the region, which is one of the UK's best for stargazing. Meteor showers, nebula, strings of constellations and the Milky Way can be seen in the night sky above the national park. Visitor centres throughout the park can give you information about stargazing events, or visit www.breconbeacons.org/stargazing.

final climb right at the end to the summit where you'll be rewarded with extravagant views.

Sugar Loaf MOUNTAIN

(Mynydd Pen-y-Fâl) The cone-shaped pinnacle of Sugar Loaf (596m) is a 4½-mile round trip from the Mynydd Llanwenarth viewpoint car park. Take the middle track that follows a stone wall, skirts a wood and climbs steeply uphill, turning right to bisect a grassy ridge before a final steep summit scramble. The descent route flanks the head of the valley.

To reach the car park, head west from Abergavenny on the A40. At the edge of town turn right for Sugarloaf Vineyards, then go left at the next two junctions.

St Issui's Church CHURCH

(Patrishow) Halfway up a hillside on a narrow country lane, 5 miles northwest of Llanvihangel Crucorney, this tiny 11th-century church contains a remarkable, finely carved wooden rood screen and loft, dating from around 1500. On the walls are medieval frescoes of biblical texts, coats of arms and a red-ochre skeleton (once believed to have been painted with human blood) bearing an hourglass and scythe – the figure of Death. The church is usually open; leave a donation in the box.

Down the hill from the church at the corner of the road is a spring, with flowers, toys and other offerings strewn about and ribbons tied to an overhanging tree. Known as the Holy Well of St Issui, it is believed to have healing powers and has long been a pilgrimage site. One of the steps leading down to the spring is carved with a Maltese Cross.

Llanthony Priory RUINS

(Cadw; www.cadw.gov.wales; ⏲10am-4pm) FREE Halfway along the Vale of Ewyas lie the atmospheric ruins of this Augustinian priory, set among grasslands and wooded hills by the River Honddu. The buildings were completed in 1230 but were abandoned after Henry VIII dissolved Britain's monasteries in 1538. Though not as grand as Tintern Abbey, the setting is even more romantic. JMW Turner painted the scene in 1794.

Activities

The Black Mountains' heath-covered summits and verdant valleys are ideally explored on foot, hoof or two wheels. The **Offa's Dyke Path** runs along the easternmost ridge between Pandy and Hay-on-Wye. **Llanvihangel Crucorney** (meaning 'Church of St Michael at the Corner of the Rock') makes a good base for an ascent of Ysgyryd Fawr; it's a 4-mile round trip from the village's famous pub to the summit. From **Llanthony**, several paths lead up to the top of the Hatterall ridge to the east; it's a stiff climb, but straightforward (2 to 3 miles round trip). For a more ambitious hike, follow the ridge north for 4 miles then descend to Vision Farm, then walk back along the valley road (9 miles round trip).

Black Mountains Cycle Centre MOUNTAIN BIKING

(☎07779 243099; www.blackmountainscyclecentre.com; Great Llwygy Farm; day pass push-up/uplift £6/30; ⏲10am-dusk) Located in farmland near Llanvihangel Crucorney, this centre has a range of downhill tracks complete with berms, bridges and jumps. Four are rated blue (moderate), four red (difficult) and five black (severe). On weekends you can pay extra for 'uplift' transport to the top of the trailheads (includes 10 to 12 transfers).

Grange Trekking Centre HORSE RIDING

(☎01873-890215; www.grangetrekking.co.uk; Capel-y-Ffin; per hour/half-day/day £17/32/52; 👪) The Griffiths family offers pony trekking in the Vale of Ewyas to suit all abilities. B&B accommodation (£38 per person) and camping (£6 per person) are also available.

Sleeping & Eating

★**Celyn Farm** B&B ££

(☎01873-890894; www.celynfarm.co.uk; Forest Coal Pit; s/d from £60/75) Set in 120 hectares of farmland reached by narrow lanes from either Llanvihangel Crucorney or

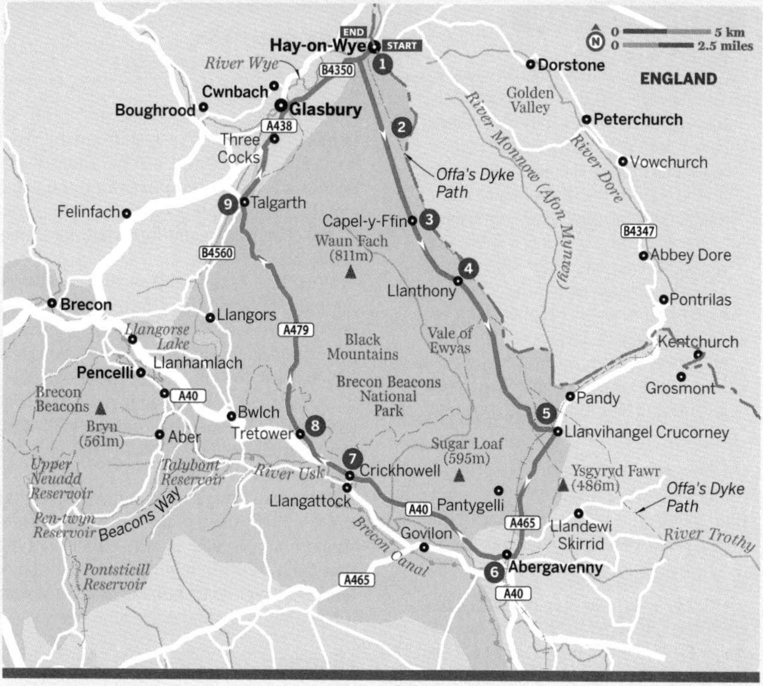

Driving Tour
Black Mountains Circuit

START HAY-ON-WYE
END HAY-ON-WYE
LENGTH 49 MILES; ONE DAY

This slow-paced drive takes you through a remote section of the Black Mountains on a narrow back road, climbing to dizzying heights (don't attempt it in winter weather!) and descending into a lush valley. It returns via a much easier route, visiting the charming village of Crickhowell and an intriguing stately home.

The route starts at the handsome little border town of **1 Hay-on-Wye**, which plays host to a famous literary festival as well as umpteen secondhand bookshops. However, you could just as easily jump ahead and start the circuit at Abergavenny or Crickhowell, if that's where you're based.

From Hay-on-Wye head south on Church St but turn sharply left onto Forest Rd at the edge of town. The road narrows to a single lane (you'll need to take it very slowly and pull over if you encounter another car) and quickly leads up to desolate moors as it crosses the **2 Gospel Pass**. The views of the forbidding Black Mountains are epic and it's quite possible that you'll encounter wild ponies on this stretch.

The country gets greener as you head down the other side into the Vale of Ewyas, via a couple of remote little churches in **3 Capel-y-Ffin** and on to the elegant ruins of **4 Llanthony Priory**.

Consider a pause at the unfeasibly ancient and creepy Skirrid Inn (p98) at **5 Llanvihangel Crucorney**. Beyond the village, turn right onto the A465, the main road into **6 Abergavenny**, where the sights include a priory church with graceful effigies, a ruined castle and a busy market hall. Take the A40 west out of town and stop to have a look at **7 Crickhowell**, one of the Brecon Beacons' most attractive towns. Continue along the A40 and turn right onto the A479. After a short while you'll come to **8 Tretower Court & Castle** (p109).

Head back onto the A479 and stop to visit the handsome stone town of **9 Talgarth**, with its restored mill and bakery cafe. From Talgarth, follow the signs back into Hay-on-Wye via the A4078, A438 and the B4350.

OFF THE BEATEN TRACK

BEACONS WAY

The 95-mile, eight-day Beacons Way trail wends its way across the national park from Ysgyryd Fawr in the Black Mountains to the village of Bethlehem on the edge of the Black Mountain, knocking off all the highest summits.

Needless to say, this is a stretching walk and requires proper walking gear as well as a good Ordnance Survey (OS) map – the moorland sections can be hard to navigate. The route is manageable in eight days, but you may want to take a little longer to make it more enjoyable and less of an endurance test.

Crickhowell (make sure you print out the directions), this remote country house offers four handsome rooms, excellent breakfasts and idyllic views over Sugar Loaf.

Llanthony Priory Hotel HOTEL ££
(01873-890487; www.llanthonyprioryhotel.co.uk; Llanthony; s/d from £70/90, mains lunch £4.50-9, dinner £11-12; food noon-2.30pm & 7-9pm; P) Seemingly growing out of the priory ruins and incorporating some of the original medieval buildings, this hotel is wonderfully atmospheric, with four-poster beds, stone spiral staircases and rooms squeezed into turrets. Bathrooms are shared, and there's no TV or wi-fi. The bar in the undercroft serves simple meals and a good selection of Welsh beers.

Skirrid Inn PUB FOOD ££
(01873-890258; www.skirridmountaininn.co.uk; Hereford Rd, Llanvihangel Crucorney; lunch £4-7, dinner £8-13; 5.30-11pm Mon, 11am-2.30pm & 5.30-11pm Tue-Fri, 11.30am-11pm Sat, noon-5pm Sun; P) Those with a taste for the macabre and ghostly will love this place. Wales' oldest inn (pre 1110) once doubled as a court and over 180 people were hanged here. Just so you don't forget, a noose dangles from the well-worn hanging beam, outside the doors to three old-fashioned bedrooms (r £90). Downstairs they serve hearty food in front of roaring fires.

Getting There & Away

Bus X4 between Abergavenny (£4.60, 16 minutes) and Hereford (£5.30, 40 minutes) stops in Llanvihangel Crucorney seven times a day; no Sunday services.

Hay-on-Wye (Y Gelli Gandryll)

POP 1600

Hay-on-Wye, a pretty little town on the banks of the River Wye, just inside the Welsh border, has developed a reputation disproportionate to its size. First came the explosion in secondhand bookshops, a charge led by the charismatic and forthright local maverick Richard Booth.

With Hay established as the world's secondhand-book capital, a festival of literature and culture was founded in 1988, growing in stature each year to take in all aspects of the creative arts. Today the Hay Festival is a major attraction in its own right, famously endorsed by former US president Bill Clinton, a high-profile guest in 2001, as 'the Woodstock of the mind'.

The small town centre is made up of narrow sloping lanes, peppered by interesting shops and peopled by the differing types that such individuality and so many books tend to attract. Even outside of festival time, it has a vaguely alternative ambience.

History

Hay has had a tempestuous history, due to its borderlands position. In fact, at the time of the Norman Conquest it was administered separately as English Hay (the town proper) and Welsh Hay (the countryside to the south and west). For the next three-and-a-half centuries Hay changed hands many times. Following the Tudor Acts of Union it settled down as a market town, and by the 18th century it had become a centre of the flannel trade.

Sights

Hay Castle CASTLE
(www.haycastletrust.org; Castle St) Standing in considerable decrepitude in the town centre, Hay's battered castle is closed to the public but there are various interesting shops to explore in its grounds, including an honesty book stall (50p per book). This was one of the earliest Norman castles to be built in Wales. A grand manor house was grafted on in the 17th century, but this too is in a precarious state.

Richard Booth became king of this castle, buying the dilapidated remains in 1961. It's now owned by a trust who are intending to restore the complex and convert it into an arts centre.

Activities

It's easy for a bibliophile to drift into insolvency here, but Hay is also an excellent base for active pursuits, whether you wish to mount Lord Hereford's Knob (aka Twmpa) or become better acquainted with Offa's Dyke.

Want to Canoe? CANOEING
(☎01497-820604; www.canoehire.co.uk; Racquety Farm, Wyecliff; half/full day £25/30) Take to the Wye waters at Hay and get collected further downstream.

Drover Holidays CYCLING, HIKING
(☎01497-821134; www.droverholidays.co.uk; 🐾) If you're tackling a long-distance cycling or walking route anywhere in Wales, this Hay-based crowd will take care of the logistics for you (transfers, bags, bikes and accommodation).

Hay-on-Wye

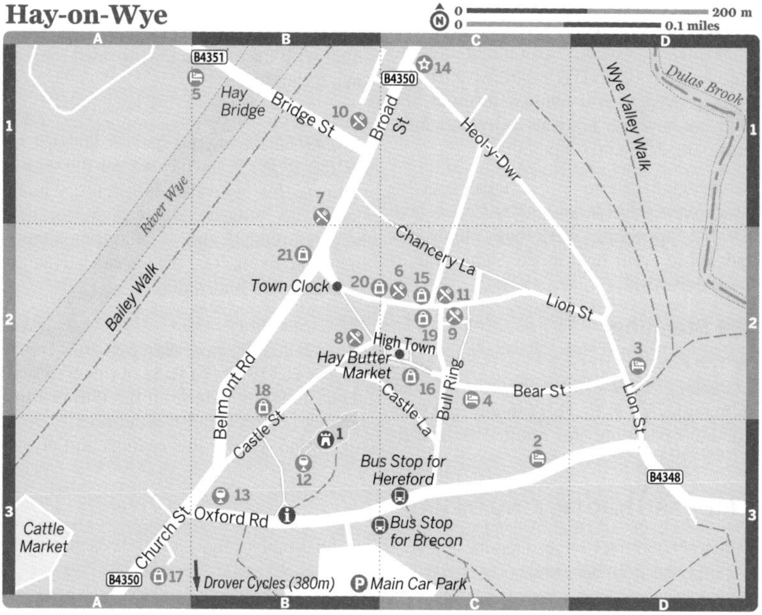

Hay-on-Wye

Sights
1 Hay Castle.......B3

Sleeping
2 Hay Stables.......C3
3 Old Black Lion.......D2
4 The Bear.......C2
5 The Start.......B1

Eating
6 Bookshop Cafe.......C2
Old Black Lion.......(see 3)
7 Old Electric Shop.......B1
8 Shepherds Ice Cream Parlour.......B2
9 St John's Place.......C2
10 Three Tuns.......B1
11 Tomatitos Tapas Bar.......C2

Drinking & Nightlife
12 Beer Revolution.......B3
13 Blue Boar.......B3

Entertainment
14 Globe at Hay.......C1

Shopping
15 Addyman Books.......C2
16 Hay Antique Market.......C2
17 Hay Cinema Bookshop.......A3
18 Mostly Maps.......B2
19 Murder & Mayhem.......C2
20 Richard Booth's Bookshop.......B2
21 Rose's Books.......B2

Festivals & Events

Hay Festival LITERATURE
(01497-822629; www.hayfestival.com; May-Jun) The 10-day Hay Festival has become Britain's leading festival of literature and the arts – a kind of bookworms' Glastonbury or, according to Bill Clinton, 'the Woodstock of the mind'. Like those legendary music festivals, it pulls more than its fair share of the leading exponents of its genre.

As well as readings, workshops, book signings, concerts and club nights, there's also a very successful children's festival called **Haydays**. There are shuttle buses from Hay-on-Wye and surrounding towns to the site, in fields on Hay's southwest fringe.

It's proved such a popular formula that there are now Hay Festivals in Ireland, Mexico, Spain, Peru and Colombia.

HowtheLightGetsIn MUSIC, PHILOSOPHY
(www.howthelightgetsin.org; May-Jun) A low-key but appealing week-long philosophy and music event held at the same time as the Hay Festival.

Sleeping

★ **The Bear** B&B ££
(01497-821302; www.thebearhay.com; 2 Bear St; s/d from £55/80; P) This friendly and well-run 1590 coaching inn retains its historic ambience and combines it with interesting art, sisal floors and bathrooms with tubs – bliss for tired hikers. One of the three chic bedrooms has a four-poster bed, and the excellent breakfasts include imaginative vegetarian options. Curl up with a book by the immense fireplace.

Hay Stables B&B ££
(01497-820008; www.haystables.co.uk; Oxford Rd; s/d from £45/70; P) Three modern en suite rooms decked out in neutral tones await you at this friendly guesthouse. There's a common area for guests and a large, fully equipped kitchen. Breakfast is a self-serve affair with the ingredients provided for your own fry-up.

The Start B&B ££
(01497-821391; www.the-start.net; Bridge St; s/d £60/80; P) Peacefully set on the fringes of town, this renovated 18th-century house boasts an unbeatable riverside location, homely rooms and a flagstone-floored breakfast room. The owner can advise on local activities and walks.

Old Black Lion PUB ££
(01497-820841; www.oldblacklion.co.uk; Lion St; s/d from £55/99; P) Parts of this traditional coaching inn date from the 13th century, making it Hay's most atmospheric sleeping option. Expect low ceilings and creaky,

RICHARD BOOTH, KING OF HAY

Richard Booth is a larger-than-life character and the dynamic force behind Hay's metamorphosis from declining border town into eminent book capital. A provocative character, he's been called a monarchist, anarchist, socialist and separatist – all of which have some element of truth. And he's definitely a superb self-publicist.

In the 1960s, after graduating from Oxford, he bought Hay's old fire station and turned it into a secondhand bookshop. He bought whole libraries from all over the world and sold in bulk to new universities. He's had setbacks, becoming bankrupt in 1984, but never lost his instinct for a good story. He first hit the headlines when he offered books for burning at £1.50 a car-boot load.

Booth established the world's largest bookshop in the old cinema before opening Booth Books and Hay Castle Books. His success attracted other booksellers and nowadays there are over two dozen bookshops in tiny Hay-on-Wye.

The idea for a separate state blossomed during a liquid lunch in 1976. Booth announced that Hay would declare independence on 1 April 1977 (April Fools' Day). Breconshire Council fiercely dismissed the idea as a Booth publicity stunt, which only fuelled the media hype. On declaration day, three TV stations, eight national newspapers and the world's press covered the event. Booth was crowned king (King Richard, *Coeur de Livre*) and the Hay navy sent a gunboat (a rowing boat) up the Wye, firing blanks from a drainpipe. Many of the king's drinking pals gained cabinet posts.

All this comedy has a serious undercurrent, and Booth continues to campaign against the causes of rural decline – with particular contempt reserved for rural development boards, supermarkets and factory farming.

uneven floors. The accumulated weight of centuries of hospitality is cheerfully carried by the current staff. The food is excellent as well.

Eating

★Tomatitos Tapas Bar SPANISH £
(01497-820770; www.haytomatitos.co.uk; 38 Lion St; tapas £2.25-5.95; 11am-11pm Mon-Sat, to 4pm Sun;) Friendly, bustling Tomatitos combines the atmosphere of everyone's favourite pub with an *España*-centric menu. Staples such as *patatas bravas* and chorizo aside, daily specials feature guest stars such as mushrooms stuffed with Cabrales cheese and lamb tagine, washed down with Spanish, Portuguese and French wine by the glass.

Old Electric Shop VEGETARIAN £
(01497-821194; www.oldelectric.co.uk; 10 Broad St; mains £5-8; 10am-5pm Wed-Sun;) Hay's hippest cafe inhabits an eclectic junk-shop-like space crammed with studios selling new and vintage clothing, furniture and, of course, books. The blackboard menu includes tasty vegetarian soups, salads and curries. Periodically they open at night as a pop-up cocktail bar, often with live music.

Bookshop Cafe CAFE £
(01497-820322; www.boothbooks.co.uk; 44 Lion St; mains £6-10; 9.30am-4.30pm) Set around a courtyard at the rear of Richard Booth's Bookshop, this light-filled eatery serves upmarket cafe fare such as smoked haddock and crayfish fishcakes and their own fancy take on a Welsh rarebit.

Shepherds Ice Cream Parlour ICE CREAM £
(01497-821898; www.shepherdsicecream.co.uk; 9 High Town; scoop £2.20; 9.30am-5.30pm) Nobody should leave Hay without trying the home-made ice cream from Shepherds. It's mainly made from sheep's milk for a lighter, smoother taste. They also serve soup, sandwiches and cake.

★St John's Place MODERN BRITISH ££
(07855 783799; www.stjohnsplacehay.tumblr.com; Lion St; mains £18; 6-10pm Fri & Sat) St John's Place is only open two nights a week and the menu is limited to three choices for each course, but this narrow focus seems to allow the kitchen plenty of room for passionate experimentation and refinement. The complexity of the food is offset by the simple elegance of the decor. Adventurous diners will be amply rewarded.

Three Tuns PUB FOOD ££
(01497-821855; www.three-tuns.com; Broad St; mains £12-19; 11am-2pm & 6.30-9pm;) Rebuilt and expanded after a fire partially destroyed the 16th-century building, this smart gastropub is a welcoming and atmospheric place. The menu has an Italian edge to it, including delicious pasta, Roman-style thin-crust pizza and, during the day, ciabatta sandwiches. The back garden is a great spot for a post-walk beverage.

Old Black Lion PUB FOOD ££
(01497-820841; www.oldblacklion.co.uk; Lion St; mains lunch £9-10, dinner £13-20; noon-2.30pm & 6.30-9pm) Walkers, book browsers and the literary glitterati all flock to this creaky, part-13th-century inn, with heavy black beams and low ceilings. The atmosphere is as cosy as you'd hope such a place would be and the food is a hearty but refined take on pub fare.

Drinking & Entertainment

Beer Revolution BEER HALL
(07870 628097; www.beerrevolution.co.uk; Old Storeroom, Hay Castle, Castle St; 10am-5pm Mon-Sat Mar-Oct, Wed-Sat Nov-Feb;) Within the castle grounds, this boozy Aladdin's cave is stacked to the rafters with Welsh craft beer and cider. Settle in to sample the range, either alfresco or in one of the handful of seats upstairs. As well as bottled beer there's always something interesting on tap. They also sell vintage women's clothes and books about beer.

Blue Boar PUB
(01497-820884; www.facebook.com/blueboarhay; cnr Castle St & Oxford Rd; 9am-11pm) This ivy-clad, family-run, traditional pub is ideal for whiling away a wet afternoon with a pint of Timothy Taylor's ale, a hearty meal and a good book.

Globe at Hay LIVE PERFORMANCE
(01497-821762; www.globeathay.org; Newport St; 9.30am-late Tue & Thu-Sun;) This converted Methodist chapel wears many hats: cafe, bar, live-music venue, theatre, club and all-round community hub. It's a wonderfully intimate place to watch a band, catch a comedian or listen to a sabre-rattling political debate.

Shopping

There are dozens of secondhand and antiquarian bookshops in Hay, with hundreds of thousands of tomes stacked floor to ceiling across town – 500,000 in Booth's alone. Each shop is profiled on a free map, available from the tourist office and from venues around town. However, Hay's shopping potential doesn't stop with books. There are also excellent stores selling antiques, craft, art and historic maps.

Richard Booth's Bookshop BOOKS
(☎01497-820322; www.boothbooks.co.uk; 44 Lion St; ⏲9.30am-5.30pm) The most famous and still the best, Booth's is a thing of beauty – from the exquisite tiling on the outside to the well-presented shelves within. There's a sizeable Anglo-Welsh literature section, a Wales travel section and a great little cafe and an arthouse cinema attached.

Mostly Maps MAPS
(☎01497-820539; www.mostlymaps.com; 2 Castle St; ⏲10.30am-5.30pm Tue-Sat) Exquisite antiquarian maps and illustrative plates, many hand-coloured.

Rose's Books BOOKS
(☎01497-820013; www.rosesbooks.com; 14 Broad St; ⏲10am-5pm) Rare children's and illustrated books.

Murder & Mayhem BOOKS
(☎01497-821613; www.hay-on-wyebooks.com; 5 Lion St; ⏲10am-5.30pm) This specialist branch of Addyman Books has a body outline on the floor, monsters on the ceiling and stacks of detective fiction, true crime and horror.

Hay Antique Market ANTIQUES
(☎01497-820175; www.hayantiquemarket.co.uk; 6 Market St; ⏲10am-5pm) Seventeen little shops in one, this is a great place to look for a memento with an extra bit of mileage on it.

Hay Cinema Bookshop BOOKS
(☎01497-820071; www.haycinemabookshop.co.uk; Castle St; ⏲9am-6pm) Hay's oldest and one of its biggest bookshops, this converted cinema is jam-packed with books on all manner of obscure subjects. There's also an antiquarian department and plenty of foreign-language titles.

Addyman Books BOOKS
(☎01497-821136; www.hay-on-wyebooks.com; 39 Lion St; ⏲10am-5.30pm) A rabbit warren of a shop spread over several levels, with rooms devoted to sci-fi, myths, horror, music and art, among other subjects.

Information

Police Station (☎101; www.dyfed-powys.police.uk; Heol-y-Dwr)

Tourist Office (☎01497-820144; www.hay-on-wye.co.uk; Oxford Rd; ⏲noon-4pm Mar-Nov, 10am-1pm Dec-Jan) Stocks a map showing all of Hay's bookshops.

Getting There & Away

There are six buses per day (except on Sunday) to/from Brecon (£6.40, 37 minutes), Talgarth (£5.10, 18 minutes) and Felinfach (£5.90, 30 minutes); and three a day to/from Hereford (£8.40, 50 minutes).

Talgarth

POP 1730

A handsome little market town of grey stone buildings set around a gurgling stream at the head of the Black Mountains (the name means 'end of the ridge'), Talgarth has some interesting historic buildings to explore, along with woods and waterfalls in its hinterland. In the 5th century it was the royal capital of the kingdom of Brycheiniog.

Talgarth fell on hard times after the closure of its hospital and nursing college in the 1980s and '90s, but the restoration of its historic mill and the opening of a live-music venue with rock-star connections herald an upturn in its fortunes.

Sights

Talgarth Mill HISTORIC BUILDING
(☎01874-711352; www.talgarthmill.com; High St; adult/child incl tour £4/1; ⏲11am-4pm Tue-Sun) Restored with the assistance of the BBC's *Village SOS* television show, Talgarth's 17th-century watermill is back in business for the first time since 1946, grinding wheat into flour, which is used by the neighbouring bakery and sold in the little craft shop at the front. Thirty-minute guided tours depart on the hour, except on Sunday. Otherwise, grab a pamphlet and show yourself around. If you're extremely lucky, you might even spot an otter in the pretty mill garden.

Bronllys Castle CASTLE
(Cadw; www.cadw.gov.wales; Bronllys Rd; ⏲10am-4pm) FREE Looking like it's slid straight off a chess board, Bronllys' circular tower was built in 1230 on the site of an earlier Norman motte-and-bailey castle. You can climb up inside, wander around its three floors

and gaze out over the verdant countryside through its little Gothic windows. It's located just outside of town, on the A479 heading northwest.

Sleeping & Eating

The Draen B&B ££

(☎01874-713102; www.thedraen.co.uk; Llanfilo; s/d/ste from £65/75/95; P 📶) Set down a narrow lane 3 miles west of Talgarth near the village of Llanfilo, this old stone farmhouse is the very picture of Welsh country comfort. There are only three guest bedrooms, the most substantial of which has its own sitting room. All have en suite bathrooms and floral feature wallpaper.

Bakers' Table CAFE £

(☎01874-711125; www.talgarthmill.com; Talgarth Mill, High St; mains £4.50-7; ⏰11am-4pm Tue-Sun; 📶 👪) Housed within Talgarth Mill, this cafe uses its own artisanal stone-ground flour to bake beautiful scones, *bara brith* (Welsh tea bread) and crusty bread. All of the food and drink sold is sourced locally, including a delicious array of sandwich fillings from the likes of Crickhowell's Black Mountains Smokery.

Entertainment

Tabernacle LIVE MUSIC

(www.thetabernacle.co.uk; Regent St) What happens when Creation Records boss Alan McGee, the man who unleashed Oasis on the world, decides to renovate an 1837 Baptist chapel in your little town? You get a gorgeous, intimate venue with a roster of top-league musicians dropping by to play. It only holds a hundred people, so check the website and book ahead.

Information

Tourist Office (☎01874-712226; www.visittalgarth.co.uk; High St; ⏰10.30am-1pm Sun & Mon, to 3.30pm Tue-Sat; 📶)

Getting There & Away

There are seven buses per day to/from Brecon (£6.40, 20 minutes), six to/from Hay-on-Wye (£5.10, 18 minutes) and a daily bus to/from Merthyr Tydfil (£4.65, 60 minutes), Builth Wells (£2.70, 37 minutes) and Llandrindod Wells (£3.50, 50 minutes). There are no Sunday services.

Brecon (Aberhonddu)

POP 8250

The handsome market town of Brecon stands at the junction of the River Usk and the River Honddu. For centuries the town thrived as a centre of wool production and weaving. Today you'll find Brecon Beacons hikers rubbing shoulders with soldiers from the town's large military base in the bars, eateries and outdoor shops that dominate the old stone streets.

History

An Iron Age hill fort on Pen-y-Crug (331m), northwest of town, and the remains of a Roman camp at Y Gaer, to the west, testify to Brecon's antiquity. After the Romans, the area was ruled by the Irish-born king Brychan, who married into a Welsh royal house in the 5th century. The town takes its name from him, and his kingdom, Brycheiniog (anglicised to Brecknock), gave its name to the old county of Brecknockshire. The town of Merthyr Tydfil was named for Brychan's daughter, St Tudful.

It was not until Norman times that Brecon began to burgeon. The local Welsh prince, Rhys ap Tewdwr, was defeated in 1093 by Bernard de Neufmarché, a Norman lord, who then built the town's castle and monastery (which is now the cathedral).

Sights

★**Brecon Cathedral** CHURCH

(☎01874-623857; www.breconcathedral.org.uk; Cathedral Close; ⏰8.30am-6pm) Perched on a hill above the River Honddu, Brecon Cathedral was founded in 1093 as part of a Benedictine monastery, though little remains from the original Norman church except the vividly carved font. Most of the Gothic structure standing today dates from the early 13th century. Modern additions include an ornate 1937 altarpiece and a cross that seems to hover in mid-air at the end of the nave.

The cathedral hosts regular choral concerts and is very visitor-friendly, with information points scattered about providing details about key features. Look out for the stone cresset just inside the main door. This ancient lighting device is the only one of its kind in Wales; the 30 cups were filled with oil and lit to illuminate dark corners or steps. Make sure you visit the Harvard Chapel, the regimental chapel of the South Wales Borderers, draped with banners from the Zulu wars.

In the cathedral grounds is a **Heritage Centre** (☎01874-625222; www.breconcathedralshop.co.uk; ⌚11am-3pm Mon-Sat) FREE, cafe and gift shop housed in a restored tithe barn.

Monmouthshire & Brecon Canal CANAL

Brecon is the northern terminus of this canal, built between 1799 and 1812 for the movement of coal, iron ore, limestone and agricultural goods. The 33 miles from Brecon to Pontypool is back in business, transporting a generally less grimy cargo of holidaymakers and river-dwellers. The busiest section is around Brecon, with craft

Brecon

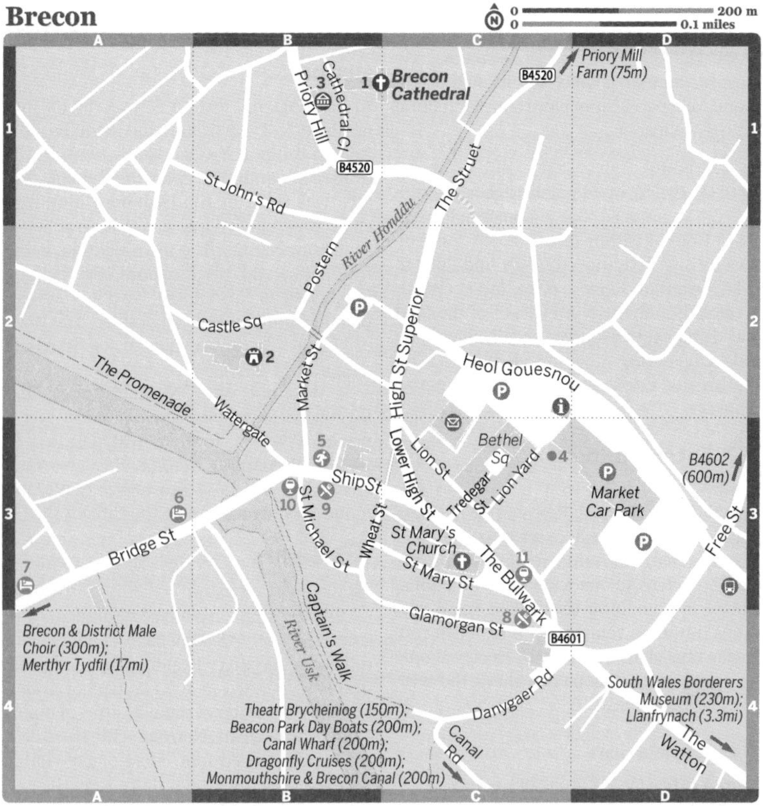

Brecon

Top Sights

1 Brecon Cathedral B1

Sights

2 Brecknock Castle B2
3 Heritage Centre B1

Activities, Courses & Tours

4 Bikes + Hikes C3
5 Biped Cycles B3

Sleeping

6 Bridge Cafe A3
7 Coach House A3

Eating

8 Gurkha Corner C4
9 The Hours B3

Drinking & Nightlife

10 Boar's Head B3
11 Brecon Tap C3

WORTH A TRIP

HIT YOUR PEAK

Ascending **Pen-y-Fan** (886m), the tallest peak in the Brecon Beacons, is one of the most popular hikes in the national park (around 120,000 people each year make the climb, giving it the nickname 'the motorway'). The shortest route begins at the Pont ar Daf car park on the A470, 10 miles southwest of Brecon. It's a steep but straightforward slog up to the summit of Corn Du (873m), followed by a short dip and final ascent to Pen-y-Fan (4.5 miles round trip; allow three hours).

A slightly longer (5.5 miles round trip) but just as crowded path starts at the Storey Arms outdoor centre, 1 mile to the north. The T4 bus stops here; note, the Storey Arms is not a pub! You can avoid the crowds by choosing one of the longer routes on the north side of the mountain, which also have the advantage of more interesting views on the way up. The best starting point is the Cwm Gwdi car park, at the end of a minor road 3.5 miles southwest of Brecon. From here, you follow a path along the crest of the Cefn Cwm Llwch ridge, with great views of the neighbouring peaks, with a final steep scramble up to the summit. The round trip from the car park is 7 miles; allow three to four hours. Starting and finishing in Brecon, the total distance is 14 miles.

departing from the canal basin, 400m south of the town centre.

A peaceful 8.5-mile walk along the towpath leads to the picturesque village of Talybont-on-Usk. You can return on the X43 bus (two daily, no Sunday service).

South Wales Borderers Museum MUSEUM
(☎01874-613310; www.royalwelsh.org.uk; The Barracks, The Watton; adult/child £5/1; ⊙10am-5pm Mon-Sat Easter-Sep, Mon-Fri Oct-Easter) Based at Brecon's military barracks (built 1805), this museum commemorates the history of the Royal Welsh – a newish British Army infantry regiment comprising the Borderers and other historic Welsh regiments. The highlight is the Zulu War Room – the Borderers fought in the 1879 Anglo–Zulu war in South Africa, inspiration for the 1964 film *Zulu* starring Michael Caine. The collection of artefacts recalls the defence of Rorke's Drift, when 150 Welsh soldiers held out against 4000 Zulu warriors.

This is still an active military base. Many of the soldiers are Gurkhas (Nepalese soldiers fighting in the British Army), often seen in their civvies around the town.

Activities

The conical hill of **Pen-y-Crug** is a good option for a short hike (2.5 miles round trip). There's a superb view of the Brecon Beacons from the summit. The tourist office sells national-park walking cards.

Brecon Beacons' classic off-road mountain-biking route is **The Gap**, following a 24-mile loop from Brecon that takes in a high pass close to Pen-y-Fan and an easy return along the canal.

The **Taff Trail** cycling and hiking trail heads south from Brecon to Cardiff. For much of its length it forms part of **National Cycle Network Route 8 (Lôn Las Cymru)**, which also heads north to Holyhead.

Dragonfly Cruises BOATING
(☎07831-685222; www.dragonfly-cruises.co.uk; Canal Basin, Canal Rd; adult/child £7.80/4.50, hire per 1/2/3 hours £15/25/40; ⊙Mar-Oct) Runs 2½-hour narrowboat cruises on the Monmouthshire & Brecon Canal. There are two to three departures on Wednesday, Saturday and Sunday, and on additional days from June to August. They also hire small boats.

Beacon Park Day Boats BOATING, CANOEING
(☎0800 612 2890; www.beaconparkdayboats.co.uk; Toll House, Canalside; per hour/half-day/day boats from £20/45/70, canoes from £15/25/40; ⊙10am-5pm Easter-Oct) Rents six- to eight-seater electric-powered boats and three-seater Canadian canoes. In a day, you can cruise southeast to Llangattock and back. It also has a fleet of luxury narrowboats for longer live-in voyages.

Bikes + Hikes OUTDOORS
(☎01874-610071; www.bikesandhikes.co.uk; Lion Yard; bikes per half/full day £18/25, canoes per 2hr £20) Hires canoes, mountain bikes and trail bikes (child seats available) and provides free delivery locally. Also offers guided rides, paddle and pedal packages, caving, gorge walking, rock climbing and more.

Biped Cycles CYCLING
(01874-622296; www.bipedcycles.co.uk; 10 Ship St; per half/full day £20/25; 9am-5pm Mon-Sat Jun-Aug, 9am-5.30pm Mon, Tue & Thu-Sat, 9am-1pm Wed Sep-May) Rents mountain and road bikes, performs repairs and can arrange guided rides.

Festivals & Events

Brecon Fringe Festival MUSIC
(www.breconfringe.co.uk; Aug) Started as an alternative to the famous Brecon Jazz Festival (which sadly blew its last note in 2015), Brecon Fringe brings a wide range of musical styles to pubs in and around town over four days in August.

Brecon Beast SPORTS
(www.breconbeast.co.uk; Sep) A gruelling mountain-bike challenge over 44 or 68 miles, held in mid-September. The entry fee (£35) covers camping, refreshments on the route, a 'pasta party' and a T-shirt.

Sleeping

Town Centre

Coach House B&B ££
(07974 328437; www.coachhousebrecon.com; 12 Orchard St; r £83-104, ste £142;) This hospitable 19th-century coaching inn is well attuned to the needs of walkers, with a drying room for hiking gear, generous breakfasts (including good vegetarian options) and packed lunches put together by the hosts. The six stylish, modern rooms, decorated in soothing creams, have ultra-comfy beds and good showers.

Bridge Cafe B&B ££
(01874-622024; www.bridgecafe.co.uk; 7 Bridge St; s/d with bathroom £60/70, without £45/55;) Owned by keen mountain bikers and hill walkers who can advise on local activities, the Bridge has three plain but attractive and comfortable bedrooms, with down-filled duvets and crisp cotton sheets. Only one has an en suite; the other two share a bathroom.

Around Brecon

Priory Mill Farm CAMPSITE £
(www.priorymillfarm.co.uk; Hay Rd; sites per adult £8; Easter-Oct; P) With a cobbled courtyard, ancient mill building, free-range chickens and a lush camping meadow, this small campground is pretty much camping heaven, and it's just a five-minute riverside walk from Brecon. It supplies local wood and charcoal so you can have your very own campfire.

★ **Peterstone Court** HOTEL £££
(01874-665387; www.peterstone-court.com; Llanhamlach; r from £150; P) At this elegant Georgian manor house, the rooms are large and comfortable, and the views across the valley to the Beacons are superb. The boutique spa centre is a big drawcard, pampering guests with organic beauty products. They also have an excellent restaurant. Llanhamlach is 3 miles southeast of Brecon, just off the A40.

Felin Fach Griffin PUB £££
(01874-620111; www.felinfachgriffin.co.uk; Felinfach; s/d from £110/130; P) Set above an acclaimed gastropub in Felinfach village 5 miles northeast of Brecon (just off the A470), the Griffin's quietly elegant rooms offer comfortable beds, fancy toiletries and homeimade biscuits. Old-fashioned radios take the place of TVs and there are plenty of books to read. A dinner-inclusive rate is available.

Eating

There are a couple of good cheap eateries in Brecon itself, but the best options are a little out of town, such as **Peterstone Court** (01874-665387; www.peterstone-court.com; A40, Llanhamlach; breakfast £8-14, lunch £15-17, dinner £14-21; 7.30-9.30am & noon-9.30pm), the White Swan (p109) and the **Felin Fach Griffin** (01874-620111; www.felinfachgriffin.co.uk; Felinfach; mains lunch £14-17, dinner £20-21; noon-2.30pm & 6-9pm).

Gurkha Corner NEPALESE £
(01874-610871; www.gurkhacorner.co.uk; 12 Glamorgan St; mains £6-10; noon-2.30pm & 5.30-11pm Tue-Sun;) Rustic scenes of the Himalayas brighten the windowless dining room of this friendly Nepalese restaurant. The food – curries, fried rice, lentils and rich veg side dishes – is delicious.

The Hours CAFE £
(01874-622800; www.the-hours.co.uk; 15 Ship St; mains £5.75-8.25; 10am-4.30pm Tue-Sat;) This cute combined bookshop and cafe serves excellent home baking, sandwiches, soup and snacks. It's located in an endearingly wonky olive-green cottage.

Drinking & Nightlife

Brecon Tap BAR

(☎01874-620800; www.breconinns.co.uk; 4 The Bulwark) Crowdfunded into being by the lads at Brecon Brewing, the Brecon Tap is a treasure trove of craft beer, traditional cider, estate wines and locally baked meat pies.

Boar's Head PUB

(☎01874-625569; www.facebook.com/boarsbrecon; Ship St; ⊙11am-11pm) The Boar's Head is a lively local pub, with sofas in the back room, sports on the TV in the front bar, a sunny beer garden overlooking the river, and a good selection of craft beer and real ales on tap. There's often live music on the weekends.

Entertainment

Brecon & District Male Choir TRADITIONAL MUSIC

(www.breconchoir.co.uk; Llanfaes Primary School, Orchard St; ⊙7-9pm Fri) For booming harmonies, head to the practice sessions of the local male choir; visitors are most welcome. Since its formation in 1937, the choir has performed at London's Royal Albert Hall 10 times and has even released its own CD.

Theatr Brycheiniog THEATRE

(☎01874-611622; www.brycheiniog.co.uk; Canal Wharf) This attractive canalside theatre complex is the town's main venue for drama, dance, comedy and music. It's worth checking what's on, as it sometimes hosts surprisingly big-name touring acts. The Brecon Jazz Club hosts a night here each month.

Information

Breconshire War Memorial Hospital (☎01874-622443; www.powysthb.wales.nhs.uk/brecon-hospital; Cerrigcochion Rd; ⊙24hr)

Tourist Office (☎01874-622485; www.midwalesmyway.com; Market car park; ⊙9.30am-5pm Mon-Sat, 10am-4pm Sun)

Getting There & Away

Direct bus services run to/from Brecon's **bus interchange** (Heol Gouesnou). Destinations include Cardiff (£8.30, 1¾ hours, eight daily), Abergavenny (£3.40, 45 minutes, 12 daily), Crickhowell (£2.60, 25 minutes, 12 daily), Hay-on-Wye (£6.40, 37 minutes, six daily) and Llandrindod Wells (£4.65, one hour, seven daily). No Sunday services.

The Market car park offers short-stay pay-and-display parking. There are long-stay lots on Hoel Gouesnou and near the canal basin.

Regular taxi services as well as a walkers shuttle are offered by **Ride & Hike** (☎07989-242550; www.rideandhike.co.uk). Indicative fares for the six-seater shuttle: National Park Visitor Centre (£20), Merthyr Tydfil (£45), Cardiff (£100).

Llanfrynach

POP 571

Tucked away in the countryside only 3 miles southeast of Brecon, sleepy little Llanfrynach feels much more remote than it really is, due in part to its only road access being narrow country lanes. It makes a good target for a short walk or bike ride from Brecon, or a quiet place to decamp to for a few days.

Activities

Cantref Adventure Farm & Riding Centre HORSE RIDING

(☎01874-665223; www.cantref.com; Upper Cantref Farm, Llanfrynach; height over/under 93cm £9.25/free, horse treks per hour/half-day/day £21/35/60; ⊙10.30am-5.30pm Easter-Oct, weekends & school holidays only Nov-Easter; 👪) This child-focused fun farm entertains the littlies with pig races, lamb and goat feeding, and indoor play areas. The adjoining riding centre offers equestrian lessons, pony rides and treks into the Brecon Beacons. Bunkhouse accommodation (from £15) and basic camping (per site £20) is also available. It's located in farmland west of Llanfrynach; follow the horseshoe signs.

Sleeping & Eating

★**Pencelli Castle Caravan & Camping Park** CAMPSITE £

(☎01874-665451; www.pencelli-castle.com; Pencelli; tent per adult/child £13/6.80, caravans £25) Near the canal in Pencelli, 1½ miles east of Llanfrynach, this award-winning site's plaudits include Loo of the Year (when we last visited there were roses in the gents!). There's a well-stocked shop, a pub down the road, a nature trail and a playground.

Camp Cynrig Tipi Village CAMPSITE ££

(☎07790 043202; www.breconbeaconstipis.co.uk; per weekend/week tepee £175/300, cabin £230/400; ⊙Easter-Oct; P) A taste of the Great Plains in the verdant Welsh countryside, this little campsite offers comfortable lodging in Sioux-style tepees near the gurgling River Cynrig, just over a mile west of Llanfrynach. Each has futon beds, a fire pit

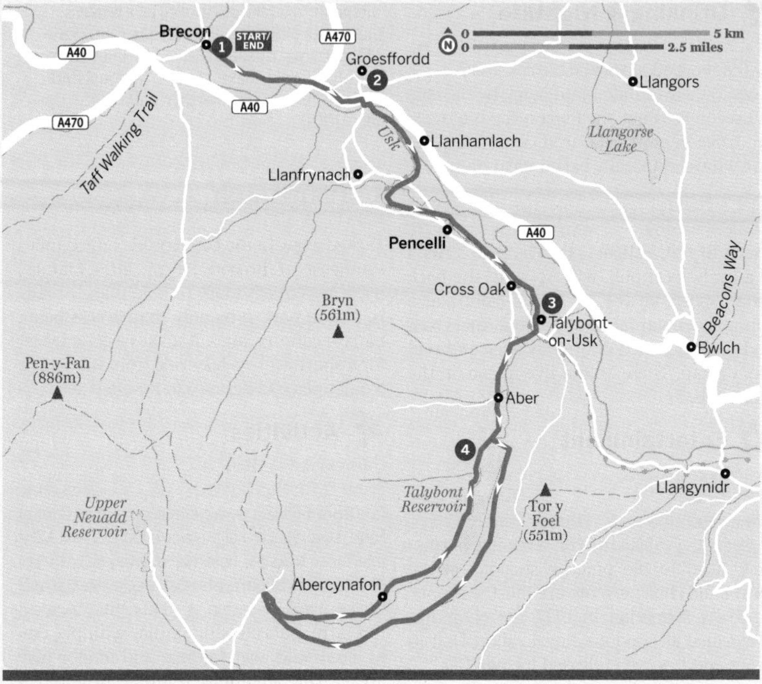

Cycling Tour
Talybont Reservoir & Return

START BRECON
END BRECON
LENGTH 26 MILES; ONE DAY

This is very much a cycling route of two halves. The first leg takes you along the canal to the little village of Talybont-on-Usk, where there's a choice of refreshment stops. This is the easy part. Beyond Talybont, a much more stretching circular loop takes you round the vast Talybont Reservoir.

Bike hire is available in 1 **Brecon**. The cycle route proper starts near Theatr Brycheiniog with its cluster of canal boats. As you leave town, the number of houses dwindles and the scene grows increasingly rural.

At the first lock at 2 **Groesffordd**, ignore cycle-route signs and continue on the canal towpath – note that the signed Taff Trail follows a similar route, but it's nicer to stick to the canal. For the next few miles you simply follow the left-hand bank of the tranquil tree-lined waterway, which at points offers a view of the sinuous and rushing River Usk. You pass the small settlements of Llanfrynach, Pencelli and Cross Oak, but these are barely perceptible from the path.

Eventually you come to 3 **Talybont-on-Usk**. Opposite the village shop, leave the path and join the lane over the drawbridge. There are various eating and drinking options at Talybont, from the handy little Talybont Stores with its cafe to a cluster of pubs (the best is the Star Inn).

Follow the country road through Aber, beyond which is the 4 **Talybont Reservoir**. Follow the signs left off the road towards Danywenallt YHA; once you have crossed the water take the lane to the right, which makes a loop right round the reservoir. At the furthest point you're on the fringes of the Taf Fechan Forest – a very steep incline takes you back to the west bank of the reservoir.

The return route – back along the canal the way you came – is easy. Nearing home, at the bridge numbered 162, just remember to cross the canal, following the signs to Brecon.

and a gas cooking stove. There's also a pleasant little wooden cabin, sleeping up to six.

The Lodge B&B ££
(☎01874-665714; www.thelodgebreconbandb.co.uk; s/d from £60/75; P 📶) Blissfully located on the rural fringes of the village, this charming B&B has four guest rooms, each with modern bathroom and countryside views. Relax in the gazebo in the lovingly tended garden while the owners' two friendly little dogs charge around the lawn.

White Swan PUB FOOD ££
(☎01874-665277; www.whiteswanbrecon.co.uk; mains £10-15; ⏱11.30am-11pm Wed-Mon; P 📶) Whitewashed, hung with flower baskets and with a wisteria-draped back terrace, the White Swan is as pretty a village pub as you could wish for. The food is excellent too, with hearty serves of fish and chips, burgers, meat pies, and daily fish, meat and vegetarian specials.

Getting There & Away

Buses stop in Llanfrynach seven times a day (except Sundays), heading to Brecon (£1.55, 11 minutes), Talybont-on-Usk (£1.55, seven minutes), Llangattock (£2.30, 30 minutes), Crickhowell (£2.40, 35 minutes) and Abergavenny (£3.20, 50 minutes).

Talybont-on-Usk

POP 720

Tiny Talybont-on-Usk has a venerable transport heritage for its size: an aqueduct takes the canal over the Caerfanell River here, and a disused railway bridge cuts dramatically across the village. Just to the south is the epic Talybont Reservoir. A hostel and a handful of decent pubs make the village a pleasant – if uneventful – holiday base.

Sleeping

Danywenallt YHA HOSTEL £
(☎0800 0191700; www.yha.org.uk; site/dm/r from £12/20/59; P) Ideally located for hiking and biking around Talybont Reservoir, this secluded converted farmhouse lacks a guest kitchen but has a cafe. Camping is available in the orchard. To get here, cross over the dam at the head of the reservoir and turn left.

Getting There & Away

Three buses a day (except on Sunday) head to Talybont-on-Usk from Abergavenny (£2.70, 38 minutes), Crickhowell (£2.10, 28 minutes), Llangattock (£2, 22 minutes), Llanfrynach (£1.55, seven minutes) and Brecon (£1.85, 19 minutes). From the bus stop it's still a 2-mile walk to the YHA.

Llangorse Lake

Reed-fringed Llangorse Lake may be Wales' second-largest natural lake (after Llyn Tegid), but it's barely more than a mile long and half a mile wide. Despite its diminutive size, it's Brecon Beacons National Park's main watersports location, used for sailing, windsurfing, canoeing and water-skiing.

Close to the northern shore is a **crannog**, a lake dwelling built on an artificial island. Such refuges were used from the late Bronze Age until early medieval times. Tree-ring dating shows that this one (of which only the base remains) was built around AD 900, probably by the royal house of Brycheiniog. Among the artefacts found here are a dugout canoe, now locked away in Brecon's Brecknock Museum; other finds can be seen at the National Museum Cardiff. There's a reconstruction of a crannog house on the shore.

Activities

Llangorse Multi Activity Centre ADVENTURE SPORTS
(☎0333 600 20 20; www.activityuk.com; The Gilfach, Llangors; half/full day £26/47; ⏱9am-10pm Mon-Sat, to 5pm Sun) Set on a hillside overlooking the lake, this centre offers a range of indoor and outdoor adventure activities, as well as horse riding for beginners and pros. The outdoor 'challenge' course involves clambering up cargo nets, balancing along logs, swinging on tyres and using Indian rope bridges. There's also a set of 14 linked zipwires that stretch for over 3km.

The indoor facility has rock-climbing walls, a log climb, an abseil area, a rope bridge and even an artificial caving area.

Sleeping

New Inn & Beacons Backpackers HOSTEL £
(☎01874-730215; www.beaconsbackpackers.co.uk; Bwlch; dm £20-22; P 📶) The one thing better than a good hostel is a good hostel inside a 14th-century pub. This compact, friendly place comes with comfy bunks, reliable hot showers, a crackling wood fire and a warm welcome from knowledgeable owners. With a couple of good hikes at its doorstep, it's a

great place to mingle with fellow ramblers and local drinkers.

Getting There & Away

The lake is accessed from the village of Llangors. To get here, turn off the A40 at Bwlch. There's no public transport to Llangors.

Crickhowell (Crughywel)

POP 2070

This prosperous, picturesque, flower-bedecked village grew up around a Norman motte-and-bailey castle and a ford on the River Usk. All that remains of the **castle** are a few tumbledown towers, and the ford was superseded in the 17th century by the elegant **stone bridge** leading to the neighbouring village of Llangattock. The bridge is famous for having 12 arches on one side and 13 on the other.

There's not a lot to see in Crickhowell itself, but it's a pleasant place for an overnight stop and there's a good clutch of independent shops to peruse. The town's fiercely protective of its locally owned stores, banding together to prevent a supermarket chain opening a branch here in 2015. That rebellious spirit continued with a highly publicised tax revolt, protesting against the ability of large companies to make use of offshore tax havens by grouping together and setting up one of their own.

Sights & Activities

Crug Hywel MOUNTAIN

(Table Mountain) Distinctive flat-topped Crug Hywel (Hywel's Rock; 451m), better known as Table Mountain, rises to the north of Crickhowell and gave the town its name. You can make a steep but satisfying hike to the impressive remains of an Iron Age fort at the top (3 miles round trip). The tourist office has a leaflet detailing the route.

Old Market Hall HISTORIC BUILDING

(High St) Built in the 1830s by the Duke of Beaufort, Crickhowell's small but grandiose open-fronted market hall hosts an arts-and-craft market most Saturdays. Upstairs there's a cafe in a space that originally served as the town hall.

Golden Castle Riding Stables HORSE RIDING

(☎01873-812649; www.golden-castle.co.uk; 1hr lesson £20, pub ride £60;) Offers pony trekking, hacking and trail riding in the countryside surrounding Llangattock.

Festivals & Events

Crickhowell Walking Festival SPORTS

(www.crickhowellfestival.com; ⏲Mar) Held in the week wrapped around St David's Day (1 March), this nine-day festival features guided treks, workshops on outdoorsy themes and music.

Green Man Festival MUSIC

(www.greenman.net; Glanusk Park; adult/child £175/20; ⏲mid-Aug;) This four-day music festival has a sterling reputation for its mellow vibe, green ethos and for catering well to children and people with disabilities. It consistently attracts the current 'it' bands of the indie, alternative and folk music firmament, along with the occasional dead-set rock legend. Tickets include onsite camping. It's held 2 miles west of Crickhowell via the B4558.

Sleeping

Riverside Caravan Park CAMPSITE £

(☎01873-810397; www.riversidecaravanscrickhowell.co.uk; New Rd; sites from £18; ⏲Mar-Oct; P) Next to the Crickhowell bridge, this grassy site is well kept and very central, but it can get crowded in high summer. No under-18-year-olds allowed.

Gwyn Deri B&B ££

(☎01873-812494; www.gwynderibedandbreakfast.co.uk; Mill St; s/d/f £40/70/100; P) The friendly couple who run this homely B&B keep its three modern guest bedrooms immaculately clean, and are more than happy to share their knowledge of the area. Bonuses include fresh fruit in the rooms and an excellent breakfast selection. Connecting rooms are available for family groups.

Dragon Inn HOTEL ££

(☎01873-810362; www.dragoninncrickhowell.com; 47 High St; s/d from £55/80; P) Though set in an 18th-century listed building, the Dragon's 15 moderately sized bedrooms have a fresh, modern feel. The cheaper rooms at the top have sloping roofs, resulting in shower heads positioned over bathtubs rather than full, stand-up showers. There's a good restaurant and bar on the ground floor.

Tŷ Gwyn B&B ££

(☎01873-811625; www.tygwyn.com; Brecon Rd; s/d from £40/72; P) Once the home of Regency architect John Nash, Tŷ Gwyn is a lovely old Georgian house with four spacious en suite rooms, each themed around a Welsh literary figure. It's five minutes' walk from the town centre.

Bear Hotel PUB ££

(☎01873-810408; www.bearhotel.co.uk; Beaufort St; s/d from £84/104, mains £10-20; P 📶) The Bear is a local institution, a fine old coaching inn with a range of old-fashioned rooms – the more expensive ones with four-posters and spa baths. The rooms across the courtyard in the converted stables have a more modern look. Downstairs they serve a huge variety of quality pub grub in low-ceilinged rooms with stone fireplaces and blackened timber beams.

Gliffaes Hotel HOTEL £££

(☎01874-730371; www.gliffaeshotel.com; r £135-290; P 📶) This Victorian mansion makes quite an impression with its Romanesque towers rising through its thickly wooded grounds on the banks of the Usk. The rooms are not overly luxurious for the price, but it is a wonderful building in a very pleasant setting. It's about 4 miles northwest of Crickhowell, off the A40.

Eating & Drinking

There are a few daytime cafes to choose between. The Bear Hotel is your best bet for an evening meal.

Number Eighteen CAFE £

(☎01873-810337; www.number-eighteen.com; 18 High St; mains £4-8; 9am-6pm; 📶) The best of Crickhowell's cafes, this bright, contemporary eatery serves better-than-average coffee, freshly made sandwiches, burgers and bistro-style lunches. There's always a tempting array of cakes in the counter cabinet, too.

Bridge End Inn PUB

(☎01873-810338; www.thebridgeendinn.com; Bridge St; 11am-11pm) This cosy, traditional pub serves a range of real ales to a cast of local characters amid old timber beams and angling paraphernalia. Try counting the confounding arches of Crickhowell's stone bridge from the riverside beer garden.

Information

Tourist Office (☎01873-811970; www.visitcrickhowell.co.uk; Beaufort St; 10am-5pm Mon-Sat, to 1.30pm Sun; 📶) Shares a building with an art gallery and stocks leaflets for local walks.

WORTH A TRIP

TRETOWER

Originally the home of the Vaughan family, **Tretower Court & Castle** (Cadw; www.cadw.gov.wales; Tretower; adult/child £6/4.20; 10am-5pm Apr-Oct, to 4pm Wed-Fri Nov-Mar) gives you two historic buildings for the price of one – the sturdy circular tower of a Norman motte-and-bailey castle, and a 15th-century manor house with a fine medieval garden. Together they illustrate the transition from military stronghold to country house that took place in late medieval times.

Some domestic clutter has been added to bring the kitchens and banqueting hall to vivid and surprisingly colourful life, but otherwise the rugged authenticity of the place is left intact. Film buffs may like to know that Tretower featured in *Restoration* starring Robert Downey Jnr, and the Johnny Depp vehicle *The Libertine*.

Tretower is situated 3 miles northwest of Crickhowell on the A479.

Getting There & Away

Direct bus services to/from Crickhowell include Abergavenny (£1.85, 11 minutes, 12 daily), Llanfrynach (£2.40, 35 minutes, seven daily), Brecon (£2.60, 25 minutes, 12 daily), Talgarth (£2.40, 27 minutes, weekdays) and Builth Wells (£4.65, 56 minutes, weekdays). No Sunday services.

Fforest Fawr & Black Mountain

The western half of Brecon Beacons National Park is sparsely inhabited and devoid of any towns of note. **Fforest Fawr** (Great Forest) was once a Norman hunting ground and is now a Unesco geopark (www.fforestfawrgeopark.org.uk), famed for its varied landscapes ranging from bleak moorland to flower-flecked limestone pavement and lush wooded ravines choked with moss and greenery. Further west is the **Black Mountain** (Y Mynydd Du), a lonely expanse of barren peaks that throws down an irresistible gauntlet to intrepid hikers.

THE PHYSICIANS OF MYDDFAI

About 8 miles southeast of Llandovery, nestled beneath the high escarpment of the Black Mountain, is a beautiful lake called **Llyn y Fan Fach** (Lake of the Little Peak); it's accessible from a car park just beyond the Llanddeusant YHA (p114).

In the mid-13th century, a young man grazing his cattle beside the lake saw a woman, the loveliest he had ever seen, sitting on the surface of the water, combing her hair. He fell madly in love with her, coaxed her to shore with some bread and begged her to marry him. Her fairy father agreed, on the condition that if the young man struck her three times she would return to the fairy world. As dowry she brought a herd of magic cows and for years the couple lived happily near Myddfai, raising three healthy sons.

Naturally the three-strikes-and-you're-out story ends badly. After three abusive incidents, she and her cattle returned forever to the lake. Her sons often visited the lake and one day their mother appeared. She handed the eldest, Rhiwallon, a leather bag containing the secrets of the lake's medicinal plants, and informed him that he should heal the sick.

From this point, legend merges with fact. Historical records confirm that Rhiwallon was a well-known 13th-century physician, and his descendants continued the tradition. The last of the line, Rice Williams, MD, died in 1842.

The Pant-y-Meddygon (Physicians' Valley) on Mynydd Myddfai is still rich in bog plants, herbs and lichens, and is well worth visiting for the scenery alone.

Sights

Penderyn Distillery DISTILLERY
(☎01685-810651; www.welsh-whisky.co.uk; Penderyn; tours £8.50; ⏰9.30am-5pm) Though Wales has a long history of spirit distillation, this boutique distillery released its first malt whisky only in 2004, marking the resurgence of Welsh whisky-making after an absence of more than 100 years due to the popularity of the temperance movement in the late 19th century. Visitors can witness the creation of the liquid fire that's distilled with fresh spring water in a single copper still, then matured in bourbon casks and finished in rich Madeira wine casks. Tours include tastings.

Besides three single-malt whiskies, the distillery also produces two award-winning gins, a vodka and Merlyn cream liqueur. Tours generally leave on the hour, but it pays to book ahead. Tickets include two tastings and enthusiasts can take a 2½-hour Master Class, which includes a guided tour and tastings (per person £45, bookings essential).

Waterfall Country WATERFALL
A series of dramatic waterfalls lies between the villages of Pontneddfechan and Ystradfellte, where the Rivers Mellte, Hepste and Pyrddin pass through steep forested gorges. The finest is **Sgwd-yr-Eira** (Waterfall of the Snow), where you can actually walk behind the torrent. At one point the River Mellte disappears into **Porth-yr-Ogof** (Door to the Cave), the biggest cave entrance in Britain (3m high and 20m wide), only to reappear 100m further south.

Walks in the area are outlined in the national park's *Waterfall Country* publication (£1), available from visitor centres. The **Elidir Trail** (2½ miles each way) starts from Pontneddfechan and connects up with various other trails. Take special care – the footpaths can be slippery, and there are several steep, stony sections.

Dan-yr-Ogof National Showcaves Centre for Wales CAVE
(☎01639-730284; www.showcaves.co.uk; A4067, Abercraf; adult/child £14/9.50; ⏰10am-3pm Easter-Oct) The limestone plateau of the southern Fforest Fawr is riddled with some of the largest and most complex cave systems in Britain. Most can only be visited by experienced cavers, but this set of three caves is well lit, spacious and easily accessible, even to children. The complex is just off the A4067, north of Abercraf.

The highlight of the 1.5-mile self-guided tour is the **Cathedral Cave**, a high-domed chamber with a lake fed by two waterfalls that pour from openings in the rock. Nearby is the **Bone Cave**, where 42 Bronze Age skeletons were discovered. **Dan-yr-Ogof Cave**, part of a 10-mile complex, has glistening limestone formations.

Somewhat at odds with the natural attractions are the plexiglas dinosaurs peeking through the trees, some of them locked in mortal combat, and a recreated Iron Age farm with mushroom-like huts. The admission fee covers other child-friendly draws, including a petting zoo and a shire-horse centre.

Beneath the hillside to the east lies the twisting maze of subterranean chambers known as **Ogof Ffynnon Ddu** (Cave of the Black Spring), the deepest and third-longest cave system in the UK (308m deep, with 30 miles of passages). This one is for expert potholers only, but you can explore it virtually at www.ogof.net.

Fan Brycheiniog MOUNTAIN

The finest feature (and the highest point) of the Black Mountain is the sweeping escarpment of Fan Brycheiniog (802m), reached via a fairly strenuous 11.5-mile loop from Glyntawe on the A4067.

The initial precipitous ascent of the Fan Hir ridge eases into a spectacular ridge walk, with views of the Llyn y Fan Fawr glacial lake to the east. A steep path climbs up to Fan Brycheiniog and it's worth detouring to climb Fan Foel for the views of Llyn y Fan Fach before following the almost level Bannau Sir Gaer ridge to the Waun Lefrith summit. Head west across pathless terrain to the rocky Carreg yr Ogof, and descend the path to the east of it across a wild landscape of limestone sinkholes, marshland and streams.

Red Kite Feeding Centre BIRD SANCTUARY

(☎01550-740617; www.redkiteswales.co.uk; Llanddeusant; adult/child £4/2; ⏲3pm Apr-Oct, 2pm Nov-Mar) A multitude of majestic birds of prey swoop in daily for their afternoon meal at this remote feeding centre. You're likely to see upwards of 50 red kites, alongside buzzards and ravens.

Garn Goch RUINS

FREE You're likely to have the remains of Garn Goch to yourself, despite their impressiveness. It's one of the largest Iron Age hill forts in Wales. Two distinct, immense, circular, stone ramparts can be discerned as you wander the hilltop, which offers endless views of the surrounding countryside. To get here, follow the signs from Llangadog through Bethlehem village and into the hills beyond.

★Carreg Cennen CASTLE

(Cadw; ☎01558-822291; www.carregcennencastle.com; Trapp; adult/child £4/3.50; ⏲9.30am-6.30pm Apr-Oct, to 4pm Nov-Mar) Dramatically perched atop a steep limestone crag, high above the River Cennen, are the brooding ruins of Wales' ultimate romantic castle, visible for miles in every direction. Originally a Welsh castle, the current structure dates back to Edward I's conquest of Wales in the late 13th century. It was partially dismantled in 1462 during the War of the Roses. It's well signposted from the A483, heading south from Llandeilo.

The castle's most unusual feature is a stone-vaulted passage running along the top of the sheer southern cliff, which leads down to a long, narrow, natural cave; bring a torch or hire one from the ticket office (£1.50).

Sleeping & Eating

There are some good hostels and campgrounds scattered about this section of the national park. Alternatively you could base yourself in Llandovery, Llandeilo or Merthyr Tydfil.

RED KITES

Even the least diligent birdwatcher is sure to spot red kites in the Brecon Beacons. The birds are magnificent and pleasingly easy to identify, with their rust-red plumage, forked tails, 2m wingspan and easy gliding motion. Red kites have a small body in relation to their long wings, meaning they can stay airborne for long periods.

The birds were eradicated from England, Scotland and most of Wales by landowners who thought them responsible for preying on livestock. In fact, the kites are primarily scavengers. In 1934 there were only two breeding pairs left in Wales. Their reintroduction across the UK has been a great success, with separate populations spreading and breeding with each other, thus strengthening the gene pool.

Wales alone now has around 900 breeding pairs, whose great presence and grace will enhance your visit to the Brecon Beacons. You can watch them close up during feeding time at the Red Kite Feeding Centre.

★**Coed Owen Bunkhouse** HOSTEL £
(☎01685-722628; www.breconbeaconsbunkhouse.co.uk; Cwmtaff; dm/r £30/60; P) Set on a working sheep farm just up the road from the Garwnant Visitor Centre, this excellent custom conversion of an old barn offers smart six- and 10-bed bunkrooms and one small, private double. There's also an excellent kitchen. On the weekends it's usually booked up by groups, but solo travellers shouldn't have trouble midweek.

Brecon Beacons YHA HOSTEL £
(☎0800 0191 700; www.yha.org.uk; Libanus; site/dm £10/19, r with/without bathroom from £55/49; ⊙daily Feb-Oct, Wed-Sun Nov-Jan; P) Set in 6 hectares of woodland, 6 miles southwest of Brecon on the A470, this 18th-century farmhouse hostel has had its facilities smartened up but it still has plenty of historic character courtesy of flagstone floors and rough stone walls. The location is ideal for hikers – particularly for ascents of Pen-y-Fan.

Llanddeusant YHA HOSTEL £
(☎0800 0191 700; www.yha.org.uk; Llanddeusant; site/dm/r from £11/20/79; P) A former inn nestled in the foothills of the Black Mountain, this wonderfully remote hostel and campground has no TV, wi-fi or mobile-phone reception. It does, however, have some wonderful walks on its doorstep, including the track to Llyn y Fan Fach. There's a large kitchen but you'll need to bring all your own food.

Dan-yr-Ogof CAMPSITE £
(☎01639-730284; www.showcaves.co.uk; A4067, Abercraf; sites per adult/child £7/5; ⊙Apr-Oct; 🐾) Part of the Dan-yr-Ogof cave (p112) attraction, this is a verdant family-friendly site with a play barn for kids. It's also a great spot for walkers, and includes riverside woodland pitches as well as space for motorhomes.

Mandinam CABIN ££
(☎01550-777368; www.mandinam.com; Llangadog; cabin £100; ⊙Easter-Oct; P) This wonderfully remote estate on the northwestern fringe of the national park offers a bohemian back-to-nature experience in little wagon-like huts, complete with kitchens and wood-fired hot tubs for a spot of romantic star-gazing. You needn't worry about privacy as the huts are positioned well apart from each other within the vast property.

Carreg Cennen Tearoom WELSH £
(☎01558-822291; www.carregcennencastle.com; Trapp; mains £4-8; ⊙9.30am-5.30pm) Possibly the best castle tearoom anywhere. The farmer/owner's longhorn beef is on the menu in the form of cottage pie and beef salad, plus they serve warming *cawl* (traditional Welsh stew) and excellent home-made cakes. The location is an impressive converted barn, which sits just below the castle.

ℹ Information

Garwnant Visitor Centre (☎01685-722481; www.naturalresourceswales.gov.uk/garwnant; parking £2; ⊙9am-5pm; 👪) Natural Resources Wales' visitor centre sits at the head of the Llwyn-on Reservoir, 5 miles north of Merthyr Tydfil on the A470. It's the starting point for a couple of easy forest walks. It also has a cafe, a mini mountain-bike course, an adventure play area and a rope course for kids.

ℹ Getting There & Away

The only useful bus routes through this region are bus 63 between Brecon and Ystradgynlais, which stops at the Dan-yr-Ogof National Showcaves Centre when it's open; and bus T3 between Cardiff and Newtown (via Merthyr Tydfil, Brecon and Llandrindod Wells), which stops near the Garwnant Visitor Centre.

SOUTH WALES VALLEYS

The valleys fanning northwards from Cardiff and Newport were once the heart of industrial Wales. Although the coal, iron and steel industries have withered, the valley names – Rhondda, Cynon, Rhymney, Ebbw – still evoke a world of tight-knit working-class communities, male voice choirs and rows of neat terraced houses set amid a scarred, coal-blackened landscape. Today the region is fighting back against its decline by creating a tourist industry based on industrial heritage – places such as the Rhondda Heritage Park, Big Pit and Blaenavon Ironworks are among Wales' most impressive tourist attractions.

History

The valleys' industrial economy emerged in the 18th century, based on the exploitation of the region's rich deposits of coal, limestone and iron ore. At first the iron trade dictated the need for coal, but by the 1830s coal was finding its own worldwide markets and people poured in from the countryside looking for work. The harsh and dangerous working conditions provided fertile ground for political radicalism – Merthyr Tydfil elected Britain's first ever Labour Party MP in 1900, and many locals went to fight in the Spanish Civil War in the 1930s.

Merthyr Tydfil (Merthyr Tudful)

POP 43,900

Merthyr Tydfil (*mur*-thir *tid*-vil) occupies a spectacular site, sprawled across a bowl at the head of the Taff Valley, ringed and pocked with quarries and spoil heaps. It was even more spectacular 200 years ago when the town was at the heart of the Industrial Revolution, and this bowl was a crucible filled with the fire and smoke of the world's biggest ironworks.

Perhaps unusually for such an industrial town, Merthyr Tydfil has produced two internationally famous fashion designers – the late Laura Ashley (famed for her flowery, feminine designs in the 1970s) and Julien Macdonald (of the shimmery, figure-hugging dresses favoured by Kylie and Britney).

The Taff Trail follows the river that runs along the western edge of town, crossed by the handsome railway viaducts of Cefn Coed (the third biggest in Wales) and Pontsarn, both completed in 1866.

History

Merthyr Tydfil means 'the place of Tydfil's martyrdom' – the town was named in honour of a Welsh princess who, according to legend, was murdered for her Christian beliefs in the 5th century. St Tydfil's Church is said to mark the spot where she died.

Merthyr remained a minor village until the late 18th century, when its proximity to iron ore, limestone, water and wood led to it becoming a centre of iron production. The subsequent discovery of rich coal reserves upped the ante, and by 1801 a string of settlements, each growing around its own ironworks – Cyfarthfa, Penydarren, Dowlais, Pentrebach and others – had merged together to become the biggest town in Wales (population 10,000, eight times the size of Cardiff at that time). Immigrants flooded in from all over Europe, and the town's population peaked at 81,000 in the mid-19th century.

By 1803 Cyfarthfa was the world's biggest ironworks. Ever more efficient ways to make iron were pioneered, on the backs of overworked labourers (including, until 1842, women and children as young as six) who lived in appalling, disease-ridden conditions.

By the 19th century Merthyr was a centre of political radicalism. The Merthyr Rising of 1831 was the most violent uprising in Britain's history – 10,000 ironworkers, angry over pay cuts and lack of representation, faced off against a handful of armed soldiers, and rioting continued for a month. During the protest a red flag was raised; it went on to become an international symbol of the workers' movement.

As demand for iron and steel dwindled in the early 20th century, one by one the ironworks closed down. Unemployment soared, reaching as high as 60% in 1935. In 1939 a Royal Commission even suggested that the whole town should be abandoned, but community ties were strong and people stayed on. Today unemployment still runs at 8%, nearly twice the UK average.

Sights & Activities

Cyfarthfa Castle CASTLE
(01685-727371; www.cyfarthfa.com; Brecon Rd; adult/child £2/free; 10am-5.30pm Mon-Fri, noon-5.30pm Sat & Sun Apr-Sep, 10am-4.30pm Tue-Fri, noon-4.30pm Sat & Sun Oct-Mar; P) For a measure of the wealth that accumulated at the top of the industrial pile, check out this castle, built in 1825 by William Crawshay II, overlooking his ironworks. The house is now jam-packed with interesting stuff, from ancient Egyptian and Roman artefacts, to Laura Ashley and Julien Macdonald frocks. The basement houses an excellent exhibition on Merthyr's gritty history, taking in the struggles of the Chartists, trade unions and suffragettes. The house is surrounded by a beautiful public park.

Set into the hillside across the river from the castle are all that remains of the Cyfarthfa blast furnaces.

Joseph Parry's Cottage HISTORIC BUILDING
(01685-727371; www.cyfarthfa.com; 4 Chapel Row; 2-5pm Sat & Sun Apr-Sep) FREE A half-mile to the south of Cyfarthfa Castle, a row of pint-sized 19th-century ironworkers' houses built by the Crawshays stands in bold contrast to their own ostentatious house. Number 4 was the birthplace of

Welsh composer and songwriter Joseph Parry (1841–1903). It's now an offshoot of the castle museum, furnished in 1840s style and devoted to his life.

Brecon Mountain Railway RAIL
(☎01685-722988; www.breconmountainrailway.co.uk; adult/child £14/6.75) Between 1859 and 1964 this narrow-gauge railway hauled coal and passengers between Merthyr and Brecon. A 5.5-mile section of track, between Pant Station and Torpantau at the head of Pontsticill Reservoir, has been restored and steam locomotives operate on the line. The trip takes 65 minutes with a 20-minute stop at Pontsticill (you can stay longer if you like and return on a later train). Check the timetable online. Pant Station is 3.5 miles north of Merthyr bus station; take bus 35 (20 minutes, departs every 15 minutes, hourly on Sunday) to the Pant Cemetery stop.

BikePark Wales MOUNTAIN BIKING
(☎07730 382501; www.bikeparkwales.com; Gethin Woods, Abercanaid; day pass £7, incl uplift £32, bike hire per half/full day from £40/60; ⏲9am-6pm Fri-Wed, to 9pm Thu May-Sep, to 5pm Oct-Apr) One of Wales' premier mountain-biking complexes, this site has dozens of tracks to suit beginners, pros and all folks in between. Also offers bike hire, repairs, coaching and a cafe.

Sleeping

Imperial Hotel PUB £
(☎01685-722555; www.imperialhotelmerthyrtydfil.co.uk; High St; s/d £40/55; P 📶) A good cheapie right in the centre of town, the Imperial offers clean en suite rooms above an old-fashioned pub. Shortcomings include wi-fi that only works downstairs and a car park that requires the removal of a padlock every time you need to access it.

Winchfawr Lodges RENTAL HOUSES ££
(☎01685-385071; www.winchfawrlodge.co.uk; Winchfawr, Heolgerrig; 2 nights/week £220/595; P 📶) Overlooking Merthyr Tydfil from the slopes to its west, this trio of self-contained, detached, brick houses offers comfortable home-style accommodation, each sleeping three to four people. The spacious grounds have barbecues, plenty of parking and a kids playset.

Eating

Old Barn Tea Room CAFE £
(Ystradgynwyn; mains £5-10; ⏲11am-5pm Mar-Nov) A beautiful 18th-century barn, decked out with vintage furniture, that serves great cream teas and a fine Sunday lunch. To find it, head north out of town on the back road that leads through Brecon Beacons National Park along the west of the Pontsticill Reservoir.

★ **Mango House** INDIAN ££
(91 High St, Cefn Coed; mains £7-13; ⏲6-10.30pm; 🖉) Bringing the subcontinent to the suburbs, this snazzy Indian eatery serves up a huge menu of delicious and complex curries, including an extensive vegetarian selection. Don't confuse the address with High St in the town centre; this High St is the continuation of Brecon Rd west of Cyfarthfa Castle.

Plas Coffi BURGERS, PIZZA ££
(☎01685-359435; www.plascoffi.co.uk; 62 High St; mains £8-18; ⏲10am-10pm Mon-Sat, to 5pm Sun; 🖉) Bringing a dose of industrial-chic to Merthyr's tired shopping strip, this cool-looking cafe-bar serves fancy burgers and wood-fired pizza, along with savoury pies, ribs, steaks and lamb racks. Not everything lives up to its promise (our chips were a little soggy), but it's still one of our favourite Merthyr hang-outs.

Getting There & Away

Merthyr Bus Station is in Victoria St, in the town centre, although there is talk of moving it a couple of blocks south to Swan St. Direct buses head to/from Cardiff (£5.20, 60 minutes, frequent), Abergavenny (£6.40, 1½ hours, 13 daily), Brecon (£3.20, 35 minutes, 10 daily), Llandrindod Wells (£7.75, 1¾ hours, every two hours) and Hereford (£9.40, 2½ hours, five daily).

Trains head to/from Cardiff (£5.70, one hour) every half hour. The station is right in the centre of town, by the giant Tesco supermarket on Tramroadside North.

For cyclists, the Taff Trail heads south from here to Cardiff and north to Brecon.

Blaenavon (Blaenafon)

POP 6060

Of all the valley settlements that were decimated by the demise of heavy industry, the one-time coal and iron town of Blaenavon shows the greenest shoots of regrowth, helped in large part by the awarding of Unesco World Heritage status in 2000 to its unique conglomeration of industrial sites. Its proximity to Brecon Beacons National Park and Abergavenny doesn't do it any harm either.

Sights & Activities

Blaenavon World Heritage Centre MUSEUM
(☎01495-742333; www.visitblaenavon.co.uk; Church Rd; ⏰10am-5pm Tue-Sun) FREE Housed in an artfully converted old school, this centre contains a cafe, tourist office, gallery, gift shop and, more importantly, excellent interactive, audiovisual displays that explore the industrial heritage of the region.

Blaenavon Ironworks HISTORIC SITE
(Cadw; www.cadw.gov.wales; North St; ⏰10am-5pm Easter-Oct, to 4pm Tue-Thu Nov-Easter) FREE When it was completed in 1789, this ironworks was among the most advanced in the world. Today the site is one of the best preserved of all its Industrial Revolution contemporaries, with a motion-activated audiovisual display within the hulking remains of one of the blast furnaces serving to rattle the ravens that now call it home. Also on display are the ironworkers' tiny terraced cottages, furnished as they would have been at different points in history.

Blaenavon Ironworks' three huge coal-fired blast furnaces were provided with air by a steam engine, making them much more powerful than older, smaller furnaces fired with charcoal and blasted with air from waterwheel-powered bellows. Within a few years of construction it was the world's second-biggest ironworks, after Cyfarthfa at Merthyr Tydfil. Innovation and development continued here until 1904, when the last furnace was finally shut down.

You can follow the whole process of production, from the charging of the furnaces to the casting of molten iron in the casting sheds. The surrounding hillsides are pitted with old tramlines, mines, tunnels and 'scouring' sites, where water was released from holding ponds to wash away topsoil and expose ore seams.

Pontypool & Blaenavon Railway RAIL
(☎01495-792263; www.pontypool-and-blaenavon.co.uk; day pass adult/child £10/5) Built to haul coal and passengers, this railway has been restored by local volunteers, allowing you to catch a steam train from the town centre to Furnace Sidings (near Big Pit) and on to Whistle Halt, which at 396m is one of the highest stations in Britain. Check online for timetables.

★**Big Pit National Coal Museum** MINE
(☎0300 111 2333; www.museumwales.ac.uk; car park £3; ⏰9.30am-5pm, guided tours 10am-3.30pm; P) FREE Fascinating Big Pit provides an opportunity to explore a real coal mine and get a taste of what life was like for the miners who worked here up until 1980. Tours descend 90m into the mine and explore the tunnels and coalfaces in the company of an ex-miner guide. Above ground, you can visit various colliery buildings including the 1939 pithead baths, filled with displays on the industry and the evocative reminiscences of ex-miners.

It's sobering to experience something of the dark, dank working conditions below ground, particularly considering that children once worked here by candlelight. If you choose to head underground you'll be decked out in a hard hat, power pack and other safety gear weighing some 5kg, and won't be allowed to bring matches or anything electrical down with you (including photo equipment and watches). It's cold down here, so take extra layers and wear sturdy shoes. Children must be at least 1m tall. Disabled visitors can arrange tours in advance.

Paraventure Paragliding PARAGLIDING
(☎01495-790961; www.paraventureparagliding.co.uk; 1-/2-/4-day course £150/295/595) Learn how to paraglide and enjoy a red kite's perspective of the valleys.

Tours

Mountain Tours CYCLING
(☎01495-793123; www.chunkofwales.co.uk; 80 Broad St; bike hire per half-/full-day £14/20) Operated in conjunction with the folks at Blaenavon Cheddar Company, this crew hires bikes and can arrange guided walking and mountain-biking tours to suit all abilities (book well in advance).

Sleeping & Eating

Oakfield B&B ££
(☎01495-792829; www.oakfieldbnb.com; 1 Oakfield Tce, Varteg Rd; s/d £42/69; P 📶) The clued-up owners of this spick-and-span B&B are a fount of local knowledge. Their three well-appointed rooms have a fresh, modern feel to them. Two have en suite bathrooms, while the third is an interconnected family suite with a bathroom on the landing.

Coffi 1860 CAFE £
(☎01495-790127; 76 Broad St; mains £6; ⏰8am-3pm; 📶) With leadlight windows, art deco fixtures and shamrock tiling on the walls,

WORTH A TRIP

RHONDDA VALLEY

Until its last pit closed in 1990, the Rhondda Valley was synonymous with coal mining. That industrial heritage is celebrated at **Rhondda Heritage Park** (☎01443-682036; www.rhonddaheritagepark.com; Trehafod; tour adult/child £3.75/2.65; ⏲10.30am-4.30pm Tue-Sat, tours 11.30am & 1.30pm) within the buildings of the Lewis Merthyr coal mine, which was closed in 1983. The highlight is the 40-minute **Underground Experience** (bookings advised), where you don a miner's helmet and lamp and, accompanied by an ex-miner, descend to the coalface. The compelling commentary vividly re-creates the experience of mine workers, and hammers home the social impact of the coal industry.

Other displays include recreated domestic interiors and shops, and a sobering section on the Tynewydd Colliery disaster of 1877. Upstairs there's a cafe and an art space.

The mine is located just off the A4058 in Trehafod, between Pontypridd and Porth. There are trains every half hour from Cardiff Central station to Trehafod (£6.90, 35 minutes), from where it's a 10-minute walk to the heritage park.

this lovely old converted shop is a great place to soak up local life. The food stretches to cooked breakfasts, sandwiches, jacket potatoes, stews, curries, quiches, cakes and proper Sunday lunches.

Butterflies PUB FOOD ££
(☎01495-791044; www.butterfliesblaenavon.co.uk; 31 Old Queen St; mains £11-23; ⏲6-10pm Tue, Wed & Sat, noon-2.30pm & 6-10pm Thu & Fri, 1-4pm Sun; 🅥) Serving surprisingly sophisticated food for a small-town pub in a former mining town, cosy Butterflies has meaty offerings that stretch to an excellent *boeuf en croute* (beef in a mushroom-lined pastry crust) and chateaubriand. If that all sounds a bit too fancy, there are pub favourites to fall back on (lasagne, burgers, steak-and-ale pie), along with fish and vegetarian options.

Shopping

Blaenavon Cheddar Company FOOD & DRINKS
(☎01495-793123; www.chunkofcheese.co.uk; 80 Broad St; ⏲10am-5pm Mon-Sat) Showcasing the company's range of award-winning handmade cheese, some of which is matured down in the Big Pit mine shaft, this little store also stocks a range of Welsh specialty ale, chutney, mustard and other local produce.

Getting There & Away

Bus X24 heads to/from Newport (£7.10, one hour) several times per hour.

Caerphilly (Caerffili)

POP 30,400

The town of Caerphilly, with its fairy-tale castle, guards the entrance to the Rhymney Valley to the north of Cardiff. Its name is synonymous with a popular variety of mild, slightly crumbly, hard white cheese that was once made in farmhouses all over South Wales.

Its other claim to fame was as the birthplace of Tommy Cooper, a much-loved British comedian who died while performing a live TV show in 1984. A statue of Cooper in his trademark fez and with a rabbit at his feet overlooks the castle from near the tourist office.

Sights

★**Caerphilly Castle** CASTLE
(Cadw; www.cadw.gov.wales; adult/child £6/4.20; ⏲9.30am-5pm Mar-Oct, 10am-4pm Nov-Feb) You could be forgiven for thinking that Caerphilly Castle – with its profusion of towers and crenellations reflected in a duck-filled lake – was a film set rather than an ancient monument. While it is often used as a film set, it is also one of Britain's finest examples of a 13th-century fortress with water defences.

Most of the construction was completed between 1268 and 1271 by the powerful English baron Gilbert de Clare (1243–95), Lord Marcher of Glamorgan, in response to the threat of attack by Prince Llywelyn ap Gruffydd, prince of Gwynedd (and the last Welsh Prince of Wales), who had already united most of the country under his control.

Edward I's subsequent campaign against the Welsh princes put an end to Llywelyn's ambitions and Caerphilly's short-lived spell on the front line came to an end. The leaning tower at the southeast corner is a result of subsidence rather than battle.

In the 13th century Caerphilly was state-of-the-art, being one of the earliest castles to use lakes, bridges and a series of concentric fortifications for defence. To reach the inner court you had to overcome no fewer than three drawbridges, six portcullises and five sets of double gates. In the early 14th century it was remodelled as a grand residence and the magnificent great hall was adapted for entertaining, but from the mid-14th century onward the castle began to fall into ruin.

Much of what you see today is the result of restoration by the castle-loving Bute family. The third marquess of Bute purchased and demolished houses built up against the walls, and in 1870 the great hall was given a magnificent wooden ceiling. The fourth marquess instituted a major restoration from 1928 to 1939, giving jobs to many Great Depression-affected locals in the process. Work continued after 1950, when the fifth marquess gifted the castle to the state. In 1958 the dams were reflooded, creating its current fairy-tale appearance.

You can enter through the outside gate and into the first tower before reaching the ticket office. Upstairs, there are detailed displays about the castle's history. A cartoonish film projected onto the walls of one of the inner towers tells a truncated version of the same story.

On the south dam platform you can see reconstructions of medieval siege weapons; they are working models that lob stone projectiles into the lake during battle re-enactments. Fans of toilet humour should seek out the communal latrine in a small tower nearby.

Festivals & Events

Big Cheese FOOD, FAIR

(www.caerphilly.gov.uk; Caerphilly; Jul) Any festival that includes a Cheese Olympics and a Tommy Cooper Tent has got to be worth a look. On the last weekend of July, Caerphilly welcomes more than 80,000 people to three days of family-oriented fun and games that offer everything from fireworks to falconry, comedy acts to cheese tasting, and a traditional fun fair.

Information

Caerphilly Tourist Office (029-2088 0011; www.visitcaerphilly.com; The Twyn; 10am-5pm) Not only is this friendly office a good place to stock up on information, it's also the only place in town selling Caerphilly cheese – along with Penderyn spirits and locally made chocolates. There's a small cafe attached.

Getting There & Away

The easiest way to reach Caerphilly from Cardiff is by train (single/return £4.40/6.90, 19 minutes, at least two per hour).

Frequent buses head to/from Cardiff (£3.80, 39 minutes) and Newport (£3.80, 40 minutes). Bus 26 from Cardiff stops near Castell Coch en route, making it possible to visit both castles in one day. Sunday services are less frequent.

Swansea, Gower & Carmarthenshire

Includes ➜

Best Places to Eat

- ➜ Mosaic (p126)
- ➜ Favourite (p127)
- ➜ Dolaucothi Arms (p145)
- ➜ Ginhaus Deli (p144)
- ➜ Wright's Food Emporium (p143)

Best Places to Sleep

- ➜ Larkhill Tipis (p146)
- ➜ Christmas Pie B&B (p125)
- ➜ Llethryd Barns (p131)
- ➜ New White Lion (p144)
- ➜ Port Eynon YHA (p133)

Why Go?

A smorgasbord of experiences is on offer in this corner of Wales, with physical proximity being the only thing linking its three main dishes, each with its own distinct flavour. Try a taste of each or gorge yourself on whatever you think sounds yummiest.

Swansea delivers something approaching big-city sophistication, with a glorious stretch of sand arcing between a slowly regenerating city centre and its beach suburb, attractive little Mumbles. On its doorstep are the craggy coastline and epic sandy beaches of the Gower Peninsula, which offer surfing, watersports of all sorts and undulating hikes. Inland, the fecund heartland of rural Carmarthenshire is little touristed but a treat for the green-fingered traveller, with nationally significant parks and gardens scattered about.

If that's whetted your appetite, this area's regional specialities are some of the most famous in all of Wales: salt-marsh lamb, Penclawdd cockles, laver bread and Carmarthen ham. Tuck in.

When to Go

➜ Beach lovers might want to brave July and August on the Gower to make the most of the best weather, though be aware that the narrow country roads – and the B&Bs and campgrounds – are likely to be crammed during this time.

➜ Many hostels and campgrounds don't open till after Easter, and the winter period is pretty quiet. If you're hiking you might prefer to aim for May, June, September or October. Come prepared for rain showers whatever time of year you visit.

➜ October sees both the classical-music-dominated Swansea International Festival (p124) and the Dylan Thomas Festival (p124) hit Swansea. Music and poetry fans might also like to plan around the Laugharne Weekend (p140) at the beginning of April.

SWANSEA (ABERTAWE)

POP 239,000

Dylan Thomas called Swansea an 'ugly, lovely town', and that remains a fair description of Wales' second-largest city today. It's currently in the grip of a Cardiff-esque bout of regeneration that's slowly transforming the drab, postwar city centre into something more worthy of its setting on the glorious 5-mile sweep of Swansea Bay.

The city's Welsh name, Abertawe, describes its location at the mouth of the Tawe, where the river empties into the bay. The Vikings named the area Sveins Ey (Swein's Island), probably referring to the sandbank in the river mouth.

Swansea makes up for some visual shortcomings with a visceral charm. A hefty student population takes to the city's bars with enthusiasm, and pockets of hipness have emerged in inner suburbs such as Sketty and Uplands, which is, conveniently, where all the best B&Bs are located.

History

The Normans built a castle here, but Swansea didn't hit its stride until the Industrial Revolution, when it developed into an important copper-smelting centre. Ore was first shipped in from Cornwall, across the Bristol Channel, but by the 19th century it was arriving from Chile, Cuba and the USA in return for Welsh coal.

By the 20th century the city's industrial base had declined, although Swansea's oil refinery and smaller factories were still judged a worthy target by the Luftwaffe, which devastated the city centre in 1941. It was rebuilt as a rather drab retail development in the 1960s, '70s and '80s, but gradual regeneration is slowly imbuing it with more soul.

Sights

National Waterfront Museum MUSEUM

(☎0300 111 2333; www.museumwales.ac.uk; South Dock Marina, Oystermouth Rd; ⏲10am-5pm) FREE Housed in a 1901 dockside warehouse with a striking glass and slate extension, this museum's 15 hands-on galleries explore Wales' industrial history and the impact of industrialisation on its people, making much use of interactive computer screens and audiovisual presentations. The effect can be a bit overwhelming but there is a lot of interesting stuff here, including displays on the Welsh music industry (artefacts include Bonnie Tyler's gold and Duffy's platinum discs) and a section on 'women's work'.

Swansea Museum MUSEUM

(☎01792-653763; www.swanseamuseum.co.uk; Victoria Rd; ⏲10am-5pm Tue-Sun) FREE Dylan Thomas referred to this august institution as 'the museum which should have been in a museum'. Founded in 1834, it remains charmingly low-tech, from the eccentric Cabinet of Curiosities to the glass cases of archaeological finds from Gower caves. Pride of place goes to the Mummy of Hor at the top of the stairs, which has been resting here since 1887 – a video in the display room explains the process of its repair and conservation.

Dylan Thomas Centre MUSEUM

(☎01792-463980; www.dylanthomas.com; Somerset Pl; ⏲10am-4.30pm) FREE Housed in the former guildhall, this unassuming museum contains absorbing displays on the Swansea-born poet's life and work. It pulls no punches in examining the propensity of Dylan Thomas for puffing up his own myth; he was eventually trapped in the legend of his excessive drinking. Aside from the collection of memorabilia, what really brings his work to life are the recordings of performances of his work.

The centre runs a high-powered calendar of talks, drama and workshops.

Glynn Vivian Art Gallery GALLERY

(www.swansea.gov.uk/glynnvivian; Alexandra Rd) FREE The seemingly never-ending refurbishment of Swansea's main art gallery was still in progress when we last visited. By the time you read this, the elegant Italianate building will probably have reopened and the public will once again have access to its prestigious collection of Welsh art – Richard Wilson, Gwen John, Ceri Richards, Shani Rhys James – along with works by Claude Monet and Lucien Freud and a large ceramics collection.

Dylan Thomas Birthplace HOUSE

(☎01792-472555; www.dylanthomasbirthplace.com; 5 Cwmdonkin Dr, Uplands; adult/child £8/6; ⏲tours 11am, 1pm & 3pm) The bad boy of Welsh poetry was born in this unassuming Uplands house and it's here that he wrote two-thirds of his poetry. The house has been lovingly restored and furnished in period style, and can be visited on a guided tour (bookings advised). You can even stay the night if you're really keen (rooms £150).

Swansea, Gower & Carmarthenshire Highlights

❶ **Rhossili** (p133) Wandering along the golden sand and watching the waves crash over the mighty Worms Head.

❷ **National Botanic Garden of Wales** (p142) Marvelling at Norman Foster's intriguing sunken greenhouse dome and the rare and endangered plants that it harbours.

❸ **Aberglasney Gardens** (p143) Channelling your inner Jane Austen within walled gardens and yew tunnels.

❹ **Dinefwr** (p143) Roaming around expansive grounds, a ruined castle and a stately manor house.

❺ **Swansea** (p121) Uncovering hidden bars, ethnic eateries and engaging museums in Wales' second-biggest city.

❻ **Laugharne** (p139) Finding inspiration in the castle-guarded coastal town that so stimulated Dylan Thomas.

❼ **The Mumbles** (p129) Tracing the broad arc of Swansea Bay to its wine-swilling, beer-supping, ice-cream-licking, pinball-playing, beach-going, well-caffeinated apotheosis.

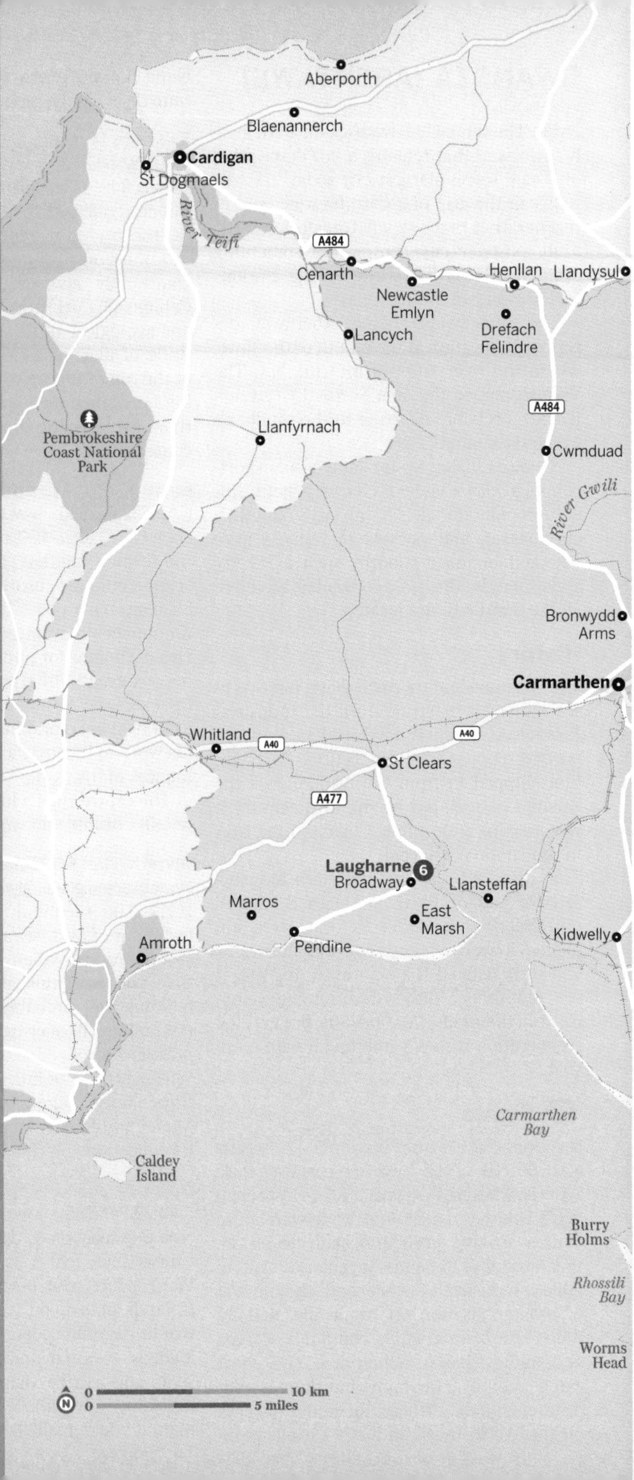

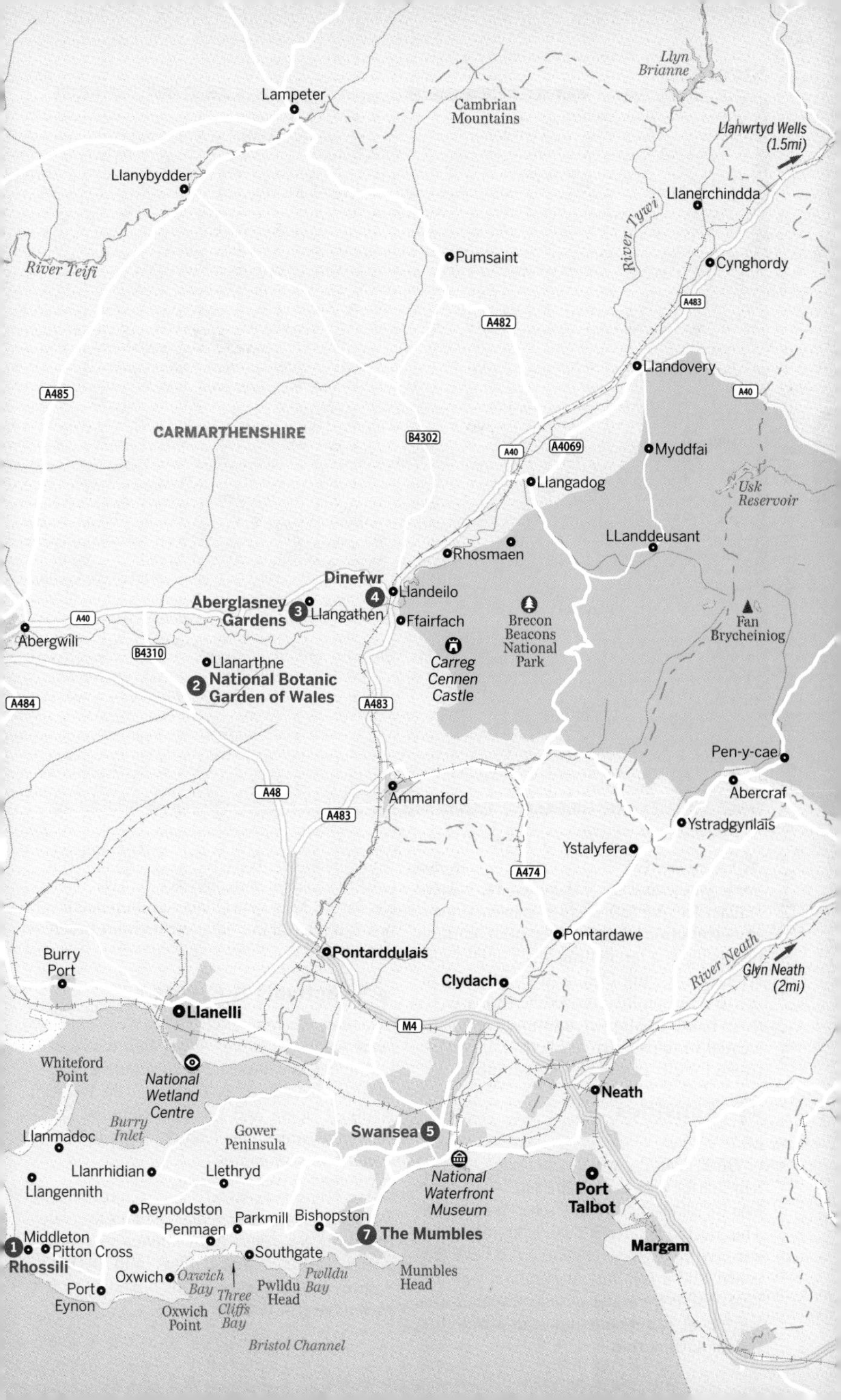
Llyn Brianne
Lampeter
Cambrian Mountains
Llanwrtyd Wells (1.5mi)
Llanybydder
Llanerchindda
River Tywi
River Teifi
Pumsaint
Cynghordy
A483
A482
Llandovery
A485
A40
CARMARTHENSHIRE
B4302
A40
A4069
Myddfai
Llangadog
Usk Reservoir
LLanddeusant
Rhosmaen
Dinefwr
4 Llandeilo
Aberglasney Gardens
3 Llangathen
Ffairfach
Brecon Beacons National Park
Fan Brycheiniog
A40
Abergwili
B4310
Carreg Cennen Castle
Llanarthne
2 National Botanic Garden of Wales
A484
A483
Pen-y-cae
A48
Ammanford
Abercraf
A483
Ystradgynlais
Ystalyfera
A474
Pontardawe
Burry Port
Pontarddulais
River Neath
Glyn Neath (2mi)
Clydach
Llanelli
M4
Whiteford Point
National Wetland Centre
Neath
Burry Inlet
Gower Peninsula
Swansea 5
Llanmadoc
Llanrhidian
Llethryd
National Waterfront Museum
Port Talbot
Llangennith
Reynoldston
Parkmill
Bishopston
Penmaen
7 The Mumbles
Margam
Middleton
1 Pitton Cross
Rhossili
Southgate
Oxwich
Oxwich Bay
Three Cliffs Bay
Pwlldu Head
Pwlldu Bay
Mumbles Head
Port Eynon
Oxwich Point
Bristol Channel

Swansea

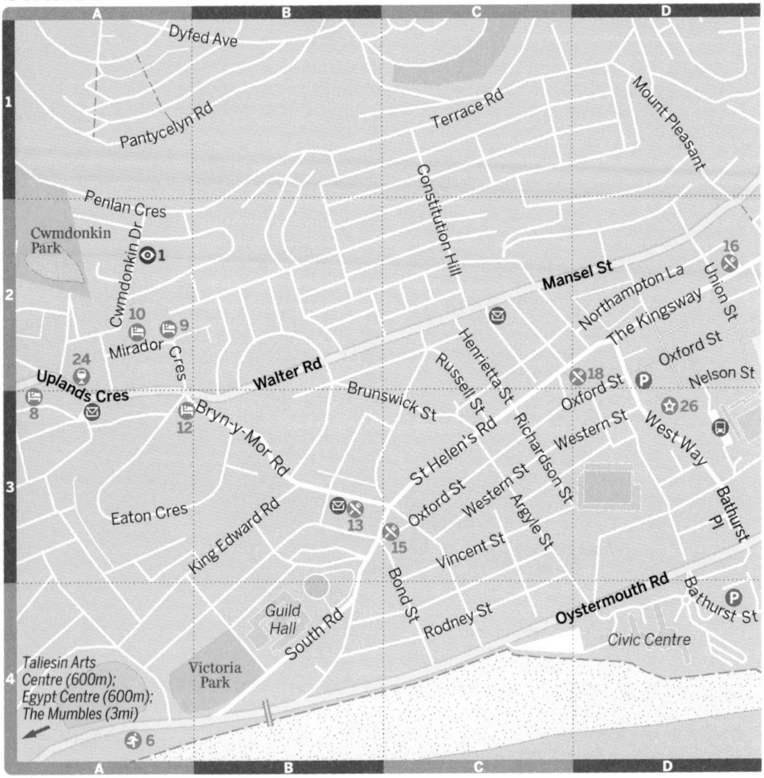

★ Egypt Centre MUSEUM
(www.egypt.swan.ac.uk; Mumbles Rd, Sketty; 10am-4pm Tue-Sat) FREE Swansea University's collection of ancient Egyptian antiquities includes a fascinating array of everyday artefacts, ranging from a 4000-year-old razor to a mummified crocodile. Kids can try their hand at Muppet mummification. It's located in the suburb of Sketty, halfway between the city centre and the Mumbles.

Activities

LC2 SWIMMING
(01792-484672; www.thelcswansea.com; Oystermouth Rd; water park adult/child £7/4; 4-8pm Mon-Fri, 9am-8pm Sat, Sun & school holidays;) The Marine Quarter's flash £32-million leisure centre includes a gym, a toddler's play centre and a 10m indoor climbing wall, but best of all is the water park, complete with a wave pool, water slides and the world's first indoor surfing ride.

360 Beach & Watersports WATER SPORTS
(01792-655844; www.360swansea.co.uk; Mumbles Rd; 8.30am-7pm) Offers stand-up paddle-boarding, kayaking, kite surfing and beach volleyball.

Festivals & Events

Swansea International Festival MUSIC
(www.swanseafestival.org; Oct) Two weeks of mainly classical-music performances and lectures, held in early October. The Welsh National Opera and the BBC National Orchestra of Wales may feature, as well as international companies.

Dylan Thomas Festival LITERATURE
(www.dylanthomas.com; Oct-Nov) This festival celebrates Swansea's most famous son with poetry readings, talks, films and performances from 27 October (his birthday) to 9 November (the date he died).

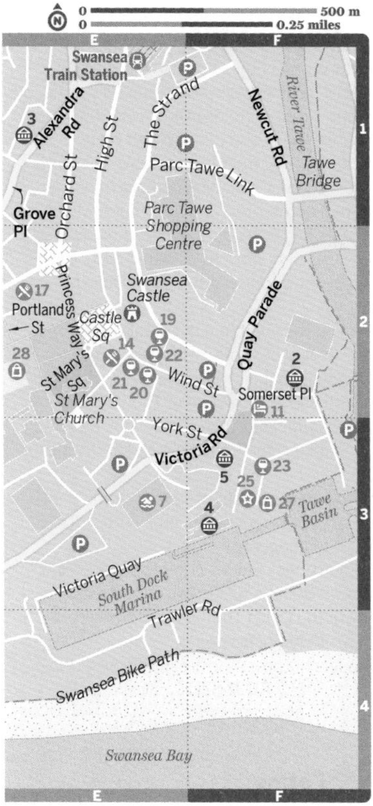

Swansea

Sights
1 Dylan Thomas Birthplace A2
2 Dylan Thomas Centre F2
3 Glynn Vivian Art Gallery E1
4 National Waterfront Museum F3
5 Swansea Museum F3

Activities, Courses & Tours
6 360 Beach & Watersports A4
7 LC2 .... E3

Sleeping
8 Alexander A3
9 Christmas Pie B&B A2
10 Mirador Town House A2
11 Morgans F2
12 White House A3

Eating
13 Favourite B3
14 Hanson at the Chelsea E2
15 Joe's Ice Cream Parlour C3
16 La Fina D2
17 Madeira E2
18 Mosaic D2

Drinking & Nightlife
19 Kon-Tiki E2
20 No Sign Bar E2
21 Perch E2
22 Prohibition E2
23 Queen's Hotel F3
24 Uplands Tavern A2

Entertainment
25 Dylan Thomas Theatre F3
26 Swansea Grand Theatre D3

Shopping
27 Mission Gallery F3
28 Swansea Market E2

Sleeping

Premier Inn Swansea Waterfront HOTEL £
(0871-527 9212; www.premierinn.com; Langdon Rd; r from £35;) It's hard to beat the value offered by this shiny new waterfront hotel, just across the river from the town centre. The rooms are generically smart, comfortable and well-equipped. Book early to take advantage of the cheapest rates and request a room with a view. If you're driving, be aware that the parking lot next door is relatively pricey.

★ **Christmas Pie B&B** B&B ££
(01792-480266; www.christmaspie.co.uk; 2 Mirador Cres, Uplands; s/d £53/82; P) The name suggests something warm and comforting, and this suburban villa does not disappoint. The three en suite bedrooms are all individually decorated. Plus there's fresh fruit and an out-of-the-ordinary, vegetarian-friendly breakfast selection.

Mirador Town House B&B ££
(01792-466976; www.themirador.co.uk; 14 Mirador Cres, Uplands; s/d from £60/80;) Kooky and kitsch in the extreme, all seven B&B rooms here are well kitted out and elaborately themed – Roman, Mediterranean, African, Venetian, Egyptian, Asian and French – with murals on the walls and sometimes the ceilings as well. The exuberant hosts are enthusiastic cheerleaders for the area.

Alexander HOTEL ££
(01792-470045; www.alexander-hotel.co.uk; 3 Sketty Rd, Uplands; s/d from £35/75;) Perfectly positioned for the Uplands strip of bars and eateries, this oversized B&B/small hotel has 10 attractive rooms and a very friendly host. The rooms at the rear have

DYLAN THOMAS

Dylan Thomas is a towering figure in Welsh literature, one of those poets who seemed to embody what a poet should be: chaotic, dramatic, drunk, tragic and comic. His work, although written in English, is of the bardic tradition – written to be read aloud, thunderous, often humorous, with a lyrical sense that echoes the sound of the Welsh voice.

Born in Swansea in 1914, he lived an itinerant life, shifting from town to town in search of cheap accommodation and to escape debt. He married Caitlin Macnamara (a former dancer, and lover of Augustus John) in 1936, but had numerous infamous affairs. Margaret Thomas, who was married to the historian AJP Taylor, was one of his admirers and paid the rent on his house in Laugharne (mysteriously enough, AJP detested him). His dramatic inclinations sometimes spilt over into real life: during a stay in New Quay he was shot at by a jealous local captain.

Thomas was also a promiscuous pub-goer, honing the habit that eventually killed him in an astonishing number of taverns. By 1946 he had become an immense commercial success, making regular book tours to America, but his marriage was suffering. In December 1952 his father died – his failing health had inspired one of Thomas' most resonant poems, *Do Not Go Gentle into That Good Night*. Less than a year later, a period of depression while in New York ended in a heavy drinking spell, and he died shortly after his 39th birthday.

Whether you're a fan or you're just interested to know what all the fuss is about, you'll find plenty of sites in Swansea to stalk the shade of the maverick poet and writer. When you've exhausted them all, you can always head on to Laugharne.

Start at the Dylan Thomas Centre (p121) and then check out his statue gazing across the marina outside the **Dylan Thomas Theatre** (☎01792-473238; www.dylanthomastheatre.org.uk; Gloucester Pl). In Uplands you can visit the Dylan Thomas Birthplace (p121), an unassuming terraced house where he wrote two-thirds of his poetry.

Perhaps the places where you're most likely to feel his presence are his beloved drinking haunts, which include No Sign Bar, **Queen's Hotel** (☎01792-521531; Gloucester Pl; ⏲10am-11pm) and Uplands Tavern (p128).

terrific views over rooftops and water to the Mumbles.

White House HOTEL ££
(☎01792-473856; www.thewhitehousehotel.co.uk; 4 Nyanza Tce, Bryn-y-Mor Rd, Uplands; s/d £49/79; 📶) More modest than its name suggests, this three-storey suburban house has an old-fashioned vibe, with chandeliers downstairs and colourful leadlights. The rooms are reasonably priced and all have their own bathrooms and lots of considerate extras such as bottled water, ironing facilities, safes and sewing kits.

Morgans HOTEL £££
(☎01792-484848; www.morganshotel.co.uk; Somerset Pl; r £65-250; P 📶) The city's first boutique hotel, set in the gorgeous red-brick and Portland-stone former Ports Authority building, Morgans combines historic elegance with contemporary design and a high pamper factor. An annexe across the road has lower ceilings but similar standards. On the downside, the reception can be starchy and the large central bar noisy.

Eating

★ **Square Peg** CAFE £
(☎01792-206593; www.squarepeg.org.uk; 29b Gower Rd, Sketty; mains £5; ⏲8am-7pm Mon-Fri, to 5pm Sat) With mismatched stools reupholstered in recycled denim and kooky local photography blanketing the walls, this is exactly the hip kind of place you'd expect to deliver seriously good coffee. With two blends on the go at any given time, it doesn't disappoint. The menu includes tasty light breakfasts, wraps, salads, soups, sandwiches and home baking.

Joe's Ice Cream Parlour ICE CREAM £
(www.joes-icecream.com; 85 St Helen's Rd; cones/sundaes from £1.45/4.10; ⏲11am-9pm) For an ice-cream sundae or a cone, locals love Joe's, a Swansea institution founded in 1922 by Joe Cascarini, son of immigrants from Italy's Abruzzi mountains.

★ **Mosaic** TAPAS ££
(☎01792-655225; www.mosaicswansea.com; 11 St Helen's Rd; tapas £3.50-8.50, platters £15-20; ⏲noon-2.30pm Fri & Sat, 6-11pm Wed-Sat; 🌱)

Set back from the road in an old brick warehouse, and with a menu as eclectic as its decor, this chic eatery specialises in 'world fusion tapas'. This translates to small plates and tasty platters designed to be shared, including a deliciously smoky red-capsicum hummus and juicy garlic king prawns. The attached cocktail bar is very cool indeed.

★ Favourite CHINESE ££
(☎01792-515230; www.favouritechinese.co.uk; 87 Bryn-y-Mor Rd; mains £7-14; ⏲noon-3pm & 5-10pm Tue-Fri, noon-10pm Sat & Sun;) Opened by expats frustrated by what passed for their national cuisine in these parts, this characterful, intimate restaurant focuses on authentic, MSG-free Chinese dishes, including a wide range of seafood, vegetable and tofu concoctions. The staff are absolutely delightful and more than willing to guide you down unfamiliar menu paths.

Hanson at the Chelsea SEAFOOD ££
(☎01792-464068; www.hansonatthechelsea.co.uk; 17 St Mary's St; mains £14-22, 2-/3-course lunch £15/18; ⏲noon-2pm daily, 7-9pm Mon-Sat) Perfect for a romantic liaison, this elegant little dining room is discreetly tucked away behind the frenzy of Wind St. Seafood's the speciality, although the menu also contains plenty of meaty dishes, and blackboard specials are chalked up daily.

Madeira PORTUGUESE ££
(☎01792-470000; www.madeirarestaurantswansea.co.uk; 46 The Kingsway; mains £9-21; ⏲noon-10pm Mon-Sat) The hooks hanging from the aged beams are there to hold the *espetadas* – traditional skewers of barbecued lamb, beef, pork, chicken or monkfish that add an extra dose of authenticity to this friendly, family-run restaurant. If you'd prefer your food on your plate, there are plenty of other delicious traditional Portuguese dishes to choose from.

La Fina SPANISH ££
(☎01792-412062; www.lafina.co.uk; 32-33 The Kingsway; tapas £3-5.50, mains £13-16; ⏲noon-2.30pm & 6-9.30pm) Specialising in tapas and *espetadas* (skewers of barbecued meat hung from hooks above the table), this convivial oak-beamed restaurant offers big flavours and plenty of atmosphere. As for value, the half-price Tapas Tuesdays are hard to beat.

Gilligan's EUROPEAN ££
(☎01792-203767; www.gilligansrestaurant.com; 100 Eversley Rd, Sketty; 2-/3-course lunch £16/19, dinner £20/24; ⏲noon-2pm Sat & Sun, 5.30-9pm Wed-Sat) You'd be pretty darned happy to have Gilligan's as your local neighbourhood bistro. Expect simple French- and Mediterranean-influenced dishes served in pleasant surrounds, with friendly and attentive service.

Slice MODERN BRITISH £££
(☎01792-290929; www.sliceswansea.co.uk; 73-75 Eversley Rd, Sketty; 3 courses £39; ⏲noon-2pm Fri-Sun, 6.30-9pm Wed-Sun) The simple decor – wooden floors and furniture, and pale walls – stands in contrast to the elaborate dishes emanating from Slice's kitchen. Its elegantly presented food is terrific: locally sourced meat, fish, cheese and beer, plus home-made bread and home-grown herbs.

Drinking & Nightlife

In a city synonymous with Dylan Thomas you'd expect some hard drinking to take place…and you'd be right. Swansea's main boozing strip is Wind St (rhymes with 'blind', as in drunk), and on weekends it can be a bit of a zoo, full of generally good-natured alcopop-fuelled teens teetering around on high heels. *Buzz* magazine (free from cafes and bars around town) has its finger on the local scene's pulse.

Prohibition COCKTAIL BAR
(www.prohibition-bar.co.uk; Green Dragon Lane; ⏲9pm-late Wed-Sat) Slink down a side lane from Wind St, give a knowing nod to the bouncer lurking in the shadows, enter the corridor, push back the bookcase and enter an illicit world where attractive mixologists dispense charm and first-rate cocktails in equal serves to an appreciative in-the-know clientele. There's no sign: look for it two doors up from Kon-Tiki bar.

Kon-Tiki COCKTAIL BAR
(☎01792-462896; 10 The Strand; ⏲6pm-midnight Sun-Thu, to 1.30am Fri & Sat) Hidden down the hill from Wind St, cool Kon-Tiki offers all the requisite elements for a tropical beach fantasy: faux Polynesian statues, cocktails served in tiki cups, flax matting on the walls and Bob Marley on the stereo. On the weekends it adopts a clubby vibe and a £1 cover charge.

No Sign Bar BAR
(☎01792-465300; www.nosignwinebar.com; 56 Wind St; ⏲11am-midnight) Once frequented by Dylan Thomas (it appears as the Wine Vaults in his story *The Followers*), the No Sign is the only vaguely traditional bar left on Wind St. It's a long, narrow haven of dark-wood

panelling, friendly staff, good pub grub and a seasonal beer selection. On weekends there's live music downstairs in the Vault.

Uplands Tavern PUB
(☎01792-458242; www.facebook.com/theuplandstavern; 42 Uplands Cres, Uplands; ⏲11am-11pm) A former Thomas hang-out, Uplands still serves a quiet daytime pint in the Dylan Thomas snug. Come nightfall, it turns into a different beast altogether as the hub of the city's live-music scene, attracting a mixed crowd of students and local regulars.

Perch COCKTAIL BAR
(☎01792-644611; www.theperchswansea.co.uk; 66 Wind St; ⏲6pm-midnight Wed & Thu, 2pm-midnight Fri, noon-midnight Sat & Sun) Arguably the classiest spot on Swansea's trashiest strip, the Perch swizzles up moreish cocktails and a good selection of wine and boutique beer. Graffiti-style murals and interesting neon art lend it a hip, bohemian edge despite the clientele being anything but.

☆ Entertainment

Taliesin Arts Centre PERFORMING ARTS
(☎01792-602060; www.taliesinartscentre.co.uk; Swansea University, Mumbles Rd) Part of Swansea University, this vibrant arts centre named after a 6th-century bard stages live music, theatre, dance and film. It also has an art gallery and an excellent gift store.

Swansea Grand Theatre THEATRE
(☎01792-475715; www.swanseagrand.co.uk; Singleton St) The city's largest theatre stages a mixed roster of ballet, opera, musicals, theatre and pantomimes, plus a regular comedy club.

Shopping

★ Swansea Market MARKET
(www.swanseaindoormarket.co.uk; Oxford St; ⏲8am-5.30pm Mon-Sat) There's been a covered market in Swansea since 1652 and at this site since 1830. Rebuilt in 1961 after being bombed in WWII, the current version is a buzzing place to sample local specialities, like cockles, laver bread and Welsh cakes hot from the griddle.

Mission Gallery ARTS & CRAFTS
(www.missiongallery.co.uk; Gloucester Pl; ⏲11am-5pm Tue-Sun) Set in a beautifully converted 19th-century seamen's chapel, this modestly sized gallery stages some of Swansea's most striking exhibitions of contemporary art. It also sells glassware, ceramics, jewellery, and art books and magazines.

ℹ Orientation

The compact city centre clusters around Castle Sq and pedestrianised Oxford St on the west bank of the River Tawe. To its south and east are the redeveloped docklands of the Maritime Quarter, linked to the new SA1 district on the Tawe's east bank by the graceful Sail Bridge (2003).

Uplands, where many of the city's guesthouses are found, is 1 mile west of the city centre, along Mansel St and Walter Rd. From the southern edge of the city centre, Oystermouth Rd runs for 5 miles west and then south along Swansea Bay, becoming Mumbles Rd.

ℹ Information

Morriston Hospital (☎01792-702222; www.wales.nhs.uk; Heol Maes Eglwys, Morriston) Accident and emergency department, 5 miles north of the city centre.

Police Station (☎101; www.south-wales.police.uk; Grove Pl)

ℹ Getting There & Away

BUS

Swansea's **bus station** (Plymouth St) is on the western edge of the city centre, by the Quadrant shopping centre.

National Express (☎0871 781 8181; www.nationalexpress.com) coaches head to/from Tenby (from £5, 1½ hours, two daily), Cardiff (£3.50, one hour, four daily), Chepstow (from £11, two hours, four daily), Bristol (£11, 2½ hours, six daily) and London (from £7, five hours, five daily).

Other direct bus services head to/from Cardiff (£4.50, 1¼ hours, at least hourly), Llanelli (£5.70, 40 minutes, half-hourly), Carmarthen (£9.20, 50 minutes, hourly), Llandeilo (£5.70, 1½ hours, seven daily) and Aberystwyth (£12, 2¾ hours, two daily).

TRAIN

The train station is 600m north of Castle Sq along Castle St and High St. Direct train services to/from Swansea include London Paddington (from £47, three hours, hourly), Abergavenny (£25, 1½ hours, hourly), Cardiff (£9.20, one hour, half-hourly), Tenby (£15, 1½ hours, seven daily) and Llandrindod Wells (£13, 2½ hours, four daily).

ℹ Getting Around

BICYCLE

Part of the Celtic Trail (National Cycle Network Route 4) hugs the bay for the lovely stretch from downtown Swansea to the Mumbles.

BUS

First Cymru (www.firstgroup.com) runs most of the local services, including buses to the Mumbles and as far as the Pennard Cliffs car park in Southgate on the Gower Peninsula. Drivers take cash for single fares, or you can pay via a mobile-phone app (see the website for details).

THE MUMBLES (Y MWMBWLS)

POP 16,600

Strung out along the shoreline at the southern end of Swansea Bay, the Mumbles has been Swansea's seaside retreat since 1807, when the Oystermouth Railway was opened. Built for transporting coal, the horse-drawn carriages were soon converted for paying customers, and the now defunct Mumbles train became the first passenger railway service in the world.

Once again fashionable, with bars and restaurants vying for trade along the promenade, the Mumbles received a boost to its reputation when its most famous daughter, Hollywood actor Catherine Zeta-Jones, built a £2-million luxury mansion at Limeslade, on the south side of the peninsula. Singer Bonnie Tyler also has a home here.

The origin of the Mumbles' unusual name is uncertain, although one theory is that it's a legacy of French seamen who nicknamed the twin rounded rocks at the tip of the headland *Les Mamelles* – 'the breasts'.

Sights

Going west from Mumbles Head there are two small bays, **Langland Bay** and **Caswell Bay**, which are shingly at high tide but expose hectares of golden sand at low water. Both are popular with families and surfers. About 500m west of Caswell, along the coast path, is beautiful **Brandy Cove**, a tiny secluded beach away from the crowds.

★Clyne Gardens GARDENS

FREE Spanning 20 hectares, these magnificent gardens are particularly impressive in spring when the azaleas and rhododendrons are at their most spectacular. Plus there are bluebell woods, wildflower meadows and a bog garden to explore. The entrance is by the Woodman Pub at the Swansea end of the Mumbles Rd strip.

Oystermouth Castle CASTLE

(☎01792-635478; www.swansea.gov.uk/oystermouthcastle; Castle Ave; adult/child £3/1.50; ⏲11am-5pm Easter-Sep) It wouldn't be Wales without a castle, hence the trendy shops and bars of Newton Rd are guarded by a majestic ruin. Once the stronghold of the Norman lords of Gower, it's now the focus of summer Shakespeare performances. There's a fine view over Swansea Bay from the battlements.

Mumbles Pier PIER

(☎01792-365225; www.mumbles-pier.co.uk; Mumbles Rd) The Mumbles' mile-long strip of pastel-painted houses, pubs and restaurants comes to a picturesque denouement with a rocky headland, a pretty sandy beach and two tiny islands, the furthermost one topped with a lighthouse. Built in 1898, Mumbles Pier juts out jauntily from the headland, housing the usual amusement arcade and a once-grand cafe festooned with chandeliers.

Tours

Gower Coast Adventures CRUISE

(☎01792-348229; www.gowercoastadventures.co.uk) Speedboat trips from the Mumbles to Three Cliffs Bay and Oxwich (adult/child £34/20, 1½ hours return), or to Worms Head (adult/child £54/32, three hours return). Boats also blast from Oxwich to Worms Head (adult/child £42/24, two hours return).

Sleeping

Tides Reach Guest House B&B ££

(☎01792-404877; www.tidesreachguesthouse.com; 388 Mumbles Rd; s/d from £65/79; P wifi) Our favourite Mumbles B&B, Tides Reach was for sale when we visited, so we're hoping the new owners maintain the same friendly service and delicious breakfasts. Some rooms have sea views; the best is suite-like room 9, where the dormer windows open out to create a virtual deck from within the sloping roof.

Patricks with Rooms BOUTIQUE HOTEL £££

(☎01792-360199; www.patrickswithrooms.com; 638 Mumbles Rd; r £120-175; wifi) Patricks has 16 individually styled bedrooms in bold contemporary colours, with art on the walls, fluffy robes and, in some of the rooms, roll-top baths and sea views. Some are set back in a separate annexe. Downstairs there's an upmarket restaurant and bar.

Eating

Front Room CAFE £
(☎01792-362140; 618 Mumbles Rd; mains £5-8; ⊙10am-4pm Tue-Sun;) With seashell chandeliers and local art on the walls, this convivial little cafe is a pleasant place to tuck into a cooked breakfast, Welsh rarebit, ploughman's lunch, sandwich (of the toasted or doorstop variety) or traditional high tea (£15 for two people).

Joe's Ice Cream Parlour ICE CREAM £
(☎01792-368212; www.joes-icecream.com; 526 Mumbles Rd; ⊙10.30am-5.30pm) A popular branch of a Swansea institution (p126).

Munch of Mumbles MODERN BRITISH ££
(☎01792-362244; www.munchofmumbles.com; 650 Mumbles Rd; 2-/3-course lunch £16/20, dinner £25/30; ⊙noon-2.30pm Wed-Sun, 6.30-9.30pm Wed-Sat;) Small, cosy and romantic, with flowers and candles on the tables, Munch offers a top-notch bistro menu, with half a dozen choices for each course. You can bring your own wine for a small corkage charge.

Mad Hatter's CAFE, BISTRO ££
(☎01792-363838; www.madhatters.co.uk; 29 Newton Rd; mains brunch £5-9, dinner £17-19; ⊙9am-5.30pm Sun-Tue, to 10.30pm Wed-Sat) White walls offset with *Alice in Wonderland* stencils provide an elegant backdrop to an affable eatery, which transitions seamlessly from daytime cafe to after-dark bistro. Crowd-pleasing classics dominate the menu, including an excellent spaghetti carbonara and huge serves of fish and chips with mushy peas.

Drinking & Nightlife

Jones WINE BAR
(☎01792-361764; www.jonesbar.co.uk; 61 Newton Rd; ⊙4.30-11pm Tue-Thu & Sun, to 12.30am Fri & Sat) The best of the Newton Rd wine bars, Jones buzzes with 40-somethings giving the chandeliers a run for their money in the bling stakes. There's no chance Dylan Thomas ever did hang out here, or would if he still could, but there's a good wine list and a friendly vibe.

Pilot PUB
(www.thepilotofmumbles.co.uk; 726 Mumbles Rd; ⊙noon-11pm;) Stained glass, polished wood and a roaring fire set an immediately comforting tone, but it's the beer that the grizzled bunch of blokes propping up the bar are here for. Sample from the Pilot's own microbrewed range or choose from its select set of guest ales.

Getting There & Away

Buses 2, 3 and 37 head between Swansea and the Mumbles (20 minutes). Bus 2C continues on to Caswell Bay.

GOWER PENINSULA (Y GŴYR)

With its broad butterscotch beaches, pounding surf, precipitous clifftop walks and rugged, untamed uplands, the Gower Peninsula feels a million miles from Swansea's urban bustle – yet it's just on the doorstep. This 15-mile-long thumb of land stretching west from the Mumbles was designated the UK's first official Area of Outstanding Natural Beauty in 1956. The National Trust owns about three-quarters of the coast and you can hike the entire length of the coastline on the Wales Coast Path. The peninsula also has the best surfing in Wales outside of Pembrokeshire.

The main family beaches, patrolled by lifeguards during the summer, are Langland Bay, Caswell Bay and Port Eynon. The most impressive, and most popular with surfers, is the magnificent 3-mile sweep of Rhossili Bay at the far end of the peninsula. Much of Gower's northern coast is salt marsh, which provides an important habitat for wading birds and wildfowl.

Parkmill & Around

Some of the Gower's best and most secluded beaches are on the stretch between the Mumbles and Oxwich Bay, particularly in the area around the small tourist village of Parkmill.

Sights

Three Cliffs Bay BEACH
Three Cliffs Bay is named for the pyramid-like, triple-pointed crag pierced by a natural arch that juts out into the water at its eastern point. It's regularly voted one of the most beautiful beaches in Britain, and it's particularly impressive when viewed from the impossibly picturesque ruins of 13th-century **Pennard Castle**. Glinting below, the Pennard Pill stream empties into the bay, creating dangerous currents for

swimmers at high tide. The craggy headland is a popular rock-climbing site.

The only way to reach the beach is on foot. For the castle view, look for the path across the road and down a bit from Shepherd's Coffee Shop in Parkmill. Once you cross the bridge, turn right and then take the next left-hand fork heading up the hill. You'll skirt some houses and a golf course before reaching the castle. For a flatter, quicker path, take the right-hand fork instead and follow the stream. Another approach is via the mile-long track along Pennard Cliffs from the National Trust car park in Southgate.

Gower Heritage Centre HISTORIC BUILDING
(01792-371206; www.gowerheritagecentre.co.uk; Parkmill; adult/child £6.80/5.80; 10am-5.30pm;) Housed in a restored mill with a working waterwheel, this complex has plenty to keep the kids entertained when the weather drives you off the beaches. There's a puppet theatre, craft workshop, petting zoo, fish pond, bouncy castle, medieval armour display, gold panning and 'Wales' smallest cinema', housed in a converted railway carriage. Adults might be more interested in the mill itself, which served as both a cornmill and a sawmill, and the non-operational heritage-listed toilet.

Parc-le-Breos PARK
(Parkmill) Nestled in a tiny valley between wooded hills, this verdant park contains the **Long Cairn**, a 5500-year-old burial chamber consisting of a stone entryway, a passageway and four chambers. It once contained the skeletons of 40 people, but these were removed, along with its protective earth mound, after it was dug out in 1869. Nearly opposite is a lime kiln, used until a century ago for the production of quicklime fertiliser.

Further into the park, a natural limestone fissure houses **Cathole Rock Cave**, home to hunter gatherers up to 20,000 years ago. Flint tools were found in the cave, alongside the bones of bears, hyenas and mammoths.

The turn-off for Parc-le-Breos is right beside the Gower Heritage Centre in Parkmill; the park is less than half a mile further on.

Sleeping

Nicholaston Farm CAMPSITE £
(01792-371209; www.nicholastonfarm.co.uk; Penmaen; site from £16; Easter-Sep) This working farm overlooking Oxwich Bay offers field camping with a view. There's also an attractive little farm shop/cafe and an excellent ablutions block.

★ **Llethryd Barns** B&B ££
(01792-391327; www.llethrydbarns.co.uk; Llethryd; ste £80-100; P) Set in a U-shape around a central courtyard, this venerable set of stone farm buildings has been converted into seven guest suites, each with a mezzanine bedroom. They all have their own courtyard entrance, so there's no sense that you're intruding in someone else's house. It's located 2 miles north of Parkmill on the B4271.

Parc-le-Breos House HOTEL ££
(01792-371636; www.parc-le-breos.co.uk; Parkmill; r from £98; P) Set in its own private estate north of the main road, Parc-le-Breos offers en suite B&B accommodation in a Victorian hunting lodge. The majestic lounge, games room and dining room downstairs have grand fireplaces that crackle into action in winter.

Drinking & Nightlife

Joiners Arms PUB
(01792-232658; www.thejoiners.info; 50 Bishopston Rd, Bishopston; 3-10pm Mon & Tue, 11.30am-11pm Wed-Sun) Pop into the slate-floored Joiners for a pint from the pub's own on-site microbrewery. A drop of the hoppy Three Cliffs Gold Ale is *the* one to try. It also does decent pub food.

Getting There & Away

Buses head to/from Swansea (36 minutes, 10 daily), Oxwich (15 minutes, seven daily), Reynoldston (14 minutes, eight daily), Port Eynon (27 minutes, four daily) and Rhossili (31 minutes, eight daily).

Oxwich Bay

Oxwich Bay is a windy, 2.5-mile-long curve of sand backed by dunes. Road access and a large car park (per day £4) make it popular with families and watersports enthusiasts (there's no lifeguard, but otherwise it's good for beginner surfers). Behind the beach lies **Oxwich Nature Reserve**, an area of salt and freshwater marshes, oak and ash woodlands and dunes; it is home to a variety of bird life and dune plants.

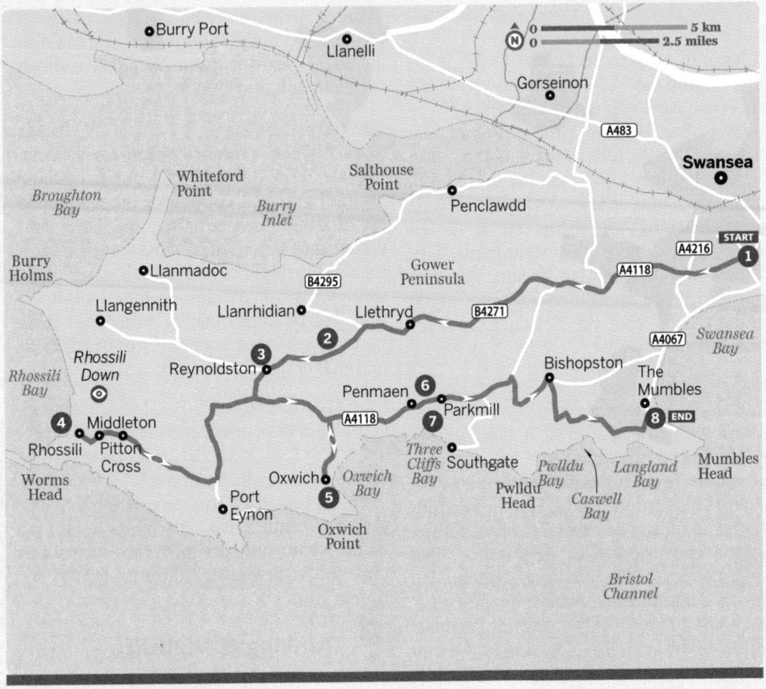

Driving Tour
Gower Circuit

START SWANSEA
END THE MUMBLES
LENGTH 40 MILES; ONE DAY

This drive takes you onto the Gower's narrow back roads, which are crowded in holiday season but otherwise have an enjoyably remote feel. The itinerary explores the area's ancient past, taking in a neolithic tomb and cairn, and brings you to two sweeping sandy beaches and a Tudor castle, winding up in picture-perfect Mumbles.

Take the A4118 (the continuation of Uplands Cres and Sketty Rd) west from 1 **Swansea** and turn right onto the B4271, the secondary road running through the centre of the Gower Peninsula. After 4.5 miles turn left on the back road signposted to Reynoldston. Before you descend to the village itself, look for a rough parking area to the right of the road and stop here to take a walk across the heath to the neolithic tomb known as 2 **Arthur's Stone** (p135), with its mighty capstone. The 3 **King Arthur Hotel** (p135) down the hill in Reynoldston makes for a great pub lunch stop: as well as real ales it serves home-cooked Welsh specialities.

Continue down to the dramatic beach at 4 **Rhossili**, where the wide sand beach is a haven for surfers. Take time to walk down to the undulating headland of Worms Head; if the tide is right you can walk onto the head itself. Backtrack to Oxwich and visit its romantically ruined 5 **Tudor castle**. Turn off at Parkmill to view another mesmerising prehistoric monument: the Long Cairn at 6 **Parc-le-Breos** (p131). The meadow here, enclosed by trees, also features an early lime kiln and a cave that once sheltered mesolithic hunters. Then walk down to nearby 7 **Three Cliffs Bay** (p130), one of Britain's most beautiful beaches, only accessible on foot.

After a dip or a stroll, meander along to the 8 **Mumbles**, a gorgeously picturesque seaside town with a castle, a pier and a long promenade featuring enticing cafes, pubs, a long-established ice-cream parlour and an attractive backdrop of green cliffs ending in a picturesque headland with a lighthouse.

Sights

Oxwich Castle CASTLE
(www.cadw.wales.gov.uk; Oxwich; adult/child £3.50/2.50; ⏲10am-5pm Wed-Sun Apr-Sep) Set on a hillside above the beach, the stately grey ruin of Oxwich Castle is less a castle and more a sumptuous 16th-century, mock-military Tudor mansion.

Sleeping

Oxwich Camping Park CAMPSITE £
(☎01792-390777; www.sites.google.com/site/oxwichcampingpark; Oxwich; site from £20; ⏲Easter-Sep; P) A tree-fringed campground on the edge of Oxwich within easy reach of the beach, and with its own outdoor pool. It doesn't allow caravans or motorhomes, but small campervans are fine.

Getting There & Away

Buses head to/from Port Eynon (26 minutes, three daily) and Parkmill (15 minutes, seven daily).

Port Eynon

The three-quarter-mile stretch of rock-strewn beach at Port Eynon is Gower's busiest – in summer, at least.

Around the bay's southern point is **Culver Hole**, a curious stone structure built into the cliff. Legend has it that it was a smugglers' hiding place, but the mundane truth is that it served as a dovecote (pigeons were a valuable food source in medieval times; the name comes from Old English *culufre*, meaning 'dove'). It's quite tricky to find – the easiest route is signposted from the YHA – and is only accessible for three hours either side of low tide; make sure you don't get caught out by the rising waters.

The coastal walk between Port Eynon and Rhossili (7 miles) is along the wildest and most dramatic part of the Gower coast, and is fairly rough going. Halfway along is a cave called Goats Hole, where the Red Lady of Paviland (p303) was found.

Sleeping

★**Port Eynon YHA** HOSTEL £
(☎0800 019 1700; www.yha.org.uk; Port Eynon; dm/r from £18/39; ⏲Easter-Oct;) Worth special mention for its spectacular location, this former lifeboat station is as close as you get to the sea without sleeping on the beach itself. It's cosier than your average hostel, with sea views from the lounge and friendly owners. There are washbasins in the rooms but most share bathrooms.

Culver House APARTMENT ££
(☎01792-720300; www.culverhousehotel.co.uk; Port Eynon; apt £90-125;) A renovated 19th-century house offering eight self-contained apartments with all the mod cons. The upper apartments have balconies, while most of those on the ground floor open onto cute little gardens.

Drinking & Nightlife

Ship Inn PUB
(☎01792-390204; www.shipinngower.co.uk; Port Eynon; ⏲noon-11.30pm;) A large rusty anchor sets an appropriately nautical tone for this appealing local pub, which serves the Gower Brewery's range of real ales.

Getting There & Away

Buses head to/from Swansea (one hour, four daily), Parkmill (27 minutes, four daily), Reynoldston (15 minutes, five daily), Rhossili (13 minutes, daily) and Llangennith (one hour, three daily).

Rhossili

Saving the best for last, the Gower Peninsula ends spectacularly with the 3 miles of golden sand that edges Rhossili Bay. Facing nearly due west towards the very bottom of Ireland, this is one of Britain's best and most popular surfing beaches. When the surf's up, swimming can be dangerous. At low tide the stark, ghostly ribs of the *Helvetica*, a Norwegian barque wrecked in a storm in 1887, protrude from the sand in the middle of the beach.

South of the village is the Viel (pronounced 'vile'), a rare surviving example of a patchwork of strip-fields first laid out in medieval times.

Sights

★**Worms Head** ISLAND
The southern extremity of Rhossili Bay is guarded by a promontory, which turns into an island at high tide. Worms Head takes its name from the Old English *wurm*, meaning 'dragon' – a reference to its snaking, Loch Ness monster profile. Seals bask around its rocks, and the cliffs are thick with razorbills, guillemots, kittiwakes, fulmars and puffins during nesting season (April to July).

There is a five-hour window of opportunity (2½ hours either side of low tide) when you can walk out across a causeway and along the narrow crest of the Outer Head to the furthest point of land. Check the tide tables posted at the Rhossili Visitor Centre carefully, as people are regularly rescued after being cut off by the rising waters. Among those who have spent a cold, nervous night trapped here was the young Dylan Thomas, as he relates in the story 'Who Do You Wish Was With Us?', from *Portrait of the Artist as a Young Dog*. If you do get stuck, do not try to wade or swim back. The currents are fierce and the rocks treacherous.

Rhossili Down HILL

Rhossili beach is backed by the steep slopes of this humpbacked, heather-covered ridge (193m), whose updraughts create perfect soaring conditions for hang-gliders and paragliders. On the summit are numerous **Iron Age earthworks**, a burial chamber called **Sweyne's Howe** and the remains of a WWII radar station. At its foot, behind the beach, is the **Warren**, the sand-buried remains of an old village.

The path to the top is easily accessed from the village; it starts steeply but flattens out at the summit.

Sleeping & Eating

Rhossili Bunkhouse HOSTEL £

(01792-391509; www.rhossilibunkhouse.com; Rhossili Village Hall, Middleton; dm £20; P) In the village of Middleton, within easy walking distance of Rhossili, this community-run bunkhouse is very well equipped, clean and comfortable. There's no food on site, but the kitchen is excellent.

West Pilton House B&B ££

(01792-391364; www.the-gower.com/bandb/westpilton/westpilton.htm; Pilton; r £70; P) Two miles east of Rhossili, this cream-painted Georgian house has two double rooms with views of the sea and the lush surrounding farmland. It's near the coastal path, and well set up for walkers, with Ordnance Survey (OS) maps and drying facilities.

Bay Bistro & Coffee House BISTRO £

(01792-390519; www.thebaybistro.co.uk; mains £6-12; 10am-5.30pm;) A buzzy beach cafe with a sunny terrace, good surfy vibrations and the kind of drop-your-panini views that would make anything taste good – although the roster of burgers, sandwiches, cakes and coffee stands up well regardless. On summer evenings it opens for alfresco meals.

Information

Rhossili Visitor Centre (01792-390707; www.nationaltrust.org.uk/gower; Coastguard Cottages, Rhossili; 10.30am-4pm) The National Trust's centre has information on local walks and wildlife, and an audiovisual display upstairs.

Getting There & Away

Buses head to/from Swansea (one hour, 10 daily), Parkmill (31 minutes, eight daily), Port Eynon (13 minutes, one daily) and Reynoldston (17 minutes, six daily).

Llangennith

Surfers flock to this pretty village at the northern end of Rhossili Bay where there's a good local pub and a large campsite right by the beach.

Sights & Activities

St Cenydd's Church CHURCH

Local hermit Cenydd (pronounced Kenneth) lends his name to both the village and this Norman church, topped with a blunt stone tower. Inside there's a 12th-century limestone effigy of a local knight and a 9th-century stone carved with Celtic knot patterns, traditionally believed to be the saint's gravestone.

Progress Surf SURFING

(01792-550019; www.swanseasurfing.com; lessons 2hr/day £25/50) Offers introductory surf lessons at either Caswell Bay or Llangennith, depending on conditions.

PJ's Surf Shop SURFING

(01792-386669; www.pjsurfshop.co.uk; Llangennith; wetsuits/surfboards/body boards per day £11/11/6; 9am-5pm) Run by former surf champion Peter Jones, this is a centre of activity for local surfers. It also operates a 24-hour surfline (0901 603 1603; calls per minute 60p).

Sleeping & Eating

Hillend CAMPGROUND £

(01792-386204; www.hillendcamping.com; Llangennith; sites from £20; Easter-Oct; P) As close to the beach as you can get, this large camping ground can accommodate 300 tents and motor homes. On-site surfy-style Eddy's Restaurant has brilliant views, and rustles up meals for under a tenner.

King's Head HOTEL ££

(☎01792-386212; www.kingsheadgower.co.uk; Llangennith; r £99-150; P 📶 🐾) Up the hill behind the **pub** (mains £5-11; ⏰11am-10pm) of the same name, these two stone blocks have been simply but stylishly fitted out with modern bathrooms and pale stone tiles. As well as the 20 rooms here, there are a further seven in a nearby house.

Getting There & Away

There are direct buses to/from Swansea (1½ hours, three daily), Port Eynon (one hour, three daily), Reynoldston (30 minutes, three daily) and Llanmadoc (10 minutes, five daily).

Reynoldston

At the heart of the Gower Peninsula is Cefn Bryn, a ruggedly beautiful expanse of moorland that rises to a height of 186m. Tucked just below it is this lost-in-time collection of stone houses and a popular pub, gathered around a village green.

Sights

Arthur's Stone TOMB

(Coeten Arthur) On a fittingly desolate ridge near Reynoldston stands this mysterious neolithic burial chamber capped by a 25-tonne quartz boulder. The view from here is fantastic: you can see out to the edges of the Gower in every direction, and on a clear day you can see south to Lundy Island and the Devon and Somerset coast. It's a great spot to watch the sunset.

In legend the capstone is a pebble that Arthur removed from his boot; the deep cut in the rock was either made by Excalibur or by St David; and the muddy spring beneath the stone grants wishes. Local lore also says that a woman who crawls around the stone at midnight during the full moon will be joined by her lover – if he is faithful.

To find it, turn right on the road leaving the King Arthur Hotel in Reynoldston and look out for a rough parking area on your left. Looking north, you can see the stone on the horizon. The walk to the stone can be very muddy, so wear sensible shoes.

Sleeping & Eating

King Arthur Hotel PUB ££

(☎01792-390775; www.kingarthurhotel.co.uk; Higher Green, Reynoldston; s/d/cottage from £70/80/120, mains £9-14; P 📶) As traditional as swords in stone and ladies of the lake, the King Arthur serves real ales in a cosy wood-panelled bar and offers a lengthy menu of tasty, rustic dishes in the nearby bistro. Accommodation is split between the pub's 1st floor and a neighbouring annexe, and it also rents a handful of romantic, stone-walled cottages in the village.

Fairyhill HOTEL £££

(☎01792-390139; www.fairyhill.net; s/d from £180/200, mains £28; ⏰restaurant noon-2pm & 6.30-9.30pm daily Easter-Oct, Wed-Sun Nov-Easter; P 📶) Hidden (as any proper fairy place should be) down a narrow lane northwest of Reynoldston, this Georgian country house has a suitably magical setting and extensive grounds. The eight bedrooms are stylishly furnished and there's an upmarket restaurant downstairs serving the likes of Gower salt-marsh lamb and Pembrokeshire duck.

Getting There & Away

Buses head to/from Swansea (45 minutes, eight daily), Parkmill (14 minutes, eight daily), Port Eynon (15 minutes, five daily), Rhossili (17 minutes, six daily) and Llangennith (30 minutes, three daily).

Llanmadoc

Little Llanmadoc sits on the edge of Whiteford Burrows, a nature reserve composed of sand dunes and pines. Check the tide tables before walking to the lighthouse on the point, the only cast-iron lighthouse in the UK. The cooperatively owned village store and post office has an attractive cafe, selling tea and cake to walkers.

Eating

Brittania PUB FOOD ££

(☎01792-386624; www.britanniainngower.co.uk; Llanmadoc; mains £8-12; ⏰noon-11pm; P 👪 🐾) This plain 18th-century inn may not be the most picturesque on the Gower, but the food is a cut well above average pub grub. Options include a sublime steak-and-ale pie, a local salt-marsh lamb burger and a lamb tagine. On a sunny day, head out to the rear lawn, where there's a play area and an aviary.

Getting There & Away

There are direct buses to/from Swansea (one hour, three daily), Port Eynon (one hour, three daily), Reynoldston (30 minutes, three daily) and Llangennith (10 minutes, five daily).

MIKE CHARLES / SHUTTERSTOCK ©

1. Three Cliffs Bay (p130)
One of the most beautiful beaches in the UK.

2. National Waterfront Museum (p121)
A statue of Swansea-born poet Dylan Thomas sits outside the museum.

3. Swansea (p121)
The Sail Bridge (2003) over the River Tawe.

4. Oystermouth Castle (p129)
A majestic ruin offering views over Swansea Bay.

3

BECKY STARES / SHUTTERSTOCK ©

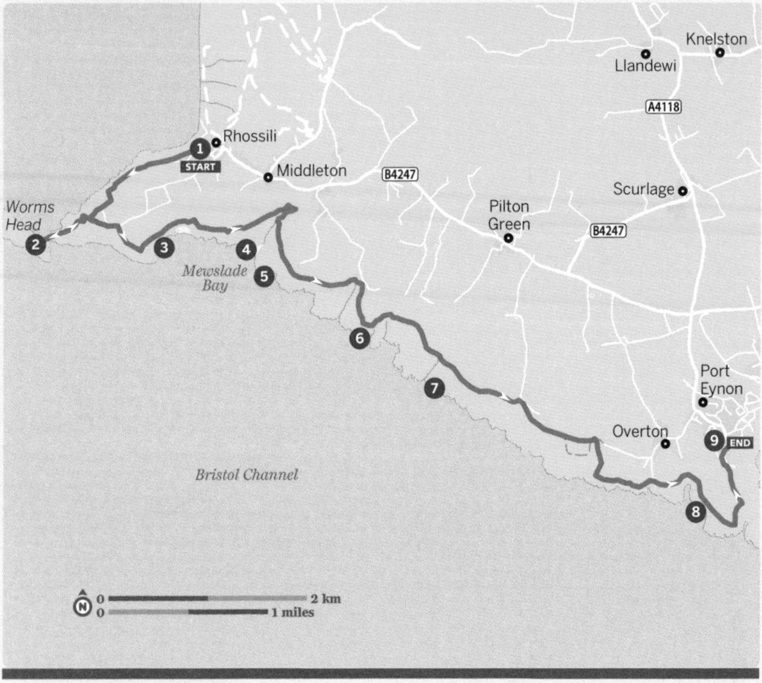

Coastal Walk A Wild Stretch

START RHOSSILI
END PORT EYNON
LENGTH 7 MILES; THREE HOURS

This wonderful walk takes in a precipitous stretch of Gower coastline, topped with ancient hill forts and punctuated by beautiful sandy coves. There's no refreshments en route so take food and water.

The walk starts at 1 **Rhossili**, a high vantage point overlooking a beach that's been voted one of the best in the world. Follow the path down to the 2 **Worms Head** (p133) – it is possible to walk out to the headland, but only at low tide or it will be partly submerged. On the high point facing the head is a Victorian coastguard station, still very much in use.

The route follows the coast above the golden beaches of 3 **Fall** and 4 **Mewslade** bays. Beyond, 5 **Thurba Head** has been in National Trust hands since 1933. More ancient history is evident at the 6 **Knave Promontory Fort**, the largest of several Iron Age structures you'll see on the walk. Built 10,000 years ago, it would originally have been edged by a fence constructed from wooden stakes. Beyond is the fossil-rich Horse Cliff. Shortly after you'll pass above the 7 **Goats Hole**, a cave in the cliff (only accessible from the water) that was the site of a hugely significant prehistoric burial: the Red Lady of Paviland.

Beyond this point the cliffs descend and the going is easier for a long stretch until you begin to climb to Port Eynon Point. There's an interesting detour near the summit – a steep descent to 8 **Culver Hole**, a ruined medieval dovecote crammed into a fissure in the cliff. Bear in mind though that it's unsigned, a little hard to find, and the path is vertiginous.

On the fringes of 9 **Port Eynon** you'll pass the Salt House, a salt-extraction unit built in the 16th century. In the village you can stop for a celebratory drink or meal in the pub. Note: only one bus a day heads between Port Eynon and Rhossili, so you may need to change in Reynoldston if you've left your car at the starting point.

CARMARTHENSHIRE (SIR GAERFYRDDIN)

Castle-dotted Carmarthenshire has gentle valleys, deep-green woods and a small, partly sandy coast. Caught between dramatic neighbours – Pembrokeshire to the west and the Brecon Beacons to the east – it remains much quieter and less explored. If your interests stretch to gardens, stately homes and all things green, add this quiet county to your itinerary.

Llanelli

POP 49,600

Carmarthenshire's largest town is a nondescript kind of place; nonetheless, it offers a couple of enticements to stop if you're travelling northwest from Swansea.

Llanelli's obsession is rugby union and the local team has produced many famous players over the years. In 1972 they achieved the unthinkable, defeating New Zealand's national squad, the mighty All Blacks, at Stradey Park – an event still remembered in these parts as 'the day the pubs ran dry'.

Sights

Llanelli Wetland Centre BIRD SANCTUARY

(☎01554-741087; www.wwt.org.uk/llanelli; Llwynhendy; adult/child £9.20/5; ⏰9.30am-5pm; P 👪) Covering 97 hectares on the northern shore of the Burry Inlet, across from the Gower Peninsula, this is one of Wales' most important habitats for waders and waterfowl. Winter is the most spectacular season, when up to 60,000 birds converge on the salt marsh and mudflats. There are plenty of hides and observation points, and you can hire binoculars (£5) if you don't have your own.

Species include oystercatchers, greylag geese, gadwalls, widgeons, teals and black-tailed godwits. The big attraction for birdwatchers is the resident population of little egret, whose numbers have increased from a solitary pair in 1995 to around 400. Flashiest of all are the resident flock of nearly fluorescent pink Caribbean flamingos.

There's always plenty on for kids during the school holidays. Late spring's Duckling Days are filled with downy cuteness, while during the summer holidays there are canoes and bikes to borrow.

Approaching from the southeast, take the A484 and turn left onto the B4304. The centre's a 2.5-mile walk from Llanelli train station.

Eating

Sosban WELSH ££

(☎01554-270020; www.sosbanrestaurant.com; North Dock; mains £14-26; ⏰noon-2.30pm Tue-Sun, 5.30-9pm Tue-Sat) A winning collaboration between some Welsh rugby internationals and a food writer, this upmarket restaurant occupies the cavernous, church-like confines of a Victorian industrial building that once controlled the dock's hydraulic lock gates. Expect bistro-style dishes created using top-notch Welsh products such as lamb, cod, cockles and Perl Wen cheese.

Getting There & Away

Llanelli's train station is on Great Western Cres, south of the town centre. Direct connections include London Paddington (from £61, 3½ hours, daily), Abergavenny (from £11, two hours, hourly), Cardiff (£14, 1½ hours, hourly), Swansea (£5.60, 20 minutes, at least hourly) and Tenby (£15, 1¼ hours, six daily).

The bus station is on Stepney Pl, right in the centre of town. There are direct services to/from Swansea (£5.70, 40 minutes, half-hourly), Kidwelly (£4.10, 35 minutes, at least hourly) and Carmarthen (£3, one hour, half-hourly).

National Express (☎0871 781 8181; www.nationalexpress.com) coaches head to/from London (from £16, 5½ hours), Cardiff (from £7.10, 1¾ hours) and Swansea (from £2.50, 40 minutes) daily.

Laugharne (Talacharn)

POP 1220

Handsome little Laugharne (pronounced 'larn') sits above the tide-washed shores of the Taf Estuary, overlooked by a Norman castle. Dylan Thomas, one of Wales' greatest writers, spent the last four years of his life here, during which time he produced some of his most inspired work, including *Under Milk Wood*. The town is one of the inspirations for this play's fictional village of Llareggub (spell it backwards and you'll get the gist).

On Thomas' first visit to Laugharne he described it as the 'strangest town in Wales', but returned repeatedly throughout his restless life. Dylan and Caitlin Thomas are buried in a grave marked by a simple, white, wooden cross in the churchyard of medieval St Martin's Church, on the northern edge of the town.

WORTH A TRIP

KIDWELLY

Rising above a narrow waterway dotted with gliding swans, the forbidding grey **Kidwelly Castle** (Cadw; www.cadw.gov.wales; Castle Rd, Kidwelly; adult/child £4/3; 9.30am-5pm Mar-Oct, 10am-4pm Nov-Feb) was founded by the Normans in 1106, but most of the system of towers and curtain walls was built in the 13th century in reaction to Welsh uprisings. If it looks at all familiar, that may be because it featured in the opening scene of *Monty Python and the Holy Grail*.

The castle is located in the small town of Kidwelly, 8 miles northwest of Llanelli at the mouth of the River Gwendraeth Fach. Buses and trains head to Kidwelly from both Llanelli and Carmarthen.

Sights

★ **Dylan Thomas Boathouse** MUSEUM
(01994-427420; www.dylanthomasboathouse.com; Dylan's Walk; adult/child £4.20/2; 10am-5pm May-Oct, 10.30am-3pm Nov-Apr) Dylan Thomas, his wife Caitlin and their three children lived in this cliff-clinging house from 1949 to 1953. It's a beautiful setting, looking out over the estuary that Thomas, in his *Poem in October*, described as the 'heron-priested shore'. The parlour has been restored to its 1950s appearance, with a desk that once belonged to Thomas' schoolmaster father. Upstairs are photographs, letters, a video about his life, and his death mask, which once belonged to Richard Burton.

Along the lane from the Boathouse is the old shed where Thomas did most of his writing. It looks as if he has just popped out, with screwed-up pieces of paper littered around the sea-facing table where he wrote *Under Milk Wood* and poems such as *Over Sir John's Hill* (which describes the view).

Laugharne Castle CASTLE
(Cadw; www.cadw.gov.wales; Wogan St; adult/child £3.80/2.85; 10am-5pm Apr-Oct) Built in the 13th century, picturesque Laugharne Castle was converted into a mansion in the 16th century for John Perrot, thought to be the illegitimate son of Henry VIII. It was landscaped with its current lawns and gardens in Victorian times.

The adjoining **Castle House** was leased in 1934 by Richard Hughes, author of *A High Wind in Jamaica*. It was Hughes who first invited Dylan Thomas to Laugharne. Thomas stayed with Hughes at Castle House and wrote some of his short-story collection, *Portrait of the Artist as a Young Dog*, in the little gazebo looking out over the estuary.

Activities

Marros Riding Centre HORSE RIDING
(01994-453777; www.marros-farm.co.uk; Marros; lessons/treks from £17/25) Based 7 miles west of Laugharne, past the broad sands of Pendine, this riding centre offers lessons and treks, including beach rides.

Laugharne Heritage Walk WALKING
(www.laugharnetownship-wcc.gov.uk) This scenic 1.7-mile loop starts at the foreshore car park and skirts the bottom of the castle before heading up to Dylan Thomas' writing shed and Boathouse. It then cuts inland to St Martin's Church and returns via the main street. It's clearly signposted, and a brochure can be downloaded from the town's website.

Festivals & Events

Laugharne Weekend LITERATURE, MUSIC
(http://s452743659.websitehome.co.uk; Apr) This vibrant small-scale festival held over the first weekend in April concentrates on music and writing by artists with a Welsh connection.

Sleeping

Carpenter's Arms PUB £
(01994-427435; www.carpentersbroadway.co.uk; Broadway; r £50; P) Nobody says the neon lights are bright in this Broadway, the tiny village immediately south of Laugharne, and it's arguable whether there's magic in the air. But this community pub has four small but tidy and extremely well-priced rooms upstairs, and a cast of local characters to share a yarn with below.

Boat House B&B ££
(01994-427263; www.theboathousebnb.co.uk; 1 Gosport St; s/d £60/80;) Friendly, homely and tastefully decorated, this is the smartest B&B in town, offering four well-appointed guest rooms. The building was formerly the Corporation Arms pub, where Dylan Thomas told stories in exchange for free drinks. The current owner's exceptional home-

cooked breakfasts would surely assuage even Thomas' legendary hangovers.

Keepers Cottage B&B ££
(☎01994-427404; www.keepers-cottage.com; A4066; s/d from £60/85; P) Sitting on the top of the hill by the main approach to town, this pretty cottage has simply decorated but very comfortable rooms. Complimentary bottled water and chocolates are a nice touch.

Eating

Castle View FISH & CHIPS £
(☎01994-427445; Grist Sq; fish & chips £4.40-9.50; ⊙noon-2pm & 5-7.30pm Mon-Sat, noon-6pm Sun) For a serve of cod, chips and mushy peas bigger than your head, you can't do better than this upmarket chippie. There's a pleasant dining area for those customers who aren't keen on battling the seagulls on the waterfront. All the fish is sustainably caught and the menu also stretches to meat pies, faggots and curry.

Brown's Hotel PIZZA £
(☎01994-427688; www.browns-hotel.co.uk; King St; pizza £8-10; ⊙11am-11pm) Numerous pubs across South Wales lay claim to a Dylan Thomas connection, but the poet was such a regular here that he famously gave out its phone number as his own. Built in 1752 but recently renovated, it's still a cosy spot for a drink, and the pizza is excellent – especially the one topped with cockles and laver bread.

Cors MODERN BRITISH £££
(☎01994-427219; www.thecors.co.uk; Newbridge Rd; mains £19-24, r £80; ⊙7pm-midnight Thu-Sat; P) Tucked away in a rambling old house behind a wonderful bog garden ('cors' means bog), this colourful and pleasantly eccentric restaurant-with-rooms serves excellent local, seasonal meals. The three bedrooms upstairs are spacious and brimming with character.

Getting There & Away

Bus 222 runs between Carmarthen and Laugharne (30 minutes, five daily).

Carmarthen (Caerfyrddin)

POP 14,200

Carmarthenshire's county town is a place of legend and ancient provenance, but it's not the kind of place you'll feel inclined to linger in. It's a handy transport and shopping hub, but there's not a lot to see. The Romans built a town here, complete with a fort and amphitheatre, and a **castle** (Nott Sq; ⊙9.30am-4.30pm Mon-Sat) FREE followed in 1106, courtesy of Henry I.

Most intriguingly, Carmarthen is reputed to be the birthplace of the most famous wizard of them all (no, not Harry Potter) – Myrddin of the Arthurian legends, better known in English as Merlin. An oak tree planted in 1659 for Charles II's coronation came to be called 'Merlin's Tree' and was linked to a prophecy that its death would mean curtains for the town. The tree died in the 1970s and the town, while a little down at heel, is still standing.

Sights & Activities

Carmarthenshire County Museum MUSEUM
(☎01267-228696; www.carmarthenmuseum.org.uk; Abergwili; ⊙10am-4.30pm Tue-Sat) FREE Located in a 13th-century country house, which served as the bishop's palace right up until 1972, this museum is a musty emporium of archaeology, Egyptology, pottery and paintings, with recreations of a Victorian schoolroom and a collection of carved Roman stones. It's located 2 miles east of Carmarthen on the A40.

Oriel Myrddin GALLERY
(☎01267-222775; www.orielmyrddingallery.co.uk; Church Lane; ⊙10am-5pm Mon-Sat) FREE Housed in a former art college, this stylish little gallery stages changing exhibitions of contemporary art. The shop sells a nice range of craft and jewellery.

Creepy Carmarthen WALKING
(☎01267-231557; www.thespookymagiccompany.co.uk; adult/child £7.50/5; ⊙7pm Wed) Stroll around the town's darker corners while being regaled with ghost stories and the more gruesome parts of the town's history.

Gwili Railway RAIL
(☎01267-238213; www.gwili-railway.co.uk; adult/child £11/5) Take a ride on a standard-gauge steam train along the lovely Gwili valley on a defunct passenger line. The round trip takes about an hour and departs from Bronwydd Arms, 3.5 miles north of Carmarthen on the A484. The trains run daily in July and August and less frequently in other months; check the website for a full timetable.

✕ Eating

Carmarthen's contribution to Welsh gastronomy is a salt-cured, air-dried ham. Local legend has it that the Romans liked the recipe so much, they took it back to Italy with them, where it is now known as Parma ham. Look for it at the market.

Waverley Stores　　　　VEGETARIAN £
(☑ 01267-236521; www.waverleyonline.co.uk; 23 Lammas St; mains £6; ⊘ 11.30am-2pm Mon-Sat; ☑) Hiding at the rear of a wholefoods store, this cheap-and-cheerful eatery serves up simple vegetarian meals such as soups, salads, quiches, lasagne and jacket potatoes.

Cafe at No 4　　　MODERN BRITISH ££
(☑ 01267-220461; 4 Queen St; 3 courses £30; ⊘ 6-9pm Thu-Sat) This chic and friendly little bistro excels at well-priced and delicious set dinners. Expect lots of Welsh produce, lovingly cooked.

❶ Information

Tourist Office (☑ 01267-231557; www.discovercarmarthenshire.com; Old Castle House; ⊘ 9.30am-4.30pm Mon-Sat)

❶ Getting There & Away

Carmarthen's bus station is on Blue St. There are direct services to/from Cardiff (2¼ hours, two daily), Swansea (50 minutes, hourly), Llandeilo (42 minutes, 10 daily), Haverfordwest (58 minutes, three daily) and Aberystwyth (2¼ hours, hourly).

National Express (☑ 0871 781 8181; www.nationalexpress.com) coaches head to/from London (from £16, six hours), Bristol (£18, three hours), Cardiff (£11, two hours), Swansea (from £3.70, 50 minutes) and Tenby (from £3.10, 45 minutes) at least daily.

The train station is 300m south of town across the river. There are direct services to/from London Paddington (from £61, four hours, daily), Abergavenny (from £12, 2½ hours, hourly), Cardiff (from £7.50, 1¾ hours, hourly), Swansea (£9.20, 50 minutes, hourly) and Tenby (£9.30, 45 minutes, nine daily).

Llanarthne

POP 765

Little Llanarthne is as pleasantly rural and slow-paced as dozens of other Carmarthenshire villages, and would have remained indistinguishable from the pack if it wasn't for the opening of the National Botanic Garden

of Wales nearby. Fancy accommodation and a celebrity-helmed eatery have followed in the garden's wake.

◉ Sights

★**National Botanic Garden of Wales**　　　GARDENS
(☑ 01558-667149; www.botanicgarden.wales; Llanarthne; adult/child £8.90/4.50; ⊘ 10am-6pm Apr-Sep, to 4.30pm Oct-Mar) Concealed in the rolling Tywi valley countryside, this lavish complex opened in 2000 and is still maturing. Formerly an aristocratic estate, the garden has a broad range of plant habitats, from lakes and bogs to woodland and heath, with lots of decorative areas and educational exhibits. The centrepiece is the Norman Foster–designed **Great Glasshouse**, a spectacular glass dome sunken into the earth. The garden is 2 miles southwest of Llanarthne village, signposted from the main roads.

The garden's themed spaces include a historic double-walled garden, a **Japanese garden** and an **apothecaries' garden**, and there are fascinating displays on plant medicine in a re-created chemist shop. The 110m-wide Great Glasshouse shelters endangered plants from Mediterranean climes sourced from all over the world.

This estate once belonged to Sir William Paxton, the man responsible for the transformation of Tenby into a tourist resort. His grand manor house, built in the 1790s, burnt down in 1931, but you can still see the outline of the foundations, and the old servants' quarters, which are pretty impressive in themselves. The original Regency-era landscaping comprising a chain of decorative lakes was in the process of being restored at the time of research. On the hill in the distance, look out for **Paxton's Tower**, a castle-like structure once used for entertaining.

🛏 Sleeping & Eating

Llwyn Helyg Country House　　B&B £££
(☑ 01558-668778; www.llwynhelygcountryhouse.co.uk; r £119-145; ℗ 🕏) Although there's a Georgian look to this huge stone house on the edge of the village, it's actually a modern build. The three guest bedrooms are luxuriously decked out with dark wooden furniture, white Italian marble en suites and spa baths, and to preserve the rarefied atmosphere, it doesn't take bookings for children under 16.

★**Wright's Food Emporium** DELI, CAFE ££
(☎01558-668929; www.wrightsfood.co.uk; B4300; mains £6.50-13; ⊙11am-5pm Sun, 11am-7pm Mon, 9am-7pm Wed & Thu, 9am-late Fri & Sat; P 📶 🐾) Sprawling through the rooms of an old village pub, this hugely popular deli-cafe serves sandwiches, salads and massive antipasto platters packed full of top-notch local and imported ingredients. Wash it all down with a craft beer or something from its range of small-estate, organic wine.

Getting There & Away

Up to two buses a day stop here en route between Carmarthen (30 minutes) and Llandeilo (20 minutes). Some also stop at the botanic garden.

Llandeilo

POP 1800

Set on a hill encircled by the greenest of fields, Llandeilo is little more than a handful of narrow streets lined with grand Georgian and Victorian buildings and centred on a picturesque church and graveyard. The surrounding region was once dominated by large country estates, and though they have long gone, the deer, parkland, trees and agricultural character of the landscape are their legacy.

Used by many travellers as a springboard for the wilder terrain of Brecon Beacon National Park, it's within a short drive of magical Carreg Cennen castle (p113).

Sights

★**Dinefwr** HISTORIC BUILDING
(NT, Cadw; ☎01558-824512; www.nationaltrust.org.uk; adult/child £6.50/3.50, parking £6; ⊙house 11am-6pm daily Easter-Oct, 11am-4pm Fri-Sun Nov-Easter; P) This idyllic, 324-hectare, beautifully landscaped estate, immediately west of Llandeilo, incorporates a **deer park**, pasture, woods, an **Iron Age fort**, the hidden remains of a **Roman fort**, a 12th-century castle and **Newton House**, a wonderful 17th-century manor with a Victorian facade. The house is presented as it was in Edwardian times, focusing particularly on the experience of servants in their downstairs domain. Other rooms recall Newton's WWII incarnation as a hospital, and the former Billiard Room is now a tearoom.

Dinefwr Castle is set on a hilltop in the southern corner of the estate and offers fantastic views from its walls and towers across the Tywi to the foothills of the Black Mountain. In the 17th century it suffered the indignity of being converted into a picturesque garden feature.

There are several marked walking routes around the grounds, some of which are accessible to visitors with disabilities. Keep an eye out for fallow deer and the rare herd of White Park cattle.

WORTH A TRIP

ABERGLASNEY GARDENS

Wandering through the formal walled **Aberglasney Gardens** (☎01558-668998; www.aberglasney.org; Llangathen; adult/child £7.30/3.70; ⊙10am-6pm Apr-Oct, 10.30am-4pm Nov-Mar) feels a bit like walking into a Jane Austen novel. They date from the 17th century and contain a unique cloister built solely as a garden decoration. There's also a pool garden, a 250-year-old yew tunnel and a 'wild' garden in the bluebell woods to the west.

At its heart stands a semi-restored **Elizabethan manor house**, where you can watch a video on the estate's history and view temporary art exhibitions. The derelict kitchens have been converted into a glass-roofed atrium garden full of subtropical plants such as orchids, palms and cycads.

Out on the terrace, a whitewashed and flagstoned tearoom sells cakes and snacks.

Aberglasney is in the village of Llangathen, just off the A40, 4 miles west of Llandeilo.

Sleeping

Cawdor HOTEL ££
(☎01558-823500; www.thecawdor.com; Rhosmaen St; r £65-150, ste/apt £200/210; P 📶) Grey-and-pink-striped carpet leads to well-appointed rooms with marble-clad bathrooms in this grand Georgian inn. The downstairs bar serves tasty meals, or you can opt for a more formal feed in the restaurant.

Plough HOTEL ££
(☎01558-823431; www.ploughrhosmaen.com; s/d from £75/95; P 📶 🐾) On the A40, just north of Llandeilo, this baby-blue inn offers hip, contemporary rooms with countryside

views. The standard rooms are spacious enough but the corner-hogging executives have cat-swinging space and then some.

Eating

★ Ginhaus Deli DELI £
(☎ 01558-823030; www.ginhaus.co.uk; Market St; mains £6.50-9; ⏲ 8am-6pm Mon-Thu, to 8pm Fri & Sat; 📶) Specialising in the very finest things in life, namely gin and cheese, this hip deli-cafe also serves cooked breakfasts, filled baguettes, quiches, tarts, fresh juices and delicious oddities such as laver bread and cockle crostini. On Friday and Saturday nights it branches out to pizza.

Heavenly SWEETS £
(☎ 01558-822800; www.heavenlychoc.co.uk; 60 Rhosmaen St; chocolates from £2; ⏲ 11.30am-4.30pm Sun, 1-5pm Mon, 9.30am-5pm Tue-Sat) Believe the name and enter an Aladdin's cave stacked with handcrafted chocolates, artisanal ice cream and enticing pastries and cakes. Grab something yummy to take away, or take a seat and settle in with a hot chocolate.

Y Capel Bach Bistro at the Angel BISTRO ££
(☎ 01558-822765; www.angelbistro.co.uk; 62 Rhosmaen St; mains lunch £7-9, dinner £11-15; ⏲ 11.30am-3pm & 6-11pm Mon-Sat; 👪) Focusing on hearty bistro-style meals, this popular gastropub chalks up daily specials on a blackboard hung between an unusual display of historical wedding photos. A set-price *table d'hôte* menu is offered most evenings (one/two/three courses £10/13/15).

Getting There & Away

Buses head to/from Swansea (£5.70, 1½ hours, seven daily), Carmarthen (42 minutes, 10 daily), Llanarthne (20 minutes, two daily), Llangathen (six minutes, eight daily) and Llandovery (40 minutes, eight daily).

Llandeilo is on the Heart of Wales line, with direct trains to/from Cardiff (from £20, 2¼ hours, two daily), Swansea (£7.30, one hour, five daily), Llandovery (£3.50, 20 minutes, five daily), Llandrindod Wells (£7.90, 1½ hours, four daily) and Shrewsbury (£14, three hours, four daily).

Llandovery (Llanymddyfri)

POP 2070

Lovely Llandovery is an attractive market town that makes a good base for exploring the western fringes of Brecon Beacons National Park. The name means 'the church among the waters', and the town is indeed surrounded by rivers, sitting between the Tywi and the Bran, and with the smaller Bawddwr running through it.

It was once an important assembly point for drovers taking their cattle towards the English markets. The Bank of the Black Ox – one of the first independent Welsh banks – was established here by a wealthy cattle merchant.

Sights

Llandovery Castle CASTLE
(Castle St) The shattered ruin of motte-and-bailey Llandovery Castle looms ineffectually over the town centre. Built in 1100 and then rebuilt in stone in the 1160s, it changed hands many times between the Normans and the Welsh, and between one Welsh prince and another, taking a severe beating in the process. Owain Glyndŵr had a good go at it in 1403, and it was finally left to decay in 1490.

The castle is fronted by an eerie disembodied stainless-steel statue commemorating Llywelyn ap Gruffydd Fychan, who was gruesomely hung, drawn and quartered by Henry IV for refusing to lead him to Owain Glyndŵr's base.

Sleeping

Drovers B&B ££
(☎ 01550-721115; www.droversllandovery.co.uk; 9 Market Sq; s/d £65/110; P 📶) This attractive Georgian house on the town's main square has a comfortably old-fashioned feel with its ancient stone hearth, antique furniture and simply decorated bedrooms. You can take breakfast in front of a roaring fire in winter.

Llanerchindda Farm HOTEL ££
(☎ 01550-750274; www.cambrianway.com; Cynghordy; s/d from £55/80; P 📶 🐾) In a spectacular rural setting with views over a historic rail aqueduct to the Black Mountain, this friendly guesthouse offers plenty of peace and seclusion. Rooms are simple, tidy and a little old-fashioned, and the large dining room downstairs serves evening meals on request. It's located 7 miles northeast of Llandovery, off the A483.

★ New White Lion BOUTIQUE HOTEL £££
(☎ 01550-720685; www.newwhitelion.com; 43 Stone St; r £120-160; P 📶) With its exterior an inviting chocolate-milkshake colour and

its opulent interiors just shy of over-the-top, this boutique hotel is a stylish proposition indeed. There are only six rooms, so book ahead.

Drinking

Castle Hotel PUB

(☎01550-720343; www.castle-hotel-llandovery.co.uk; Kings Rd; ⏰8am-11pm) This large, handsome, family run pub has a rambling sequence of low-ceilinged rooms with log fires, along with 15 guest bedrooms and a restaurant. The Red Giraffe shop, selling Welsh blankets and African artefacts, is an unexpected bonus. Plus the local history society has a mini-museum upstairs.

Information

Tourist Office (☎01550-720693; Kings Rd; ⏰10am-5pm Easter-Oct; 📶)

Getting There & Away

Buses head to/from Carmarthen (1½ hours, eight daily), Llangathen (50 minutes, eight daily), Llandeilo (40 minutes, eight daily) and Pumsaint (23 minutes, daily).

Llandovery is on the Heart of Wales line, with direct trains to/from Cardiff (from £20, 2½ hours, two daily), Swansea (£8.70, 1½ hours, five daily), Llandeilo (£3.50, 20 minutes, five daily), Llandrindod Wells (£6, one hour, four daily) and Shrewsbury (£14, 2¾ hours, four daily).

Pumsaint

A cluster of stone houses on the surprisingly busy A482 between Lampeter and Llanwrda, Pumsaint is an obscure kind of place distinguished largely by one important historical site and a truly excellent pub. The name means 'five saints', which is a reference to five mysterious hollows on a standing stone positioned near its famous goldmines. The reality is far less saintly: the stone was simply an anvil used by the Romans.

Sights

Dolaucothi Gold Mines MUSEUM

(NT; ☎01558-650177; www.nationaltrust.org.uk; Pumsaint; adult/child £8/3.95; ⏰11am-5pm Easter-Oct) Set in a beautiful wooded estate, this is the only known Roman goldmine in the UK. The exhibition and the mining machinery above ground are interesting, but the main attraction is the chance to go underground on a guided tour of the old mine workings. Back at the surface, there's a sediment-filled water trough where you can try your hand at panning for gold.

The Romans left around AD 120, but the locals carried on for a couple of hundred more years. Mining recommenced with the Victorians, and by the time the mine was finally closed down in 1938 the works employed more than 200 men.

Eating

★**Dolaucothi Arms** PUB FOOD ££

(☎01558-650237; www.thedolaucothiarms.co.uk; A482; mains £8-15; ⏰5-11pm Tue-Thu, noon-11pm Fri & Sat, noon-8pm Sun; P📶🐾) Even hardened city slickers might be tempted to village life if a local pub this good could be guaranteed. This 16th-century drovers' inn has a friendly front bar, complete with board games and an open fire, and upstairs there are three comfortable bedrooms. However it's the restaurant that draws the crowds, serving country cuisine with a contemporary twist.

Getting There & Away

The 289 bus between Lampeter and Llandovery stops here at least once a day on weekdays.

Newcastle Emlyn & Around

POP 1190

Most travellers head west from Carmarthen, leaving the lush green hills and valleys of northern Carmarthenshire relatively unexplored. The River Teifi forms much of the border with Ceredigion, and a particularly pretty stretch of the river passes through this historic market town. Although there's not much to see in the town itself, there's a cluster of interesting sights in the surrounding countryside.

Three miles downstream, the village of **Cenarth** occupies a picturesque spot by an old stone bridge, at the foot of a stretch of rapids. Near the south side of the bridge is Ffynnon Llawddog, a holy well linked to an early Celtic saint. It's one of many such sites throughout Wales that were popular during medieval times for their supposedly curative powers, although many have ancient pre-Christian origins.

Sights

Castell Newydd Emlyn CASTLE

(Castle St) FREE Perched above a languid loop in the River Teifi, this ruined fortress holds the distinction of being the first stone castle to be built by a Welshman. Dating from around 1240, it was captured by Owain Glyndŵr in 1403 and then thoroughly trashed in 1648 during the Civil War. Now only the remains of the gatehouse are still standing.

Local legend has it that an English soldier killed the last-ever dragon here. This story is commemorated in the 'Spirit of the Dragon', a large throne-like wooden seat set within a mosaic behind the castle, and in plaques in the pretty riverside park below.

Caws Cenarth FACTORY

(01239-710432; www.cawscenarth.co.uk; Fferm Glyneithinog, Pontseli, Lancych; 10am-5pm Mon-Sat; P) FREE One of Wales' most acclaimed organic cheesemakers, Caws Cenarth produces all the well-known Welsh cheeses (Caerphilly, Perl Wen, Perl Las) as well as the washed-rind Golden Cenarth, which won the supreme prize at the British Cheese Awards in 2010. On weekdays you can watch the cheese being made from a mezzanine overlooking the factory. There are interesting displays to peruse, plus a short video explaining the process. It's located in the countryside, 4 miles southwest of Newcastle Emlyn.

National Wool Museum MUSEUM

(0300 111 2333; www.museumwales.ac.uk; Drefach Felindre; 10am-5pm daily Apr-Sep, Wed-Sat Oct-Mar) FREE The Cambrian Mills factory, world famous for its high-quality woollen products, closed in 1984 and this surprisingly interesting museum has taken its place. Former mill workers are often on hand to get the machines clickety-clacking, but there's also a working commercial mill next door where you can watch the operations from a viewing platform. There's a cafe on site, along with a gift shop selling snugly woollen blankets.

The museum is positioned in verdant countryside at Drefach Felindre, 3.5 miles east of Newcastle Emlyn, signposted from the A484.

Sleeping & Eating

★ **Larkhill Tipis** CAMPSITE ££

(01559-3715881; www.larkhilltipisandyurts.co.uk; Cwmduad; tents from £70) Puffed-up American turkeys escort guests around the fairy-lit grounds of this off-the-grid glamping site. Five different styles of tent are available, each from a different part of the world, and all are comfortably furnished with their own beds, gas cookers and wood fires. It's in a remote spot, 7 miles southeast of Newcastle Emlyn.

Gwesty'r Emlyn Hotel HOTEL ££

(01239-710317; www.gwestyremlynhotel.co.uk; Bridge St; s/d from £80/120; P) This 300-year-old coaching inn has been transformed into a slick little hotel with well-presented rooms, a restaurant and a 'fitness suite', with gym equipment, a spa pool and a sauna.

Yasmin's INDIAN £

(01239-711681; Sycamore St; mains £8-10; 5-11pm;) The winner of various Welsh curry awards over the years, Yasmin's offers a massive menu of fairly traditional Indian dishes. In the warmer months, the restaurant reaps the rewards of its own large kitchen garden out the back.

Getting There & Away

There are direct bus services departing hourly for Carmarthen (one hour), Henllan (16 minutes), Cenarth (five minutes) and Cardigan (26 minutes).

St Davids & Pembrokeshire

Includes ➡

Best Places to Eat

- Coast (p150)
- Grove (p164)
- Canteen (p183)
- Cliff (p150)
- Food at Williams (p161)

Best Places to Sleep

- Pentower (p179)
- Tŵr y Felin (p174)
- Old School Hostel (p175)
- Cliff House (p150)
- Max & Caroline's (p164)

Why Go?

The Pembrokeshire coast is what you imagine the world would look like if God were a geology teacher. There are knobbly hills of volcanic rock, long thin inlets scoured by glaciers, and stratified limestone pushed up vertically and then eroded into arches, blowholes and sea stacks. All along the shoreline towering red and grey cliffs play leapfrog with perfect sandy beaches.

This wild and incredibly beautiful landscape is the county's greatest asset and in summer people flock here from all over Britain to enjoy the spectacular walking, surfing, coasteering and sea kayaking, as well as the glorious beaches and abundant marine life.

On top of its natural assets, Pembrokeshire offers a wealth of Celtic and pre-Celtic sites, forbidding castles, fascinating islands and little St Davids – the magical mini-city with its chilled vibe, spectacular cathedral and abiding association with Wales' patron saint.

When to Go

- A good time to be in St Davids is 1 March, when the whole country celebrates their patron saint.
- Fishguard serenades summer with some serious sessions at its Folk Festival in late May.
- Hoards of holidaymakers descend during the peak season months from June to August, but this is also the best time for walking the coast path and hitting the beach.
- The kids go back to school but Tenby bursts into life all over again for its annual arts festival in September.
- Surfers will catch the best swells between September and February on Pembrokeshire's rugged beaches.

St Davids & Pembrokeshire Highlights

1 St Davids (p170) Exploring the laid-back little city with the spectacular cathedral and gnarly surf beach.

2 Pembrokeshire Coast Path (p151) Tracing the breathtaking collision of rock and sea on a trail that encompasses the county's entire coast.

3 Tenby (p152) Joining the summer fun in a colourful seaside resort flanked by velvety-sand beaches.

4 Newport (p180) Discovering the culinary joys of a little gem of a town surrounded by beaches and hill walks.

5 Watersports (p158) Experiencing excellent surfing at Freshwater West, sea kayaking at Fishguard and coasteering at Abereiddi.

6 Skomer Island (p167) Observing the locals in one of the richest wildlife habitats in Britain.

7 Castell Henllys (p181) Entering the Iron Age in this reconstructed Celtic fort.

8 Pentre Ifan (p181) Soaking up the views from Wales' loftiest dolmen, a prehistoric chamber tomb formed from the same rock as Stonehenge.

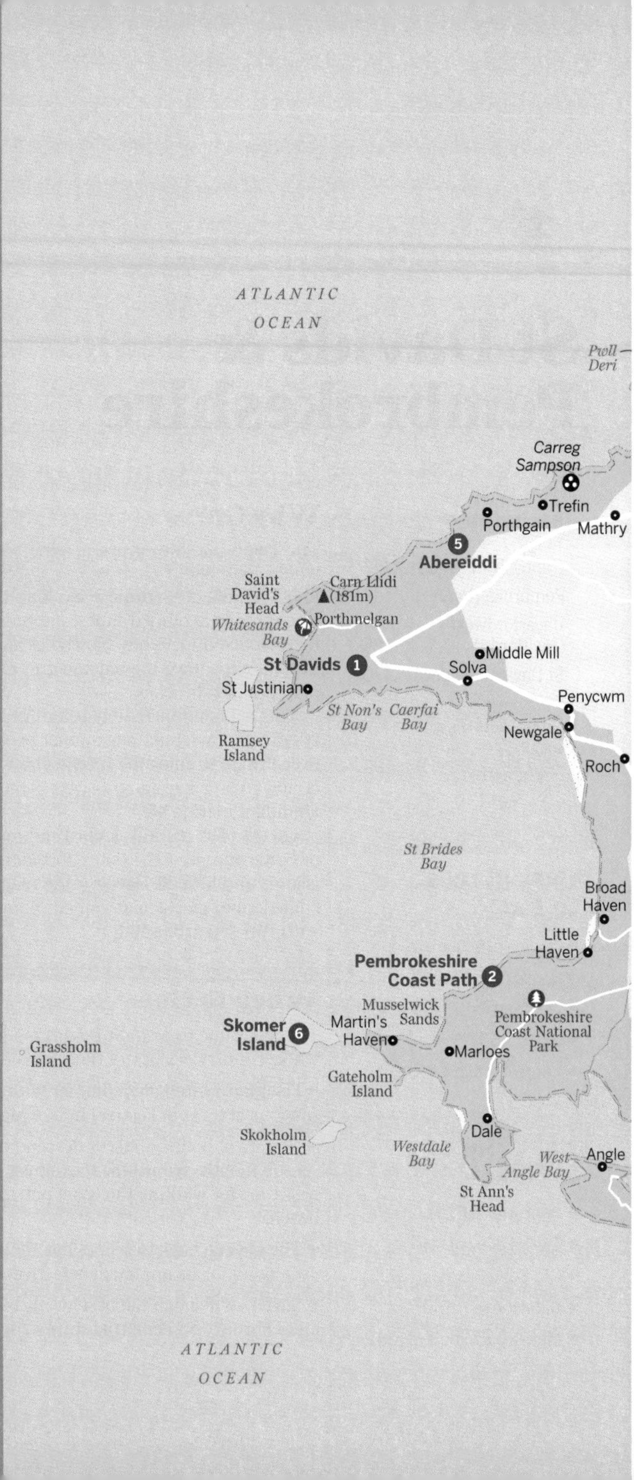

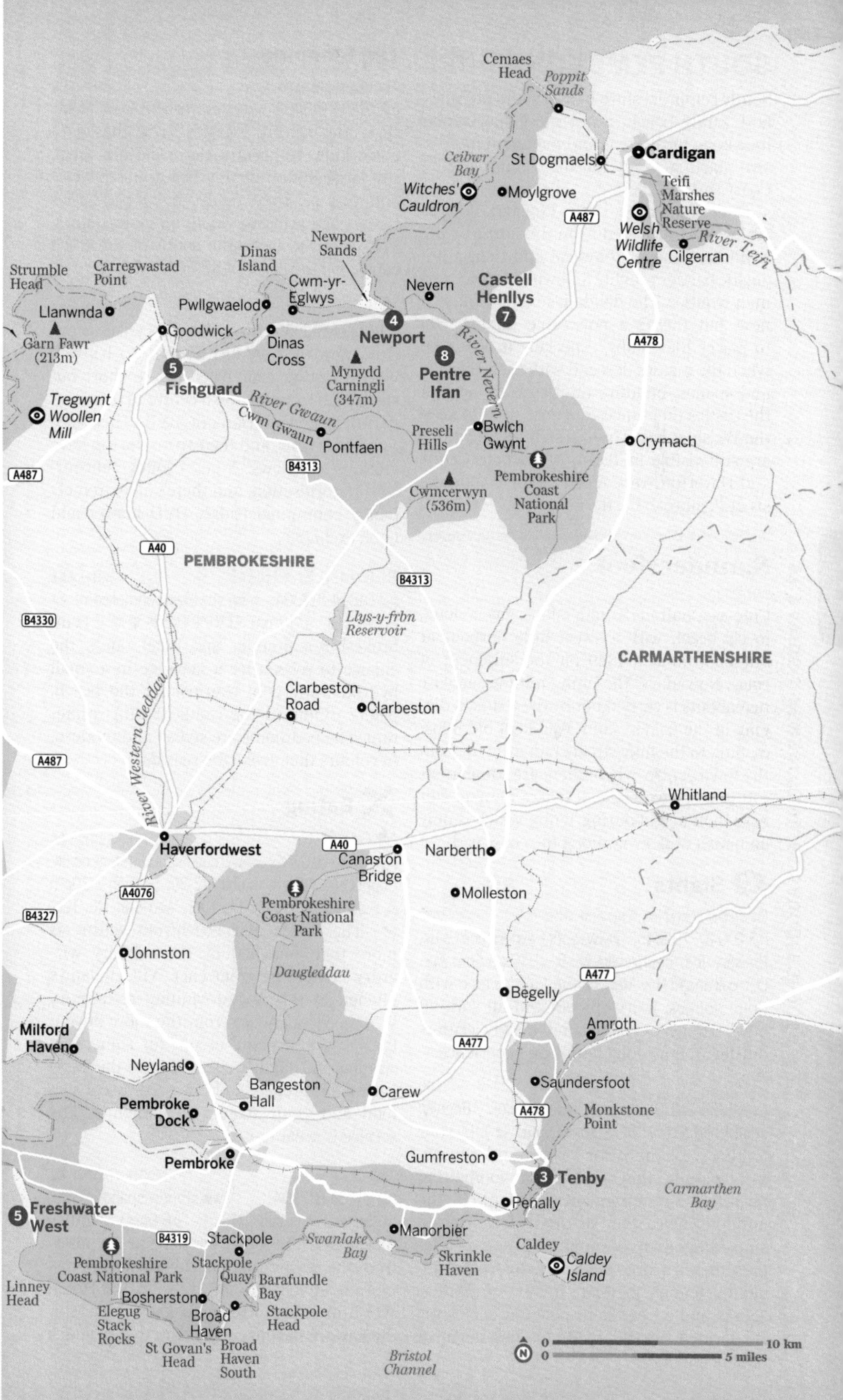

Cemaes Head
Poppit Sands
Cardigan
St Dogmaels
Ceibwr Bay
Witches' Cauldron
Moylgrove
Teifi Marshes Nature Reserve
Welsh Wildlife Centre
River Teifi
Cilgerran
A487
Newport Sands
Dinas Island
Strumble Head
Carregwastad Point
Cwm-yr-Eglwys
Nevern
Castell Henllys
7
Pwllgwaelod
Llanwnda
Goodwick
4
Newport
Dinas Cross
Garn Fawr (213m)
5
Fishguard
Mynydd Carningli (347m)
8
Pentre Ifan
River Nevern
A478
Tregwynt Woollen Mill
River Gwaun
Cwm Gwaun
Pontfaen
Preseli Hills
Bwlch Gwynt
Crymach
B4313
Pembrokeshire Coast National Park
Cwmcerwyn (536m)
A40
PEMBROKESHIRE
B4330
Llys-y-frbn Reservoir
CARMARTHENSHIRE
Clarbeston Road
Clarbeston
River Western Cleddau
Whitland
Haverfordwest
Canaston Bridge
Narberth
Molleston
A4076
B4327
Johnston
Daugleddau
A477
Begelly
Amroth
Milford Haven
Neyland
Saundersfoot
Bangeston Hall
Carew
Pembroke Dock
Monkstone Point
Pembroke
Gumfreston
3
Tenby
Carmarthen Bay
Penally
Freshwater West
B4319
Stackpole
Swanlake Bay
Manorbier
Caldey
Caldey Island
Stackpole Quay
Skrinkle Haven
Pembrokeshire Coast National Park
Linney Head
Barafundle Bay
Bosherston
Elegug Stack Rocks
Broad Haven
Stackpole Head
St Govan's Head
Broad Haven South
Bristol Channel
0 10 km
0 5 miles
N

SOUTH PEMBROKESHIRE

South Pembrokeshire boasts some of Wales' best sandy beaches and most spectacular limestone formations and makes an impressive starting point for the Pembrokeshire Coast Path (PCP).

Once known as Little England Beyond Wales, it was divided from the north by the Landsker Line – a physical and then a linguistic barrier roughly following the old Norman frontier. The divide is less pronounced now, but there's a noticeable English feel to places like Tenby, especially in summer, when the masses descend with their buckets and spades, building miniature replicas of the castles their ancestors once used to keep the Welsh at bay. Those sturdy fortifications are still visible in Tenby, Manorbier, Carew and Haverfordwest, reaching their apotheosis at Pembroke Castle.

Saundersfoot

POP 2630

Cute-as-a-button Saundersfoot has a long, lovely beach with a sweet little harbour at one end, built in 1829 for the shipment of coal. Nowadays the only mining activity hereabouts is carried out by the toddlers digging in the golden sand. Well-kept old houses cling to the hilly streets radiating up from the town centre, where there are some interesting shops to peruse. It makes for a quieter base than neighbouring Tenby, which is only an hour's walk away along the coast path.

Sights

Dragon Reptile Experience ZOO

(07940 793845; www.reptile-experience.co.uk; Brewery Tce; adult/child £8/5; 10am-5pm Apr-Oct, call ahead Nov-Mar) Come face to face with huge snakes, hairy spiders and all sorts of other slippery, creepy and crawly critters during an hour-long hands-on experience.

Folly Farm ZOO

(01834-812731; www.folly-farm.co.uk; Begelly; adult/child £11/9.25; 10am-5pm;) If your toddler's tolerance for castles and churches is waning, this combination zoo/petting farm/fun fair/amusement park could be the antidote. Once they've tired of the pirate ship, dragon playground and ride-on diggers, there's a large menagerie to explore, including lemurs, meerkats, monkeys, giraffes, zebras and an excellent penguin enclosure. It's located on the A478, 3 miles north of Saundersfoot.

Sleeping

Trevayne Farm CAMPSITE £

(01834-813402; www.trevaynefarm.co.uk; Monkstone; sites from £11; Easter-Oct;) Based on a working 40-hectare permaculture farm, this large clifftop site has beautiful sea views and two separate fields so back-to-basics tenters can avoid the looming motorhomes. The campsite is a mile south of the town centre via the coast path, or 2 miles by road.

★**Cliff House** B&B ££

(01834-813931; www.cliffhousebbsaundersfoot.co.uk; Wogan Tce; s/d from £57/75;) It's well worth lugging your bags up the short but steep road from the town centre to this wonderful little Victorian-era B&B. There are only five rooms, and the two on the top have glorious sea views. A guest lounge encourages fraternisation, and there's an extremely handy communal fridge, DVD library and book exchange.

St Brides Spa Hotel HOTEL £££

(01834-812304; www.stbridesspahotel.com; St Brides Hill; s/d from £130/160; P) Pembrokeshire's premier spa hotel offers the chance to relax after a massage in a small hydrotherapy pool overlooking the beach, before dining in the candlelit Cliff restaurant. The bedrooms are stylish and modern, in colours that evoke the seaside.

Eating

★**Coast** MODERN BRITISH ££

(01834-810800; www.coastsaundersfoot.co.uk; Coppet Hall Beach; mains £12-26; noon-2.30pm & 6.30-9.30pm daily Mar-Oct, Wed-Sun Nov-Feb;) The spectacular beachfront setting is more than matched by the culinary wizardry emanating from chef Will Holland's kitchen at this award-winning restaurant. Whether you choose from the more adventurous 'Will's menu' or opt for something simpler and slightly cheaper from the 'market menu', prepare to be wowed. Local seafood and game feature prominently. The service is great too.

★**Cliff** MODERN BRITISH ££

(01834-812304; www.stbridesspahotel.com; St Brides Hill; mains £16-21; 6-9pm) Candles flicker and the views stretch out for miles from the dining room of this upmarket restaurant, attached to the St Brides Spa Hotel. Welsh produce mixes with Asian and Middle Eastern flavours on a menu that includes

DON'T MISS

PEMBROKESHIRE COAST PATH

Straddling the line where Pembrokeshire drops suddenly into the sea, the Pembrokeshire Coast Path is one of the most spectacular long-distance routes in Britain. Established in 1970, it meanders along 186 miles of Britain's most dramatic coastal scenery running from Amroth to St Dogmaels, taking in vertiginous clifftops and endless beautiful beaches.

The route takes you from popular holiday spots to long stretches where the only evidence of human existence are the ditches of numerous Celtic forts. Marine life is plentiful, and rare birds make the most of the remote cliffs, where peregrine falcons, red kites, buzzards, choughs, puffins and gannets can be spotted.

If you don't have the time or the stamina for the full route, it can easily be split into smaller chunks. You can walk the trail in either direction but a south–north route allows an easy start in populated areas and builds up to longer, more isolated stretches. Skip from Angle to Dale by bus to avoid two days of industrial landscapes around Milford Haven.

Some sections look deceptively short but expect endless steep ascents and descents where the trail crosses harbours and beaches. Referring to a tide table is essential if you want to avoid lengthy delays in places.

The weather can be quite changeable and mobile-phone coverage is unreliable; come prepared, bring wet-weather gear and something warm, even in summer.

Maps

The route is covered by Ordnance Survey (OS) Explorer 1:25,000 maps No 35 (North Pembrokeshire) and No 36 (South Pembrokeshire). *Pembrokeshire: Wales Coast Path Official Guide* by Vivienne Crow and *Pembrokeshire Coast Path* by Brian John have detailed route descriptions. Ten *Pembrokeshire Coast Path National Trail* cards with basic maps also cover the route and are available from tourist offices and national-park centres (50p each).

When to Walk

Spring and early summer are good times to walk, when wildflowers litter the hills, bird life is abundant and the school holidays are yet to begin in earnest. Late summer tends to be drier and you might spot migrating whales out to sea, but it can be busy and hard to find a bed for a single night. In autumn the crowds die down and seals come ashore to give birth to their pups. Many hostels and campgrounds close from October to Easter and buses are far less frequent at this time. Although walking in winter can be exhilarating, it may not be the most enjoyable or safest experience. High winds can easily turn a backpack into a sail, which can be extremely dangerous on the clifftop sections.

Best Sections

Marloes Sands to Broad Haven (4½ to six hours, 13 miles) A wonderful walk along dramatic clifftops ending at an impressive beach. Many access points and regular public transport make it good for short circular walks too.

Whitesands to Porthgain (four to five hours, 10 miles) A beautiful but taxing section worth tackling if your time is limited. It's within easy reach of St Davids and offers the reward of some excellent nosh at the end of your day.

Porthgain to Pwll Deri (four to six hours, 12 miles) An exhilarating section with sheer cliffs, rock buttresses, pinnacles, islets, bays and beaches but some steep ascents and descents in between. Magnificent views of St Davids and Strumble Head.

Newport to St Dogmaels (six to eight hours, 15.5 miles) A tough, roller-coaster section with frequent steep hills but spectacular views of the wild and rugged coast and its numerous rock formations, sheer cliffs and caves.

several fish dishes, local lamb and beef, and a couple of vegetarian options.

Information

Tourist Office (☎01834-842402; www.visitpembrokeshire.com; Saundersfoot Library, Regency Hall; ⏲10am-4pm Mon-Wed & Sat, to 6pm Thu & Fri Apr-Oct, 10am-1pm Wed & Sat, 2.30-5pm Thu & Fri Nov-Mar)

Getting There & Away

Saundersfoot's train station is a mile from the centre of town. Direct services head to/from Newport Gwent (from £12, three hours, daily), Cardiff (from £10, 2¾ hours, daily), Swansea (£15, 1½ hours, seven daily), Tenby (£3.40, seven minutes, nine daily) and Pembroke (£7.40, 37 minutes, nine daily).

Direct buses head to/from Tenby (10 minutes, hourly), Narberth (34 minutes, 10 daily) and Haverfordwest (one hour, 10 daily).

Tenby (Dinbych Y Pysgod)

POP 4700

Perched on a headland with sandy beaches either side, Tenby is a postcard-maker's dream. Houses are painted from the pastel palette of a classic fishing village, interspersed with the white elegance of Georgian mansions. The main part of town is still constrained by its Norman-built walls, funnelling holidaymakers through medieval streets lined with pubs, ice-cream parlours and gift shops.

Without the tackiness of the promenade-and-pier beach towns, it tastefully returns to being a sleepy little place in the low season. In summer it has a boisterous, boozy, holiday-resort feel.

History

Tenby flourished in the 15th century as a centre for the textile trade, exporting cloth in exchange for salt and wine. Cloth making declined in the 18th century, but the town soon reinvented itself as a fashionable watering place. The arrival of the railway in the 19th century sealed its future as a resort, and William Paxton (owner of the Middleton estate in Carmarthenshire, now home to the National Botanic Garden of Wales; p142) developed a saltwater spa here. Anxiety over a possible French invasion of the Milford Haven waterway led to the construction in 1869 of a fort on St Catherine's Island.

Among those who have taken inspiration or rest here are Horatio Nelson, Jane Austen, George Eliot, JMW Turner, Beatrix Potter and Roald Dahl. The artist Augustus John was born here, and he and his sister Gwen lived here during their early life.

Tenby

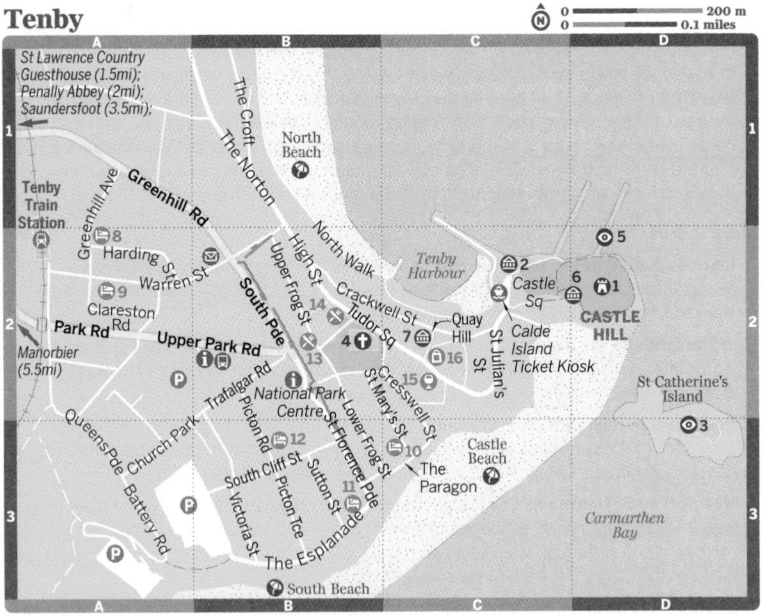

Sights

St Mary's Church CHURCH

(www.stmaryschurchtenby.co.uk; High St) The graceful arched ceiling at the centre of this 13th-century triple-naved church is studded with fascinating wooden bosses, mainly dating from the 15th century and carved into flowers, cheeky faces, mythical beasts, fish and even a mermaid holding a comb and mirror. There's a memorial here to Robert Recorde, the 16th-century writer and mathematician who invented the 'equals' sign, and an eerie cadaver-topped tomb intended to remind the viewer of their own mortality.

The young Henry Tudor (later to become King Henry VII) was hidden here before fleeing to Brittany. It's thought he left via a tunnel into the cellars under Mayor Thomas White's house across the road.

Tudor Merchant's House HISTORIC BUILDING

(NT; ☎01834-842279; www.nationaltrust.org.uk; Quay Hill; adult/child £5/2.50; ⏰11am-5pm Wed-Mon Easter-Jul, Sep & Oct, daily Aug, Sat & Sun Nov-Easter) This handsomely restored 15th-century town house is set up as it would have been in its heyday, with colourful wall hangings, period-style beds and kitchen implements. The curators have drawn the line at recreating the scent of the open cesspit next to the kitchen though.

Tenby

Sights

1 Castle Hill D2
2 Laston House C2
3 St Catherine's Island D3
4 St Mary's Church B2
5 Tenby Lifeboat Station D2
6 Tenby Museum & Art Gallery D2
7 Tudor Merchant's House C2

Sleeping

8 Ivy Bank A2
9 Langdon Villa Guest House A2
10 Myrtle House C3
11 Panorama B3
12 Southside B3

Eating

13 Blue Ball Restaurant B2
14 Mooring B2
Plantagenet House .... (see 7)

Drinking & Nightlife

15 Tenby House C2

Shopping

16 Caldey Abbey Shop C2

Laston House HISTORIC BUILDING

(1 Castle Sq) This unassuming building was built by William Paxton in the late 18th century to house Tenby's original saltwater baths. The Greek writing on the pediment translates as the optimistic 'The sea will wash away all the evils of man'. It's no longer open to the public.

Tenby Lifeboat Station NOTABLE BUILDING

(www.tenbyrnli.co.uk; Castle Hill; ⏰8.30am-5.30pm) FREE It's worth popping into this swanky lifeboat station to see the boat, watch footage of it being launched and learn a little about one of the UK's busiest lifeboat crews. Planned training launches are posted on noticeboards, a spectacle well worth seeing if you happen to be in town.

Castle Hill CASTLE

Separating North Beach from Castle Beach, this modest headland is capped by the scanty remains of Tenby's 11th-century Norman **castle**. On the very top is a large memorial to Prince Albert (captioned 'Albert Dda', meaning Albert the Good).

Tenby Museum & Art Gallery MUSEUM

(☎01834-842809; www.tenbymuseum.org.uk; Castle Hill; adult/child £4.95/free; ⏰10am-5pm daily Apr-Dec, Tue-Sat Jan-Mar) Housed within the ruins of Tenby's Norman castle, this museum covers the town's development from a fishing village into a 19th-century seaside resort bigger than Blackpool (summarised in a short film), with interesting exhibits ranging from delicate Roman vases to a Victorian antiquarian's study. There's also a recreated pirate's cell and a gallery including paintings by Augustus and Gwen John.

St Catherine's Island ISLAND

At low tide you can walk across the sand to little St Catherine's Island, but it's a long, cold wait if you get trapped by the tide – check tide tables in *Coast to Coast* or online, or ask at the tourist office. The Victorian fort on the island is closed to the public.

Caldey Island ISLAND

(☎01834-844453; www.caldey-island.co.uk; adult/child £12/6; ⏰Mon-Sat May-Sep, Mon-Thu Apr & Oct) Connected to Tenby by a seasonal boat service, Caldey Island is home to grey seals, sea birds and a red-topped, whitewashed monastery that houses a community of around a dozen Cistercian monks. Join a free guided tour or wander around at your own pace. Make sure you visit sandy **Priory**

DON'T MISS

PEMBROKESHIRE COAST NATIONAL PARK

Established in 1952, Pembrokeshire Coast National Park (Parc Cenedlaethol Arfordir Sir Benfro) takes in almost the entire coast and its offshore islands, as well as the moorland hills of Mynydd Preseli in the north. Pembrokeshire's sea cliffs and islands support huge breeding populations of sea birds, while seals, dolphins, porpoises and whales are frequently spotted in coastal waters.

There are three national-park information centres (in Tenby, St Davids and Newport) and the local tourist offices scattered across Pembrokeshire are well stocked with park paraphernalia. The free annual publication *Coast to Coast* (online at www.pembrokeshirecoast.org.uk) has lots of information on park attractions, a calendar of events and details of park-organised activities, including guided walks, themed tours, cycling trips, pony treks, island cruises, canoe trips and minibus tours. It's worth getting it for the tide tables alone – they're a necessity for many legs of the coast path.

Bay, the **lighthouse**, the village **museum**, the **old priory** and **St Illtyd's Church**, with its oddly shaped steeple. Inside is a stone with inscriptions in Ogham (an ancient Celtic script).

The monks live an austere life here but make various luxurious products for sale, including essential oils, soaps and perfumes that are derived from the island's wildflowers and herbs. You can buy these products on the island or in the Caldey Abbey Shop in Tenby.

Little **St Margaret's Island** at the western tip of Caldey is a nature reserve (landings are prohibited); it's home to grey seals and Wales' biggest colony of cormorants.

From Tenby, the boats to Caldey Island depart half-hourly from about 10.30am during opening days. They leave from the harbour at high tide and from Castle Beach at low tide. Tickets are sold from a **kiosk** (Castle Sq) at the harbour slipway.

Tours

Guided Tours Wales WALKING
(☎01834-845841; www.guidedtourswales.co.uk; adult/child £5/3.50, private tour £40; ⏲Mar-Oct) Marion Davies brings Tenby's history to life with a variety of guided town tours. Adults with an interest in history will get a great insight into the town's past from the Story of Tenby walk, while families will enjoy the tales of smugglers and shipwrecks on the Pirates tour, and those of fairies, apparitions and witches on the Ghost Walk.

Festivals & Events

Tenby Arts Festival PERFORMING ARTS
(☎01834-845277; www.tenbyartsfest.co.uk; ⏲late Sep) A week-long celebration in a variety of venues around town, the annual arts fest features everything from poetry readings by Caldey Island monks to sandcastle competitions. Expect classical concerts, talks on seaweed, piano recitals and Tenby's fine male voice choir in between.

Sleeping

Centre

Southside HOTEL ££
(☎01834-844355; www.southsidetenby.co.uk; Picton Rd; s/d £45/80; 📶) Rooms are spacious, comfortable and not at all chintzy at this friendly little private hotel just outside the town walls. Three of the four rooms have en suites, while the other has a private bathroom accessed from the corridor.

Myrtle House HOTEL ££
(☎01834-842508; www.myrtlehousehoteltenby.com; St Mary's St; r £70; 📶) There's an old-fashioned feel to this friendly, family-run hotel in a Georgian town house in the old part of town. Don't expect anything in the way of views, but it's well located not far from the steps leading down to Castle Beach.

Ivy Bank B&B ££
(☎01834-842311; www.ivybanktenby.co.uk; Harding St; s/d £45/66) Subtle swagged curtains, tasselled lampshades and bold floral wallpapers are the order of the day in this Victorian B&B close to the train station. Room sizes vary – some are very small – but all are cosy and comfortable, and children are welcome.

Langdon Villa Guest House B&B ££
(☎01834-849467; www.langdonguesthousetenby.co.uk; 3 Warren St; r £70; 📶) A traditional and very comfortable B&B with a variety

of rooms, Langdon Villa has tasteful decor, great breakfasts, and incredibly friendly and accommodating owners.

Panorama HOTEL **££**
(☑01834-844976; www.panoramahotel.co.uk; The Esplanade; s/d from £55/95; 🐾) The pink slice of a pastel row of town houses, this convivial, family-run hotel has eight guest rooms of various configurations, each with its own bathroom. There's a bit of peeling paint here and there, but your eyes are inevitably drawn out to sea from the front rooms anyway.

🛏 Around Tenby

St Lawrence Country Guesthouse B&B **££**
(☑01834-849727; www.stlawrencecountryguest house.co.uk; Gumfreston; r from £96; P🐾) Set in seven hectares of gardens, pasture and woodland, this tranquil B&B offers five comfortable rooms and wonderful sea views. It's located 1.5 miles west of Tenby, off the B4318. Make sure you check out the ancient church and holy well right next door.

Penally Abbey HOTEL **£££**
(☑01834-843033; www.penally-abbey.com; Penally; r from £145; P🐾🐕) Set on a hillside overlooking Carmarthen Bay, this country-house hotel is built on the site of an ancient monastery in the village of Penally, 2 miles southwest of Tenby along the A4139. The 11 bright and comfortable rooms are spread between the main house and the neighbouring coach house, and there's an impressive restaurant attached.

🍴 Eating & Drinking

Mooring CAFE **££**
(☑01834-842502; www.themooringtenby.com; 15 High St; mains breakfast £3.50-6.50, lunch £6.50-9.25, dinner £13-19; ⊙8.30am-9pm; 🐾🐕) Although it's anchored to the High St, this fresh, modern eatery drifts breezily from a daytime cafe serving comfort food (cooked breakfasts, sandwiches, bangers and mash, mac cheese) into a sophisticated bistro after dark. The coffee's good too.

Blue Ball Restaurant INTERNATIONAL **££**
(☑01834-843038; www.theblueballrestaurant.co.uk; Upper Frog St; mains £15-20; ⊙6-9pm Wed-Sat, 12.30-2.30pm Sun) Polished wood, old timber beams and exposed brickwork create a rustic atmosphere in this cosy restaurant. The menu makes good use of local produce, veering from Asian-influenced dishes to traditional Welsh faggots (offal-filled meatballs).

Plantagenet House MODERN BRITISH **£££**
(☑01834-842350; www.plantagenettenby.co.uk; Quay Hill; lunch £10-12, dinner £20-38; ⊙noon-2.30pm & 5.30-9.30pm, reduced hours winter; 🖉) Atmosphere-wise, this place instantly impresses; it's perfect for a romantic, candlelit dinner. Tucked down an alley in Tenby's oldest house, it's dominated by an immense 12th-century Flemish chimney hearth. The menu ranges from acclaimed seafood to organic beef.

Tenby House PUB
(☑01834-842000; www.tenbyhousehotel.com; Tudor Sq; ⊙10am-12.30am; 🐾) This lively pub has DJs on the weekends, and a sunny, flower-bedecked courtyard for summer afternoon sessions.

🛍 Shopping

Caldey Abbey Shop GIFTS & SOUVENIRS
(www.caldey-island.co.uk; Quay Hill; ⊙10am-4pm) Along with religious paraphernalia, this little shop sells locally made honey and jam, and essential oils, soaps and perfumes made by the monks on Caldey Island (p153).

ℹ Information

National Park Centre (☑01834-845040; www.pembrokeshirecoast.org.uk; South Pde; ⊙9.30am-5pm daily Apr-Sep, 10.30am-3.30pm Mon-Sat Oct-Mar) Information and interesting displays about Pembrokeshire Coast National Park.

Police Station (☑101; www.dyfed-powys.police.uk; Warren St)

Tourist Office (☑01437-775603; www.visit pembrokeshire.com; Upper Park Rd; ⊙9am-5pm Mon-Sat Sep-May, daily Jun-Aug)

ℹ Getting There & Away

BUS
The **bus station** (Upper Park Rd) is next to the tourist office on Upper Park Rd. There are direct buses to/from Narberth (47 minutes, 11 daily), Saundersfoot (10 minutes, hourly), Manorbier (20 minutes, hourly), Pembroke (45 minutes, hourly) and Haverfordwest (1¼ hours, hourly).

National Express (☑0871 781 8181; www.nationalexpress.com) coaches head to/from London (from £18, 6¾ hours, daily), Birmingham (£40, 5¾ hours, daily), Cardiff (£18, 2¾ hours, daily), Swansea (from £5, 1½ hours, two daily) and Pembroke (£2, 20 minutes, daily).

CAR
If you come in high season, expect to pay for parking.

TRAIN

There are direct trains to/from Newport Gwent (from £12, three hours, daily), Cardiff (from £10, 2¾ hours, daily), Swansea (£15, 1½ hours, seven daily), Narberth (£4.90, 19 minutes, nine daily) and Pembroke (£5.50, 20 minutes, nine daily).

Manorbier (Maenorbŷr)

POP 1330

Manorbier (man-er-*beer*) is a little village of leafy, twisting lanes with an impressive castle and 12th-century church nestled above a lovely sandy beach. If the beach at Manorbier gets busy, it's worth walking west along the coast path to remote and tranquil Swanlake Bay, where there is a fine stretch of sand at low tide.

Sights

Manorbier Castle CASTLE

(01834-871394; www.manorbiercastle.co.uk; adult/child £5.50/3; 10am-5pm Apr-Sep) Craggy, lichen-spotted Manorbier Castle was the birthplace of Giraldus Cambrensis (Gerald of Wales; 1146–1223), one of the country's greatest scholars and patriots. The 12th- to 19th-century castle buildings are grouped around a pretty garden. If they look familiar, it may be because they starred in the 2003 film *I Capture the Castle.*

Medieval music plays in the Great Hall and there's a murky dungeon, a smuggler's secret passage and a tableaux of wax figures in period costume – apparently rejects from Madame Tussauds in London.

King's Quoit TOMB

This simple neolithic dolmen fashioned from slabs of rock has sat here overlooking shell-shaped Manorbier Bay since around 3000 BC. The enormous capstone is supported by an earth bank and two small sidestones. To find it, head to the beach at Manorbier and turn left onto the coast path. You will see the dolmen before you round the headland.

A COTTAGE OF YOUR OWN

Pembrokeshire is blessed with a wealth of self-catering cottages that make a good base for a longer stay in the area.

Coast & Country Holidays (01239-821910; www.welsh-cottages.co.uk) Holiday accommodation in well-kept cottages throughout the area.

Coastal Cottages (01437-765765; www.coastalcottages.uk) Something to suit everyone in this huge range of Pembrokeshire cottages.

National Trust Cottages (www.nationaltrustcottages.co.uk) Lets 20 quaint and historic cottages in the county.

Welsh Country Cottages (03452-688734; www.welsh-country-cottages.co.uk) A collection of mostly rural cottages across Pembrokeshire.

Sleeping & Eating

Manorbier YHA HOSTEL £

(0800 019 1700; www.yha.org.uk; site/dm/r from £10/16/39; P) Looking like a cross between a space station and a motorway diner, this futuristic ex–Ministry of Defence building is 1.5 miles east of the village centre, close to the beach at Skrinkle Haven. It's a terrific, remote spot and the facilities are good.

Castle Inn PUB FOOD £

(01834-871268; Main St; mains £7-11; 11am-10pm;) This classic village pub has a rhododendron-shaded beer garden, a jukebox and live music on Saturday nights, as well as a decent range of pub grub.

Getting There & Away

Manorbier is 5.5 miles southwest of Tenby. It's served by bus 349, which heads to Tenby (20 minutes), Pembroke (27 minutes), Pembroke Dock (42 minutes) and Haverfordwest (1¼ hours) hourly, except on Sunday.

There's also a train station, a mile north of the village, with direct services to Swansea (£14.90, two hours, five daily), Carmarthen (£9.30, one hour, eight daily), Narberth (£7.40, 37 minutes, eight daily), Tenby (£3.20, nine minutes, nine daily) and Pembroke (£3.60, 11 minutes, nine daily).

Stackpole (Stagbwll)

The villages of Stackpole and Bosherston bookend the National Trust–run **Stackpole Estate** (NT; 01646-661359; www.nationaltrust.org.uk; dawn-dusk) FREE, a vast, formerly aristocratic property encompassing beaches, woodland and lakes. The coastline heading west from the estate is some of the most ruggedly beautiful in the entire country, with sheer cliffs dropping 50m into churning, thrashing surf. Unfortunately, much of it lies within the army's Castlemartin firing range and it's regularly closed to the public.

Sights

Stackpole Elidor Church CHURCH

This pretty little church is nestled in a wooded valley. Its earliest parts date back to the 12th century, with 14th-century vaulting in the transepts and a 6th-century memorial stone set beneath the window in the side chapel. Stackpole was the seat of the Campbells, earls of Cawdor, and the church contains elaborate effigies of Elidor de Stackpole and his wife, and Lord Cawdor, who featured in the French invasion of Fishguard.

Stackpole Quay HARBOUR

The tiny picturesque harbour of Stackpole Quay marks the point where pink and purple sandstone gives way to the massive grey limestone that dominates the South Pembrokeshire coast from here to Freshwater West. There's a large car park and a good tearoom, and in the warmer months it's possible to partake in kayaking or coasteering here. The quay itself isn't well signposted; instead look for signs pointing to the Boathouse.

Barafundle Bay BEACH

Regularly voted one of Britain's most beautiful beaches, Barafundle Bay is a scenic 10-minute walk south along the coast path from Stackpole Quay (turn right). It is a gorgeous spot but its reputation has put paid to seclusion, so on summer weekends it can get pretty crowded despite the lack of road access. Come out of high season and you may just have the whole place to yourself, though.

If you're up for more walking, follow the coast path south of the beach out onto **Stackpole Head** with its impressive cliffs and rock arches.

Bosherston Lily Ponds LAKE

FREE Criss-crossed by a network of footpaths and wooden bridges, these famous ponds are a wonderfully tranquil spot for a stroll. The lilies bloom in June and July but the surrounding woodlands are full of wildlife year-round. The ponds are home to otters, herons and more than 20 species of dragonfly, while the ruins of the manor house are inhabited by the greater horseshoe bat.

The main car park for the ponds is in Bosherston village, but walking trails connect them to Broad Haven South (30 minutes) and Barafundle Bay (1¾ hours).

Broad Haven South BEACH

A mile southeast of Bosherston village, this beautiful golden-sand beach is framed by grey limestone cliffs and pointed sea stacks. The beach was formed in the 1860s by the erection of the dam that created the Bosherston Lily Ponds.

St Govan's Chapel CHURCH

One of the most dramatic sights on this extraordinary stretch of coast is this 13th-century chapel, wedged into a slot in the cliffs, just out of reach of the sea. Steps hacked into the rock lead down through the empty shell of the structure and on to the rocks below, where there's a particularly picturesque rock arch, perpetually pounded by the waves.

The chapel is named for a 6th-century Irish preacher who, according to legend, was being pursued by pirates when the cliff conveniently opened and enfolded him, protecting him from his attackers. In gratitude he built the original chapel and lived here until his death in 586. The waters from St Govan's Well (now dried out), just below the building, were reputed to cure skin and eye complaints. St Govan's is well signposted from Bosherston and there's a car park at the top of the cliffs.

Huntsman's Leap LANDMARK

A spectacular gash in the cliffs with near-vertical walls, Huntsman's Leap is famed as one of Britain's best sea-cliff climbing locations. The sheer sides are often dotted with rock climbers and it makes a good short walk if you're in the area. Park at the St Govan's Head car park and walk west along the coast path for about 10 minutes to get here.

Elegug Stack Rocks LANDMARK

Picturesque in the extreme, these two isolated pillars of rock rise steeply from the sea. The rocks are an important nesting site for guillemots and kittiwakes, which can be seen throughout spring and early summer. Nearby is the **Green Bridge of Wales**, the biggest natural arch in the country. The access road to the Stack Rocks car park is off the B4319 between Stackpole and Castlemartin.

Sleeping & Eating

St Govan's Country Inn PUB ££

(☎01646-661311; www.stgovansinn.co.uk; Bosherston; s/d from £53/85; P 📶 🐾) This friendly village pub in sleepy Bosherston has simple, bright B&B accommodation above a

PEMBROKESHIRE ADVENTURES

With all that wild, rugged coastline it's no surprise that watersports are a big deal in Pembrokeshire. All across the region you'll find sailing, surfing, windsurfing, kite surfing, diving and kayaking operators, as well as Pembrokeshire's very own home-grown invention, **coasteering**. A combination of rock climbing, gully scrambling, cave exploration, wave riding and cliff jumping, this demanding activity is the mainstay of the local adventure-sports scene.

The notorious **Bitches** in Ramsey Sound are known as one of Britain's best white-water play spots. This tidal race offers massive whirlpools, eddies, big wave trains and stoppers, and standing waves on higher tides. It's a dangerous place to play, however, so consider hiring a guide for your first attempt. You'll find more information and safety advice at www.the-bitches.co.uk.

West Wales Watersports (☑ 01646-636642; www.surfdale.co.uk; Dale) Windsurfing, sailing and kayaking lessons for adults (per hour/half-day/day £25/65/120) and kids (£20/55/100). It also hires windsurfers (per hour/day £15/60), kayaks (£8/20), wetsuits (£5/20) and sailing dinghies (£25/85).

Outer Reef Surf School (☑ 01646-680070; www.outerreefsurfschool.com; from £35) Learn to surf at Newgale Sands or Manorbier before hitting the big breaks at Freshwater West. Stand-up paddleboarding also offered.

convivial bar decorated with hair-raising photos of rock climbs on the local sea cliffs.

Stackpole Inn PUB FOOD **££**
(☑ 01646-672324; www.stackpoleinn.co.uk; Jasons Cnr, Stackpole; mains £12-20; ⊙ noon-3pm & 6.30-11pm Sun-Fri, noon-11pm Sat; 🅿 🛜 👪) This wonderful country pub is a cosy place on a wet day, with a gas fire, beamed ceilings and whitewashed walls, while the garden is perfect for a summer's pint. However, it's the food that really draws people here – hearty, rustic dishes made from the best Welsh seasonal produce. Four simple but stylish bedrooms (single/double from £60/90) are housed in a neighbouring building.

ℹ Getting There & Away

The Coastal Cruiser (p160) stops at Stackpole Quay, Stackpole village, Bosherston and Broad Haven South, with additional stops at St Govan's Head and Elegug Stack Rocks on the weekends.

When the army's Castlemartin firing range is in use, the roads heading south to the coast at St Govan's Head and Stack Rocks, and the section of coast path that links them, are usually closed. The firing times are posted in Bosherston, or you can check online at www.gov.uk (search for Castlemartin). Keep an eye out for the red flags, which indicate that firing is taking place.

Angle

At the southern head of the Milford Haven waterway, the village of Angle feels a long way off the beaten track. The main attraction is the nearby surf beach of Freshwater West, but there's also a tiny beach in West Angle Bay that looks across the mouth of Milford Haven to St Ann's Head. The peninsula offers good coastal walks with lots of rock pools to explore.

If you're walking the coast path, consider catching the Coastal Cruiser bus from Angle to Dale to skip two grim days passing the giant oil refineries lining Milford Haven.

◉ Sights

Freshwater West BEACH
Wild and windblown, this 2-mile strand of golden sand and silver shingle backed by acres of dunes is Wales' best surf beach, sitting wide open to the Atlantic rollers. But beware – although it's great for surfing, big waves, powerful rips and quicksand make it dangerous for swimming. Lifeguards patrol the beach from mid-June to August; swim only between the flags.

If it looks familiar, it may be because it was the setting for Dobby's sad demise in *Harry Potter and the Deathly Hallows*. Keys scenes from Ridley Scott's *Robin Hood* were also filmed here.

🍷 Drinking & Nightlife

Old Point House PUB
(☑ 01646-641205; Angle Point; ⊙ noon-10pm daily Apr-Sep, Wed-Sat Mar & Oct; 🐾) Warm and welcoming but rough around the edges, this

15th-century cottage pub sits at the end of a deeply rutted road, looking out over the water and marooned by spring tides. It was partly built with shipwreck timbers, and its battered furniture, ancient navigational charts and roaring fire lend it plenty of charm.

Getting There & Away

The seasonal Coastal Cruiser (p160) bus stops at Freshwater West, Angle and West Angle Bay.

Pembroke (Penfro)

POP 7550

Pembroke is not much more than a single street of neat Georgian and Victorian houses guarded by a whopping great castle. This mighty fortress fell only once – in 1648, following a 48-day siege by Cromwell during the English Civil War. After this, the town was stripped of its encircling walls.

Nowadays more people live in Pembroke Dock, a sprawling expanse of grim housing abutting a commercial port, just down the hill from the historic town. In 1154 local traders scored a coup when a Royal Act of Incorporation made it illegal to land goods anywhere in the Milford Haven waterway except at Pembroke Dock. Between 1814 and 1926 more than 260 Royal Navy ships were built here, and the dock served as a Royal Air Force base for flying boats during WWII. Aside from a 19th-century Martello tower in the harbour, there's nothing to see down here.

Sights

★Pembroke Castle CASTLE

(☎01646-684585; www.pembroke-castle.co.uk; Main St; adult/child £6/5; ⏲10am-5pm; 👪) This spectacular and forbidding castle was the home of the earls of Pembroke for over 300 years and the birthplace of Henry VII, the first Tudor king. A fort was established here in 1093 by Arnulph de Montgomery, but most of the present buildings date from the 13th century. It's a great place for both

Pembroke

Top Sights

1 Pembroke Castle A2

Sleeping

2 Penfro C3

3 Woodbine C2

Eating

4 Food at Williams B2

5 Waterman's Arms B1

Pembroke

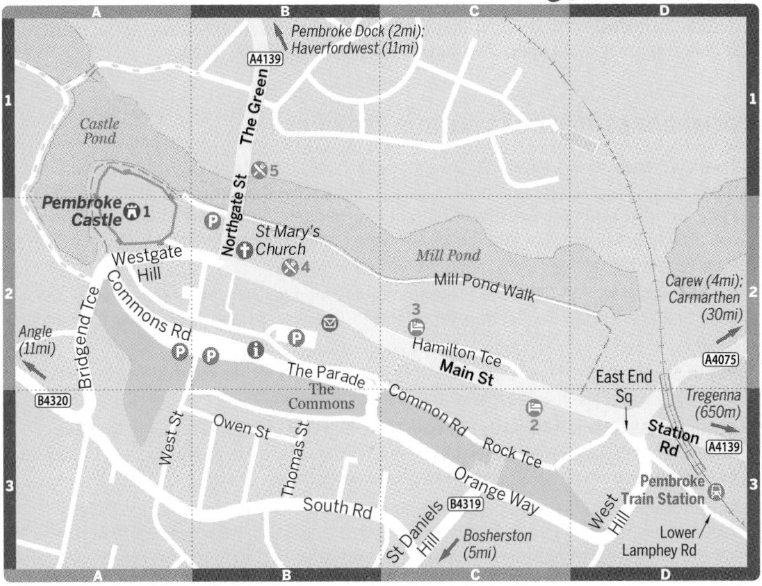

kids and adults to explore – wall walks and passages run from tower to tower, and there are vivid exhibitions detailing the castle's history.

The oldest part of the complex is the sinister, looming **keep**, completed in 1204. One hundred steps lead to the top, from where there are great views over the town. Next to the keep is the **Dungeon Tower**, where you can peer into a dank, dark prison cell. Nearby, with access through the **Northern Hall**, are steps to the creepy **Wogan Cavern**, a large natural cave that was partially walled in by the Normans and probably used as a store and boathouse.

In the room in which he is believed to have been born, in 1457, a tableau commemorates Henry Tudor (Harri Tudur), who defeated Richard III at the Battle of Bosworth Field in 1485 to become King Henry VII.

Free guided tours are offered daily; check the website for times. Falconry displays and costumed re-enactments are held in summer.

Sleeping

Centre

Woodbine B&B ££

(☎01646-686338; www.pembrokebedandbreakfast.co.uk; 84 Main St; s/d from £50/65; 📶) This well-kept, forest-green Georgian town house presents a smart face to Pembroke's main drag. The three pretty guest rooms are tastefully furnished, with original fireplaces and contemporary wallpaper. Two have en suites, while the family room has its bathroom out on the corridor.

Penfro B&B ££

(☎01646-682753; www.pembroke-bed-and-breakfast.co.uk; 111 Main St; s/d from £65/75) Austerely elegant from the outside, this large Georgian town house is a delight inside, retaining many of its original 18th-century features, including 250-year-old glass, Georgian wood panelling, moulded plaster ceilings and period fireplaces. Rooms are not en suite, as the owner has chosen not to destroy original features.

Around Pembroke

Tregenna B&B ££

(☎01646-621525; www.tregennapembroke.co.uk; 7 Upper Lamphey Rd; s/d £50/65; P📶) If your image of B&Bs is tainted by creaky-floored, chintz-filled cottages run by cranky empty-nesters, prepare to have it challenged by this large, friendly, modern establishment on the eastern edge of Pembroke. Each of the five guest rooms has its own bathroom and there's a large sun-filled breakfast room at the rear.

Lovesgrove HOTEL ££

(☎01646-687514; www.lovesgrove.com; A477, Bangeston Hall; s/d from £65/75; P📶) Is it a small hotel, a large B&B or an upmarket motel? Whatever label you settle on, Lovesgrove is a handsome choice, with 12 large, modern rooms and a rural setting on the main road east of Pembroke Dock.

PEMBROKESHIRE COASTAL BUS SERVICES

The hiker's best friend, Pembrokeshire's coastal buses operate on four main routes three times a day in each direction from May to September. For the remainder of the year the Puffin Shuttle, Strumble Shuttle and Poppit Rocket operate two services a day on Thursday and Saturday only. For timetables, see www.pembrokeshiregreenways.co.uk or pick up a copy of the national park's *Coast to Coast* magazine.

Coastal Cruiser (364/388/387) Loops around Pembroke Dock, Pembroke, Freshwater East, Stackpole Quay, Bosherston, Broad Haven, St Govan's Head, Freshwater West and Angle.

Puffin Shuttle (400) Heads between St Davids and Martin's Haven, stopping in Solva, Newgale, Broad Haven, Little Haven and Marloes.

Strumble Shuttle (404) Heads between Fishguard and St Davids, calling at Goodwick, Strumble Head, Tregwynt Woollen Mill, Trefin, Porthgain and Abereiddi. The first bus of the day starts from Newport and the last terminates there.

Poppit Rocket (405) Heads between Fishguard and Cardigan. Stops include Pwllgwaelod, Newport, Moylgrove, Poppit Sands and St Dogmaels. From October to April it only covers the stops between Newport and Cardigan.

WORTH A TRIP

CAREW

This pretty little village situated on the tidal reaches of the River Carew between Tenby and Pembroke is completely dominated by its imposing castle. It's a pretty slice of rural Wales, with a few fascinating historic sights to explore.

Looming romantically over the River Carew, its gaping windows reflected in the glassy water, the craggy **Carew Castle** (☎01646-651782; www.carewcastle.com; adult/child £4/3, incl mill £5/3.50; ⏲10am-5pm Apr-Oct, 11am-3pm Nov-Mar; P) is an impressive sight. The rambling limestone ruins range from functional 12th-century fortifications to Elizabethan country house, and there are plenty of towers, wall walks and dank basements to explore. A summer program of events includes archery, falconry, battle re-enactments and open-air theatre. Also in summer, a combined ticket can be purchased, which allows admission to the castle's **Tidal Mill**.

The castle was built by Gerald de Windsor (Henry I's constable of Pembroke) and his wife, the wonderfully named Princess Nest (daughter of the Welsh king of Deheubarth), on the site of an ancient Celtic fort. Abandoned in 1690, it's now inhabited by a large number of bats, including the protected greater horseshoe variety.

The mill at the castle is the only intact mill of this kind in Wales. The incoming tide would be trapped in a pond, which was then released through sluice gates to turn the waterwheels. For 400 years until 1937, the mill ground corn for the castle community, although the present building only dates from the early 19th century.

Near the castle entrance is the 11th-century **Carew Cross**. Covered in intricate Celtic carvings and standing 4m tall, it's one of the grandest of its kind.

Eating

★ **Food at Williams** CAFE £

(☎01646-689990; www.foodatwilliams.co.uk; 18 Main St; mains £5-8.50; ⏲9am-4.30pm Mon-Sat, 10am-3pm Sun; 📶) Pop into this bright and cheerful cafe in the morning for a cooked breakfast or in the afternoon for a glass of wine and Welsh cheese platter on the terrace.

Waterman's Arms PUB FOOD ££

(☎01646-682718; www.watermansarmspembroke.co.uk; 2 The Green; mains £8-18; ⏲noon-11pm; 🖊) The Waterman's crowd-pleasing menu includes the likes of lamb shanks, burgers, steaks, curries and giant Yorkshire puddings laden with meat and gravy. The outdoor terrace is a suntrap on a summer afternoon, with fine views across the Mill Pond to the castle. There's often live music on the weekends.

Information

Tourist Office (☎01437-776454; www.visitpembrokeshire.com; Library, Commons Rd; ⏲10am-5pm Mon-Wed, Fri & Sat, to 7pm Thu Apr-Oct, 11am-5pm Tue, Thu & Fri, to 1pm Sat Nov-Mar)

Getting There & Away

BOAT

Irish Ferries (☎08717 300 500; www.irishferries.com; car & driver from £74) has two sailings a day on the four-hour route between Pembroke Dock and Rosslare in the southeast of Ireland.

BUS

There are direct buses to/from Tenby (45 minutes, hourly), Manorbier (27 minutes, hourly), Pembroke Dock (10 minutes, half-hourly) and Haverfordwest (29 minutes, half-hourly). The seasonal Coastal Cruiser loops in both directions between Pembroke, Angle, Freshwater West, Bosherston and Stackpole, terminating at Pembroke Dock.

National Express (☎0871 781 8181; www.nationalexpress.com) coaches head to/from London (from £26, seven hours, daily), Birmingham (£40, six hours, daily), Cardiff (£18, 3½ hours, daily), Swansea (£8, two hours, two daily) and Tenby (£2, 20 minutes, daily).

TRAIN

Trains stop in both Pembroke and Pembroke Dock. There are direct services to/from Newport Gwent (from £12, 3½ hours, daily), Cardiff (from £10, 3¼ hours, daily), Swansea (£15, two hours, seven daily), Narberth (£8.40, 48 minutes, eight daily) and Tenby (£5.50, 20 minutes, nine daily).

1

IAN WOOLCOCK / SHUTTERSTOCK ©

2

1. Saundersfoot (p150)
The beach town's harbour was originally built to transport coal.

2. Carreg Samson (p175)
An ancient dolmen in a farmer's field, overlooking Strumble Head.

3. St Govan's Chapel (p157)
A 13th-century chapel wedged into the cliffs near Stackpole.

4. Pembrokeshire Coast Path (p151)
Clifftops and beaches dominate this spectacular long-distance route.

4

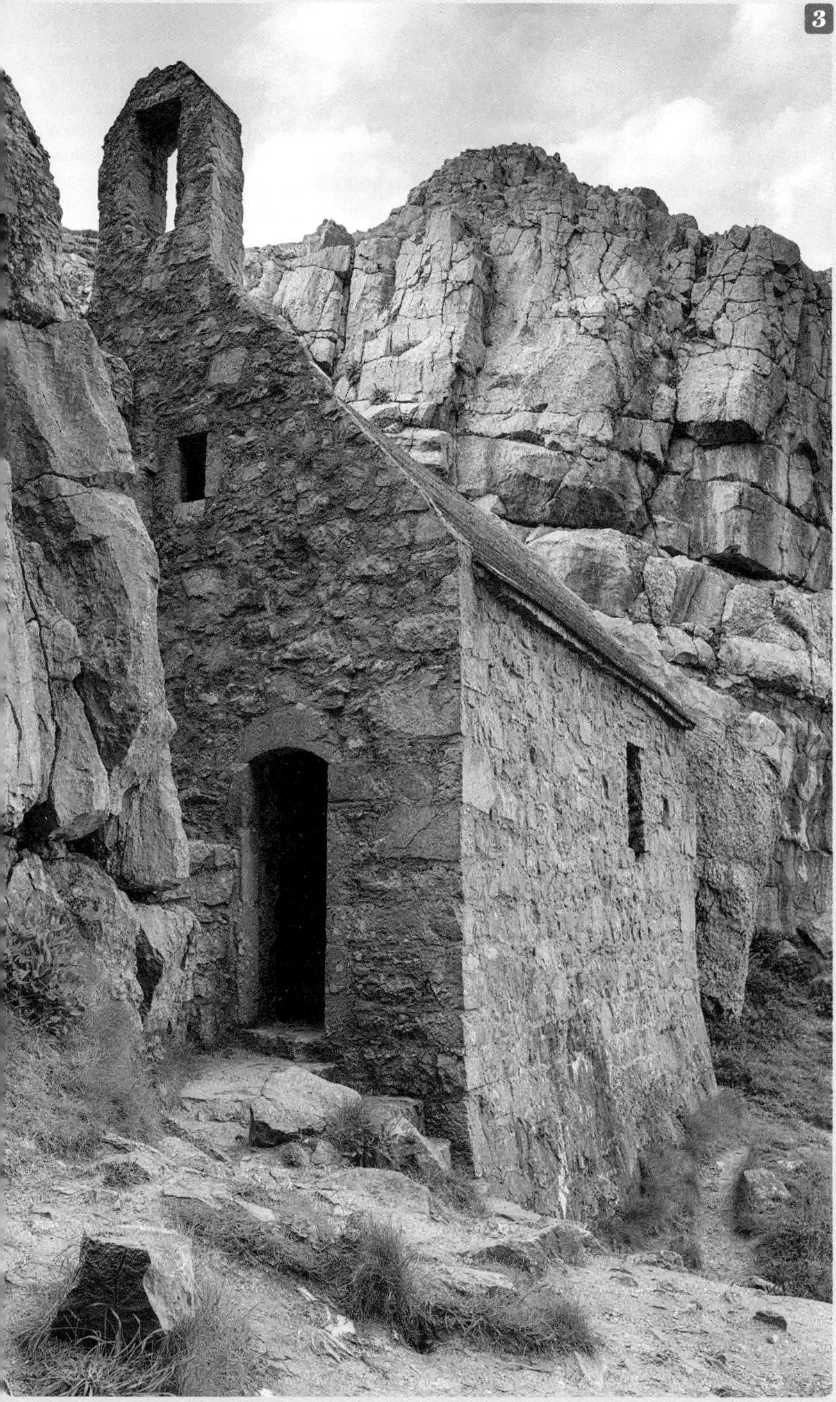

HELEN HOTSON / SHUTTERSTOCK ©

Narberth (Arberth)

POP 1930

An arty little town full of independent shops, cafes, restaurants and galleries, Narberth is a gem. Despite being light on specific sights, it's well worth a stop en route west for its lively vibe, passion for food and thriving retail scene. Somehow managing to beat the economic odds, butchers, delis, antique shops and boutiques line the streets. There's also a friendly food festival in September, a ruined Norman castle and an interesting town hall with a double stairway.

Sights

Narberth Museum MUSEUM

(☎01834-860500; www.narberthmuseum.co.uk; Church St; adult/child £3.50/2; ⏲10am-5pm Wed-Sat) Housed in a wonderfully atmospheric restored bonded-stores building, this whizbang museum celebrates the rich history of Narberth and the surrounding area. You can learn about medieval siege warfare and Narberth Castle through models and interactive games; walk historic streets and visit the shops; or listen to Welsh folk stories in the story-telling chair.

There are lots of hands-on activities and dressing-up for children, as well as a well-stocked museum shop with interesting local crafts. It also doubles as Narberth's tourist office.

Festivals & Events

Narberth Food Festival FOOD & DRINK

(www.narberthfoodfestival.com; ⏲Sep) A wonderful celebration of Welsh produce, fine food, good wine and the joy of cooking, this small but incredibly friendly weekend festival offers everything from master classes and tutored tastings to free cookery demonstrations, workshops and talks, alongside food stalls, live music, street theatre and children's activities.

Sleeping

★ **Max & Caroline's** GUESTHOUSE £

(☎01834-861835; www.maxandcarolines.com; 2a St James St; s/d £40/60; Wi-Fi) Why bother serving breakfast when you're situated directly above Narberth's best cafe? That's the philosophy at this excellent family-run guesthouse, and it means that its two handsomely furnished guest rooms can be rented a little more cheaply than you'd otherwise expect for the high standards on offer.

Canaston Oaks HOTEL ££

(☎01437-541254; www.canastonoaks.co.uk; Canaston Bridge; r/ste from £113/122; P Wi-Fi) Set alongside a working farm 3 miles west of Narberth (near the intersection of the A40 and A4075), this mini-hotel has eight en suite rooms positioned around a Celtic-cross-shaped garden. The larger rooms have spa baths. Expect hearty breakfasts and charming Welsh hospitality.

★ **Grove** HOTEL £££

(☎01834-860915; www.thegrove-narberth.co.uk; Molleston; r from £189, 3-course lunch/dinner £29/59; ⏲restaurant noon-2.30pm & 6-9.30pm; P Wi-Fi) A truly magical place to stay, this luxurious country house hotel is secluded south of Narberth, surrounded by manicured lawns, mature trees and wildflower meadows. The sumptuous rooms blend period character with contemporary style, while the renowned restaurant is Pembrokeshire's finest, serving a creative menu of modern Welsh cuisine.

Eating

Narberth's town centre offers an excellent array of eateries, and nearby hotel Grove houses our favourite Pembrokeshire restaurant.

Plum Vanilla CAFE £

(☎01834-862762; www.plumvanilla.com; 2a St James' St; mains £6-12; ⏲9am-5pm Mon-Sat) Adorned with technicolor chandeliers and vividly painted walls, this friendly little bohemian cafe has a loyal local clientele who flock here for the cooked breakfasts, homemade soups, interesting salads, luscious desserts and daily specials. Be prepared to wait for a table at lunchtime.

Ultracomida SPANISH £

(☎01834-861491; www.ultracomida.co.uk; 7 High St; tapas £4-6.50; ⏲10am-6pm Mon-Sat) The aroma of cured meats, fine cheeses, olives and freshly baked bread greets you as you walk in the door of this wonderful little deli and cafe. Stock up on supplies for a gourmet picnic or tuck into the delicious tapas.

Dragon Inn PUB FOOD ££

(☎01834-860257; www.thedragonnarberth.com; Water St; mains £8-12; ⏲11am-11pm) Stone walls, slab floors and low ceilings all hint at the venerable age of this old village pub. While seafood is the chef's speciality, it's hard to go past the slow-roasted beef with all the trimmings for Sunday lunch.

Entertainment

Queen's Hall PERFORMING ARTS

(☎01834-861212; www.thequeenshall.org.uk; High St) Narberth's artsy image is given full expression in this vibrant venue, which incorporates a gallery and a cafe. If it's music you love, any given month's roster might include jazz, pop or hip-hop. It also hosts theatre, dance, a regular comedy club and DJ nights.

Shopping

Giddy Aunt VINTAGE

(☎01834-861335; www.giddyauntclothes.co.uk; 11 Market Sq; ⏲10.30am-5pm Tue-Sat) There's nothing musty or moth-eaten about the kooky-cool threads on sale at this cute little boutique, proud winner of the UK National Vintage Awards 2015. Along with recycled clothing and an interesting assortment of mid-century homewares, it also tailors 'bespoke retro' clothes using vintage-style prints; think flirty rockabilly frocks and extremely loud men's shirts.

Getting There & Around

Bus destinations include Carmarthen (37 minutes, three daily), Saundersfoot (34 minutes, 10 daily), Tenby (47 minutes, 11 daily), Haverfordwest (24 minutes, hourly) and Cardigan (£4.05, one hour, three daily).

There are direct trains to/from Newport Gwent (from £12, 2¾ hours, daily), Cardiff (from £10, 2½ hours, two daily), Swansea (from £15, 1¼ hours, eight daily), Tenby (£4.90, 19 minutes, nine daily) and Pembroke (£8.40, 48 minutes, eight daily).

Haverfordwest (Hwlffordd)

POP 12,000

A workaday town rather than a tourist hot spot, Haverfordwest is Pembrokeshire's main transport and shopping hub. Though it retains some fine Georgian buildings, many are in dire need of repair and it lacks the prettiness and historic atmosphere of most of its neighbours.

Founded as a fortified Flemish settlement by the Norman lord Gilbert de Clare in about 1110, its castle became the nucleus for a thriving market and its port remained important until the railway arrived in the mid-19th century.

Today the Riverside Quay is the main focus of activity and home to an excellent farmers market with organic and local produce stalls every Friday from 9am to 2pm.

Sights

Haverfordwest Castle CASTLE

(Castle St) The meagre ruins of Haverfordwest Castle consist of little more than three of its 13th-century walls. The castle survived an onslaught by Owain Glyndŵr in 1405, but according to one dubious local story it was abandoned by its Royalist garrison during the English Civil War, when its soldiers mistook a herd of cows for Roundheads.

Haverfordwest Town Museum MUSEUM

(☎01437-763087; www.haverfordwest-town-museum.org.uk; Castle House, Castle St; adult/child £2/free; ⏲10am-4pm Mon-Sat Easter-Oct) The museum is housed in the residence of the governor of the prison, which once stood in Haverfordwest Castle's outer ward. It was here that the unsuccessful French invasion force was incarcerated in 1797 (p177). Displays cover the town's history.

Eating

Georges CAFE ££

(☎01437-766683; www.thegeorges.uk.com; 24 Market St; mains £5.50-15; ⏲10am-5.30pm Tue-Sat; 🖉) Gargoyles on leashes guard the door of this trippy, hippy gift shop that doubles as an offbeat cafe. The Georges has cosy nooks of stained glass and candlelight, lanterns and fairy lights, along with a simple menu of home-cooked food ranging from steak to pasta to curry.

Shopping

Wickedly Welsh Chocolate Company FOOD

(☎01437-557122; www.wickedlywelsh.co.uk; Withybush Rd; ⏲10.30am-4pm Sun-Fri Easter-Oct, reduced hours other months) Set among an otherwise drab industrial estate on the northern edge of town, this purply-pink den of temptation is hard to miss and even harder to resist. All of the truffles, Easter eggs and other sweet goodies are made on site, and in the warmer months there are chocolate-making demonstrations twice a day. It also has a choc-heavy cafe.

Information

Haverfordwest Library & Information Centre
(☎01437-775244; www.visitpembrokeshire.com; off Dew St; ⏲10am-5pm Mon, Wed & Fri, to 7pm Tue, to 1pm Sat)

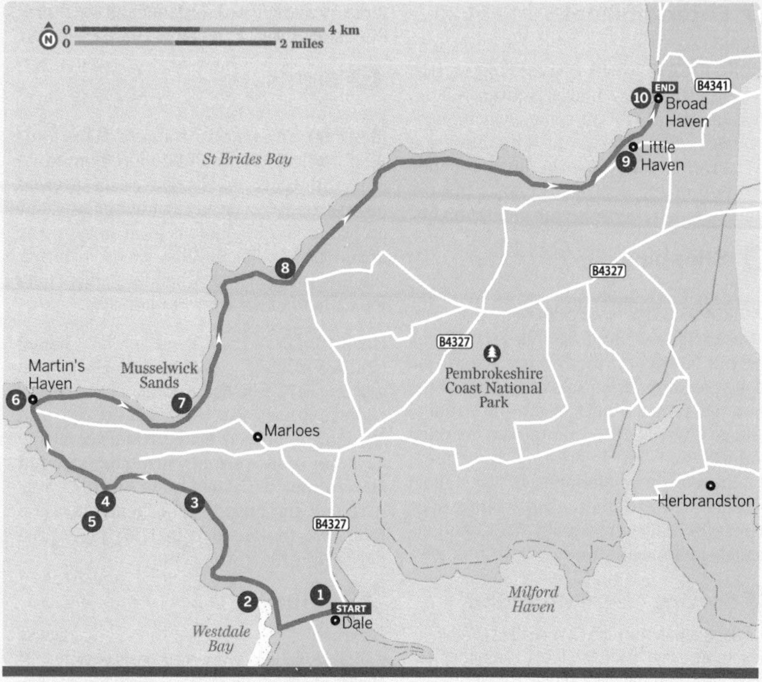

Coastal Walk
Dale to Broad Haven

START DALE
END BROAD HAVEN
LENGTH 15.4 MILES; SIX HOURS

A wonderful but not too challenging walk along dramatic clifftops, this section of the Pembrokeshire Coast Path (PCP) is close to villages, bus routes and road access points, making it ideal for more leisurely walking but, particularly in midsummer, potentially busier than more remote sections of the path.

Start at 1 **Dale** and cut across country to pick up the Coast Path in 2 **Westdale Bay**. As you head up around the northern headland you'll skirt a disused WWII airfield before reaching the long curving stretch of beach at 3 **Marloes Sands**. At the end of the beach you'll pass 4 **Gateholm Island**, a major Iron Age Celtic settlement where the remains of 130 hut circles have been found. Although the island appears accessible at low tide, it is surrounded by slippery jagged rocks and steep cliffs. Walk on, though, and you'll soon pass the earthwork ramparts of a 5 **promontory fort**. Atlantic storms batter this section of coast and active erosion threatens the sheer red cliffs streaked with yellow algae.

Continue on, enjoying views over Skomer and Skokholm islands, to 6 **Martin's Haven**. This tiny harbour is the base for Skomer Island boat trips and the office of the Skomer Marine Nature Reserve, which has an interesting display on the underwater environment. Set into the wall next to the office is a Celtic cross, which may date from the 7th century.

Around the headland the cliffs change from red to black, and after an hour you'll reach the lovely beach at 7 **Musselwick Sands**. There are fine views over St Brides Bay and across to St Davids and Ramsey Island. 8 **St Brides Haven** is a further 2 miles down the track, with the headland dominated by a Victorian faux-castle.

A reasonably easy 5-mile stretch leads to 9 **Little Haven**, a pretty village with restaurants and B&Bs. It's separated by a rocky headland from 10 **Broad Haven**; from the path you'll be able to assess the tide and decide whether to follow the busy road or cross via the beach.

Police Station (☎101; www.dyfed-powys.police.uk; Merlin's Hill)

Withybush General Hospital (☎01437-764545; www.wales.nhs.uk; Fishguard Rd)

Getting There & Away

Direct buses head to Tenby (1¼ hours, hourly), Pembroke (29 minutes, half-hourly), St Davids (£3.30, 40 minutes, 10 daily), Carmarthen (58 minutes, three daily) and Aberystwyth (£6, 3¼ hours, eight daily).

National Express (☎0871 781 8181; www.nationalexpress.com) coaches head to/from Tenby (£3.20, 50 minutes, daily), Swansea (from £6, 2½ hours, twice daily), Cardiff (from £18, four hours, daily), Birmingham (from £40, 6½ hours, daily) and London (from £22, 7½ hours, daily).

There are direct trains to/from Newport Gwent (from £12, three hours, five daily), Cardiff (from £10, 2½ hours, eight daily), Swansea (£16, 1½ hours, eight daily), Llanelli (£16, one hour, eight daily) and Carmarthen (£9.50, 37 minutes, eight daily).

Skomer, Skokholm & Grassholm Islands

The rocky islands that lie in the turbulent, tide-ripped waters at the south end of St Brides Bay form one of the richest wildlife environments in Britain. In the nesting season, Skomer and Skokholm Islands are home to more than half a million sea birds, including guillemots, razorbills, puffins, storm petrels and a significant colony of Manx shearwaters. These unusual birds nest in burrows and after a day spent feeding at sea return to their nests under the cover of darkness. Grey seals are also plentiful on Skomer, especially in the pupping season (September).

Eleven miles offshore, Grassholm Island has one of the largest gannet colonies in the northern hemisphere, with 39,000 breeding pairs. Landing is not permitted.

Tours

Dale Sailing BOATING

(☎01646-603123; www.pembrokeshire-islands.co.uk; ⏲10am, 11am & noon Tue-Sun Easter-Sep) Heads to Skomer (adult/child £11/7) on a first-come, first-served basis, departing from Martin's Haven. If you go ashore, there's an additional landing fee (£10/5). Other options include one-hour round-the-island trips (£12/8), and an evening cruise (£16/10) that offers the opportunity to see (and hear – the noise can be deafening) the huge flocks of Manx shearwaters returning to their nests.

It also runs three-hour, round-the-island trips to Grassholm (£35), two-hour Historic Haven cruises (adult/child £20/10) and a series of 'sea safaris' on high-speed rigid inflatable boats. There are no day trips to Skokholm, but Dale Sailing lands on the island twice a week (£28 return).

Sleeping

Skomer Bunkhouse HOSTEL ££

(☎01656-724100; www.welshwildlife.org; dm/s/d £45/90/120; ⏲Easter-Sep) For avid birdwatchers, the Wildlife Trust has basic but comfortable bunkhouse accommodation on Skomer. It's a great way to enjoy the isolation and tranquillity of the island after the day trippers have left; book well ahead. It also runs a similar house on Skokholm, although boats travel there less frequently, so you'll need to commit to a three- or four-night stay.

Getting There & Away

The Puffin Shuttle (p160) heads to Martin's Haven, which is where the island cruises depart from.

Little & Broad Havens

Tucked into the southern corner of St Brides Bay, these two beaches are joined at low tide but separated by a rocky headland otherwise. Little Haven is the upmarket neighbour, with a tiny shingle beach and a village vibe formed by a cluster of pastel-painted holiday cottages and some nice pubs. The beach is both bigger and better at Broad Haven, backed by tearooms, gift shops, and places selling rubber rings, water wings and body boards.

Activities

Haven Sports WATER SPORTS

(☎01437-781354; www.havensports.co.uk; Marine Rd, Broad Haven; ⏲10am-5pm) Haven Sports, at the south end of the prom behind the Galleon Inn, rents wetsuits (per hour/day £3/15), body boards (£3/15), surfboards (£5/20) and kayaks (£6/30).

West Wales Dive Company DIVING

(☎01646-278260; www.westwalesdivers.co.uk; Broad Haven; guided dives per day from £50) Offers PADI dive courses and, for certified divers, guided boat and shore dives.

Sleeping

Broad Haven YHA HOSTEL £

(☎0800 019 1700; www.yha.org.uk; dm from £16, r with/without bathroom £65/59; ⊙Apr-Oct; P@⊜) This excellent purpose-built, well-kept hostel is close to the beach and has wonderful sea views from its dining room and deck. It closes completely in winter and only opens on weekends outside of the busiest months.

Mill Haven Place CAMPSITE £

(☎01437-781633; www.millhavenplace.co.uk; Talbenny; yurt weekend/week from £175/390, cottage per week £300-975) This charming campground is decked out with bunting, brightly coloured tablecloths, solar-powered fairy lights and paper lanterns, and there's a small beach and plenty of rock pools nearby. Only Camping & Caravanning Club members can pitch a tent here, but there are five well-equipped yurts and three self-catering cottages for hire. Talbenny is 1.4 miles west of Little Haven.

Getting There & Away

The 311 bus connects Broad Haven with Haverfordwest (20 minutes, six daily except Sunday). The seasonal Puffin Shuttle (p160) stops in both Little and Broad Havens.

Newgale (Niwgwl)

Newgale is the biggest beach in St Brides Bay, stretching for 2.5 miles and backed with a massive bank of pebbles. It's a good spot for beginner surfers, particularly on an incoming tide. As you pass over the bridge by the pub near the north end of Newgale, you're officially crossing the Landsker Line into North Pembrokeshire.

Activities

Newsurf WATER SPORTS

(☎01437-721398; www.newsurf.co.uk; ⊙10am-4pm Sat & Sun Jan-Mar, 9am-5pm Mon-Fri, to 8pm Sat & Sun Apr-Dec) Hires surfboards (£5/15 per hour/day), wetsuits (£4/12) and kayaks (£10/25 per two hours/day), and offers 2½-hour group surfing lessons (£35), and four-hour kayak tours (£58) as well as coasteering (£45).

Sleeping & Eating

Accommodation is limited, but there are rooms at the pub and a campsite right next door. Plus there are further options inland at Roch and Penycwm.

Ty Coed De B&B ££

(☎01437-711340; www.tycoedde.co.uk; A487, Roch; s/d from £40/70; P⊜) A mile up the hill on the road to Roch, this friendly little B&B has three clean and comfortable but thin-walled en suite rooms in a little cottage set on the edge of farmland. Served in the conservatory, the excellent breakfast selection is accompanied by views over the fields and out to sea. The sunsets here are spectacular.

OFF THE BEATEN TRACK

CYCLING THE CELTIC TRAIL

The Celtic Trail (National Cycle Network Route 4; www.sustrans.org.uk) is arguably the best cycle touring route in South Wales, taking in large sections of Pembrokeshire Coast National Park and passing in the shadow of numerous imposing castles. Starting in Fishguard, it follows a mixture of off-road coastal paths, riverside trails, old railway lines and quiet lanes on its way to Chepstow, 220 miles away.

The main route shadows the coast southwest from Fishguard, passing through St Davids and Broad Haven before cutting inland to skirt Haverfordwest and then veering down through Pembroke, Tenby and Saundersfoot. Leaving Pembrokeshire and entering Carmarthenshire, there's an optional diversion to Laugharne before the route cuts up to Carmarthen. It then meanders south through Kidwelly to Llanelli and on to Swansea. From here it skirts the bottom of the valleys and passes through Caerphilly and Newport before arriving in Chepstow.

In several towns along the way it intersects with National Route 47, offering a high-country alternative route with more traffic-free cycling.

The Celtic Trail is best ridden from west to east to make use of the prevailing westerly winds and is generally broken into six days' riding.

THE LANDSKER LINE

The Landsker Line takes its name from a Norse word for frontier. It marks the edge of the lands conquered by the Normans in West Wales in the 11th century. The south of Pembrokeshire became Anglicised (roughly the area below the A40 highway), leaving the north a bastion of Welsh identity.

Asheston Eco Barns CABIN ££
(☎01348-831781; www.eco-barns.co.uk; Penycwm; per week from £740) A collection of five stylishly converted two- to three-bedroom barns sleeping four to seven people. They're located 3 miles inland from Newgale's beach.

Duke of Edinburgh PUB FOOD ££
(☎01437-720586; mains £6-14; ⏰noon-3pm & 6-9pm; P 📶) Although on the face of it the menu at Newgale's beachfront boozer reads as pub-grub-by-numbers (fish and chips, chicken tikka, gammon steak etc), the burgers and hot chips are surprisingly good, and everything comes with a mountain of salad or coleslaw.

Getting There & Away

Both the Puffin Shuttle (p160) and bus 411 between St Davids, Solva and Haverfordwest (10 daily except Sunday) stop here.

NORTH PEMBROKESHIRE

The Welsh language may not be as ubiquitous in North Pembrokeshire as it once was but there's no escaping the essential Welshness of the region. It's a land of Iron Age hill forts, holy wells and Celtic saints – including the nation's patron, Dewi Sant (St David). Predating even the ancient Celts are the remnants of an older people, who left behind them dolmens and stone circles – the same people who may have transported their sacred bluestones all the way from the Preseli Hills to form the giant edifice at Stonehenge. Much of the coastline from St Davids onwards is inaccessible by car. If you're only going to walk part of the Pembrokeshire Coast Path (PCP; p151), this is an excellent section to tackle.

Solva (Solfach)

POP 865

With its colourfully painted cottages, art galleries and inviting pubs, Solva is a North Pembrokeshire gem. Lower Solva sits at the head of a peculiar L-shaped harbour, where the water drains away completely at low tide leaving its flotilla of yachts tilted on the sand. Clifftop walks provide wonderful views over the village and surrounding coastline.

Sights & Activities

Solva Woollen Mill HISTORIC BUILDING
(☎01437-721112; www.solvawoollenmill.co.uk; Middle Mill; ⏰9.30am-5.30pm Mon-Fri Oct-Jun, 9.30am-5.30pm Mon-Sat, 2-5.30pm Sun Jul-Sep) FREE It's a pleasant walk of just over a mile upriver from Solva to Middle Mill, where you'll find the oldest working woollen mill in Pembrokeshire. You can see the weavers at work, browse in the shop, or enjoy tea and cake in the cafe.

Solva Sailboats BOATING
(☎01437-720972; www.solvasailboats.co.uk; Trinity Quay; sailing per 3 people 3hr/5hr/day £90/130/170, tour adult/child £15/10) Set sail in a 9m yacht or take an hour-long coastal tour in a powerboat. It also offers a water-taxi service within St Brides Bay and dinghy sailing courses.

Sleeping & Eating

Haroldston House B&B ££
(☎01437-721404; www.haroldstonhouse.co.uk; 29 High St; r £80-90; P 📶) Set in a lovely old Georgian merchant's house, this wonderful B&B offers chic modern style. The simple but tastefully decorated rooms feature art by owner Ian McDonald as well as other Welsh or Wales-based artists. There's a free electric-car charging point, discounts for guests arriving by public transport, and tasty, inventive breakfast options.

Cambrian Inn PUB FOOD ££
(☎01437-721210; www.thecambrianinn.co.uk; 6 Main St; mains £11-21, s/d £70/95; ⏰noon-3pm & 6-9pm; ✍) The Cambrian Inn blends old and new with exposed stonework and original beams but a decidedly contemporary style. It serves an interesting menu of upmarket pub classics, including meat pies, steaks, seafood and delicious gourmet burgers (try

the Fat Cow). It also has five bright and colourful guest rooms upstairs, and others in a neighbouring building.

Getting There & Away

Both the Puffin Shuttle (p160) and bus 411 between Haverfordwest and St Davids stop here. Alternatively, you can walk along the coast path from St Davids and then bus it back. Join the coast path at Caerfai Bay (signposted from Oriel y Parc), then pick up the eastbound path. It's about 5 miles in total.

St Davids (Tyddewi)

POP 1840

Charismatic St Davids (yes, it has dropped the apostrophe from its name) is Britain's smallest city, its status ensured by the magnificent 12th-century cathedral that marks Wales' holiest site. The birth and burial place of the nation's patron saint, St Davids has been a place of pilgrimage for 1500 years.

The setting itself has a mystical presence. The sea is just beyond the horizon on three sides, so you're constantly surprised by glimpses of it at the ends of streets. Then there are those strangely shaped hills in the distance, sprouting from an ancient landscape.

Today St Davids attracts hordes of non-religious pilgrims too, drawn by the town's laid-back vibe and the excellent hiking, surfing and wildlife-watching in the surrounding area.

History

Dewi Sant (St David) founded a monastic community here in the 6th century, only a short walk from where he was born at St Non's Bay. In 1124 Pope Callistus II declared that two pilgrimages to St Davids were the equivalent of one to Rome, and three were equal to one to Jerusalem. The cathedral has seen a constant stream of visitors ever since.

Sights

City Centre

★ **St David's Cathedral** CATHEDRAL

(www.stdavidscathedral.org.uk; suggested donation £3, tours £4; ⌚8.30am-6pm Mon-Sat, 12.45-5.30pm Sun) Hidden in a hollow and behind high walls, St David's Cathedral is intentionally unassuming. The valley site was chosen in the vain hope that the church would be overlooked by Viking raiders, but it was ransacked at least seven times. Yet once you pass through the gatehouse separating it from the town and its stone walls come into view, it's as imposing as any of its contemporaries.

Built on the site of a 6th-century chapel, the building dates mainly from the 12th to the 14th centuries. Extensive works were carried out in the 19th century by Sir George Gilbert Scott (architect of London's Albert Memorial and St Pancras) to stabilise the building. The distinctive **west front**, with its four pointed towers of purple stone, dates from this period.

The atmosphere inside is one of great antiquity. As you enter the **nave**, the oldest surviving part of the cathedral, the first things you'll notice are the sloping floor and the outward lean of the massive, purplish-grey pillars linked by semicircular Norman Romanesque arches, a result of subsidence. Above is a richly carved 16th-century oak ceiling, adorned with pendants.

At the far end of the nave is a delicately carved 14th-century Gothic **pulpitum** (screen), which bears a statue of St David dressed as a medieval bishop, and contains the tomb of Bishop Henry de Gower (died 1347), for whom the Bishop's Palace was built.

Beyond the pulpitum is the magnificent **choir**. Check out the mischievous carved figures on the 16th-century misericords (under the seats), one of which depicts pilgrims being seasick over the side of a boat. Don't forget to look up at the colourfully painted lantern tower above (those steel tie rods around the walls were installed in the 19th century to hold the structure together).

Between the choir and the high altar is the object of all those religious pilgrimages – a **shrine** containing the bones of St David and St Justinian. Destroyed during the Reformation, it was restored and rededicated in 2012, adorned with five new Byzantine-style icons by artist Sara Crisp.

Accessed from the north wall of the nave, the **Treasury** displays vestments and religious paraphernalia crafted from precious metals and stones. Just as valuable are the treasures in the neighbouring **library** (entry £1), the oldest of which dates to 1505.

Towards the rear of the cathedral is the low-lit **Holy Trinity Chapel**, distinguished by a superb fan-vaulted ceiling dating from the early 16th century, and the light-filled **Lady Chapel**.

Lord Rhys ap Gruffydd, the greatest of the princes of South Wales, and his son Rhys Gryg are known to be buried in the cathedral, although their effigies in the south choir aisle date only from the 14th century. Gerald of Wales, an early rector of the cathedral, has a gravestone here, but scholars suggest he is actually buried at Lincoln Cathedral.

In August there are hour-long guided tours at 11.30am Monday and 2.30pm Friday; at other times, tours can be arranged in advance.

★St Davids Bishop's Palace RUINS

(Cadw; www.cadw.gov.wales; adult/child £3.50/2.65; ⏲9.30am-5pm Mar-Oct, 10am-4pm Nov-Feb) This atmospheric ruined palace was begun at the same time as the neighbouring cathedral, but its final, imposing Decorated Gothic form owes most to Henry de Gower, bishop from 1327 to 1347. The most distinctive feature is the arcaded parapet that runs around the courtyard, adorned with a chequer-board pattern of purple and yellow stone blocks. The corbels that support the arches are richly adorned with a menagerie of carved figures – animals, grotesque mythical creatures and human heads.

Interesting displays within the basements and ruined rooms bring each part of the palace to life. The distinctive purple sandstone, also used in the cathedral, comes from Caerbwdy Bay, a mile southeast of St Davids.

The palace courtyard provides a spectacular setting for open-air plays in summer.

★Oriel y Parc GALLERY

(Landscape Gallery; ☎01437-720392; www.orielyparc.co.uk; cnr High St & Caerfai Rd; ⏲10am-4pm) Occupying a bold, semicircular, environmentally friendly building on the edge of

St Davids

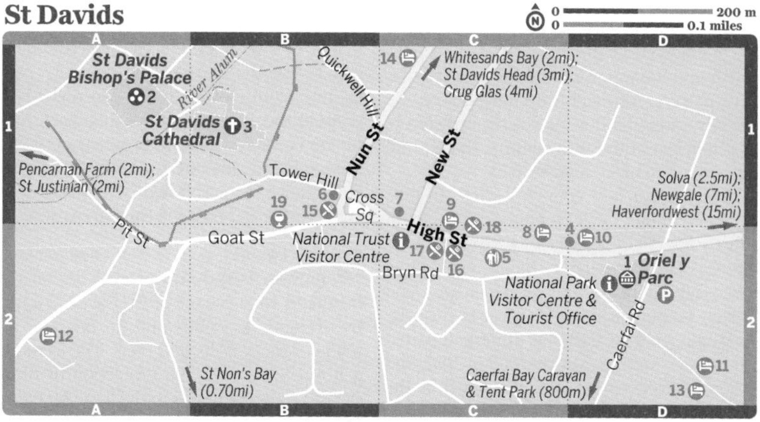

St Davids

Top Sights
1 Oriel y Parc D2
2 St Davids Bishop's Palace A1
3 St Davids Cathedral B1

Activities, Courses & Tours
4 Aquaphobia D2
5 Ma Sime's Surf Hut C2
6 Thousand Islands Expeditions B1
7 TYF Adventure C1
Voyages of Discovery (see 7)

Sleeping
8 Bryn Awel C2
9 Coach House C1
10 Grove D2
11 Moorings D2
12 Ramsey House A2
13 Tŵr y Felin D2
14 Y Glennydd C1

Eating
15 Bishops B1
16 Cwtch C2
17 Sound Cafe C2
18 St Davids Food & Wine C2

Drinking & Nightlife
19 Farmer's Arms B1

town, Oriel y Parc is a winning collaboration between the Pembrokeshire Coast National Park Authority and the National Museum Wales. Not only does it function as a tourist office and national-park visitor centre, it houses changing exhibitions from the museum's art collection. The focus is on landscapes, particularly Pembrokeshire scenes.

Around St Davids

St Non's Bay RUINS, CHURCH

Immediately south of St Davids, this ruggedly beautiful spot is named after St David's mother and traditionally accepted as his birthplace. A path leads to the 13th-century ruins of St Non's Chapel. Only the base of the walls remains, along with a stone marked with a cross within a circle, believed to date from the 7th century. Standing stones in the surrounding field suggest that the chapel may have been built within an ancient pagan stone circle.

On the approach to the ruins is a pretty little holy well. The sacred spring is said to have emerged at the moment of the saint's birth and the water is believed to have curative powers. Although pilgrimages were officially banned following the suppression of Catholicism in the 16th century, the faithful continued to make furtive visits.

The site has now come full circle. In 1935 a local Catholic, Cecil Morgan-Griffiths, built the Chapel of Our Lady & St Non out of the stones of former religious buildings that had been incorporated into local cottages and farms. Its dimensions echo those of the original chapel. The Catholic Church repaired the stone vaulting over the well in 1951, and Morgan-Griffiths' house is now used by the Passionist Fathers as a retreat centre.

Whitesands Bay BEACH

(Porth Mawr) This mile-long sandy beach is a popular surfing, swimming and strolling spot. At extremely low tide you can see the wreck of a paddle tugboat that ran aground here in 1882, and the fossil remains of a prehistoric forest. If Whitesands is really busy – and it often is – you can escape the worst of the crowds by walking north along the coastal path for 10 to 15 minutes to the smaller, more secluded beach at Porthmelgan.

Whitesands is 2 miles northwest of St Davids. If you drive, expect to pay an extortionate amount for parking (£5 even for a short stop in winter!). Otherwise catch the Celtic Coaster bus or walk, but you're well advised to stop in at the tourist office for directions.

St Davids Head AREA

This atmospheric heather-wreathed promontory was fortified by the ancient Celts. The jumbled stones and ditch of an Iron Age rampart are still visible, as are rock circles, which once formed the foundations of huts. The tip of the headland is a series of rock and turf ledges, a great place for a picnic or wildlife-spotting – in summer you can see gannets diving and choughs soaring. Adding to the ancient ambience, wild ponies can often be spotted.

Further along the grassy path, an even older structure stands. The simple burial chamber known as Coetan Arthur (Arthur's Quoit) consists of a capstone supported by a rock at one end and dates to about 3500 BC.

The rocky summit of Carn Llidi (181m) rises behind, offering panoramic views that take in Whitesands Bay, Ramsey and Skomer Islands and, on a clear day, the coast of Ireland on the horizon. Look for the remains of two neolithic chambered tombs just below the start of the concrete path leading to the lower of the two rocky outcrops at the very top. Rather than backtrack on the Coast Path, another route leads down the landward side of Carn Llidi, past Upper Porthmawr Farm, joining the main road to Whitesands just past the caravan park.

Ramsey Island BIRD SANCTUARY

Ramsey Island (Ynys Dewi) lies off the headland to the west of St Davids, ringed by dramatic sea cliffs and an offshore armada of rocky islets and reefs. The island is a Royal Society for the Protection of Birds (RSPB) reserve famous for its large breeding population of choughs – members of the crow family with glossy black feathers and distinctive red bills and legs – and for its grey seals.

You can reach the island by boat from the tiny harbour at St Justinian, 2 miles west of St Davids. Longer boat trips run up to 20 miles offshore, to the edge of the Celtic Deep, to spot whales, porpoises and dolphins. What you'll see depends on the weather and the time of year: July to September are the best months. Porpoises are seen on most trips, dolphins on four out of five, and there's a 40% chance of seeing whales. The most common species is the minke, but pilot whales, fin whales and orcas have also been spotted.

Thousand Islands Expeditions is the only operator permitted to land day trippers on the island. Voyages of Discovery, Aquaphobia and Venture Jet head out to the island but don't land there.

Activities

Thousand Islands Expeditions BOATING
(☎01437-721721; www.thousandislands.co.uk; Cross Sq; ⊙Apr-Oct) The only operator permitted by the RSPB to land day trippers on Ramsey Island (adult/child £18/8.50); it also offers 90-minute cruises around it (£25/12, including landing £38/18). Other boat trips include hour-long blasts in a high-speed inflatable boat (£25/12), 2½-hour whale- and dolphin-spotting cruises around Grassholm Island (£60/30), and one-hour jet-boat trips (£25/12). Book in advance.

Voyages of Discovery BOATING
(☎01437-721911; www.ramseyisland.co.uk; 1 High St; ⊙Easter–mid-Nov) Offers trips to the waters around Ramsey Island (adult/child £25/13), as well as 2½-hour whale- and dolphin-watching trips (adult/child £60/30) and evening birdwatching excursions (£32/19).

Aquaphobia BOATING
(☎01437-720471; www.aquaphobia-ramseyisland.co.uk; Grove Hotel, High St; ⊙Easter-Oct) Wildlife-spotting powerboat trips to the coast of Ramsey (adult/child from £25/10) and Grassholm (£50/25) islands.

Venture Jet BOATING
(☎01348-837 7764; www.venturejet.co.uk; ⊙May-Oct) Bills itself as a 'New Zealand jet, Pembrokeshire-style'. Trips range from the 90-minute Wet & Wild ride to the waters around Ramsey Island (adult/child £30/17) to a three-hour Offshore Adventure (£60/32). Most trips depart from St Justinian, but some leave from Whitesands beach in the summer school holidays.

Ma Sime's Surf Hut SURFING
(☎01437-720433; www.masimes.co.uk; 28 High St; 2hr group lesson £35; ⊙10am-5pm Easter-Oct) Rents wetsuits (£8), surfboards (£15) and body boards (£8) from both its shop in St Davids and, in the summer holidays, from the beach at Whitesands. Also runs a surf school at Whitesands from May to October.

TYF Adventure ADVENTURE
(☎01437-721611; www.tyf.com; 1 High St) Organises coasteering, surfing, sea-kayaking and rock-climbing trips from its St Davids base.

Festivals & Events

St Davids Cathedral Festival MUSIC
(www.stdavidscathedralfestival.co.uk; St David's Cathedral; ⊙May-Jun) Ten days of classical-music performances, starting on the Spring Bank Holiday weekend at the end of May. The Irish-oak ceiling gives the cathedral fine acoustics, so if you're not here for the festival it's well worth checking out one of the many other concerts performed here throughout the year.

Sleeping

City Centre

Ramsey House B&B ££
(☎01437-720321; www.ramseyhouse.co.uk; Lower Moor; tw/d £110/120; P ᯤ) The young owners have created a fashionable boutique-style B&B from their house on the outskirts of the little city. The six rooms are all different but feature bold wallpapers, matching chandeliers, silky throws, goose-down duvets and stylish bathrooms.

Moorings B&B ££
(☎01437-720876; www.waterings.co.uk; Anchor Dr; s/d from £70/90; P ᯤ) Offering more privacy than your typical B&B, the Moorings has only two rooms in the main house but a further five in an attached outbuilding opening on to the garden. The garden rooms are large and suite-like, with a semi-separated sitting area and their own external entrances. Breakfasts are excellent.

Coach House B&B ££
(☎01437-720632; www.thecoachhouse.biz; 15 High St; s/d from £70/95; ᯤ) The bright, simple rooms at the Coach House are just part of its appeal. Friendly and helpful hosts, great breakfasts and the central location all conspire to make it one of St Davids' better options.

Bryn Awel B&B ££
(☎01437-720082; www.brynawel-bb.co.uk; 45 High St; s/d £85/90; ᯤ) A pretty little terraced house on the main street, Bryn Awel has small but cosy rooms (all en suite). The owners are keen outdoors enthusiasts, and can

advise on the best local spots for walking and birdwatching.

Y Glennydd HOTEL ££
(☎01437-720576; www.glennyddhotel.co.uk; 51 Nun St; s/d from £50/75;) Decorated with maritime memorabilia, this 1880s terraced house was built to accommodate coast guard officers and has a traditional, bordering on old-fashioned, feel. Some of the 11 smallish, unfussy bedrooms have views over Whitesands, and there's a cosy lounge-bar downstairs.

Grove PUB ££
(☎01437-720341; www.grovestdavids.com; High St; r £105-120;) Offering upmarket pub accommodation, the Grove's rooms have all been refurbished, giving them a fresh, up-to-the-moment look. The downstairs rooms are particularly large and stylish, while they're simpler and smaller upstairs. Expect a bit of noise from the bar, but it's closed by midnight and rarely raucous – pack earplugs or join in.

★ **Tŵr y Felin** HOTEL £££
(☎01437-725555; www.twryfelinhotel.com; Caerfai Rd; r/ste from £160/240) Incorporating an odd circular tower that was once a windmill, this chic boutique hotel is St Davids' most upmarket option. The entire building is lathered with contemporary art, with dozens of pieces in the lounge-bar and restaurant alone. The 21 bedrooms are all luxurious, but the most spectacular is the three-level circular suite in the tower itself.

Around St Davids

St Davids YHA HOSTEL £
(☎0800 019 1700; www.yha.org.uk; Llaethdy; dm from £19, r with/without bathroom from £89/39; Apr-Sep;) If you're an enthusiastic walker or you have your own transport, this former farmhouse tucked beneath Carn Llidi, 2 miles northwest of St Davids, is a wonderful option. The cow sheds now house snug dorms and twins, and an inviting communal kitchen. En suite rooms sleep four people.

Caerfai Bay Caravan & Tent Park CAMPSITE £
(☎01437-720274; www.caerfaibay.co.uk; Caerfai Rd; 2-person sites from £16; Mar-Nov;) A 15-minute walk south of St Davids, this large campground has good facilities and exceptional views across St Brides Bay. It's set on the edge of a dairy farm, practically right on the coast path.

Pencarnan Farm CAMPSITE £
(☎01437-720580; www.pencarnanfarm.co.uk; sites per adult/child £17/6.50) Set on a large working farm with a miniature-horse stud, this campground is the most westerly in Wales. There are 60 level pitches within walking distance of an almost private beach. Kayaks and stand-up paddleboards are available for rent. The site is 2 miles from St Davids; head in the direction of St Justinian and follow the signs.

Eating & Drinking

St Davids Food & Wine DELI £
(☎01437-721948; www.stdavidsfoodandwine.co.uk; High St; mains £2.75-4.50; 9am-5pm Mon-Sat) You can stock up on picnic supplies at this delicatessen, which specialises in local organic produce. Or you can grab a pastry or a made-to-order sandwich and enjoy it at the tables out the front.

Sound Cafe CAFE £
(☎01437-721717; 18 High St; mains £4-11; 10am-4pm Sun-Tue & Thu, to 8pm Wed, Fri & Sat) This cosy, chilled-out cafe has a low-ceilinged interior and a pleasant front terrace where you can devour a hearty lunch, a gourmet burger or pizza in the evenings. It's fully licensed so is equally good for quenching your thirst after a day's walking.

Bishops PUB FOOD ££
(☎01437-720422; www.thebish.co.uk; 22-23 Cross Sq; mains £9-12; 11am-midnight;) A friendly, rambling pub full of locals, walkers and blow-ins, this place serves hearty pub grub with a smile. There's a roaring fire in winter, a decent pint on offer and great views of the cathedral from the beer garden.

Cwtch MODERN BRITISH £££
(☎01437-720491; www.cwtchrestaurant.co.uk; 22 High St; 2/3 courses £26/33; 6-9.30pm Wed-Sat, noon-2.30pm Sun Feb, Mar & Nov, 6-11pm daily Apr-Sep, 6-9.30pm Mon-Sat, noon-2.30pm Sun Oct, 6-11pm Mon-Sat Dec) Stone walls and wooden beams mark this out as a 'sense of occasion' place, yet there's a snugness that lives up to its name (*cwtch* means 'a cosy place' or 'a cuddle'). Dishes showcase local produce such as lamb, laver bread, cockles and Solva crab, although the execution isn't always flawless. There's a discounted menu for early diners.

Farmer's Arms PUB
(☎01437-721666; www.farmersstdavids.co.uk; 14 Goat St; 4pm-midnight Mon-Fri, noon-midnight

Sat & Sun;) Even though St Davids is a bit of a tourist trap, you'd be hard-pressed finding a more authentic country pub. There's real ale and Guinness on tap, and it's *the* place to be when the rugby's playing.

Information

National Park Visitor Centre & Tourist Office (01437-720392; www.orielyparc.co.uk; High St; 9.30am-5pm) Located at Oriel y Parc.

National Trust Visitor Centre (01437-720385; High St; 10am-4pm Mon-Sat Jan-Easter, 9am-5.30pm Mon-Sat, 10am-4pm Sun Easter-Dec) Sells gifts, local-interest books, Ordnance Survey maps and guides to NT properties in Pembrokeshire.

Getting There & Away

Public transport is limited, especially on Sundays and in winter.

The main Pembrokeshire Coastal Bus Services (p160) stopping here are the Strumble and Puffin shuttles. From 25 March to 25 September, there's also the Celtic Coaster, which circles between St Davids, St Non's Bay, St Justinian and Whitesands.

Other buses head to/from Haverfordwest (£3.30, 40 minutes, 10 daily), Newgale (£2.45, 21 minutes, nine daily), Solva (£1.50, 10 minutes, nine daily) and Fishguard (£3.70, 45 minutes, six daily).

Getting Around

The Celtic Trail (National Cycle Network Route 4) passes through St Davids. There's pleasant cycling on minor roads around the peninsula but no off-road action (the coast path is for walkers only).

St Davids and the surrounding area suffer from parking problems and congestion in summer.

Tony's Taxis (01437-720931; www.tonystaxis.net) provides a luggage-transfer service for Pembrokeshire Coast Path walkers, covering the area from Little Haven to Fishguard.

Porthgain & Around

For centuries the tiny harbour of Porthgain consisted of little more than a few sturdy cottages wedged into a rocky cove. From 1851 it began to prosper as the port for shipping out slate quarried just down the coast at Abereiddi, and by 1889 its own deposits of granite and fine clay had put it on the map as a source of building stone and brick. The post-WWI slump burst the bubble, and the sturdy stone quays and overgrown brick storage 'bins' are all that remain.

Despite having been an industrial harbour, Porthgain is surprisingly picturesque and today it is home to a couple of art galleries and eateries.

Sights

Blue Lagoon BAY

(Abereiddi) Slate was quarried at this site on the water's edge in Abereiddi right up until 1910 and then transported by tramway to the harbour at Porthgain. After the mining stopped, a channel was blasted through to the sea, flooding the pit and creating a brilliantly blue-green pool surrounded by a bowl of sheer stone walls. You can certainly swim here but be aware that the water is very deep and commensurately cold.

From Porthgain, the Blue Lagoon is best reached via a spectacular 30-minute walk west along the coast path.

Carreg Samson TOMB

FREE Sitting in a farmer's field, with terrific views of Strumble Head, this dolmen is quite remarkable. The massive capstone seems to be only just touching the stones that it is balanced on. It's off the minor road between Trefin and Abercastle, 3 miles east of Porthgain. Look out for the small walker's signpost pointing to the farm.

Activities

Celtic Quest ADVENTURE SPORTS

(01348-881530; www.celticquestcoasteering.com; coasteering £44) Coasteering specialists, taking to the cliffs at Abereiddi all year round.

Preseli Venture ADVENTURE

(01348-837709; www.preseliventure.co.uk; Parcynole Fach, Mathry;) Has its own excellent backpackers' lodge near Abermawr, 6 miles east of Porthgain. Activities include coasteering, sea kayaking, surfing and coastal hiking.

Sleeping

★**Old School Hostel** HOSTEL £

(01348-831800; www.theoldschoolhostel.co.uk; Ffordd-yr-Afon, Trefin; s/d £25/40;) Set in a rambling old school building, this is one of the new breed of independent, brightly painted, personably run backpackers. The six rooms have en suite showers but share communal toilets. A good-quality self-service breakfast is included in the price. The hostel's in the village of Trefin, 2 miles east of Porthgain.

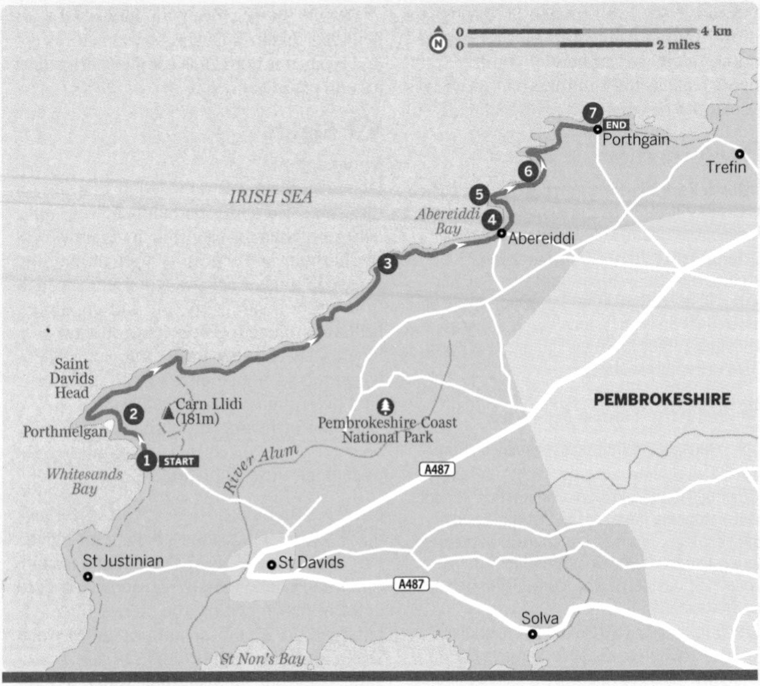

Walking Tour
Whitesands to Porthgain

START WHITESANDS
END PORTHGAIN
LENGTH 10 MILES; FOUR TO SIX HOURS

Covering a beautiful but remote stretch of coast from popular Whitesands Bay near St Davids to the historic port of Porthgain, this rewarding walk takes you over rugged headlands and past dramatic cliffs, pretty coves and flooded quarries. It's a taxing route with several steep descents and ascents but it's well worth the effort. Bring provisions, as it's a long way between villages.

Start out at busy ❶ **Whitesands Bay** (p172) and head west onto wild and rocky St Davids Head. The start of the route is fairly easy with a good path, wide open views and craggy volcanic outcrops to admire. The only signs of human habitation here are ancient, with the simple ❷ **neolithic burial chamber** on the headline predating the surrounding remnants of Celtic forts.

The path soon becomes more rugged, with a rock scramble down to and up from the lovely little cove at ❸ **Aberpwll**. Continue on past crumbling cliffs to ❹ **Abereiddi**, looking out for seals in the coves, gannets and possibly porpoises diving for fish out at sea. The beach at Abereiddi is famous for its black sand full of tiny fossils. Ruined quarry buildings and slate workers' cottages flank the path beyond the beach that leads to the ❺ **Blue Lagoon** (p175), a deep turquoise flooded slate quarry now popular with coasteerers and, in early September, cliff divers from all over the world who compete here, diving 27m into the icy water below.

The 45-minute walk from Abereiddi to Porthgain is one of the best stretches along the entire coast path, following a clifftop plateau past the often deserted beach at ❻ **Traeth Llyfn**. A flight of steep stairs leads down to the golden sand, but beware of strong undercurrents and the tide, which can cut off parts of the beach from the steps.

Continue on for the last descent into the tiny harbour of ❼ **Porthgain** (p175), where you can reward yourself with some superb seafood at the Shed or a cold beverage at the welcoming Sloop Inn.

Crug Glâs HOTEL £££
(☎01348-831302; www.crug-glas.co.uk; r £150-190; P 📶) Set on a big working farm, this opulent country house offers rooms decked out in a grand manner with rich fabrics, ornate beds, enormous bathrooms and elegant period grandeur. Five rooms are in the main house while two are in converted farm buildings. There's also a top-notch restaurant. Crug Glâs is 3 miles south of Porthgain, off the A487.

Eating & Drinking

The Shed SEAFOOD ££
(☎01348-831518; www.theshedporthgain.co.uk; mains £11-18; ⏱10am-9pm Apr-Oct, call ahead Nov-Mar; 📶) Housed in a beautifully converted machine shop right by the harbour, this simple little bistro is renowned as one of Pembrokeshire's best seafood restaurants. Fish and chips get their own separate menu, while the main menu relies heavily on the day's fresh catch alongside favourites such as Porthgain lobster.

Sloop Inn PUB FOOD ££
(☎01348-831449; www.sloop.co.uk; mains £9-19; ⏱11.30am-11pm Mon-Fri, 9.30am-11pm Sat & Sun; 📶) With wooden tables worn smooth by many a bended elbow, old photos of Porthgain in its industrial heyday, and interesting nautical clutter all over the place, the Sloop is a cosy and deservedly popular pub. The hearty, home-cooked meals will satisfy even the hungriest Coast Path walker.

Farmers Arms PUB
(☎01348-831284; www.farmersarmsmathry.co.uk; Mathry; ⏱noon-11pm; 📶🐾) If you're a lover of village pubs, this ivy-clad tavern in the hilltop village of Mathry, 5 miles east of Porthgain, is well worth seeking out. There's nothing fancy about it, just rugby memorabilia on the walls, hard rock on the jukebox, good honest food and a rotating selection of hand-pulled guest ales.

Getting There & Away

The only bus heading here is the Strumble Shuttle, one of the Pembrokeshire Coastal Bus Services (p160).

Fishguard (Abergwaun)

POP 5400

Perched on a headland between its modern ferry port and former fishing harbour, Fishguard is often overlooked by travellers, many of them rushing through on the ferries to and from Ireland. It doesn't have any sights as such, but it's an appealing little town and it holds the quirky distinction of being the setting for the last foreign invasion of Britain.

Fishguard is split into three distinct areas. In the middle of it all is the main town, centred on the Town Hall in Market Sq. To the east is the picturesque harbour of the Lower Town (Y Cwm), which was used as a setting for the 1971 film version of *Under Milk Wood* (starring Richard Burton, Peter O'Toole and Elizabeth Taylor). The train station and ferry terminal lie a mile northwest of the town centre, down on the bay in Goodwick (Wdig; *oo*-dig).

THE LAST INVASION OF BRITAIN

While Hastings in 1066 may get all the press, the last invasion of Britain was actually at Carregwastad Point, northwest of Fishguard, on 22 February 1797. A ragtag collection of 1400 French mercenaries and bailed convicts, led by an Irish-American named Colonel Tate, had intended to land at Bristol and march to Liverpool, keeping English troops occupied while France mounted an invasion of Ireland. Bad weather blew them ashore at Carregwastad where, after scrambling up a steep cliff, they set about looting for food and drink.

The invaders had hoped that the Welsh peasants would rise up to join them in revolutionary fervour but, not surprisingly, their drunken pillaging didn't endear them to the locals. The French were quickly seen off by volunteer 'yeoman' soldiers, with help from the people of Fishguard, including, most famously, one Jemima Nicholas who single-handedly captured 12 mercenaries armed with nothing more than a pitchfork.

The beleaguered Tate surrendered and a mere two days after their arrival the invaders laid down their weapons at Goodwick and were sent off to the jail at Haverfordwest.

History

In 1078, the marshy plain of Goodwick was the site of a battle between the northern and southern Welsh lords (as if they didn't have enough to worry about from the encroaching Normans), culminating in a bloody massacre of the southerners.

Sights

Last Invasion Gallery GALLERY
(☎01437-776638; www.pembrokeshire.gov.uk/libraries; Fishguard Library, Town Hall, Market Sq; ⊙10am-5pm Mon-Thu & Sat Apr-Sep, 10am-5pm Mon-Thu, to 1pm Sat Oct-Mar) FREE Inspired by the *Bayeux Tapestry,* which recorded the 1066 Norman invasion at Hastings, the *Fishguard Tapestry* was commissioned in 1997 to commemorate the bicentenary of the failed Fishguard invasion (p177). It uses a similar cartoonish style as the *Bayeux* (albeit with fewer rude bits) and tells the story in the course of 37 frames and 30m of cloth. A film about its making demonstrates what a huge undertaking it was. Some relics of the invasion are also on display.

St Gwyndaf's Church CHURCH
(Llanwnda) At the heart of the tiny village of Llanwnda, 2 miles northwest of Goodwick, 8th-century St Gwyndaf's showcases its antiquity in the carved stones, inscribed with crosses and Celtic designs, set into the outside walls. Inside, look up at the timber roof beams; at the far end of the third beam from the west (door) end, facing the altar, is a 15th-century carving of a tonsured monk's head.

While you're here, check out the neighbouring cottage, a higgledy-piggledy hippy shack covered in recycled objects, slogans and solar panels. Head inside and help yourself to a tea or coffee; donations are welcome.

A mile-long track leads from Llanwnda to Carregwastad Point, the site of the infamous 1797 invasion (p177).

Strumble Head VIEWPOINT
On wild and rocky Strumble Head, a lighthouse beams out its signal as high-speed ferries thunder past on their way to Ireland. The headland makes a good vantage point for spotting dolphins, seals, sharks and sunfish; below the parking area is a WWII lookout that now serves as a shelter for observing wildlife. It's located 4 miles northwest of Goodwick and the route is well marked.

Activities

Marine Walk WALKING
This path follows the coast from the car park on the Parrog in Goodwick and traces the cliffs flanking Fishguard, offering great views of the harbour, the Lower Town and along the coast to Dinas Head. There's an option to take a detour into the Lower Town before heading up and circling back to Goodwick.

Kayak-King KAYAKING
(☎07967 010203; www.kayak-king.com; tours £45) Twice-daily sea-kayaking tours, tailored to either family groups or adults.

Mayberry Kayaking KAYAKING
(☎01348-874699; www.mayberrykayaking.co.uk; ⊙May-Sep) Offers two-day sea-kayaking courses (£197) and guided kayaking tours suitable for either adults (half/full day £70/117) or families (half day £127).

Festivals & Events

Fishguard Folk Festival MUSIC
(www.pembrokeshire-folk-music.co.uk; ⊙late May) A four-day festival of music and dance held over the holiday weekend at the end of May, this is a wonderful way to experience Welsh musical traditions as well as modern-day interpretations of this ancient craft. Most performances are free and they include pub sessions, dance displays, open-mic events, workshops and a rip-roaring festival *twmpath* (traditional community dance).

Fishguard International Music Festival MUSIC
(www.fishguardmusicfestival.co.uk; ⊙Jul-Aug) A two-week festival of mainly classical-music performances starting in late July, including opera, choirs, solo pianists, string quartets and other ensemble groups.

Aberjazz MUSIC
(www.aberjazz.com; ⊙Aug) A five-day jazz and blues festival held in local theatres, pubs and cafes.

Sleeping

Fishguard has some excellent B&Bs, and staying in the main part of town will give you easy access to the better bars and eateries. Goodwick is full of budget hotels and B&Bs catering to passengers catching the Irish ferries. There are also some memorable camping options in the surrounding countryside.

Centre

★Pentower B&B ££
(☎01348-874462; www.pentower.co.uk; Tower Hill; s/d from £55/85; P) Built by Sir Evan Jones, the architect who designed the harbour, this rambling turreted home is perched on a hill at the edge of town, overlooking his creation. The house is pretty and unassuming, apart from the grand tiled atrium. The three en suite guest rooms are spacious and romantic.

Fern Villa B&B ££
(☎01348-874148; www.fernvillafishguard.co.uk; Church Rd, Goodwick; s/d from £45/70;) Situated on the slopes in Goodwick (head towards the church), this large Victorian house offers clean en suite rooms, some with exposed stone walls and sea views. It's a great option if you want to be close to the train station and ferry port.

Around Fishguard

Pwll Deri YHA HOSTEL £
(☎0845-371 9536; www.yha.org.uk; Castell Mawr, Trefasser; dm/r from £18/45; P) Perched atop a 120m-high cliff overlooking the sea, this hostel has one of the finest locations in Britain. The views from the dining room would rival those from any top hotel and the sunsets are spectacular. The private rooms all have their own bathrooms.

Fishguard Bay Resort CAMPSITE £
(☎01348-811415; www.fishguardbay.com; site for 2 incl car £20, pod £65, caravan/house per week from £435/695;) Dramatically positioned on a clifftop overlooking Fishguard Bay, this large complex offers a wide range of accommodation including tent sites, static caravans, self-contained cottages, luxury lodges and barrel-shaped 'glamping pods'. There's also a shop, a small playground and a 'pamper pod' used for massage. It's located 2.5 miles east of Fishguard, signposted from the A487.

Manor Town House B&B ££
(☎01348-873260; www.manortownhouse.com; 11 Main St; s/d from £75/85;) This graceful Georgian house has a lovely garden terrace where you can sit and gaze over the harbour. The young owners are charm personified and the house has been very tastefully renovated, with continual improvements being made to the six smart en-suite rooms.

Eating

Gourmet Pig DELI, CAFE £
(☎01348-874404; www.gourmetpig.co.uk; 32 West St; mains £4-8; ⏲9.30am-5.30pm Mon-Sat, 11am-3pm Sun;) Delicious sandwiches, samosas, deli platters, pies and pastries are the main attractions at this relaxed deli-cafe, along with barista-made Coaltown coffee (roasted in Ammanford). Grab a window seat and watch Fishguard go about its business.

Number 3 ITALIAN ££
(☎01348-871845; www.number3restaurant.co.uk; 3 Main St; mains £12-18; ⏲6-9.30pm Wed-Sat;) This simple restaurant with bare wooden floors, leather chairs and a mellow vibe turns out excellent pasta, pizza and risotto, but the fare's not all Italian by any means. A range of gourmet burgers rubs shoulders with rustic mains such as beef cheeks, pork belly and roast chicken.

Drinking & Entertainment

Peppers BAR
(☎01348-874540; www.peppers-hub.co.uk; 16 West St; ⏲10am-10pm Fri & Sat, daily summer) This hip hub includes an interesting art gallery and an excellent restaurant, but what we really love about Peppers is its little burgundy-walled bar. There's a good selection of Welsh craft beer and cider, a decent choice of wine, and the staff know their way around a cocktail shaker. There are regular live gigs as well, particularly jazz.

Ship Inn PUB
(☎01348-874033; Old Newport Rd, Lower Town; ⏲6pm-midnight Wed-Fri, noon-midnight Sat & Sun) This lovely little 250-year-old pub has an open fire in winter and walls covered in memorabilia, including photos of Richard Burton filming *Under Milk Wood* outside (the street and nearby quay have not changed a bit).

Ffwrn LIVE MUSIC
(☎01348-875412; Main St; ⏲10.30am-2.30pm Thu-Sun) Call into this very cool converted church hall during the day for the delicious pastries and crêpes, but keep a look out for the posters advertising an eclectic range of events. It's easily Fishguard's most interesting live-music venue, and there are regular themed DJ nights, poetry readings and talks.

Shopping

Melin Tregwynt ARTS & CRAFTS
(☎01348-891288; www.melintregwynt.co.uk; ⌚9.30am-5pm Mon-Fri, 11am-4.30pm Sat & Sun) Since 1912 the same family has run this traditional woollen mill, which churns out some of Wales' best blankets, cushions and upholstery fabrics. New designs have brought the traditional weaves bang up to date and the full range includes clothing and bags, all of which are on display in the mill shop.

You can watch the looms and giant waterwheel in action on weekdays and there's also a small cafe on site.

The mill is reached by narrow country lanes, 5 miles southwest of Goodwick, but it's very well signposted. You'll know you're here when you see the giant yarn and knitting-needle sculpture.

Information

Tourist Office (☎01437-776636; www.visitpembrokeshire.com; Town Hall, Market Sq; ⌚9am-5pm Mon-Fri) As well as this helpful tourist office, the Town Hall contains the library (handy for free internet access) and the market hall, which hosts a general market on Thursday and a farmers market on Saturday mornings.

Getting There & Away

BOAT

Stena Line (☎08447 707 070; www.stenaline.co.uk; car & driver from £79, foot passenger £34; 📶) has two ferries a day, year-round between Rosslare in the southeast of Ireland and Fishguard Harbour.

BUS

Direct services to/from Fishguard include Haverfordwest (£3.40, 31 minutes, hourly), St Davids (£3.70, 45 minutes, six daily), Newport (£2.45, 15 minutes, hourly), Cardigan (£3.75, 37 minutes, hourly) and Aberystwyth (£6, 2½ hours, nine daily). The Pembrokeshire Coastal Bus Services (p160) are also useful.

TRAIN

There are direct trains to both Fishguard & Goodwick Station and Fishguard Harbour (both of which are actually in Goodwick) from destinations including Carmarthen (£9.30, 56 minutes, four daily), Swansea (£16, two hours, daily), Cardiff (from £10, three hours, two daily), Newport (£12, three hours, daily) and Manchester (£30, 6½ hours, daily).

Cwm Gwaun

The narrow, wooded valley of the River Gwaun curves southeast from Fishguard to its source in the Preseli Hills. Despite its proximity to Fishguard, Cwm Gwaun (Gwaun Valley; pronounced 'cum gwine') feels strangely remote and mysterious. Numerous ancient sites litter the valley and, famously, its inhabitants retain a soft spot for the Julian calendar, which was abandoned by the rest of Britain in 1752. During their New Year's celebrations (on 13 January, according to the usual calendar), local children walk from house to house singing traditional Welsh songs and are rewarded with sweets and money.

The valley's narrow lanes are best explored by bicycle or on foot. The valley has no public transport links.

Sights

St Brynach's Church CHURCH
(www.fishguardanglicanchurch.org.uk; Pontfaen) Located in tiny Pontfaen, this little church was founded in AD 540. Ruined and then rescued in the late 19th century, it has two 9th-century stone crosses in the graveyard.

Drinking & Nightlife

Dyffryn Arms PUB
(☎01348-881305; Pontfaen; ⌚11am-10pm) If the step-back-in-time feel of Cwm Gwaun isn't visceral enough, drop into the Dyffryn Arms. Better known as Bessie's after its legendary octogenarian landlady, this rare survivor of yesteryear occupies what's basically the front room of her house. Beer is served from jugs filled straight from the barrel; no hand pumps here!

Newport (Trefdraeth)

POP 1160

In stark contrast to the industrial city of Newport near the English border, the Pembrokeshire Newport is a pretty cluster of flower-bedecked cottages huddled beneath a small Norman castle (now a private residence). It sits at the foot of Mynydd Carningli, a large bump on the seaward side of the Preseli Hills, and in recent years it has gained a reputation for the quality of its restaurants and guesthouses.

Newport makes a pleasant base for walks along the coastal path or south into the Preseli Hills, but it does get crowded in summer. At the northwest corner of the town is little Parrog Beach, dwarfed by Newport Sands (Traeth Mawr) across the river.

History

Newport Castle was founded by a Norman nobleman called William FitzMartin – who was married to a daughter of Lord Rhys ap Gruffydd – after his father-in-law drove him out of nearby Nevern in 1191. Newport grew up around the castle, initially as a garrison town.

Sights

Carreg Coetan TOMB

(Pen-y-Bont) FREE It's now surrounded by houses but this little dolmen has been here for 6000 years. At first glance it looks like the capstone is securely supported by the four standing stones. A closer inspection suggests that some old magic has held it together all these thousands of years as it's balanced on only two of them. Archaeological investigations have uncovered the remains of cremated bones and urns. It's well signposted down a side road on the town's eastern edge.

St Brynach's Church CHURCH

(Nevern) With its overgrown castle and atmospheric church, the little village of Nevern, 2 miles east of Newport, makes a good objective for an easy walk or ride. St Brynach's beautifully melancholic churchyard dates from around the 6th century, predating the church itself. Its supremely gloomy alley of yew trees is estimated to be upwards of six centuries old. The second yew on the right is the so-called bleeding yew, named after the curious reddish-brown sap that oozes from it.

Among the gravestones is a tall Celtic cross, one of the finest in Wales, decorated with interlace patterns and dating from the 10th or 11th century. According to tradition, the first cuckoo that sings each year in Pembrokeshire does so from atop this cross on St Brynach's Day (7 April).

Inside the church, the Maglocunus Stone, thought to date from the 5th century, forms a window sill in the south transept. It is one of the few carved stones that bears an inscription in both Latin and Ogham. Stones like these were important tools for deciphering the meaning of the ancient Celtic script.

Up on the wooded hill behind the church you'll find the scant remains of Nevern Castle, a Norman motte-and-bailey destroyed by the Welsh in 1195.

★ Pentre Ifan TOMB

The largest dolmen in Wales, Pentre Ifan is a 5500-year-old neolithic burial chamber set on a remote hillside with superb views across the Preseli Hills and out to sea. The huge, 5m-long capstone, weighing more than 16 tonnes, is delicately poised on three tall, pointed, upright stones, made of the same bluestone that was used for the menhirs at Stonehenge. The site is about 3 miles southeast of Newport, on a minor road south of the A487; it's signposted.

Preseli Hills AREA

(Mynydd Preseli) The only upland area in Pembrokeshire Coast National Park, these hills rise to a height of 536m at Foel Cwmcerwyn. They encompass a fascinating prehistoric landscape, scattered with hill forts, standing stones and burial chambers, and are famous as the source of the mysterious bluestones of Stonehenge (p182). The ancient Golden Road track, once part of a 5000-year-old trade route between Wessex and Ireland, runs along the crest of the hills, passing prehistoric cairns and the stone circle of Bedd Arthur.

★ Castell Henllys HISTORIC SITE

(☎01239-891319; www.castellhenllys.com; Meline; adult/child £5/3.50; ⏰10am-5pm Apr-Oct, reduced hours Nov-Mar) If you've ever wondered what a Celtic village looked, felt and smelt like, take a trip back in time to this Iron Age fort, 4 miles east of Newport. From about 600 BC and right through the Roman occupation there was a thriving Celtic settlement here, and the whole thing has been reconstructed on its original foundations. Costumed staff bring the site to life, stoking the fires and performing traditional crafts.

The name Castell Henllys means Castle of the Prince's Court. For 27 years students from around the world, supervised by the University of York archaeology department, spent their summers digging and sifting at the site and in the process learned enough to build this remarkable recreation of the settlement, complete with educated guesses about the clothing, tools, ceremonies and agricultural life of that time.

The buildings include four thatched roundhouses, animal pens, a smithy and a grain store – all of which you can enter and touch. There are even Iron Age breeds of cattle and reconstructions of Celtic gardens.

Buses between Newport and Cardigan stop nearby.

Activities

If you keep walking past Carreg Coetan (p181), you'll come to an iron bridge over the **Nevern Estuary**, a haven for birds, especially in winter. Cross the bridge and turn left for an easy walk along the shoreline to the beach at **Newport Sands**.

It's said that in the 6th century, St Brynach of Nevern used to head up **Mynydd Carningli** (347m) to commune with angels, which is the likely derivation of the name. You can climb to the summit from town (a 3.5-mile round trip) via Market St then Church St, keeping the castle on your right. At a fork in the lane called College Sq, go right (uphill), following narrow tracks past a couple of farms and houses to reach a gate leading onto the open hillside. Work your way up on grassy paths to the summit, the site of an Iron Age **hill fort**, with great views of Newport Bay and Dinas Head. On a fine day you might spot Ireland.

Carningli Bike Hire CYCLING

(01239-820724; www.carninglibikehire.com; Carningli Centre, East St; per half-day/day/week £15/22/60; 10am-5.30pm Mon-Sat) Offers bike rental with free delivery within the local area, provides route maps and leads guided rides.

Sleeping & Eating

Newport YHA HOSTEL £

(0800 019 1700; www.yha.org.uk; Lower St Mary's St; dm/r from £15/35; Apr-Aug) Set in a converted Victorian school, this hostel has a lovely common room under the vaulted ceiling and a variety of bunk rooms of different sizes.

Cnapan B&B ££

(01239-820575; www.cnapan.co.uk; East St; s/d £65/95; Easter–mid-Dec; P) This listed Georgian town house has a flower-filled garden and five light-filled rooms above a popular **restaurant** (2-/3-course dinner £27/33; 6.30-8.45pm Wed-Sun Easter–mid-Dec). A recent renovation has freshened up the decor and left brand new bathrooms in its wake. Ask for room 4 – it's a little bigger than the others.

Llys Meddyg HOTEL ££

(01239-820008; www.llysmeddyg.com; East St; s/d from £100/120; P) This converted doctor's residence takes contemporary big-city cool and plonks it firmly by the seaside. Bedrooms are large and bright and decked out in an unassuming but very stylish manner. Original artworks adorn the walls, locally woven blankets and cushions add a splash of colour, and the bathrooms are spacious. Plus there's an upmarket **restaurant** (mains £15-23; noon-2.30pm & 6.30-9pm;) and snug bar downstairs.

Golden Lion PUB ££

(01239-820321; www.goldenlionpembrokeshire.co.uk; East St; s/d from £80/100; P) This

BLUESTONE MYSTERY

There are 31 bluestone monoliths (plus 12 'stumps') at the centre of Stonehenge, each weighing around 4 tonnes. Geochemical analysis shows that the Stonehenge bluestones originated from outcrops around Carnmenyn and Carn Goedog at the eastern end of the Preseli Hills. Stonehenge scholars have long been of the opinion that Preseli and the bluestones held some religious significance for the builders of Stonehenge, and that they laboriously dragged these monoliths down to the River Cleddau, then carried them by barge from Milford Haven, along the Bristol Channel and up the River Avon, then overland again to Salisbury Plain – a distance of 240 miles.

In 2000 a group of volunteers tried to re-enact this journey, using primitive technology to transport a single, 3-tonne bluestone from Preseli to Stonehenge. They failed – having already resorted to the use of a lorry, a crane and modern roads – with the stone slipping from its raft and sinking just a few miles into the sea journey.

An alternative theory is that the bluestones were actually transported by Ice Age glaciers, and dumped around 40 miles to the west of the Stonehenge site some 12,000 years ago – although there is no evidence of any similar glacial transportation in southern Britain.

warm and cosy country inn has 13 bright, clutter-free rooms with simple but contemporary decor in restful colours. They vary in size from snug doubles to more spacious family rooms. In contrast to the modern bedrooms, there's a snug traditional bar with a log fire and low ceilings downstairs, serving real ales and good-quality **meals** (mains £12-17; ⏲noon-2.30pm & 6.30-9pm; 👪).

★Canteen PIZZA, BURGERS £
(☎01239-820131; www.thecanteennewport.com; cnr Market & East Sts; mains £6-11; ⏲9.30am-2.30pm & 6-9pm Wed-Mon;) With names like *The Red Dragon*, *Land of my Fathers* and *Costa del Newport*, the Canteen's lip-smacking range of thin, crispy, stone-baked pizza has been suitably Welshified with the addition of quality, locally sourced toppings. It also serves burgers, salads and sandwiches, better-than-average coffee and a range of Welsh craft beer.

Drinking & Nightlife

Llwyngwair Arms PUB
(☎01239-821554; East St; ⏲noon-11pm) With its aged stone walls and red-and-black chequer-board tiles, this is a proper locals' pub – and the best place in Newport to watch the rugby. There's a pool table upstairs and a beer garden at the rear.

Shopping

Carningli Centre ANTIQUES
(☎01239-820724; www.carninglicentre.com; East St; ⏲10am-5.30pm Mon-Sat) This rabbit warren of a shop is packed with interesting oddments, including art, antique homewares, books and loads of railway paraphernalia. It also hires bikes.

Newport Collective ARTS & CRAFTS
(☎01239-821056; www.newportcollective.co.uk; East St; ⏲10am-5pm Mon-Sat) The showcase for nearly two dozen North Pembrokeshire artists, this interesting little store sells jewellery, pottery, clothing, paintings, photography and hand-turned wooden objects.

Wholefoods of Newport FOOD & DRINKS
(☎01239-820773; www.wholefoodsofnewport.co.uk; East St; ⏲8.30am-5.30pm Mon-Sat) The place to go to stock up on picnic supplies and planet-friendly provisions. There's a selection of ethical gifts at the rear, including Pembrokeshire wool, pottery and hippyish knick-knacks.

Information

National Park Information Centre & Tourist Office (☎01239-820912; Long St; ⏲10am-5.30pm Mon-Sat Easter-Oct, 10am-3.30pm Mon, Wed, Fri & Sat Nov-Easter) As well as friendly staff and stacks of information, there are interesting displays on Pembrokeshire Coast National Park.

Getting There & Away

BUS

Direct services to/from Newport include Haverfordwest (£4.45, 50 minutes, 10 daily), Fishguard (£2.45, 15 minutes, hourly), Dinas Cross (£1.50, six minutes, hourly), Cardigan (£3.35, 23 minutes, 12 daily) and Aberystwyth (£6, 2¼ hours, nine daily). The Pembrokeshire Coastal Bus Services (p160) are also useful.

CAR

Most visitors arrive by car. Expect to pay for, and possibly fight over, parking from April to September.

St Dogmaels (Llandudoch)

POP 1360

Just across the River Teifi from Cardigan, this large village marks the end of the Pembrokeshire Coast Path. From as early as the 5th or 6th century there was a Celtic monastic community here, which the Normans replaced with French Tironian monks. The remains of their beautiful abbey still stand today.

Sights

Centre

St Dogmaels Abbey RUINS
(☎01239-615389; www.stdogmaelsabbey.org.uk; ⏲10am-4pm) FREE Built in 1120 on the site of the already ancient Celtic monastery, in 1538 St Dogmaels was dissolved along with all of Britain's monasteries by Henry VIII and subsequently fell into artful ruin. The visitor centre in the Coach House tells the abbey's story and includes a popular cafe and gallery. A vibrant **Local Producers Market** (⏲9am-1pm Tue) is held here weekly.

St Thomas the Martyr CHURCH
St Dogmaels' parish church houses several ancient stones from the original Celtic community founded by the local saint, including the Sagranus Stone, inscribed in Latin and Ogham. The stone was instrumental in

deciphering the ancient Ogham script in the 19th century. The church's altar was originally from St Dogmaels Abbey and is one of the oldest in Britain.

Y Felin HISTORIC BUILDING
(☎01239-613999; www.yfelin.co.uk; tours adult/child £2.50/1; ⏰10am-5.30pm Mon-Sat, 2-5.30pm Sun) A working watermill dating from the 1640s, Y Felin is still used to make flour, which you can purchase at the mill door.

Around St Dogmaels

Poppit Sands BEACH
Right at the end of the road that follows the river north from St Dogmaels, this big, broad, sandy beach offers terrific views over the estuary to Cardigan Island and out to sea. It's an extremely popular spot for swimmers, surfers, sun seekers and dog walkers. Lifeguards patrol here at the height of summer and facilities include a cafe and toilets. It's about 2 miles north of the main part of sprawling St Dogmaels; the Poppit Rocket bus (p160) stops here.

Cilgerran Castle CASTLE
(Cadw; www.cadw.gov.wales; adult/child Apr-Oct £3.50/2.65, Nov-Mar free; ⏰10am-4pm) Originally built in timber and earth in around 1100 to control a crossing on the River Teifi, this sturdy stone incarnation with two massive round towers dates from the 13th and 14th centuries. Climb to the top for views over the wooded river valley. Cilgerran is 4 miles southeast of St Dogmaels.

Welsh Wildlife Centre WILDLIFE RESERVE
(☎01239-621600; www.welshwildlife.org; Cilgerran; parking £3; ⏰10am-4pm) FREE Bordering the River Teifi just south of Cardigan, the **Teifi Marshes Nature Reserve** is a haven for birds, otters, badgers and butterflies. You can find out more about the critters that live in the surrounding river, marsh and woodland habitats at this striking glass-walled information centre, which also houses a shop and cafe. There are several short waymarked trails nearby, most of them wheelchair accessible.

Sleeping & Eating

Poppit Sands YHA HOSTEL £
(☎0800 019 1700; www.yha.org.uk; dm £15, r with/without bathroom from £69/39) Tucked into a hillside overlooking the bay, this fully renovated hostel has superb views and an excellent kitchen and dining area. The en suite rooms sleep up to five people, but private twins and doubles without a bathroom are also available. The location is quite isolated, and be prepared for a flight of 56 steps down to the hostel.

★ **Fforest Camp** CAMPSITE ££
(☎01239-623751; www.coldatnight.co.uk; Cilgerran; per 3-night stay from £280; 🐾) On the edge of Teifi Marshes Nature Reserve, Fforest challenges the notion that camping means roughing it. Stay in large tents, tepees or geodesic domes and enjoy the country air. Simple, wholesome breakfasts are served at the lodge, and the owners run a second site further up the coast at Manorafon. There's a seven-night minimum stay during summer holidays.

Ferry Inn PUB FOOD ££
(☎01239-615172; www.ferry-inn.com; Poppit Rd; mains £11-14; ⏰noon-10pm; P 🖉 👪 🐾) This great old pub has grafted on a glassed-in pavilion to make the most of its extraordinary riverside views. The food is excellent, particularly the Sunday roasts and the pastry-less Ferry Fish Pie, which comes crammed with salmon, prawns, scallops, mussels and cockles in a béchamel sauce, topped with a cheesy, bread crumb.

Getting There & Away

The Poppit Rocket (p160) stops here, as does the 407 bus (Poppit Sands–Cardigan; hourly, no Sunday service).

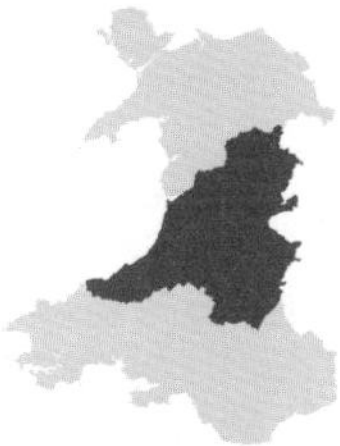

Aberystwyth & Mid-Wales

Includes ➡

Best Places to Eat

- ➡ Ynyshir Hall (p201)
- ➡ Carlton Riverside (p206)
- ➡ Checkers (p216)
- ➡ Drawing Room (p207)
- ➡ Ultracomida (p196)

Best Places to Sleep

- ➡ Harbour Master (p192)
- ➡ Beudy Banc (p200)
- ➡ Glandyfi Castle (p200)
- ➡ Gwesty Cymru (p195)

Why Go?

Bordered by the dramatic landscapes of two national parks, Mid-Wales is often overlooked. Yet this region of plunging coastline, wooded river valleys and small market towns is something of a well-kept secret. As devotees of the bilingual detective series *Hinterland* (or *Y Gwyll*, filmed throughout the region) know, this is Wales at its most rural, a sweep of undulating hills that the Industrial Revolution bypassed. Criss-crossed with country lanes and dedicated cycling and walking routes, it's an excellent area to explore under your own steam.

Apart from exuberant, student-populated Aberystwyth, you won't find much excitement in the urban areas, but in any case, it's the places in between, and the people who live in them, that are far more interesting. From struggling farmers to pioneers of sustainable development and the weird and wacky minds of Britain's smallest town, the region reveals more about the Welsh than you may ever have imagined.

When to Go

➡ Long days and the promise of fine weather make June to September the best time to tackle long-distance walking routes such as Offa's Dyke Path (p211), while the wonderful foliage colours make autumn perfect for walking or cycling the wooded trails around the Elan Valley.

➡ Festivals abound in the summer months with oddballs taking part in some of the weirdest sporting events on the planet in Llanwrtyd Wells in May, June and July; a massive celebration of rural life at the Royal Welsh Show (p206) at the beginning of July; and a look back in time at the Victorian Festival (www.victorian-festival.co.uk) in Llandrindod Wells in late August.

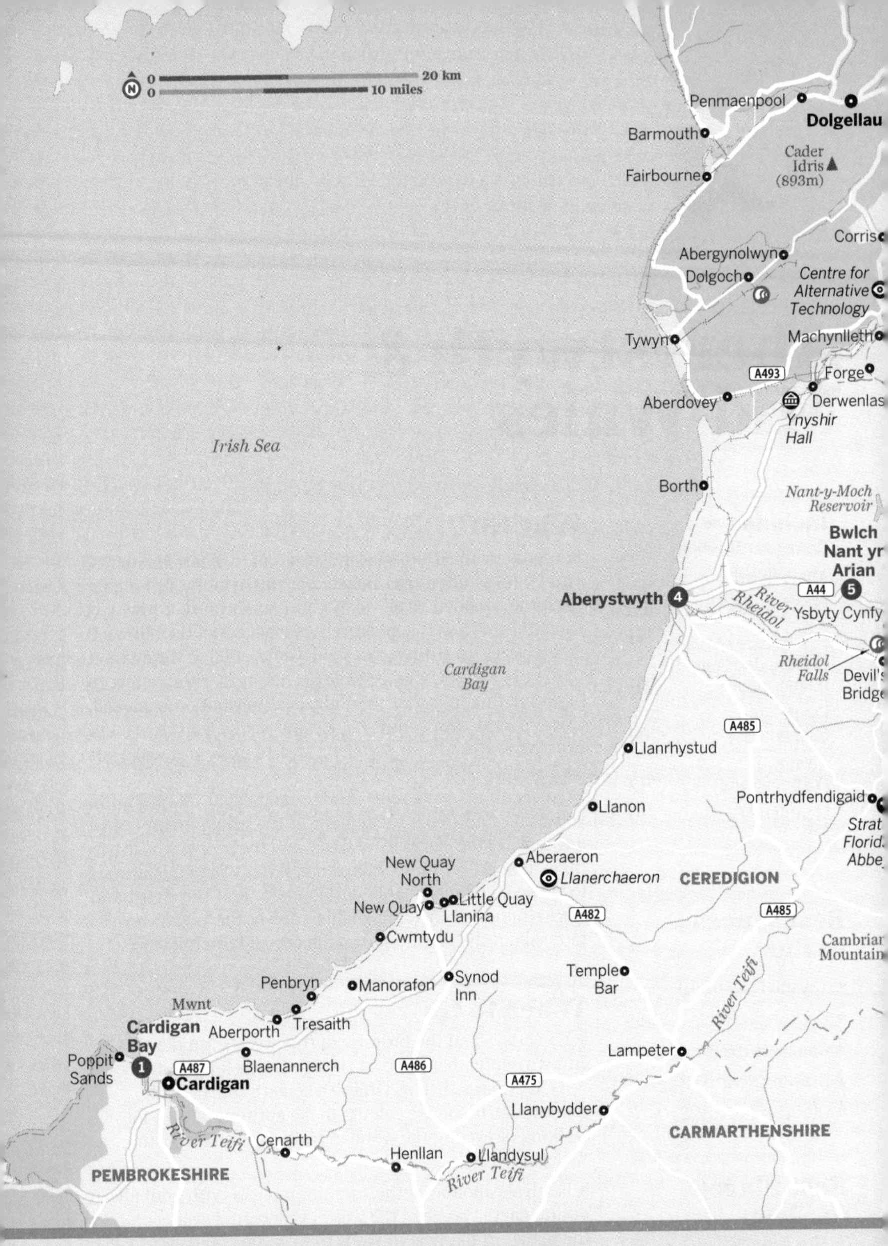

Aberystwyth & Mid-Wales Highlights

1 Cardigan Bay (p189) Kayaking with dolphins and seals along this gloriously rugged stretch of coast.

2 Cambrian Mountains (p203) Enjoying the splendid isolation and utter tranquillity of the Cambrian Mountains' deserted moorlands.

3 Elan Valley (p204) Exploring mighty Victorian dams and picking wild berries in this lovely valley.

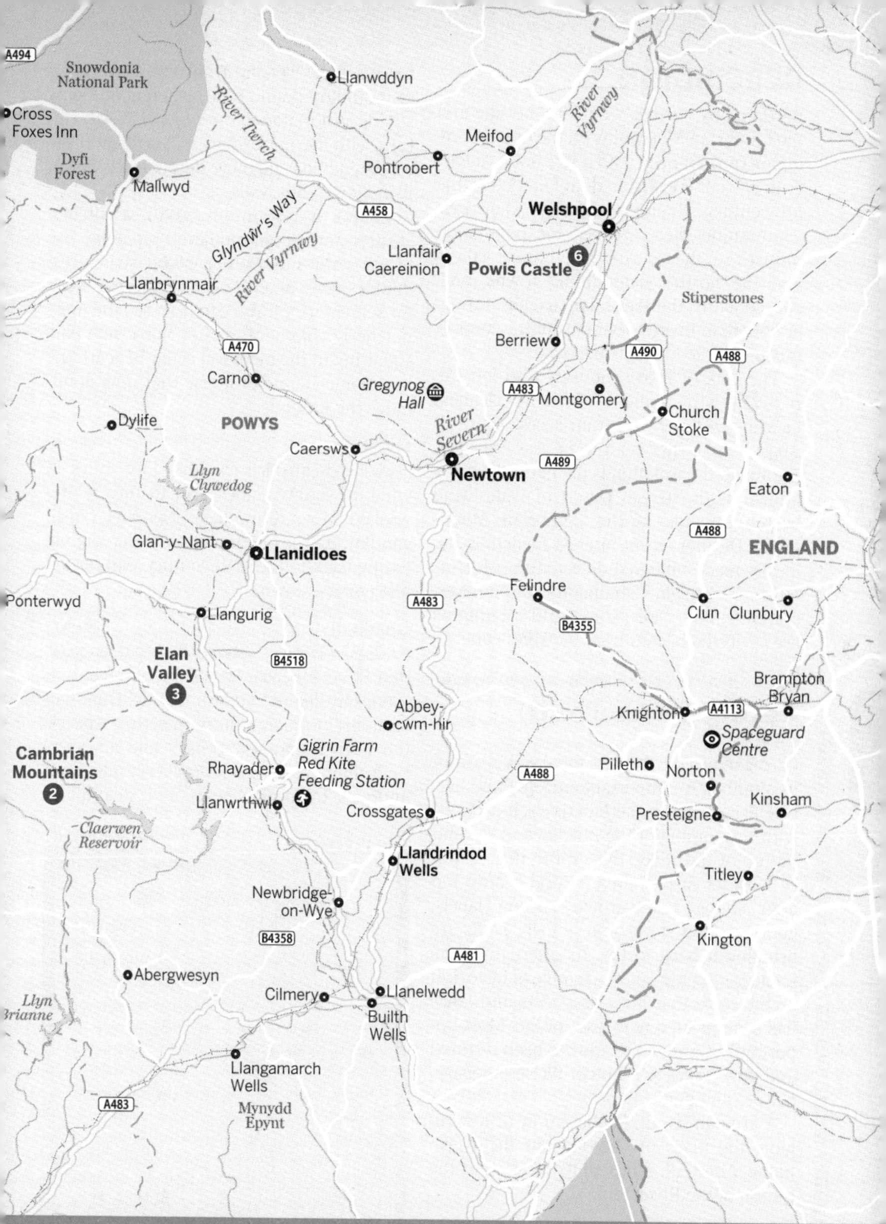

4 Aberystwyth (p192)
Experiencing a collision of high culture and student high jinks in Aberystwyth, a colourful seaside university town.

5 Bwlch Nant yr Arian (p198) Watching the birds of prey swoop down for a lakeside feast in this picturesque woodland and lake setting.

6 Powis Castle (p217)
Discovering the magnificent gardens and ornate interiors of this castle near Welshpool.

CEREDIGION

Bordered by Cardigan Bay on one side and the Cambrian Mountains on the other, Ceredigion (pronounced with a 'dig' not a 'didge') is an ancient Welsh kingdom founded by the 5th-century chieftain Ceredig. The rural communities here escaped the population influxes of the south's coal-mining valleys and the north's slate-mining towns, and, consequently, the Welsh language is stronger here than in any other part of the country except Gwynedd and Anglesea.

The lack of heavy industry also left Ceredigion with some of Britain's cleanest beaches and, with no train access south of Aberystwyth, they tend to be less crowded. Adding to the isolation is the natural barrier known as the 'Green Desert of Wales' (the barren uplands of the Cambrian Mountains). Despite recent interest fuelled by the locally made bilingual detective series *Hinterland/Y Gwyll*, Ceredigion's sandy coves, sea cliffs, river valleys and arid mountains are as off-the-beaten-track as Wales gets.

Cardigan (Aberteifi)

POP 4184

Cardigan has the feel of a town waking from its slumber. An important entrepôt and herring fishery in Elizabethan times, it declined with the coming of the railway and the silting up of the River Teifi in the 19th century. Now its surrounding natural beauty, hip craft shops, home-grown fashion labels, gourmet food stores and homely B&Bs are bringing it back to life. Its alternative arts scene is growing and the jumble of historical architecture that lines its streets and lanes has been given a new lease of life. Most importantly, Cardigan Castle has been restored and now serves as a hub of Welsh language, culture and performance.

'Cardigan' is an Anglicisation of Ceredigion, the place of Ceredig, but the Welsh name, Aberteifi, refers to its location at the mouth of the River Teifi.

Sights

★Cardigan Castle CASTLE

(Castell Aberteifi; ☎01239-615131; www.cardigancastle.com; 2 Green St) Cardigan Castle holds an important place in Welsh culture, having been the venue for the first competitive National Eisteddfod, held in 1176 under the aegis of Lord Rhys ap Gruffydd. Neglected for years, it's sprung from the ashes via a multimillion-pound refurbishment and now stands as a major centre of local Welsh culture, with live performances, language classes, eisteddfods and more taking place within its hollowed-out walls.

There's a restaurant (p190), a kitchen garden and accommodation (making use of old stables and other extant structures; doubles start at £90 or it's £420 per week for self-catering). You can even see the most northerly colony of greater horseshoe bats squatting in the medieval cellar beneath the handsome Georgian house that now dominates the grounds.

Mwnt Church CHURCH

(www.friendsofmwntchurch.co.uk) Five miles of winding country lanes lead to tiny, whitewashed Mwnt Church, overlooking Cardigan Bay. It's the oldest church in Ceredigion, dating back to the 14th century. Signposted just north of town.

Guildhall MARKET

(☎01239-615554; www.guildhall-cardigan.co.uk; High St; ⏲9am-5pm Mon-Sat) Completed in 1860, Cardigan's 'modern Gothic' Guildhall is home to community meeting spaces, the **Corn Exchange gallery** and an eclectic indoor market, selling everything from antiques to local cheeses and steampunk

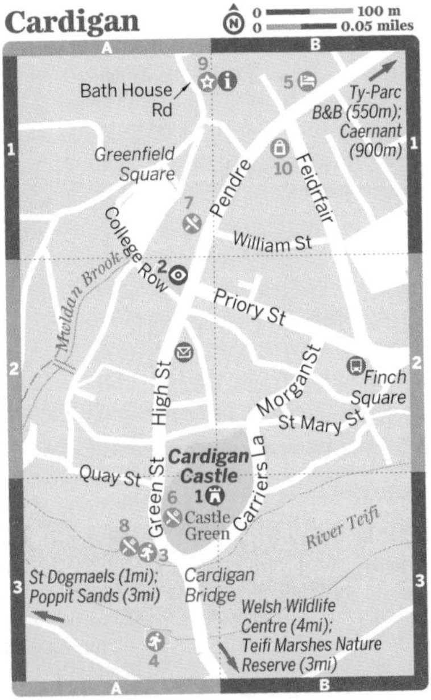

fashions. The field cannon outside, commemorating local losses in the Charge of the Light Brigade in 1854, was actually used at Balaclava.

Activities

Set between the Pembrokeshire Coast Path (PCP) and the Ceredigion Coast Path (CCP), Cardigan offers plenty of options for walkers as well as anyone keen to try out some adventure sports.

Walking

For a challenging but spectacular day's walk, head to St Dogmaels Abbey (p183) and tackle the last leg of the PCP in reverse, catching the bus back from Newport. In the other direction, the first day of the CCP is shorter, ending up in Aberporth where you can catch the 552 bus back.

If you don't fancy a full day's trek, you can walk or cycle from Cardigan through the **Teifi Marshes** to the Welsh Wildlife Centre (p184; WWC). From the High St head downhill to the river, cross over the footbridge to Castle St and then cross the road. Take the pedestrian walkway leading onto the riverbank and follow it out of town past the reed beds and along a wooded trail to the wildlife centre. The walk is about 1 mile long, but it's 4 miles by road.

The tourist office (p191) stocks the *Walking the Teifi Estuary* brochure, outlining five other graded walks in the area, including a 10-mile circular walk to the gorgeous hidden cove at **Mwnt**. Here a small arc of golden sand sits between folds of the cliffs, and a simple whitewashed church overlooks the sea where you'll often spot dolphins, seals and porpoises.

CARDIGAN BAY'S DOLPHINS

Cardigan Bay is home to an amazingly rich variety of marine animals and plants, but the star attraction is Europe's largest pod of bottlenose dolphins. With reliable sightings from May to September, there are few places where these sociable creatures are more easily seen in the wild. Along with the dolphins, harbour porpoises, Atlantic grey seals and a variety of bird life are regularly seen, as well as seasonal visitors such as sunfish, basking sharks and leatherback turtles.

Some of the best places to spot bottlenose dolphins from the shore are the beaches around New Quay: New Quay North, Little Quay, Cwmtydu and Llanina are good bets, as are the beautiful sandy beaches at Penbryn and Tresaith north of Cardigan. Aberystwyth, Aberporth and Mwnt also have regular sightings.

You can learn more about Cardigan Bay's marine life at the **Cardigan Bay Marine Wildlife Centre** (01545-560032; http://cbmwc.org; Glanmore Tce, New Quay; 9am-5pm Easter-Oct) FREE, in New Quay.

Cardigan

Other Activities

A Bay to Remember WILDLIFE WATCHING
(01239-623558; www.baytoremember.co.uk; Prince Charles Quay; 1hr trip adult/child £25/12; Mar-Oct) Running one- and two-hour trips into Cardigan Bay from St Dogmaels, Gwbert and Poppit Sands, this operation takes groups out in rigid-hulled inflatable boats to spot bottlenose dolphins, harbour porpoises, grey seals and seabirds. The booking office is at Prince Charles Quay, on the Teifi.

Cardigan Bay Active ADVENTURE SPORTS
(01239-612133; www.cardiganbayactive.co.uk; Granary Warehouse, Teifi Wharf, Castle St; 9.30am-5pm Mon-Sat) CBA offers guided canoe or kayak trips through Cilgerran Gorge as well as climbing, coasteering, surfing, white-water rafting expeditions and

bushcraft trips. Sea kayaking in Cardigan Bay, always a great spot to encounter bottlenose dolphins and Atlantic grey seals, is £40 per person.

Sleeping

Caernant B&B £

(01239-612932; www.caernant.co.uk; Gwbert Rd; s/d £40/60; P wi-fi) Big, bright, spacious rooms are on offer at Caernant, a delightful modern B&B just outside Cardigan. With tea and scones on arrival, incredible breakfasts (including smoked salmon and buttered kippers) and heartfelt hospitality, it's well worth the short trip from town (less than a mile from the centre of Cardigan on the B4548).

Ty-Parc B&B B&B ££

(01239-615452; www.ty-parc.com; Park Ave; s/d £50/65; P wi-fi) This appealing Edwardian house north of downtown Cardigan offers five bright en-suite rooms decked out in cream shades and blond-wood furnishings. Extra thoughtful touches include radios in the shower, fresh flowers and packed lunches on request.

Llety Teifi B&B ££

(01239-615566; www.lletyteifi-guesthouse.co.uk; Pendre; s/d from £45/75; P wi-fi) Well-appointed and stylish, this large Victorian guesthouse has plenty of period character, despite the lurid pink exterior. Expect bold patterned fabrics and wallpapers, giant windows and spacious bathrooms. Breakfast is served next door and altogether it's a very good deal.

Eating

Fforest Pizzatipi PIZZA £

(01239-612259; www.pizzatipi.co.uk; Cambrian Quay; pizza £7-9; 4-10pm daily Jul & Aug, Sat & Sun late Jun & Sep) Brought to you by the hip folks at Cardigan's Fforest empire, this seasonal pop-up venue is the hottest ticket in town on summer nights. Pizzas pumping from two wood-fired ovens, craft beer, music and a buzzing atmosphere all set under a candlelit tepee in a hidden riverside courtyard: what more could you ask for?

Cafe Food for Thought CAFE £

(01239-621863; 13 Pendre; mains £6-8; 9am-5pm Mon-Sat; vegetarian) A consistent local favourite, this simple cafe delivers an interesting menu that ranges from light bites to Welsh lamb, gourmet burgers, local seafood, specialist teas and coffees, homemade cakes and plenty of options for vegetarians. Arrive early at lunchtime or be prepared to wait for a table.

1176 BISTRO ££

(01239-562002; www.cardigancastle.com/dining; Cardigan Castle; mains £15-18; 10am-4pm daily, 6.30-9.30pm Fri & Sat) Named for the year of Wales' first National Eisteddfod, held at Cardigan Castle, this gleaming new bistro is an integral part of the monument's 2015 rebirth. Popular for lunch and afternoon tea (£12 per person), it also opens for dinner on Fridays and Saturdays, when the produce of the castle's kitchen garden stars.

OFF THE BEATEN TRACK

CEREDIGION COAST PATH

Running for 60-odd miles up and down wave-tormented headlands, past sweeping bays and through Cardigan Bay's principal settlements, **Ceredigion Coast Path** (www.ceredigioncoastpath.org.uk) is one of Wales' classic walks. At moderate pace, it takes around a week to complete, with plenty of accommodation available along the way. Taxis can also be booked to cart baggage ahead, under Ceredigion's 'Cab a Bag' scheme (www.ceredigion.gov.uk).

A sensible six-day itinerary would see you stopping overnight in Aberporth (12 miles from Cardigan), New Quay (14 miles), Aberaeron (6.5 miles), Llanrhystud (7.5 miles), Aberystwyth (11 miles) and Borth (12 miles); each has its own sandy beach to relax on at the end of the day. The truly hardcore enthusiast could tack this on to the end of the 13- to 15-day Pembrokeshire Coastal Path – a total of 249 continuous coastal miles.

The **Cardi Bach bus** (Fri & Sat late Mar-late May, daily except Thu late May-late Sep, Thu only late Sep-late Mar) – the 552 – covers the coast between Cardigan and New Quay year-round, making it easy to split this stretch into day-long walks.

Entertainment

Theatr Mwldan THEATRE
(☎01239-621200; www.mwldan.co.uk; Bath House Rd; ⏲from 5pm Mon, from 10am Tue-Sat, from noon Sun until last performance) Located in the former slaughterhouse, Theatr Mwldan stages comedy, drama, dance, music and films, and has an art gallery and a good cafe. In summer there are open-air productions.

Shopping

Pendre Art ART
(☎01239-615151; 35 Pendre; ⏲10am-5pm Mon-Sat; 📶) Not only a great place to buy local art, Pendre has an excellent coffee shop serving sandwiches, crêpes, baguettes and home-baked scones. Bring your laptop and lurk in one of the numerous retro niches, taking advantage of the free wi-fi.

Information

Cardigan & District Memorial Hospital (☎01239-612214; Pont-y-Cleifion) Has no accident and emergency department.

Tourist Office (☎01239-613230; www.discoverceredigion.co.uk; Theatr Mwldan, Bath House Rd; ⏲10am-4pm Tue, Wed, Fri & Sat) In the lobby of the Theatr Mwldan.

Getting There & Away

Bus routes include X50 to Aberystwyth (1½ hours); 407 to St Dogmaels (eight minutes) and Poppit Sands (15 minutes); 460 to Carmarthen (90 minutes); and the Poppit Rocket (405) to Fishguard (90 minutes). The bus station is on Finch Sq.

Bikes can be hired from **New Image Bicycles** (☎01239-621275; www.bikebikebike.co.uk; 29-30 Pendre; per half day/day £15/20; ⏲10am-5pm Mon-Sat) for cycling around Cardigan Bay and the Teifi Valley.

Aberaeron

POP 1422

The elegant port of Aberaeron with its brightly painted Georgian houses was once a busy port and ship-building centre, its genteel architecture the result of planned expansion in the early 19th century. With heavy industry long gone, today Aberaeron is quietly bucking the trends of economic decline; its stylish streets and much-admired harbour are lined with independent shops and cafes, chic B&Bs and boutique hotels, and a number of excellent restaurants.

LÔN TEIFI & LÔN CAMBRIA

Two long-distance cycling routes that are part of the **Sustrans** (☎02920-650602; www.sustrans.org.uk) National Cycle Network cut clear through Mid-Wales. The Lôn Teifi (Route 82) heads 100 miles from Fishguard through Cardigan, Lampeter and Tregaron to Aberystwyth. From here the 113-mile Lôn Cambria (Route 81) kicks in, passing through Rhayader, Newtown and Welshpool en route to Shrewsbury.

Sights & Activities

Llanerchaeron HISTORIC BUILDING
(NT; ☎01545-570200; www.nationaltrust.org.uk/llanerchaeron; Ciliau Aeron; adult/child £7.60/3.80; ⏲10.30am-5.30pm, villa 11.30am-4pm) This beautifully maintained Georgian country estate offers a fascinating insight into the life of the Welsh gentry and their staff 200 years ago. The villa itself was designed by John Nash and is one of his most complete early works, featuring curved walls, false windows and ornate cornices.

The estate was self-sufficient and remains virtually unchanged in that respect, with staff in period dress tending to the fruit, veg and herbs in the walled garden and looking after the Welsh Black cattle, Llanwenog sheep and rare Welsh pigs. You can join in and have a go at beating rugs, washing clothes and baking Georgian style, or simply stroll around the ornamental lake and pleasure gardens or buy some of the estate produce at the well-stocked farm shop.

Llanerchaeron is 2.5 miles southeast of Aberaeron along the A482.

SeaMôr Boat Trips BOATING
(☎07795-242445; www.seamor.org; Pen Cei; adult/child £20/10; ⏲May-Sep) New Quay–based SeaMôr also runs one-hour boat trips from Aberaeron's Quay Promenade past the dolphin-feeding sites of Llanina Reef and New Quay Bay. Grey seals, bottlenose dolphins and harbour porpoises are commonly seen and there are occasional sightings of sunfish, basking sharks, minke whales and

even humpback whales. Departures are tide-dependent: enquire at the tourist office or call SeaMôr directly.

Sleeping & Eating

3 Pen Cei B&B ££

(☑ 01545-571147; www.pen-cei-guest-house.co.uk; 3 Pen Cei; d £105-160; 🛜) The affable owners John and Lesley have refurbished this grand Georgian shipping office beautifully, with crisp linens, bold colour schemes and fresh flowers. The larger rooms have super-king beds (one also has a free-standing bath) and the hosts go out of their way to make guests feel welcome.

★ Harbour Master BOUTIQUE HOTEL £££

(☑ 01545-570755; www.harbour-master.com; Pen Cei; s/d from £75/145; 🛜) Commanding Aberaeron's harbour entrance, this small, hip hotel offers food and accommodation worthy of any chic city bolthole. The striking, violet-painted Georgian buildings hold 13 quirky rooms featuring Frette linens, vintage Welsh blankets, bold colour schemes and high-tech bathrooms. Those in the newly restored grain warehouse have the same contemporary styling with excellent harbour views.

Downstairs its renowned restaurant (two-/three-course dinner £27.50/35) champions local ingredients with lobster and crab, and Welsh beef, lamb and cheeses whisked into imaginative and extremely satisfying dishes. The lively bar offers the same outstanding food in a more casual setting (mains from £10.50).

Hive BISTRO ££

(☑ 01545-570445; www.thehiveaberaeron.com; Cadwgan Pl; mains £10.50-14; ☺ 9am-4pm Sun-Tue, to 11pm Wed-Sat; 🛜) Set in a converted warehouse and coal yard overlooking the inner harbour, Hive has an eclectic modern menu featuring BBQ, burgers and plenty of seafood from the attached fishmonger (open 10am to 5pm, Wednesday to Saturday). It also has a large courtyard with outdoor seating, a friendly, lively vibe and incredible honey ice cream – don't leave without trying it!

ℹ Getting There & Away

Between Monday and Saturday, buses T5 and X50 go regularly to Aberystwyth (45 minutes) and Cardigan (55 minutes).

Aberystwyth

POP 13,040

Sweeping around the curving shore of Cardigan Bay, the lively university town of Aberystwyth (aber-*ist*-with) has a stunning location but a bit of an identity crisis. Student bars and cheap restaurants line the streets, the flashing lights of traditional amusements twinkle from the pier, and tucked away in the side streets are a handful of chichi boutiques and organic, wholefood cafes. During term time the bars are buzzing and students play football on the promenade, while in the summer the bucket-and-spade brigade invades and enjoys the beach.

Meanwhile the trappings of this once-stately seaside resort remain in the terrace of grand Georgian houses painted in subtle pastel hues that line the promenade.

Welsh is widely spoken here and locals are proud of their heritage. Catching a show at the Arts Centre (p196), hearing the male voice choir (p196) perform or simply soaking up the sunset over Cardigan Bay are quintessential local experiences.

History

Aberystwyth's now mainly ruined castle was erected in 1277; like many other castles in Wales it was captured by Owain Glyndŵr at the start of the 15th century and slighted by Oliver Cromwell in the 17th. By the beginning of the 19th century, the town's walls and gates had completely disappeared and much of the stone was repurposed by locals.

The town developed a fishing industry, and silver and lead mining were also important here. With the arrival of the railway in 1864, the town reinvented itself as a fashionable seaside destination. In 1872 Aberystwyth was chosen as the site of the first college of the University of Wales (Aberystwyth University now has over 9000 students) and in 1907 it became home to the National Library of Wales.

◉ Sights

Marine Tce, with its impressive sweep of imposing pastel-hued houses overlooking North Beach, harks back to the town's halcyon days as a fashionable resort. When you reach the bottom of the 1.5-mile prom, it's customary to kick the white bar, although the locals can't seem to explain the rationale behind this ritual.

North Beach is lined by somewhat shabby Georgian hotels, albeit with a couple of notable exceptions. Royal Pier, the grand Old College and the enigmatic, sparse ruins of Aberystwyth Castle are the major sights here.

The prom pivots before leading along **South Beach** – a more desolate but still attractive seafront. Many locals prefer the stony but emptier **Tanybwlch Beach**, just south of the harbour where the Rivers Rheidol and Ystwyth meet. Pen Dinas, the upland rising behind Tanybwlch, is the site of the important Iron Age hill fort **Dinas Maelor**. While the outline of the fort is still visible, the peak is now dominated by a monument to Wellington.

Aberystwyth Castle CASTLE

FREE Erected in 1277, Aberystwyth Castle was captured by Owain Glyndŵr at the start of the 15th century, then retaken by the future Henry V using 'The Messenger' – a two-ton cannon that unfortunately self-destructed. Later slighted by Oliver Cromwell, the castle retains three partial towers and some outer wall and offers lovely seaward views along the Llŷn Peninsula to Bardsey Island.

A stone circle planted in the centre of the castle is a relic of a 1915 eisteddfod, while the large war memorial in front of it features a surprisingly raunchy nude.

Old College HISTORIC BUILDING

(King St) Reminiscent of a French chateau, this Gothic-revival building with castellated towers, conical spires and flamboyant gargoyles was originally built as a hotel but was sold to Aberystwyth University's founders before it ever opened. The uni plans to have a museum, restaurant, artists' spaces and other facilities in place for the building's sesquicentennial in 2022.

Royal Pier LANDMARK

(www.royalpier.co.uk; Marine Tce; 10am-9pm) The top-heavy Royal Pier lumbers out to sea under the weight of a pub, nightclub, pizzeria and cheerfully tacky amusement arcade.

Ceredigion Museum MUSEUM

(01970-633088; www.ceredigion.gov.uk; Terrace Rd; 10.30am-4pm Tue-Sat, noon-4pm Sun Apr-Sep) FREE This museum is in the Coliseum, which opened in 1905 as a theatre, then served as a cinema promising 'amusement without vulgarity' from 1932 onwards. The elegant interior retains its stage, around which are entertaining exhibitions on Aberystwyth's history – everything from old chemist furnishings and hand-knitted woollen knickers to a mini puppet theatre and re-creation of an 1850s cottage.

The museum is due for a major redevelopment in 2017, when it will expand; the tourist office (p197) below will also receive an upgrade.

Constitution Hill HILL

Constitution Hill rises from the northern end of the seafront promenade; on a clear day you can see the Llŷn Peninsula from its blustery top. Having either walked or ridden the Cliff Railway (p195) up, there's a cafe, ten-pin bowling and the world's largest **Camera Obscura** (01970-617642; www.aberystwythcliffrailway.co.uk; adult/accompanied child £1/free; 11am-4pm Apr-Oct) to divert you. A re-created 'relic' of the Victorian era, the camera obscura is an immense pinhole camera allowing you to see practically into the windows of the houses below or spy on friends on the beach.

National Library of Wales LIBRARY

(01970-632800; www.llgc.org.uk; A487; 9.30am-6pm Mon-Fri, to 5pm Sat) FREE Sitting proudly on a hilltop half a mile east of town, the National Library is a cultural powerhouse. Founded in 1911, it holds millions of books in many languages – as a copyright library it has copies of every book published in the UK. The **Hengwrt Room** holds gems such as the 12th-century Black Book of Carmarthen (the oldest existing Welsh text), a text of Chaucer penned by his scribe Adam Pinkhurst and a first edition of Milton's *Paradise Lost*.

Other galleries display an always stimulating set of changing exhibitions. The entrance to the library is off Penglais Rd (the A487); take a right just past the hospital.

Activities

Vale of Rheidol Railway RAIL

(Rheilffordd Cwm Rheidol; 01970-625819; www.rheidolrailway.co.uk; Park Ave; adult/child return £20/8; up to 5 daily late Mar-Oct, Sat & Sun Nov, closed late Dec–mid-Feb) This scenic narrow-gauge railway is one of Aberystwyth's most popular attractions. Steam locomotives built between 1923 and 1938 have been lovingly restored by volunteers and chug for almost 12 miles up the beautiful wooded valley of the River Rheidol to Devil's

Bridge. The line opened in 1902 to bring lead and timber out of the valley.

Rheidol Cycle Trail CYCLING

Sticking mainly to designated cycle paths and quiet country lanes, the 17-mile Rheidol Cycle Trail heads from Aberystwyth Harbour to Devil's Bridge through the beautiful Rheidol Valley. Along the way it passes the Woodland Trust's Coed Geufron, and side routes lead to Bwlch Nant yr Arian (p198), Rheidol Power Station and Rheidol Mines. The last section is very steep.

Aberystwyth

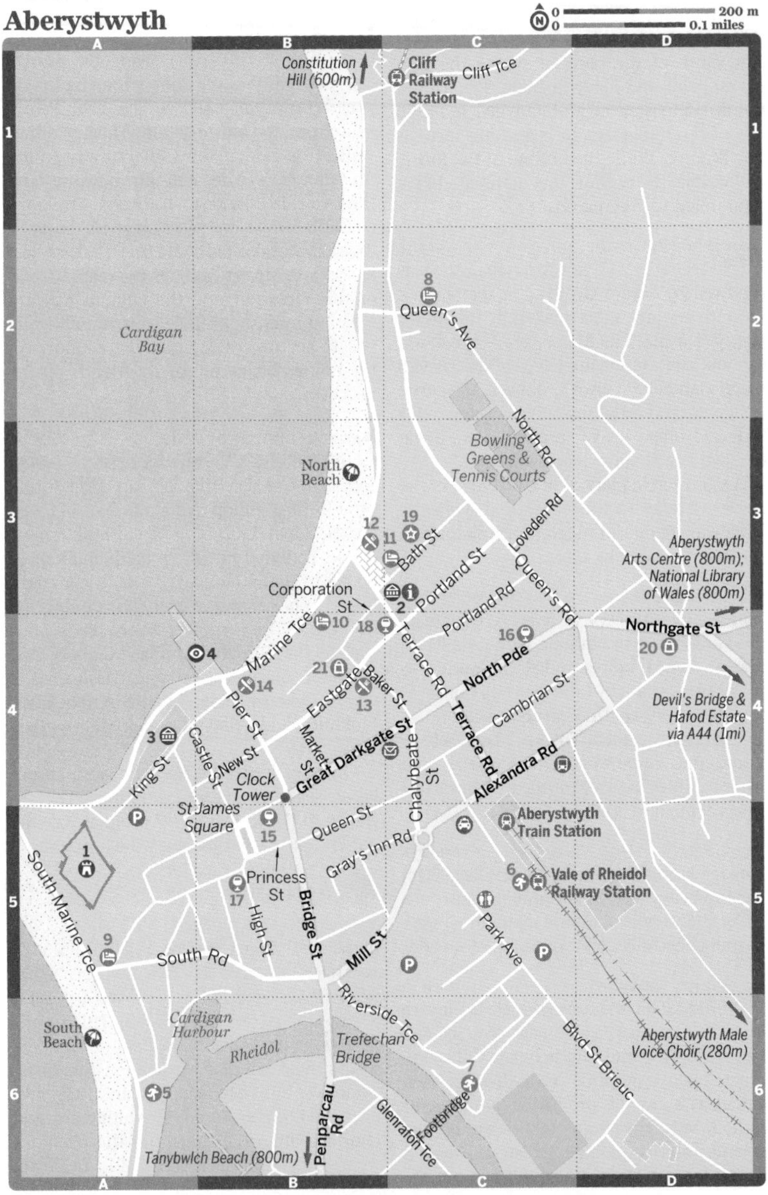

Ystwyth Trail CYCLING

Suitable for cyclists and walkers, this 21-mile waymarked route mainly follows an old rail line from Aberystwyth southeast to Tregaron, shadowing the River Ystwyth for the first 12 miles and ending in the Teifi Valley. Pick up the trail from the footbridge on Riverside Tce in Aberystwyth or start from Tregaron if you prefer heading downhill.

Cliff Railway CABLE CAR

(Rheilffordd y Graig; ☎01970-617642; www.aberystwythcliffrailway.co.uk; Cliff Tce; adult/child one way £3/2, return £4/2.50; ⏰10am-5pm Apr-Oct, shorter hours Nov-Mar) If your legs aren't up to the climb of Constitution Hill (p193); 130m), you can catch a lift on the trundling little Cliff Railway, the UK's longest electric funicular and possibly its slowest too, at a breakneck 4mph. It must have been glacial when first built, in 1896, when it was powered by a water-balance system.

Sleeping

Maes-y-Môr GUESTHOUSE £

(☎01970-639270; www.maesymor.co.uk; 25 Bath St; s/d £35/55; P 📶) Yes, that is a laundrette. But don't be fooled: venture upstairs from the drying machine and you will find nine clean, bright rooms and a warm welcome. Breakfast is not included but there's a kitchen for guest use and a locked shed for bicycles.

★**Gwesty Cymru** HOTEL ££

(☎01970-612252; www.gwestycymru.com; 19 Marine Tce; s/d from £70/95; ⏰restaurant noon-2.30pm & 6-9pm Tue-Sun; 📶) A real gem, the 'Wales Hotel' is a charismatic boutique property right on the waterfront with a strong sense of Welsh identity. Local slate features throughout, paired with rich aubergine carpets and contemporary styling. Of the eight en-suite rooms, those on the top floor offer baths with sea views.

The hotel's small restaurant (mains £16 to £20) has an enviable reputation and serves a good choice of local produce as well as international dishes. Meat lovers should try the succulent Welsh steak or lamb shank. Book ahead.

Bodalwyn B&B ££

(☎01970-612578; www.bodalwyn.co.uk; Queen's Ave; s/d £55/80; 📶) Simultaneously upmarket and homely, this handsome Edwardian B&B offers tasteful rooms with sparkling new bathrooms and a hearty cooked breakfast (with vegetarian options). Five of the rooms have sea views, but ask for room 3, with the bay window.

Glyn Garth B&B ££

(☎01970-615050; www.glyngarth.pages.qpg.com; South Rd; s/d from £33/66; 📶) A stone's throw from the sea (literally!), this friendly B&B is a boon for budget and solo travellers. Chintzy decor aside, all rooms are cosy and spotless; cheaper rooms share facilities and the cooked breakfast is suitably hearty.

Eating

Treehouse CAFE £

(☎01970-615791; www.treehousewales.co.uk; 14 Baker St; mains £8-10; ⏰10am-5pm Mon-Fri, from 9am Sat; 🖉) Spread over two floors of a Victorian house above an organic grocer, this excellent cafe uses local produce in a wide range of tempting dishes catering equally to vegetarians, vegans and meat lovers.

Aberystwyth

Perhaps the best bet in town for lunch (noon to 3.30pm), it serves imaginative fare such as harissa roast chicken or rice noodles with greens, gyoza and shiitake broth.

★**Ultracomida** TAPAS ££
(☎01970-630686; www.ultracomida.co.uk; 31 Pier St; tapas £1.50-6; ⏲10am-5pm Mon, to 9pm Tue-Sat, noon-4pm Sun; ✎) This is a foodie's idea of nirvana: out front, a delicatessen with Spanish, French and Welsh goodies and a cheese counter to die for; out back, communal tables to sample the produce with an appropriate glass of wine. Favourite tapas can be eaten as mains (£10), while the *pintxos* plate – including two glasses of wine (£14) – is excellent value.

Baravin ITALIAN ££
(☎01970-611189; www.baravin.co.uk; Terrace Rd, Llys y Brenin; mains £10-15; ⏲10am-late Mon-Sat; ⓦ) If you've ever wondered how Italian food tastes when made with Welsh ingredients – think pizzas and calzones with Welsh pork sausage or Perl Wen cheese – this stylish bistro by the bay can help satisfy your curiosity.

Drinking & Nightlife

Thanks to its large student population, during term time Aberystwyth has a livelier nightlife than anywhere else in the northern half of the country.

Ship & Castle PUB
(☎07773-778785; 1 High St; ⏲2pm-midnight Mon-Thu & Sun, 2pm-1am Fri, noon-1am Sat; ⓦ) A sympathetic renovation has left this 1830 pub as cosy and welcoming as ever, while adding big screens to watch the rugby on. It is the place to come for real ales, with a large, constantly revolving selection on tap, plus a few ciders.

White Horse PUB
(☎01970-615234; www.whitehorseaberystwyth.co.uk; Upper Portland St; ⏲10am-midnight Sun-Thu, 9am-1am Fri & Sat; ⓦ) Spacious, simple and student-friendly, the Horse has an open, modern feel and big windows for watching activity on the street. It's packed on weekend nights and relaxing during the daytime, when you can make the most of the free wi-fi.

Academy BAR
(☎01970-636852; Great Darkgate St; ⏲noon-1am Sun-Fri, to 2am Sat) An incongruous setting for a booze palace, perhaps, but an incredibly beautiful one. This former chapel has Victorian tiles on the floor, a mezzanine supported by slender cast-iron columns, red lights illuminating a wooden staircase leading to an eagle-fronted pulpit and organ pipes behind the bar.

Harry's PUB
(☎01970-612647; www.harrysaberystwyth.com; 40-46 North Pde; ⏲bistro noon-9pm, bar noon-midnight, to 1am Fri & Sat) Billing itself as hotel, bar and bistro, Harry's comprises a series of rooms wrapped around the central bar, ranging from a large screen-festooned sports bar to a small clubby lounge. The bistro serves up satisfying pastas, grills and other pub staples (£9 to £14).

☆ Entertainment

Aberystwyth Arts Centre PERFORMING ARTS
(Canolfan Y Celfyddydau; ☎box office 01970-623232; www.aberystwythartscentre.co.uk; Penglais Rd; ⏲8am-11pm Mon-Sat, noon-8pm Sun) One of the largest arts centres in Wales, this happening place stages excellent opera, drama, dance and concerts, plus it has a bookshop, an art gallery, a bar and a cafe. The cinema shows a good range of cult and foreign-language movies. Part of Aberystwyth University, the centre is on the Penglais campus, half a mile east of town.

Aberystwyth Male Voice Choir TRADITIONAL MUSIC
(☎01970-623800; www.aberchoir.co.uk; Plascrug Ave; ⏲7-8.30pm Thu) Harmonising since 1962, the Aber Male Choir rehearses at the Aberystwyth Rugby Club from 7pm to 8.30pm most Thursdays.

Commodore Cinema CINEMA
(☎01970-612421; www.commodorecinema.co.uk; Bath St) This traditional single-screen shows current mainstream releases and runs a bar for a pre-flick beer.

Shopping

Treehouse2 HOMEWARES, BEAUTY
(☎01970-625116; www.treehousewales.co.uk; 3 Eastgate; ⏲10am-5.30pm Mon-Sat) This little boutique specialises in organic and fair-trade homewares, cosmetics and baby goods.

Andy's Records MUSIC
(☎01970-624581; 16 Northgate St; ⏲11.30am-6pm Mon, Tue & Thu-Sat) A handy indie record shop that also sells tickets for gigs at the university.

Information

Bronglais Hospital (☎01970-623131; Caradoc Rd) Has a 24-hour accident and emergency department.

Tourist Office (☎01970-612125; www.discoverceredigion.co.uk; Terrace Rd; ⊙10am-5pm Mon-Sat; 📶) Below the Ceredigion Museum, this office stocks maps and books on local history, has free wi-fi and the helpful staff can arrange accommodation. It's due for an upgrade, as part of the museum's 2017 expansion.

Getting There & Away

BUS

Routes include the X28 to Machynlleth (45 minutes); T2 to Dolgellau (1¼ hours), Porthmadog (2¼ hours), Caernarfon (three hours) and Bangor (3½ hours); 701 to Carmarthen (two hours), Swansea (2¾ hours) and Cardiff (4¼ hours); Thursday-only X18 to Rhayader (one hour), Llandrindod Wells (1½ hours) and Llanwrtyd Wells (2½ hours); and X50 to Aberaeron (45 minutes) and Cardigan (1½ hours).

A daily National Express coach heads to/from Newtown (£10, 80 minutes), Welshpool (£12, 1¾ hours), Shrewsbury (£15, 2¼ hours), Birmingham (£28, four hours) and London (£38, seven hours).

TRAIN

Aberystwyth is the terminus of the Arriva Trains Wales Cambrian Line, which crosses Mid-Wales every two hours en route to Birmingham (£30, three hours) via Machynlleth (£6.50, 35 minutes), Newtown (£13, 1¼ hours), Welshpool (£15, 1½ hours) and Shrewsbury (£20, two hours).

Getting Around

The **bus station** (Alexandra Rd) and taxi stand are immediately in front of the train station, while the Cliff Railway (p195) leaves from the northern end of Marine Tce.

Around Aberystwyth

The area around Aberystwyth is rural, with around half the population speaking Welsh. It has come to recent attention as the setting for the bilingual detective series *Hinterland/Y Gwyll*.

Sights

Forest of Borth FOREST

(Borth) Low tide on the beach at Borth, 7 miles north of Aberystwyth, exposes the gnarled stumps of a prehistoric forest linked in local lore to the 'drowned kingdom' of Cantre'r Gwaelod. In 2014 the Forest of Borth, swallowed by the waves 4500 years ago, was resurrected when ferocious storms swept away thousands of tons of sand.

Ysbyty Cynfyn CHURCH

(A4120) Ysbyty Cynfyn (es-*bet*-ty *kun*-vin) is a fascinating example of the grafting of the Christian onto the pagan, so widely evident in Wales. Here, the remains of a stone circle are clearly visible within Georgian churchyard walls. Earlier, the site was a hospice *(ysbyty)*, run by the Knights Hospitaller for travellers making their way to Strata Florida abbey (p198).

Devil's Bridge BRIDGE

(www.devilsbridgefalls.co.uk; adult/child £3.75/2; ⊙9.30am-5pm) Mysterious Devil's Bridge spans the Rheidol Valley on the lush western slopes of Plynlimon (Pumlumon Fawr; 752m) where the Rivers Mynach and Rheidol tumble together in a narrow gorge. Just above the confluence, the Rheidol drops 90m in a series of spectacular waterfalls. Devil's Bridge is itself a famous crossing point, where three bridges are stacked above each other. The lowest was supposedly built by the Knights Templar before 1188, the middle one in 1753 and the uppermost road-bridge in 1901.

It's one of many bridges associated with an arcane legend that involves the devil building a bridge on the condition that he gets to keep the first living thing that crosses the bridge. An old lady then outwits the devil by throwing some food over, which her dog chases and everybody's happy – except the devil and, presumably, the dog.

WORTH A TRIP

LLANFIHANGEL Y CREUDDYN

The main reason to visit the pretty hamlet of Llanfihangel y Creuddyn, 7 miles southeast of Aber, is to visit the outstanding pub **Y Ffarmers** (☎01974-261275; www.yffarmers.co.uk; Llanfihangel y Creuddyn; mains £15-18; ⊙6-11pm Tue-Fri, noon-11pm Sat, noon-3pm Sun, extended hours in high season). Ostensibly another snug, white-brick house of assembly, it does fantastic Welsh pub food: cockle cakes with laverbread sauce, guinea fowl with tarragon and shallots, and other lip-smacking creations. Take the A4340 to the village of New Cross and follow the signs.

Access to the waterfalls and the old bridges is from beside the top-most bridge. There are two possible walks: one, just to view the three bridges, takes only 10 minutes (£1); the other, a half-hour walk, descends 100 steps (Jacob's Ladder), crosses the Mynach and ascends the other side, passing what is said to have been a robbers' cave. It's beautiful but steep and can be muddy; wear sensible footwear.

Hafod Estate GARDENS
(☎01974-282568; www.hafod.org) FREE Nearly 200 hectares of sublime, picturesque grounds await at Hafod Estate, a lovely Georgian park not far from Devil's Bridge. Five walks of between 1 mile and 4 miles weave around the landscape, showing off its different aspects. Open all year round, and free to access, Hafod is off the B4574 between Pontrhydygroes and Cwmystwyth; park at the church and walk from there.

Strata Florida MONASTERY
(Ystrad Fflur; Cadw; www.cadw.gov.wales/daysout/strata-florida-abbey; Abbey Rd, Pontrhydfendigaid; £3.50, Nov-late Mar free; ⏲10am-5pm late Mar-Oct, to 4pm Nov-late Mar) On an isolated, peaceful site southeast of Aberystwyth lies this ruined Cistercian abbey. The best preserved remnant is a simple, complete arched doorway, decorated with lines like thick rope. At the rear of the site a roof has been added to protect two chapels, which still have some of their 14th-century tiling, including one depicting a man admiring himself in a mirror.

The community at Strata Florida (Ystrad Fflur or 'Valley of the Flowers') was founded in 1164 by a Norman lord named Robert FitzStephen. After Welsh resurgence in the southwest, however, the Cistercians won the support of the Welsh princes, and their abbeys became a focus for literary activity and influence. The present site was established under Lord Rhys ap Gruffydd, and a number of princes of Deheubarth, as well as the great 14th-century poet Dafydd ap Gwilym, are buried here.

The site is a mile down a rural road from the village of Pontrhydfendigaid (pont-reed-*ven*-dee-guide) on the B4343; the village is 15 miles from Aberystwyth or 9 miles south of Devil's Bridge (p197).

Activities

Bwlch Nant yr Arian BIRDWATCHING
(☎01970-890453; www.naturalresources.wales; Ponterwyd; parking 2hr £1.50; ⏲visitor centre & cafe 10am-5pm) Part of Natural Resources Wales, Bwlch Nant yr Arian (*bull*-kheh nant ear *arr*-ee-en) is a picturesque piece of woodland set around a lake, ringed with mountain-bike and walking tracks. The main drawcard, however, is the red kite feeding, which takes place at 2pm daily year-round (3pm British Summer Time).

Even outside mealtimes you'll quite often see majestic birds of prey circling above. You can watch all the action from the terrace of the attractive turf-roofed visitor centre and cafe. It's 9 miles east of Aberystwyth on the A44.

Getting There & Away

The Vale of Rheidol Railway (p193) heads to Devil's Bridge from Aberystwyth, as does the Rheidol Cycle Trail. Bus T21 runs to Pontrhydfendigaid (35 minutes) from Aber and there are regular trains to Borth (11 minutes).

POWYS

Small villages, quiet market towns and an abundance of sheep litter the undulating hills and moorland of rural Powys, by far Wales' biggest county. Named after an ancient Welsh kingdom, this modern entity was formed in 1974 from the historic counties of Montgomeryshire, Radnorshire and Brecknockshire.

It's an overwhelmingly rural place, ideal for walking and cycling, but this county isn't just green in a literal sense – Machynlleth has become a focal point for the nation's environmentally friendly aspirations, and all over the county efforts to restore the threatened red kite have been met with outstanding success. The bird is now the very symbol of Powys, the county at Wales' green heart.

Machynlleth

POP 2235

Little Machynlleth (ma-*hun*-khleth) punches well above its weight. Saturated in historical significance, it was here that nationalist hero Owain Glyndŵr established the country's first parliament in 1404. But even that legacy is close to being trumped by Machynlleth's reinvention as the green capital of Wales – thanks primarily to the Centre for Alternative Technology (CAT), 3 miles north of town.

Machynlleth

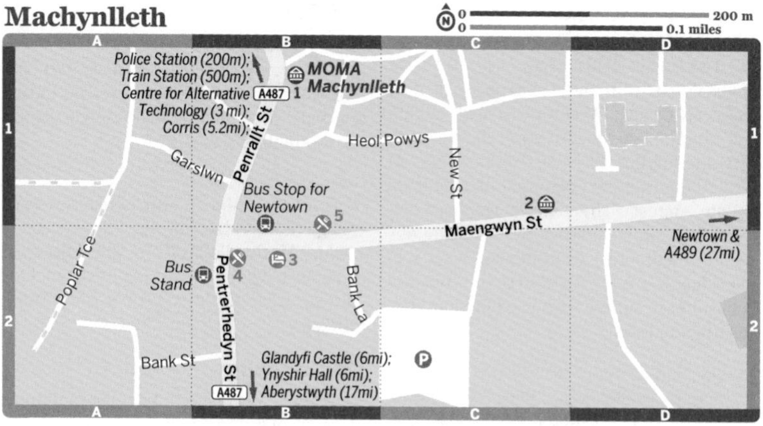

The centre has given Machynlleth an eco-magneticism that attracts alternative lifestylers from far and wide. If you want to get your runes read, take up yoga or explore holistic dancing, Machynlleth is the ideal place for you. Unfortunately, it hasn't been enough to protect the town from failing fortunes, with some much-loved shops and cafes succumbing to economic pressures in recent years. Still a surprisingly cosmopolitan local town, Machynlleth is surrounded by serene countryside, particularly suited to mountain biking.

Machynlleth

Top Sights
1 MOMA Machynlleth B1

Sights
2 Owain Glyndŵr Centre C1

Sleeping
3 Wynnstay Wales B2

Eating
4 Market B2
5 Number Twenty One B1

Sights

★Centre for Alternative Technology — LANDMARK

(CAT; Canolfan y Dechnoleg Amgen; ☎01654-705950; www.cat.org.uk; Pantperthog; adult/child £8.50/4; ⏲10am-5pm; P ♿) A small but dedicated band of enthusiasts have spent 40 years practising sustainability at the thought-provoking CAT, set in a beautiful wooded valley 3 miles north of Machynlleth. Founded in 1974 (well ahead of its time), CAT is an education and visitor centre that demonstrates practical solutions for sustainability. There are 3 hectares of displays dealing with topics such as composting, organic gardening, environmentally friendly construction, renewable energy sources and sewage treatment and recycling.

To explore the whole site takes about two hours – take rainwear as it's primarily outdoors. Kids love the interactive displays and adventure playground and there's a great organic wholefood restaurant. The visit starts with a 60m ride up the side of an old quarry in an ingenious water-balanced cable car (closed in winter to save water). A drum beneath the top car fills with stored rainwater and is then drawn down while the bottom car is hauled up. At the top you disembark by a small lake with great views across the Dyfi Valley.

There are workshops and games for children during the main school holidays and an extensive program of residential courses for adults throughout the year (day courses start at around £45). A new purpose-built education centre also offers postgraduate programs on sustainability, renewable energy and sustainable architecture. Volunteer helpers are welcome, but you'll need to apply.

To get to the CAT from Machynlleth (seven minutes) you can take the 34 bus. Buses T2 and X27 go to the village of Pantperthog, a 10-minute walk away.

★**MOMA Machynlleth** GALLERY
(☎01654-703355; www.moma.machynlleth.org.uk; Penrallt St; ⏲10am-4pm Mon-Sat) FREE Housed partly in the **Tabernacle**, a neoclassical former Wesleyan chapel (1880), the Museum of Modern Art exhibits work by contemporary Welsh artists as well as an annual international competition (mid-July to late August). The small permanent collection is supplemented by a continuous roster of temporary exhibitions. The chapel itself has the feel of a courtroom, but the acoustics are superb – it's used for concerts, theatre and talks.

Owain Glyndŵr Centre MUSEUM
(Canolfan Owain Glyndŵr; ☎01654-702932; www.canolfanglyndwr.org; Maengwyn St; ⏲10am-4pm Easter-Sep) FREE Housed in a rare example of a late-medieval Welsh townhouse, the Owain Glyndŵr Centre houses a new exhibition telling the rip-roaring story of the Welsh hero's fight for independence. Although it's called the Old Parliament Building, it was probably built around 1460, some 50 years after Glyndŵr instituted his parliament on this site, but it's believed to closely resemble the former venue.

Activities

The rolling wooded hills that surround Machynlleth shelter some of the best mountain biking in the country, with numerous tracks and bridleways criss-crossing the hills and four excellent trails to follow. See Dyfi Mountain Biking for information and maps.

There's also Sustrans National Cycle Network Route 8, leading off the A487 just north of the train station, following a countryside path, crossing the Millennium Bridge and leading you towards the Centre for Alternative Technology by the greenest possible form of transport.

Dyfi Mountain Biking MOUNTAIN BIKING
(www.dyfimountainbiking.org.uk) This local collective has waymarked four mountain-bike routes from Machynlleth: the Mach 1, 2, 3 and 4, each longer and more challenging than the last. In the Dyfi Forest, near Corris, is the custom-built, 9-mile, ClimachX loop trail. In May the same crew runs the **Dyfi Enduro**, a noncompetitive, 37-mile mountain-bike challenge attracting over 1000 riders.

Festivals & Events

Machynlleth Comedy Festival COMEDY
(www.machcomedyfest.co.uk; ⏲April/May) This long weekend of laughs also involves theatre and kids' shows and is increasingly attracting top-flight UK comics.

Gŵyl Machynlleth MUSIC
(Machynlleth Festival; www.momawales.org.uk; ⏲Aug) Takes place in the Tabernacle at MOMA Machynlleth during the third week of August, with music ranging from kids' stuff to cabaret, plus there's a lively fringe festival.

Sleeping

Downtown Machynlleth has a good number of guesthouses and pubs with rooms, while out of town you'll find a campsite and more glamorous, secluded options.

★**Beudy Banc** CAMPGROUND £
(☎01650-511495; www.beudybanc.co.uk; Abercegir; sites/d from £20/75) Set on a working sheep farm nestled in the folds of the Dyfi Valley, this wonderful place offers back-to-basics camping in grassy meadows with glorious views. There are hot showers and composting toilets, campfires are allowed and, with a limited number of pitches, it never feels too crowded.

If you feel like a little more comfort, you can choose from excellent-value, fully furnished bell tents sleeping four (£40 per night), a simple but quirky cabin (£75 per night) or a gorgeous green-powered barn, which can sleep up to eight (prices start at £85 for two people).

A walking trail across the farm links up with Glyndŵr's Way, but the real joy here are the two excellent mountain-bike descents and the network of tracks and bridleways around the farm. Beudy Banc is about 3 miles northeast of Machynlleth off the A489.

★**Glandyfi Castle** BOUTIQUE HOTEL ££
(☎01654-781238; www.glandyficastle.co.uk; A487, Glandyfi; r £90-250; P 📶) Built in 1820 as a fashionable statement of wealth, this quirky Regency Gothic castle has been brought back to life as a gloriously indulgent hotel. The eight excellent-value rooms blend classical styling with modern sensibilities, while the turrets, towers, octagonal rooms and superb views over the vast grounds make it feel like an incredibly special place to stay.

A three-course set menu (£35 per head) is served in the evening, and afternoon tea can be arranged (£18 per head). The castle is 6 miles southwest of Machynlleth, off the A487.

Sunny View B&B ££

(☎01654-700387; www.sunnyviewbandb.weebly.com; Forge; s/d £50/70) Set in a quiet village 1 mile from Machynlleth, this bungalow has two immaculate en-suite rooms decorated in an unfussy modern style. The breakfasts are good, there's a very warm welcome and it's a great option for cyclists as the trails of Dyfi Mountain Biking pass through the village.

To get here head out of Machynlleth on the A489 towards Newtown and turn right onto Forge Rd just opposite the hospital. If you arrive by train, the owners are happy to pick you up at the station.

Wynnstay Wales HOTEL ££

(☎01654-702941; www.wynnstay.wales; Maengwyn St; s/d from £59/90; P) This erstwhile Georgian coaching inn (1780) remains the best all-rounder in town, with 22 charming older-style rooms, one with a four-poster bed, and creaky, uneven floors. Downstairs there's a good restaurant and, in the courtyard, a wood-fired pizzeria (pizzas £8).

★**Living Room Treehouses** CABIN £££

(☎01172-047830; www.living-room.co; 3-day, 2-night double/family £349/379; P) Wonderfully designed, these six, cosy, rustic-glam tree houses blend organically into an enchanted forest off the A470. You're as close to nature as can be (up a tree!), yet the beds are luxurious, insulation and wood-burning stoves keep you warm all year and the seclusion is glorious. Arrival days are Sundays, Wednesdays and Fridays.

It may sound hackneyed, but these electricity-free tree houses really do make for perfect romantic getaways (as long as your sweetie loves the great outdoors). Our favourite is Gwdy Hw (pronounced 'Goody-Hoo'), but Bryn Meurig, lower to the ground, is the best choice for families.

Eating

Market MARKET £

(www.machynllethmarket.co.uk; Maengwyn St; Wed) Chartered by Edward I himself, in 1291, the Wednesday street market has been going ever since and remains a lively affair.

Number Twenty One WELSH ££

(☎01654-703382; www.numbertwentyone.co.uk; 21 Maengwyn St; mains £13-17; noon-10pm Wed-Sun;) Run by a passionate young foodie couple with ambitions that exceed the usual small-town bistro, Number Twenty One has been popular since the day it opened. The food is imaginative without being fussy, the service is friendly but professional, children are welcome and nothing seems too much trouble. Space is limited so book ahead.

★**Ynyshir Hall** GASTRONOMY £££

(☎01654-781209; www.ynyshirhall.co.uk; Eglwysfach; 5-course lunch/dinner menu £39.50/55, tasting menus £89/120; noon-2pm & 7-9pm) Foraged wild foods, the best local meat and seafood and its own kitchen garden produce give the kitchen at Ynyshir Hall the foundations to concoct some of Wales' most fancied fare. A Michelin-starred restaurant within a luxurious country retreat that once belonged to Queen Victoria, it offers set menus studded with delights such as scampi with black garlic and rhubarb.

Ynyshir Hall is off the A487, 6 miles southwest of Machynlleth.

Getting There & Away

If you're on a bike, Lôn Las Cymru (Sustrans National Cycling Network Route 8) passes through Machynlleth, heading north to Corris and southeast to Rhayader.

Bus routes include X28 to Aberystwyth (45 minutes); T2 to Dolgellau (30 minutes), Porthmadog (90 minutes), Caernarfon (2¼ hours) and Bangor (2¾ hours); X85 to Newtown (55 minutes); and 34 to the Centre for Alternative Technology (seven minutes) and Corris (15 minutes).

The bus stops for Newtown (Maengwyn St) and other destinations (Pentrerhedyn St) are either side of the market cross in the centre of town.

By train, Machynlleth is on the Cambrian and Cambrian Coast Lines. Destinations include Aberystwyth (£6.50, 35 minutes), Porthmadog (£13.20, 1¾ hours), Pwllheli (£15.30, 2½ hours), Newtown (£9.10, 38 minutes) and Birmingham (£20.90, 2¼ hours).

Corris

POP 723

Tucked beneath looming slopes of pine on the edge of Snowdonia National Park, Corris is a peaceful former slate village, 5 miles north of Machynlleth. With a steam railway, craft centre, theatre, great bike trails and subterranean tours of the village's old slate mine and caves, it's well worth a stop.

Activities

Corris Mine Explorers TOURS

(01654-761244; www.corrismineexplorers.co.uk; tours by appointment) The harsh working conditions and cramped depths of the slate mines are brought vividly to life on these tours. Braich Goch was abandoned about 40 years ago but everything is left just as it was when the miners last walked out. A reasonable level of fitness and a willingness to get wet and dirty are required. Bookings are essential.

There are three tour options: a one-hour taster (adult/child £12.50/8.50; minimum age eight), a two-hour explorer (£25/25; minimum age 10) and a four-hour expedition (£48/48; minimum age 13).

King Arthur's Labyrinth TOURS

(01654-761584; www.kingarthurslabyrinth.com; adult/child £9.95/6.65; 10am-5pm Easter-Oct;) Child-focused King Arthur's Labyrinth is an underground boat ride and walking tour through caves and tunnels where a sound-and-light show, manikins and a hooded guide bring old Celtic tales and Arthurian legends to life.

Corris Railway RAIL

(01654-761303; www.corris.co.uk; Station Yard; adult/child £6/3; see website for days of operation) Built in the 1850s to transport slate, the narrow-gauge Corris Railway now offers 50-minute trips, which include a guided tour of the sheds. Trains run every hour from 11am to 4pm and the attached museum is free to enter.

Bike Corris MOUNTAIN BIKING

(01654-761456; www.bikecorris.co.uk) This operation is your passport to the trails of the Dyfi Valley and Southern Snowdonia, host to some of the UK's most challenging downhill mountain-bike races. Packages including guided riding, accommodation and meals are available.

Sleeping

Corris Hostel HOSTEL £

(01654-761686; www.corrishostel.co.uk; Old School; dm/s/d from £16/23/35) Occupying an old slate schoolhouse uphill from the centre of town, this ecofriendly independent hostel is popular with walkers and mountain bikers. There's a self-catering kitchen or meals can be arranged (dinner is only offered to groups).

Eco Retreats CAMPGROUND ££

(01654-781375; www.ecoretreats.co.uk; A487, Furnace; d 2 nights tepee/yurt from £195/215) Eco Retreats offers superchilled accommodation in beautifully furnished tepees and yurts. It's a low-tech experience, with wood burners, compost toilets and outdoor showers set in a remote location up a rough forest track. The tents are well spaced and the views are glorious, making it an incredibly tranquil place to unwind.

Reiki, meditation, kinesiology and elemental medicine sessions are also available on site. It's tricky to find; the owners will give you directions to the campground when you make your booking.

Eating & Drinking

Andy & Adam's Shop CAFE

(01654-761391; www.andyandadam.co.uk; Bridge St; 9.30am-6.30pm) From paddock to plate, the eponymous, hands-on owners here oversee the production of dishes such as the 'local bap' (with sausage made from pork they reared themselves) and a kale-and-bacon 'superfood stack'. The coffee here is excellent and the walls are teeming with top-notch groceries.

Slaters Arms PUB

(01654-761324; www.theslatersarms.com; Bridge St) A convivial and old-fashioned Welsh village pub, the Slaters does simple pub food (mains £8) and has a range of real ales from craft brewer the Celt Experience.

Shopping

Corris Craft Centre ARTS & CRAFTS

(01654-761584; www.corriscraftcentre.co.uk; 10am-5pm) A hive of interconnected hexagonal workshops for potters, glassblowers, gin distillers, wood turners, candle-makers and chocolatiers, along with a cafe to keep everyone productive, the Corris Craft Centre is an excellent place to see artists and craftspeople at work, join a short workshop or pick up some souvenirs. It's just outside Corris, on the A487.

Information

Post Office (Corris Institute, Bridge St; 9-11.30am Mon, Tue, Fri & Sat) Essentially a desk in the half-timbered Corris Institute (the old cultural centre for the town's miners), this terrifically friendly post office is an unofficial wealth of information for visitors to the area. Local crafts and preserves are sold, too.

Getting There & Away

Buses T2 and X27 from Machynlleth (15 minutes) stop in Corris.

Rhayader (Rhaeadr Gwy)

POP 1824

Rhayader is a handsome, small and fairly uneventful livestock-market town revolving around a central crossroads marked by a war-memorial clock. It's a place that appeals to walkers visiting the nearby Elan Valley and tackling the 136-mile Wye Valley Walk. Distinguished by several extremely venerable timber buildings, it's largely deserted on Thursdays (when businesses trade for only half a day) but fills out on Wednesday – market day.

Sights & Activities

Rhayader Museum & Gallery MUSEUM
(☎01597-810561; www.carad.org.uk; East St; adult/child £4/free; ⏰10am-4pm Tue-Sat) Focusing on local history and life in and around Rhayader, this small museum uses artefacts, film and more than 50 oral histories to explore everything from folk tales to sheep farming. The attached shop sells local craft, toys and books, and has plenty of information for visitors to the area, while the theatre houses dance, drama and music.

Gigrin Farm Red-Kite Feeding Station BIRDWATCHING
(☎01597-810243; www.gigrin.co.uk; South St (A470); adult/child £5/3; ⏰12.30-5pm daily Jan-Oct, to 4pm Sat & Sun Nov & Dec) There's been a dramatic Mid-Wales resurgence in the UK's threatened population of red kites, and hundreds arrive at Gigrin Farm every day at 2pm (3pm during British Summer Time) to gorge on meat scraps. First come crows, then ravens, then the super-agile kites – often mugging the crows to get the meat – and lastly the buzzards.

There's an interpretive centre with information on red kites and other local wildlife, a cafe and picnic area, recorded night-time footage of badgers, a camera overlooking the feeding site and marked nature trails. For £15 you can also access special photographers' and disabled-access hides. Gigrin is a working farm on the A470, half a mile south of Rhayader town centre (or 1 mile from the Wye Valley Walk).

OFF THE BEATEN TRACK

CAMBRIAN MOUNTAINS

The Cambrian Mountains are a rather desolate but starkly beautiful area of uplands covering the region roughly between Snowdonia and the Brecon Beacons. Largely unpopulated and undeveloped, this wild, empty plateau of high moorland is the source of both the Rivers Severn and Wye. Hidden in the folds of the hills are lakes, waterfalls and deserted valleys as well as hill farms home to thousands of sheep. The region sees relatively few visitors except for around the Elan Valley; if you wish to get away from it all there is no finer place in Wales in which to hike or bike in solitude. Many tracks criss-cross the area, including the 83-mile Cambrian Way; you can find details of routes at www.walkingbritain.co.uk or more information about the region at www.cambrian-mountains.co.uk.

Clive Powell Mountain Bike Centre MOUNTAIN BIKING
(☎01597-811343; www.clivepowell-mtb.co.uk; West St; ⏰9am-1pm & 2-5.30pm) This centre is run by a former cycling champion and coach. You can hire a mountain/off-road bike here (£24/16 per day, including helmet and puncture kit), or take it easier with an electric bike (£30 per day).

Sleeping

Wyeside Caravan & Camping Park CAMPGROUND £
(☎01597-810183; www.wyesidecamping.co.uk; Llangurig Rd; site/adult/child £3/8/3.50; ⏰Feb-Nov) A short walk from the centre of Rhayader, this relaxed, grassy campsite has river views, lots of trees, two shower blocks and a shop.

Horseshoe Guesthouse B&B ££
(☎01597-810982; www.rhayader-horseshoe.co.uk; Church St; s/d £44/68; P📶) This 18th-century former inn, once the Butcher's Arms, now offers comfortable modern rooms (five of seven are en suite) and plenty of communal space in the large dining room, garden, conservatory and walled courtyard. There's also a 20-seater restaurant (three courses for £16) and packed lunches for £6 per person.

✖ Eating & Drinking

Old Swan Tearooms CAFE £

(☑ 01597-811060; www.oldswantearooms.co.uk; West St; mains £5-6; ⊙10am-5pm) Using every cranny of a low-ceilinged, half-timbered, crooked-chimneyed 17th-century former inn in the dead centre of Rhayader, the Old Swan is great for breakfast, afternoon tea or something more substantial (chilli con carne, Welsh cawl and the like).

Triangle Inn PUB

(☑ 01597-810537; www.triangleinn.co.uk; Cwmdauddwr; mains £8-12; ⊙6.30-11pm daily year-round, noon-3pm Tue-Sat May-Aug, noon-3pm Thu-Sat Sep-Apr; 🕏) This tiny 16th-century inn, just over the bridge to Cwmdauddwr (the village adjoining Rhayader), is the pick of the local places to drink. It's so small that its toilets are across the road and there's a trapdoor in the floor for darts players (so they don't bang their heads on the extremely low ceiling). A very welcoming place, it serves real ales and hearty pub classics.

❶ Getting There & Away

Bus X16 goes to Builth Wells (25 to 40 minutes, one daily schooldays and Saturdays) and the X47 to Llandrindod Wells (25 minutes).

Elan Valley

The Elan Valley is filled with strikingly beautiful countryside, split by imposing Victorian and Edwardian feats of civil engineering. In the late 19th century, dams were built on the River Elan (pronounced 'ellen'), west of Rhayader, mainly to provide a reliable water supply for Birmingham. Around 100 people had to move, but only landowners received compensation. During WWII, the earliest of the dams was used to perfect the 'bouncing bomb' used in the storied Dambusters raid on targets in Germany's Ruhr Valley. In 1952 a fourth, large dam was inaugurated on the tributary River Claerwen. Together their reservoirs now provide over 70 million gallons of water daily for Birmingham and parts of South and Mid-Wales.

The need to protect the 70-sq-mile watershed (called the Elan Valley Estate) has turned it and adjacent areas into an important wildlife conservation area. The dams and associated projects also produce some 4.2 megawatts of hydroelectric power.

Unless you have your own transport, the only way into the Elan Valley is a taxi from Rhayader.

🏃 Activities

The **Elan Valley Trail** is an 18-mile (return) traffic-free walking, horse-riding and cycling path that mostly follows the line of the long-gone Birmingham Corporation Railway alongside the River Elan and its reservoirs. It starts just west of Rhayader at Cwmdauddwr.

🛏 Sleeping & Eating

Elan Valley Hotel HOTEL ££

(☑ 01597-810448; www.elanvalleyhotel.co.uk; B4518; s/d £57/75; 🅿🕏) This pleasant little hotel, with 11 bedrooms and a decent restaurant (mains £13 to £15) makes a good base for walking, cycling and birdwatching in the valley. It's on the B4518, 2.5 miles southwest of Rhayader.

Elan Valley ACCOMMODATION SERVICES

(☑ 01597-810880; www.elanvalley.org.uk) Has a handful of accommodation options, including the wonderfully isolated farmhouse of Tynllidiart.

Penbont House TEAHOUSE £

(☑ 01597-811515; ⊙11am-5pm Fri-Mon Mar-Jul, Sep & Oct, daily Aug; 🔁) Delightfully situated on a verdant hillside below the Pen y Garreg dam, these traditional Welsh tearooms are definitely worth a stop when driving in the Elan Valley. *Bara brith* (a rich, fruit tealoaf), Welsh cakes, properly brewed tea and light lunches can be taken on the lawn, or in the charming house itself.

The B&B accommodation (£70 for a quad or double) is outstanding value.

❶ Information

Elan Valley Visitor Centre (☑ 01597-810880; www.elanvalley.org.uk; B4518; ⊙10am-5pm Easter-Oct) The visitor centre houses a new exhibit on the Water Scheme (complete with photos of houses being inundated), native wildlife and local history. It also provides leaflets on the estate's 80 miles of nature trails and footpaths, rents bicycles (£6/24 per hour/day) and offers activities such as birdwatching safaris and helicopter tours over the lakes and moorland.

The centre is just downstream of the lowest dam, 3 miles from Rhayader on the B4518. Parking is £2.

Llanwrtyd Wells (Llanwrtyd)

POP 630

Llanwrtyd (khlan-*oor*-tid) Wells is an odd little town – mostly deserted except during one of its unconventional festivals, when it's packed to the rafters with crazy contestants and their merrymaking supporters.

Apart from this recent status as the capital of wacky Wales, Llanwrtyd Wells has long been surrounded by beautiful walking, cycling and riding country, with the Cambrian Mountains to the northwest and the Mynydd Epynt to the southeast.

Theophilus Evans, the local vicar, first discovered the healing properties of the Ffynon Droellwyd (Stinking Well) in 1732 when he found it cured his scurvy. The popularity of the waters grew and Llanwrtyd became a spa town. Nowadays, however, its wells have been capped and, outside of the festivals, it's hard to find much by way of vital signs.

Activities

Sustrans National Cycle Route 43 passes through Llanwrtyd Wells, heading east to Builth Wells (from where Route 8, Lôn Las Cymru, continues north to Machynlleth or south to the Wye Valley). There's excellent mountain biking in the surrounding hills; enquire at the Drovers Rest (p206).

Festivals & Events

While mulling over how to enourage tourism in Llanwrtyd in the dark winter months, some citizens started an inspired roll call of unconventionality. There's something on every month (see www.green-events.co.uk for more details).

Saturnalia Real Ale Ramble & Chariot Racing Championship SPORTS
(www.green-events.co.uk; ramble/chariot race £11/20; ⌚Jan) Roman-themed festival in mid-January including a 'best dressed Roman' competition, the devouring of stuffed bulls' testicles, rambling the course of old Roman roads and a race between bike-drawn chariots. And plenty of ale, of course.

Man vs Horse Marathon SPORTS
(www.green-events.co.uk; ⌚mid-Jun) The event that kicked off all the craziness in Llanwrtyd Wells, the Man vs Horse Marathon has been held every year since 1980 and has resulted in some tense finishes. Two-legged runners have won only twice, most recently in 2007. Held mid-June, the prize money jackpots each year a biped fails to win.

World Bog Snorkelling Championships SPORTS
(www.green-events.co.uk; adult/child £15/12; ⌚bank holiday Aug) The most famous of all Llanwrtyd's wacky events. Competitors are allowed wetsuits, snorkels and flippers to traverse a trench cut out of a peat bog, using no recognisable swimming stroke and surfacing only to navigate. Spin-off events include Mountain Bike Bog Snorkelling ('like trying to ride through treacle') and the Bog Snorkelling Triathlon, both held in July.

Real Ale Wobble & Ramble SPORTS
(www.green-events.co.uk; 1-/2-day ride £18/25; ⌚Nov) In conjunction with the Mid-Wales Beer Festival, every November cyclists and walkers follow waymarked routes (10, 15 or 25 miles for ramblers; 15 or 28 miles for the wobblers), supping real ales at the 'pint stops' along the way.

Mari Llwyd NEW YEAR
(New Year Walk In; www.green-events.co.uk; ⌚New Year's Eve) A revival of the ancient practice of parading a horse's skull from house to house on New Year's Eve while reciting Welsh poetry. The procession leaves from the centre of Llanwrtyd Wells at 10.30pm.

Sleeping & Eating

Plasnewydd B&B B&B £
(☎01591-610293; www.plasnewydd90.co.uk; Irfon Tce; s/d £35/60; P 📶) Located in the heart of town, this spick-and-span B&B has won numerous fans thanks to its warm, cosy, individually styled rooms, an extensive breakfast spread (including Glamorgan – leek-and-cheese – sausages for vegetarians) and the accommodating attitude of its owners. Wet biker gear is given a place to dry, and nice touches include delicious homemade Welsh cakes.

Lasswade Country House B&B ££
(☎01591-610515; www.lasswadehotel.co.uk; Station Rd; s/d from £65/90; P 📶) This excellent restaurant-with-rooms makes great use of a handsome, three-storey Edwardian house looking over the Irfon Valley towards the Brecon Beacons. Committed to green tourism (it's won a slew of awards, sources hydroelectric power and even offers electric vehicle recharging), it's also big on gastronomy: the chef/owner's three-course menu

(£35) features Cambrian lamb, venison, Towy salmon and other delights.

Ardwyn House B&B ££
(☎01591-610768; www.ardwynhouse.co.uk; Station Rd; s/d £60/80; P 📶) The young owners have been busy restoring the Arts-and-Crafts grandeur of this once derelict house. Some rooms have claw-foot baths and rural views, and there is parquet flooring and period wallpaper and furnishings. There's also an oak-panelled guest lounge with a pool table and bar.

★**Carlton Riverside** WELSH ££
(☎01591-610248; www.carltonriverside.com; Irfon Cres; mains £15-21; ⏲7-10.30pm Tue-Sat; P 📶) This upscale restaurant has a boutique feel and a mantelpiece groaning under its many awards. There's a basement bar (open Tuesday to Sunday evenings) but the real star here is the restaurant and its superb menu featuring plenty of local produce. Lunch can be organised with at least a day's notice, from Tuesday to Saturday.

The rooms (single/double from £50/75) are modern, simple and tasteful, and with late breakfasts and checkouts, it's well set up for bon vivants. Ask about all-inclusive foodie breaks.

Drovers Rest WELSH ££
(☎01591-610264; www.food-food-food.co.uk; Y Sgwar; 3 courses £30; ⏲10.30am-3.30pm & 7-9.30pm Tue & Thu-Sat, 12.30-2.30pm Sun; 📶) Increasingly recognised as one of Mid-Wales' best dining venues, this charming restaurant does fantastic things with local produce. Snugly perched by the Irfon, it has a new riverside terrace and a few simple-but-cosy rooms (single/double £40/80, some en suite). The owners also run regular one-day cooking courses (£165 to £195) featuring Welsh cuisine, game and other delights.

Drinking & Nightlife

★**Neuadd Arms Hotel** PUB
(☎01591-610236; www.neuaddarmshotel.co.uk; Y Sgwar; ⏲8.30am-midnight Sun-Thu, 8.30am-1am Fri & Sat) Like any good village pub, the Neuadd Arms is a focal point for the community. There's an interesting menu (mains £7 to £11), half- and full-board rooms (single/double £58/106 and £65/130) and excellent beers brewed in the stables. It's also Llanwrtyd's tourist information point, with everything you'll need to know about mountain biking, pony trekking or hiking in the area.

It was here that former landlord Gordon Green and his punters cooked up many of the kooky events that have put Llanwrtyd Wells on the tourist trail. Today its jumble of bric-a-brac, peeling paint and friendly staff give it the charm of a bygone era long lost in most parts of the country. During winter you might join one of the farmers' dogs on the couch in front of the fire.

Getting There & Away

Bus 48 heads to Builth Wells (30 minutes).

Llanwrtyd is on the Heart of Wales Line (www.heart-of-wales.co.uk), with direct services to Swansea (£11.10, two hours), Llandeilo (£5.20, 45 minutes), Llandrindod Wells (£4.20, 31 minutes) and Shrewsbury (£13.90, 2¼ hours).

Builth Wells (Llanfair-Ym-Muallt)

POP 2829

Builth (pronounced 'bilth') Wells is by far the liveliest of the former spa towns, with a bustling, workaday feel. Once the playground of the Welsh working classes, it has a pretty location on the River Wye and prominence as a local farming centre. While there are no attractions per se, it's a handy base for walkers or cyclists tackling any of the long-distance paths that pass through.

Festivals & Events

Royal Welsh Show FAIR
(www.rwas.co.uk; Llanelwedd; adult/child per day £26/5; ⏲Jul; 👪) Over 200,000 people descend on Builth for four days every July for the Royal Welsh Show (founded in Aberystwyth in 1904) to see everything from gussied-up livestock to lumberjack competitions and a food hall bursting with farm produce. The showgrounds – actually just over the Wye in Llanelwedd – host numerous other events throughout the year, from antiques fairs and garden shows to equestrian events.

Sleeping & Eating

Bronwye B&B £
(☎01982-553587; www.bronwye.co.uk; Church St; s/d from £40/60; P 📶) Overlooking the River Wye, this imposing 19th-century house has five comfortable, modern rooms with good beds and bathrooms. It's cosily modern, rather than rich with period character, but there's a warm welcome and excellent breakfasts, which, at these rates, make it a bargain.

Caer Beris Manor HOTEL £££
(☎01982-552601; www.caerberis.com; A483; s/d from £74/143) Once home to Lord Swansea, this half-timbered country manor lies at the end of a long driveway, winding through 11 hectares of parkland on the River Irfon. Classic styling, log fires and spacious rooms with swag curtains, heavy fabrics and tasslied lamps await. The oak-panelled Restaurant 1896 serves a fine seasonal menu featuring plenty of local produce (mains £19 to £25).

The hotel is on the west side of Builth Wells, on the A483.

Cosy Corner WELSH ££
(☎01982-552795; 55 High St; mains £9-12; ⊙11am-4pm Mon & Thu, to 10pm Wed, Fri & Sat) This timber-windowed, low-ceilinged tea-room lives up to its sobriquet, providing excellent homemade cakes and sandwiches alongside more elaborate dishes such as lasagne and *cawl* (Welsh stew). Welsh high tea is served from 3pm and special dinner menus mark occasions such as St David's Day.

★**Drawing Room** MODERN WELSH £££
(☎01982-552493; www.the-drawing-room.co.uk; 3 courses £40; ⊙from 7pm, last orders 8.30pm; 📶) Set in a Georgian country house, this two-rosette restaurant-with-rooms is one of the region's finest. Prime Welsh black beef, Brecon Mountain lamb and Cardigan Bay crab feature on the locally sourced menu, while the beautifully refurbished rooms are well worth considering (£125 to £150, including breakfast). It's 3 miles north of Builth, on the A470.

☆ Entertainment

Wyeside Arts Centre PERFORMING ARTS
(☎01982-552555; www.wyeside.co.uk; Castle St; ⊙12.30-9pm Tue-Fri, from 2pm Sat & Sun) A great little venue with a bar, exhibition space, cinema and live shows ('from Pinter to panto').

Builth Male Voice Choir PERFORMING ARTS
(www.builthmalechoir.org.uk; ⊙from 8pm Mon) You can catch a rehearsal from 8pm on Monday nights in the upper room of the Greyhound Hotel on Garth Rd, which is also one of the town's better pubs. Formed at the local rugby club in 1968, the choir now sings internationally.

ℹ Information

Builth Wells Library (20 High St; ⊙10am-1pm & 2-5pm Mon & Tue, 10am-1pm & 2-6pm Thu, 10am-1pm Fri, 10am-12.30pm Sat) There's no tourist office in Builth any more, but the library acts as a local information point.

ℹ Getting There & Away

Buses stopping here include the T4 to Llandrindod Wells (20 minutes), Brecon (45 minutes) and Newtown (70 minutes); the X16 and X17 to Rhayader (25 to 40 minutes, one daily schooldays and Saturdays); and the 48 to Llanwrtyd Wells (30 minutes, Monday to Saturday).

Llandrindod Wells (Llandrindod)

POP 5309

The Victorian and Edwardian glory days of this pleasantly faded spa town live on in its delightful architecture – Queen Anne and Edwardian baroque hotels and terraces that are arrestingly grand to this day. However, once the allure of the iron-, sulphur- and saline-rich waters dwindled, Llandrindod relaxed into sleepy obscurity. Now you'd need to prod it with a sharp stick to rouse it on a Wednesday afternoon, when most of the shops close.

Roman remains at nearby **Castell Collen** show that it wasn't the Victorians who first discovered the healthy effects of the local spring waters, but it was the arrival of the Central Wales Railway (now the Heart of Wales Line) in 1865 that brought visitors en masse.

⊙ Sights

National Cycle Museum MUSEUM
(☎01597-825531; www.cyclemuseum.org.uk; Temple St; adult/child £5/2; ⊙10am-4pm Tue-Fri Apr-Oct) Housed in the art nouveau Automobile Palace, the National Cycle Museum comprises more than 250 bikes. The exhibits show the progression from clunky boneshakers and towering penny-farthings to bamboo bikes from the 1890s and the vertiginous 'Eiffel Tower' of 1899 (used to display billboards), as well as slicker, modern-day versions.

Great effort has been made to put the bikes in context, with re-created Victorian and Edwardian cycle shops, photos and signboards – it's run with infectious enthusiasm. The building was constructed by Tom Norton, a local entrepreneur who started as a bicycle dealer and became the main Austin distributor.

Rock Park PARK

Rock Park, the site of the earliest spa development, is an artfully wild, well-strewn oasis at the centre of town. The bathhouse is now a complementary **health centre** (☎01597-824102; www.actionteam.org.uk; Winter Gardens Pavillion; ⏲9am-5pm Mon-Fri) and the pump room a conference centre. Fill your bottle at the rusty-looking, salty **Chalybeate Spring** (donated to the public by the Lord of the Manor in 1879) beside the Arlais Brook – apparently the iron-rich water is good for treating gout, rheumatism, anaemia and more.

Llandrindod Wells

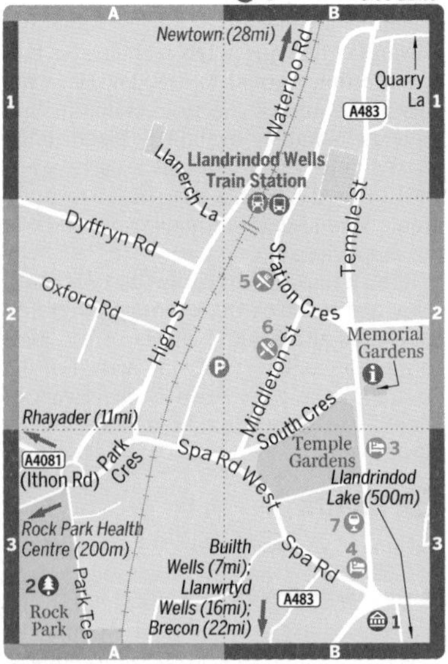

Llandrindod Wells

Sights

1 National Cycle Museum....B3
2 Rock Park....A3

Sleeping

3 Metropole Hotel....B3
4 The Cottage....B3

Eating

5 Herb Garden Cafe....B2
Spencer's Bar & Brasserie....(see 3)
6 Van's Good Food Shop....B2

Drinking & Nightlife

7 Arvon Ale House....B3

Llandrindod Wells Lake LAKE

Just southeast of the centre is a sedately pretty, tree-encircled lake, built at the end of the 19th century to allow Victorians to take their exercise without appearing to do so. The lake's centrepiece is a sculpture of a water-spouting Welsh dragon.

Sleeping

The Cottage B&B ££

(☎01597-825435; www.thecottagebandb.co.uk; Spa Rd; s/d £45/68) A really top-notch B&B making great use of a large, Arts and Crafts–style Edwardian house, the Cottage has a flower-adorned garden, and comfortable rooms decorated in period style with heavy wooden furniture and lots of original features. All rooms are either en suite or have private bathrooms and the only TV is in the guest lounge.

Metropole Hotel HOTEL ££

(☎01597-823700; www.metropole.co.uk; Temple St; s/d from £98/111; P 📶 🏊) This grand, turreted, late-Victorian hotel has spacious, corporate-style rooms and an excellent leisure complex with a swimming pool, sauna and gym. The Rock Spa offers a full range of treatments (£65 for a one-hour hot-stone massage) and there are two restaurants: **Spencer's Bar & Brasserie** (☎01597-823700; www.metropole.co.uk; Temple St; mains £15) for light bistro fare and the swankier Radnor & Miles Restaurant (menus £25).

Eating & Drinking

Van's Good Food Shop DELI £

(☎01597-823074; www.organicfoodpowys.co.uk; Middleton St; ⏲9am-5.30pm Mon-Sat; ✎) This excellent vegetarian deli features the best of local produce, including organic fruit, cheese and wine, plus ecofriendly cleaning products and other ethically selected goods. It's been in business for nearly 40 years, so it must be doing something right.

Herb Garden Cafe CAFE £

(☎01597-823082; www.herbgardencafe.co.uk; 5 Spa Centre; mains £4-7; ⏲9.30am-5pm Mon-Sat; 📶✎) Tucked away in a shopping arcade just off Station Cres, the Herb Garden Cafe serves tasty organic, wholefood meals such as smoked chicken, mango and avocado salad. While not strictly vegetarian, it makes an effort to cater for various dietary requirements. It also gets busy at lunchtime, so book ahead.

Arvon Ale House PUB

(☎07477-627267; Temple St; ⏲4-10pm Wed-Sun) A haven for lovers of real ale and cider, this snug, welcoming little taproom with hop-festooned, baby-blue walls is easily the best house of refreshment in Llandrindod. Contented regulars enjoy folk nights (on the second and fourth Sundays of the month), the sale of local hen and duck eggs, book swaps and locally sourced, frequently rotated tipples.

Information

Llandrindod Wells Memorial Hospital (☎01597-822951; Temple St; ⏲24hr) Has a minor injuries unit and is open 24 hours.

Tourist Office (☎01597-822600; www.llandrindod.co.uk; Temple St; ⏲10am-5pm Mon-Sat) The tourist office is in the old town hall in the Memorial Gardens.

Getting There & Away

Bus routes include T4 to Builth Wells (20 minutes), Newtown (55 minutes) and Brecon (70 minutes); the X47 to Rhayader (25 minutes); and the infrequent X18 to Aberystwyth (1½ hours, once a week in summer).

The **bus station** (Station Cres) is right next to the train station. For places not served, call a **cab** (☎01597-822877).

By train, Llandrindod is on the Heart of Wales Line, with direct services to Swansea (£12.70, 2½ hours), Llandeilo (£7.90, 1¼ hours), Llanwrtyd Wells (£4.20, 28 minutes), Knighton (£4.70, 36 minutes) and Shrewsbury (£11.70, 1½ hours).

Presteigne (Llanandras)

POP 2056

At the far east of the vanished county of Radnorshire, pressed right up against the English border, is Presteigne – its former county town. It's a very appealing little place, lined with handsome old buildings, studded with tearooms, craft shops and farmers' pubs and surrounded by beautiful countryside.

Sights

Judge's Lodging HISTORIC BUILDING

(☎01544-260650; www.judgeslodging.org.uk; Broad St; adult/child £7.95/3.95; ⏲10am-5pm Tue-Sun Mar-Oct, 10am-4pm Wed-Sun Nov, 10am-4pm Sat & Sun Dec) The Judge's Lodging offers an intimate glimpse into Victorian times through an audioguided wander through the town's 19th-century courthouse and lock-up. The tour is enlivened by narrations from an array of Victorian characters and you'll explore the apartments where circuit judges used to stay and where the servants who tended them lived.

Sleeping

★**Old Vicarage** B&B ££

(☎01544-260038; www.oldvicarage-nortonrads.co.uk; Norton; s/d from £78/112; P) This three-room, gay-friendly boutique B&B features Victorian fittings, making you feel like you've wandered onto the set of a period drama. Opulent, rich colours dominate and the peace of your sojourn is only interrupted by the chiming of antique clocks. Sumptuous three-course dinners (£34.95) need to be booked in advance. Norton is 1.5 miles north of Presteigne on the B4355.

Wegnalls House B&B ££

(☎01544-267710; www.kingsturning.co.uk; Kingsturning; s/d £50/80; P) This substantial early Edwardian redbrick house, right on the brook that marks the England/Wales border in these parts, is the venue for a very pleasant guesthouse. The friendly owners are from Shropshire farming backgrounds and are happy to discuss walks, dining and other distractions in the area.

Eating

Moroccan Delicatessen DELI £

(☎01544-598351; High St; mains £5-10; ⏲9am-2pm Tue-Sat) Run by a French/North African couple who cut their teeth on the London restaurant trade, this delightful deli is the best place in Presteigne to get a coffee and the only place for homemade baklava, *harira* (Moroccan soup, £4.75) and mezze platters (for one/two £9.90/15). It will also open on Friday and Saturday evenings by appointment.

Duck's Nest MODERN BRITISH ££

(☎01544-598090; www.theducksnest.com; 10 High St; mains £14-17; ⏲noon-2pm & 6-10pm Tue-Sat) The provenance board on the wall reflects the diligence with which this excellent new restaurant scours Powys, Hereford and Shropshire for great local produce. Whether it's the early (6pm to 7pm) prix fixe menu or later à la carte, you'll choose from simple, delightful dishes such as coley with crab, ginger and puy lentils or aubergine with pomegranate, feta and pearl barley.

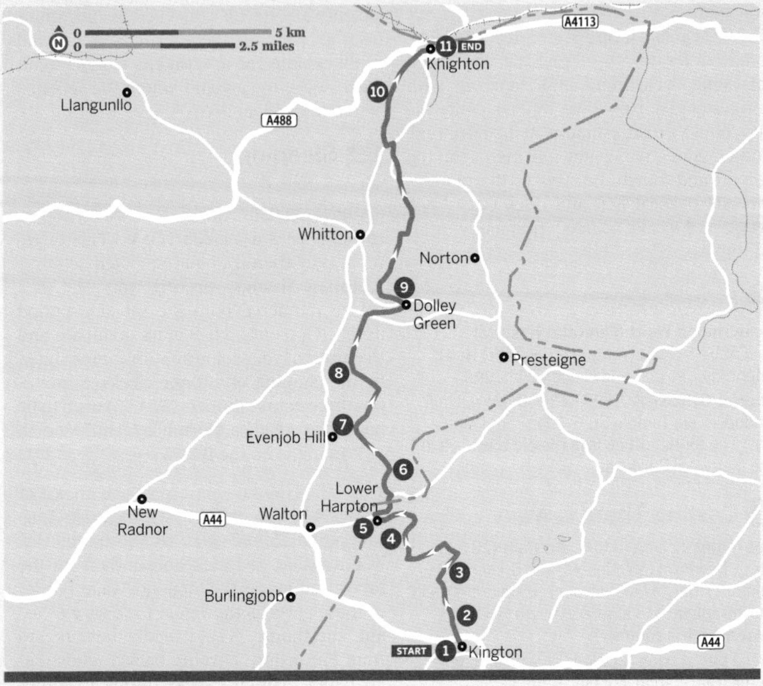

Walking Tour
Offa's Dyke Path

START KINGTON (ENGLAND)
END KNIGHTON
LENGTH 13.5 MILES; FIVE TO SEVEN HOURS

One of the most rewarding sections of Offa's Dyke Path, this route offers glorious views of the surrounding hills and passes some particularly well-preserved sections of the 8th-century defensive earthwork. The walk begins across the border in Herefordshire and weaves between the two countries crossing remote hills to Knighton (Tref-Y-Clawdd; the town on the dyke).

From ❶ **Kington Museum** head towards the clock tower, turning left onto Church St and then right onto Doctor's Lane, which soon becomes Prospect Rd. Follow the narrowing road around until you cross a footbridge over a stream. Continue straight across the busy A44 and start your first ascent towards ❷ **Bradnor Green**. Skirt the edge of the golf course and continue the climb along the edge of Bradnor Hill and then ❸ **Rushock Hill**, enjoying wonderful views across the undulating landscape. Follow the path as it runs along a section of the dyke round a field edge to reveal another impressive vista southwest to the Hergest Ridge and East Radnor Hills. Here the dyke heads up near the summit of ❹ **Herrock Hill** but the path runs down the side of the hill to ❺ **Lower Harpton** where you cross into Wales over an old packhorse bridge.

Follow the leafy lane uphill past the scant remains of ❻ **Burfa Camp**, an ancient hill fort. The path then heads up ❼ **Evenjob Hill** where the dyke remains in remarkable condition with wonderful westerly views. As you head up and over ❽ **Pen Offa** the easterly hills are revealed. It's downhill from here to the Lugg Valley past magnificent, towering sections of the dyke. Cross the field to the River Lugg, a small but beautiful river with deep pools and plenty of shade. From nearby ❾ **Dolley Green** it's a steep but scenic climb up ❿ **Furrow Hill** where you'll get great views to the west. The dyke here is little more than a raised mound of earth. From here on it's a gentle stroll down into ⓫ **Knighton**.

Getting There & Away

Bus 41, otherwise known as the 'Offa Hopper', heads to Knighton (17 minutes) every day except Sunday.

Knighton (Tref-Y-Clawdd)

POP 3007

Hilly Knighton (Tref-Y-Clawdd; the town on the dyke) is a lively, handsome town of winding streets and half-timbered houses midway along the Offa's Dyke Path National Trail and at one end of the Glyndŵr's Way National Trail. A popular stopover for walkers, it is so close to the border that its train station is actually in England.

The coming of the railway in 1861 and the growth of livestock farming saw Knighton's fortunes rise, but they fell again with the decline in population post WWII and failed attempts to turn it into a spa town. One disturbing piece of local folklore suggests that it was possible for a man to obtain a divorce by 'selling' his wife at the square where the 1872 clock tower now stands. Husbands would bring their spouse to the square at the end of a rope; the last wife was sold in 1842.

Sights

Spaceguard Centre OBSERVATORY

(☎01547-520247; www.spaceguarduk.com; Llanshay Lane; adult/child £7/4; ⊙mandatory tours 2pm & 4pm Wed-Sun year-round & 10.30am May-Sep) The hilltop Spaceguard Centre is the UK's National Near Earth Objects Information Centre, keeping an eye out for any potential *Judgment Day* scenarios. As well as telescopes watching for asteroids and comets, there's a camera obscura and planetarium shows. Take the A4113 east from Knighton, follow the sign up Llanshay Lane and the centre is 1.5 miles further on.

Sleeping & Eating

Offa Dyke House B&B ££

(☎01547-528886; www.offadykehouse.com; 4 High St; s/d from £64/99; P 📶) Reached through a passageway from High St, this B&B consists of three sumptuous rooms, all decorated with great attention to detail and with the comfort of hikers in mind. Offa Dyke Room and Glyndŵr Room feature views of the eponymous trails, baths in two of the rooms soothe aching bodies, and guests' needs are anticipated with cheerful efficiency.

OFF THE BEATEN TRACK

OFFA'S DYKE PATH

The true purpose of Offa's Dyke, Britain's longest ancient monument, isn't known, although one theory is that the 2.4m-high earthwork was thrown up in the 8th century by the Anglian king, Offa, to defend his kingdom (Mercia) from Welsh Powys. Running for 176 miles across river valleys and through handsome market towns, the Offa's Dyke Path (http://nationaltrail.co.uk/offas-dyke-path) is best tackled in 12 stages.

Horse & Jockey Inn B&B ££

(☎01547-520062; www.thehorseandjockeyinn.co.uk; Station Rd; s/d £60/85; 📶) This former 14th-century coaching inn is still in the eating-drinking-sleeping game, with a bar that opens all day and restaurant serving lunch and dinner seven days, year-round. The eight upmarket en-suite rooms in the hayloft mix modern fittings with ancient exposed stone walls and flash bathrooms.

★**Red Lion** PUB FOOD ££

(☎01547-428080; www.redlionknighton.co.uk; West St; 4 tapas £12.50; ⊙kitchen 6-9pm Tue, noon-3pm & 5-9pm Wed-Sat, noon-4.30pm Sun; 📶) With upcycled furniture, a tapas-oriented menu (largely making use of produce sourced within 30 miles) and carefully curated drinks (12 whites, 12 reds and beers from 14 different breweries), the Red Lion is a next-level addition to Knighton's dining scene. A fully refurbished 19th-century coaching inn, it also has four immaculate, carpeted bedrooms, two with baths and corner views (single/double £55/85).

Information

Tourist Office & Offa's Dyke Centre (☎01547-528753; www.offasdyke.demon.co.uk; West St; ⊙10am-5pm Apr-Oct, to 4pm Mon-Sat Nov-Mar; 📶) While austerity threatens to cut its funding, this wonderful two-in-one tourist office and Offa's Dyke Centre is full of information for walkers with interactive displays about the dyke, a section of which runs behind the centre. There's also a basic cafe with free wi-fi.

Transport

Knighton is one of the stops on the lovely Heart of Wales Line. Destinations include Swansea (£16.40, 3¼ hours), Llandeilo (£11.30, 2¼ hours), Llanwrtyd Wells (£7.30, 80 minutes), Llandrindod Wells (£4.70, 38 minutes) and Shrewsbury (£9.80, 54 minutes). Bus 41 (the 'Offa Hopper') heads to Presteigne (17 minutes) every day except Sunday.

Newtown (Y Drenewydd)

POP 11,537

A former mill town and once major UK textile centre, Newtown, on the Severn and dating back to 1279, has lots of history but is quiet today. You'll struggle to find much life on a Sunday, although it wakes up for the Tuesday and Saturday markets. Its big claim to fame is that Robert Owen, the factory reformer, founder of the cooperative movement and 'father of Socialism', was born here in 1771, though he left at the age of 10 and only returned just before his death in 1858. Monuments to his esteemed memory abound in the town centre.

Newtown is almost the home of Laura Ashley (she opened her first shop in Carno, 10 miles west of the centre).

History

Newtown was once the home of Welsh flannel and a major UK textile centre. When competition began driving wages down, Wales' first Chartist meeting was held here in October 1838. Pryce Jones, the world's first-ever mail-order firm, got its start here on the back of the textile trade. By the end of the 19th century Newtown's boom days were over – and they've never been back. There are several small museums devoted to those long-gone salad days.

Sights

Gregynog Hall GARDENS

(☎01686-650224; www.gregynog.wales.ac.uk; Tregynon; formal garden admission £3; ⊙dawn-dusk) While Gregynog Hall has been here in some form for 800 years, its current mock-Tudor manifestation – notable as one of the first uses of concrete in modern construction – dates to 1840. It's now the 300-hectare Grade 1-listed garden, dating to at least the 16th century, that's the major attraction. Walking tracks trace avenues of sculpted yews, banks of rhododendrons and azaleas, 300-year-old oaks and bird-filled beech woodlands. Admission to the grounds is unrestricted; parking costs £2.50.

From 1924 Gregynog was the home of the Davies sisters, Gwendoline and Margaret, who bequeathed an extraordinary collection of paintings to the National Museum. The sisters intended to make the house an arts centre, founding a fine-arts press in the stables and holding an annual Festival of Music and Poetry. In the 1960s the estate was given to the University of Wales, which uses it as a conference centre and venue for the Gŵyl Gregynog, an annual classical music festival held in mid-June. The house, largely unchanged since Margaret's death in 1963, opens for group tours by appointment and houses a cafe and shop (10am to 4.30pm from mid-February to December).

The hall is 5 miles north of Newtown and is signposted from the B4389.

Oriel Davies Gallery GALLERY

(☎01686-625041; www.orieldavies.org; The Park; ⊙10am-5pm Mon-Sat) FREE One of Wales' leading contemporary spaces hosting often edgy national and international exhibitions, Oriel Davies is the largest visual-arts venue in the region and offers a range of talks, courses and workshops. Its sunny, glassed-in cafe (open 10am to 4pm) is popular, vegetarian-friendly and the best place for a light meal, such as homemade soup, quiche or baked potatoes.

In summer you can eat overlooking the leafy riverside park, which contains a mound that is all that remains of Newtown's 13th-century castle and a *gorsedd* (druidic) stone circle dating from the Royal National Eisteddfod of 1965.

Robert Owen Museum MUSEUM

(☎01686-622544; www.robert-owen-museum.org.uk; The Cross, Broad St; ⊙11am-3pm Mon-Fri) FREE Housed in Newtown's Edwardian library and council chambers, this sober museum is the best place to bone up on Robert Owen's legacy. The son of a saddler who became a successful cotton-mill owner, Owen introduced radical reforms including a 10- to 12-hour workday, a minimum working age of 10 and schools for his employees' children. Combining plenty of text with artefacts and pictures, the exhibits are rich in detail. The museum's front desk also serves as Newtown's tourist information point.

Owen is considered a founding father of the cooperative and the trade union movements. At the corner of Gas and Short Bridge Sts, a statue and garden herald him as a 'pioneer, social reformer and philanthropist'.

St Mary's Old Parish Church RUINS

(Old Church St) Dating from at least 1253, St Mary's was allowed to fall into ruin after a bigger church was built in 1856; it's now a public garden, thanks to the local cooperative union. It's also the peaceful, poignant site of both founding socialist Robert Owen's grave and a memorial to Thomas Powell, a disciple of Owen who led Welsh Chartist demands for universal male suffrage in the 1830s and '40s.

WH Smith Museum MUSEUM
(☎01686-626280; 24 High St; ⏰9am-5.30pm Mon-Sat) Newtown's WH Smith bookshop has been lovingly restored to its original 1929 look, complete with wooden furniture, mirrors, signage and skylights. Upstairs is a free (but not always open) little company museum telling the history of one of Britain's biggest household names.

Festivals & Events

Gŵyl Gregynog Festival MUSIC
(☎01686-207100; www.gwylgregynogfestival.org; ⏰Jun) Since 1933 this festival has brought classical music to various historic locations across rural northern Powys. The epicentre of it all is the eponymous Gregynog Hall near Newtown, the historic seat of the Blayney family, gifted to the University of Wales in 1960.

Sleeping & Eating

Old Vicarage Dolfor B&B ££
(☎01686-629051; www.theoldvicaragedolfor.co.uk; Dolfor; s/d from £70/95; P wifi) A handsome rural Victorian house, the Old Vicarage offers pretty rooms with muted colour schemes, subtle floral wallpapers, claw-foot bath-tubs and an incredibly warm welcome. If you book, you can also dine here: the accomplished two-course dinner menu (£25) features plenty of local produce. The Old Vicarage is 4 miles south of Newtown by the busy A483.

Elephant & Castle Hotel HOTEL ££
(☎01686-626271; www.elephantandcastlehotel.co.uk; Broad St; s/d from £60/90; P wifi) Occupying a sweet, central spot by the Severn, this refurbished stone pub offers five en-suite rooms with king-size beds in the hotel proper (will it be the 'Robert Owen' or the 'Laura Ashley'?) and another 10 in the bothy (hut) out back. There's also the in-house Riverside Restaurant, making a good fist of a standard pub menu (mains £12 to £14).

High Street Delicatessen DELI £
(☎01686-610491; www.thehighstreetdelicatessen.com; 13 High St; panini £3.50; ⏰9am-5pm Mon-Fri, to 2pm Sat; wifi) Fantastic locally roasted coffee, homemade cakes, panini and soups, Welsh smallgoods and carefully chosen wines and beers are just for starters at this excellent, imaginative addition to Newtown's food landscape. Barrie and Jojo, the charming owners, are also experimenting with mezze nights (5.30pm to 7.30pm on the first Thursday of the month), wine tastings, hampers and more.

Mirrens STEAK ££
(☎01686-621120; www.mirrenssteakandtapasbar.co.uk; 17 Parkers Lane; mains £12-16; ⏰noon-3pm daily, 6-9pm Mon-Thu, to 11pm Fri & Sat) Scrubbed up in 2016, adding a 2nd-level cocktail bar, Mirrens still sources beef from local farmers who feed their Japanese Wagyu cattle with beer and treat them to the odd massage. Tapas is another speciality; the three-dish £10 tapas lunch is good value.

Shopping

Market Hall MARKET
(☎01686-622388; www.glanhafren.org; Market St; ⏰9am-5pm Tue-Sat) Dating to 1870, Newtown's handsome brick market hall has been extensively restored by the Mid-Wales Food and Land Trust. Run by Glanhafren (meaning 'by the banks of the Severn'), it now houses stalls selling organic food, handicrafts and the like.

Street Market MARKET
(⏰from 7am Tue & Sat) Around 50 stalls selling food, trinkets and hardware line the centre of Newtown on Tuesday and Saturday from around 7am.

Getting There & Away

Bus routes include X75 to Welshpool (40 minutes) and Shrewsbury (1½ hours); X85 to Machynlleth (55 minutes); and T4 to Llandrindod Wells (55 minutes), Builth Wells (70 minutes) and Brecon (two hours).

The daily National Express (www.nationalexpress.com) coach from Aberystwyth (£10, 80 minutes) to London (£31.50, 5½ hours), via Welshpool (£4.50, 25 minutes), Shrewsbury (£7.90, one hour) and Birmingham (£10.60, 2½ hours) stops here.

By train, Newtown is on the Cambrian Line, which crosses from Aberystwyth (£13, 1¼ hours) to Birmingham (£19.60, 1¾ hours) every two hours via Machynlleth (£9.10, 38 minutes), Welshpool (£5.20, 15 minutes) and Shrewsbury (£7.40, 40 minutes).

ANTB / SHUTTERSTOCK ©

1. Cardigan Bay (p188)
A stretch of coastal walk on the Ceredigion Coast Path (p190).

2. Aberystwyth Castle (p193)
One of the three remaining towers of the ruined castle, built in 1277.

3. Elan Valley (p204)
The River Elan flows through some of Wales' most beautiful countryside.

4. Aberystwyth (p192)
The pastel houses of Marine Tce overlook North Beach.

ALLEN PAUL PHOTOGRAPHY / SHUTTERSTOCK ©

Montgomery

POP 986

Set around a market square lined with handsome stone and brick houses, and overlooked by the ruins of a Norman castle FREE, genteel Montgomery is one of the prettiest small towns in the country. A charming mixture of Georgian, Victorian and timber-framed houses (many marked by helpful historical plaques) lines the streets and there are a number of excellent places to eat.

A curiosity, for travellers, is **Bunners** (01686-668308; www.bunners.co.uk; Arthur St; 9am-5pm Mon-Sat), an old-fashioned ironmongers that seems to sell everything under the sun and which attracts customers from miles away. A mile east of town is one of the best-preserved sections of Offa's Dyke, with 6m-high ditches flanking the B4386.

Sights

St Nicholas' Church CHURCH

(Church Bank; 9am-dusk) Evocative Norman St Nicholas' Church dates from 1226 and boasts a vaulted ceiling decorated with intricate coloured bosses, a beautifully carved pre-Reformation rood screen and striking mid-19th-century stained-glass windows. Look out for the elaborate canopied tomb of local landowner Sir Richard Herbert and his wife Magdalen, parents of Elizabethan poet George Herbert.

In the churchyard is the **Robber's Grave**, the final resting place of John Davies of Wrexham who was sentenced to death by hanging in 1821 for highway robbery. He vehemently protested his innocence and declared that grass would not grow on his grave for 100 years. It remained bare for at least a century.

Cloverlands Model Car Museum MUSEUM

(www.montgomeryinstitute.co.uk; Montgomery Institute, Arthur St; adult/child £2.50/75p; 2.15-5pm Fri & Sun, 10.30am-12.45pm Sat) With over 3000 exhibits, Cloverlands is a must for model-car lovers. Around half the cars are on loan from one collector, Gillian Rogers, including quarter-scale, working models of a Fiat 1936 Topolino and a 1935 Singer Le Mans, built especially for the collector and her sister. Appointments can be made for out-of-hours openings.

Sleeping & Eating

Dragon Hotel INN ££

(01686-668359; www.dragonhotel.com; Market Sq; s/d from £56/79; P) Popular with walkers, this 17th-century half-timbered coaching inn has 20 en-suite rooms, a common snug (the Den), a pool and a restaurant run by Bistro 7, formerly of Welshpool (mains £13 to £18). The bar is as good a place as any to try ales brewed at Monty's, just down the road.

Castle Kitchen CAFE £

(01686-668795; www.castlekitchen.org; 8 Broad St; mains £4-8; 9am-4.30pm Mon-Sat, 11am-4.30pm Sun) This lovely little deli-cafe overlooking Monty's picturesque heart is perfect for stocking up on bottles, butter, charcuterie and other supplies for a picnic on Offa's Dyke or in the surrounding hills. Or you can just relax in-house, enjoying a wonderful selection of soups, breads, sandwiches, daily specials and, of course, luscious cakes.

Ivy House Cafe CAFE £

(01686-668746; Church Bank; mains £5-7; 9am-5pm;) A warm, homely place with local art on the walls and a fine line in home baking, Ivy House offers a good selection of hearty and wholesome classic cafe fare with plenty of choice for vegetarians and not a chip in sight.

★ **Checkers** MODERN BRITISH £££

(01686-669822; www.thecheckersmontgomery.co.uk; Broad St; 5/8 courses £55/75; dinner Tue-Sat;) It's no exaggeration to say that one of the main drawcards of Montgomery is this truly excellent restaurant-with-rooms. The modern French menu, put together from fresh, locally sourced ingredients, and first-rate service have earned it a Michelin star and a loyal fan base. Upstairs, the five contemporary rooms are quietly stylish, with extra-comfy beds, iPod docks and blissful bathrooms. Bed and dinner packages are available from £245.

Information

Library (01686-668937; Montgomery Institute, Arthur St; 10am-noon & 3-5pm Mon, Wed & Fri, 10am-5pm Tue & Thu, 9.30am-noon Sat) Has a tourist information point.

Getting There & Away

Bus X71 runs to Welshpool (18 minutes) and Newtown (21 minutes).

Berriew

POP 1334

Shortly before the River Rhiw empties into the Severn, it gurgles through this pretty village of black-and-white houses, grouped around an ancient oval churchyard. Tiny Berriew is the unlikely location for the Andrew Logan Museum of Sculpture; when it's closed there's not much to do here except stroll around and take in the scenery.

Sights

Andrew Logan Museum of Sculpture GALLERY

(☎01686-640689; www.andrewloganmuseum.org; adult/child £3/1.50; ⊙noon-4pm Sat & Sun Jun-Sep) The supremely flouncy and fascinating Andrew Logan Museum of Sculpture is a surprise find in this tiny village. Occupying a former squash court, it's a glorious celebration of the beautiful, frivolous, and humorous, including the huge, glittering Cosmic Egg and a larger-than-life portrayal of fashion designer Zandra Rhodes. Logan has been running the Alternative Miss World contest since 1972 ('a parade of freaks, fops, show-offs and drag queens') and the museum contains many relics of the shows.

Eating

Lychgate Cottage CAFE £

(☎01686-640750; mains £5-6; ⊙9am-4.30pm Mon-Sat) This little tearoom and delicatessen by the village church serves delicious Welsh cheese and pâté platters, Ludlow olives, sandwiches, baguettes and cakes. It's very much the local hub.

Getting There & Away

Berriew is 6 miles south of Welshpool, just off the A483; take bus X75 from Newtown (25 minutes) or Welshpool (15 minutes) or bus 89 from Welshpool.

Welshpool (Y Trallwng)

POP 5948

The English originally called this place Pool, after the 'pills' – boggy, marshy ground (long since drained) along the nearby River Severn. It was changed in 1835 to Welshpool, so nobody would get confused with Poole in Dorset. Set below a steeply wooded hill, it's a handsome market town with a mixture of Tudor, Georgian and Victorian buildings along its main streets but few other distractions in the town centre and a dearth of places to stay or eat. More compelling, however, are the peripheral sights such as glorious Powis Castle and the narrow-gauge Welshpool & Llanfair Light Railway (p218).

Sights & Activities

★**Powis Castle** CASTLE

(NT; ☎01938-551944; www.nationaltrust.org.uk; adult/child castle & gardens £12/6, gardens only £9.90/4.95; ⊙gardens 10am-6pm, castle 11-5pm) Surrounded by magnificent gardens, the redbrick Powis Castle was originally constructed in the 13th century by Gruffydd ap Gwenwynwyn, prince of Powys, and subsequently enriched by generations of the Herbert and Clive families. The castle's highlight, the **Clive Museum**, houses exquisite treasures brought back from India and the Far East by Clive of India (British conqueror of Bengal at the Battle of Plassey in 1757) and his son Edward, who married the daughter of the 1st Earl of Powys.

The extravagant mural-covered, wood-panelled interior, the mahogany beds, tiger skins and one of Wales' finest collection of paintings proclaim the family's wealth, while the Clive Museum, with its cache of armour, bejewelled weapons, precious stones, textiles, diaries and letters, is testimony to a life richly lived in colonial India. You may spot a gold tiger's head encrusted with rubies and diamonds – one of only two to survive from the throne of Tipu Sultan – as well as a Chinese sword with snakeskin scabbard and finely carved ivory chess pieces.

The baroque gardens are peerless, dotted with ornamental lead statues and an orangery, formal gardens, wilderness, terraces and orchards.

The castle is just over a mile south of Welshpool off Berriew Rd.

Powysland Museum & Montgomery Canal MUSEUM

(☎01938-554656; www.powys.gov.uk; Canal Wharf; adult/child £1/free; ⊙11am-1pm & 2-5pm Mon-Fri, 11am-1pm Sat, closed Wed Sep-May) The Montgomery Canal originally ran for 35 miles, starting at Newtown and ending at Frankton Junction in Shropshire, where it joined the Llangollen Canal. Beside the canal wharf in Welshpool is the Powysland Museum, marked outside by a big blue handbag (an Andy Hancock sculpture to commemorate the Queen's jubilee). Inside, the museum tells the story of the county,

OFF THE BEATEN TRACK

GLYNDŴR'S WAY

Named for the last native Prince of Wales, Glyndŵr's Way (http://nationaltrail.co.uk/glyndwrs-way) meanders some 135 miles from Welshpool, near the English border, to Machynlleth on the southern cusp of Snowdonia National Park. It then returns cross-country to Knighton, just below the dreamy Shropshire Hills.

with fascinating details such as beautifully painted narrow-boat gear and the Roman recipe for stuffed dormouse.

After sections of canal banks burst in 1936, the canal lay abandoned until a group of volunteers and the British Waterways Board began repairing it in 1969.

Welshpool & Llanfair Light Railway RAIL
(01938-810441; www.wllr.org.uk; Raven Sq; adult/child £12.80/4; Mar-Oct, check times online) This sturdy narrow-gauge railway, completed in 1902 to bring livestock to market, runs through the pretty Banwy Valley. It's an 8-mile, 50-minute journey up steep inclines from Raven Square Station to Llanfair Caereinion. Closed in 1956, the line was reopened seven years later by enthusiastic volunteers and now even offers courses in steam-engine driving (£395).

Festivals & Events

Welshpool Country Music Festival MUSIC
(www.countrywestern.org.uk; weekend ticket £25; Jul) In mid-July, the county showground near Powis Castle (p217) becomes the unlikely venue for a weekend hoedown. Proceeds benefit children with disabilities, through the Heulwen Trust. There's free camping and caravanning sites, food stalls, beer tents and lots of knee-slapping.

Sleeping & Eating

Royal Oak HISTORIC HOTEL ££
(01938-552217; www.royaloakwelshpool.co.uk; The Cross; s/d £80/100; P) Occupying a lovely Georgian coaching inn and known by the honorific 'Royal' ever since Queen Victoria visited, the Oak is easily the grandest hotel-restaurant in Welshpool. Adorned in bright patterns, the rooms are comfortably modern, while the public bar and restaurant serve the town both for casual trysts and destination dining (mains around £15).

Long Mountain B&B ££
(01938-553456; www.longmountainbandb.co.uk; Hope Rd, Little Hope; s/d £64/86; P) A purpose-built B&B located 2 miles from Welshpool, Long Mountain is a modern extension to a 400-year-old timber-frame house. The three guest rooms all have top-quality fittings with solid oak furniture, king-sized beds with Egyptian cotton bed linen and marble bathrooms. Offa's Dyke Path runs almost past the guesthouse and there are wonderful views. No children under 16. To get here head east on the B4381, turning left onto the B388 and then right onto Hope Rd.

Corn Store INTERNATIONAL ££
(01938-554614; 4 Church St; mains £12-16, 2-course menu £15; noon-3pm & 6-11pm Tue-Sun) If Welshpool has a dining institution, this is it. Run by chef-proprietor Rebecca for over 25 years, its avocado walls and cheery, round, rainbow mirrors overlook families of regulars tucking into Euro-Med-Asian dishes such as hake with leeks and rarebit or goat's-cheese tart with roasted red pepper and pesto. The best and friendliest place in town.

Information

Tourist Office (01938-552043; www.welshpool.org/tic.html; 1 Vicarage Gardens, Church St; 9.30am-5pm Mon-Sat, 10am-4pm Sun) Has a bed-booking service and plenty of information on sights, activities and the rest in Welshpool.

Victoria Memorial Hospital (01938-558900; Salop Rd) Has a 24/7 Minor Injuries Department.

Getting There & Away

Bus X75 runs to Newtown (40 minutes) and Shrewsbury (48 minutes).

The daily National Express (www.nationalexpress.com) coach through Welshpool runs from Aberystwyth (£12, 1¾ hours) to London (£31.50, 5½ hours), via Shrewsbury (£4.80, 35 minutes) and Birmingham (£9.90, 2¼ hours).

Welshpool is on the Cambrian Line, which heads east from Aberystwyth (£15, 1½ hours) to Birmingham (£17.70, 1½ hours) and Shrewsbury (£6.10, 22 minutes) every hour or two and, in the other direction, Machynlleth (£12.70, 52 minutes) and Newtown (£5.20, 15 minutes).

Snowdonia & the Llŷn

Includes ➡

Best Places to Eat

- Soul Food (p239)
- Coconut Kitchen (p260)
- Bistro Bermo (p238)
- Tyddyn Llan Restaurant (p230)
- Gallt-y-Glyn (p248)

Best Places to Sleep

- Ffynnon (p234)
- Ruthin Castle Hotel (p223)
- mh Townhaus (p227)
- Tŷ Newydd (p262)
- Coed-y-Celyn Hall (p244)

Why Go?

This part of Wales really packs it in, from rugged mountain trails to coastal paths, old industrial sites and heritage train lines. The gem in this diadem is Snowdonia National Park, where the mightiest peaks south of Scotland scrape glowering skies. With such a formidable mountain shield, it's little wonder that the northwestern county of Gwynedd has held tightly to Cymraeg language and culture. More than 65% speak the ancient mother tongue here – the highest proportion in the country.

Along with the mountains there's the sea – battering the rocks at Braich-y-Pwll, producing surfer-friendly swells at Porth Neigwl and cooling the bathers at Barmouth. And all those bracing sea breezes seem to have blown much of the stuffiness or British reserve from the local populace. In many ways, this slice of the country distils the very essence of Welshness – just don't mention that to the folks in Cardiff!

When to Go

- April to July are the driest months, while July and August are the warmest. The best months to hit the mountains are June and July for their combination of higher temperatures and lower wind and rain.
- In June the Three Peaks Yacht Race hits Barmouth, while the hardcore put on their fell-running shoes for the Snowdon Race in July, the same month Llangollen holds its International Musical Eisteddfod and Fringe Festival.
- September is the big month for events, with Bala's triathlon, Barmouth's arts and walking festivals and Portmeirion's wonderful Festival No 6. Snow starts to fall in the mountains in October and lingers on the paths until May.

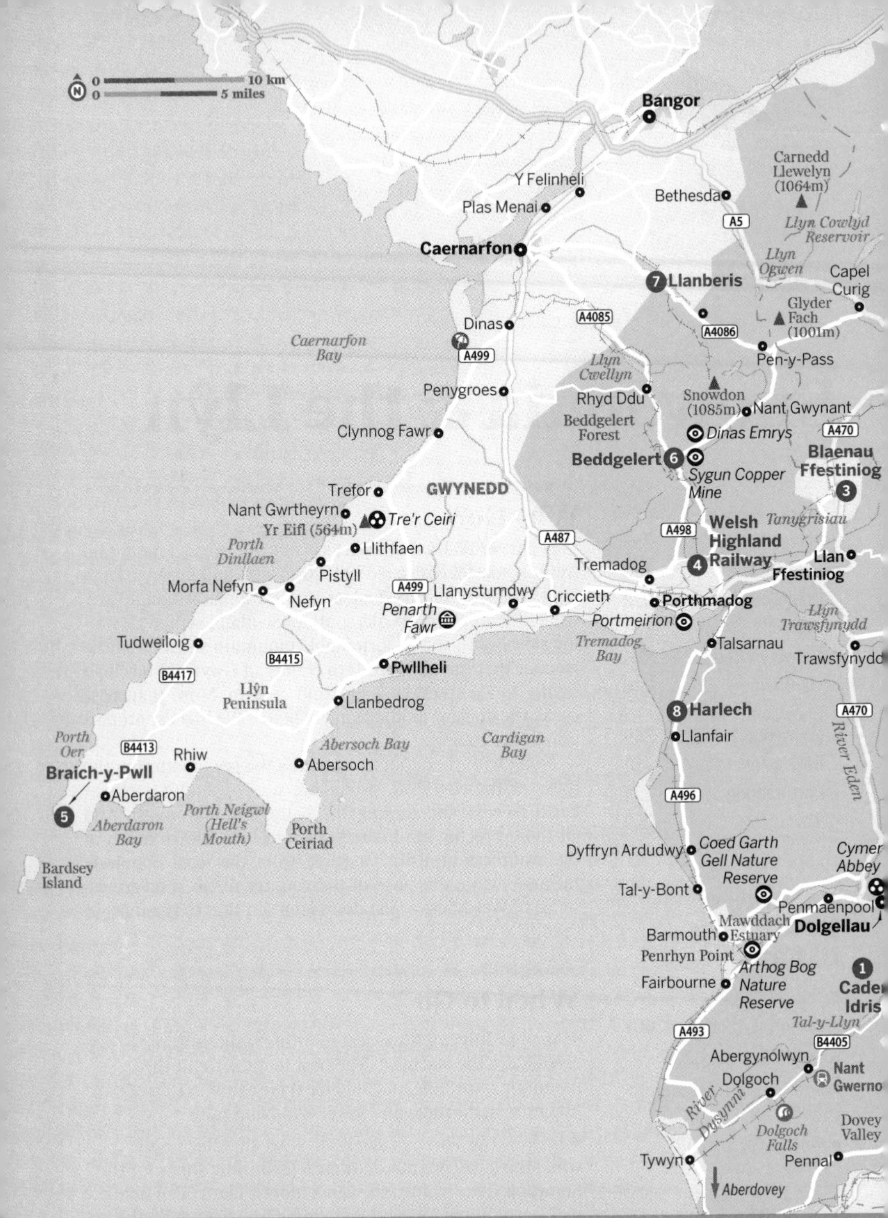

Snowdownia & the Llŷn Highlights

1 Cader Idris (p235) Climbing Snowdonia's second-most-famous peak, a legendary haunt of giants.

2 Pontcysyllte Aqueduct (p224) Floating through the air across this pinnacle of Georgian civil engineering.

3 Blaenau Ffestiniog (p240) Testing your claustrophobia in gloomy slate caverns.

4 Welsh Highland Railway (p255) Taking a coast-to-coast journey on a narrow-gauge railway.

5 Braich-y-Pwll (p261) Gazing towards a magical

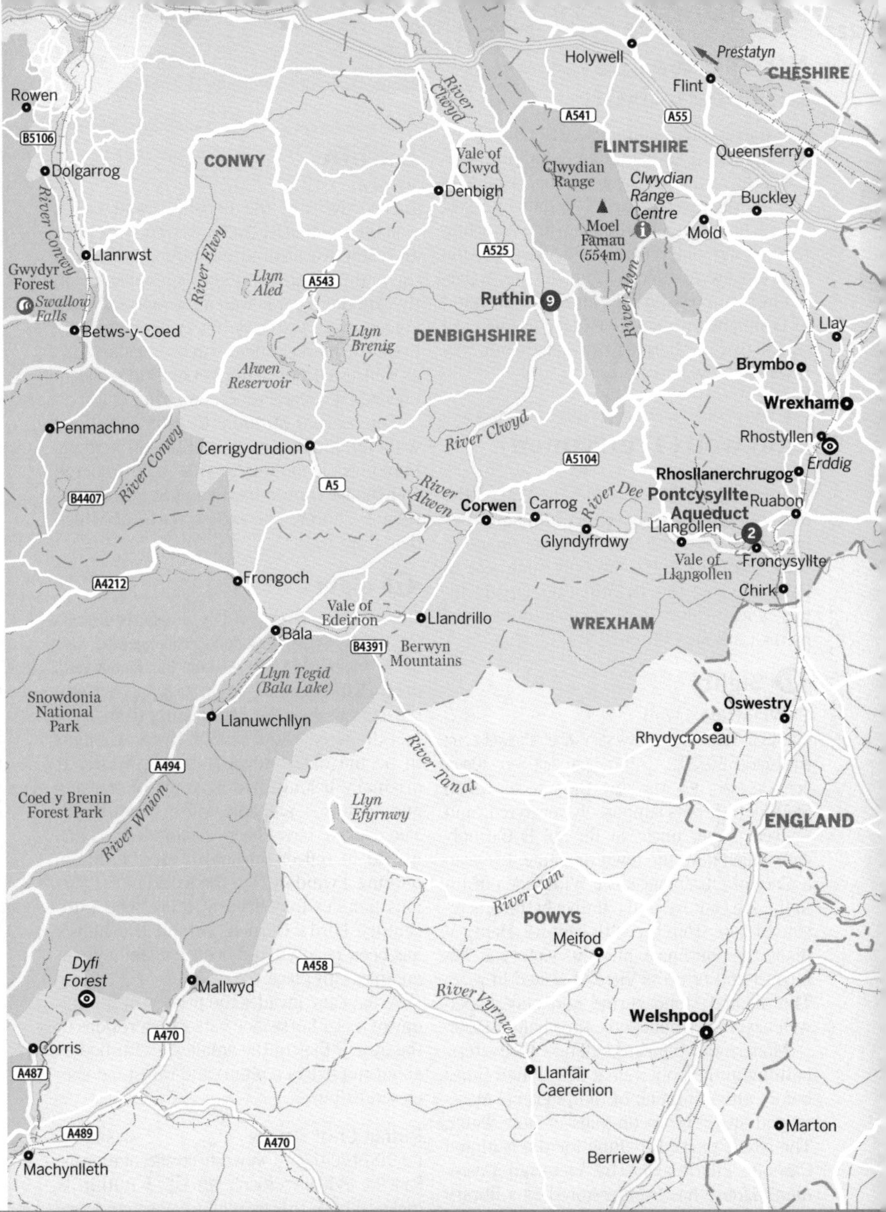

isle from an end-of-the-world headland.

6 Beddgelert (p251) Wandering among the cottages, rivers and looming hills of beautiful Beddgelert.

7 National Slate Museum (p246) Hearing stories at this fascinating museum in Llanberis.

8 Harlech Castle (p239) Enjoying cliff-edge views of Cardigan Bay and Snowdon, Wales' highest peak, from the castle's battlements.

9 Ruthin (p222) Soaking up the countryside vibe of historic market town Ruthin.

NORTH WALES BORDERLANDS

The northeastern counties of Denbighshire, Wrexham and Flintshire are a baffling jumble of the gritty and the gorgeous. From 1974 to 1996 they were all part of the county of Clwyd, before being broken up and reverting to their far older names. Surprisingly, the best bits are furtherest from the coast, particularly in the wild hills and lush farmland of Denbighshire's southern reaches. It's well worth pausing here as you make your way towards Snowdonia.

Holywell (Treffynnon)

POP 9808

Trumpeted as 'The Lourdes of Wales', the market town of Holywell in Flintshire has been a revered site of pilgrimage for more than 1300 years. It's the only such site to have survived the Reformation largely intact, and it's now once again administered by the Catholic Church.

Sights

St Winefride's Well SHRINE

(01352-713054; www.saintwinefrideswell.com; adult/child 80/20p; 9am-5pm Apr-Sep, 10am-4pm Oct-Mar; P) Marking the site at which St Winefride was supposedly martyred (and revived by her uncle, St Bueno) is the holy well which gave the town its name. It's been a place of pilgrimage since Winefride's death in the 7th century, and curative bathing is recorded here from the 12th century. Henry V made the pilgrimage after his victory at Agincourt and Princess Victoria visited in 1828. The vaulted stone shrine and star-shaped well basin were built some time before 1509.

Modern-day pilgrims still take the waters, bathing in the holy well at designated times before attending one of the pilgrims' Masses and stocking up on vials of holy water. The site is packed in June for the National Catholic Pilgrimage. The Victorian Custodian's House has been restored as a library and museum, documenting the history of the well and its pilgrims. It's open noon to 4pm Wednesdays and weekends from April to September.

Getting There & Away

Buses head to/from Rhyl (route 11G, one hour), Prestatyn (route 11G, 40 minutes), Mold (route 126, 25 minutes), Flint (route 11/18; 15 to 30 minutes) and Chester (route 11, one hour).

Ruthin

POP 5461

Tucked away in the bucolic Clwyd valley, well off any tourist route, Ruthin (rith-in) is an attractive lost-in-time hilltop town and the administrative hub of Denbighshire. In the Middle Ages it was an important market town and textile producer. There are still livestock markets held three times a week, as well as a produce market on Friday mornings and a general market on Thursdays.

The heart of Ruthin is St Peter's Sq, lined with an impressive collection of heritage buildings, including a 1401 half-timbered courthouse (now a bank) and St Peter's Collegiate Church, the oldest parts of which date from 1310.

Sights

Nantclwyd y Dre HISTORIC BUILDING

(01824-709822; www.denbighshire.gov.uk; Castle St; adult/child £5/4; 11am-4pm Mon & Wed, to 5pm Sat, to 3pm Tue & Sun Jul & Aug, see website for hours Apr-Jun & Sep) Dating from 1435, half-timbered Nantclwyd y Dre is thought to be the oldest town house in Wales. It originally belonged to a family of weavers and retains a palpable sense of antiquity. The rooms have been restored and furnished to reflect the era of each addition, offering a window into the world of the various families that lived in them. The 13th-century Lord's Garden, behind the house, has been restored and is once again a green and pleasant place.

A 'bat-cam' invades the privacy of the colony of lesser horseshoe bats which resides in the attic – they're the smallest (with bodies about the size of a plum) and rarest bat species in Britain.

Ruthin Craft Centre ARTS CENTRE

(01824-704774; www.ruthincraftcentre.org.uk; Park Rd; 10am-5.30pm; P) FREE Ruthin is lucky to have this excellent gallery and arts hub. Aside from the galleries – which do great work bringing the best of local photography, painting and sculpture to light, and show many pieces for sale – the complex includes artists' studios, public workshops and talks, a very nice cafe and shop and an unstaffed information centre.

Ruthin Gaol HISTORIC BUILDING

(☎01824-708281; www.denbighshire.gov.uk; 46 Clwyd St; adult/child £5/4; ⏲10am-5pm Wed-Mon Apr-Sep) This sombre building is the only Pentonville-style Victorian prison that is open to visitors. A free audio guide allows you to follow the prison sentence of a mystical prisoner, while information panels in the cells fill you in on all the fascinating and grisly details of day-to-day prison life and the daring escapes of John Jones, the 'Welsh Houdini', who was a guest here in the 1870s.

Sleeping

★ **Ruthin Castle Hotel** HISTORIC HOTEL ££

(☎01824-702664; www.ruthincastle.co.uk; Castle St; r/ste from £129/189; P 📶) The forlorn cries of peacocks strutting the gardens of this wonderful hotel are the first hint of the off-beat luxury within. Making unabashed use of a Victorian 'castle' built amid the ruins of the real thing (built in the 13th century by an ally of Edward I), its over-the-top grandeur includes a spa, a wood-panelled library/bar, and even a medieval banqueting hall.

Manorhaus BOUTIQUE HOTEL ££

(☎01824-704830; www.manorhaus.com; 10 Well St; s/d from £75/150; 📶) This boutique restaurant with rooms has eight gorgeously styled bedrooms in a dignified Georgian townhouse, each decorated by a different local or national artist. With a spa, library and film room, it's one of Ruthin's best sleeps, while the in-house restaurant (open 6pm to 9pm Tuesday to Saturday; two/three courses £25/30) certainly dishes up some of its best food.

Eating

Leonardo's DELI £

(☎01824-707161; www.leonardosdeli.co.uk; 4 Well St; pies £4; ⏲8.30am-5pm Mon-Sat) This drool-inducing deli is well stocked with local cheeses, preserves and top-notch pies (its Persian lamb, coriander and apricot concoction was a 2016 British Pie Awards winner). Their 'Ruthin honeybuns', made to a 16th-century recipe, are delicious.

★ **On the Hill** MODERN BRITISH ££

(☎01824-707736; www.onthehillrestaurant.co.uk; 1 Upper Clwyd St; mains £14-17, 1-/2-/3-course lunch £13/16/19; ⏲noon-2pm Mon-Sat, 6.30-9pm nightly) The low ceilings and exposed beams of this 16th-century house near the square make a memorable setting for sophisticated country cooking. Classics such as duck breast with celeriac and redcurrant or sole stuffed with prawns and lobster and blanketed in sherry and cream sauce, sit alongside more contemporary creations, but all hit the mark. The lunch menu is fantastic value.

> WORTH A TRIP
>
> **MOLD CULTURE**
>
> The unfortunately named town of Mold, 10 miles east of Ruthin, is the unlikely home of Wales' leading theatre company, **Clwyd Theatr Cymru** (☎box office 01352-701521; www.clwyd-theatr-cymru.co.uk). Founded in 1976, Clwyd Theatr Cymru has five performance spaces and stages a year-round program of old and new drama, mainly in English, including works for children and young people. It also offers opera, live music, dance, comedy, poetry and films. It's signposted off the A5119, a mile outside Mold, in Flintshire.

Getting There & Away

Bus X50 heads to/from Denbigh (20 minutes) and Wrexham (50 minutes).

Llangollen

POP 3466

Huddled around the banks of the tumbling River Dee (Afon Dyfrdwy) and with the mysterious hilltop ruins of Castell Dinas Brân as a backdrop, picturesque little Llangollen (khlan-goth-len) has long been recognised as a scenic gem. The riverside walk, heading west from the 14th-century bridge, has been a popular promenading spot since Victorian times.

In summer, Llangollen has a burgeoning walking and white-water-rafting scene, while in winter, under a thick blanket of snow, it just sits there and looks pretty. Two major arts festivals boost tourism, as do railway and engineering enthusiasts interested in the area's industrial legacy. That legacy accounts for the town's present layout: much of the original housing was relocated to make way for locomotives.

Llangollen takes its name from St Collen, a 7th-century monk who founded a religious community *(llan)* here. Centuries later it became an important stop on the London-to-Holyhead stagecoach route, linking the British capital to Ireland.

DON'T MISS

'YOU RANG, M'LORD?'

For a glimpse into the life of the British upper class in the 18th and 19th centuries, and the 'upstairs-downstairs' social hierarchy of their bygone world, the stately house and gardens of **Erddig** (NT; ☎01978-355314; www.nationaltrust.org.uk/erddig; adult/child £11.25/5.60, grounds only £7.20/3.60; ⏱house 12.30-3.30pm, grounds 10am-5pm; Ⓟ) are highly recommended. The house, the earliest parts of which date from 1680, has hardly been altered since the early 20th century; there's no electricity and it still has extensive outbuildings.

Erddig was the Yorke family's ancestral home for more than two centuries (until 1973). It provides a unique insight into the relationship that existed between masters and their servants, with the best archive of servant material of any house in Britain. There are even oil paintings and poems in honour of some of the favourites.

Today the property is managed by the National Trust, which has added a decent cafe and a gift shop. The house and outbuildings trace the historical element of the Yorke family's story, while the country estate includes a walled garden, restored in Victorian style, rare fruit trees, a canal and the National Ivy Collection. Best of all, however, Erddig now hosts a huge program of family-friendly activities, school-holiday events and themed days out, ranging from autumnal apple days to Easter-egg trails and a Christmas fair.

Erddig is about 12 miles northeast of Llangollen in the village of Rhostyllen, signposted off the A483.

Sights

Centre

Plas Newydd HISTORIC BUILDING
(☎01978-862834; www.denbighshire.gov.uk/heritage; Hill St; adult/child £6/5; ⏱10am-5pm Wed-Mon Mar-Oct, plus Tue Jun-Aug) The 18th-century home of the Ladies of Llangollen, Plas Newydd is an atmospheric step back in time. The celebrated couple transformed the house into a hybrid of Gothic and Tudor styles, complete with stained-glass windows, carved oak panels and the romantic, picturesque formal gardens. Admission to the house includes a good self-guided audio tour of the house, and the tranquil gardens are free to explore.

Llangollen Museum MUSEUM
(☎01978-862862; www.llangollenmuseum.org.uk; Parade St; ⏱10am-4pm Thu-Tue) FREE Staffed by committed volunteers of the best sort, this diverting little museum of local history occupies a hexagonal building retaining some of the air of the library it once was. Filled to the brim with artefacts relating Llangollen's journey through the years, its crowning glory (unless you're a kid and into dress-ups) is the gravestone of the Ladies of Llangollen.

Around Llangollen

★**Pontcysyllte Aqueduct & Canal World Heritage Site** CANAL
(☎01978-292015; www.pontcysyllte-aqueduct.co.uk; guided tours £3; ⏱visitor centre 10am-4pm daily Easter-Oct, plus long weekends in Nov, Dec & late Feb–Easter) FREE The preeminent Georgian engineer, Thomas Telford (1757–1834) built the Pontcysyllte Aqueduct in 1805 to carry the canal over the River Dee. At 307m long, 3.6m wide, 1.7m deep and 38m high, it is the most spectacular piece of engineering on the entire UK canal system and the highest canal aqueduct ever built. In recognition of this, the aqueduct and an 11-mile stretch of the canal have been declared a Unesco World Heritage Site.

In the 18th century the horse-drawn canal barge was the most efficient way of hauling goods over long distances but, with the advent of the railway, most of them fell into disrepair. The Llangollen Canal fared better than most because it was used for many more years to carry drinking water from the River Dee to the Hurleston Reservoir in Cheshire. Today it's again in use, carrying visitors up and down the Vale of Llangollen. In addition, the old towpaths offer miles of peaceful, traffic-free walking.

Telford's goal was to connect up the haulage routes between the Rivers Dee, Severn and Mersey. To collect water for the canal from the River Dee, he also designed an elegant curving weir called Horseshoe Falls. The adjacent riverbank is a tranquil picnic spot.

Blue-badge guides run guided tours from near the aqueduct visitor centre, while canal boats offer trips along the 'stream in the sky' from the nearby quay and from Llangollen wharf. Otherwise you can simply stroll across, free of charge. Whichever way you choose, you'll need a head for heights.

Horseshoe Falls is about 2 miles west of Llangollen (take the A5 west and after about 1.5 miles turn right across the river), while the aqueduct is 4 miles east, near the village of Trevor (on the A539 Ruabon road). Both are easily reached by the canal towpath, if you're in no hurry.

Castell Dinas Brân CASTLE

FREE The ever-visible ragged arches and tumbledown walls of Dinas Brân (Crow Castle) mark the remnants of a short-lived 13th-century castle of which it was said 'there was not a mightier in Wales nor a better in England'. It was burnt by Edward I after it was surrendered to him in advance of his invasion. Its fabulous 360-degree views over the Dee and surrounding countryside are well worth the 1½-hour return walk up the steep track from town.

Valle Crucis Abbey RUINS

(Abaty Glyn y Groes; Cadw; www.cadw.wales.gov.uk; A542; adult/child £3.50/2.50 Apr-Oct, free Nov-Mar; 10am-5pm, to 4pm Nov-Mar) The dignified ruins of this Cistercian abbey are a 2-mile walk north of Llangollen. Founded in 1201 by Madog ap Gruffydd, ruler of northern Powys, its largely Gothic form predates its more famous sibling at Tintern (which, on the eve of Valle Crucis's 1537 dissolution, was its only rival as the richest Cistercian abbey in the land). A small interpretation centre brings the monks' daily routines to life, and plays and other events sometimes animate the peaceful grounds.

Activities

Welsh Canal Holiday Craft BOATING

(01978-860702; www.horsedrawnboats.co.uk; Llangollen Wharf; mid-Mar–Oct) Peaceful horse-drawn narrowboats depart on

Llangollen

Sights

1 Llangollen Museum B2

Activities, Courses & Tours

2 Llangollen Outdoors B2
3 Llangollen Railway B1
4 Welsh Canal Holiday Craft B1

Sleeping

5 Cornerstones Guesthouse C2
6 Llangollen Hostel B3
7 mh Townhaus C3

Eating

8 Corn Mill B2
9 Dee Side Caffe Bistro B2
10 Gales of Llangollen C2

Llangollen

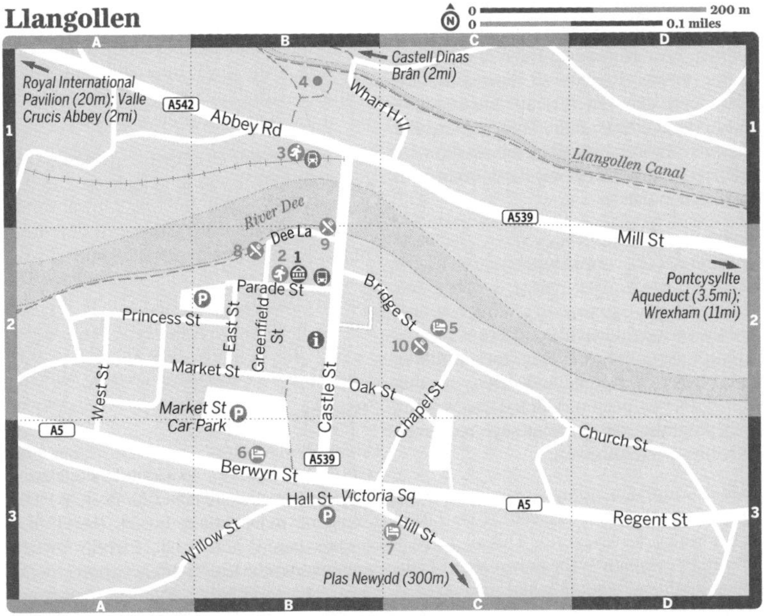

THE LADIES OF LLANGOLLEN

Lady Eleanor Butler and Miss Sarah Ponsonby, the 'Ladies of Llangollen', lived in **Plas Newydd** (New Home; p224) from 1780 to 1829 with their maid, Mary Carryl. They had fallen in love in Ireland but their aristocratic Anglo-Irish families discouraged the relationship. In a desperate bid to be allowed to live together, the women eloped to Wales, disguised as men, and set up home in Llangollen to devote themselves to 'friendship, celibacy and the knitting of stockings'.

Their romantic friendship became well known yet respected and they were visited by many national figures of the day, including the Duke of Wellington, William Wordsworth and Sir Walter Scott. Wordsworth was even suitably moved to pen the following words: 'Sisters in love, a love allowed to climb, even on this earth above the reach of time'.

The ladies' relationship with their maid, Mary, was also close. Mary managed to buy the freehold of Plas Newydd and left it to the 'sisters' when she died. They erected a large monument to her in the graveyard at St Collen's Parish Church in Llangollen, where they are also buried. Lady Eleanor died in 1829; Sarah Ponsonby was reunited with her soulmate just two years later.

45-minute trips (adult/child £13/8) from Llangollen Wharf every half hour during the school holidays, and hourly otherwise (adult/child £7/3.50). Two-hour journeys head to the Horseshoe Falls and back, and motorised boats take you up to Pontcysyllte Aqueduct (p224) with the return journey by coach (adult/child £14/12). Self-drive boats are £130/180 per day/weekend.

Llangollen Railway RAIL
(☎01978-860979; www.llangollen-railway.co.uk; Abbey Rd; adult/child return £15/8; ⏲daily Apr-Sep, reduced services rest of year) Now extended, the 10-mile jaunt through the Dee Valley via Berwyn (near Horseshoe Falls) and Corwen on the former Ruabon to Barmouth Line is a superb day out for rail fans, families and heritage lovers alike. There are regular *Thomas the Tank Engine* theme days for children, and murder-mystery excursions are also popular.

Llangollen Outdoors OUTDOORS
(☎01978-897220; www.llangollenoutdoors.co.uk; Parade St, Fringe Shed; tubing & rafting £55; ⏲8.30am-5pm) Catering to the recreational and the serious alike, this outfit runs rafting, tubing, canyoning, canoeing, rock climbing and bushcraft tasters and trips, starting from £45 per person. Offered year-round, their program even contains such recherché activities as axe-throwing.

Safe & Sound Outdoors ADVENTURE SPORTS
(☎01978-860471; www.sasoutdoors.co.uk; Chapel St; bike hire half/full day £20/22) This all-purpose adventure company is the only place in Llangollen that hires mountain and road bikes. It also does rafting, gorge walking, rock climbing, paintball and…err…stag dos.

Festivals & Events

International Musical Eisteddfod PERFORMING ARTS
(☎01978-862000; www.international-eisteddfod.co.uk; events from £5, full season ticket £210; ⏲Jul) The International Musical Eisteddfod was established after WWII to promote international harmony. Every July it attracts 4000 participants and 50,000 spectators from around 50 countries, transforming lovely Llangollen into a global village. In addition to folk music and dancing competitions, gala concerts at the Royal International Pavilion feature international stars. It was nominated for the Nobel Peace Prize in 2004.

Llangollen Fringe Festival PERFORMING ARTS
(☎08001-455779; www.llangollenfringe.co.uk; festival ticket £85; ⏲Jul) This small-town, volunteer-run arts festival, held over 11 days from mid-July, manages to attract some surprisingly big names: 2016's line-up included The Selecter and Gang of Four. There are also poetry readings, a jazz narrowboat cruise, special musical train services and a final concert in the ruins of Valle Crucis Abbey.

Sleeping

Llangollen Hostel HOSTEL £
(☎01978-861773; www.llangollenhostel.co.uk; Berwyn St, Isallt; dm/d from £20/45; P 📶) This excellent independent hostel, based in a former family home, has friendly owners and a cared-for feel. It offers various rooms, from private en suite doubles to a six-bed

dorm, as well as an orderly kitchen and cosy lounge. It actively welcomes cyclists, walkers and canoeists, offering laundry facilities and bike/boat storage. Prices include a self-service cereal-and-toast breakfast.

Cornerstones Guesthouse B&B ££
(☎01978-861569; www.cornerstones-guesthouse.co.uk; 19 Bridge St; r £90-140; P 📶 🐾) All stripped floorboards and oak beams, this converted 16th-century house has charm and history in spades. It's now a five-star gold B&B with fires in winter, fantastic breakfasts and three beautifully appointed rooms.

Abbey Farm FARMSTAY ££
(☎01978-861297; www.theabbeyfarm.co.uk; cottage per week £240-490; ⊙Feb-Dec; P) With three sweet stone self-catering cottages (the largest sleeping up to 14), a campsite in the lee of the impressive ruins of Valle Crucis Abbey, a farm shop and tearoom-cum-bistro, Abbey Farm covers many bases. If setting up your own tent seems like just too much trouble, their semifixed camping 'pods' make life a little easier.

★ **mh Townhaus** B&B ££
(☎01978-860775; www.manorhaus.com; Hill St; s/d £76/111; 📶) Sster to the well-established Ruthin Manorhaus, this ultrastylish guesthouse boasts six clean-cut rooms, a lounge and bar, and even a rooftop hot tub. Originally opened in 2012 as a restaurant with rooms, it now focuses more on accommodation (including a new six-bed room) but can still do wonderful three-course meals for groups (by arrangement).

Eating

Dee Side Caffe Bistro CAFE £
(☎07466-699269; www.deesidebistro.co.uk; Dee Lane; mains £7-13; ⊙9am-9pm) Serving a crowd-pleasing menu of burgers, baked potatoes, pies and pasta, this cheap-and-cheerful little riverside eatery is as traditional as they come. Try to grab a table overlooking the kayaks as they shoot the rapids below.

Corn Mill PUB FOOD £
(☎01978-869555; www.brunningandprice.co.uk/cornmill; Dee Lane; light meals £7-11, mains £10-18; ⊙kitchen noon-9.30pm; 📶) The water wheel still turns at the heart of this converted mill, now a cheerful, bustling pub and eatery. The deck is the best spot in town for an unfussy al fresco lunch, with views over the River Dee to the steam railway. The bar stays open for an hour or two longer than the kitchen.

Gales of Llangollen EUROPEAN ££
(☎01978-860089; www.galesofllangollen.co.uk; 18 Bridge St; mains £12-15; ⊙noon-2pm & 6-9.30pm Mon-Sat) Equal parts wine bar and bistro, Gales is something of a Llangollen institution. It boasts an ever-changing seasonal menu best enjoyed with a good glass from the extensive wine list. The owners – who took a punt in the late 1970s by opening this, the first wine bar in North Wales – also run the wine shop next door.

Information

Tourist Office (☎01978-860828; www.northeastwales.co.uk; Castle St, The Chapel; ⊙9.30am-5pm) Helpful tourist office, well stocked with maps, books and gifts. It doubles as an art gallery. Pick up the *Llangollen History Trail* brochure, which details a 9.5km walking circuit taking in Valle Crucis and Dinas Brân.

Getting There & Away

Bus T3 heads to Wrexham (30 minutes), Llandrillo (35 minutes), Bala (55 minutes), Dolgellau (1½ hours) and Barmouth (1¾ hours). National Express coaches head to Wrexham (£3.60, 25 minutes), Shrewsbury (£9.40, one change, 2½ hours) and Birmingham (£17, one change, four hours). Buses leave from Parade St, near the museum.

Parking is at a premium in Llangollen. If your accommodation doesn't have its own, check whether it can provide a pass for the council car parks.

WORTH A TRIP

BRIDGE END INN

If you're prepared to make a pilgrimage for a good pub, seek ye out Ruabon's **Bridge End Inn** (☎01978-810881; www.mcgivernales.co.uk; 5 Bridge St, Ruabon; ⊙5-11pm Mon-Fri, noon-11pm Sat & Sun). In 2012 this unassuming little place became the first Welsh pub to win the coveted Campaign for Real Ale (CAMRA) pub-of-the-year award. Run by the McGivern family, it's home to the McGivern microbrewery and also showcases craft beers from around the nation. Ruabon is 6 miles east of Llangollen, on the way to Wrexham.

STOCKER1970 / SHUTTERSTOCK ©

1. Snowdon Mountain Railway (p249)
Catch the UK's highest rack-and-pinion railway up to the summit of Snowdon.

2. Llangollen (p223)
A scenic gem with a popular riverside walk.

3. Dolbadarn Castle (p247)
A ruined keep between two lakes, with wonderful views.

4. Snowdonia National Park (p230)
Wales' first and best-known national park embraces coastline, forests, valleys, rivers and lakes.

NATURAL EARTH IMAGERY / SHUTTERSTOCK ©

DON'T MISS

TYDDYN LLAN

The glowing reputation of this Michelin-starred **Tyddyn Llan Restaurant** (☎01490-440264; www.tyddynllan.co.uk; Llandrillo; 2-/3-course dinner £50/60; ⏲lunch Fri-Sun, dinner daily; P) is well deserved. We are still salivating at the memory of our last visit – some dishes went beyond merely good and approached extraordinary. The pairings of ingredients are classical rather than off-the-wall – spring asparagus, for example, with morels and duck egg. It's set among gardens near the pretty Georgian village of Llandrillo (located on the secondary B4401 route between Llangollen and Bala).

SNOWDONIA NATIONAL PARK (PARC CENEDLAETHOL ERYRI)

Wales' best-known and most visited slice of nature became the country's first national park in 1951. Every year more than 350,000 people walk, climb or take the train to the 1085m summit of Snowdon. Yet the park is more than just Snowdon – its 823 sq miles embraces stunning coastline, forests, valleys, rivers, bird-filled estuaries and Wales' biggest natural lake.

Like Wales' other national parks, this one is lived-in, with sizeable towns at Bala, Dolgellau, Harlech and Betws-y-Coed, and a population in excess of 26,000. Two-thirds of the park is privately owned, with more than three-quarters used for raising sheep and cattle.

The Welsh name for Snowdonia is Eryri (eh-*ruh*-ree) meaning highlands.

The park is the only home to two endangered species, an alpine plant called the Snowdon lily and the rainbow-coloured Snowdon beetle. The *gwyniad* is a species of whitefish found only in Llyn Tegid (Bala Lake), which incidentally also has probably the UK's only colony of glutinous snails.

Bala (Y Bala)

POP 1980

Kayakers, canoeists, windsurfers, sailors, rafters and hikers will appreciate the quiet Welsh-speaking town of Bala. Here you'll find Wales' largest natural lake, Llyn Tegid (Bala Lake), as well as the River Tryweryn, hallowed in whitewater kayaking circles.

Bala was a centre for the Welsh wool industry during the 18th century, but today it's better known as a gateway to Snowdonia National Park and the park's main watersports hub. The main street is dotted with adventure sports and outdoors shops, and bustles with visitors in summer.

The Romans had a camp here, the remains of which have been found on private land near the river. Just behind the high street is a Norman motte (castle mound) that would once have supported a wooden castle.

Welsh remains the language of everyday commerce and conversation for 76% of its residents.

Sights & Activities

Llyn Tegid LAKE

(Bala Lake) Llyn Tegid was formed during the last Ice Age when glaciers blocked the valley of the River Dee with debris. The resulting rectangular lake is 4 miles long, three-quarters of a mile wide and, in places, more than 42m deep. It's also the only home of the gwyniad, an endemic fish isolated in the glacial lake.

Local folk tales record an alternative to the geological version of events. Once upon a time the valley was home to a cruel and dissolute prince named Tegid Foel. One night the harpist at a banquet thrown by the prince kept hearing a small bird urging him to flee the palace. He did so, fell asleep on a hilltop, and awoke at dawn to find the palace and principality drowned beneath the lake.

National White Water Centre RAFTING

(Canolfan Dŵr Gwyn Genedlaethol; ☎01678-521083; www.ukrafting.co.uk; Frongoch; 1/2hr trip £35/66; ⏲9am-4.30pm Mon-Fri) Due to the damming of the River Tryweryn in the 1960s, this and the River Dee are among the few Welsh rivers with fairly reliable white water year-round (water releases mean rafting is possible around 200 days per year). Rafting, kayaking and canoeing trips traverse a 1.5-mile stretch of the Tryweryn with abundant class-III white water and class IV sections.

Bookings are best made at least two days in advance and are subject to cancellation in the event of insufficient releases from the dam – call to check the day before. The centre's Adventure Breaks schedule marries rafting with another activity, such as rock climbing, mountain biking, pony trekking, high ropes, 4WD off-road driving, canyoning, clay-pigeon shooting or quad biking; prices start at £140 and include bed and breakfast.

Bala Adventure & Watersports Centre WATER SPORTS
(☑ 01678-521059; www.balawatersports.com; Pensarn Rd; ☺ 9am-5pm, later in summer) This one-stop activity-and-hire centre, behind the leisure centre by the lake shore, offers windsurfing, sailing, canoeing, kayaking, mountain biking, rock climbing and abseiling courses (most cost £40/80 per half/ full day). Rental gear includes kayaks (£12), canoes (£25), rowboats (£27), pedalos (£15), windsurfers (£19) and sailing boats (from £28); all prices are per hour.

It offers courses only (no equipment hire) October to March.

Bala Lake Railway RAIL
(☑ 01678-540666; www.bala-lake-railway.co.uk; adult/unaccompanied child return £10.50/5.50; ☺ Feb-Oct) Built in 1868 and shut down in 1965, this narrow-gauge railway was rescued by volunteers, who reopened the 4.5-mile stretch from Bala to Llanuwchllyn in 1971. Up to four vintage locomotives depart from the little station at Penybont each day, skirting the lake for a scenic 90-minute return journey. Penybont is half a mile from Bala, off the B4391.

🛏 Sleeping

Bala Backpackers HOSTEL £
(☑ 01678-521700; www.bala-backpackers.co.uk; 32 Tegid St; dm/tw from £21/49; ☺ reception 8-10am & 5-10pm; 🛜) Spread over two restored 19th-century houses facing each other across Tegid St, Bala Backpackers has brightly painted dorms (with a maximum of four single beds), private twins and renovated kitchen and bathrooms. The owner also serves good home-cooked food at nearby Eco Caffe (21 Tegid St; mains £6.50; ☺ 11am-4pm long weekends & bank holidays).

★ Abercelyn Country House B&B ££
(☑ 01678-521109; www.abercelyn.co.uk; Llanycil; s/d from £60/80; 🅿 🛜) Luxurious rooms, excellent breakfasts and a lovely setting in gardens with a gurgling brook make this former rectory (1729) a great option – the more luxurious rooms even have whirlpool baths. The owner is a mountain guide and

white-water enthusiast. It's quietly situated on the A494, a mile along the lake from the town.

🍴 Eating

Eagles Inn (Tafarn Yr Eryrod) PUB FOOD £
(☑ 01678-540278; www.yr-eagles.co.uk; Llanuwchllyn; mains £9-17.50; ☺ 11am-11pm Sun-Wed, to midnight Thu-Sat, closed lunch Mon; 🅿) In Llanuwchllyn, the village at the other end of the lake from Bala, this handsome stone pub is known for its Welsh-speaking regulars and great food. Most of the vegetables and some of the meat comes from the family farm, and for dessert there's a delicious array of home-made pies and puddings.

Plas-yn-Dre PUB FOOD ££
(☑ 01678-521256; www.plasyndre.co.uk; 23 High St; mains £12-14; ☺ kitchen noon-2pm & 6-8.30pm; 🛜) With a terraced pub on one side and a large country-style dining room on the other, this is the best eating option on the main strip. The menu is unadventurous but hearty, with burgers, steaks, fish, pasta and daily vegetarian specials.

🛍 Shopping

Stori FOOD & DRINKS
(☑ 01678-520501; www.storibeers.wales; 101 High St; ☺ 10.30am-8pm) This cracking craft-beer shop takes localism very seriously, stocking an enormous range of North Welsh beers,

THE LEGEND OF TEGGIE

Sightings of the beast of Llyn Tegid have been reported since at least the 1920s and it has been variously likened to a crocodile or a small dinosaur. Affectionately known as Teggie, this Welsh answer to the Loch Ness monster prompted a three-day search by a Japanese film crew in 1995, but their minisubmarine failed to find any sign of the elusive beast.

One man who claims to have seen the creature from the deep is Rhodri Jones, whose sheep farm extends to the landlocked lake's foreshore. He says in summer 2006 he saw a crocodile-sized creature moving through the waters on a still night.

Since then Jones has spoken to other local farmers and found other stories of mysterious sightings.

and focusing on the *stori* (story) of their production. With a tiny tap room out back, casks to fill your growler (1.85L bottle) for as little as £6, plus Welsh spirits and cider and imported wine, it's the off-licence *in excelsis*.

Information

Bala Information Point (www.visitbala.org; Pensarn Rd, Penllyn Leisure Centre; 10am-9pm Mon-Thu, to 7.30pm Fri, to 4pm Sat & Sun;) Located inside the large leisure centre by the lake (where there's also a cafe and an indoor pool with water slides) this unstaffed information point might be supplemented by the helpful leisure-centre staff, if they're not busy.

Getting There & Away

Buses stop on the High St. Bus T3 heads to/from Barmouth (one hour), Dolgellau (35 minutes), Llangollen (52 minutes) and Wrexham (1½ hours).

Coed y Brenin Forest Park

Covering 16 sq miles, this woodland park (8 miles north of Dolgellau off the A470) is the premier location for mountain biking in Wales. Ever-expanding, it's laced with more than 70 miles of purpose-built cycle trails, divided into eight graded routes to suit everyone from beginners to guns. Guidance is at hand in the form of old-fashioned waterproof trail cards or downloadable geocaches and MP3 audio files. Some of the more gung-ho trails – such as the Dragon's Back and the Beast of Brenin – are used for major mountain-biking events.

Wildlife here includes fallow deer; they're hard to spot but you're most likely to see them early in the morning.

Activities

Beics Brenin CYCLING

(01341-440728; www.beicsbrenin.co.uk; per day from £25; 9am-5pm) Housed under the Coed y Brenin Visitor Centre, this bike shop has plenty of technicians, gear and bikes for hire, from simple hardtail mountain bikes to adaptive bikes and motor-assisted pedal 'e-bikes'.

Information

Coed y Brenin Forest Park Visitor Centre (01341-440747; www.naturalresources.wales/coedybrenin; car park per hour/day £1/5; 9.30am-5pm) Has a cafe (offering a 10% discount to anyone arriving by public transport), toilets, showers and a children's play area, as well as trail and forest information. It's also the hub for foraging and survival-skills walks, craft workshops, races and other events.

Getting There & Away

The T2 bus from Bangor to Aberystwyth stops at Coed y Brenin and the nearby villages of Ganllwyd and Bronaber. The centre is also on National Cycle Network route 82, Lon Las (North) and Lon Las Cymru.

Dolgellau

POP 2688

Dolgellau (dol-*geth*-lye) is a charming little market town, steeped in history and boasting the highest concentration of heritage-listed buildings in Wales (more than 200). Once the county town of bygone Merionethshire, it was a regional centre for Wales' prosperous wool industry in the 18th and early 19th centuries and many of its finest buildings, sturdy and unadorned, were built at that time. Local mills failed to keep pace with mass mechanisation, however, and decline set in – preserving the town centre much as it was then.

The region bounced back when the Romantic Revival made Wales' wild landscapes popular with genteel travellers. There was also a minor gold rush in the 19th century. Famous for its pink tinge, Dolgellau gold became associated with royalty and the gold for the wedding rings of the current crop of senior royals was mined here. Today Dolgellau relies heavily on tourism.

Sights

One of Snowdonia's premier peaks, bulky Cader Idris, rises to the south, the lovely Mawddach Estuary lies to the west and, to the north, the Coed y Brenin Forest offers glorious mountain biking. Altogether, it's one of the most appealing bases from which to explore the national park.

Tŷ Siamas CULTURAL CENTRE

(01341-421800; www.tysiamas.com; Eldon Sq, Neuadd Idris; 10am-4pm Tue-Fri, to 1pm Sat;) Dolgellau has been a Welsh folk-music hub since holding the first national folk festival in 1952. The town's former market hall now houses the volunteer-run National Centre for Welsh Folk Music, named after Dolgellau-born Elis Sîon Siamas, harpist to Queen Anne and the first Welshman to build a triple harp (now known as the

'Welsh harp'). There's a recording studio, workshops and lessons on traditional instruments and a cafe and shop. Check the website for upcoming performances.

Mawddach Estuary NATURE RESERVE
(www.mawddachestuary.co.uk) The Mawddach Estuary is a striking sight, flanked by woodlands, wetlands and the mountains of southern Snowdonia. There are two Royal Society for the Protection of Birds (RSPB) nature reserves in the valley, both easily reached on foot or by bike from Dolgellau or Barmouth via the Mawddach Trail. Arthog Bog is 8 miles west of Dolgellau on the access road to Morfa Mawddach station, off the A493, while Coed Garth Gell is 2 miles west, on the A496.

On the south side, Arthog Bog is a small wetland reserve favoured by cuckoos, grasshopper warblers, lesser redpolls, reed buntings and siskins. Set in oak woodlands along the northern side, Coed Garth Gell has two circular walking trails; one 1.25 miles, the other 1.5 miles. Spring visitors include redstarts, wood warblers and pied flycatchers, while in summer you might spot dippers and in winter, woodcocks.

Cymer Abbey RUINS
FREE This Cistercian abbey, founded in 1198, was never especially grand but the ruined walls and arches are still picturesque, especially when the daffodils are in bloom. There are walks in the vicinity and nice picnic spots near the river. It's 2 miles northwest of Dolgellau, signposted from the A470.

Activities

Precipice Walk HIKING
If you're not up to scaling Cader Idris, this 3.5-mile circular walk through the private Nannau estate is surprisingly varied and offers plenty of beautiful scenery. It leads you through woodland, along the side of a steeply sloped mountain and beside a lake (Llyn Cynwch). The walk starts from Saith Groesffordd car park, Llanfachreth, around 2.5 miles from Dolgellau.

Walk the loop anticlockwise for the best views of Cader Idris, Snowdon and the Mawddach Estuary.

Mawddach Trail HIKING
(www.mawddachtrail.co.uk) The 9.5-mile Mawddach Trail is a flat (and in places wheelchair-accessible) walking and cycling path that follows an old train line through woods and past wetlands on the southern side of the beautiful Mawddach Estuary, before crossing over the train viaduct to Barmouth (where you can catch the bus back). The trail starts in the car park beside the bridge.

Mawddach Way HIKING
(www.mawddachway.co.uk) Mawddach Way is a 30-mile two- to three-day track looping through the hills on either side of the bird-filled and extremely scenic Mawddach

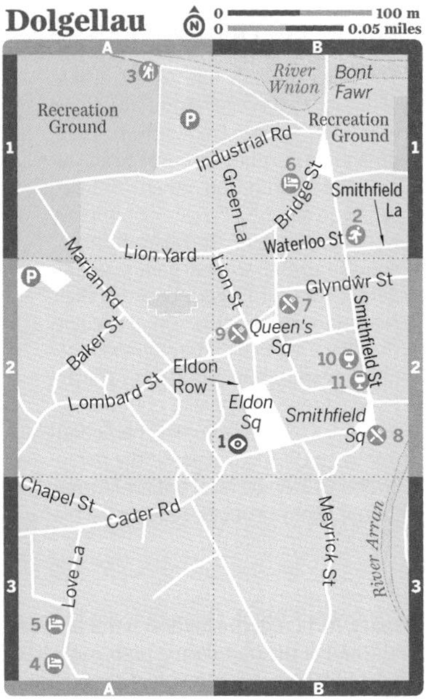

Dolgellau

Sights
1 Tŷ Siamas ... B2

Activities, Courses & Tours
2 Dolgellau Cycles ... B1
3 Mawddach Trail ... A1

Sleeping
4 Bryn Mair House ... A3
5 Ffynnon ... A3
6 HYB Bunkhouse ... B1

Eating
7 TH Roberts ... B2
8 Y Meirionnydd ... B2
9 Y Sospan ... B2

Drinking & Nightlife
10 Dylanwad Da ... B2
11 Torrent Walk ... B2

THE DOLGELLAU QUAKERS

The Dolgellau area has historical links with the Society of Friends (the Quakers). After George Fox visited in 1657, preaching his philosophy of direct communication with God, free from creeds, rites and clergy, a Quaker community was founded here. Converts, from simple farmers to local gentry, were persecuted with vigour because their refusal to swear oaths – in particular to the king – was considered treasonous. Many eventually emigrated to William Penn's American Quaker community, in 1689. *Y Stafell Ddirgel* (The Secret Room), a 1969 novel about the persecution written by local author Marion Eames, was curricular reading for many a Welsh schoolchild.

Estuary. Although the highest point is 346m, by the end of the undulating path you'll have climbed 2226m. An A5 booklet on the route in available online for £5.

The official guide splits the route into three legs: Barmouth to Taicynhaeaf (10 miles, five to six hours), Taicynhaeaf to Penmaenpool (9 miles, four to five hours) and Penmaenpool to Barmouth (11 miles, six to seven hours). Fit walkers should be able to do it in two days, with pit stops at Barmouth and Dolgellau.

Dolgellau Cycles CYCLING
(☎01341-423332; www.dolgellaucycles.co.uk; Smithfield St, The Old Furnace; half-/full-day rental £15/20) Rents bikes, performs repairs and offers advice on local cycle routes, including Lôn Las Cymru (Welsh National Cycle Route 8, which passes through Dolgellau). Helmets are included, trailers and seats are available for £5, and the friendly owner is happy to do deals for families.

Sleeping

Centre

HYB Bunkhouse HOSTEL £
(☎01341-421755; www.medi-gifts.com; 2-3 Bridge St; dm/r £21/84; P wi-fi) Attached to the ground-floor Medi Gift Shop, this bunkhouse has a series of oak-beamed rooms, each sleeping four people (in bunk beds, each group separated where possible), with handy kitchenettes. On the downside, there's no lounge, only one room is en suite and, during busy periods it's charged by the room rather than by the bed.

Bryn Mair House B&B ££
(☎01341-422640; www.brynmairbedandbreakfast.co.uk; Love Lane; s/d from £95/105; P wi-fi) This impressive stone house – a former Georgian rectory no less – sits among gardens on wistfully monikered Love Lane. Its three luxurious B&B rooms are all kitted out with Egyptian cotton sheets, DVD players and iPod docks; room 1 has sublime mountain views.

★**Ffynnon** B&B £££
(☎01341-421774; www.ffynnontownhouse.com; Love Lane; s/d from £100/150; P wi-fi) With a keen eye for contemporary design and a super-friendly welcome, this award-winning boutique B&B manages to be homey and stylish. French antiques are mixed in with modern chandeliers, claw-foot tubs and electronic gadgets, and each room has a seating area for admiring the stunning views in comfort. There's a bar, library and even an outdoor hot tub.

Around Dolgellau

Kings YHA HOSTEL £
(☎08453-719327; www.yha.org.uk; Penmaenpool; dm/r £17/46; P wi-fi) Occupying slightly foreboding and spartan slate buildings, this remote woodland hostel has a gorgeous setting beside a stream, 2 miles from the Ty-Nant Path (Pony Path) trailhead up Cader Idris. Follow the signposts from the A493, west of Penmaenpool. The wi-fi is patchy and not free.

Pandy Isaf B&B ££
(☎01341-423949; www.pandyisaf-accommodation.co.uk; s/d from £75/85; P) This extended country house, set alongside the River Clewedog, started life as a 16th-century fulling mill. It's now a peaceful retreat straight out of the pages of *Country Living*, offering spotless bedrooms, a large guest lounge full of books and DVDs, and amazing breakfasts. It's located 2 miles northeast of Dolgellau off the A494; turn left after the petrol station.

Penmaenuchaf Hall HOTEL £££
(☎01341-422129; www.penhall.co.uk; Penmaenpool; s/d £130/180; P wi-fi pets) With grand furnishings, sculpted gardens and superb views, this upscale country hotel is the former pile of Bolton cotton magnate, James

Leigh. The 14 rooms have a lavish old-world air with all the 21st-century conveniences. Standards are similarly high in Llygad yr Haul, the hotel's garden restaurant. It's located 2 miles west of Dolgellau, off the A493.

Eating

TH Roberts CAFE £
(☎01341-423552; Glyndŵr St, Parliament House; light mains £4-5; ⏰9am-5.30pm Mon-Sat; 📶) Occupying a Grade-II-listed building fitted with its original counter, glass cabinets and wooden drawers, this charismatic cafe still looks a lot like the ironmonger's it once was. The coffee and tea are proudly the best in Dolgellau, there's a reading room with books and papers, and the soup, sandwiches and rarebit (and Nan's scones) are all first rate.

Mawddach Restaurant EUROPEAN ££
(Bwyty Mawddach; ☎01341-421752; www.mawddach.com; Llanelltyd; mains £16-22; ⏰noon-2.30pm Thu-Sun, 6.30-9pm Thu-Sat) Occupying a smartly renovated former barn with views of Cader Idris and the estuary valley, Mawddach sits 2 miles west of Dolgellau on the A496. Tasteful slate floors and leather seats are matched by excellent food: slow-cooked local pork belly with confit fennel, or roasted hake with greens, garlic and anchovies. The Sunday lunch menu (two/three courses £21/24) is great value.

Y Sospan BISTRO ££
(☎01341-423174; www.ysospan.co.uk; Queen's Sq; breakfast & lunch £5-9, dinner £13-17; ⏰8.30am-9.30pm; 📶) In a book-lined, flag-stoned and rough-beamed 1606 building that once served as a prison, this relaxed local serves fry-up breakfasts, sandwiches, jacket potatoes and light meals during the day. Lamb and beef play a starring role on the more ambitious bistro menu available in the evenings, and most of the desserts have been on the booze.

Y Meirionnydd EUROPEAN £££
(☎01341-422554; www.themeirionnydd.com; Smithfield Sq; 2/3 courses £23/27; ⏰7-10pm Tue-Sat) Making atmospheric use of the medieval cellar of the former county jail (anyone over 5ft, 10in will have to stoop to move around the room), this prix fixe restaurant takes good local ingredients and gives them the pan-European treatment. So you might follow a first course of gravlax cured in beetroot and brandy with Welsh lamb rump on rösti.

Drinking & Nightlife

Dylanwad Da WINE BAR
(☎01341-422870; www.dylanwad.co.uk; Finsbury Sq; snacks £5-7; ⏰10am-6pm Tue-Thu, to 11pm Fri & Sat) Relocation to a slickly renovated new premises (one of Dolgellau's oldest) has seen this local institution shift emphasis from food to owner Dylan Rowlands' main interest – wine. Cheeses, serrano ham and other small plates are still available but – as the title of Dylan's book, *Rarebit and Rioja*, suggests – they're there as supporting cast to a star-studded list of wines.

Torrent Walk PUB
(☎01341-422858; Smithfield St; ⏰11am-midnight; 📶) Real ales, real ciders and plenty of locals catching up under the low, twisted roof-beams of this 18th-century pub in the narrow-laned heart of Dol. Plenty of walkers, too, in season.

Getting There & Away

Buses stop on the western side of Eldon Sq in the heart of town. Destinations include Machynlleth (route T2, 30 minutes), Betws-y-Coed (route X1, 1¼ hours, one daily Monday to Saturday), Llangollen (route T3, 1½ hours), Porthmadog (route T2, 50 minutes) and Caernarfon (route T2, 1½ hours). Note that some services, such as the 28 to Tywyn (55 minutes), stop on the southern side of the square.

Cader Idris (Cadair Idris)

Cader Idris (893m), or the 'Seat of Idris' (a legendary giant), is a hulking, menacing-looking mountain with an appropriate mythology attached. It's said that hounds of the underworld fly around its peaks, and that strange light effects are often sighted in the area. It's also said that anyone who spends the night on the summit will awake either mad or a poet – although perhaps you'd have to be a little mad or romantic to attempt it in the first place. Regardless of its repute, it's popular with walkers and it's the park's favourite locale for rock climbers.

Activities

The usual route to the summit of Cader Idris is the 'Tŷ Nant' or **Pony Path** (6 miles return, five hours), which begins from the Tŷ Nant car park, 3 miles southwest of Dolgellau. It's a rocky but safe, straightforward route.

The easiest but longest route is the 'Tywyn' or **Llanfihangel y Pennant Path** (10 miles return, six hours), a gentle pony track that heads northeast from the hamlet of Llanfihangel y Pennant, joining the Tŷ Nant Path at the latter's midpoint. Llanfihangel is 1.5 miles from the terminus of the Talyllyn Railway at Abergynolwyn.

The shortest but steepest route is the **Minffordd Path** (6 miles return, five hours), which begins from the Dol Idris car park (four hours/day £2/4), 6 miles south of Dolgellau at the junction of the A487 and the B4405. This route requires the most caution, especially on the way back down, but there's the added incentive of a hot beverage awaiting at the tearoom, near the car park.

Whichever route you choose, wear stout shoes, carry protective clothing and check the weather conditions on the Met's website (www.metoffice.gov.uk). Printable maps can be downloaded from the Snowdonia National Park website (www.eryri-npa.gov.uk).

Near the Minffordd trailhead is **Tal-y-llyn**, a tranquil lake hemmed in by the encroaching mountains. It's stocked with trout and popular with both anglers and otters.

Sleeping

★ **Old Rectory on the Lake** B&B ££

(☎01654-782225; www.rectoryonthelake.co.uk; Tal-y-Llyn; s/d from £45/90, 4-course meal £40; P 📶) If you think you might need a little pampering after your Cader Idris ascent – perhaps a gourmet meal, a complimentary glass of sherry or a soak in a hot tub – this wonderful adults-only B&B could be just the ticket. It's located on the shores of Tal-y-llyn, less than 2 miles from the Minffordd trailhead.

Getting There & Away

Bus 30 connects Dolgellau with Minffordd (15 minutes), Tal-y-llyn (20 minutes) and Abergynolwyn (27 minutes) once daily from Monday to Saturday. The easiest way to reach the trailheads is with your own wheels.

Tywyn

POP 3097

While the town falls just outside the national park, Tywyn's long sandy Blue Flag beach is one of the most popular in the region. Its other major drawcard is the narrow-gauge Talyllyn Railway, famous as the inspiration for Rev W Awdry's *Thomas the Tank Engine* stories. Beyond these diversions it's a quiet, pleasant town, surrounded by salt-marsh sheep pastures and strung out along a meandering High St.

Sights & Activities

Narrow Gauge Railway Museum MUSEUM

(www.ngrm.org.uk; Tywyn Wharf; ⏰10.30am-4.30pm Apr-Sep) FREE At Tywyn Wharf Station, the terminus of the Talyllyn Railway, this museum is one for steam-locomotive buffs. Its 1000-plus artefacts date as far as 200 years back, telling the stories of British narrow-gauge railways and the volunteers who fought to preserve Talyllyn. There are regular temporary exhibitions, and opening hours are coordinated with the train timetable.

Talyllyn Railway RAIL

(Rheilffordd Talyllyn; ☎01654-710472; www.talyllyn.co.uk; Wharf Station; adult/accompanied child return £18/2; ⏰Easter-Oct, varies rest of year) A must for railway buffs, the narrow-gauge Talyllyn Railway opened in 1865 to carry slate and was saved in 1950 by the world's first railway-preservation society. One of Wales' most enchanting railways, it puffs 7.3 miles up the Fathew Valley to Nant Gwernol. There are five stations along the way, each with waymarked walking trails. Tickets are valid all day.

Eating

Salt Marsh Kitchen BISTRO ££

(☎01654-711949; 9 College Green; mains £12-15; ⏰5-9pm) Bare timber and blue paint give this ambitious little bistro an appropriately maritime feel, given the good things it does to fish. Inspiration is drawn from around the globe, with dishes such as crisp bream with scallop butter and risotto, smoked haddock chowder and a Thai-style curry bristling with mussels and prawns.

Proper Grander MODERN BRITISH ££

(☎01654-712169; www.propergandertywyn.com; 4 High St; mains £13-15; ⏰noon-3pm & 6-9pm Tue-Sat) Crustacea from Cardigan Bay, including crab and lobster from Tywyn and Aberdyfi, are sometimes highlights of the locally focused menu at this pleasant little bistro. Welsh cheese, beer, gin and meat are also given their chance to shine.

Getting There & Away

Train Tywyn is on the Cambrian Coast Line, with direct trains to/from Machynlleth (£5.90, 27 minutes), Fairbourne (£4, 20 minutes), Barmouth (£5.90, 30 minutes), Porthmadog (£12, 1½ hours) and Pwllheli (£14, two hours).

Bus Buses head to/from Dolgellau (route 28/30, 55/40 minutes), Fairbourne (route 28, 30 minutes) and Machynlleth (route X29, 35 minutes).

Barmouth (Abermaw)

POP 2315

With a Blue Flag beach and the beautiful Mawddach Estuary on its doorstep, the seaside resort of Barmouth has been a popular tourist destination since the coming of the railway in 1867. In summer it becomes a typical seaside resort – chip shops, dodgem cars, donkey rides and crabbing – catering to thousands from England's West Midlands. Outside of the brash neon of high summer it's considerably mellower, allowing space to appreciate its Georgian and Victorian architecture, beautiful setting and superb walking trails.

The main commercial strip is spread out along the A496; as it passes through town it's known as Church St, High St and King Edward's St.

Sights & Activities

The oldest part of Barmouth is around the quay. The unusual round building, Tŷ Crwn (The Quay; 10.30am-5pm) FREE, was once a jail where drunk and disorderly sailors could cool off until morning. In the 15th century, supporters of Henry Tudor met in nearby Tŷ Gwyn to plot his ascension to the throne (the building now houses a bar and restaurant).

Barmouth Bridge — BRIDGE

You're unlikely to miss Barmouth's foremost landmark: in fact, you'll probably arrive on it, either by train, on foot or on two wheels. Curving scenically into town, spanning 700 metres of the Mawddach Estuary mouth, it was built in 1867 for the new railway and is one of the longest wooden viaducts in Britain. Originally incorporating a drawbridge, it now has a swing bridge to allow tall shipping into the estuary.

Plans were afoot in 2015/16 to close the bridge to foot and cycle traffic, saving Gwynnedd Council the 10% of maintenance costs it pays to Network Rail. Not only is the viaduct an iconic and picturesque feature of the town, but its closure would force users of the Welsh Coastal Path and National Cycle Network on an 18-mile detour including busy sections of road. For the moment the Council seems to have responded to fierce local opposition and the path remains open.

Last Haul — MONUMENT

(Church St) This pockmarked slab of marble salvaged from the *Bronze Bell*, a famous local shipwreck of 1709, has been sculpted by local Franck Cocksey to depict three fishermen straining to haul in a catch.

Dinas Oleu — HILL

Rising behind Barmouth, rocky Dinas Oleu (258m) made history in 1895 by becoming the first property ever bequeathed to the National Trust, kick-starting a movement dedicated to preserving Britain's best landscapes and buildings. A network of trails covers the 4.5 gorse-covered acres of the 'Fortess of Light', including the popular Panorama Walk (signposted from the A496 on the eastern edge of town), which has the best views of Mawddach Estuary.

Otherwise, scramble up any one of several alleys running off Barmouth's High St, where you'll find the town gets more and more vertical, with better and better views, until the old houses are nearly on top of one another.

Taith Ardudwy — WALKING

(Ardudwy Way; www.taithardudwyway.com) Running 24 miles from Barmouth to Llandecwyn, this upland path crosses the Harlech Dome and other ancient rock formations as it traverses the medieval commote (administrative region) of Ardudwy, along Cardigan Bay. The way is marked with the trail's icon – the buzzard.

Festivals & Events

Three Peaks Yacht Race — SPORTS

(www.threepeaksyachtrace.co.uk; late Jun) The arduous Three Peaks Yacht Race runs from Barmouth to Fort William, with crew members running up Snowdon, Scafell Pike and Ben Nevis – the highest peaks of Wales, England and Scotland – en route. In all, that's 389 nautical miles of sailing, 29 miles of cycling and 59 miles of fell running.

The record time for the race thus far is two days, 14 hours and four minutes, achieved in 2002.

Barmouth Walking Festival WALKING
(www.barmouthwalkingfestival.co.uk; per walk £8.50; ⊙Sep) If you fancy a hike but would prefer some companions, this festival takes place over 35 graded walks and 10 days in September.

Sleeping

Hendre Mynach Caravan Park CAMPGROUND £
(☎01341-280262; www.hendremynach.co.uk; sites from £19; P🐾) Right by the beach, this well-kept park has caravan sites marked out between manicured hedges and a couple of flat camping fields protected by windbreaks. It's just off the A496, immediately north of Barmouth.

Richmond House B&B ££
(☎01341-281366; www.barmouthbedandbreakfast.co.uk; High St; s/d £65/80; P📶) Undergoing renovation at the time of research, this handsome town house has big, contemporary rooms (two with sea views) and an attractive garden area for summer lounging on chunky wooden furniture. It's very handy for both the town centre and the beach.

Eating

Ebeneezer Chapel Cafe & Emporium CAFE £
(☎01341-388100; High St; mains £5-6; ⊙9.30am-5pm) Making unorthodox use of a Georgian Wesleyan chapel on the High St is this offbeat cafe, its sky-blue ceiling awash with stars and the alcoves crammed with handicrafts from India, Thailand, Indonesia and beyond. Its main line of trade – soups, fishcakes, jacket potatoes, cakes, hot chocolate and coffee – is pretty good.

★**Bistro Bermo** EUROPEAN ££
(☎01341-281284; www.bistrobarmouth.co.uk; 6 Church St; mains £15-19; ⊙6.30-10pm Tue-Sat, plus noon-2pm Wed-Sat Apr-Oct) Discreetly hidden behind an aqua-green shopfront, this intimate restaurant delivers a sophisticated menu chock-full of Welsh farm produce and fresh fish. Featuring dishes such as red bream with scallops and seafood bisque, the cooking is classical, rather than experimental, and generally excellent. There are only half a dozen tables, so book ahead.

Drinking & Entertainment

Last Inn PUB
(☎01341-280530; www.lastinn-barmouth.co.uk; Church St; ⊙noon-11pm; 👪) In a 15th-century cobbler's home now lives Barmouth's most characterful pub, full of old ship timber and other eclectic nautical memorabilia. Most unusually, the hillside forms the rear wall, with a spring emerging to form a gaudily decorated pond inside the building itself. Kids are welcome, the menu's full of crowd-pleasers and there's live music on Tuesday and Friday nights.

Dragon Theatre PERFORMING ARTS
(Theatr y Ddraig; ☎01341-281697; www.dragontheatre.co.uk; Jubilee Rd) Since 1959 the cultural life of the town has centred on this 1890s chapel and its year-round schedule of live performances, cinema and exhibitions.

Getting There & Away

Train Barmouth is on the Cambrian Coast Line, with direct trains to Machynlleth (£9.30, one hour), Fairbourne (£2.80, seven minutes), Harlech (£4.90, 24 minutes), Porthmadog (£7.30, 50 minutes) and Pwllheli (£12, 1¼ hours).

Bus Buses stop on Jubilee Rd, across Beach Rd from the train station. Destinations include Harlech (route 38, 30 minutes), Dolgellau (route 38/T3, 20 minutes), Bala (route T3, one hour), Llandrillo (route T3, 1½ hours) and Llangollen (route T3, two hours).

Bicycle Cycle path Lôn Las Cymru passes through Barmouth, heading north to Harlech and east to Dolgellau.

Harlech

POP 1762

Hilly Harlech is best known for the mighty, grey stone towers of its castle, framed by gleaming Tremadog Bay and with the mountains of Snowdonia as a backdrop. Some sort of fortified structure has probably surmounted the rock since Iron Age times, but Edward I removed all traces when he commissioned the construction of his castle. Finished in 1289, Harlech Castle is the southernmost of four fortifications included in the 'Castles and Town Walls of King Edward in Gwynedd' Unesco World Heritage Site.

Harlech is such a thoroughly pleasant place that it has become one of the more gentrified destinations in Snowdonia – every other shop seems to sell antiques or tea. While it's bustling in summer, it can be deliciously sleepy otherwise. It makes a great base for a beach holiday or for day trips into the national park – and those views never get boring.

Sights & Activities

★Harlech Castle CASTLE

(Cadw; www.cadw.wales.gov.uk; Castle St; adult/child £6/4.20; ⏲9.30am-5pm Mar-Jun & Sep-Oct, to 6pm Jul & Aug, to 4pm Nov-Feb) Edward I finished this intimidating yet spectacular building in 1289, the southernmost of his 'iron ring' of fortresses designed to keep the Welsh firmly beneath his boot. The grey sandstone castle's massive, twin-towered gatehouse and outer walls are still intact and give the illusion of impregnability even now. A new visitor centre, with interactive displays, kids' activities and films, was opened in 2015, where the Castle Hotel once stood.

A drawbridge leads through the gatehouse to the compact inner ward, where four gloomy round towers guard the corners. Some of the ramparts are partly ruined and closed off, but you can climb up other sections for views in all directions. The fortress' great natural defence is the seaward cliff face. When it was built, ships could sail supplies right to the base.

Despite its might, this fortress has been called the 'Castle of Lost Causes' because it has been lucklessly defended so many times. Owain Glyndŵr captured it after a long siege in 1404. He is said to have been crowned Prince of Wales in the presence of envoys from Scotland, France and Spain during one of his parliaments in the town. He was, in turn, besieged here by the future Henry V.

During the Wars of the Roses the castle is said to have held out against a siege for seven years and was the last Lancastrian stronghold to fall. The siege inspired the popular Welsh hymn Men of Harlech, which is still played today in regimental marches and sung with patriotic gusto at rugby matches. The castle was also the last to fall in the English Civil War, finally giving in to Cromwell's forces in 1647.

The finest exterior view of the castle (with Snowdon as a backdrop) is from a craggy outcrop on Ffordd Isaf, opposite Maelgwyn House.

Snowdonia Adventure Activities OUTDOORS

(☎01341-241511; www.snowdoniaadventureactivities.co.uk; 2 Sarn Hir, Llanbedr; adult/child £70/40) This young couple offers customised adventures within the national park, including rock climbing, abseiling, canyoning, gorge scrambling, canoeing, kayaking, mountain biking and guided hiking: a full day's program combines two activities. You'll find Llanbedr 3 miles south of Harlech, on the A496.

Sleeping

★Maelgwyn House B&B ££

(☎01766-780087; www.maelgwynharlech.co.uk; Ffordd Isaf; r £70-95; P 📶) A model B&B in an art-bedecked former boarding school, Maelgwyn has interesting hosts, delicious breakfasts and a small set of elegant rooms with tremendous views across the bay, and stocked with DVD players and tea-making facilities. Bridget and Derek can also help arrange birdwatching trips and fungus forays. Full marks.

Castle Cottage HOTEL £££

(☎01766-780479; www.castlecottageharlech.co.uk; Ffordd Pen Llech; r from £135; P 📶) Within arrow's reach of the castle, this 16th-century cottage has spacious bedrooms in a contemporary style, with exposed beams, in-room DVD players and a bowl of fresh fruit for each guest. The award-winning fine-dining restaurant (two-/three-/five-course dinner £35/40/45) is a great showcase for Welsh produce: bacon from the Llŷn Peninsula, Rhydlewis salmon, Brecon venison and other delights.

Eating

Cemlyn Tea Shop TEAROOM £

(☎01766-780425; www.cemlynteashop.co.uk; High St; snacks around £5; ⏲10am-5pm Wed-Sun; 🐾) The Coles (Jan and Geoff) may be merry old souls but it's tea that's king here. There are more than 30 varieties on offer, along with homemade cakes and a cosy, lemon-tinted dining room in which to enjoy them. When the weather's good, the rear terrace at this award-winning tearoom offers spectacular views of the castle and beyond.

★Soul Food CARIBBEAN ££

(☎01766-780416; www.soulfoodcaribbeanrestaurant.co.uk; High St; mains £13-15; ⏲5.30-9pm Tue-Sat) Slaty Harlech is an unlikely locale for an authentic Tobagan joint, let alone the best Caribbean restaurant in Wales. But the locals – hungrily snapping up Trinidadian roti with goat and potato curry, caramelised lime chicken, jerk lamb, vegetarian pepper pot and other spicy delights – don't seem to notice anything incongruous.

As.Is INTERNATIONAL ££

(☎075082-68276; www.asisatharlech.com; The Square; mains £12-14; ⏱5.30-9pm Thu-Tue) A young chef couple have hung out their shingle in the lee of the castle, offering a short menu of Italian palate-ticklers, alongside more adventurous fare (pigeon with asparagus, perhaps, or leek and mushroom strudel). The space is stylish – naked wires, oversized light bulbs and rough timber tables – and the patrons are very eager to please.

☆ Entertainment

Theatr Ardudwy PERFORMING ARTS

(☎01766-780667; www.theatrardudwy.cymru; Ffordd Newydd) An impressive cultural asset for a town of this size, Theatr Ardudwy is a lively local arts centre that stages dance, theatre and music, and screens a well-considered assortment of films, from Hollywood blockbusters to artier offerings.

Getting There & Away

Train Harlech is on the Cambrian Coast Line, with direct trains to Machynlleth (£12.60, 1½ hours), Fairbourne (£6, 34 minutes), Barmouth (£4.90, 25 minutes), Porthmadog (£4, 24 minutes) and Pwllheli (£8.40, 47 minutes). The station is at the base of the rocks below the castle; it's a strenuous 20-minute climb on one of several stepped tracks up to High St or about half a mile by road.

Bus Bus 38 to Barmouth (30 minutes) stops on High St; some buses continue on to Dolgellau (one hour).

Bicycle National Cycle Network path 8 (Lôn Las Cymru North) passes through Harlech, heading north to Porthmadog and south to Barmouth.

Blaenau Ffestiniog

POP 3662

Most of the slate used to roof 19th-century Britain came from Wales, and much of that came from the mines of Blaenau Ffestiniog. However, only about 10% of mined slate is usable, so for every tonne that goes to the factory, 9 tonnes remain as rubble. Despite being in the centre of Snowdonia National Park, the grey mountains of mine waste that surround Blaenau (*blay*-nye) prevented it from being officially included in the park – a slap in the face for this close-knit but impoverished town in the days before Wales' industrial sites were recognised as part of its heritage.

Although slate mining continues on a small scale, it's the abandoned workings of this once-mighty industry that are now Blaenau's attraction. By no means a 'pretty' town, opportunities to explore the slate caverns or tickle your adrenal gland with extreme sports make it a great day trip from Porthmadog, via the historic Ffestiniog Railway.

Sights

★ **Llechwedd Slate Caverns** MINE

(☎01766-830306; www.llechwedd-slate-caverns.co.uk; tours £20; ⏱9.30am-5.30pm) Blaenau's main attraction takes you down into the bowels of a Victorian slate mine. You descend the UK's steepest mining cable railway into the 1846 network of tunnels and caverns, while 'enhanced-reality technology' brings to life the harsh working conditions of the 19th-century miners – be prepared to duck and scramble around dark tunnels. There's also a tour of the quarry in a military truck (an extra £20 per person). Check the website for tour times and prebooking.

Cellb ARTS CENTRE

(☎01766-832001; www.cellb.org; Park Sq; ⏱cafe/bar 10am-3pm Tue-Sat, 7-11pm Wed-Sat) Recently opened in the Edwardian-era police station (hence 'Cell B'), this multifunction centre hosts everything from yoga and Welsh-language classes to live bands and film screenings. It's also the town's most appealing dining and drinking space, with a cafe-bar and a cocktail bar. At the time of writing, they were putting the finishing touches to a new, 50-seat digital cinema and hostel accommodation.

Activities

Zip World Blaenau Ffestiniog ADVENTURE SPORTS

(☎01248-601444; www.zipworld.co.uk; Llechwedd Slate Caverns; ⏱booking office 8am-6.30pm; 👪) If you've ever wanted to practise trampoline tricks in a slate mine (and who hasn't?) then Bounce Below – a 'cathedral-sized' cavern with bouncy nets, walkways, tunnels and slides – is your chance (one hour, £25). There's also Titan – 8000m of zip wires over deep open pits (£50 per two hours) – and zip wires through the caverns (£60 for two hours).

Antur Stiniog MOUNTAIN BIKING

(☎01766-832214; www.anturstiniog.com; 1 uplift £17-19, day pass £29-33; ⏱10am-4pm Thu-Mon) If you're a serious mountain biker and don't know the meaning of fear, check out these six new blue and black runs down the mountainside near the slate caverns. There's a minibus uplift service, a cafe (9am to 4.30pm) and plans to introduce a 'velorail' (a pedal-powered vehicle running on the abandoned train line leading to Llan Festiniog).

The same crew can organise tailored activity-based holidays (walking, kayaking, climbing and wild camping) and has a shop on Blaenau Ffestiniog's High St.

❶ Getting There & Away

Train Both the Conwy Valley Line from Betws-y-Coed (£5.20, 34 minutes) and Llandudno (£8.70, 1¼ hours), and the steam-powered Ffestiniog Railway (p255) from Porthmadog terminate here.

Bus Buses head to/from Porthmadog (route 1B, 30 minutes); Dolgellau (route 35, 47 minutes); Betws-y-Coed (route X1, 25 minutes); and Llandudno (route X1, 1¼ hours).

Penmachno

POP 617

Tucked away in the valley of the River Machno, the picturesque village of Penmachno dates to at least Roman times, but it's a sleepy place these days. It's edged by the Gwydyr Forest, a leafy paradise for mountain bikers and horse riders.

◉ Sights & Activities

St Tudclud's Church CHURCH
(www.churchinwales.org.uk/bangor) After 12 years of closure, little St Tudclud's reopened in 2009 after the community rallied to save it. It isn't particularly old (1859), but inside are five Latin-inscribed stones dating from the 5th century, a 12th-century font, and a 13th-century gravestone which may have belonged to the father of Llywelyn the Great. It's usually open; call in and help yourself to a cup of coffee.

Penmachno Trails MOUNTAIN BIKING
(www.penmachnobiketrails.org.uk; requested donation £2) The southern part of the Gwydyr Forest (p243) has two red-graded mountainbiking loops – the 12-mile Dolen Machno (1½ to three hours) and the 7-mile Dolen Eryri (one to two hours) – which can be combined into the 19-mile Penmachno Trail. They offer a good mix of descents and forest climbs, with some sections of boardwalk.

Gwydyr Stables HORSE RIDING
(☑ 01690-760248; www.horse-riding-wales.co.uk; half/full day £40/70) Offering rides on the plentiful bridle trails of the surrounding Gwydyr Forest throughout the year, Gwydyr is also know for its pub rides, which afford plenty of scope for refreshment along the way. To find the stables, turn right at the Eagles inn and follow the signs towards Tŷ Mawr.

🛏 Sleeping

The Eagles HOSTEL £
(☑ 01960-760177; www.eaglespenmachno.co.uk; dm £18.50-20.50; ☺ pub 7pm-late Wed-Fri, 2pm-late Sat & Sun; 🛜) A hand-painted sign depicting three black eagles hangs above the door of the village pub, popular for its cask-conditioned ales, banter and (on Saturdays, plus Fridays from February to November) evening meals. Upstairs there's simple bunkhouse accommodation in nine private rooms, plus a self-catering kitchen. It's well suited to mountain bikers, with a drying room and secure bike storage.

Penmachno Hall B&B ££
(☑ 01690-760140; www.penmachnohall.co.uk; d £95, 2-night minimum; 🅿🛜) Just over the bridge on the way to Tŷ Mawr, this ivy-draped 1860s stone house has three vibrant colour-coded guest rooms and a separate coach-house cottage for longer stays. 'Yellow' has a sleigh bed and 'Orange' has the best views, but both have claw-foot tubs. Welsh suppers can be prepared on request (£17.50 per person, minimum of two people).

❶ Getting There & Away

Penmachno is 5 miles south of Betws-y-Coed; take the A5 and then turn right on to the B4406. From Monday to Saturday, bus 64 heads to/from Betws-y-Coed (10 minutes).

Betws-y-Coed

POP 2253

Betws-y-Coed *(bet-*us-ee-*koyd)* sits at the junction of three river valleys (the Llugwy, the Conwy and the Lledr) and on the verge of the Gwydyr Forest. With around seven outdoor shops for every pub, walking trails leaving right from the centre and guesthouses occupying a fair proportion of its slate Victorian buildings, it's the perfect base for exploring Snowdonia.

The town has been Wales' most popular inland resort since Victorian times, when a group of countryside painters founded an artistic community to record the diversity of the landscape. The arrival of the railway in 1868 cemented its popularity, and today Betws-y-Coed is as busy with families and coach parties as it is with walkers.

Sights

One of the joys of Betws is wandering its riverbanks and criss-crossing its historic bridges. The main road crosses the Conwy at the 32m-wide **Waterloo Bridge**: known locally as the 'iron bridge', it bears a large inscription celebrating its construction in the year of Wellington's victory over Boney (1815). Behind the information centre a pleasant path leads around the tongue of land framed by the convergence of the Rivers Conwy and Llugwy, and back past St Michael's Church. Nearby, **Sapper's Bridge** is a white suspension footbridge (1930) that crosses the Conwy and leads through the fields up to the A470.

At the other end of the village, the 15th-century stone **Pont-y-Pair** (Bridge of the Cauldron) crosses a set of rapids on the Llugwy. A riverside path leads about a mile downstream to the **Miners' Bridge**, named for the route miners took on their way to work in nearby lead mines. This was the oldest crossing of the Llugwy, but the original bridge is long gone.

The Rivers Conwy and Llugwy are rich with salmon in autumn. Outdoors shops are strung out along Holyhead Rd, selling equipment and specialist references for walkers, climbers and cyclists.

Centre

Conwy Valley Railway Museum MUSEUM
(☎01690-710568; www.conwyrailwaymuseum.co.uk; The Old Goods Yard; adult/child £1.50/1; ⏰10am-5pm) If you're the sort who's fascinated by dioramas and model train sets, this tiny museum is for you. In which case the model shop you have to pass through in order to enter might pose an unfair tempta-

Betws-y-Coed

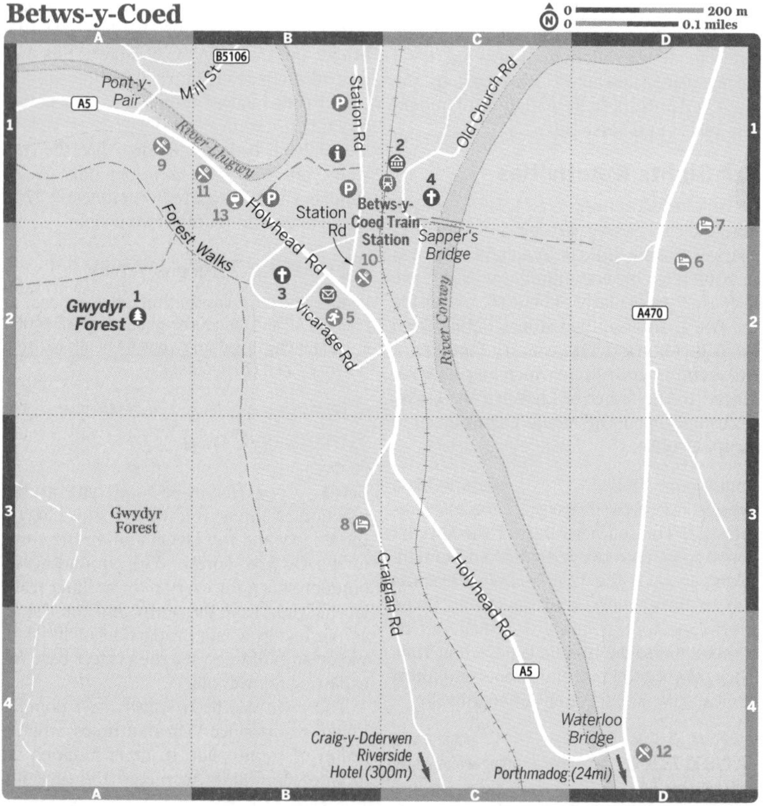

tion. The big attraction for kids is the miniature steam-train ride (the 1-mile round trip through manicured gardens costs £2, and is sometimes diesel-powered) and there's a cafe in a full-sized carriage.

St Michael's Church CHURCH
(www.stmichaelsbyc.org.uk; Old Church Rd; ⏲10am-5pm Sun Easter-Sep) The name Betws is thought to be derived from 'bead house', meaning a place of prayer (*y coed* – in the woods). It's likely that 14th-century St Michael's Church, the town's oldest building, stands on the site of that early sanctuary. The main item of interest inside is a stone effigy of Gruffydd ap Dafydd Goch, possibly the grandnephew of Llywelyn ap Gruffydd, the last native Prince of Wales. If it's locked, ask for the key at the Railway Museum.

In 1873 it was replaced as the parish church by the much larger St Mary's Church, but it's still used on St Michael's Day (29 September) and for the occasional funeral.

Around Betws-y-Coed

★**Gwydyr Forest** FOREST
The 28-sq-mile Gwydyr Forest, planted since the 1920s with oak, beech and larch, encircles Betws-y-Coed and is scattered with the remnants of lead and zinc mine workings. Named for a more ancient forest in the same location, it's ideal for a day's walking, though it gets very muddy in wet weather.

Betws-y-Coed

Walks Around Betws-y-Coed (£5), available from the National Park Information Centre, details several circular forest walks.

The northern section of the park is home to the Marin Trail, a challenging 15.5-mile mountain-biking loop, starting immediately southwest of Llanrwst, 3.5 miles north of Betws.

Swallow Falls WATERFALL
(Rhaeadr Ewynnol; £1.50) Betws-y-Coed's main natural tourist trap is located 2 miles west of town alongside the A5. It's a beautiful spot, with the torrent, Wales's highest, weaving through the rocks into a green pool below. Outside seasonal opening hours, bring a £1 coin for the turnstile.

Ugly House HISTORIC BUILDING
(Tŷ Hyll; www.theuglyhouse.co.uk; ⏲10.30am-4.30pm daily Easter-Oct, Mon-Fri Nov & Feb-Mar) The Ugly House isn't actually ugly at all. This unusual cottage is constructed from huge boulders and is home to a characterful tearoom and, upstairs, the Honeybee Room, with displays devoted to the beleaguered insect. Visitors can wander through the grounds and gardens, even when the house is closed. It's located half a mile past Swallow Falls on the A5.

The origins of the house are steeped in folklore. One yarn suggests it was built in 1475 by two local bandits as their hideout; according to another, there was a Welsh law that allowed any man who built on common land after sunset and had smoke coming out of the chimney by daybreak to stake a claim for the freehold as far as he could throw an axe around the property. The Snowdonia Society, a charity working to protect and enhance Snowdonia's heritage and wildlife, rescued the property from dereliction and turned it into its headquarters in 1988 following painstaking renovations by a team of dedicated volunteers.

Activities

Go Below Underground Adventures ADVENTURE SPORTS
(☎01690-710108; www.go-below.co.uk; adult/child from £49/39) Head into the depths of an old slate mine and try your hand ziplining across lakes and abseiling down shafts. You don't have to have caving experience, or squeeze through tiny spaces, but claustrophobes may demur. The booking office is based at Conwy Falls, on the A5 south of Betws at the turn-off to Penmachno.

WORTH A TRIP

MOUNTAIN SURFING

Lying just outside the National Park's eastern border, in the lush Conwy Valley, is this unexpected little slice of Maui: **Surf Snowdonia** (01492-353123; www.surfsnowdonia.co.uk; Conway Rd, Dolgarrog; free; 8am-11pm;), an adventure park centred on a vast artificial wave pool (open 10am until sunset). If learning to surf (adult/child £50/35) doesn't excite, there are lagoon 'crash and splash' sessions (£25 per hour), kayaking, walking and a soft-play centre for kids.

There's also a cafe/bar, restaurant and on-site fixed camping, if you want to dally. Surf Snowdonia is signposted off the A470 from Llandudno Junction to Betws-y-Coed.

Zip World Fforest ADVENTURE SPORTS
(01248-601444; www.zipworld.co.uk; A470; 2hr 'Safari' £40; 9am-4pm) Tree-top fun in the Fforest includes the 'Safari' – a network of rope ladders and zip-lines high in the tree tops – the 'Plummet' – which uses a 'power fan' to simulate a parachute drop – and Skyride – a giant, five-person swing that reaches jaw-clenching velocity. There's a cafe for a nice, soothing hot chocolate afterwards.

Beics Betws CYCLING
(01690-710766; www.bikewales.co.uk; Vicarage Rd; 9.30am-5pm Mar-Nov, call ahead at other times) Advises on local cycling trails, has Marin Trail maps, performs repairs and hires mountain bikes (including helmet and tool bag from £28 per day).

Snowdonia Safaris TOURS
(07511-749673; www.snowdoniasafaris.co.uk; per person from £35; Apr-Nov) Offers personalised 4WD tours to 'hidden gems' within a 6-mile radius of Betws, including neolithic tombs, abandoned quarries and villages, and natural beauty spots.

Sleeping

★ **Coed-y-Celyn Hall** APARTMENT £
(07821-099595; www.snowdonia-self-catering.co.uk; A470, Coed-y-Celyn; apt per week from £300;) Built in the 1850s for a mining magnate, this grand pile on the banks of the Conwy was auctioned off in the 1950s and half of it has been converted into apartments. They're all different, but they're all huge – and terrifically good value. We particularly love apartment 4 for its moulded ceilings, grand windows and views over the front lawns.

Vagabond HOSTEL £
(01690-710850; www.thevagabond.co.uk; Craiglan Rd; dm from £19;) Sitting on the slopes below a forested crag, from which spills its own 'private' waterfall, the Vagabond is Betws's best hostel – and the only one within the town. It's a simple set-up, with freshly decorated dorm rooms, shared bathrooms and an appealing bar (4.30pm to 11pm), kitchen and common room downstairs. The obligatory £24 weekend rate includes a cooked breakfast.

Betws-y-Coed YHA HOSTEL £
(01690-710796; www.swallowfallshotel.co.uk; Holyhead Rd, Swallow Falls; dm/tw £19/40, site per adult/child £8/4;) Part of the Swallow Falls Complex – a bustling traveller hub which includes a hotel, tavern and campground – this no-frills hostel occupies an unattractive building plonked in the middle of the car park. We prefer the terraced camping area at the rear.

Tyn-y-Fron B&B ££
(01690-710449; www.snowdoniabedandbreakfast.co.uk; Lon Muriau, off A470; s £70, d £78-110;) The best of a clump of B&Bs over the fields from the town, this gracious old stone house has five guest rooms, all of which have been given a plush, modern makeover, and some of which have divine valley views. Mike and Lesley, the friendly, rugby-mad owners, serve an excellent breakfast, including award-winning sausages and bacon from the local butcher.

Maes-y-Garth B&B ££
(01690-710441; www.maes-y-garth.co.uk; Lon Muriau, off A470; r £75-130;) Accessible from Betws by a footpath across the river and the fields (starting behind St Michael's Church), this newly built home has earned itself a legion of fans. Inside you'll find a warm welcome and five quietly stylish guest rooms with gorgeous views – perhaps the nicest is room 4, which has its own balcony and views of the valley.

Bod Gwynedd B&B ££
(01690-710717; www.bodgwynedd.com; Holyhead Rd; s/d from £60/75;) On the west-

ern edge of town, this friendly B&B offers tastefully furnished bedrooms in a mid-Victorian slate house. The friendly owners keep everything spick-and-span and have plenty of local knowledge to impart.

Afon Gwyn B&B ££
(☎01690-710442; www.guest-house-betws-y-coed.com; A470, Coed-y-Celyn; r from £81; P 📶) Down in the valley, this old stone house has been skillfully converted into a grand boutique guesthouse. The decor is faultlessly tasteful, with hushed tones, white-painted wood panelling, glittering chandeliers, and bathrooms bedecked in Italian tiles and marble. While all the rooms are spacious, the Alice Suite, complete with free-standing bath and canopied bed, is massive.

Eating & Drinking

Cwmni Cacen Gri CAFE £
(☎01690-710006; www.cwmnicacengri.co.uk; Station Approach; Welsh cakes 50p; ⏲9am-4.30pm Tue-Sun; 🅥) At this pint-sized spot, local ladies Jen and Jo serve Welsh cakes straight from the griddle – from traditional fare to unusually flavoured sweet and savoury ones; all are made with organic Welsh eggs and butter. Pies, homemade cakes and good coffee are also available: all ideal picnic fodder.

★**Bistro Betws-y-Coed** WELSH ££
(☎01690-710328; www.bistrobetws-y-coed.com; Holyhead Rd; lunch £6-9, dinner £13-20; ⏲noon-3pm & 6.30-9.30pm daily Jun-Sep, Wed-Sun Mar-May, 6.30-9.30pm Wed-Sun Dec-Feb) This cottage-style eatery's statement of intent is 'Traditional and Modern Welsh' and the menu features some interesting adaptations of Welsh recipes from the 18th and 19th centuries. Watch out for possible shot pellets in the sautéed breast of wild wood pigeon with blueberry pancakes and crispy bacon! And book in summer as it gets absolutely packed.

Tŷ Gwyn Hotel EUROPEAN ££
(☎01690-710383; www.tygwynhotel.co.uk; A5; mains £15-19; ⏲noon-2pm & 6-9pm; 🅥) This 400-year-old coaching inn oozes character from every one of its numerous exposed beams. The menu is full of intriguing modern takes on age-old local ingredients (locally reared suckling pig, whole lake trout from Llyn Brenig) and a decent number of veggie options (the wild mushroom and pine-nut stroganoff is as good as it sounds). Book ahead.

Olif BISTRO ££
(☎01690-733942; www.olif-betws.co.uk; Holyhead Rd; tapas £5-7; ⏲6-8.30pm Tue-Sun, noon-3pm Sat & Sun May-Oct, closed Mon-Wed Nov-Apr) Breakfast first up, burgers at lunch, tea in the afternoon and tapas in the evening – Olif morphs to please throughout the day. The tapas has a distinctly Welsh flavour, without straying too far into fusion territory (the croquettes are made with Perl Wen cheese and the ham's from Camarthen) and there are several smart en suite rooms available, too.

Stables Bar PUB
(☎016907-10219; www.stables-bistro.co.uk; A5; ⏲11.30am-11pm; 📶) Attached to the grander Royal Oak, and doing a roaring trade in lasagne, curries and pints for weary walkers, the Stables (Y Stablau) is the only pub per se in Betwys. It's a long, low-ceilinged, tile-floored barn of a place, but very welcoming. There's also music, including Dixieland, blues and Welsh male choirs.

Information

Snowdonia National Park Information Centre (☎01690-710426; www.eryri-npa.gov.uk; Royal Oak Stables; ⏲9.30am-5.30pm Easter-Oct, to 4pm rest of year) More than just a repository of books, maps and local craft, this office is an invaluable source of information about walking trails, mountain conditions and more.

Getting There & Away

Betws-y-Coed is on the Conwy Valley Line (www.conwyvalleyrailway.co.uk), with trains every day but Sunday to Llandudno (£6.30, 54 minutes) and Blaenau Ffestiniog (£5.20, 34 minutes).

Snowdon Sherpa bus services head to Swallow Falls (route S2, seven minutes), Capel Curig (route S2, 12 minutes), Pen-y-Pass (route S2, 25 minutes), Llanberis (route S2, 35 minutes) and Bangor (route S6, in summer, one hour); all trips are £1.50.

Other buses head to Llandudno (route X1/19, one hour), Conwy (route 19, 45 minutes), Blaenau Ffestiniog (route X1, 25 minutes) and Dolgellau (route X1, one daily Monday to Saturday, 1¼ hours).

Capel Curig

POP 206

Tiny Capel Curig, 5 miles west of Betws-y-Coed, is one of Snowdonia's oldest hill stations and has long been a magnet for walkers, climbers and other outdoor junkies. It's a heady setting, ringed by looming mountains. A popular track heads south from Plas y Brenin to the summit of Moel Siabod (872m). Capel Curig village spreads out along the A5 but the main clump of activity is at the intersection of the A4086.

Activities

Plas y Brenin National Mountain Sports Centre OUTDOORS
(☎01690-720214; www.pyb.co.uk; A4086) At the western edge of the village, this multi-activity centre has excellent facilities and a huge array of year-round courses on both land and water, ranging from basic rock climbing and summer and winter mountaineering, to kayaking, canoeing and abseiling. Book ahead for 'Taster Days' throughout the school holidays, introducing youngsters to adventure activities (£25/40 per half/full day).

Sleeping

★**Plas Curig** HOSTEL £
(☎01690-720225; www.snowdoniahostel.co.uk; A5; dm/d/f from £20/50/90; P) Plas Curig is an exceptional hostel that wears its five stars with pride. Paying as much attention to comfort as decor, it has comfortable bunks with privacy curtains, a large, well-equipped kitchen and a drying room for soggy hiking gear.

Bryn Tyrch Inn HOTEL ££
(☎01690-720223; www.bryntyrchinn.co.uk; A5; s/d from £75/90; P) Downstairs there's a restaurant and bar with a roaring fire – Capel Curig's liveliest spot after dark, with mains from £15 to £19. Upstairs the rooms have all been prettied up, with feature wallpaper, exposed stonework and modern bathrooms. It also does packed lunches for walkers (£7.50 per person).

Getting There & Away

Snowdon Sherpa bus S2 heads to/from Betws-y-Coed (10 minutes), Pen-y-Pass (15 minutes) and Llanberis (35 minutes). Single trips start from £1.50.

WORTH A TRIP

LLYN OGWEN & LLYN IDWAL

Despite the A5 being the main road to Anglesey, the section of the national park west of Capel Curig is often overlooked. It's a gorgeous drive, with the slate-hued shore of Llyn Ogwen on one side and the Glyderau mountains on the other. You couldn't ask for a more beautiful setting for the **Idwal Cottage YHA** (☎08453-719744; www.yha.org.uk; Nant Ffrancon; dm/tw £22/56; daily Mar-Oct, Fri & Sat Nov-Feb), near the western end of the lake. From here a track leads up to Cwm Idwal, an amphitheatre-shaped hanging valley sheltering another impossibly scenic lake, Llyn Idwal. Keep an eye out for feral goats, descended from herds farmed here in the distant past.

Llanberis

POP 1844

Llanberis is a mecca for walkers and climbers, attracting a steady flow of rugged polar-fleece wearers year-round but especially in July and August (when accommodation is at a premium). It's positioned just outside the national park but functions as a hub, partly because the Snowdon Mountain Railway leaves from here. While not the most attractive town in the area, its offbeat charm complements the appeal of its glorious surrounds.

Llanberis originally housed workers from the Dinorwig slate quarry; the massive waste tips are hard to miss. While tourism is the cornerstone of life these days, the town proudly wears its industrial heritage on its sleeve. Dinorwig, which once boasted the largest artificial cavern in the world, is now part of Europe's biggest pumped-storage power station. Some of the old quarry workshops have been reincarnated as a slate-industry museum, and the narrow-gauge railway that once hauled slate to the coast now transports excited toddlers along Llyn Padarn.

Sights

★**National Slate Museum** MUSEUM
(☎03001-112333; www.museumwales.ac.uk/en/slate; 10am-5pm Easter-Oct, to 4pm Sun-Fri Nov-Easter) FREE A slate museum sounds dull; ii isn't. Even if you're not enraptured by industrial museums, this one's well worth checking out. At Llanberis much of the slate was carved out of the open mountainside – leaving behind a jagged, sculptural cliff-face that's fascinating if not quite beautiful. The museum occupies the Victorian workshops beside Llyn Padarn. It features video clips, a huge working water wheel, workers' cottages (each furnished in a progression from

1861 until 1969, when the quarries closed) and demonstrations.

The turn-off is along the A4086 between the Electric Mountain exhibition centre and the Snowdon Mountain Railway station. The museum is part of the Padarn Country Park.

Quarry Hospital Museum MUSEUM
(⌚10am-5pm Easter-Oct, to 4pm Sun-Fri Nov-Easter) FREE Built in 1860 to minister to workers injured in rockfalls and the other mishaps inseparable from slate mining, this museum provides a vivid insight into the sometimes gruesome medical care provided in Victorian times. The hospital is part of Padarn Country Park, on the northeastern shore of Llyn Padarn.

Electric Mountain MUSEUM
(☎01286-870636; www.electricmountain.co.uk; tour adult/child £8.50/4.35; ⌚10am-4.30pm Jan-May & Sep-Dec, 9.30am-5.30pm Jun-Aug) More than just Dinorwig Power Station's public interface, Electric Mountain is a tourist hub incorporating a gallery, cafe, children's playground, climbing wall and souvenir shop. It also has interactive exhibits on hydropower and is the starting point for a fascinating guided tour into the power station's guts, 750m under Elidir mountain.

The Dinorwig pumped-storage power station is the largest scheme of its kind in Europe. Spanning 16km of tunnels deep within the mountain, its construction required one million tonnes of concrete, 200,000 tonnes of cement and 4500 tonnes of steel, and incorporates the largest human-made cavern in Europe, big enough to house St Paul's Cathedral (should you wish to do so). The station uses surplus energy to pump water from Llyn Peris up to Marchlyn Reservoir; when half the population switches on their kettles for tea during a TV ad break, the water is released to fall through underground turbines. Dinorwig's reversible turbine pumps are capable of reaching maximum generation in less than 16 seconds.

The centre is by the lakeside on the A4086, near the south end of High St.

Dolbadarn Castle CASTLE
(Castell Dolbadarn; www.cadw.gov.wales; ⌚10am-4pm) FREE Built before 1230 by the Princes of Gwynedd, the keep of Dolbardarn rises like a perfect chessboard rook from a green hilltop between the two lakes, Llyn Padarn and Llyn Peris. If it seems spartan, spare a thought for Owain ap Gruffydd, imprisoned here for 20 years in the mid-13th century by his younger brother Llewellyn the Last. It's a brief stroll from town and you'll be rewarded with wonderful views of the lakes, quarries and Snowdon itself.

Activities

Padarn Adventures ADVENTURE SPORTS
(☎01286-872310; www.padarnadventures.com; Padarn Country Park;) Right by the slate museum, this outfit offers a high ropes course (adult/child £27/22 for two hours), a giant swing, abseiling, mountain walks, kayaking, or a mixture of activities. While the high ropes are aimed at ages 'eight to infinity', there's also a special low course for four to eight year olds. Call ahead for opening times.

Vivian Diving Centre DIVING
(☎01286-870889; www.viviandivecentre.co.uk; Padarn Country Park; member/nonmember per day £10/12; ⌚9am-5pm Wed-Mon Apr-Nov, 10am-4pm Nov-Mar) Tucked underneath the cliffs near the slate museum, the 18m-deep water-filled Vivian Quarry offers diving year-round. Beneath the inky-looking but quite clear waters are two boats, a quarryman's house and plenty of fish.

Snowdon Star CRUISE
(☎07974-716418; www.snowdonstar.co.uk; Padarn Country Park jetty; adult/child £7/4; ⌚May-Oct) Float beneath the sculpted cliffs of the Dinorwig Quarry on this 45-minute Llyn Padarn cruise. The *Star* departs from the jetty near the National Slate Museum car park on the hour from noon until 4pm, with additional sailings at 11am and 5pm in July and August; call ahead to confirm.

Lake Padarn is home to the most southerly population of Arctic char, a type of fish that's survived in the depths since the last Ice Age.

Llanberis Lake Railway RAIL
(☎01286-870549; www.lake-railway.co.uk; adult/child £8.20/4.50; ⌚Feb-Nov) If you need something to placate the kids on days that the Snowdonia Mountain Railway isn't operating, this little steam train might be just the ticket. It departs on a 5-mile return jaunt along the route used from 1843 to 1961 to haul slate to the port on the Menai Strait.

The gentle, scenic one-hour return trip heads alongside Llyn Padarn, past the National Slate Museum and through Padarn Country Park to the terminus at Penllyn. The starting point is either Llanberis Station (across the A4086 from the Snowdon

Mountain Railway station) or Gilfach Ddu Station (in Padarn Country Park).

Boulder Adventures OUTDOORS
(01286-870556; www.boulderadventures.co.uk; Ty Du Rd; session/full day £45/65) Small groups and families can work with Boulder to devise their own adventure from a list including rock climbing, abseiling, gorge walking, coasteering, orienteering and kayaking. It also offers hostel-style accommodation within the Bryn Du Mountain Centre, a spacious Victorian house on the slopes above Llanberis (£22 per person).

Sleeping

Brynteg RESORT £
(01286-871374; www.brynteg.co.uk; Llanrug; caravan/lodge per week from £279/649; P) Tucked away near a privately owned castle halfway between Llanberis and Caernarfon, this large holiday park rents out static caravans (some with central heating and double-glazing) and lodges (with hot tubs). Facilities include a swimming pool, climbing wall, adventure playground, 'country club with brasserie' and the dubious-sounding 'Teen Room'.

YHA Snowdon Llanberis HOSTEL £
(0845 371 9645; www.yha.org.uk; Capel Goch Rd; dm/r from £15/39; reception 8-10am & 5-10pm; P) Originally a quarry manager's house, this no-frills hostel offers great views (from an admittedly scrappy hillside locale), a self-catering kitchen and a drying room. It's about a 10-minute walk above the town, signposted from the High St.

★**Beech Bank** B&B ££
(01286-871085; www.beech-bank.co.uk; 2 High St; s/d £60/80; P) First impressions of this double-gabled, wrought iron–trimmed stone house are great, but step inside and it just gets better. A stylish renovation has left beautiful bathrooms and exuberant decor, which matches the gregarious nature of the host. Highly recommended, although not set up for children.

Plas Coch Guest House HOTEL ££
(01286-872122; www.plascochsnowdonia.co.uk; High St; s £60, d £80-90; P) More like a little hotel than a B&B, this large ivy-draped 1865 house is operated by a friendly couple with lots of local knowledge to impart. The rooms are stylishly renovated, very comfortable and, in some cases, large enough to qualify as suites.

Glyn Afon B&B ££
(01286-872528; www.glyn-afon.co.uk; 72 High St; s/d from £50/70; P) Rooms are clean, warm and homey at this midrange guesthouse, renovated in 2015. The hearty breakfast will set you up well for a day of mountain striding, and the owners are happy to help with information on walks (and will even lend you a compass or rucksack if you haven't brought one with you).

Eating

Y Pantri CAFE £
(High St; mains £4-6; 10am-5pm) Good coffee! After that, everything else this cruisy, pastel-hued little cafe does is a bonus. But those extras – homemade cakes, sandwiches, soups and the like – are also from the top drawer.

Pete's Eats CAFE £
(01286-870117; www.petes-eats.co.uk; 40 High St; mains £3-7; 8am-8pm;) Pete's Eats is a local institution – a busy, primary-coloured cafe where hikers and climbers swap tips over monster breakfasts and under photos of their knee-trembling forebears. There's bunkhouse accommodation upstairs, a huge noticeboard full of travellers' information, a book exchange, a map and guidebook room, and computers for internet access.

Llygad yr Haul CAFE £
(01286-870814; 90 High St; mains from £5; 10am-5pm;) The delicious homemade bread and cakes have won this friendly little cafe a local fan base, while walkers crowd in for the generous helpings of jacket potato with ample toppings, and panini-and-soup meal deals.

★**Gallt-y-Glyn** PUB FOOD ££
(01286-870370; www.gallt-y-glyn.co.uk; A4086; mains £8-15; 6-9pm Wed-Sat;) Sure, it serves pasta, pies, steaks and salads too, but almost everyone comes for the pizza and the free-pint-with-every-main deal. Simply tick what you want on the paper menu and hand it over at the bar. You'll find Gallt-y-Glyn on the A4086, half a mile towards Caernarfon. It's a bit shabby, slightly eccentric, very family friendly and utterly brilliant.

Peak Restaurant INTERNATIONAL ££
(Bwyty'r Copa; 01286-872777; www.peakrestaurant.co.uk; 86 High St; mains £13-17; 7-10pm Wed-Sat;) A chef-patron who once clattered the pans at the legendary Chez Panisse in California is behind this restaurant's

popularity and longevity. The open kitchen allows you to see her at work, turning good Welsh produce into internationally inspired dishes such as Anglesey sea bass with coriander butter and Welsh lamb shanks with white-onion puree.

Shopping

Snowdon Honey Farm & Winery FOOD & DRINKS
(www.snowdonhoneyfarmandwinery.co.uk; High St; cakes £3-5; ⏲10am-4pm) All manner of honey-related goodies are sold here, including a range of mead, graded Roman, Celtic or Medieval, depending on sweetness. There's also honey liqueur, homemade fudges, preserves and fruit wine and, if you ask nicely, the engaging owner may let you sip before you commit. There's an attached tearoom, serving ice cream and cakes.

Information

Joe Brown (☎01286-870327; 63 High St; ⏲9am-5.30pm) A climbing shop that sells all things outdoors; its noticeboard includes weather forecasts and lots of information and advice for walkers.

Getting There & Away

Snowdon Sherpa buses stop by Joe Brown's on the High St. S1 heads to Pen-y-Pass (15 minutes), while S2 continues on to Capel Curig (35 minutes) and Betws-y-Coed (47 minutes).

Other buses head to Caernarfon (route 88, 25 minutes) and Bangor (route 85/86, 50 minutes).

Snowdon (Yr Wyddfa)

No Snowdonia experience is complete without coming face-to-face with Snowdon (1085m), one of Britain's most awe-inspiring mountains and the highest summit in Wales (it's actually the 61st highest in Britain, with the higher 60 all in Scotland). 'Yr Wyddfa' in Welsh (pronounced uhr-*with*-vuh, meaning 'the Tomb'), it's the mythical resting place of the giant Rhita Gawr, who demanded King Arthur's beard for his cloak and was killed for his temerity. On a clear day the views stretch to Ireland and the Isle of Man over Snowdon's fine jagged ridges, which drop away in great swoops to sheltered *cwms* (valleys) and deep lakes. Even on a gloomy day you could find yourself above the clouds. Thanks to the Snowdon Mountain Railway it's extremely accessible when the weather is clement. In fact, the summit and some of the tracks can get frustratingly crowded.

Sights & Activities

Just below the cairn that marks Snowdon's summit is Hafod Eryri (p251), a striking piece of architecture that opened in 2009 to replace the dilapidated 1930s visitor centre that Prince Charles famously labelled 'the highest slum in Europe'.

★ **Snowdon Trails** HIKING
Six paths of varying length and difficulty lead to the summit, all taking around six hours return. Just because Snowdon has a train station and a cafe on its summit, doesn't mean you should underestimate it. No route is completely safe, especially in winter. People regularly come unstuck here and many have died over the years, including experienced climbers.

The most straightforward route to the summit is the **Llanberis Path** (9 miles return) running beside the train line. The two paths starting from Pen-y-Pass require the least amount of ascent but are nevertheless tougher walks: the **Miner's Track** (8 miles return) starts off wide and gentle but gets steep beyond Llyn Llydaw and the more interesting **Pyg Track** (7 miles return) is more rugged still.

Two tracks start from the Caernarfon–Beddgelert road (A4085): the **Snowdon Ranger Path** (8 miles return) is the safest route in winter, while the **Rhyd Ddu Path** (8 miles return) is the least-used route and boasts spectacular views. The most challenging route is the **Watkin Path** (8 miles return), involving an ascent of more than 1000m on its southerly approach from Nantgwynant and finishing with a scramble across a steep-sided, scree-covered slope.

The classic **Snowdon Horseshoe** (7.5 miles return) branches off from the Pyg Track to follow the precipitous ridge of **Crib Goch** (one of the most dangerous routes on the mountains and only recommended for the very experienced) with a descent over the peak of Y Lliwedd and a final section down the Miner's Track.

Allow six or seven hours for any of these trails.

★ **Snowdon Mountain Railway** RAIL
(☎01286-870223; www.snowdonrailway.co.uk; Llanberis; adult/child return diesel £29/20, steam £37/27; ⏲9am-5pm mid-Mar–Nov) If you're not physically able to climb a mountain, short on time or just plain lazy, those industrious, railway-obsessed Victorians have gifted you an alternative. Opened in 1896, the

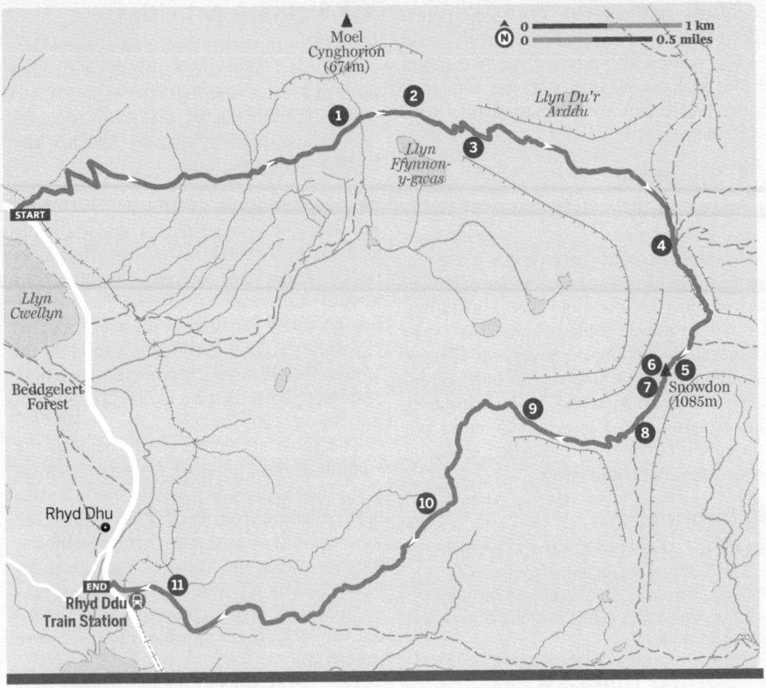

Mountain Walk
Up Snowdon Ranger, Down Rhyd Ddu

START SNOWDON RANGER YHA
END RHYD DDU TRAIN STATION
LENGTH 8 MILES, SIX HOURS

This particular Snowdon route is reasonably straightforward, quiet and doesn't involve difficult scrambles (that said, in snowy and icy conditions, the descent on the Rhyd Ddu Path should only be undertaken by experienced mountaineers equipped with crampons and ice picks; everyone else should double back on the Snowdon Ranger Path). Both trailheads are connected by buses and trains to accommodation in Caernarfon, Beddgelert and Porthmadog.

The original 'Snowdon Ranger' was John Morton, an English mountain guide who built an inn on the site of the current YHA in the early 1800s and led guests to the summit along this track. The path climbs gently along the lower slopes of 1 **Moel Cynghorion** to 2 **Bwlch Cwm Brwynog**, before it steepens and heads above 3 **Clogwyn Du'r Arddu**. Eventually it draws parallel with the Snowdon Mountain Railway. The path crosses the tracks at a 4 **standing stone**, turns right and merges with the Llanberis Path for the final approach to the 5 **summit**.

When you're ready to descend, pick up the Rhyd Ddu Path below the 6 **Hafod Eryri** visitor centre. After 200m a 7 **standing stone** marks the point where the Watkin Path veers off; continue straight ahead. The next section, along 8 **Bwlch Main** (meaning 'Slender Path'), is a narrow track with steep slopes on either side: if there's ice, snow or wind, this can be genuinely dangerous and is only for properly equipped and experienced walkers. Near the end of this stretch the path splits into two; keep on the right-hand track. From here the path broadens as it zigzags down and then edges along the 9 **Llechog ridge**. It starts to flatten out after it passes the 10 **ruins** of an old refreshment hut. The final stretch continues alongside the abandoned 11 **Ffridd Slate Quarry** before terminating near the Rhyd Ddu train station.

Snowdon Mountain Railway is the UK's highest – and its only public – rack-and-pinion railway. Vintage steam and modern diesel locomotives haul carriages from Llanberis up to Snowdon's summit in an hour.

Return trips involve a scant half-hour at the top before heading back down again. Single tickets can only be booked for the journey up (adult/child £22/17); if you want to walk up and ride down, you'll have to hope there's space. Tens of thousands of people take the train to the summit each season: make sure you book well in advance or you may miss out. Departures depend on customer demand and are weather dependent. From March to May (or during high winds) the trains can only head as far Clogwyn Station (adult/child £19/13) – an altitude of 779m.

Sleeping

YHA Snowdon Pen-y-Pass HOSTEL £
(☎08453-719534; www.yha.org.uk; A4086; dm/tw £29/55) This superbly situated hostel has three of Snowdon's trails literally on its doorstep. Comprehensively refurbished in 2014, it has a new kitchen, Mallory's Cafe/Bar (named for a past patron who perished on Everest) and some of the best rooms of any of the park's YHAs (half of which are en suite). It's 5.5 miles up the A4086 from Llanberis.

YHA Snowdon Bryn Gwynant HOSTEL £
(☎08453-719108; www.yha.org.uk; Nantgwynant; dm/tw £29/55; ⏲Mar-Oct; P📶) Bryn Gwynant has the most impressive building and the most idyllic setting of all Snowdonia National Park's youth hostels, occupying a slate Victorian mansion overlooking Lake Gwynant to Snowdon. It's located 4 miles east of Beddgelert, near the start of the Watkin Path.

YHA Snowdon Ranger HOSTEL £
(☎08453-719659; www.yha.org.uk; Rhyd Ddu; d/tw £29/55; P📶) On the A4085, 5 miles north of Beddgelert at the trailhead for the Snowdon Ranger Path, this former inn has its own adjoining lakeside beach, and is close to Llanberis too. Accommodation is basic but dependable.

Pen-y-Gwryd HOTEL ££
(☎01286-870211; www.pyg.co.uk; Nant Gwynant; s/d from £45/90; P📶🐾) Eccentric but full of atmosphere, this Georgian coaching inn was used as a training base by the 1953 Everest team, and memorabilia from their stay includes signatures on the restaurant ceiling. TV, wi-fi and mobile-phone signals don't penetrate here; instead, there's a comfy games room, sauna and a lake for those hardy enough to swim.

You'll find the hotel below Pen-y-Pass, at the junction of the A498 and A4086.

> **VISITOR NEWS**
>
> The Park Authority (www.eryri-npa.gov.uk) publishes a free annual visitor newspaper, which includes information on getting around, organised walks and other activities.

Information

Hafod Eryri (⏲10am–20min before last train departure; 📶) Clad in granite and curved to blend into the mountain, Hafod Eryri houses a cafe, toilets and ambient interpretative elements built into the structure itself. A wall of picture windows gazes down towards the west, while a small row faces the cairn. Closed in winter or if the weather's terrible, it's open whenever the train is running.

Getting There & Away

It's worth considering public transport: car parks can fill up quickly and Pen-y-Pass car park costs £10 per day.

Before you decide which route you'll take to the summit, study the bus and train timetables. If you're based in Llanberis, you'll find it easiest to get to and from the Llanberis, Pyg and Miner's paths. The Snowdon Ranger and Rhyd Ddu paths are better connected to Beddgelert and Caernarfon.

The Welsh Highland Railway stops at the trailhead of the Rhyd Ddu Path and there is a request stop (Snowdon Ranger Halt) where you can alight for the Snowdon Ranger Path.

All the trailheads are accessible by Snowdon Sherpa bus services S1, S2, S4 or S97 (single/day ticket £1.50/5).

Another option is to take the Snowdon Mountain Railway (p249) from Llanberis to the top and walk back down. It's more difficult to do this the other way around as the train will only take on new passengers at the top if there is space.

Beddgelert

POP 453

Charming Beddgelert is a conservation village of dark stone cottages overlooking the River Colwyn and its ivy-covered bridge, just upstream from where it meets the

River Glaslyn. Flowers festoon the village in spring and the surrounding hills are covered in a purple blaze of heather in summer, reminiscent of a Scottish glen. Scenes from Mark Robson's 1958 film, *The Inn of the Sixth Happiness* starring Ingrid Bergman, were shot here.

Beddgelert, meaning 'Gelert's Grave', is said to refer to the dog of 13th-century Llywelyn the Great, Prince of Gwynedd. Thinking his dog Gelert had savaged his baby son, Llywelyn slaughtered the dog, only to discover that Gelert had fought off the wolf that had attacked the baby. More likely, the name Beddgelert comes from a 5th-century Irish preacher, Celert, who is believed to have founded a church here. Regardless, Gelert's 'grave' is a popular attraction, reached by a pretty riverside trail. It's believed to have been constructed by an unscrupulous 18th-century hotelier to boost business.

Sights & Activities

Sygun Copper Mine — MINE

(www.syguncoppermine.co.uk; A498; adult/child under 15 £8.95/6.95; ⏲9.30am-5pm in British Summer Time, 10am-4pm Nov-Feb) This mine dates from Roman times, although extraction was stepped up in the 19th century. Abandoned in 1903, it has since been converted into a museum, with a half-hour self-guided underground tour containing dioramas that evoke the life of Victorian miners. You can also try your hand at metal detecting (£2.50) or panning for gold (£2). It's located a mile northeast of Beddgelert, along the A498.

Open during British Summer Time (last Sunday of March to the last Sunday of October).

Craflwyn & Dinas Emrys — WALKING

(NT; ☎01766-510120; www.nationaltrust.org.uk/craflwyn-and-beddgelert) A mile northeast of Beddgelert, near Llyn Dinas, National Trust-owned Craflwyn Farm is the starting point for several short walks, including a path to Dinas Emrys, one of the most significant yet largely unheralded sites in Welsh mythology. To stay at Pretty Craflwyn Hall contact HF Holidays (www.hfholidays.co.uk), which leases it on behalf of the Trust.

According to legend, Dinas Emrys was the hill where King Vortigern – son-in-law of Britain's last Roman ruler, Magnus Maximus – tried to build a castle. It kept collapsing until the young wizard Merlin (Myrddin Emrys) liberated two dragons in a cavern under the hill – a white one representing the Saxons (the Germanic ancestors of the English) and a red one representing the Britons (today's Welsh) – and prophesied that they'd fight until the red dragon was triumphant. The two dragons have been at each other's throats ever since.

It takes about half an hour to walk through fields, alongside a stream, past a waterfall and through woods to the summit. At the top there are the remains of 12th-century and Roman-era fortifications and wonderful views over the lake and the valley of Nantgwynant.

Aberglaslyn Gorge & Moel Hebog — WALKING

The Aberglaslyn Gorge trail runs from Beddgelert, through the pretty Glaslyn river gorge to the main road at Pont Aberglaslyn (3 miles return, two hours). The ascent of Moel Hebog hill (783m) is more strenuous (8-mile loop, five hours), and includes a lovely scenic ridge walk over two more peaks. Beddgelert's tourist office has leaflets on both hikes.

Beddgelert Forest — MOUNTAIN BIKING

Within this forestry commission block (2 miles northwest of Beddgelert along the A4805) is a popular campground and two mountain-bike trails: the 6-mile Hir Trail and the easier 2.5-mile Byr Trail. A section of the Lon Las Gwyrfai cycle trail also runs through the forest, from Beddgelert to Rhyd Ddu.

Beddgelert Bikes — CYCLING

(Beics Beddgelert; ☎01766-890434; www.beddgelertbikes.co.uk; per 2/4/8hr £15/21/28) Located near the train station, this outfit rents out mountain bikes, tandems and child seats, and can advise on the many trails in the area.

Sleeping

Beddgelert Campsite — CAMPGROUND £

(☎01766-890288; www.campingintheforest.co.uk/wales/beddgelert-campsite; sites from £23; P 🐾) This site is well equipped, with a shop for contingencies, and situated in the beautiful Beddgelert Forest. The campsite is 1 mile north of Beddgelert, signposted from the A4085.

Sygun Fawr Country House — HOTEL ££

(☎01766-890258; www.sygunfawr.co.uk; s/d from £43/86; P 📶) A warm welcome awaits at this sturdy stone manor house, tucked away at the end of a narrow lane. Bits have been grafted on to the 1660s core over the centuries (including a conservatory), so each of the 12 comfortable bedrooms are quite different; some have spectacular mountain views. It's well signposted from the A498, immediately northeast of the village.

Colwyn Guest House B&B ££
(☎01766-890276; www.beddgelertguesthouse.co.uk; Carenarfon Rd; s/d £37.50/75;) Coleen, who also works at the National Trust shop at the other end of the town's much-photographed central bridge, is a consummate host. Her floral rooms are large, spotless and very comfortable. Those at the front of this 18th-century stone house look out over the murmuring Colwyn and surrounding hills.

Tanronnen Inn HOTEL ££
(☎01766-890347; www.tanronnen.co.uk; s/d £60/110; P) Right at the centre of things, this attractive stone coaching inn offers busily carpeted 1st-floor rooms that are comfortable, if a little dated. Downstairs, polished brass, deep armchairs and crackling fires set the scene for a hearty pub menu (mains £10 to £13), ranging from sausage and chips to chickpea curry.

Eating

Glaslyn Ices & Cafe Glandwr ICE CREAM £
(☎01766-890339; www.glaslynices.co.uk; mains £6-10; ⏲9.30am-5.30pm Sun-Fri, to 8.30pm Sat; P) In summer this excellent ice-cream parlour is the busiest place in the village. It serves at least 24 homemade flavours (more when things get busy) and is attached to a family restaurant offering simple meals, such has pizza.

★**Hebog Beddgelert** BISTRO ££
(☎01766-890400; www.hebog-beddgelert.co.uk; Fford Caernarfon; mains £18-20;) A welcome addition to Beddgelert's dining (and sleeping) scene, Hebog is an upmarket cafe that morphs into a sleek bistro by night, serving the likes of monkfish tails in parma ham with prawns and lobster velouté. A self-catering apartment and summer terrace overlooking the babbling Glaslyn seal the deal.

★**Beddgelert Bistro & Antiques** BISTRO ££
(☎01766-890543; www.beddgelert-bistro.co.uk; Smith St; mains £12-15; ⏲9am-5pm & 6.30-9pm;) An eccentric gem, this hybrid bistro/antique store offers exceptional home cooking. By day it's more like a tearoom, but at night the tiny dining room at the heart of the 17th-century cottage fills up with happy diners enjoying specials such as goose breast in orange and Triple Sec, and Welsh black beef in creamy peppercorn sauce. Good wines, too.

There are also three en suite bedrooms above (£30 per person with breakfast).

Information

National Trust Shop (☎01766-890545; Stryd Yr Eglwys; ⏲11am-5pm, shorter hours winter weekdays) Tŷ Isaf, a Grade II–listed 17th-century cottage on the south side of the central bridge, contains Beddgelert's National Trust shop. Along with crafts made from local materials, regional produce and literature, there are kids' activity packs and walking guides to the local area.

Tourist Office (☎01766-890615; www.eryri-npa.gov.uk; Canolfan Hebog; ⏲9.30am-5pm Easter-Oct) Great for information on walks, cycling and accommodation in the area.

Getting There & Away

Snowdon Sherpa bus S4 heads to/from Caernarfon (30 minutes), Snowdon Ranger (10 minutes), Rhyd Ddu (six minutes) and Pen-y-Pass (20 minutes).

Bus S97 heads to Porthmadog (21 minutes), Tremadog (13 minutes) and Pen-y-Pass (18 minutes).

Beddgelert is a stop on the historic Welsh Highland Railway, which runs between Caernarfon (£29.10 return, 1½ hours) and Porthmadog (£20.90, 40 minutes) from Easter to October, with limited winter service, and stops at the Rhyd Ddu and Snowdon Ranger trailheads.

LLŶN PENINSULA

Jutting into the Irish Sea from the Snowdonia mountains, the Llŷn (pronounced 'khleen' and sometimes spelt 'Lleyn') is a green finger of land some 30 miles long and averaging 8 miles wide. This peaceful and largely undeveloped region has isolated walking and cycling routes, Iron-Age forts, beaches, a scattering of small fishing villages and 70 miles of wildlife-rich coastline (much of it in the hands of the National Trust, with almost 80% designated an Area of Outstanding Natural Beauty). Over the centuries the heaviest footfalls have been those of pilgrims heading to Bardsey Island.

Welsh is the everyday language. Indeed, this is about as Welsh as it gets. The Llŷn Peninsula and Anglesey were the last stops for the Romans and Normans, and both have maintained a separate identity.

This isolated place has been an incubator of Welsh activism. It was the birthplace of David Lloyd George, the first Welsh prime minister of the UK, and of Plaid Cymru (the Party of Wales), which was founded in Pwllheli in 1925 and now holds 18% of the seats in the Welsh Assembly.

Porthmadog

POP 4185

Despite a few rough edges, busy little Porthmadog (port-*mad*-uk) has an attractive estuarine setting and a conspicuously friendly, mainly Welsh-speaking populace. It straddles both the Llŷn Peninsula and Snowdonia National Park, and has the fantastical village of Portmeirion at its doorstep. Throw in abundant transport connections and you have a handy place to base yourself for a couple of days.

Porthmadog is a mecca for railway buffs. There are 'little trains' all over Wales, a legacy of Victorian industry, but Porthmadog is triply blessed. It forms the southern terminus for two of Wales' finest narrow-gauge train journeys and has a third steam-train line connected to a rail heritage centre.

Mullet abound in the shallow Traeth Bach estuary, which in turn attract ospreys. Keep an eye out for these large birds of prey as you walk around the cliffs of Borth-y-Gest and Porthmeirion.

History

Both Porthmadog and the neighbouring village of Tremadog (the latter now virtually a suburb of the former) were founded by and named after reforming landowner William Alexander Madocks. In the early 19th century he laid down the mile-long Cob causeway, drained the 400 hectares of wetlands that lay behind it and created a brand-new harbour. After his death, the Cob became the route for the Ffestiniog Railway: at its 1873 peak, it transported more than 116,000 tonnes of slate from the mines of Blaenau Ffestiniog to the harbour. In 1888 TE Lawrence (Lawrence of Arabia) was born in Tremadog, although the Lawrence family moved to Oxford 12 years later; look for his family home (marked with a plaque) near the church.

Sights

★Portmeirion Village VILLAGE

(☎01766-770000; www.portmeirion-village.com; adult/child £11/8; ⏲9.30am-7.30pm; P) Set on its own tranquil peninsula reaching into the estuary, Portmeirion Village is a fantastical collection of colourful buildings with a heavy Italian influence, masterminded by the Welsh architect Sir Clough Williams-Ellis. Starting in 1925, Clough collected bits and pieces from disintegrating stately mansions and set them alongside his own creations to create this weird and wonderful seaside utopia. Today the buildings are all heritage-listed and the site is a conservation area.

Fifty years after he began, and at the ripe old age of 90, Sir Clough deemed Portmeirion to be complete.

It's really more like a stage set than an actual village and, indeed, it formed the ideally surreal set for cult TV series, *The Prisoner*, which was filmed here from 1966 to 1967. It still draws fans of the show in droves, with

IS AMERICA REALLY NEW WEST WALES?

Porthmadog may be named after William Alexander Madocks, but there's another legendary namesake associated with the area. The story goes that in 1170 Madog ab Owain Gwynedd, a local prince, set off from here and 'discovered' America. The tale was dusted off during Elizabeth I's reign to justify the English crown's claim on the continent over Spain's; America's indigenous occupants weren't canvassed for their opinion. The story gained further traction during Wales' 18th-century Romantic renaissance when it was deployed to give the Welsh a sense of pride in their past.

Madog and his followers were said to have intermarried with Native Americans and formed their own Welsh-speaking tribe. After America's 'rediscovery', explorers returned with stories of meeting Welsh-speaking clans in Virginia and Kentucky. In 1796 John Evans, the leader of a party that helped map the Missouri River, sought and failed to find any evidence of them. Given that many small Native American tribes disappeared soon after colonisation, the Madog story still has some traction among hardcore Welsh patriots.

rival *Prisoner* conventions held annually in March and April. The giant plaster of Paris Buddha, just off the piazza, also featured in the 1958 film, *The Inn of the Sixth Happiness,* starring Ingrid Bergman.

A documentary on Williams-Ellis and Portmeirion screens on the hour in a building just above the central piazza. Sir Clough's lifelong concern was with the whimsical and intriguing nature of architecture, his raison d'être to demonstrate how a naturally beautiful site could be developed without defiling it. His life's work now stands as a testament to beauty, something he described as 'that strange necessity'. He died in 1978, having campaigned for the environment throughout his life. He was a founding member of the Council for the Protection of Rural Wales in 1928 and served as its president for 20 years.

Most of the kooky cottages and scaled-down mansions scattered about the site are available for holiday lets, while other buildings contain cafes, restaurants and gift shops. Portmeirion pottery (the famously florid tableware designed by Susan, Sir Clough's daughter) is available, even though these days it's made in Stoke-on-Trent (England). A network of walking paths thread along the coast and through the private forested peninsula, which includes the ruins of a castle (a real one, not one of Sir Clough's creations), and a profusion of exotic plants, nourished by the warm microclimate of the peninsula. Free guided tours of the village are held most days, and from April to October the 'forest train' tours the woodlands.

Portmeirion is 2 miles east of Porthmadog; public transport isn't great, so if you don't fancy the walk, you're best to catch a taxi. Admission is reduced by 15% after 3.30pm.

Borth-y-Gest VILLAGE

The best views over the estuary are from Porthmadog's Terrace Rd, which becomes Garth Rd above the harbour. At its end a path heads down to Borth-y-Gest, a pretty horseshoe of candy-coloured houses overlooking a sandy bay. At the other end of the crescent the path continues around the cliffs; if you look carefully, you should be able to spot Harlech Castle in the distance.

Activities

★Welsh Highland Railway RAIL

(☎01766-516000; www.festrail.co.uk; adult/child return £38/34.20; ⏲Easter-Oct, limited winter service) Leaving from the Porthmadog Harbour Station, as does the Blaenau-Ffestiniog Railway, the Welsh Highland runs to Caernarfon (£38 return, 2½ hours) via Rhd Ddu (£25.10 return) and Beddgelert (£20.90 return).

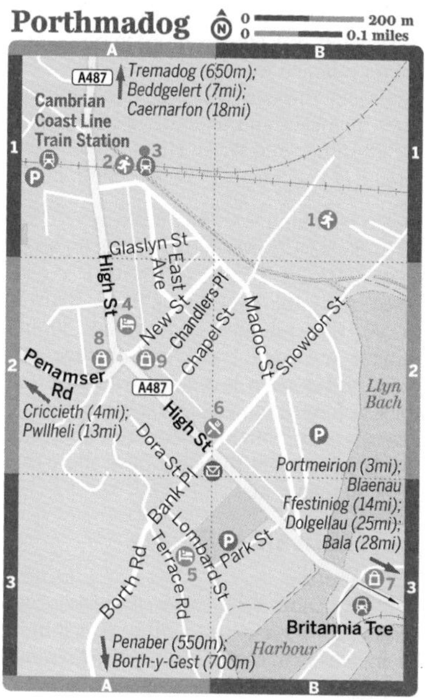

Porthmadog

Activities, Courses & Tours
1 Ffestiniog Railway B1
2 Welsh Highland Heritage Railway A1
3 Welsh Highland Railway A1

Sleeping
4 Royal Sportsman Hotel A2
5 Yr Hen Fecws A3

Eating
6 Big Rock Cafe B2

Shopping
7 Cob Records B3
8 Kerfoots A2
9 Purple Moose A2

★Ffestiniog Railway RAIL

(Rheilffordd Ffestiniog; ☎01766-516024; www.festrail.co.uk; adult/child return £23/21; ⏲daily Easter-Oct, reduced service rest of year; 👪) The world's oldest surviving narrow-gauge railway, the Ffestiniog wends its way from the slate-mining town of Blaenau Ffestiniog to

Porthmadog. Long past its industrial heyday, its 150-year-old steam locomotives and monogrammed wooden carriages now ferry sightseers through oak woodlands, under towering peaks and by flashing rivers. Both the Ffestiniog and Welsh Highland lines terminate at Porthmadog Harbour Station.

Welsh Highland Heritage Railway RAIL
(☎01766-513402; www.whr.co.uk; High St; adult/child £8.50/4.25; ⏲Easter-Oct) Not to be confused with the Welsh Highland Railway (p255), this volunteer-run railway doesn't provide any useful transport link. Steam or diesel trains chug less than a mile up the track before heading back via the rail heritage centre and engine sheds. You can swap to a miniature railway here for a short ride through the woods.

Festivals & Events

PortmeiriCon CULTURAL
(Prisoner Convention; www.portmeiricon.com; Portmeirion; ⏲Apr) One to either pencil in or avoid, fans of the cult TV show *The Prisoner* converge on Portmeirion in April for a weekend of dress ups and human chess. Indoor events are only open to members of the Six of One (the *Prisoner* Appreciation Society) but anyone can catch outdoor shows or glimpses of celebrities bussed in for the occasion.

★ **Festival No 6** PERFORMING ARTS
(☎08449-670002; www.festivalnumber6.com; ⏲Sep) Started in 2012, this rock and dance-music festival with arts, culture and comedy components has topped many best-festival lists and makes imaginative use of Portmeirion's varied and dreamlike environment. Headliners have included New Order, Fleetwood Mac and Cassius. It's held over a long weekend in September.

Sleeping

Penaber B&B £
(☎01766-512041; www.porthmadog.co.uk/penaber; Morfa Bychan Rd; r from £50; P 📶) Sitting between Porthmadog and Borth-y-Gest, about half a mile from either, Penaber is a large, modern house offering scrupulously clean and very comfortable pastel-coloured rooms at a bargain rate. Within walking distance of the beach, you can find it by veering right off Borth Rd before it curves down to the bay.

Golden Fleece Inn PUB £
(☎01766-512421; www.goldenfleeceinn.com; Market Sq, Tremadog; s/d from £45/55; P 📶) Hop flowers hang from the ceiling of this inviting and friendly old inn, which offers real ales in a cave-like beer cellar, pub grub, an open fire on cold nights and live acoustic music on Tuesdays. The rooms above the pub are comfortable and atmospheric; however, be prepared for noise until closing. Ask about quieter rooms in neighbouring buildings.

★ **Yr Hen Fecws** B&B ££
(☎01766-514625; www.henfecws.com; 16 Lombard St; s/d from £65/80; P 📶) Probably Porthmadog's nicest digs, this stylishly restored stone cottage has seven simply decorated en suite rooms with exposed-slate walls and fireplaces. Breakfast is served within the marigold walls and exposed beams of the cosy cafe downstairs (mains £6 to £10; open 8am to 4pm Monday to Saturday).

Royal Sportsman Hotel HOTEL ££
(☎01766-512015; 131 High St; s/d from £70/100; P 📶 🐾) It's not about to win any awards for its decor but this old charmer (constructed in 1862 as a coaching inn) has clean and comfortable rooms and a staff that's eager to please. 'Courtyard' rooms open onto an enclosed walkway at the rear.

Hotel Portmeirion & Castell Deudraeth HOTEL £££
(☎01766-770000; www.portmeirion-village.com; Portmeirion; hotel s/d £204/219, castle & village s/d from £139/169; P ≋) You can live the fantasy and stay within the famous fairy-tale village itself in one of 17 whimsical cottages. Over-the-top Hotel Portmeirion, dating to 1850 but extended by Clough Ellis, has a plum spot by the water, with a terraced bar for afternoon tippling. Fanciful Castell Deudraeth is a more modern alternative, despite also dating to Victoria's reign.

Eating

Big Rock Cafe CAFE £
(Y Graig Fawr; ☎01766-512098; 71 High St; mains £4-6; ⏲8.30am-5pm Mon-Sat) Although this cool cafe is church-run, you needn't fear any morals being served with your morning mocha and the coffee is excellent by Welsh standards. The wholefood-oriented menu stretches to cooked breakfasts, soups, falafel wraps, sandwiches and sweets, and there are plenty of newspapers to peruse.

★Y Sgwâr BISTRO £££

(☎01766-515451; www.ysgwar-restaurant.co.uk; 12-16 Market Sq; mains £15-25; ⊙noon-2pm & 6-9pm) On the edge of Tremadog's main square, this French-accented Welsh restaurant has the best food in Porthmadog or Tremadog. The service is super-attentive and friendly, and dishes such as scallops with crispy belly pork, cauliflower puree and black pudding are a delight. There's value in the set menu (two/three courses £18/22) offered at lunch or between 6pm and 7pm.

Shopping

Purple Moose DRINK

(Bragdy Mŵs Piws; ☎01766-512777; www.purplemoose.co.uk; 129 High St; ⊙9.30am-5.30pm Mon-Sat, plus 10.30am-4.30pm Sun Aug) The retail front for Purple Moose, an award-winning brewer supplying the better North Welsh pubs. Tipples include Snowdonia Ale, Madog's Ale, Glaslyn Ale, Dark Side of the Moose and the newest addition, Decadence (aged in Islay whisky casks). Ale aficionados can arrange a tour of the nearby brewery (£7.50; noon to 1pm Tuesday to Thursday), which includes free tastings.

Kerfoots DEPARTMENT STORE

(136-140 High St; ⊙10am-4pm Mon-Fri & Sun, to 5pm Sat) Established in 1874, this independent store is a local institution. It stocks a limited range of household goods and clothing, but is worth checking out for its upstairs coffee shop and the stained-glass dome above the staircase.

Cob Records MUSIC

(☎01766-512170; www.cobrecords.com; 1-3 Britannia Tce; ⊙9am-5.30pm Mon-Sat) A great little independent record shop (established in 1967) with a healthy collection of Welsh music, plenty of vinyl and a big mail-order presence.

Information

Ysbyty Alltwen (☎01766-510010; A487, Tremadog) The local hospital treats minor injuries but doesn't have a full emergency department.

Getting There & Away

Train Porthmadog is on the Cambrian Coast Line, with direct trains to Machynlleth (£14, two hours), Barmouth (£7.30, 50 minutes), Harlech (£4, 24 minutes), Criccieth (£2.80, seven minutes) and Pwllheli (£5.10, 25 minutes). See also the Ffestiniog & Welsh Highland Railways (www.festrail.co.uk) for steamy services to Blaenau Ffestiniog, the Snowdon trailheads and Caernarfon.

Bus Buses stop on High St and most services pass through Tremadog. Routes head to/from Machynlleth (route T2; 1½ hours), Dolgellau (route T2; 50 minutes), Beddgelert (route S97; 25 minutes), Pwllheli (route 3; 40 minutes) and Caernarfon (route 1/1A, 45 minutes).

Bicycle The Lôn Las Cymru (National Cycle Route 8) passes through Porthmadog, heading west to Criccieth and south to Harlech.

Criccieth

POP 1753

This genteel slow-moving seaside town sits above two sand-and-stone Blue Flag beaches, 5 miles west of Porthmadog. Its main claim to fame is ruined Criccieth Castle, perched up on the clifftop and offering views stretching along the peninsula's southern coast and across Tremadog Bay to Harlech.

Sights

Criccieth Castle CASTLE

(Cadw; www.cadw.wales.gov.uk; Castle St; adult/child £3.50/2.50; ⊙10am-5pm daily Mar-Oct, 9.30am-4pm Fri & Sat, from 11am Sun Nov-Mar) Ruined Criccieth Castle is perched on the clifftop and offers views stretching along the southern coast and across Tremadog Bay to Harlech. Constructed by Welsh prince Llywelyn the Great in 1239, it was overrun in 1283 by Edward I's forces and recaptured for the Welsh in 1404 by Owain Glyndŵr, whose forces promptly sacked it. Today there is a small but informative exhibition centre at the ticket office.

Lloyd George Museum MUSEUM

(☎01766-522071; http://gwynedd.gov.uk/museums; Llanystumdwy; adult/child £5/4; ⊙10.30am-5pm Mar-Oct) Tiny Llanystumdwy, 1.5 miles west of Criccieth, was the boyhood home of David Lloyd George. The video, photos, posters and personal effects at the museum introduce the fiery orator and ladies' man who was largely responsible for introducing National Insurance in a two-pronged attack on unemployment and poverty. Later on in his career, his loyalty to Wales was challenged by his ambitions in Westminster and, though a friend of Churchill, by WWII Lloyd George became a shameless war apologist.

Lloyd George grew up in his uncle's house, Highgate, which is 50m away and forms part of the museum. His mortal remains moulder in a boulder-topped grave about 150m away, by a babbling brook.

Sleeping

Bron Eifion HISTORIC HOTEL ££
(☎01766-522385; www.broneifion.co.uk; r £95-175; P) The former palace of a slate magnate, set in 2 hectares of fabulously formal gardens, grand old Bron Eifion has been refurbished with flat-screen TVs sitting alongside faux-Gothic carvings and wooden panels. The hotel is half a mile west of Criccieth, on the A497.

Glyn-y-Coed HOTEL ££
(☎01766-522870; www.gychotel.co.uk; Porthmadog Rd; s/d from £65/85; P) While the name alludes to a wooded glen, this 10-bedroom Victorian house is plonked right on the main road, gazing out to sea. The views through the bay windows in the elegant front rooms encompass the castle, the bay and the mountains of Snowdonia, while inside you'll find individually styled rooms with quality beds.

Eating

Castle Fish & Chips FISH & CHIPS £
(☎01766-522081; www.castlefishandchips.co.uk; 5 Castle St; mains from £7; 5.30-9pm) A local institution, this fish-and-chip shop has been serving crispy battered fish to Criccieth's residents for more than 40 years.

Dylan's INTERNATIONAL ££
(☎01766-522773; www.dylansrestaurant.co.uk; Maes y Mor; mains £12-17; noon-10pm; P) Making great use of Morannedd – a light-filled, 1950s deco-style beachside pavilion, designed by Portmeirion architect Sir Clough Williams-Ellis and once used by Butlin's for afternoon tea dances – Dylan's is the slickest place in Criccieth. Like its sibling in Menai Bridge, it offers fantastic sea views to complement a globe-trotting bistro menu including pizzas, curries and seafood.

Poachers Restaurant INTERNATIONAL ££
(☎01766-522512; www.poachersrestaurant.co.uk; 66 High St; 2-course menu £18; 6-8.30pm Mon-Sat) A likeable little family restaurant, Poachers sits in a converted grocer's on the High St. Local produce, especially Welsh black beef, features in a menu that takes much from Europe (lasagne, pickled herring salad), a little from Asia (fish cakes with sweet chilli) and a little more from America (jambalaya and a cajun-spiced seafood risotto).

Tir a Môr BRASSERIE ££
(☎01766-523084; www.tiramor-criccieth.co.uk; 1 Mona Tce; mains £15-18; 6-9.30pm Tue-Sat mid-Feb–Nov) The name means 'Land and Sea' but don't worry, this isn't a throwback 'surf and turf' restaurant: think more flank steak with red wine and shallots, or smoked haddock tart. Picked out in maritime cream and blue, it's an intimate place and popular, too – bookings are advised.

Getting There & Away

Train Criccieth is on the Cambrian Coast Line, with direct trains to Machynlleth (£16, two hours), Barmouth (£8.10, one hour), Harlech (£6, 35 minutes), Porthmadog (£2.80, seven minutes) and Pwllheli (£3.60, 15 minutes).

Bus Buses head to/from Pwllheli (route 3; 24 minutes), Llanystumdwy (route 3; four minutes), Porthmadog (routes 1 and 3; 17 minutes) and Caernarfon (routes 1/1A, 45 minutes).

Bicycle The Lôn Las Cymru (National Cycle Route 8) passes through Criccieth, heading north to Caernarfon and east to Porthmadog.

Pwllheli

POP 4076

The Llŷn's main market town, public-transport hub and unofficial capital, Pwllheli (poolth-*heh*-lee; meaning 'Salt-Water Pool') has a long sandy beach (blue-flagged Marian y De), a busy marina and a staunchly Welsh population. It's also home to an unusual colony of herons that has chosen to nest in willows near the town centre; look for them upstream from Bont Solomon, on Cardiff Rd west of the marina.

Sights & Activities

Penarth Fawr HOUSE
(☎01766-810880; www.cadw.gov.wales; Chwilog; 10am-5pm Apr-Oct) FREE Surrounded by stone farm buildings that time forgot, Penarth Fawr is a 15th-century manor that has somehow survived into the 21st century. Basically one large hall with an open hearth, stone flagging and a roof still supported by its original oak 'spere-truss', it gives a sense of how the Llŷn's better-heeled families lodged themselves in years gone by. Keep a third eye open for the resident ghost. It's on a country lane, signposted from the A497 between Criccieth and Pwllheli.

Glasfryn Parc AMUSEMENT PARK
(☎01766-810000; www.glasfryn.co.uk; Y Ffôr, Pwllheli; go-karts per 6min £6, other activities variously

WORTH A TRIP

ART BY THE BEACH

A diverse collection of work by contemporary Welsh artists – all available for purchase – is only part of the attraction of **Oriel Plas Glyn-y-Weddw** (☎01758-740763; www.oriel.org.uk; ⊙10am-5pm Wed-Mon, daily school holidays), Wales's oldest gallery. It's worth visiting just to gape at the flamboyant Victorian Gothic mansion it's housed in, with its exposed beams and stained glass. One room is devoted to the history of the house and a collection of porcelain. The two carved stones in the foyer date from the 5th or 6th century.

The grounds – planted with rare and exotic species and threaded by paths rolling down to National Trust–owned Llandbedrog beach – are a draw in themselves. Then there's a four-bedroom self-catering apartment in the rear of the mansion; an outdoor amphitheatre with regular music and theatre in summer; and a very decent cafe, serving panini, wraps and cakes. Plas Glyn-y-Weddw is 3 miles from Abersoch and 4 miles west of Pwllheli.

priced; ⊙9.30am-6pm; 👪) Not a bad option if the kids are suffering ancient-monument overload, Glasfryn Parc has indoor activities (bowling, play areas and a farm shop), outdoor activities (go-karting, quad-biking and archery) and even watersports (kayaking and wake-boarding) between Easter and October. It's 4 miles north of Pwllheli, on the A499 towards Caernarfon.

Offaxis Harbourside KITESURFING
(☎01758-613298; www.offaxis.co.uk; Harbourside, Pwllheli; ⊙10am-5pm Mon-Sat, to 4pm Sun) The boys from Abersoch's Offaxis have opened this quayside retail, hire and instruction centre. You can take wakeboarding, surfing and kitesurfing lessons, hire gear, or buy gear, clothing and flotation devices.

Sleeping & Eating

★**Plas Bodegroes** HOTEL £££
(☎01758-612363; www.bodegroes.co.uk; Nefyn Rd; r 2-night stay from £150, dinner £49, lunch Sun £24.50; ⊙restaurant 7-9pm Tue-Sat, noon-2pm Sun; P 📶) Set in a stately 1780 manor house, this family-run restaurant with rooms offers romantic, classically styled lodgings amid 2 hectares of immaculate gardens. The Michelin-starred restaurant slings imaginative dishes such as duck-yolk ravioli and line-caught seabass with confit chicken wing and chestnut mushrooms, and the service could not be friendlier. It's a mile inland from Pwllheli, along the A497.

Taro Deg CAFE £
(☎01758-701271; 17 New St, 3 Thomas Bldgs; mains £5-9; ⊙9am-4.30pm Mon-Sat; 📶👪) Relaxed, spacious and perennially popular, this centrally located cafe (near the train station) offers newspapers to browse and a tasty selection of cooked breakfasts, sandwiches and cakes. If you haven't tried *bara brith* (a rich, fruit tea-loaf), this is the place to do so.

Getting There & Away

BUS

A daily National Express coach heads to/from Caernarfon (£8, 40 minutes), Bangor (£8.60, one hour), Llandudno (£9, 1¾ hours) and London (£37, 10½ hours).

Most of the Peninsula's services originate or terminate at Pwllheli. Destinations include Aberdaron (route 17/17B, 40 minutes), Morfa Nefyn (route 8, 20 minutes), Criccieth (route 3, 24 minutes), Porthmadog (route 3, 40 minutes) and Caernarfon (route 12, 45 minutes).

TRAIN

Pwllheli is the terminus of the Cambrian Coast Line, with direct trains to Criccieth (£3.60, 15 minutes), Porthmadog (£5.10, 25 minutes), Harlech (£8.40, 47 minutes), Barmouth (£12, 1¼ hours) and Machynlleth (£16, 2½ hours).

Abersoch

POP 1990

Abersoch comes alive in summer with a 30,000-person influx of boaties, surfers and beach bums. Edged by gentle blue-green hills, the town's main attraction is its Blue Flag beach, one of the most popular on the peninsula. Surfers head further south for the Atlantic swell at **Porth Neigwl** (Hell's Mouth) and **Porth Ceiriad**.

Activities

Abersoch Sailing School BOATING
(07917-525540; www.abersochsailingschool.co.uk; Sat, Sun & school holidays Mar-Oct) Operating from Abersoch's main beach, weather permitting, this outfit offers sailing and powerboating lessons (from £50) and joy rides (per half hour £25). It also hires laser fun boats (one/two hours £30/40), catamarans (one-two hours £40/60), sea kayaks (per hour single/double £10/20), pedalos (per hour £20) and skippered yachts (2½ hours per person/boat £50/180).

Offaxis WAKEBOARDING, SURFING
(01758-713407; www.offaxis.co.uk; Lôn Engan; lessons incl equipment from £30; 10am-5pm Mon-Fri, 9am-6pm Sat, 10.30am-4pm Sun) This surf shop hires equipment (£10 per day for wakeboards and surfboards) and specialises in wakeboarding, kitesurfing and surfing lessons. Most of the kitesurfing and wakeboarding is run out of Offaxis Harbourside at the Pwllheli marina.

West Coast Surf Shop SURFING
(01758-713067; www.westcoastsurf.co.uk; Lôn Pen Cei; lessons incl equipment from £30; 10am-5pm Thu-Tue) Hires out boards (£10) and wetsuits (£8) year-round, and runs the not-at-all-intimidating-sounding Hell's Mouth Surf School. Its website features a live surf-cam and daily surf reports.

Sleeping

★**Venetia** HOTEL ££
(01758-713354; www.venetiawales.com; Lôn Sarn Bach; r £108-148; P) No sinking old Venetian palazzo, just five luxurious rooms in a grand Victorian house decked out with designer lighting and modern art; room Cinque has a TV above its bathtub. The restaurant specialises in the traditional tastes of Venice (mains £12 to £24), particularly seafood and pasta dishes, and serves them under twinkling modern chandeliers.

Angorfa B&B ££
(01758-712967; www.angorfa.com; Stryd Fawr; r from £60;) Everything is ship-shape in this smart, beach-themed guesthouse, run by a welcoming couple who are happy to chat about the charms of the Llŷn Peninsula as they serve your breakfast. Popular with families, it's just up the High Street (Stryd Fawr) from the centre of town.

Egryn HOTEL ££
(01758-712332; www.egryn.com; Lôn Sarn Bach; s £75-90, d £80-139; P) With tones as muted as its hosts are ebulliently welcoming, this Edwardian house has eight comfortable, modern rooms with marbled en suites and sea views, plus two spacious family suites. The downstairs restaurant, open from 5pm in summer, does much of its cooking on hot rocks (mains £12 to £16).

Eating

★**Coconut Kitchen** THAI ££
(01758-712250; www.thecoconutkitchen.co.uk; Lôn Port Morgan; mains £13-16; 5.30-10pm daily, closed Jan, Feb & Tue & Wed in low season; P) The Thai head chef and her Welsh partner started the Coconut Kitchen in a van and were quickly compelled to find a more substantial venue for their harmonious marriage of local ingredients and real Thai cuisine. Try Menai mussels in a lemongrass and chilli broth, five-spiced duck or any of the open kitchen's outstanding curries, salads and stir-fries. Book ahead.

Fresh BISTRO, BAR ££
(01758-710033; www.fresh-abersoch.co.uk; Stryd Fawr; mains £13-18; 6pm-midnight, from 11.30am Jul & Aug;) A popular surfer's hang-out, whether for a beer on the front terrace or dinner, Fresh serves hearty bistro food including lamb shanks, grilled fish, burgers and steaks. The bar sometimes has live music and can get animated.

Porth Tocyn INTERNATIONAL £££
(01758-713303; www.porthtocynhotel.co.uk; Bwlch Tocyn; 2/3 courses £40/47; noon-2.30pm & 7-9pm Easter-Oct;) Having sat for so long on top of Abersoch's dining pile, Porth Tocyn offers fine dining in swankily old-fashioned surrounds, rather than innovation. Best bets from the prix-fixe menu include dependable classics such as grilled fillet of lemon sole with Montpellier butter. Also offering 17 luxurious rooms, you'll find Porth Tocyn in Bwlch Tocyn, just south of Abersoch.

Drinking & Nightlife

The Vaynol PUB
(01758-712776; Lon Pen Cei; noon-midnight;) The local pub has been given a Hamptons-style, bleached-wood makeover. Don't despair: it still plays sports on big TVs and welcomes dogs, only now it has a better range of craft beers to enjoy on the terrace,

Aberosch's most central and ostentatious place of assembly.

Zinc Bar & Grill BAR
(☎01758-713433; www.zincabersoch.com; Lon Pen Cei; ⊙noon-3pm & 6pm-midnight) Zinc Bar is good for both a post-surf cocktail or a lunchtime burger. Its riverside deck can be one of the nicest places in town for a sundowner, when the weather's right.

Getting There & Away

Bus 18 stops on Stryd Fawr (High St), heading to/from Llanbedrog (15 minutes) and Pwllheli (25 minutes).

Aberdaron

POP 965

Aberdaron is an ends-of-the-earth kind of place with whitewashed, windswept houses contemplating the sands of Aberdaron Bay. It was traditionally the last resting spot before pilgrims made the treacherous crossing to Bardsey Island. The little Gwylan Islands, just offshore, are North Wales' most important puffin-breeding site, while choughs, peregrines, hares and grey seals all thrive in the wild splendour of the surrounding country.

Sights

Centre

St Hywyn's Church CHURCH
(www.st-hywyn.org.uk; ⊙10am-6pm Apr-Oct, to 4pm Nov-Mar) Stoically positioned above the pebbly beach, the left half of St Hywyn's Church dates from 1100 while the right half was added 400 years later to accommodate the pilgrims. Inside there's information about local history, as well as two 6th-century memorial stones and a medieval font and holy-water stoup. Welsh poet RS Thomas was the minister here from 1967 to 1978 – an appropriate setting for his bleak, impassioned work.

Porth y Swnt CULTURAL CENTRE
(☎01758-703810; www.nationaltrust.org.uk; Henfaes; adult/child £2/1; ⊙10am-4pm Oct-Mar, to 5pm Apr-Jun & Sep, to 6pm Jul & Aug) Run by the National Trust, this rather impressionistic centre takes visitors deeper into the land and culture of the Llŷn through poetry, sound, light and artefacts. Its centrepiece is the magnificent optic of Bardsey Island lighthouse, which still bears bullet marks from being strafed during WWII.

LLŶN COASTAL BUS

Between March and October the **Llŷn Coastal Bus** (☎01758-721777) runs between Nefyn and Abersoch, via Aberdaron, Porth Neigwl and Porthor, five times a day from Thursday to Sunday. At only £1 per trip, it's a boon for walkers on some of the more remote stretches of the Llŷn Coastal Path. Booking 24 hours ahead is advised.

Around Aberdaron

★**Braich-y-Pwll** OUTDOORS
(NT; www.nationaltrust.org.uk) The rugged, ethereally beautiful extremity of the Llŷn Peninsula is where the medieval pilgrims set off to reach the holy island of Bardsey: one glimpse of their destination, rising out of the gunmetal-grey sea beyond the surf-pounded rocks hints at the drama of their final voyage. A path leads down past the remains of St Mary's Abbey to a Neolithic standing stone known as Maen Melyn, suggesting this was a holy place well before the Celts or their saints arrived.

A natural freshwater spring called St Mary's Well (Ffynnon Fair)issues from a cleft in the rock below the high-tide mark; it was held to be holy and pilgrims would sip the water before setting out. There are sheer drops to the sea and high surf, so we don't recommend you attempt it.

Inland are strip fields that preserve many of the patterns of ancient land use. Keep an eye out for choughs, a cheeky red-legged relation of the crow, and the rare spotted rock rose – this is the only place on the British mainland where this yellow bloom is found.

Porth Oer BEACH
(Whistling Sands; NT; www.nationaltrust.org.uk; car park £1.50) This lovely remote scoop of beach, 2.5 miles north of Aberdaron, has sand which squeaks when you walk on it, giving it its English name, Whistling Sands. From here it's a 2-mile coastal walk southwest via the twin headlands of Dinas Bach and Dinas Fawr to the cove of Porth Orion.

St Gwynhoedl's Church CHURCH
(Llangwnnadl) Part of the chain of pilgrim's churches leading to Bardsey, pretty St

Gwynhoedl's looks like three churches fused together. It still has 15th- and 16th-century roof timbers and a Celtic Cross and bronze sanctus bell dating from around AD 600. Check out the carved font; the crowned figure represents Henry VIII. The church is 5 miles north of Aberdaron, off the B4417.

Plas-yn-Rhiw HISTORIC BUILDING
(NT; ☎01758-780219; www.nationaltrust.org.uk/plas-yn-rhiw; adult/child £5.20/2.60; ⏲noon-5pm Thu-Sun Apr, Oct & Nov, Wed-Mon May-Aug, Thu-Mon Sep) The three Keating sisters, Eileen, Lorna and Honora, came to the rescue of this little decaying 17th-century manor house in the 1930s and '40s. The lush gardens provide a sharp contrast to the surrounding moorland and the views over Porth Neigwl (Hell's Mouth) to Cardigan Bay are sublime. It's on the heights near the hamlet of Rhiw, 4 miles east of Aberdaron; follow the signposts from the B441.

Sleeping & Eating

★Tŷ Newydd HOTEL ££
(☎01758-760207; www.gwesty-tynewydd.co.uk; s/d from £60/90; 📶) The location alone would make this a top pick, even if the digs weren't so cushy. Right on the beach, this friendly hotel has fully refurbished, light-drenched, spacious rooms and wonderful sea views. The tide comes in right under the terrace off the pub restaurant (mains £12 to £17), which seems designed with an afternoon gin and tonic in mind.

Ship Hotel PUB ££
(☎01758-760204; www.theshiphotelaberdaron.co.uk; r from £99; 📶) A family-run concern for more than 30 years, the Ship has very decent rooms, some with sea views. The bar's commitment to stocking the product of small Welsh breweries has earned it the praise of the Campaign for Real Ale (Camra), and the in-house restaurant (mains £13 to £15) is a cut above the pub standard – try the locally caught crab.

Y Gegin Fawr WELSH £
(The Big Kitchen; ☎01758-760359; mains from £7; ⏲9am-6pm) With their spiritual needs sorted, the Bardsey-bound saints could claim a meal at Y Gegin Fawr, a little thick-walled building with tiny windows, just over the bridge in the centre of the village. Dating from 1300, it now dishes up locally caught crab and lobster, plus homemade cakes and scones. Even pilgrims need to pay these days, of course.

Getting There & Away

Buses head to/from Nefyn (route 8B, 30 minutes), Llanbedrog (17/17B, 30 minutes) and Pwllheli (17/17B, 40 minutes).

Bardsey Island (Ynys Enlli)

POP 4

This mysterious island, 2 miles long and 2 miles off the tip of the Llŷn, is a magical place. In fact, it's one of many candidates for the Isle of Avalon from the Arthurian legends. It's said that the wizard Merlin still sleeps in a glass castle somewhere on the island.

In the 6th or 7th century the obscure St Cadfan founded a monastery here, giving shelter to Celts fleeing the Saxon invaders, and medieval pilgrims followed in their wake. Three pilgrimages to Bardsey were said to be equivalent to one to Rome.

THE BARDSEY PILGRIMAGE

In the early Middle Ages, when journeys from Britain to Italy were long, perilous and beyond the means of most people, the Pope decreed that three pilgrimages to the holy island of Bardsey would have the same spiritual value as one to Rome. Tens of thousands of penitents took advantage of this get-out-of-Purgatory-free (or at least quickly) card and many came here to die (hence the sobriquet 'Island of 20,000 Saints'). In the 16th century, Henry VIII's ban on pilgrimages stopped the practice – although a steady trickle of modern-day pilgrims defies the late Hal to walk the route today.

The traditional path stops at ancient churches and holy wells along the way. It's broken into nine legs on the **Edge of Wales Walk** (☎01758-760652; www.edgeofwaleswalk.co.uk) website, run by a cooperative of local residents. They can help to arrange a 47-mile, self-guided walking tour, including five nights' accommodation and baggage transfers (£376 per person). A similar service is also offered for the 98-mile **Llŷn Coastal Path**.

Most modern pilgrims to Bardsey are seabird-watchers; during the summer around 17,000 Manx shearwaters nest in burrows here, emerging at night. A colony of Atlantic grey seals lives here year-round; a pile of rocks by the harbour is a popular hang-out. Other sights include 6th-century **carved stones**, the remains of a 13th-century **abbey tower** and a candy-striped **lighthouse**.

Sights

The island's Welsh name means 'Isle of the Currents', a reference to the treacherous tidal surges in Bardsey Sound, which doubtless convinced medieval visitors that their lives were indeed in God's hands. A **Celtic cross** amid the abbey ruins commemorates the pilgrims who came here to die and inspired the island's poetic epithet: the Isle of 20,000 Saints. Their bones still periodically emerge from unmarked graves; it's said that in the 1850s they were used as fencing, there were so many of them.

Sleeping

Bardsey Lodge & Bird Observatory HOSTEL
(01626-773908; www.bbfo.org.uk; adult/child per week £165/102) One option, for those keen on feathered fauna, is to stay at the dormitory-style accommodation at this Bird Observatory, which has been monitoring birdlife on Bardsey since 1953. Bookings are taken for a week – from Saturday to Saturday – and there's a kitchen, dining room and common area. Those with permits can help with the bird-ringing.

Information

Bardsey Island Trust (08458-112233; www.bardsey.org) The Bardsey Island Trust can help arrange trips to the island and holiday lets in cottages for those who wish to linger beyond a day trip.

Getting There & Away

Two private boat services are the only way to reach Bardsey. In summer **Bardsey Boat Trips** (07971-769895; www.bardseyboattrips.com; adult/child £30/20) sails to Bardsey from Porth Meudwy, near Aberdaron; **Enlli Charters** (08458-113655; www.enllicharter.co.uk; per person £45; Apr-Sep) sails from Pwllheli.

Morfa Nefyn

POP 1229

The diminutive village of Morfa Nefyn sits above a pretty crescent of sand at **Porth Dinllaen** (parking summer/winter £5/1.50, free to NT members in summer). It's hard to believe that this was once a busy cargo, shipbuilding and herring port, the only safe haven on the peninsula's north coast. Indeed, it was eyed up by slate magnate William Madocks as a possible home for ferries to Ireland, but in 1839 the House of Commons gave that job to Holyhead. Today one of its chief draws is the **Nefyn & District Golf Club** (01758-720966; www.nefyn-golf-club.co.uk; Lon Golf), which maintains a picturesque course on a headland jutting into the Irish Sea.

Eating

★ **Tŷ Coch Inn** PUB FOOD £
(01758-720498; www.tycoch.co.uk; Porth Dinllaen; mains £6-10; 11am-11pm Mon-Sat, to 5pm Sun Jun-Aug, see website for hours other months;) At the western end of Porth Dinllaen – reached either by water or by walking through the Nefyn Golf Club's course and turning beachwards once you reach the Iron Age hill fort – is the legendary Tŷ Coch Inn. Famous for its stunning views, you can sip your pint while dabbling your toes in the sea.

Getting There & Away

Buses head here from Pistyll (route 14, five minutes) and Pwllheli (route 8, 20 minutes).

Pistyll

One of the main pit stops on the Bardsey pilgrimage, the ancient hospice church **St Beuno's** sits peacefully in the middle of its oval churchyard below the village of Pistyll.

East of Pistyll are the 100m sea cliffs of **Carreg y Llam**, a major seabird site.

Sights

St Beuno's Church CHURCH
St Beuno (died 640) was to North Wales what St David was to the Welsh south (another St Beuno's sits further up the coast at Clynnog Fawr, where his religious community was based). This tiny stone church's slate roof would once have been thatched, but original features include a Celtic carved

font and a window beside the altar that allowed lepers standing outside to watch Mass. On the interior face of this wall there are rare remnants of pre-Reformation frescoes.

St Beuno's is at its most atmospheric during the Christmas, Easter and harvest seasons when the floors are covered in reeds and fragrant herbs – unless, of course, you're a hay-fever sufferer.

Sleeping

★**Natural Retreats** APARTMENT ££
(☎01625-416430; www.naturalretreats.com; Pistyll Farm; apt from £124; P 📶 🐾) Offering big-city luxury in the middle of nowhere, Natural Retreats has taken an old stone farm complex and converted it into a gorgeous set of one- to three-bedroom apartments, fully equipped with all the mod cons (including that ultimate traveller treat, the clothes washer-dryer). It's peacefully and picturesquely located on the cliffs near St Beuno's Church.

Getting There & Away

Pistyll is on the B4417, 1.5 miles northeast of Nefyn; bus 14 from Pwllheli to Tudweiliog stops here. The turn-off to the church and National Trust car park is past the village; look for the Natural Retreats sign.

Nant Gwrtheyrn

The village of Porth y Nant, now Nant Gwrtheyrn, was built for quarry workers in the 19th century, when granite was dug out of the surrounding mountains and shipped to Liverpool, Manchester and elsewhere to be used in building roads. The quarries closed after WWII and the village was gradually abandoned. After being used for the New Atlantic Commune in the 1970s, it was given a new lease of life when the **Welsh Language & Heritage Centre** (☎01758-750334; www.nantgwrtheyrn.org; weekend/3-day course incl full board £240/295; ⏱call ahead for times) opened in the restored buildings, in 1982, offering residential Welsh-language courses.

Nant Gwrtheyrn has an isolated and dramatic setting, reached by a preposterously steep road down into the valley, accessed from the village of Llithfaen (on the B4417). If you're driving, take it very slowly and be extremely careful. Otherwise it's a 25-minute walk from the car park at the top of the hill.

Sights

Nant Gwrtheyrn is a magical place – eerily quiet and ideal for a tranquil walk along world's-end cliffs. According to tradition it's the burial place of the 6th-century Celtic King Vortigern (Gwrtheyrn in Welsh), who features in many of the Arthurian legends. The old chapel has a small but compelling exhibition on the history of the village and the founding of the centre. A 10-minute film on life in the village is shown in one of the worker's cottages, which has been decked out in period furnishings. There's also a marked 3-mile loop walk heading past the pebbly beach, various quarries and abandoned infrastructure and the ruins of earlier farms. Wild goats and sheep dot the scree.

From the top car park is the start of a 30- to 50-minute track to striking **Tre'r Ceiri**, one of the best preserved Iron Age hill forts in Europe, where the remains of 150 stone huts have been discovered.

Sleeping

Nant Gwrtheyrn Cottages COTTAGE
(☎01758-750334; www.nantgwrtheyrn.org; Nant Gwrtheyrn, Llithfaen; @) Nant Gwrtheyrn's 24 terraced stone cottages have been adapted to provide cosy modern accommodation, with solid wooden furniture and under-floor heating. Breakfast is served in the nearby cafe.

Getting There & Away

The closest town to Nant Gwrtheyrn is Llithfaen (25 minutes from Pwllheli on bus 27). From there, it's a short cab ride or a 30-minute walk.

Anglesey & the North Coast

Includes ➡

Best Places to Eat

➡ Blas (p271)

➡ Osteria (p271)

➡ Hayloft Restaurant (p276)

➡ Watson's Bistro (p279)

➡ Tredici Italian Kitchen (p293)

Best Places to Sleep

➡ Victoria House (p270)

➡ Cleifiog (p292)

➡ Totters (p269)

➡ Bodysgallen Hall (p280)

➡ Château Rhianfa (p290)

Why Go?

This compact region can be boiled down to two essential things: castles and coast. Yes, there are look-at-me castles all over Wales, but few attract more admiring stares than the glamorous trio of Caernarfon, Conwy and Beaumaris, which is why they're recognised as World Heritage Sites today. As for the coast, there's a reason that Llandudno has been crowned 'the Queen of Welsh Resorts'. Its genteel appeal stands in stark contrast to the altogether more wild edges of the Isle of Anglesey, where the echoes of the ancients can be heard in the waves that batter South Stack and the breezes that eddy around clifftop barrows.

Beyond the sands and stones, this part of Wales offers rich opportunity for surfing, sailing, windsurfing, kayaking, kitesurfing, powerboating, paddleboarding, walking and birdwatching. You certainly won't be bored.

When to Go

➡ May is both the sunniest and the driest month, and Llandudno celebrates the warming weather with much Victorian merriment. Walkers will find it a good time to hit the coastal paths.

➡ Temperatures are highest in July and August, which are the best beach months, although average highs are rarely above 20°C.

➡ In October, Gwledd Conwy Feast (p278) gives foodies an excuse to start working on a warming layer of winter fat.

➡ The winter months give student musicians plenty of incentive to stay inside and practise for the Bangor Music Festival (p274) in March.

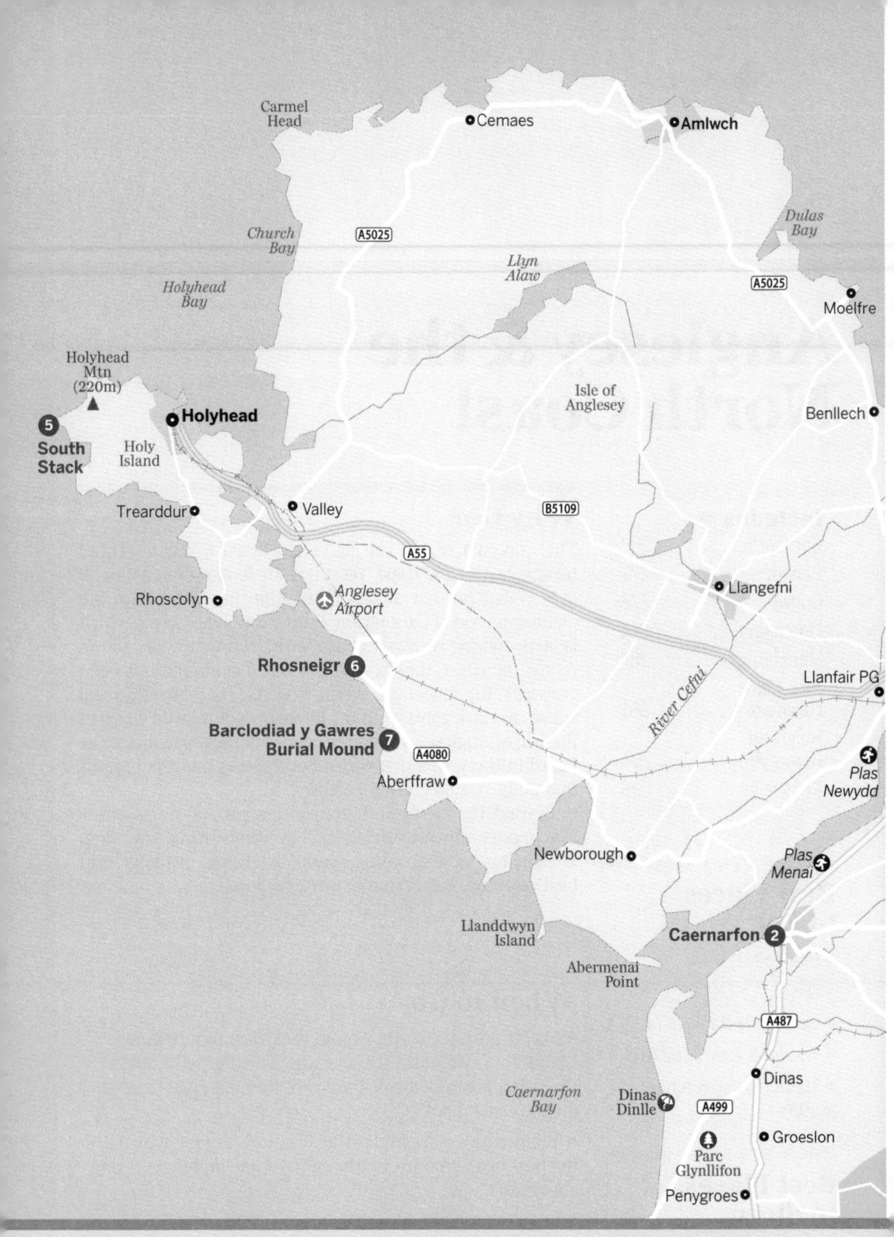

Anglesey & the North Coast Highlights

❶ **Beaumaris** (p291) Falling for the Georgian charms of Anglesey's finest town.

❷ **Caernarfon Castle** (p268) Witnessing the Byzantine beauty and strength of Caernarfon's castle.

❸ **Llandudno** (p281) Discovering vast Bronze Age mines alongside the Victoriana of this perennially popular seaside resort.

❹ **Conwy** (p276) Savouring the history of the medieval walled town, in the shadow of its mighty castle.

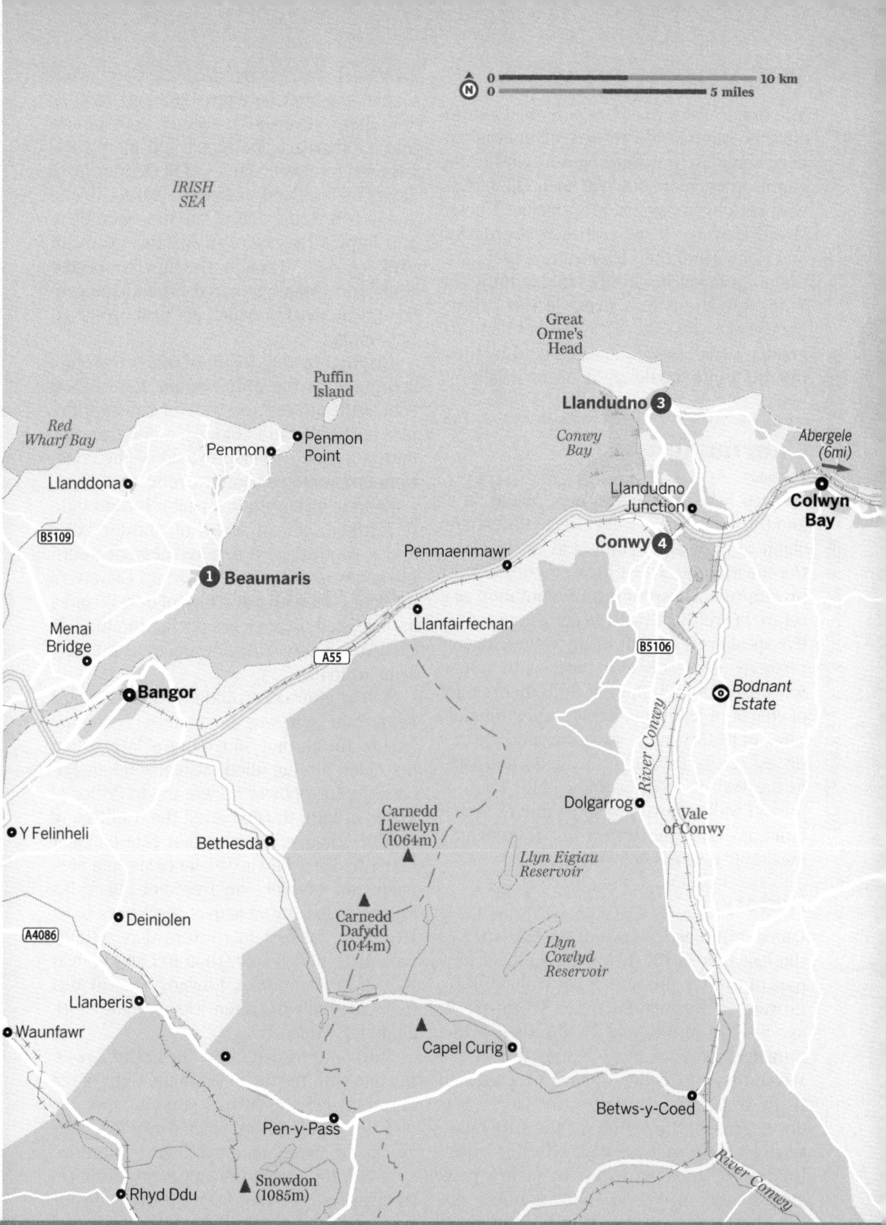

5 South Stack (p295)
Watching guillemots, razorbills and choughs wheel under the mighty cliffs.

6 Rhosneigr (p298)
Strolling along Rhosneigr's long sandy beach and watching the surfers at play.

7 Barclodiad y Gawres Burial Mound (p298)
Communing with the ancients in their tomb with a view.

THE NORTH COAST

The North Wales coast has perennial natural charms, but seaside resorts of uneven appeal: some are outstanding examples of the genre, others more down at heel. The section west of Colwyn Bay includes glorious Unesco World Heritage–listed castles at Caernarfon and Conwy and the Victorian resort of Llandudno, a favourite family holiday hub. The sands stretch along a string of less appealing resort towns east of the bay, but there are greater attractions to be discovered by turning south into the delightful Conwy Valley.

Caernarfon

POP 9493

Wedged between the gleaming Menai Strait and the deep-purple hills, Caernarfon's main claim to fame is its fantastical castle. Given the town's crucial historical importance, its proximity to Snowdonia and reputation as a centre of Welsh culture (its percentage of native speakers is as high as anywhere), it's surprisingly down-at-heel in parts, with quite a few boarded-up buildings. Still, there's a lot of charm in its untouristy air and a tangible sense of history in the streets around the castle, especially Palace St, Castle Sq and Hole in the Wall St. Within the cobbled lanes of the old walled town are some fine Georgian buildings, and the waterfront is marching inevitably towards gentrification.

History

Caernarfon Castle was built by Edward I as the last link in his 'iron ring' and it's now part of the 'Castles and Town Walls of King Edward in Gwynedd' Unesco World Heritage Site. In an attempt by the then prime minister, David Lloyd George (himself a Welshman), to bring the royals closer to their Welsh constituency, the castle was designated as the venue for the 1911 investiture of the Prince of Wales. In retrospect, linking the modern royals to such a powerful symbol of Welsh subjugation may not have been the best idea. It incensed fervent nationalists and at the next crowning, that of Prince Charles in 1969, the sentiment climaxed with an attempt to blow up his train.

Sights

★**Caernarfon Castle** CASTLE
(Cadw; www.cadw.wales.gov.uk; adult/child £7.95/5.60; ⌚9.30am-5pm Mar-Jun, Sep & Oct, to 6pm Jul & Aug, to 4pm Nov-Feb) Majestic Caernarfon Castle was built between 1283 and 1330 as a military stronghold, seat of government and royal palace. Designed and mainly supervised by Master James of St George, from Savoy, its brief and scale were extraordinary. Today it remains one of the most complete and impressive castles in Britain – you can walk on and through the interconnected walls and towers gathered around the central green, most of which are well preserved but empty.

Inspired by the dream of Macsen Wledig recounted in the *Mabinogion*, Caernarfon echoes the 5th-century walls of Constantinople (İstanbul), with colour-banded masonry and polygonal towers, instead of the traditional round towers and turrets.

Despite its fairy-tale aspect it is thoroughly fortified, with a series of murder holes and a sophisticated arrangement of multiple arrow slits. It repelled Owain Glyndŵr's army in 1404 with a garrison of only 28 men, and resisted three sieges during the English Civil War before surrendering to Cromwell's army in 1646.

A year after construction began, Edward I's second son was born here, becoming heir to the throne four months later when his elder brother died. To consolidate Edward junior's power he was made Prince of Wales in 1301, thus creating the tradition of English kings conferring that title on their heirs. As King Edward II he came to a very nasty end, possibly via a red-hot poker; his much-eroded statue is over the King's Gate. However, the first investiture that actually took place here (rather than in London) was that of his namesake, Edward VIII, in 1911 (coincidentally his reign was also cut short, albeit less violently).

Start your inspection at the **Eagle Tower**, the one with the flagpoles to the right of the entrance. On the turrets you can spot the weathered eagle from which it gets its name, alongside stone-helmeted figures intended to swell the garrison's apparent numbers (they're easier to spot from the quay). Inside there are displays on Eleanor of Castile and the Welsh 'Game of Thrones'.

There's a film tracing the history of the site since Roman times in the **North East Tower**, while in the **Queen's Tower** (named after Edward I's wife Eleanor) is the **Regimental Museum of the Royal Welch Fusiliers**, filled with medals, uniforms, weapons and historical displays.

St Mary's Church CHURCH
(Church St) Built in 1307 at the same time that the castle was going up, this pretty Gothic church once ministered to the castle's garrison. Built directly into the old town wall, its exterior was remodelled in 1811; head inside to see more masonry dating to the original construction.

Around Caernarfon

Segontium Roman Fort RUINS
(Cadw; www.cadw.wales.gov.uk; Ffordd Cwstenin; 10am-4pm Tue, Wed & Sat Apr-Oct) FREE Just east of the town centre, these low stone foundations represent the westernmost legionary fort of the Roman Empire. The fort dates back to AD 77, when General Gnaeus Julius Agricola completed the Roman conquest of Wales by capturing the Isle of Anglesey. Sadly the on-site museum is closed, and the only interpretive sign is on the side of the building.

Segontium was designed to accommodate a force of up to 1000 infantrymen, and coins recovered from the site indicate that it was an active garrison until AD 394 – a reflection of its crucial strategic position. Caernarfon's name is a reference to this site, meaning 'fort opposite Anglesey'. The site is about half a mile along the A4085 (to Beddgelert), which crosses through the middle of it.

Parc Glynllifon GARDENS
(01766-771000; www.gwynedd.gov.uk/parcglynllifon; Clynnog Rd; adult/child £4/2; 10am-5pm daily Apr-Sep, Thu-Sun Oct-Mar) Strewn with rare plants, follies, sculptures and fountains, these historic gardens once formed part of the estate of the Lords Newborough. While the grand neoclassical manor house isn't open to the public, the woodland paths that criss-cross the park are. There's also a historic steam engine and the **Adra craft centre**, where resident artisans sell their wares, and public arts classes. Parc Glynllifon is 6 miles south of Caernarfon, on the A499.

Dinas Dinlle BEACH
Dolphins and porpoises can sometimes be spotted from this long, sandy Blue Flag beach, 6 miles southwest of Caernarfon. The flatness of the surrounding land stands in contrast to the dramatically sculpted Llŷn Peninsula, visible in the distance. The exception is a solitary hill, with a path leading up to the remains of an Iron Age fort.

Activities

Plas Menai WATER SPORTS
(01248-670964; www.plasmenai.co.uk; half/full day £25/40; 8.30am-7pm) The excellent National Watersports Centre offers year-round water-based courses for all interests (sailing, power boating, kayaking, windsurfing, stand-up paddleboarding) and abilities. Advance reservations are necessary. On-site accommodation includes B&B rooms (singles/doubles £45/70) and a bunkhouse (dorms £25). It's located 3 miles along the A487 towards Bangor. Bus 1A (Caernarfon to Bangor) stops here.

GreenWood Forest Park OUTDOORS
(01248-671493; www.greenwoodforestpark.co.uk; Bush Rd, Y Felinheli; £9-14; 10am-5.30pm;) Underpinned by a strong green ethos, GreenWood has a slew of rides and activities spread over 7 hectares of parkland. There's the Green Dragon, the world's first people-powered roller coaster, the solar-powered Sun Splash, treetop walkways, archery and more. GreenWood is signposted from the A487 near Y Felinheli, 4 miles northeast of Caernarfon.

Menai Strait Pleasure Cruises CRUISE
(01286-672772; www.menaicruises.co.uk; Slate Quay; adult/child 40min £7/5, 2hr £16/8; every hour from 11.30am May-Oct) The 1937 ferry *Queen of the Sea* offers 40-minute cruises, with a full commentary, to the southwest entrance of the Menai Strait, and two-hour cruises in the other direction as far as the Menai Suspension Bridge. They leave from Slate Quay, beside the castle.

Beacon Climbing Centre CLIMBING
(08454-508222; www.beaconclimbing.com; Cibyn Estate, Lôn Cae Ffynnon; adult/child £9/6.50; 10am-10pm Mon-Fri, to 8pm Sat & Sun) This large indoor climbing centre offers one-hour taster sessions for beginners (£15) and plenty of challenging faces for experienced climbers to hone their skills on. It's located in an industrial estate off the Llanberis Rd (A4086), about a mile east of town.

Sleeping

★**Totters** HOSTEL £
(01286-672963; www.totters.co.uk; 2 High St; dm/d £18.50/50;) Modern, clean and very welcoming, this excellent independent hostel is the best-value place to stay in town. The 14th-century arched basement gives a sense of history to guests' free breakfasts

(cereal, toast and hot beverages are included in the price). In addition to dorms, there's a two-bed attic apartment, a TV room and book-swap library.

Caer Menai B&B £

(01286-672612; www.caermenai.co.uk; 15 Church St; s/d/f from £48/63/85; @ wifi) A former county school (1894), this elegant building is on a quiet street nestled against the western town wall. The seven renovated rooms are fresh, clean and snug; number 7has sunset sea views.

★ Victoria House B&B ££

(01286-678263; 13 Church St; r £90-100; @ wifi) Victoria House is pretty much the perfect guesthouse – a delightful, solid Victorian building in the middle of Caernarfon's old town, run by exceptionally welcoming and attentive hosts. The four spacious, modern rooms include lovely touches – free toiletries, a DVD on the town's history, fresh milk and a welcoming drink in the bar fridge – and breakfast is a joy.

Plas Dinas Country House B&B ££

(01286-830214; www.plasdinas.co.uk; Bontnewydd; r from £109; P wifi) Until the 1980s this large 17th-century house belonged to Lord Snowdon's family; his wife, Princess Margaret, often stayed here. Despite the ancestral photos in the hallway and the grand drawing room, the overall impression is surprisingly homey. The 10 bedrooms are filled with antiques and thoughtful touches, such as Molton Brown toiletries and fluffy bathrobes. Self-catering cottages are available, too.

It's set amid extensive grounds off the A487, 2 miles south of Caernarfon.

Celtic Royal Hotel HOTEL £££

(01286-674477; www.celtic-royal.co.uk; Bangor St; s/d £105/150; P wifi pool) This grand old sandstone building, with its impressive entrance hall and wood-panelled corridors, was built by the Earl of Uxbridge in 1794, becoming a

Caernarfon

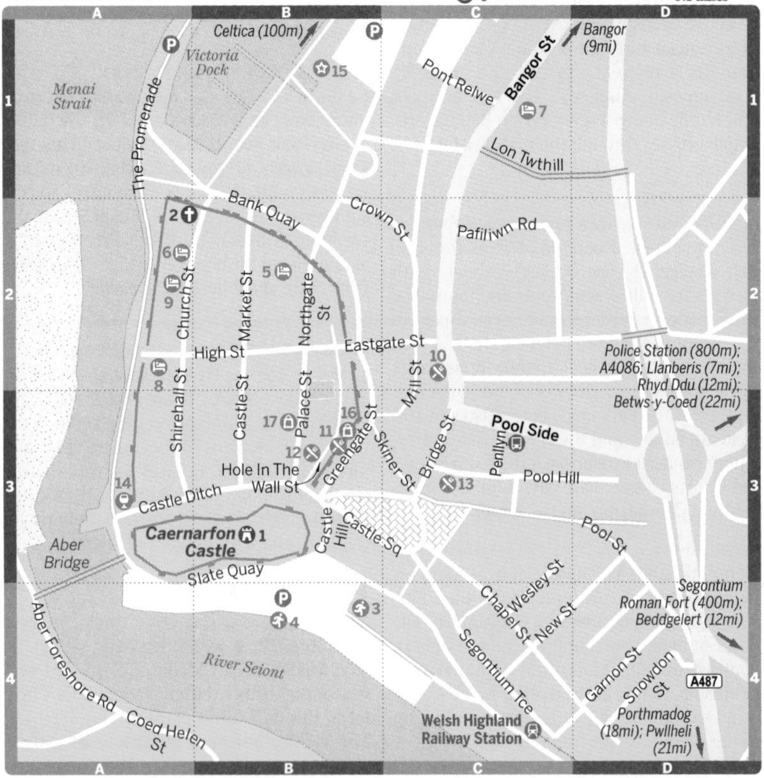

focus of local society in Georgian and Victorian times. It's hardly intimate, but it has all the advantages of a large hotel, including an indoor pool, sauna, steam room, jacuzzi, gym, restaurant and bar.

Eating

Y Gegin Fach CAFE £

(☎01286-672165; 5-9 Pool Hill; mains £5-7; ⏲9.30am-3pm) 'The Little Kitchen' is a proper old-fashioned Welsh-speaking *caffi*, right down to the net curtains and cheery red polka-dot tablecloths. It's a great spot to tuck into traditional faves like rarebit, faggots, *lobscouse* (lamb stew) and Welsh cakes, and wish you had a Welsh granny. Opens later in summer.

Ainsworth's Traditional Fish & Chips FISH & CHIPS £

(☎01286-673151; 41 Bridge St; mains £3-6; ⏲11.30am-9pm) Our favourite North Wales chippie offers a choice of crispy cod, plaice and haddock, along with burgers, pies and fried chicken. It's mainly a takeaway operation, but there are four stools by the window counter if you want to tuck straight in.

★**Blas** WELSH ££

(☎01286-677707; www.blascaernarfon.co.uk; 23-25 Hole in the Wall St; mains £18-20; ⏲10.30am-3.30pm & 6-11pm Tue-Sat, 10am-3pm Sun) Blas (taste) abounds at this slick place in one of Caernarfon's most picturesque streets. Chef Daniel ap Geraint makes skilful use of Welsh produce in dishes such as ginger and lemongrass cured salmon with Aberdaron crab, and rib of Llanfair Hall beef with confit tomato. Local beers, ciders and spirits also feature, and tea is served in the afternoon.

★**Osteria** TUSCAN ££

(☎01286-238050; 26 Hole in the Wall St; mains £11; ⏲noon-3pm Thu-Sat, 6-9pm Tue-Sat) Two Florentine partners opened this excellent addition to Caernarfon's dining scene in a compact whitewashed-stone building hard up against the city walls. Specialising in interesting carpaccios and bruschette (think wild boar or poached turkey), they import many of their ingredients and wines from Tuscany and also prepare stuffed vegetables and more substantial daily specials.

Black Boy Inn PUB FOOD ££

(☎01286-673604; www.black-boy-inn.com; Northgate St; mains £8-18; ⏲noon-9pm; 📶👪) Packed with original 16th-century features, this charismatic pub (singles/doubles from £57/86) is divided into a series of snug rooms, with low, warped roof-beams, open fires and Welsh beer on tap. Dishes such as the *lobscouse* (Caernarfon-style beef-shin stew) highlight local meats and seafood, and there are plenty of pub-grub staples such as roasts, pies, burgers, scampi and grilled fish.

Drinking & Entertainment

Anglesey Arms PUB

(☎01286-672158; Harbour Front; ⏲11am-midnight; 📶) If you're after a pint, this converted 18th-century waterfront customs house is your best bet. In summer, grab a seat outside; it's a great spot for watching the sunset.

Galeri Caernarfon THEATRE

(☎01286-685222; www.galericaernarfon.com; Victoria Dock; ⏲box office 8.30am-6pm Mon-Fri, 10am-4pm Sat) This excellent multipurpose arts centre hosts exhibitions, theatre, films and events; check online for details.

Caernarfon

Top Sights
1 Caernarfon Castle B3

Sights
2 St Mary's Church A2

Activities, Courses & Tours
3 Beics Menai B4
4 Menai Strait Pleasure Cruises B4

Sleeping
5 Black Boy Inn B2
6 Caer Menai A2
7 Celtic Royal Hotel C1
8 Totters A2
9 Victoria House A2

Eating
10 Ainsworth's Traditional Fish & Chips C2
Black Boy Inn .... (see 5)
11 Blas B3
12 Osteria B3
13 Y Gegin Fach C3

Drinking & Nightlife
14 Anglesey Arms A3

Entertainment
15 Galeri Caernarfon B1

Shopping
16 Iechyd Da! B3
17 Palas Print B3

Shopping

Iechyd Da! ALCOHOL

(☎01286-675373; www.iechyd-da.co; 19 Hole in the Wall St; ⏲10.30am-5pm Tue-Sun) Over 170 Welsh ales and ciders twinkle from the shelves of this Australian-owned hole in the wall on Hole in the Wall St, alongside Welsh whisky, gin and vodka. Open longer hours in summer, it even manages to find room for that elusive beast, a Welsh wine. Oh, and the name (pronounced ya-*kee*-da) means 'good health!'

Palas Print BOOKS

(☎01286-674631; www.palasprint.com; 10 Palace St; ⏲9.30am-6pm Mon-Sat) Everything you'd want from a local, indie book shop, this little gem stocks English and Welsh books and CDs, with emphasis on local authors, Welsh folk and the history and landscape of the area. Crochet club meets every Wednesday evening.

Celtica ARTS & CRAFTS

(☎01286-669602; www.celtica-wales.com/celtica; Doc Fictoria; ⏲8.30am-5pm Mon-Sat, 10am-4pm Sun) Love spoons and jewellery sit alongside a deli and food store, featuring local specialities such as Halen Môn salt and Snowdonia cheese, inside this gleaming venue by the yacht marina. It has a good selection of books and maps of Wales, too.

Inigo Jones Slateworks GIFTS & SOUVENIRS

(☎01286-830242; www.inigojones.co.uk; A487, Groeslon; tour per adult/child £5.50/5; ⏲9am-5pm) Built in 1861 to provide slate for schools, this workshop now earns its coin making garden ornaments, place mats, picture frames, cake stands and other knick-knacks from this most Welsh of materials. You can also take a self-guided tour of the works and get great Welsh cakes from the on-site cafe. It's on the A487, 6 miles south of Caernarfon.

Getting There & Away

BUS

Buses and coaches depart from the **bus station** (Pool Side). A daily National Express coach stops en route to Pwllheli (£8, 45 minutes) and London (£37, 10 hours) via Bangor (£7.10, 20 minutes), Llandudno (£8.40, one hour) and Birmingham (£32, 6½ hours). Other buses include 1/1A to Criccieth (45 minutes), Tremadog (45 minutes) and Porthmadog (50 minutes); 5/X5 to Bangor (30 minutes), Conwy (1¼ hours) and Llandudno (1½ hours); 12 to Parc Glynllifon (12 minutes) and Pwllheli (45 minutes); and 88 to Llanberis (30 minutes). Snowdon Sherpa bus S4 heads to Beddgelert (30 minutes) via the Snowdon Ranger (22 minutes) and Rhyd Ddu (24 minutes) trailheads.

BICYCLE

Beics Menai (☎01286-676804; www.beicsmenai.co.uk; 1 Slate Quay; half/full day £10/15; ⏲9.30am-5pm Mon-Sat) hires bikes and can advise on local cycle routes. A brochure on Gwynedd recreational cycle routes includes the 12.5-mile Lôn Eifion (starting near the Welsh Highland Railway station and running south to Bryncir) and the 4.5-mile Lôn Las Menai (following the Menai Strait to the village of Y Felinheli). Lôn Las Cymru passes through Caernarfon, heading northeast to Bangor and south to Criccieth.

CAR

Free street parking is at a premium but you might snatch a park in the walled town (try Church St) and there are highly contested free parks by the water on the south embankment of Victoria Dock.

TRAIN

Caernarfon is the northern terminus of the Welsh Highland Railway tourist train, which runs to Porthmadog (£38 return, 2½ hours) via Rhyd Ddu (£22.80 return, one hour) and Beddgelert (£29.10 return, 1½ hours) from Easter to October, with limited winter service. The station is near the river on St Helen's Rd.

Bangor

POP 17,988

While Bangor isn't the most attractive town in North Wales, it has a lively arts and cultural scene, boosted by the addition of two fantastic new venues: Pontio (p274) and Storiel. Dominated by its university and blessed with a multicultural population, it's the largest city in Gwynedd and a major transport hub for North Wales, with plenty of onward connections to Anglesey and Snowdonia.

St Deiniol established a monastery here in the 6th century, which grew up into Bangor's sweet little cathedral. The main university building sits above it on a ridge, its contours aping those of the cathedral. Bangor University was founded in 1884 and it is now rated as the best university in Wales and one of the top 15 in the UK. During term time 10,000 students swell the city's population.

Bangor

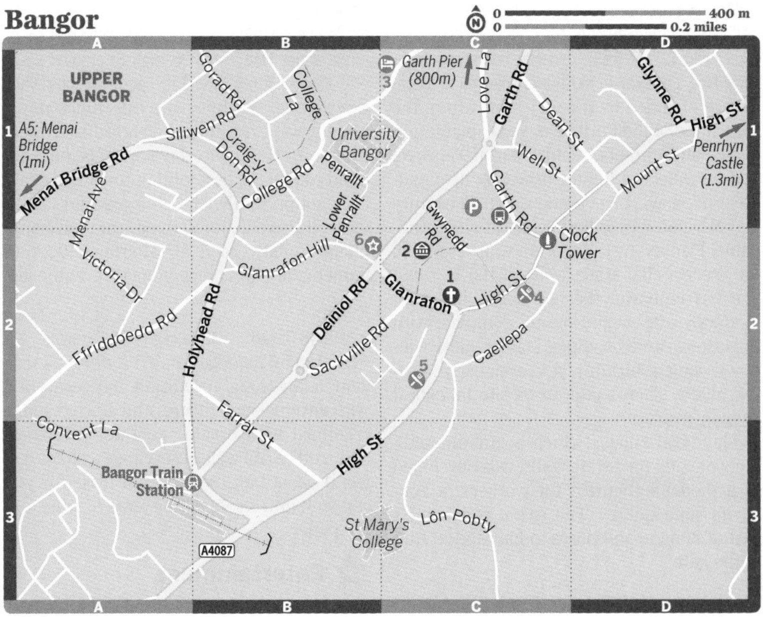

Sights & Activities

Bangor Cathedral CATHEDRAL

(http://bangor.churchinwales.org.uk; Glanrafon; 9am-4.30pm Mon-Fri, 10.30am-1pm Sat) More formally known as the Cathedral Church of St Deiniol, this building occupies one of the oldest ecclesiastical sites in Britain, dating from AD 525 when the saint founded his community here. The earliest part of today's stone church dates to the 12th century, although that building was largely destroyed in 1211 during a raid by England's King John. Much of the architecture seen today is the work of the eminent architect Sir George Gilbert Scott between 1870 and 1880.

Storiel MUSEUM

(01248-353368; www.gwynedd.gov.uk/museums; Ffordd Gwynedd; 11am-5pm Tue-Sat) FREE The former Gwynedd Museum & Art Gallery has moved into swankier premises and taken the portmanteau word 'Storiel' (a cross between the Welsh words for 'story' and 'gallery'). Essentially a folk museum for Gwynedd county, it makes great use of the former Bishop's Palace, with exhibitions of local artefacts (including the Roman 'Segontium sword'), photography, art and more. There's also a cafe and shop.

Bangor

Sights

1	Bangor Cathedral	C2
2	Storiel	C2

Sleeping

3	Management Centre	C1

Eating

4	Blue Sky	C2
5	Kyffin	C2

Entertainment

6	Pontio	B2

Garth Pier LANDMARK

(adult/child 50/20p; 8am-6pm Mon-Sat, 10am-5pm Sun) Given the large expanse of mudflats exposed at high tide (a paradise for all manner of wading birds), it's surprising that the Victorians chose to build one of Britain's longest pleasure piers here. Built in 1896, Garth Pier stretches 460m into the Menai Strait – most of the way to Anglesey. Ornate kiosks are scattered along its length and there's a tearoom at the very end. In the distance you can glimpse Thomas Telford's handsome Menai Suspension Bridge.

Penrhyn Castle
CASTLE

(NT; www.nationaltrust.org.uk; off A5, Llandygai; adult/child £11.30/5.65; ☉castle noon-5pm Mar–early Nov, grounds & museums year-round 11am-5pm; ℙ) Funded by the vast profits from the slate mine of the Caribbean sugar-plantation owner and anti-abolitionist Baron Penrhyn, and extended and embellished by his great-great-nephew, this immense 19th-century neo-Norman folly is both tasteless and formidable. Flanked by a Victorian walled garden, the creeper-clad stone walls of the Norman 'fortress' embower the neo-Gothic hall with its darkly extravagant rooms, complete with intricately carved ceilings, stained-glass windows, opulent furniture and even early flushing toilets. There's also an on-site industrial **railway museum**.

Llandygai village, which begins immediately outside the estate walls, was developed as a model settlement for workers in Penrhyn's slate quarry. The castle is 1.5 miles east of Bangor, and buses to Llandudno stop at the gate.

Zip World Bethesda
ADVENTURE SPORTS

(☑01248-601444; www.zipworld.co.uk; Penrhyn Quarry, Bethesda; single ride £60; ☉8am-6.30pm) The old Penrhyn slate quarry, nearly a mile long and 360m deep, is now home to Europe's longest (and the world's fastest) zip line – Zip World Velocity. Flying over the lake at the heart of the still-operational quarry, speeds of 100mph can be achieved. Bethesda is on the A5, about 4miles southeast of Bangor.

⚡ Festivals & Events

Bangor Music Festival
MUSIC

(☑01248-382181; www.bangormusicfestival.org.uk; ☉Mar) Trends in contemporary composition, avant-garde performances, masterclasses, talks and conferences all come together during this six-day festival, held in collaboration with Bangor University's Music School.

🛏 Sleeping & Eating

Management Centre
HOTEL ££

(☑01248-365900; www.themanagementcentre.co.uk; Bangor Business School, College Rd; s £70-80, d £90; ℙ🛜) Bangor isn't exactly blessed with accommodation options, but this university business centre has 57 modern en suite rooms and makes for a comfortable stay. There's an on-site restaurant and bar if you don't fancy the steep walk down into town and back.

Blue Sky
CAFE £

(☑01248-355444; www.blueskybangor.co.uk; Ambassador Hall, rear 236 High St; mains £5-11; ☉9.30am-5.30pm Mon-Sat, open evenings when gigs are held; ☑) Blue Sky cafe hides down an alleyway in a former Jehovah's Witness Kingdom Hall, but the secret is out: it's hands down the best joint in town for breakfasts, soups, sandwiches, burgers and salads, with all ingredients sourced from local suppliers. Equally good for afternoon tea and homemade cakes or catching an evening gig.

Kyffin
CAFE £

(☑01248-355161; 129 High St; mains £9; ☉9.30am-5.30pm Mon-Sat; ☑) Kyffin is a true gem: a fair-trade, vegetarian and vegan cafe with antique-shop fittings and a deli counter crammed with organic goodies, chocolates and truffles. As well as serving excellent coffee, it has a large selection of teas – or you can sink into a sofa with a glass of wine and the papers.

☆ Entertainment

Pontio
PERFORMING ARTS

(☑01248-383838, box office 01248-382828; www.pontio.co.uk; Deiniol Rd; ☉8.30am-11pm Mon-Sat, noon-8pm Sun) Pontio cements Bangor's place as the cultural capital of North Wales. Within the fluid, Guggenheim-esque interior of this ambitious new multimillion-pound arts and innovation centre are a 450-seat main theatre, a 120-seat studio theatre and a cinema. Run by Bangor University, it stages drama in English and Welsh, classical music and circus performances and other arts, film festivals and more.

ℹ Information

Ystyby Gwynedd (☑01248-384384; Penrhos Rd, Penrhosgarnedd) Located 2 miles southwest of the city centre, this is the regional hub for accident and emergency (A&E) treatment.

ℹ Getting There & Away

BUS

National Express coaches head to/from Caernarfon (£6.90, 25 minutes), Holyhead (£20, 50 minutes), Birmingham (£29.30, six hours) and London (£38.70, 9½ hours).

The **bus station** (Garth Rd) is located behind the Deiniol Shopping Centre. Bus routes include 5/X5 to Caernarfon (30 minutes), Conwy (40 minutes) and Llandudno (one hour); 53-58 to Menai Bridge (12 minutes) and Beaumaris (35 minutes); 85/86 to Llanberis (30 to 50 minutes);

T2 to Caernarfon (30 minutes), Porthmadog (one hour), Dolgellau (two hours), Machynlleth (2½ hours) and Aberystwyth (3¼ hours); and X4 to Menai Bridge (12 minutes), Llanfair PG (18 minutes), Llangefni (36 minutes) and Holyhead (1½ hours).

Over summer Snowdon Sherpa S6 runs three times per day on weekends and public holidays to Capel Curig (50 minutes) and Betws-y-Coed (one hour).

TRAIN

Bangor's train station is on Holyhead Rd, just off the southwest end of the High St. Direct services head to/from Holyhead (£9.40, 35 minutes), Rhosneigr (£6.70, 25 minutes), Llanfair PG (£3.10, six minutes), Conwy (£6.90, 17 minutes) and London (£91, 3¼ hours).

Bodnant Estate

Whether you're a lover of gardens or fine food, the publicly accessible attractions on this privately owned agricultural estate (www.bodnant-estate.co.uk) should not be missed. While many large country estates fell on hard times in the 20th century, the McLaren family (holders of the title Baron Aberconway) managed to keep hold of theirs. The 2nd Baron Aberconway, a keen horticulturist, donated Bodnant Garden to the National Trust in 1949, although the family continues to maintain it on the trust's behalf.

Sights & Activities

★Bodnant Welsh Food FARM
(01492-651100; www.bodnant-welshfood.co.uk; Furnace Farm, Tal-y-Cafn; farm shop 10am-6pm Mon-Sat, 10am-4pm Sun; P) On the west side of the vast Bodnant Estate, a collection of lavishly restored 18th-century farm buildings now operates as Bodnant Welsh Food. One of the big attractions here is the **Farm Shop**, a wonderful showcase for Welsh produce comprising a bakery, dairy, deli and the kind of butchery that knows the name of practically every animal that passes over the counter. Around three quarters of what's sold here is produced on site or sourced in Wales. If you want to do more than simply consume Welsh cheese, fresh produce, chocolate and ale, there's also a lively program of food-and-wine events and a cookery school above the shop.

Bodnant Garden GARDENS
(NT; 01492-650460; www.bodnant-estate.co.uk/bodnant-garden; Bodnant Estate, Tal-y-Cafn; adult/child whole property £11.25/5.60, winter £5.60/2.80; 10am-5pm Mar-Oct, to 4pm Nov-Feb, to 8pm Wed May-Aug; P) Painstakingly landscaped over 150 years and bequeathed by Lord Aberconway (of the McLaren family) to the National Trust in 1949, Bodnant is one of Wales' most beautiful gardens. Laid out in 1875, its 32 lush hectares unfurl around picturesque Bodnant Hall, the McLaren's gracious late-18th-century pile. Formal Italianate terraces overlook the River Conwy, towards Snowdonia, and rectangular ponds creep down from the house into orderly disorder, transforming themselves into a picturesque wooded valley and wild garden, complete with a rushing stream.

Spring is probably the best time to visit but there's something to see in every season. Key features are the 55m laburnum tunnel, a hair-raising howl of yellow when it blooms in late May/early June; fragrant rose gardens; great banks of azaleas and rhododendrons; and some of the tallest giant redwoods in Britain. Bodnant is 4 miles south of Conwy, just off the A470.

National Beekeeping Centre Wales FARM
(01492-651106; www.beeswales.co.uk; Furnace Farm, Tal-y-Cafn; tours adult/child £7/3.50; 10am-4pm Wed-Sun late-Mar–early Sep) This nonprofit organisation is dedicated to encouraging people to take up beekeeping. Its corner of the Bodnant Welsh Food complex has interesting displays about the plight of the honey bee, a live hive-cam and lots of bee-produced products to sample and purchase. In warm weather it runs apiary tours (minimum two people).

Bodnant Cookery School COOKING
(01492-651108; www.bodnant-welshfood.co.uk; Bodnant Welsh Food, Furnace Farm, Tal-y-Cafn; courses £10-92) The cookery school at Bodnant Welsh Food runs courses for all levels, covering many different cooking skills from its impressive group kitchen classroom. Students make the most of the farm's home-grown and homemade products.

Sleeping & Eating

Bodnant Farmhouse B&B ££
(01492-651100; www.bodnant-welshfood.co.uk/accommodation; Bodnant Welsh Food, Furnace Farm, Tal-y-Cafn; s/d from £65/100; P) Making great use of a refurbished Georgian farmhouse with views across the Conwy Valley, this six-bedroom B&B is just the place to sleep off any excesses or exertions incurred

at Bodnant Estate. Breakfast is served in the nearby Hayloft Restaurant and there's a shared kitchen should you wish to create something using the delightful produce at Bodnant Welsh Food's Farm Shop.

Furnace Tea Room CAFE £
(☎01492-651100; www.bodnant-welshfood.co.uk/furnace-tea-room; Bodnant Welsh Food, Furnace Farm, Tal-y-Cafn; mains £5-7; ⏰9am-5pm Mon-Thu, 9am-5.30pm Fri & Sat, 10am-4.30pm Sun) Set in the former stables of Furnace Farm at Bodnant Welsh Food, these tearooms are ideal for a breakfast bacon bap, a light Welsh rarebit lunch or, between 2.30pm and 4.30pm, afternoon tea. Lavish use is made of the farm's own produce, including freshly churned butter from the dairy.

★Hayloft Restaurant MODERN EUROPEAN ££
(☎01492-651102; www.bodnant-welshfood.co.uk/hayloft-restaurant; Bodnant Welsh Food, Furnace Farm, Tal-y-Cafn; mains £17-20; ⏰noon-3pm Tue-Sun, 6-9pm Tue-Sat) The in-house restaurant at Bodnant Welsh Food is more than an afterthought – offering technically refined dishes such as crab *bavarois* with smoked haddock consommé jelly and granny smith apple, it makes great use of both stand-out produce and a smart, A-framed dining room. It serves lunch, high tea (by appointment), an early evening menu, then, later, the full *carte*. On Thursday nights the restaurant hosts live Welsh folk music and harpists.

Getting There & Away

The estate is located east of the River Conwy, 4 miles south of Conwy. Bodnant Welsh Food is on the A470, while the garden is accessed by a well-signposted side road. There's no public transport to the estate, so you'll need your own wheels.

Conwy

POP 3873

A visit to Britain's most complete walled town should be high on the itinerary for anyone with even a mild crush on things historic. The World Heritage–listed castle continues to dominate the town, as it's done ever since Edward I first planted it here in the late 13th century.

Approaching from the east, the scene is given another theatrical flourish by a tightly grouped trio of bridges crossing the River Conwy, including Thomas Telford's 1826 suspension bridge (one of the first of its kind in the world) and Robert Stephenson's 1848 wrought-iron railway bridge (the first ever tubular bridge).

Sights

★Conwy Castle CASTLE
(Cadw; ☎01492-592358; www.cadw.wales.gov.uk; Castle Sq; adult/child £7.95/5.60; ⏰9.30am-5pm Mar-Jun, Sep & Oct, to 6pm Jul & Aug, to 4pm Nov-Feb; P) Caernarfon is more complete, Harlech more dramatically positioned and Beaumaris more technically perfect, yet out of the four castles that comprise the Unesco World Heritage Site, Conwy is the prettiest to gaze upon. Exploring the castle's nooks and crannies makes for a superb, living-history visit, but best of all, head to the battlements for panoramic views and an overview of Conwy's majestic complexity.

At around £15,000 (over £10 million in today's money), Conwy was Edward I's most costly Welsh stronghold. And if its crenellated turrets and towers call to mind romance and fairy tales rather than subjugation and oppression, it certainly wasn't the intention of its builders.

Constructed between 1283 and 1287, Conwy rises from a rocky outcrop with commanding views across the mountains of Snowdonia and the mouth of the River Conwy. With two barbicans (fortified gateways), eight fierce, slightly tapered towers of coarse dark stone and a great bow-shaped hall all within the elongated complex, it's very solid indeed.

After the Civil War in the 17th century, the castle fell into some disrepair and the Council of State ordered it to be partially pulled down. But today it lives on and is a must-visit for anyone with an interest in Welsh history.

Town Wall HISTORIC BUILDING
FREE The survival of most of its 1300m-long town wall, built concurrently with the castle, makes Conwy one of the UK's prime medieval sites. It was erected to protect the English colonists from the Welsh, who were forbidden from living in the town and were even cleared from the surrounding countryside. You can enter the town walls at several points and walk along the battlements.

Smallest House in Great Britain NOTABLE BUILDING
(☎07925-049786; www.thesmallesthouseingreatbritain.co.uk; Lower Gate St; adult/child £1/50p; ⏰10am-4pm Apr-Oct, longer hours summer) The Smallest House in Great Britain is a curiosity with dimensions of 72 in by 122 in and a

mention in the *Guinness Book of Records*. On the quayside, it's built hard up against the town wall and old houses, which accounts for its meagre dimensions.

Aberconwy House HISTORIC BUILDING

(NT; www.nationaltrust.org.uk; Castle St; adult/child £4/2; ⏲11am-5pm late Feb-Oct) The timber-and-plaster Aberconwy House is the town's oldest, built as one of 20 merchants' houses when the town was fortified around 1300. Over the years it has been a coffee house, temperance hotel, bakery and antique shop, but it remains surprisingly well preserved. An audiovisual presentation shows daily life from different periods of history. The National Trust shop downstairs has a good range of souvenirs and gifts.

Plas Mawr HISTORIC BUILDING

(Cadw; www.cadw.wales.gov.uk; High St; adult/child £6/4.20; ⏲9.30am-5pm Easter-Sep) Completed in 1585 for the merchant and courtier Robert Wynn, Plas Mawr is one of Britain's finest surviving Elizabethan town houses. The tall, whitewashed exterior is an indication of

Conwy

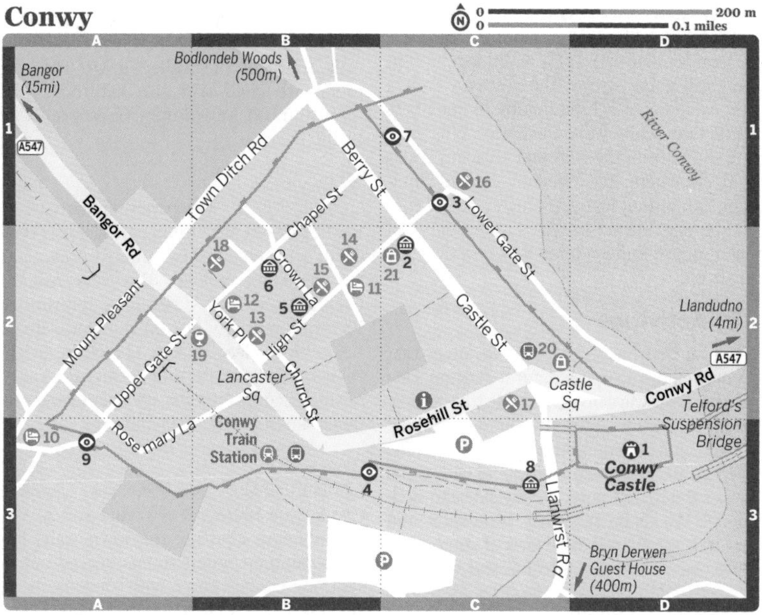

Conwy

Top Sights

1 Conwy Castle D3

Sights

2 Aberconwy House C2
3 Lower Gate C1
4 Mill Gate B3
5 Plas Mawr B2
6 Royal Cambrian Academy B2
7 Smallest House in Great Britain C1
8 Town Wall C3
9 Upper Gate A3

Sleeping

10 Bryn B&B A3
11 Castle Hotel B2
12 Gwynfryn B2

Eating

13 Alfredo's B2
14 Amelie's B2
15 Edwards of Conwy B2
16 Parisella's of Conwy Ice Cream C1
17 Press Room C2
Shakespeare's .... (see 11)
18 Watson's Bistro B2

Drinking & Nightlife

19 Albion Ale House B2

Shopping

20 Knight Shop C2
21 Potter's Gallery C2

CADW JOINT TICKET

Cadw (the Welsh historic monuments agency) offers combined tickets (adult/child £9.80/6.90) for the two historic properties it manages in Conwy: Conwy Castle and Plas Mawr.

the owner's status, but gives no clue to the vivid interior, with its colourful friezes and plasterwork ceilings. The admission price includes a helpful audioguide.

Royal Cambrian Academy GALLERY
(☎01492-593413; www.rcaconwy.org; Crown Lane; ⊙11am-5pm Tue-Sat) FREE Founded in 1881 and still going strong, the academy runs a full calendar of exhibitions by its members in its twin white-walled galleries, plus visiting shows from the National Museum Wales and elsewhere. Its excellent Annual Summer Exhibition, featuring the cream of contemporary fine art in Wales under one roof each August and September, is now over 130 years old.

Activities

With all that history, it's easy to forget that Conwy enjoys a superb natural location. One of the best ways to appreciate the simple country pleasures of Conwy life is by taking a stroll along the quay and the beach towards the marina, hugging the headland with views across the River Conwy on one side and Bodlondeb Woods on the other. It's a short and leisurely stroll with fine views of gently bobbing boats, fluttering bird life and wildflowers peeking through the grassy banks.

Festivals & Events

Gwledd Conwy Feast FOOD & DRINK
(www.gwleddconwyfeast.co.uk; ⊙Oct) Held over a weekend in late October, this food festival, spiced up with music performances and a lantern parade, is the highlight of the Conwy calendar. It incorporates the Blinc digital art festival, with images projected onto the castle walls at night. Around 25,000 people attend, so book accommodation well in advance; nearby Llandudno can accommodate spillover.

Sleeping

Conwy YHA HOSTEL £
(☎08453-719732; www.yha.org.uk; Sychnant Pass Rd, Larkhill; dm/r £22/47; P ᯤ) Perched on a hill above the town, this former hotel has been converted into a top-notch hostel. Dorms have either two or four beds, and many of the private rooms have en suites. Head up to the large dining room for awesome views of the mountains and the sea. Wi-fi only works in the common areas.

To get here, continue from Upper Gate St onto Sychnant Pass Rd; the hostel's up a long drive to the left.

Bryn Derwen Guest House B&B £
(☎01492-596134; www.conwybrynderwen.co.uk; Llanwrst Rd, Woodlands; s/d from £50/60; P ᯤ) Behind steep lawns, this six-bedroom Victorian townhouse B&B is barely a five-minute walk south of the walled town. The rear rooms are small, with tiny bathrooms, but they're priced accordingly. Guests must be 12 and over.

★**Gwynfryn** B&B ££
(☎01492-576733; www.gwynfrynbandb.co.uk; 4 York Pl; r £65-90; ᯤ) Although it seems in danger of being engulfed by butterfly ornaments and dangling mobiles, this very friendly five-bedroom B&B – set in a refurbished Victorian property just off the main square – is a great place to stay. The clean, bright rooms are filled with thoughtful extras such as small fridges, biscuits, chocolates and earplugs. Guests must be 15 and over.

Bryn B&B B&B ££
(☎01492-592449; www.bryn.org.uk; Sychnant Pass Rd; s/d £60/80; P ᯤ) This sturdy Victorian house abutting the town walls has five sumptuous guest rooms decked out in soothing creams, three with king-size beds. Breakfast is a delight, with freshly baked bread and organic/fair-trade ingredients. Special diets are accommodated and nothing is too much trouble for the congenial proprietor.

Castle Hotel HOTEL ££
(☎01492-582800; www.castlewales.co.uk; High St; s/d/ste from £77/114/216; P ᯤ) A major refit has loosened the tie on this once-stuffy coaching inn, built on the site of Conwy's vanished Cistercian Abbey. The bedrooms feature contemporary decor and Bose sound systems, while some boast castle views and free-standing baths. The Castle has hosted an impressive roll of literary visitors: William Wordsworth, Charlotte Brontë, Samuel Johnson and Robert Louis Stevenson.

Massage, beauty and therapeutic treatments are available in its 'Healing Hands' centre.

Eating & Drinking

★ Parisella's of Conwy Ice Cream ICE CREAM £
(www.parisellasicecream.co.uk; Conwy Quay; per scoop £2; ⌚10.30am-5.30pm) The kiosk on the quay sells a selection of what we consider to be the best ice cream in Wales. The best of Parisella's 50-plus flavours include mint choc chip, salted caramel, and amaretto and black cherry. It also has a **parlour** (12 High St; ⌚10am-5pm); seagulls gather outside both locations to mug unsuspecting lickers on busy days.

Edwards of Conwy DELI £
(☎01492-592443; www.edwardsofconwy.co.uk; 18 High St; pies £5; ⌚7am-5.30pm Mon-Sat) While first and foremost a butchery with a great line in Welsh meat, Edwards also sells savoury pies, local cheeses and freshly filled baps and sandwiches. Awards are continually piled on the deli for everything from its sausages to its pork pies.

Press Room CAFE £
(☎01492-592242; 3 Rose Hill St; mains £6-8; ⌚10am-4.30pm;) Located right next to the castle entrance, this arty cafe serves a tasty selection of meals, including rarebit made with ciabatta and a good choice of cakes and scones to finish up with. There's a terrace setting for an alfresco lunch and a craft shop downstairs.

★ Watson's Bistro WELSH ££
(☎01492-596326; www.watsonsbistroconwy.co.uk; Bishop's Yard, Chapel St; 2-course lunch £13, mains £18-20; ⌚noon-2pm Wed-Sun, 5.30-8pm Tue-Sun) Hidden in a verdant garden setting in the lee of the town wall, Watson's marries French bistro cooking with quality local ingredients. Everything is homemade, from the chicken-liver pâté to the ox-cheek with 'dirty carrots' to the ice cream. Book to arrive before 6.30pm for the early-bird set menu (three courses £21).

Alfredo's ITALIAN ££
(☎01492-592381; 9-10 Lancaster Sq; mains £9-23; ⌚6-9.30pm Mon-Sat;) There's something tremendously appealing about the stereotypical Italian-ness of Alfredo's (chequered tablecloths, fake ivy, fairy lights draped from the ceiling, shabby carpets and a giant menu of pasta, pizza and traditional grills) that could only be enhanced with comedy moustaches and loud exclamations of 'mamma mia'. Importantly, the food is very good.

Shakespeare's INTERNATIONAL ££
(☎01492-582800; www.castlewales.co.uk; Castle Hotel, High St; mains £15-19; ⌚noon-9.30pm;) With flocked wallpaper and gilt-framed orientalist scenes covering the walls, and dapperly dressed staff delivering tasty brasserie-style meals, Shakespeare's is Conwy's swankiest dining environment. The adjoining bar – named for the Victorian painter John Dawson Watson, an adoptive son of Conwy who designed the castle's facade – offers the same menu, wines and ales in similarly upmarket surrounds.

Amelie's FRENCH ££
(☎01492-583142; 10 High St; lunch £6-9, dinner £13-16; ⌚11.30am-2.15pm & 6-9pm Tue-Sat;) Named after the Audrey Tautou film, Amelie's has the feel of a French bistro, with wooden floors and flowers on the tables, but offers a multinational menu including shanks, curries, steaks, fish and more. It's a relaxed place, equally good for a light lunch or a more hefty evening meal.

★ Albion Ale House PUB
(☎01492-582484; www.albionalehouse.weebly.com; 1-4 Upper Gate St; ⌚noon-11pm;) Born out of a collaboration of four Welsh craft breweries (Purple Moose, Conwy, Nant and Great Orme), this heritage-listed 1920s boozer is a serious beer-drinker's nirvana. Of the 10 hand pulls, eight are loaded with real ale and two with cider. Winner of multiple Wales and North Wales pub-of the-year awards, the Albion looks after wine and whisky drinkers, too.

There's no TV or background music – just the crackle of the fire, the gentle hum of conversation and the odd contented slurp. The good news for Conwy's Camra (Campaign for Real Ale) connoisseurs is that the collective looks set to create something similar in the Bridge Inn, opposite the castle.

Shopping

Knight Shop GIFTS & SOUVENIRS
(☎01492-541300; www.theknightshop.co.uk; Castle Sq; ⌚10am-5pm) Always buying boring, samey souvenirs for your loved ones? Then why not go for a Henry VIII–era replica helmet, a ramshead heavy siege crossbow, some chain mail or perhaps a Viking drinking horn? The Knight Shop is appropriately located across the street from Conwy Castle.

Potter's Gallery
ARTS & CRAFTS

(☑ 01492-593590; www.thepottersgallery.co.uk; 1 High St; ⊙10am-5pm Mar-Dec, closed Wed Jan & Feb) Run by a cooperative of North Wales-based potters and designers, this gallery showcases the latest works from its members and is a mine of information about the local arts scene.

ℹ Information

Tourist Office (☑ 01492-577566; www.visitllandudno.org.uk; Muriau Buildings, Rose Hill St; ⊙9am-5pm Mon-Fri, 10am-4pm Sat & Sun) Extremely busy office, well stocked with pamphlets and souvenirs and staffed by very helpful local experts. There's an interesting interactive exhibition on the princes of Gwynedd in the adjoining room.

ℹ Getting There & Away

BUS
Bus routes include 5/X5 to Caernarfon (1¼ hours), Bangor (40 minutes) and Llandudno (22 minutes); 14/15 to Llandudno (20 minutes); and 19 to Llandudno (22 minutes) and Betws-y-Coed (50 minutes). Buses to Llandudno leave from the stop near Castle Sq, while those to Bangor/Caernarfon leave from outside the train station.

CAR
Through-traffic bypasses Conwy on the A55 via a tunnel under the river. The main road into town from Bangor skirts the outside of the town walls before cutting inside the walls, crawling along Berry and Castle Sts and heading across the road bridge. The rest of the narrow grid within the walls has a one-way system and restricted parking during the day.

There are pay-and-display car parks on Mt Pleasant and by the castle. If you're after a free park and don't mind a 10-minute walk, turn right off Bangor Rd on the second-to-last street before you reach the town walls, cross the narrow rail bridge and park on residential Cadnant Park.

TRAIN
Conwy's train station is just inside the town walls on Rosemary Lane. Direct services head to/from Holyhead (£14.70, one hour), Rhosneigr (£14.70, 44 minutes), Llanfair PG (£8.20, 26 minutes), Bangor (£6.90, 20 minutes) and Shrewsbury (£17.50, two hours).

Llandudno Junction
POP 10,658

Llandudno Junction, located across the estuary from Conwy, has grown around the Llandudno Junction railway station. It's here that passengers from Cardiff, London or Holyhead need to disembark and change if they're Llandudno- or Conwy-bound.

⊙ Sights

Conwy Nature Reserve
BIRD SANCTUARY

(☑ 01492-584091; www.rspb.org.uk; North Wales Expressway; adult/child £5/2.50; ⊙9.30am-5pm, closed Christmas Day; 🚻) Christmas for twitchers, this Royal Society for the Protection of Birds (RSPB) sanctuary on the lovely Conwy estuary is home to lapwings, sedge warblers, shelducks and the superbly named black-tailed godwit. Hides and wheelchair-accessible trails make for good going, while guided bird-spotting and family activities such as wildlife bingo keep interest levels high. There's a cafe (open 10am to 4pm) and easy access along the A456 from Llandudno Junction.

🛏 Sleeping

★ **Bodysgallen Hall**
HISTORIC HOTEL £££

(NT; ☑ 01492-584466; www.bodysgallen.com; s/d/ste from £160/180/435; P 🛜 🏊) Managed by the National Trust, this magnificent pink-stone 1620 country house set in spectacular French-style formal gardens lets you lose yourself in the wood-panelled world of the Jacobean gentry. The rooms, split between the main hall and outlying cottages, are traditional with a nod to mod cons, and there's a well-regarded restaurant and spa centre in the grounds.

Bodysgallen is 3 miles south of Llandudno, on the A470.

✖ Eating & Drinking

★ **Enochs**
FISH & CHIPS ££

(☑ 01492-581145; www.enochs.co.uk; 146 Conwy Rd; mains £9-17; ⊙11.30am-8.30pm, takeaway to 9.30pm; 🚻) 🍴 Customers come from miles around to sample the offerings at nautically themed Enochs, a fish-and-chip joint dedicated to sustainable fishing. The mains are a perfect blend of tender fish and crispy batter, unless you opt to have yours cooked *en papillote* (in baking paper). Locals love Enochs so much it's opened a second cafe in Valley on Anglesey.

Providero
CAFE

(148 Conwy Rd; coffee £2; ⊙8am-6pm Mon-Fri, from 9.30am Sat) What started out as a North Coast–plying coffee van has found a permanent home in this wonderful thimble-sized cafe. You may well find yourself lingering over a cup of locally roasted coffee or one of

the 30-plus types of tea, propping up the bar and watching the friendly barista work their latte-art magic.

Getting There & Away

The railway, Llandudno Junction's raison d'être, connects to Llandudno (£2.90, eight minutes), Conwy (£2.90, two minutes), Betws-y-Coed (£6.30, 28 minutes), Chester (£19.20, 55 minutes) and London Euston (£87.10, three to four hours).

Buses include the X1 to Llandudno (15 minutes), Betws-y-Coed (35 minutes) and Blaenau Ffestiniog (one hour); the A55 to Caernarfon (one hour); and the X5 to Bangor (45 minutes).

Llandudno

POP 15,371

Wales' biggest seaside resort straddles a peninsula with long sandy beaches on either side. Developed as an upmarket holiday town for Victorian visitors, Llandudno still retains much of its 19th-century grandeur, with graceful Victorian wedding-cake architecture lining its sweeping waterfront promenade. Innumerable B&Bs and small private hotels cater to mainly mature-aged travellers in the low season, while young families descend with their buckets and spades in summer.

Alongside the lost-in-time charms of the British seaside (pier, promenade, Punch and Judy shows), Llandudno's main attraction is the near-wilderness of the Great Orme (p282) on its doorstep, a striking, rough-hewn headland where there are breathtaking views of the Snowdonia range and miles of trails to explore.

A very tenuous link to *Alice In Wonderland* (Alice Liddell, the real inspiration for Lewis Carroll's fictional Alice, used to holiday here with her family) has seen statues of the book's characters sprout around the town.

Sights

Centre

Mostyn Gallery GALLERY
(www.mostyn.org; 12 Vaughan St; 10.30am-4pm Tue-Sun) FREE A sensitively restored, heritage-listed 1901 terracotta-and-brick exterior hides the sharply angled innards of North Wales' leading contemporary art gallery. Its six galleries house changing and often challenging exhibitions, and were amongst the first to exhibit female artists in Britain. Call in to explore the shop or grab a coffee upstairs, even if you find the art perplexing.

WORTH A TRIP

COUNTRY COMFORT

Kinmel Arms (01745-832207; www.thekinmelarms.co.uk; St George; ste 2-night stay from £115; Tue-Sat; P) is a rural enclave of fine food, real ales and, now, four beautifully finished boutique suites. But it's the restaurant (mains £17 to £25), one of Wales' most justly acclaimed gastropubs, that's the main attraction here. Cooked breakfasts aren't offered, but room fridges are stocked with breakfast fare the night before.

St George is near the eastern edge of Conwy and the North Wales coast. While there's not too much to entice visitors to this little hamlet, the Kinmel Arms is an exception.

Llandudno Promenade WATERFRONT
Llandudno's iconic 2-mile promenade is one of its distinctive sights. It was here that Queen Victoria herself watched Professor Codman's Punch & Judy Show (p285), performed by the same family since 1860 – we hope she was amused. Mr Punch's iconic red-and-white-striped tent sits by the entrance to the Victorian pier.

Llandudno Pier LANDMARK
(9am-6pm;) A trip to Llandudno isn't complete until you've strolled along the Victorian pier, eating ice cream and shooing away seagulls. At 670m it's Wales' longest. When it opened in 1878 its main use was as a disembarkation point for passengers from the Isle of Man steamers. Those days are long gone, and candyfloss, slot machines and views of the offshore wind farm are now the order of the day. High art it ain't, but the kids will love it.

Llandudno Cable Car CABLE CAR
(01492-877205; adult/child return £9/7; 10am-6pm Apr-Oct) Britain's longest cable car runs a mile from the Happy Valley Gardens above the pier and, if it's not too windy, whisks passengers up to the summit of the Great Orme in just 18 minutes, with superb sea views en route.

Great Orme & Around

Great Orme Tramway CABLE CAR
(01492-577877; www.greatormetramway.co.uk; Victoria Station, Church Walks; adult/child return £7/5; 10am-6pm Easter-Oct) Head to the top

of the Great Orme without breaking a sweat in an original 1902 tramcar. It's one of only three cable-operated trams in the world (the other two are in equally glamorous Lisbon and San Francisco). Trips head up the steep incline every 20 minutes, weather permitting; change to a second tram at the Halfway Station.

Marine Drive WATERFRONT

(drivers & cyclists £2.50; ⏲9am-8pm) Starting by the pier, this one-way, 4-mile narrow road loops anticlockwise around the Great Orme, with immense sea vistas opening up on your right-hand side. There are few places to pull over along the loop, but you can take the branch road that heads up to the Great Orme summit a quarter of the way along.

★Great Orme HILL

(Y Gogarth) From sea level it's difficult to gauge the sheer scale of the Great Orme (Y Gogarth), yet it stretches for around 2 miles and rises to a height of 207m. Named after a Norse word for 'worm' or 'sea serpent', this gentle giant looms benevolently over the town. Designated a Site of Special Scientific Interest (SSSI), the headland is home to a cornucopia of flowers, butterflies and sea birds and a herd of around 150 wild Kashmir mountain goats.

Three waymarked trails (of which the Haulfre Gardens Trail is the easiest to negotiate) lead to the summit and there's a neolithic burial chamber, a Bronze Age mine, the remains of an Iron Age fort, and an ancient church dedicated to Llandudno's namesake, St Tudno. At the summit there's a cafe, bar, gift shop, minigolf and other amusements, as well as the Great Orme Country Park Visitor Centre (p285), which has lots of fascinating displays including a 15-minute video. Views – across the Irish Sea and its fertile wind farms in one direction, overlooking Llandudno towards Snowdonia in the other – are stunning.

Llandudno

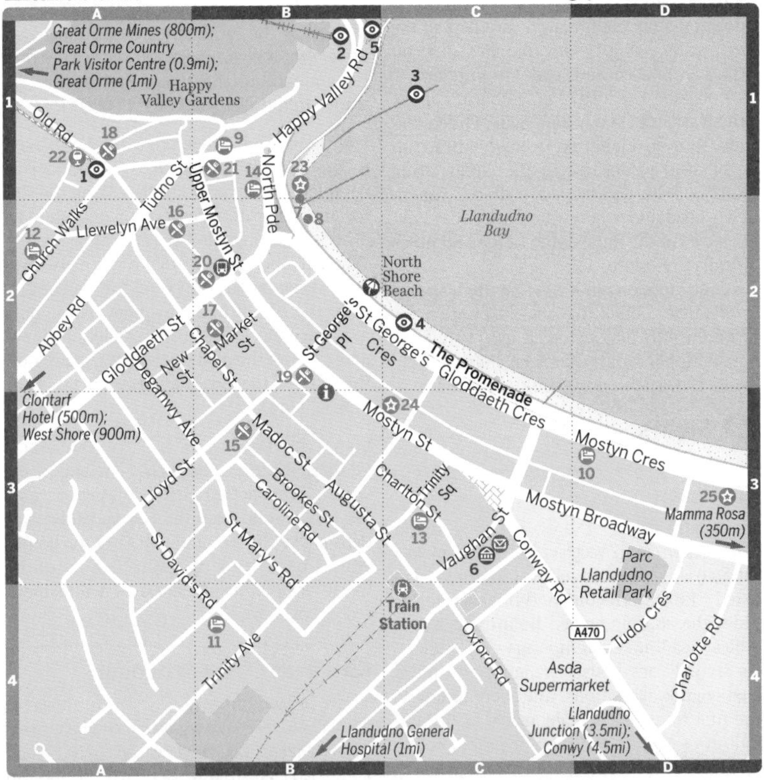

★ **Great Orme Mines** MINE
(www.greatormemines.info; adult/child £6.75/4.75; ⏲9.30am-5.30pm mid-Mar–Oct) Sitting unobtrusively near the top of the Great Orme is the largest prehistoric mine ever discovered. Nearly paved over for a car park, this site of tremendous historical importance has been developed as a must-see attraction, with a visitor centre and the chance to explore portions of the 5 miles of tunnels dug over centuries in search of copper. What is truly astounding is that 4000 years ago the tools used to excavate this maze were just stones and bones.

A 45-minute self-guided tour explains how the ancients turned rock into copper at the smelting site and then heads underground for about 200m into 3500-year-old tunnels. The site was worked again from the 17th to 19th centuries; its discovery moved Britain's metallurgic history back a cool 2000 years.

West Shore BEACH
When the main beach gets too frantic, go west to this considerably less built-up stretch on Conwy Bay. The views over Anglesey and the mountains of Snowdonia can be stunning, especially as the sun sets, and there's a model boating pool at the Orme end. It's just a shame that the water quality on this side is substandard.

Activities

Llandudno Land Train BUS
(£4; ⏲9am-5.30pm) During the school holidays this colourful trackless 'train' runs a regular shuttle from the pier to the West Shore and back. All up, with a 15-minute cafe pit stop, the circuit takes about an hour.

City Sightseeing BUS
(☎01492-879133; www.city-sightseeing.com; adult/child £9/4; ⏲Mar-Sep) Departs from the pier for a hop-on/hop-off double-decker bus tour of Llandudno and Conwy, with prerecorded commentary. Tickets are valid for 24 hours.

Festivals & Events

Victorian Extravaganza PERFORMING ARTS
(www.victorian-extravaganza.com; ⏲May) Llandudno plays dress-up for this annual event, held over the early May bank holiday weekend. It's the social event of the year, with a daily parade, strolling Victorian characters, bands, funfairs – and grossly over-inflated accommodation prices.

Sleeping

Beach Cove B&B £
(☎01492-879638; 8 Church Walks; s/d £35/65; 📶) A stone's throw from both the Great Orme and the Promenade, this eight-room B&B represents excellent value for money, particularly for single travellers. The decor is all light wood and creams, breakfast is ample and if you're travelling with your sweetie, splurge a little on the four-poster room (£75).

Llandudno Hostel HOSTEL £
(☎01492-877430; www.llandudnohostel.co.uk; 14 Charlton St; dm £25, tw £60-65, f £150; P📶) Staking out the middle ground between

Llandudno

Sights
1 Great Orme Tramway A1
2 Llandudno Cable Car B1
3 Llandudno Pier C1
4 Llandudno Promenade C2
5 Marine Drive B1
6 Mostyn Gallery C3

Activities, Courses & Tours
7 City Sightseeing B2
8 Llandudno Land Train B2

Sleeping
9 Beach Cove B1
10 Can-y-Bae D3
11 Cliffbury B4
12 Escape B&B A2
13 Llandudno Hostel C3
14 Osborne House B1

Eating
15 Candles B3
16 Characters A2
17 Cottage Loaf B2
18 Fish Tram Chips A1
19 Ham Bone Food Hall & Brasserie B2
20 Orient-Express B2
Osborne's Cafe Grill .... (see 14)
21 Seahorse B1

Drinking & Nightlife
22 King's Head A1

Entertainment
23 Professor Codman's Punch & Judy Show B1
24 St John's Methodist Church C3
25 Venue Cymru D3

hostel and budget B&B, this powder-blue Victorian townhouse offers tidy rooms, bike storage and a free continental breakfast. It's family run and very family friendly – not the kind of place for booze hounds, but then neither is Llandudno. Kitchen facilities are limited to a microwave and kettle.

★**Escape B&B** B&B ££
(01492-877776; www.escapebandb.co.uk; 48 Church Walks; r £95-149; P) Escape brought a style revolution to Llandudno with its boutique-chic ambience and magazine-spread design. Its most recent, design-led makeover then added a host of energy-saving and trendsetting features. Even if you're not a *Wallpaper** subscriber, you'll love the honesty-bar lounge, Bose iPod docks, DVD library, tasty breakfasts and atmosphere of indulgence. Unique.

Clontarf Hotel HOTEL ££
(01492-877621; www.clontarfhotel.co.uk; 2 Great Ormes Rd; s £46, d £66-89; P) The nine individually styled rooms at this small, friendly hotel come with luxurious touches: sophisticated showers in three of the rooms and a four-poster bed and whirlpool bath in the Romantic room. All rooms look out either onto the sea or the Great Orme (p282), a small bar contributes to evening relaxation and the friendly proprietor cooks up delicious breakfasts.

Can-y-Bae HOTEL ££
(01492-874188; www.can-y-baehotel.com; 10 Mostyn Cres; s/d from £40/80;) Just down the road from Venue Cymru (p285), this welcoming, gay-friendly hotel accommodates many a visiting thespian among its mainly older clientele. Signed memorabilia blankets the walls of the little residents' bar and there's a piano if anyone wants to start a sing along. It's even smarter, following a refurb in 2015.

Cliffbury B&B ££
(01492-877224; www.thecliffbury.co.uk; 34 St David's Rd; r £70-82; P) Set on a quiet backstreet, this attractive corner house has six individually styled B&B rooms; two are suites and the remaining four are almost suite-like in their proportions. The friendly owners tactfully describe the place as 'mainly catering for over 25s'.

Osborne House HOTEL £££
(01492-860330; www.osbornehouse.co.uk; 17 North Pde; ste £175-200; P) All marble, antique furniture and fancy drapes, the lavish Osborne House takes a classical approach to aesthetics and the results are impressive. The best suites are on the 1st floor with Victorian-style sitting rooms and sea views. Guests have use of the spa and swimming pools at nearby sister property, the Empire Hotel.

Eating & Drinking

Orient-Express CAFE £
(01492-879990; 8 Gloddaeth St; mains £5-10; 8am-5pm;) Brown leather, dark wood, chandeliers and tight confines conjure a faint impression of train travel's golden age, but above all this is simply a welcoming, child-friendly cafe. While it's possible to get standard British cafe food here, the best bets are the Turkish dishes that show the owner's origins – halloumi, grilled chicken, dolmas, baklava and the like.

Fish Tram Chips FISH & CHIPS £
(01492-872673; www.fish-tram-chips.co.uk; 22-24 Old Rd; mains £7-10; noon-7.30pm) Consistently serving up tasty, fresh fish and homemade side dishes with unaffected friendliness, this is where the locals head for good-value fish meals. Probably the best bargain in Llandudno, its opening hours are extended in summer.

Ham Bone Food Hall & Brasserie DELI £
(01492-860084; www.hambone.co.uk; 3 Lloyd St; mains £6-10; 8am-5pm Mon-Sat, 10am-4pm Sun;) The best deli-cafe in Llandudno serves a huge range of freshly made sandwiches, perfect for a picnic on the Promenade. Breakfast is served until 11.30am, or come in at lunchtime for burgers, fishcakes, steak-and-ale pies, huge pizzas and an ever-changing selection of specials. From July to September it stays open until 9pm Thursday to Saturday.

★**Characters** CAFE ££
(01492-872290; www.charactersllandudno.com; 11 Llewelyn Ave; lunch £5-7, dinner £15-21; 11am-4pm Mon-Thu, 11am-8.30pm Fri & Sat;) If you're wondering whether it's the place that's full of character or the people running it, it's both. Llandudno's hippest tearoom serves wonderful cream teas (£5) and three-tiered high teas (£10), along with light lunches of sandwiches, soup and jacket potatoes; avoid the coffee. Weekends sizzle with hot-stone dinners.

★Cottage Loaf PUB FOOD ££
(☎01492-870762; www.the-cottageloaf.co.uk; Market St; mains £9-16; ⊙kitchen noon-9pm; 📶) Tucked down an alleyway off Mostyn St, this charismatic pub has print-strewn walls, carpeted wooden floors and an atmosphere of genuine bonhomie. The excellent food ranges from the traditional – slow-roasted pork belly, beef-and-ale pie and their ilk – to the more exotic, and there are both plenty of good beers and a flower-strewn terrace to enhance it.

Osborne's Cafe Grill BRASSERIE ££
(☎01492-860330; www.osbornehouse.co.uk; 17 North Pde; mains £10-14; ⊙10.30am-9.30pm; 📶) If you really want to live the grand Victorian fantasy, starch your shirt and head to Osborne House (p284), where military types peer out of gilt frames from black walls offset with white columns and candle-powered chandeliers. The seafood-heavy menu values tradition over contemporary tomfoolery and the prices are very reasonable given the ambience.

Mamma Rosa ITALIAN ££
(☎01492-870070; www.mammarosa.co.uk; 11 Mostyn Ave; mains £9-15; ⊙6-9pm Wed-Sun; 🖉) The front-parlour setting of this family restaurant is a clue to the Italian home cooking on offer. The lengthy menu is full of pasta, risotto, pizza and traditional grills, although the chef gets to show off on a specials page crammed with seafood, steak and other prime ingredients.

Candles EUROPEAN ££
(☎01492-874422; www.candlesllandudno.com; 29 Lloyd St; mains £16-25, 3-/4-course menu £20/22; ⊙5.30-10pm; 🖉) Popular with locals for celebration meals, this cosy family-run cellar restaurant serves a hearty selection of British, French and Italian dishes. Staff are friendly, the set menus are good value, and there's even a four-course vegetarian alternative available (£21; look out for the chef-proprietor's inventive touch with Quorn, a meat-substitute product).

Seahorse SEAFOOD £££
(☎01492-875315; www.the-seahorse.co.uk; 7 Church Walks; mains £15-23; ⊙4.30-10pm) The chef at this, Llandudno's only dedicated seafood restaurant, is a keen fisherman and the menu reflects his passion for the local catch: specials might be local mussels, or fresh anchovies in tempura batter. The restaurant is a split-level affair: upstairs is decorated with large Mediterranean murals, while the more intimate cellar room has a cosier feel.

King's Head PUB
(☎01492-877993; www.kingsheadllandudno.co.uk; Old Rd; ⊙noon-11pm Mon-Thu & Sun, to midnight Fri & Sat; 📶) Dating from the late 18th century, Llandudno's oldest pub is a great place for a quiet pint or a hearty meal (£11 to £16), especially if you've just toiled up and down the Great Orme (p282). There's a music quiz on Tuesday and a general knowledge quiz on Wednesday.

☆ Entertainment

Professor Codman's Punch & Judy Show PERFORMING ARTS
(☎07900-555515; www.punchandjudy.com/codgal.htm; The Promenade; ⊙2pm & 4pm Sat & Sun year-round, daily school holidays Easter–mid-Sep) Queen Victoria herself watched this show, performed by the same family with the same puppets since 1860. Mr Punch's iconic red-and-white-striped tent sits near the entrance to the pier (p281). If you're not familiar with the Punch and Judy tradition, you might be surprised by the violence and puppet-spouse abuse – but the kids don't seem to mind.

Venue Cymru PERFORMING ARTS
(☎01472-872000; www.venuecymru.co.uk; The Promenade; ⊙box office 10am-7pm Mon-Sat, plus 1hr before performances) Having undergone a major expansion, Venue Cymru is one of North Wales' leading event and performance venues. The line-up covers all bases from big rock gigs to high-brow classical performances, big-name stand-ups, musicals and shows for children.

St John's Methodist Church LIVE MUSIC
(☎01492-860439; www.stjohnsllandudno.org; 53 Mostyn St; adult/Conwy-card holder £6/1) Built in 1866, this church hosts a summer season of performances (8pm, May to October) with choirs on Tuesday and Thursday and brass bands most weekends.

ⓘ Information

Great Orme Country Park Visitor Centre
(www.conwy.gov.uk/greatorme; ⊙9.30am-5.30pm Easter-Oct) The visitor centre on the summit of the Great Orme has 3D and interactive displays on the geology and flora and fauna of the area. It organises two-hour guided walks of the headland every Sunday from May to September.

Llandudno General Hospital (☎01492-860066; Hospital Rd; ⊙8am-10pm) One mile south of the town centre, off the A546. The nearest accident and emergency (A & E) department is at Ystyby Gwynedd (p274) in Bangor.

Llandudno Tourist Office (☎01492-577577; www.visitllandudno.org.uk; Mostyn St; ⊙9.30am-4.30pm) In the library building, with helpful staff and an accommodation booking service.

Getting There & Away

Llandudno's train station is centrally located on Augusta St. Direct services head to/from Betws-y-Coed (£6.30, 50 minutes), Blaenau Ffestiniog (£8.70, 1¼ hours), Chester (£20, one hour) and Manchester Piccadilly (£33, 2¼ hours); for other destinations you'll need to change at Llandudno Junction (£2.90, eight minutes).

Buses stop on the corner of Upper Mostyn St and Gloddaeth St. National Express coaches head to/from Liverpool (£14.20, 2½ hours), Manchester (£18.20, four hours), Birmingham (£35, five hours) and London (£37.50, 8¾ hours). Other bus routes include 5/X5 to Caernarfon (1½ hours), Bangor (one hour) and Conwy (22 minutes); 14/15 to Conwy (21 minutes); and 19 to Conwy (22 minutes) and Betws-y-Coed (70 minutes).

Parking is metered during the day on the main part of the Promenade, but it's free once you get past the roundabout east of Venue Cymru.

Getting Around

Llandudno Bike Hire (☎07496-455188; www.llandudnobikehire.com; Harmony House, St George's Pl; ⊙9.30am-5pm Tue-Sun) Llandudno's elongated promenade and surrounding natural attractions make it a good place to explore on two wheels, and Debbie from Llandudno Bike Hire has you covered. Standard bikes are £15 per day, electric bikes £40 and you can throw in some free advice on where to use them.

ISLE OF ANGLESEY (YNYS MÔN)

At 276 sq miles, the Isle of Anglesey is Wales' largest island and bigger than any in England. It's a popular destination for visitors with miles of inspiring coastline, hidden beaches and Wales' greatest concentration of ancient sites. A brush with royalty has given Anglesey an added cachet in recent years, with the Duke and Duchess of Cambridge setting up home here for the three years Wills served at the Royal Air Force base in Valley.

Almost all of the Anglesey coast has been designated as an Area of Outstanding Natural Beauty. The handsome Georgian town of Beaumaris is its most obviously attractive, but there are hidden gems scattered all over the island. It's very much a living centre of

THE DRUIDS

The magical mystique that the ancient druids enjoy today is assisted by a lack of evidence – coming from an oral culture, they naturally wrote down nothing about their beliefs. It is known that they had charge of Celtic religion and ritual, and were educators and healers as well as political advisors and so were vastly influential. However, the main sources of information about this spiritual aristocracy are Roman scholars, whose accounts are seen through an adversarial glass. The Romans are coloured as a civilising force and the Celts and druids as bloodthirsty and keen on human sacrifice.

Resistance to the Romans was powered by druidic influence in Britain. Anglesey was a major seat of druidic learning because of its strategic placement between Wales, Ireland and France. According to the Roman historian Tacitus, when the Romans attacked Anglesey in AD 60, they were terrified by the resident wild women and holy fanatics who greeted them with howls and prayers, and the Romans found the altars there covered in the blood of prisoners. The conquerors set about destroying the druids' shrines and sacred groves, and did all they could to impress their culture on the locals, but the result was inevitably a mix of new and old beliefs.

Druidism became a fashionable interest in the 18th century and the Welsh poetic tradition is believed to stem from the druids. In 1820 Edward Williams created druidic ceremonies to be performed during the annual Eisteddfod, which accounts for many of the long beards and solemn ceremonies still in evidence at this festival of poetry and literature today.

Welsh culture, too, as you can see for yourself at Oriel Ynys Môn.

History

From prehistoric times, Anglesey's fertile land was settled by small communities of farmers. The island was holy to the Celts and, in AD 60, it was the last part of Wales to fall to the Romans. Given its outpost status and singular character, Anglesey has as fair a claim as any to being the Welsh heartland. One ancient name for the isle, bestowed by the prelate and historian Gerald of Wales in the 12th century, was Môn mam Cymru: 'Mother of Wales'.

Llanfairpwllgwyngyllgogerychwyrndrobwllllantysiliogogogoch (Llanfair PG)

POP 3107

The small town with the absurdly long, consonant-mangling name is an unlikely hot spot for visitors, yet coaches stop by frequently, waiting while their passengers jostle for a photo opportunity on the train station platform (go on, you know you want to). The name (which means St Mary's Church in the Hollow of the White Hazel near a Rapid Whirlpool and the Church of St Tysilio near the Red Cave) was dreamt up in the 19th century to get the tourists in. And it worked. The previous name Llanfairpwllgwyngyll would have been hard enough; most locals call it Llanfairpwll but you'll often see it written as Llanfair PG.

Getting There & Away

Buses head to/from Holyhead (X4; one hour), Llangefni (4A, 44A, X4; 19 minutes), Menai Bridge (4A, 44A, X4; five minutes) and Bangor (4A, 43, 44A, X4; 18 minutes).

Direct trains head to/from Holyhead (£8.30, 29 minutes), Rhosneigr (£6.30, 18 minutes), Bangor (£3.10, eight minutes), Conwy (£8.20, 30 minutes) and Shrewsbury (£39.10, 2½ hours).

Menai Bridge

POP 4958

It's a testimony to his genius that not only does engineer extraordinaire Thomas Telford have a large town in Shropshire named after him, this small town is named after one of his creations. The industrial age arrived in Anglesey in 1826 when Telford established the first permanent link to the mainland with his innovative 174m Menai Suspension Bridge across the Menai Strait – the first bridge of its kind in the world. The central span is 30m high, allowing for the passage of tall ships. It was joined in 1850 by Robert Stephenson's **Britannia Bridge**, further south, which carried the newly laid railway.

WORTH A TRIP

LLANGEFNI

The lively arts centre of **Oriel Ynys Môn** (☎01248-724444; www.orielynysmon.info; Rhosmeirch, Llangefni; ⊙10.30am-5pm; P) is the linchpin of Anglesey's visual-arts scene. The art space hosts a program of exhibitions, the **History Gallery** explores Anglesey's past and its pivotal role in the Roman invasion, plus there's a great licensed cafe (Blas Mwy; open 10am to 4.30pm) and a children's discovery area for rainy days. But the main draw is the **Oriel Kyffin Williams**: exhibits change regularly but always feature some of the gallery's 400-plus Williams works.

Sir John 'Kyffin' Williams was a prolific artist whose portraits and landscapes provide a unique window into Welsh culture. While Oriel Ynys Môn's history museum is strangely disjointed, it's still a good place to top up your knowledge of the Roman invasion.

Sights & Activities

Thomas Telford Centre MUSEUM

(☎01248-715046; www.menaibridges.co.uk; Mona Rd; adult/child £3/free; ⊙10am-5pm Wed & Thu Apr-Oct) This small, volunteer-run museum is the best way to learn more about the feats of Victorian engineering that lie behind the iconic bridges connecting Anglesey to the mainland, and to explore the ecology of the Menai Straits. The friendly volunteers of Menai Heritage regularly arrange talks, tours and family activities to show off some of their deserved local pride.

RibRide BOATING

(☎03331-234303; www.ribride.co.uk; Water St, Porth Daniel; adult/child from £24/16) For an adrenaline kick take a blast out to sea on a rigid inflatable boat (RIB) through the Menai Strait, to Puffin Island, or past Caernarfon Castle to Llanddwyn Island.

1

TIPWAM / SHUTTERSTOCK ©

2

1. Conwy (p276)
The Smallest House in Great Britain, on Conwy's quayside.

2. Britannia Bridge (p287)
Robert Stephenson's bridge across the Menai Strait, linking the Isle of Anglesey to the mainland.

3. South Stack Lighthouse (p297)
A steep trail along a rocky islet leads to the reputedly haunted lighthouse.

4. Bodnant Garden (p275)
A peacock struts through the beautifully landscaped gardens.

4

JULIUSKIELAITIS / SHUTTERSTOCK ©

DON'T MISS

ANGLESEY'S SOUTHERN CORNER

Sights & Activities

Bryn Celli Ddu Burial Chamber (Cadw; www.cadw.gov.wales; 10am-4pm) There are neolithic burial mounds scattered all around Wales, but many have been completely stripped of their earthen covering by over-enthusiastic archaeologists and left as a stone shell. What makes Bryn Celli Ddu fascinating is that it's relatively intact; you can enter the barrow and pass into a stone-lined burial chamber that was used as a communal grave 5000 years ago. To find it, follow the signpost off the A4080 down the country lane to the marked car park.

Plas Newydd (NT; www.nationaltrust.org.uk; adult/child £9.80/4.90, garden only £7.70/3.85; house 11am-4.30pm Mar–early Nov, garden 10.30am-5.30pm Mar-Oct, 11am-3pm Nov-Feb; P) When you pull up into the car park, don't get too excited by the impressive building you can see in front of you – that's just the stables! The grand manor house of the Marquesses of Anglesey is set well back from the road, surrounded by tranquil gardens, gazing out across the Menai Strait to Snowdonia. The earliest parts date from the early 15th century, but most of the Gothic masterpiece that stands today took shape in the 1790s.

Inside, the walls are hung with gilt-framed portraits of worthy ancestors of the Paget family (William Paget was secretary of state to Henry VIII), who owned the house until 1976. A highlight is a giant painting by Rex Whistler filling an entire wall of the dining room, which magically changes perspective as you walk around the room. In the grounds there's a tearoom, a cafe, an adventure playground and a luxuriant rhododendron garden.The house is 2 miles southwest of Llanfair PG, along the A4080.

Anglesey Sea Zoo (01248-430411; www.angleseyseazoo.co.uk; Brynsiencyn; adult/concession £7.75/6.65; 10am-4.45pm Feb-Nov; P) This excellent aquarium introduces you to the denizens of the local waters: from lobster and cuckoo wrasse to tiny brine shrimp and Picasso-painting-like flatfish. Designers have gone to great pains to imitate different environments, such as quayside and shipwrecks; tidal waves crash into the glass tank that simulates life in a tidal pool. A crowning touch is a life-sized model of a basking shark – the second-largest fish in the world. Conger eel or shark feedings are held daily.

There are plenty of less educational distractions too – a bouncy 'octocastle', playground, shop and cafe. Head south along the A4080 from Llanfair PG towards Brynsiencyn and follow the signs for Anglesey Sea Zoo.

Shopping

Tŷ Halen (Halen Môn Saltcote; 01248-430871; www.halenmon.com; 10am-5pm) Used by Michelin-starred restaurants such as Fat Duck and Tyddyn Llan, Halen Môn salt is known in the most exalted of foodie circles. Sourced directly from the Menai Strait's waters, it is sold both in pure form and flavoured. The £1.25-million visitor centre explores the entire salt-making process and you can buy all seven delectable flavours at the attached shop.

Flavours include smoked, Tahitian vanilla, chilli, garlic and more, and the shop also sells other tempting side products, such as salted caramel sauce. The shop and visitor centre are located next to Anglesey Sea Zoo.

Sleeping & Eating

★ **Château Rhianfa** BOUTIQUE HOTEL £££
(01248-713656; www.plasrhianfa.com; Beaumaris Rd, Glyngarth; r from £175; P) Would-be Prince Charmings and fairy-tale princesses can indulge their fantasies in this remarkable turreted Victorian mansion, styled after a French renaissance chateau. Some rooms are chic and contemporary, while others are old-fashioned and romantic. Over-the-top touches like free-standing baths, giant sleigh beds and sculpted gardens with views across the Strait to Snowdonia complete the illusion. Glyngarth is a little over a mile northeast of Menai Bridge's centre.

Dylan's INTERNATIONAL ££
(01248-716714; www.dylansrestaurant.co.uk; St George's Rd; mains £12-17; noon-10pm;) Visible from Thomas Telford's famous suspension bridge and itself overlooking the

bird-filled shallows of the Strait, this casual, much-awarded modern restaurant is Menai's most popular. Local seafood features heavily in dishes such as roasted lobster or linguini with mussels, and there are plenty of hearty burgers, curries and the like to round out your choices.

★ Sosban & the Old Butchers GASTRONOMY £££
(☎01248-208131; www.sosbanandtheoldbutchers.com; Trinity House, 1 High St; lunch/dinner £34/59; ⏲7-11pm Thu-Sat, 12.30-2pm Sat) Still bearing cosmetic vestiges of its days as an actual butcher shop (etched mirror-tiles and a mint-green shopfront), this superb *prix-fixe* restaurant elevates Menai Bridge dining above anywhere else in Anglesey. 'The Saucepan's' married owners handle two sittings at dinner and one at Saturday lunch, lavishing a succession of surprising and delightful dishes on those lucky enough to get a booking.

Getting There & Away

Menai Bridge is Anglesey's bus hub. Destinations include Holyhead (X4; 1¼ hours), Llanfair PG (4A, 44A, X4; five minutes), Beaumaris (53-58; 18 minutes) and Bangor (4A, 44A, 53-58, X4; 12 minutes).

Beaumaris (Biwmares)

POP 1370

Anglesey's prettiest town offers a winning combination of a waterfront location, ever-present views of the mountains, a romantic castle lording it over an elegant collection of mainly Georgian buildings and a burgeoning number of boutiques, galleries, smart hotels and chic eateries. Many of the houses are extremely old; the local real estate agent occupies a half-timbered house dating from 1400 – one of the oldest in Britain (look for it on Castle St near the bottom of Church St).

The town's romantic name dates back to the time of French-speaking Edward I, who built the castle. It's a corruption of *beau marais* (meaning 'beautiful marsh') rather than *beau maris* (meaning 'good husbands') – although, unlike in French, the final 's' is sounded. Today, it's an understandably popular place for retirees.

Sights & Activities

★ Beaumaris Castle CASTLE
(Cadw; www.cadw.wales.gov.uk; Castle St; adult/child £6/4.20; ⏲9.30am-5pm Mar-Oct, to 6pm Jul & Aug, 11am-4pm Nov-Feb) Started in 1295, Beaumaris was the last of Edward I's great castles of North Wales and today it's deservedly a World Heritage Site. With swans gliding on a water-filled moat and a perfect, symmetrical design, it's what every sandcastle maker unknowingly aspires to. The four successive lines of fortifications and concentric 'walls within walls' make it the most technically perfect castle in Great Britain, even though it was never fully completed.

The overall effect may seem more fairy tale than horror story, but the massive gates with their murder holes (used to pour boiling oil on invaders) hint at its dark past. The walk along the top of part of the inner wall gives super views of the castle layout and the breathtaking scenery that surrounds it. Look out for the old latrines (marginally less unpleasant than the murder holes for those

OFF THE BEATEN TRACK

ANGLESEY AMBLES

Anglesey is a big draw for walkers thanks to the **Isle of Anglesey Coastal Path** (www.angleseycoastalpath.co.uk), a 125-mile route passing through a watery landscape of coastal heath, salt marsh, clifftops and beaches. It's well waymarked and not particularly gruelling, especially if you stick to the leisurely 12-day itinerary that's suggested (strong walkers could easily slice off a few days).

A highly recommended section passes from Red Wharf Bay to Beaumaris, via the beach at Llanddona and the ancient priory at Penmon. Another favourite section runs from Trearddur Bay to Holyhead (p296).

Anglesey Walking Holidays (☎01248-713611; www.angleseywalkingholidays.com; 3 Pen Rallt, Menai Bridge; per person from £295) offers self-guided walking and cycling packages, including accommodation, breakfast, luggage transfers and transport between trailheads.

walking below) and the arrow slits in the wall for picking off unwelcome visitors.

Beaumaris Courthouse HISTORIC BUILDING
(Llys Biwmares; www.visitanglesey.co.uk; Castle St; adult/child £3.60/2.80, incl Beaumaris Gaol £7.90/6.50; 10.30am-5pm Sat-Thu Apr-Oct) The Beaumaris Court, opposite the castle, was an instrument of justice dispensed by the English between 1614 and 1971, with Welsh-speaking defendants at a distinct disadvantage as the proceedings were held in English. An excellent audioguide (included in the price) helps to paint the picture.

Beaumaris Gaol HISTORIC BUILDING
(www.visitanglesey.co.uk; Steeple Lane; adult/child £5/4, incl Beaumaris Courthouse £7.90/6.50; 10.30am-5pm Sat-Thu Apr-Oct) This fortress-like jail, built in the early 19th century, was modern for its time, with toilets in every cell and a treadmill water pump. However, that's not enough to dispel the gloom of the windowless punishment cell, the condemned cell where prisoners awaited their demise at the gibbet or the stone-breaking yard where inmates were subjected to hard labour.

Penmon Priory CHURCH
(Cadw; www.cadw.wales.gov.uk; Penmon; parking £2.50; 10am-4pm; P) FREE Penmon, 4 miles north of Beaumaris, is Anglesey at its most numinous. An early Celtic monastery was established here in the 6th century by St Seiriol; burnt in AD 971, its last relic is the basin of the holy well, tucked behind the current simple stone church. The earliest extant parts of that church include two 10th-century Celtic crosses, a font from around the turn of the millennium and some wonderful 12th-century Romanesque arches.

The Augustinian Priory that took over the site in the 13th century survived until dissolution in 1536. The buildings then fell into ruin, with the exception of the church, which is still used as a parish church to this day. Once the monks were turfed out, the land was taken over by Beaumaris' leading family, the Bulkeleys, who, in 1600, built the gigantic **dovecote** that stands nearby. Pigeons, used for their meat and eggs, would enter through the cupola and roost in the 930 holes.

The car-parking charge includes access to a toll road leading to **Penmon Point**, where there's a cafe (open March to October) and fantastic views of the lighthouse, Puffin Island and the Great Orme (p282).

Seacoast Safaris BOATING
(07854-028393; www.seacoastsafaris.co.uk; adult/child £10/8; Apr-Oct;) Off Anglesey's eastern point, the Special Protection Area of Puffin Island is alive with puffins, cormorants and kittiwakes, while seals, porpoises and dolphins call the waters around the 28-hectare island home. Seacoast's (weather-dependent) 90-minute boat trips cruise alongside the island or through Menai Strait; book at the kiosk at the entrance to the pier or by phone.

Sleeping

Kingsbridge CAMPGROUND £
(01248-490636; www.kingsbridgecaravanpark.co.uk; Llanfaes; sites low/high season £18/24;) This well-equipped camping and caravanning site is also a haven for local wildlife and wildflowers, earning it 13 David Bellamy Conservation Awards. It's located 2 miles north of Beaumaris, signposted from the B5109.

★ **Cleifiog** B&B ££
(01248-811507; www.cleifiogbandb.co.uk; Townsend; s £85, d £90-110;) A charming little gem, this art-filled townhouse oozes character and history and boasts superb views over the Menai Strait, particularly as the morning sun streams in. The front bedrooms have their original 18th-century wood panelling, while the rear room has a 16th-century barrel ceiling; all three are stylishly decorated.

Ye Olde Bulls Head Inn & Townhouse HOTEL ££
(01248-810329; www.bullsheadinn.co.uk; Castle St; d inn/townhouse from £90/110;) These sister properties, located just across the road from each other, provide quite a contrast. Where the Bulls Head accommodation – occupying the oldest pub in town – is historic and elegant, the townhouse is contemporary, high-tech and design driven. Breakfast for both is served at the old inn.

Eating & Drinking

Red Boat Ice Cream Parlour ICE CREAM £
(01248-810022; www.redboatgelato.com; 34 Castle St; scoop £2.40; 10am-6pm Mon-Thu, 10am-7pm Fri-Sun;) This popular parlour whips up authentic Italian gelato in a range of flavours, from the exotic (strawberry, mascarpone and balsamic vinegar) to the extremely Welsh (*bara brith*, a rich, fruit

tea-loaf). It's so popular, in fact, that it's expanded and now offers breakfast, Dutch pancakes, pizzas (£8 to £10) and other light meals.

Bishopsgate Restaurant　　　EUROPEAN **££**
(☑01248-810302; www.bishopsgatehotel.co.uk; 54 Castle St; mains £15-20, 3-course menu £24.50; ⊘6-9.30pm, from noon Sun) The formal restaurant at Bishopsgate House serves well-executed, hearty pan-European dishes such as toasted goat's cheese on beetroot salad and roasted hake with chorizo crumb and red pesto cream. Get in before 7pm between Sunday and Friday to take advantage of the early bird menu (£15 for two courses).

★ Tredici Italian Kitchen　　　ITALIAN **££**
(☑01248-811230; www.tredicibeaumaris.com; 13 Castle St; ⊘6-9pm Sun-Thu, 5-10pm Fri & Sat, noon-3pm Sat & Sun) Occupying an intimate 1st-floor dining room above a quality butcher and grocer, Tredici has brought a touch of the Mediterranean to wind-blown Anglesey. While some Welsh produce is used (local lamb cutlets are pan-fried with mint and redcurrant, and the sea bass almost has the same postcode), the swordfish, figs and the like naturally come from sunnier climes.

George & Dragon　　　PUB
(☑01248-810491; Church St; ⊘11.30am-11pm, to midnight Sat; 🛜) For over 600 years drinkers have been sipping their ales within these walls and beneath these low ceilings. Join this venerable throng and while you're at it, keep an eye out for the horse brasses and 400-year-old wall paintings.

① Information

Tourist Office (www.visitbeaumaris.co.uk; Town Hall, Castle St; ⊘10am-2pm Mon-Fri) This information point is only staffed for limited hours; at other times, it's still accessible, and a handy spot to pick up brochures.

① Getting There & Away

Buses stop on Church St. Routes include the 53-58 to Menai Bridge (18 minutes) and Bangor (35 minutes); buses 57 and 58 continue on to Penmon (11 minutes).

There's a large pay-and-display car park on the waterfront by the castle. If you're prepared to walk, there are often free parks on the Menai Bridge approach to town.

Moelfre
POP 710

Moelfre, an old herring-fishing port, is the prettiest harbour village on the east coast. A stream splashes between the old stone houses before cascading down a waterfall and exiting onto the stony beach.

⊙ Sights

Gwylfan Moelfre Seawatch　　　MUSEUM
(Seawatch Centre; ☑01248-410300; ⊘10.30am-4.30pm daily mid-Feb–Oct, Sat & Sun Nov) **FREE** Anglesey's treacherous east coast has claimed numerous ships over the centuries, perhaps most famously the *Royal Charter* in 1859, which took 460 lives and £360,000 of gold. This little centre is devoted to the brave souls of the Royal National Lifeboat Institute (RNLI), including Richard Evans (1905–2001), who rescued 281 people in his 49 years stationed here; his statue stands outside, as does a schedule of lifeboat launches.

Lligwy Burial Chamber　　　ARCHAEOLOGICAL SITE
(Cadw; www.cadw.gov.wales; ⊘10am-4pm) **FREE** Sometime before 3000 BC the local people raised Lligwy's 25-tonne capstone into place, forming a stone chamber that they covered with an earthen mound. When the barrow was excavated in 1908, the bones of about 30 people were found buried within. To find it, look for the country lane marked 'Ancient Monument' near the roundabout on the approach to Moelfre. Park at the marked car park and walk back along the road; the chamber is on the right.

Din Lligwy　　　RUINS
(Cadw; www.cadw.gov.wales; ⊘10am-4pm) **FREE** In the 4th century, during the relative stability of the lengthy Roman occupation, local farmers built a small fortified settlement here consisting of stone buildings behind a large stone wall. All that remains are the foundations, but it's enough to give a good sense of the layout of the site. Nearby, across the fields, stands the photogenic remains of a 12th-century chapel. Follow the country lane marked 'Ancient Monument' near the roundabout before Moelfre to find the car park.

🛏 Sleeping & Eating

**Tyddyn Isaf Camping
& Caravan Park**　　　CAMPGROUND **£**
(☑01248-410203; www.tyddynisaf.co.uk; Lligwy Bay, Dulas; sites from £21; 🛜🐾) 🍃 With sandy,

undeveloped Lligwy Bay close at hand, this large, well-groomed campground is a repeat winner of the David Bellamy Conservation Award and makes a great base for family holidays. Facilities include a restaurant, bar and children's playground with a very cool lighthouse slide.

Ann's Pantry CAFE ££
(☎01248-410386; www.annspantry.co.uk; lunch £5-11, dinner £11-21; ⏲11am-5pm daily, 6-9pm Thu-Sat; 📶) With a pretty garden setting and a funky, beach-hut-meets-stone-cottage interior, Ann's is a gem. The lunch menu includes deli rolls, burgers, salads and local fish, while the pastel-coloured cafe walls bulge with knick-knacks for sale.

Getting There & Away

Bus 62 heads to/from Cemaes (35 minutes), Amlwch (19 minutes), Benllech (six minutes), Menai Bridge (24 minutes) and Bangor (35 minutes).

Church Bay (Porth Swtan)

Tucked away Church Bay has a fine grin of a beach, smirking at the Irish Sea. There's only a small number of houses, one of which is 17th-century Swtan.

Swtan HOUSE
(www.swtan.co.uk; adult/child £4/1; ⏲noon-4pm Tue-Sun Easter-Sep) The last surviving thatched cottage on Anglesey, Swtan has been restored to provide a glimpse of life in the 19th century, with a central living and sleeping area abutted by the grain store, hen house and other outbuildings.

Wavecrest Cafe CAFE £
(☎01407-730650; www.wavecrestcafe.co.uk; snacks £3-9; ⏲10.30am-5pm Thu-Sun, daily summer holidays) A cosy, relaxed cafe with local photography for sale, great snack lunches (try the homemade fish pie), and fluffy scones and gigantic sponges for afternoon tea.

Lobster Pot SEAFOOD £££
(☎01407-730241; www.thelobsterpotrestaurant.co.uk; mains £17-24; ⏲hours vary, see website) Seventy years old, this local institution is famous for its fresh seafood and decadent three-course lunch menus, which come in a choice of standard (£13), duck (£18) and, of course, lobster (£29). Its dedication to locavorism is admirable: the lamb, mussels, oysters and steak all come from Anglesey.

Getting There & Away

The nearest buses stop a little over a mile away at Rhydwyn. Bus 61 heads to Holyhead (32 minutes), Cemaes (12 minutes) and Amlwch (25 minutes).

Holyhead (Caergybi)

POP 11,431

In the heyday of the mail coaches, Holyhead (confusingly pronounced 'holly head') was the vital terminus of the London road and the main hub for onward boats to Ireland. The coming of the railway only increased the flow of people through town, but the recent increase in cheap flights has reduced the demand for ferries and Holyhead has fallen on hard times. Regeneration funding allowed the impressive Celtic Gateway bridge to be built (linking the train station and ferry terminal to the main shopping street) and a radical waterfront redevelopment has been promised; but for now, the town centre remains a rather moribund affair.

Holyhead isn't actually on Anglesey at all. Holy Island is divided from the west coast of Anglesey by a narrow channel, although the various bridges obstruct the views these days, and you might not realise that you're crossing onto another island.

History

The area has a rich prehistoric and Roman past, visible in the impressive herringbone walls of the 4th-century fort from which the town takes its Welsh name, Caergybi.

Sights

St Cybi's CHURCH
(Victoria Rd) FREE St Cybi, the son of a 6th-century Cornish king, became a priest and eventually washed up in North Wales, where the King of Gwynedd gave him an old Roman naval fort in which to base a religious community. The Gothic church came much later, with the oldest parts built in the 13th century. Interesting medieval carvings peer out from the walls, while inside the light is softened by beautiful stained-glass windows from William Morris' workshop.

You can still see the remains of the 4th-century Roman walls, built to repel Irish pirates, surrounding the present-day churchyard. The fort came to be known as Cybi's Fort (Caergybi, the Welsh name for Holyhead) and the island on which it stood

Holyhead

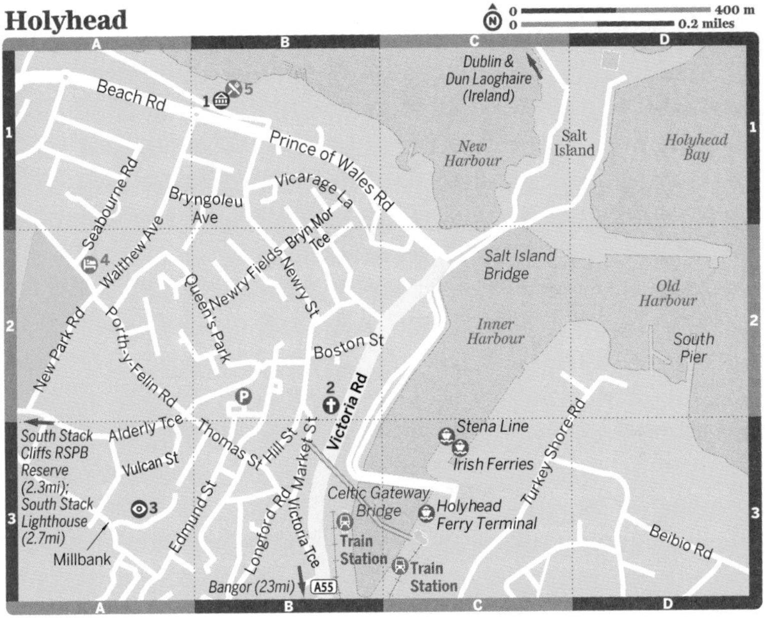

became Cybi's Island (Ynys Gybi, the Welsh name for Holy Island).

Holyhead Maritime Museum MUSEUM

(☎01407-769745; www.holyheadmaritimemuseum.co.uk; Newry Beach; adult/child £5/free; ⊙10am-4pm Tue-Sun Easter-Oct; 👪) Small but lovingly restored, this little museum is housed in what is believed to be the oldest lifeboat house in Wales (c 1858). It's a family-friendly visit with model ships, photographs and exhibits on Holyhead's maritime history from Roman times onwards. The exhibition 'Holyhead at War' occupies an adjacent WWII air-raid shelter.

Ucheldre Centre ARTS CENTRE

(Canolfan Ucheldre; ☎01407-763361; www.ucheldre.org; Millbank; ⊙10am-5pm Mon-Sat, 2-5pm Sun) Housed in a former convent chapel, now a 200-seat theatre and gallery, Ucheldre is Holyhead's artistic hub. Call in to view the latest exhibition and to find out what's coming up in the way of films, live music, drama and dance.

★South Stack Cliffs RSPB Reserve WILDLIFE RESERVE

(Ynys Lawd; ☎01407-762100; www.rspb.org.uk/wales; South Stack Rd; ⊙visitor centre 10am-5pm; P) FREE Two miles west of Holyhead, the sea vents its fury against the cliffs of South Stack, an important RSPB reserve – home to thousands of seabirds. A steep, serpentine flight of steps leads down to the suspension bridge that crosses over to the South Stack Lighthouse (p297) for tremendous cliff views. Numerous paths lead into the bracken-covered, hilly interior, climbing the 219m **Holyhead Mountain (Mynydd Twr)** and skirting Neolithic stone circles. **South Stack Kitchen**, an interpretive-centre-cum-cafe providing maps and information, is open all year.

Between May and June around 12,000 guillemots, 1200 razorbills and 15 loved-up puffin couples congregate on the cliffs here – and that's not to mention the choughs,

Holyhead

Sights

1 Holyhead Maritime Museum B1
2 St Cybi's B2
3 Ucheldre Centre A3

Sleeping

4 Yr-Hendre A2

Eating

5 Harbourfront Bistro B1
Ucheldre Kitchen .... (see 3)

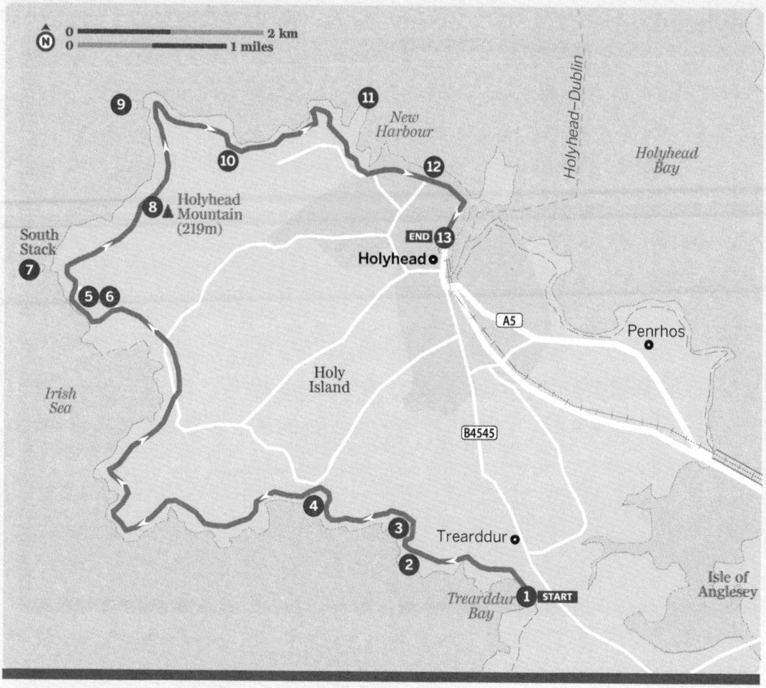

Coastal Walk
Trearddur Bay to Holyhead

START TREARDDUR BEACH CAR PARK
END ST CYBI'S CHURCH
LENGTH 12 MILES; FIVE TO SIX HOURS

This walk takes in one of the most interesting sections of the Isle of Anglesey Coastal Path, circling the northern half of Holy Island. It's also part of the Wales Coastal Path; look for the blue-and-yellow disks that point the way. To reach the start, catch bus 4 from Holyhead (13 minutes, hourly, Monday to Saturday).

Pretty scallop-shaped 1 **Trearddur Bay** has a sandy beach edged by rocks. Head right and continue along the path as it passes a succession of rocky coves. For the most part, the waymarked route hugs the road but it does cut a few corners. At 2 **Porth y Pwll**, a tiny bay with a scrap of sand, it leaves the road and rounds a headland before reaching the larger beach at 3 **Porth y Post**.

The route then follows the road before heading to the cliffs and arching back to picturesque 4 **Porth Dafarch**. From here the path takes a long amble along the cliffs, before eventually coming back to the road, crossing it and continuing parallel to it. It then joins the narrow road heading to 5 **Twr Ellin** (Ellin's Tower) and the 6 **RSPB Visitor Centre** (p295). There's a cafe and toilet here, making it the perfect pit stop. If you're making good time and feeling energetic, stop to explore 7 **South Stack Lighthouse**, but beware: it's a very steep walk back up.

Pick up the track again for the most remote section of the walk, edging alongside 8 **Holyhead Mountain** (219m) towards 9 **North Stack**. Here the path loops back and passes 10 **Breakwater Country Park** (another handy toilet and coffee stop) and then skirts the base of the 11 **breakwater** before reaching Holyhead. Walk along the promenade past the 12 **Maritime Museum** (p295) and then follow the road towards the port. Turn right onto Victoria Rd and follow it until you see the gate of 13 **St Cybi's** (p294) church on your right.

fulmars, peregrine falcons and numerous other species that can be spotted throughout the year. For a sheltered view, head to **Twr Ellin** (Ellin's Tower; April to September), a birdwatcher magnet equipped with binoculars, telescopes and a TV with a live feed from cameras on the cliffs.

Caer y Twr, one of Wales' most impressive Iron Age sites, is found at the blustery summit of Holyhead Mountain, but if you're not up to a 45-minute hike, there are also remains of Neolithic round houses a short stroll along a path that's opposite the car park.

South Stack Lighthouse LIGHTHOUSE
(☎01407-763900; www.trinityhouse.co.uk; South Stack Rd; adult/child £5.80/3.15; ⊙10.30am-5pm Sat-Thu Easter–early Sep) The rocky islet of South Stack has a gloriously end-of-the-earth feel, with waves crashing around the base of the cliffs and guillemots and razorbills nesting overhead. The trail down to the rickety old bridge anchoring it to Holy Island is not for the faint-hearted, with 400 slippery steps and the foreboding of a steep return climb. Admission includes a tour of the 28m-high lighthouse, built in 1809, reputedly haunted and still operating. Last tickets are sold at 4pm.

On a blustery day, spare a thought for model Jerry Hall who had to crawl semi naked on the rocks below dressed as a mermaid for the cover of Roxy Music's *Siren* album.

South Stack is 3 miles west of Holyhead along narrow South Stack Rd. Otherwise, head to Trearddur Bay and follow the coastal road.

Sleeping & Eating

Yr-Hendre B&B ££
(☎01407-762929; www.yr-hendre.net; Porth-y-Felin Rd; r £65-75; P@) A former minister's house set in a large garden on the quiet edge of town, Yr-Hendre is perhaps the best place to stay in Holyhead. Professionally managed and homey, the three bedrooms have a feminine touch and one has sea views. Walkers are welcomed and safe bicycle storage is available.

Ucheldre Kitchen CAFE £
(www.ucheldre.org; Millbank; mains £5-7; ⊙10am-4.30pm Mon-Sat, 2-4.30pm Sun) Avoid the greasy spoons around the high street and head up to the cafe attached to the arts centre (p295) instead. Lit by skylights and decked with art, it's a relaxed spot for light lunches (wraps, toasted sandwiches, paninis, soup) or tea and cake.

OFF THE BEATEN TRACK

HIGH-FLYING PUB

Tucked away in the southwest corner of Anglesey on Holy Island is the busy gastropub **White Eagle** (☎01407-860267; www.white-eagle.co.uk; Rhoscolyn; mains £13-16; ⊙kitchen noon-9pm, bar to 11pm;), with a huge decking area and gardens for kids to explore. The menu is surely more inventive than in its village-pub days, but the portions remain generously pub-sized and the service is friendly. There's also a good selection of beer.

Harbourfront Bistro INTERNATIONAL ££
(☎01407-763433; www.harbourfrontbistro.co.uk; Newry Beach; mains £13-16; ⊙noon-2.30pm Tue-Sun, 6-9pm Thu-Sat) For good food and sea views, this cosy little bistro adjoining the Maritime Museum (p295) is hard to beat. Sandwiches and baguettes are served alongside cooked lunches, along with coffee and pastries outside mealtimes. The deck is a relaxed spot to watch the ships approaching the harbour on summer evenings.

Information

Holyhead doesn't have a tourist information centre but some of the local stores stock brochures. The South Stack Cliffs RSPB Reserve visitor centre (p295) is a good source of advice about local walks.

Getting There & Away

When the weather's poor, it always pays to check with the ferry companies – **Irish Ferries** (☎08718 300 400; www.irishferries.com; foot passenger/motorcycle/car from £31/55/104) and **Stena Line** (☎08447 707 070; www.stenaline.co.uk; foot passenger/bicycle/car from £34/42/105) – before heading to the ferry terminal (www.holyheadport.com), as services are sometimes cancelled. Direct trains head to/from Rhosneigr (£4.50, 12 minutes), Llanfair PG (£8.30, 29 minutes), Bangor (£9.40, 30 minutes), Conwy (£1, 1¼ hours) and London Euston (£94.80, four to five hours).

National Express coaches stop at the ferry terminal, heading to/from Bangor (£20, 35 minutes), Liverpool (£31, 2¾ hours), Manchester (£36, 4¾ hours), Birmingham (£35, four hours) and London (£29, 7¼ hours). The main bus stops are on Summer Hill. Destinations include Trearddur (route 4; 13 minutes), Cemaes (61; 44 minutes), Llanfair PG (X4; one hour), Menai Bridge (X4; 1¼ hours) and Bangor (X4; 1½ hours).

Rhosneigr

POP 1008

The long sandy beach at Rhosneigr may not be Anglesey's safest, but it's certainly one of its most beautiful. It's the island's top surfing spot, but does have some rock pools and sheltered areas for swimming. The large village, a popular resort in Edwardian times, sits between the beach and a small lake, and has the rare advantage of having its own functioning train station – all of which conspire to make it one of the most desirable addresses in Anglesey.

Sights & Activities

★ Barclodiad y Gawres Burial Mound ARCHAEOLOGICAL SITE

(Cadw; ☎01407-810153; www.cadw.gov.wales; ⏰exterior 10am-4pm) FREE Squatting on a headland above gorgeous Trecastle Bay, 2 miles south of the village, Barclodiad y Gawres (the Giantess' Apronful) is the largest neolithic tomb in Wales. When it was excavated in the 1950s, archaeologists were excited to find five standing stones inside, decorated in spirals and zigzags similar to those found in Ireland's Boyne Valley, along with the cremated remains of two men.

Due to problems with vandalism, the entrance to the mound is now blocked by an iron gate, but you can still peer into the murky space. If you're keen to get inside, call into Wayside Stores in Llanfaelog (1 mile up the road) to make an appointment between noon and 4pm on Saturdays, Sundays and bank holidays, and the staff will send someone down to open up.

Funsport WATER SPORTS

(☎01407-810899; www.funsportonline.co.uk; 1 Beach Tce; ⏰9am-5pm) Right by the beach at the bottom of town, this is the hub for the shaggy-haired brigade, renting out boards and wetsuits and then providing a bragging venue with the Surf Cafe upstairs. It also offers taster courses in surfing (£20/35 for one/two hours), windsurfing (£35 to £60 for two hours) and kitesurfing (£25 to £35 for one hour).

Eating

Oyster Catcher BISTRO ££

(☎01407-812829; www.oystercatcheranglesey.co.uk; Maelog Lake; mains £12-19; ⏰10am-11pm; P) This striking, German-designed, glass-fronted structure, backed by windswept sand dunes, serves hearty, well-prepared gastropub dishes and sandwiches to hungry walkers. Oyster Catcher serves a second purpose by giving ex-offenders the chance to retrain as chefs.

Getting There & Away

AIR

Anglesey Airport (☎01407-878056) Flights to Cardiff with Citywing (www.citywing.com).

PUBLIC TRANSPORT

Direct trains head to/from Holyhead (£4.50, 12 minutes), Llanfair PG (£6.30, 18 minutes), Bangor (£6.70, 25 minutes), Conwy (£14.70, 44 minutes) and Shrewsbury (£45.60, three hours).

Bus routes include 25 to Holyhead (30 minutes) and 45 to Llangefni (35 minutes).

Understand Wales

Wales Today

Wales stormed into the new millennium with a renewed sense of optimism, buoyed by its freshly minted National Assembly, with its devolved powers, and the rejuvenation of its capital city. Since then, a global financial crisis has served to remind Wales of its position at the bottom of the UK heap economically, while Brexit has raised many questions about the future. The optimism hasn't completely disappeared, but it has taken a few knocks.

Best on Film

How Green Was My Valley (1941) Acclaimed adaptation of Richard Llewellyn's novel.

Human Traffic (1999) An edgy romp through Cardiff's clubland.

Edge of Love (2008) Dylan Thomas biopic starring Sienna Miller, Keira Knightley and Matthew Rhys.

Under Milk Wood (1972) Thomas' play about life in a fictional Welsh fishing village, adapted into a film starring Wales' most iconic actor, Richard Burton.

Best in Print

On the Black Hill (Bruce Chatwin; 1982) Traces 20th-century Welsh rural life through the lens of an oddball pair of twins.

How Green Was My Valley (Richard Llewellyn; 1939) Life in a Welsh mining community laid bare.

Collected Poems 1934–1953 (Dylan Thomas; 2003) Worth it for *Do Not Go Gentle into That Good Night* alone.

Rape of the Fair Country (Alexander Cordell; 1959) Powerful family tale.

A History of Wales (John Davies; revised 2007) Comprehensive and fascinating.

Wales: Epic Views of a Small Country (Jan Morris; 1998) Lovingly written travelogue.

Brexit

In June 2016, a slim majority of the British public voted in a referendum to leave the European Union (EU). While Scotland and Northern Ireland voted to stay by a comfortable margin, the Wales result was almost identical to England's, with 53% wanting to leave versus 47% to remain.

Before the vote, Wales' First Minister Carwyn Jones warned that the Welsh economy would 'tank' in the event of a British exit from the EU. Wales has been a net benefactor from EU funding, receiving an estimated £70 per head of population. As well as direct grants, it has benefited from farming subsidies. Indeed, the area that voted the most strongly to leave – the economically depressed Ebbw Vale in South Wales – has been one of the UK's biggest recipients of EU funds.

The anti-EU result reflects concerns about the threat of immigration on jobs and a distrust of European bureaucracy, as well as a general rejection of a status quo, which has failed to improve the lot of people living in Wales' more marginalised communities.

Interestingly, aside from cosmopolitan Cardiff, the counties voting with the highest majority to remain were two of the most strong Welsh-speaking areas: Ceredigion and Gwynedd.

The United Kingdom?

Following the Brexit vote, the Scottish First Minister, Nicola Sturgeon, signalled that if it is forced to leave the EU, Scotland would push for a second independence referendum. A previous referendum held in 2014 saw Scotland voting 55% to 45% in favour of staying within the UK. It's speculated that with the EU referendum going against the wishes of the majority of the Scottish people, support for independence will be strengthened.

The issue of Scottish independence poses interesting questions for Wales and its own status within the UK. While there is no immediate likelihood of Wales following suit, Plaid Cymru (which holds 20% of the seats in the Welsh Assembly) has independence as one of its key goals.

In the wake of the referendum, Plaid Cymru leader Leanne Wood said that the Brexit vote had 'changed everything' and that 'in all likelihood, with Scotland voting to remain, the UK will cease to exist in the near future'.

In reality, negotiations over Britain and its role in Europe are likely to roll on for years if not decades.

In the midst of all the uncertainty in the immediate wake of the Brexit referendum, Wales' totally unexpected success at the Euro 2016 football championship, reaching the semifinals, gave both sides of the debate something to cheer.

Welsh Language Woes

Although support for the Welsh language has strengthened in recent years and other minority cultures look to Wales as a shining example, in reality the threat to the language is acute. These days more people are learning Welsh as a second language and all school children are required to study Welsh up to the age of 16, but pressure on Welsh as a living first language remains.

It's thought that until the 1870s more people in Wales could speak Welsh than could speak English. Between the 2001 and 2011 censuses, the proportion of the population who could speak Welsh dropped from 20.5% to 18.6%.

Economic hardship in Welsh-speaking rural areas in Mid, West and North Wales has resulted in a drift to urban centres. At the same time, large numbers of non-Welsh speakers have been moving in, changing the cultural dynamic of rural Wales in a very short time. Historically, few of these migrants have learnt the Welsh language or become involved in local traditions, and their presence inflates house prices and forces local people out.

Today, with the advent of the Welsh Assembly, the focus has shifted from the radical opposition to the English 'invaders' that characterised Welsh nationalism from the 1960s to 1980s, towards education and the strengthening of the language's official status.

Yet, for the first time in the 2011 census, the number of Welsh speakers in Ceredigion fell below 50%, leaving Gwynedd and the Isle of Anglesey as the only counties where a majority of people can still speak the ancient mother tongue.

POPULATION: **3,070,000**

AREA: **8022 SQ MILES**

UNEMPLOYMENT: **4.8%**

HIGH STREET SHOP VACANCIES: **14%**

if Wales were 100 people

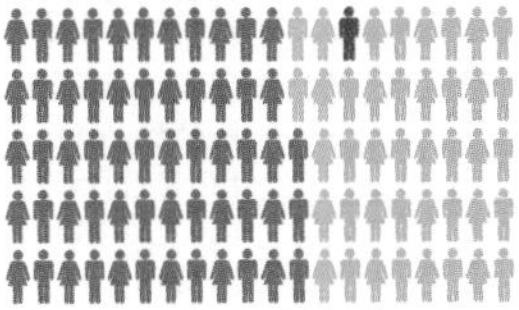

58 class themselves as Welsh only
7 class themselves as Welsh and British
1 class themselves as Welsh and another nationality
34 don't class themselves as Welsh

Welsh speaking

(% of population)

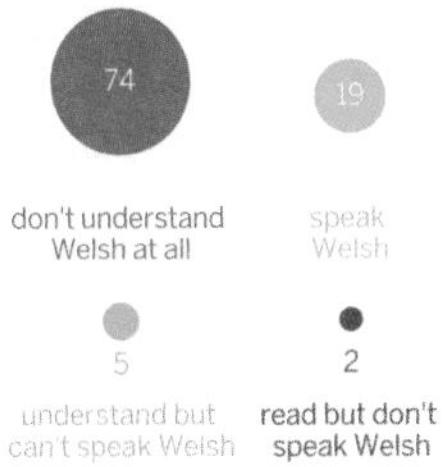

population per sq mile

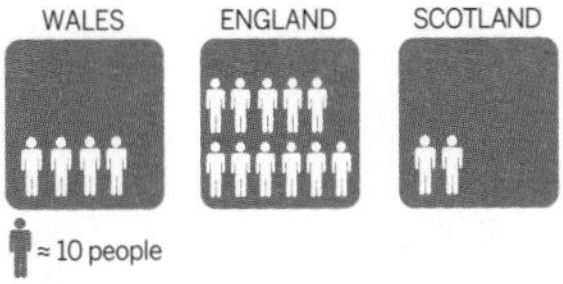

History

Everywhere you go in Wales you'll see the nation's history written large. The landscape is littered with ancient burial mounds, standing stones, earthworks, rusting machinery, sculpted mountainsides, great mounds of slag, sturdy churches, dour chapels and evocative graveyards – and everywhere castles, castles and more castles. Travel through Wales with its history in mind and you'll find it easier to understand Welsh resentment and Welsh pride.

Early History

Little is known of Britain's earliest peoples, but by 3500 BC the cromlechs, standing stones and stone circles that are evident throughout Britain today started to be raised. This is evidence of the presence of fairly large communities; for instance, it is estimated that it would have taken 200 men to raise the giant capstone at Tinkinswood, near Cardiff, into place.

It was much later, around 600 BC, that the first wave of Celts arrived on Brtiain's shores and with them their poets and priests – the druids – who were revered as much for their knowledge as for their spiritual power. By the 3rd century BC they were the dominant force in Europe, with Celtic tribes ranging from Turkey to Ireland. The Celts had a defining role in Britain, making enormous technical and artistic advances and introducing a new social hierarchy, belief system and language. The British variant on the Celtic language became known as Brythonic, which later developed into modern Welsh.

Perhaps the most intriguing glimpse into Wales' early history is the 33,000-year-old ochre-stained skeleton of the Red Lady of Paviland, the earliest known formal burial in Western Europe, found in a cave in Gower's Rhossili Bay.

The Romans

When Julius Caesar arrived in Britain in 55 BC with 10,000 Roman legionnaires, the Celtic tribes who had occupied the island for over half a millennia put up a staunch resistance. In AD 43 the Romans returned with 40,000 men and proceeded to advance through Britain. Mona (Anglesey) was the centre of Druidic power and resistance to Rome. After the druids' last stand on Anglesey in AD 60, the Romans eventually took

TIMELINE

250,000 BC

Someone loses a tooth in a cave in Denbighshire, not realising what excitement it will cause a quarter of a million years later when it becomes the earliest evidence of a human presence in Wales.

600 BC

The Celtic people begin to settle in Britain. It's unclear whether they displaced the indigenous people or whether the indigenous people adopted the Celtic culture and language.

AD 60

The Druids' last stand on Anglesey unleashes the brute force of the Roman army, who set about destroying the island's sacred groves and shrines.

DUDE LOOKS LIKE A LADY

In 1823, the Reverend William Buckland discovered a human skeleton dyed with red ochre in a cave on the Gower coast. As he also found jewellery buried along with the bones, the good vicar assumed the deceased must be a woman. Being a devout Christian, he believed she must date from the Roman era, as she could not be older than the biblical flood. The 'Red Lady', as the skeleton became known, was therefore a Roman prostitute or witch, according to Buckland.

Modern analysis shows that the Red Lady was actually a man – possibly a tribal chief – who died, aged around 21, some 33,000 years ago. Dating from before Britain was abandoned during the last Ice Age, his are the oldest human remains found in the UK, and one of the oldest known ritual burials in Western Europe. The Red Lady's peaceful seaside slumber is no more – he's now residing at Oxford University.

control of present-day Wales and England. They cemented their rule by building a series of military forts, the remains of which can still be seen in Cardiff Castle, Caernarfon and, most impressively, at the 'city of the legion' Caerleon. In true Imperial fashion they gradually Romanised the local population, while allowing them to maintain their own language, customs and gods – at least until Christianity became the official state religion in 391.

Wales is Born

In the wake of the fall of the Western Roman Empire in the 5th century, various kingdoms arose across Britain and a new threat surfaced in the form of Germanic tribes such as the Saxons and Angles. This era is shrouded in legend but it is quite possible that there was a figure such as King Arthur who briefly held the Saxon invaders at bay, inspiring romantic fables.

Eventually the Anglo-Saxons conquered most of present-day England, with native Brythonic-speakers holding on in remote places such as Wales and Cornwall. To this day, the Welsh word for the English is *Saeson* (Saxon); the English word for the Welsh derives from the old Anglo-Saxon word for foreigner. For their part, the Welsh started to refer to themselves as *cymry,* a word meaning 'fellow countrymen', and a separate Welsh identity was born – distinct for the first time from the rest of Britain.

Religion was a point of difference between the Christian Welsh and the pagan Saxons. In the 6th century religious communities were founded all over Wales. Many of these *llan* were associated with charismatic

383

Magnus Maximus, commander of Britain, becomes emperor of the Western Roman Empire. He enters Welsh mythology as Macsen Wledig, whose 'dream' inspires the architecture of Caernarfon Castle.

391

Christianity becomes the official state religion, supplanting the worship of local deities.

c 410

The Romans pull out of Britain and the empire starts to crumble. A number of disparate kingdoms emerge in Wales, including Morgannwg (Glamorgan), Gwent, Dyfed, Gwynedd and Powys.

5th century

The Saxons and other Germanic tribes arrive in Britain, eventually overrunning all of England. The Celtic Britons hold fast in the west where a separate Welsh identity starts to form.

leaders, ushering in the so-called 'Age of Saints' and bequeathing Wales with a fair share of their current place names (Llandudno – St Tudno's community; Llandeilo – St Teilo's community etc). St David became a key figure, establishing his eponymous town as a centre of religion and learning.

During the 9th and 10th centuries savage coastal attacks in the south by Danish and Norse pirates forced the small kingdoms of Wales to cooperate. Rhodri Mawr (Rhodri the Great), a charismatic leader, managed to unite most of the kingdoms, only for them to be split among his sons.

His grandson, Hywel Dda (Hywel the Good), reunified the country and then went on to consolidate its laws, decreeing communal agricultural practices and affording women and children greater rights than other legal systems of the time.

A present-day reminder of the tensions between the Anglo-Saxons (in the form of the Kingdom of Mercia, under King Offa) and the Welsh is Offa's Dyke, the 8th-century fortification marking the boundary between the two. Offa's Dyke Path national trail traces this border, which still largely aligns with Wales' border today.

Enter the Normans

When the Normans claimed England in 1066, William the Conqueror set up feudal barons, the Marcher Lords, along the Welsh border to secure his kingdom. Under sustained attack, the Welsh rulers were pushed back and it was not until Llywelyn ap Gruffydd (Llywelyn the Last) that a pan-Welsh leader again emerged. He adopted the title 'Prince of Wales' and by 1267 had forced England's Henry III to recognise him as such. But Llywelyn's triumph was short-lived and by 1277 he had lost much of what he had achieved.

Edward I fought to control the Welsh upstart and eventually killed both Llywelyn and his brother Dafydd. He then set up his 'Iron Ring' of castles to prevent further Welsh revolt. Of these, Caernarfon is the ultimate expression of military and royal authority and it was here that his infant son, the future Edward II, was born. The younger Edward was later invested with the title Prince of Wales, a title bestowed, to this day, on the eldest son of the reigning monarch.

Curiously, against this troubled backdrop Welsh storytelling and literature flourished. In 1176 Rhys ap Gruffydd (Lord Rhys), one of Wales' great leaders, convened the first bardic tournament – the original eisteddfod. The 13th-century Black Book of Carmarthen, the oldest surviving Welsh-language manuscript, also dates from this period and is today held at the National Library of Wales in Aberystwyth.

Owain Glyndŵr

Anti-English feeling was rife throughout Wales by 1400 and Owain ap Gruffydd (better known as Owain Glyndŵr), a descendant of the royal house of Powys, became the uprising's leader, declaring himself Prince of Wales and attacking neighbouring marcher lords.

6th century

Wales enters the 'Age of Saints'. Religious communities spring up all over the country, including the one founded in Pembrokeshire by Wales' patron saint, David.

9th & 10th centuries

The small kingdoms of Wales unite and join forces against attacks by Danish and Norse pirates.

1066

The Normans invade England. By 1086 the Kingdom of Gwent has fallen and there are Norman castles in Chepstow, Monmouth and Caerleon, controlled by the powerful Marcher Lords.

1134

Robert, the eldest son of William the Conqueror, dies in Cardiff Castle, where he had been imprisoned for many years by his brother, Henry I of England.

Henry IV reacted harshly and passed a series of penal laws imposing severe restrictions on the Welsh. This only increased support for the rebellion and by 1404 Glyndŵr controlled most of Wales, capturing Harlech and Aberystwyth castles and summoning a parliament at Machynlleth and at Harlech. But Glyndŵr met his match in Prince Henry, son of Henry IV and hero of the Battle of Agincourt. After a series of defeats, Glyndŵr's allies deserted him and after 1406 he faded into myth-shrouded obscurity. Glyndŵr remains a great hero to the Welsh; he is memorialised in the Owain Glyndŵr Centre in Machynlleth, devoted to his life story, and the Glyndŵr's Way National Trail, a multiday walking track connecting places associated with him.

The Acts of Union

By the later part of the 15th century the Welsh and English had learnt to coexist uneasily. With the Wars of the Roses raging, the Welsh cast their hopes on Harri Tudur (in English, Henry Tudor), viewing him as the prophesied ruler who would restore their fortunes. Born in Pembroke Castle, his claim to the English throne was through his Lancastrian mother, but his father was descended from a noble Welsh family from Anglesey. After years of exile in Brittany, Henry defeated Richard III in the Battle of Bosworth Field in 1485 and ascended the throne as Henry VII. This began the Tudor dynasty, which would reign until the death of Elizabeth I in 1603.

But it was Henry VIII who brought real change with the Tudor Acts of Union in 1536 and 1543 to establish English sovereignty over the country. Although the Welsh became equal citizens and were granted parliamentary representation for the first time, Welsh law was abolished and English was declared the official language of law and administration. The glory years of the Cistercian abbeys as centres of learning also came to an end when Henry VIII declared the independence of the Church of England in 1534 and dissolved the abbeys in 1536.

The effect of the Acts of Union was to make Wales a constituent part of England. Later, when Scotland and Ireland were brought into the fold to form the United Kingdom, Wales wasn't even represented on the Union Flag. Throughout the next two centuries, the Welsh gentry became increasingly Anglicised, while the majority of the ordinary people continued to speak Welsh.

The marcher lordships had a degree of autonomy from the English crown and maintained a separate legal status right up until the time of Henry VIII. Eventually the Marches came to cover much of the south and east of Wales and some of the neighbouring English counties.

The Reformation

Protestantism was initially slow to catch on in Wales and for many years places such as Monmouthshire and the Llŷn Peninsula had a determined Catholic underground. Under the reign of Elizabeth I, several Welsh

1178

Rhys ap Gruffydd (Lord Rhys) convenes the first bardic tournament, the original eisteddfod, as literature and storytelling flourish.

13th century

Llywelyn ap Gruffydd emerges as a unifying Welsh leader but is trounced by Edward I, who builds a ring of castles to suppress the Welsh uprising.

1301

Edward I formally invests his son Edward with the title Prince of Wales, starting the tradition where the heir-apparent to the English throne is granted that title.

1400

Welsh nationalist hero Owain Glyndŵr leads the Welsh in rebellion and is declared 'Prince of Wales' by his followers, but his rebellion is short-lived and victory fleeting.

priests were caught and executed; they're now recognised as saints by the Catholic Church. Acceptance of the Church of England was greatly assisted by the translation of the Bible into Welsh and the commencement of services in the native tongue.

In the 18th century, the Nonconformist Protestant churches – particularly the Methodists – started to make great inroads into the Welsh-speaking population, and eventually Wales became a land of chapels. Until very recently the chapel was one of the defining symbols of Welsh life, with Sundays being bookended by lengthy services accompanied by hearty hymn-singing. Wherever you go in Wales, even in quite small villages, you'll see multiple chapels – although these days many are abandoned or have been converted into museums, apartments or even bars.

In 1847 the Education Commission published a damning report on education in Wales. It questioned Welsh morality and blamed the influences of religious nonconformity and the Welsh language for allegedly lax morals. The introduction of the 'Welsh Not', a ban on speaking Welsh in schools, created a tide of anger.

Romantic Wales

Towards the end of the 18th century the influence of the Romantic revival made the wild landscapes of Wales fashionable with genteel travellers. The works of landscape painters such as Richard Wilson did much to popularise the rugged mountains and ruined castles, and the rediscovery of Celtic and Druidic traditions fuelled a growing cultural revival and sense of Welsh identity.

Scholars were increasingly concerned about the need to preserve the culture and heritage of their country and efforts were made to collect and publish literature. Edward Williams (Iolo Morganwg to use his bardic name) went on to revive ancient bardic competitions and held the first 'modern' eisteddfod in Carmarthen in 1819.

Industrialisation & Unrest

The iron industry had been growing steadily across Wales since the mid-18th century with an explosion of ironworks around Merthyr Tydfil. Industrialists constructed roads, canals and tramways, changing the face of the valleys forever. Major engineering developments from this period include Thomas Telford's spectacular Pontcysyllte Aqueduct and his graceful suspension bridge at Conwy.

As the Industrial Revolution gathered pace, workers were increasingly dissatisfied with the appalling conditions and low rates of pay. Trade unions emerged and the first half of the 19th century was characterised by calls for a universal right to vote. In 1839 the Chartist Riots broke out in towns such as Newport when a petition of more than one million signatures was rejected by Westminster. Between 1839 and 1843 the Rebecca Riots broke out in the rural southwest. The name 'Rebecca' refers to a biblical verse: 'Rebecca...let thy seed possess the gate of those who hate them'. The 'Daughters of Rebecca' (men dressed in women's clothes)

1536 & 1543
The Tudor Acts of Union introduced by Henry VIII unite Wales and England, granting equal rights and parliamentary representation, but make English the main language.

1563
Church services begin to be held in Welsh. Before then the Reformation had seen services move from one little understood foreign language (Latin) to another (English). Protestantism starts to catch on.

1642–49
Major battles are fought at St Fagans and Pembroke during the English Civil War between the forces of King Charles I and the Parliamentarians led by Oliver Cromwell.

1759–82
With the Industrial Revolution gripping the South Wales valleys, Dowlais and Merthyr Tydfil ironworks start production and Bethesda's slate quarry opens for business.

attacked the hated turnpike tollgates, which charged hefty tolls for those using the roads.

Reform & the Depression

By the second half of the 19th century, coal had superseded iron and the population of Wales exploded. In 1867 industrial workers and small tenant farmers were given the right to vote and elections in 1868 were a turning point for Wales. Henry Richard was elected as Liberal MP for Merthyr Tydfil, and brought ideas of land reform and native language to parliament for the first time.

The Secret Ballot Act of 1872 and then the Reform Act of 1884 broadened suffrage and gave a voice to the rising tide of resentment over the hardships of the valleys and the payment of tithes (taxes) to the church. In 1900 Merthyr Tydfil returned James Keir Hardie as Wales' first Labour MP.

National sentiment grew and education improved substantially. During WWI Wales boomed and living standards rose as Welsh coal and agriculture fed the economy.

THE NEWPORT RISING

Chartism, a parliamentary reform movement that arose during the early years of Queen Victoria's reign, was particularly strong in Wales. It argued for a charter of reforms, most of which we would consider to be essential to democracy today: a vote for every man in a secret ballot (up until this time only male landowners could vote); no property requirement for Members of Parliament; equal-sized electorates; and payment for MPs (making it possible for poor men to serve).

On 4 November 1839 some 5000 men from the Usk, Ebbw and Rhymney Valleys converged on Newport, intent on taking control of the town and sparking off a national uprising. They tried to storm the Westgate Hotel on Commercial St, where several Chartists were being held. Police and infantrymen inside fired into the crowd, killing at least 20 people. Five men were subsequently imprisoned and three were sentenced to death (but were instead transported to Australia). The bodies of 10 rioters were surreptitiously recovered and buried secretly in the churchyard in unmarked graves.

The rising is remembered in several plaques and monuments around town, notably near the Westgate Hotel (now the Starbucks at the corner of Stow Hill), where the masonry is still bullet-scarred. Outside, among the hurrying shoppers, is an ensemble of determined bronze figures.

Property requirements for male voters weren't completely removed until 1918. Landless women had to wait another decade for the vote.

1839
The Chartists Riots break out as workers demand reforms, including the universal right to vote.

1865
A Welsh colony is set up in Patagonia, Argentina. Welsh is the language of the courts, schools, chapels and newspapers until 1896.

1867
Industrial workers and small tenant farmers are given the right to vote. Suffrage is broadened over the following two decades.

1900
James Keir Hardie, a Scotsman, becomes the first Labour MP to enter parliament after winning a seat in the Welsh mining town of Merthyr Tydfil.

Between the world wars the country suffered the results of economic depression and thousands were driven to emigrate in search of employment. The Labour Party weathered the storm and, as the 20th century progressed, became the dominant political force in Wales. In 1925 six young champions of Welsh nationalism founded Plaid Cenedlaethol Cymru (the Welsh Nationalist Party; later shortened to Plaid Cymru) in Pwllheli and began a campaign for self-government.

Postwar Wales & Industrial Decline

The postwar years were not kind to Wales. The coal industry went into steep decline, forcing the closure of mines and a bitter struggle as unemployment levels rose to twice the UK average. The Welsh language was suffering and national pride was at an all-time low.

The final blow came in 1957 when the North Wales village of Capel Celyn, near Bala, and the surrounding valley were flooded to provide water for the city of Liverpool, despite vigorous campaigning across Wales.

DAVID LLOYD GEORGE (1863–1945)

David Lloyd George began his career as the champion of Welsh populist democracy and a critic of society and its institutions. A talented and witty orator, in 1890 he won his first seat as Liberal MP for Caernarfon Boroughs and, at 27, became the youngest member of the House of Commons.

As Chancellor of the Exchequer he launched a broad but controversial agenda of social reform, including the introduction of old-age pensions, a 1909 budget that taxed the wealthy to fund services for the poor, and the 1911 National Insurance Act to provide health and unemployment insurance. Elected prime minister in 1916 after a divisive alliance with the Conservatives, Lloyd George went on to become an energetic war leader. He excelled at a time when strong leadership was needed, dismissing red tape and forcing his opinion when necessary.

Postwar industrial unrest and economic reconstruction dogged the country, however, and he eventually agreed to Irish independence to end civil war, a solution the Conservative alliance never forgave. Accusations of corruption, financial greed and the selling of honours began to ruin his reputation. Radicals, Welsh nationalists and campaigners for women's rights all felt betrayed. In 1922 the Conservatives staged a party revolt and broke up the shaky coalition. Lloyd George resigned immediately.

His popularity faded, the Liberal Party was in disarray, political allies had abandoned him and both the Welsh and the British working class felt thoroughly deceived. Lloyd George's political career had reached a sad anticlimax.

He died in 1945 at Llanystumdwy, where there is a small museum devoted to his life.

1916

With WWI in progress, David Lloyd George becomes prime minister, the only Welshman to have ever held the role. Welsh was his first language, English his second.

1965

The Welsh Nationalist Party or Plaid Cenedlaethol Cymru (later Plaid Cymru) is formed and begins and campaign for self-government.

1939–45

WWII rages across Europe and much of Africa, Asia and the Pacific. Parts of Wales are bombed by the Germans, notably Swansea, Cardiff and the Rhondda Valley.

1955

After a ballot of members of the Welsh local authorities, Cardiff is declared the first-ever Welsh capital, garnering three times as many votes as nearest contender, Caernarfon.

THE ABERFAN DISASTER

On 21 October 1966 Wales experienced one of its worst disasters. Heavy rain loosened an already dangerously unstable spoil heap above Aberfan, 4 miles south of Merthyr Tydfil, and sent a 500,000-tonne mudslide of liquefied coal slurry down onto the village. It wiped out a row of terraced houses and ploughed into Pantglas primary school, killing 144 people, most of them children.

Today the A470 Cardiff–Merthyr Tydfil road cuts right through the spot where the spoil heap once stood. The site of the school has been turned into a memorial garden, while the village cemetery contains a long, double row of matching headstones, a mute and moving memorial to those who died.

There were too few Welsh MPs in the House of Commons to oppose the project and resentment still lingers over the issue even today.

The 1960s became a decade of protest in Wales and Plaid Cymru gained ground. Welsh pop music began to flourish and Welsh publishing houses and record labels were set up. In 1962 Cymdeithas yr Iaith Gymraeg (the Welsh Language Society) was founded. Further electoral successes by Plaid Cymru in the 1970s started people thinking about a measure of Welsh self-government. In 1976 the Welsh Development Agency (WDA) was established to foster new business opportunities across Wales in the face of the decline in traditional industry.

Margaret Thatcher's Conservative Party initiated a sweeping campaign of privatisation during the 1980s, leading to severe cuts in the coal, manufacturing and steel industries. Agriculture, too, was in a state of disarray and unemployment began to soar. Welsh living standards lagged far behind the rest of Britain and, with the collapse of the UK Miners' Strike (1984–85), Welsh morale hit rock bottom. Many mines were subsequently shut down and whole communities destroyed. Some have since reopened purely as tourist attractions, notably Big Pit at Blaenavon and the Rhondda Heritage Park.

Something good did come out of the '80s, however, with the 1982 establishment of S4C (Sianel Pedwar Cymru), the Welsh-language TV channel. Support and enthusiasm for the Welsh language increased, night courses popped up all over the country, Welsh-speaking nurseries and schools opened, university courses were established and the number of Welsh speakers started to stabilise at around 20% of the population.

1959

Wales adopts the red dragon on a white and green background as its official flag. Henry VII, the first Tudor king, used this banner at the Battle of Bosworth Field in 1485.

1962

Cymdeithas yr Iaith Gymraeg (the Welsh Language Society) is founded to campaign for legal status for the language and for Welsh-speaking radio and TV.

1966

A colliery spoil tip collapses on the village of Aberfan, near Merthyr Tydfil, killing 116 children and 28 adults. An enquiry blames the National Coal Board for extreme negligence.

1984

Margaret Thatcher's Conservative government announces the closure of 20 coal mines. The ensuing Miners' Strike ends in 1985 with the workers defeated. Further pit closures follow.

Devolution

The 1997 general election brought Tony Blair's 'New Labour' to power in the UK and the devolution process got off the ground once again. In September of that year a referendum on the establishment of the Welsh Assembly scraped through by the narrowest of margins.

A quarter of a million people were employed in Wales' coal industry in the 1920s. Remnants of this heyday can be seen in World Heritage–listed Blaenavon and dozens of other communities in the valleys.

Lacking the powers granted to the Scottish Parliament, the Assembly was always going to have a hard time convincing the world, including Wales, of its merit. The unveiling of the new National Assembly building in Cardiff Bay and the passing of the Government of Wales Act in 2006, creating a new legislature and executive, gave the assembly more teeth and helped the new seat of government to become part of the fabric of daily Welsh life.

A further referendum in 2011, asking whether the Assembly should be able to create laws in its own right, rather than having to have them rubber-stamped by the UK Parliament, passed with a much stronger affirmative vote. These law-making powers are still limited in scope, but include such important areas as housing, health, social welfare, tourism, culture and the Welsh language.

1997

A referendum asking whether a Welsh Assembly should be formed narrowly passes. The 'yes' vote is strongest in the west (except Pembrokeshire); the majority of people in the border counties vote 'no'.

1999

The first National Assembly for Wales is elected, with limited powers devolved from the UK Parliament. The Assembly is led by a coalition between the Welsh Labour Party and the Liberal Democrats.

2008

Wales' last deep coal mine closes. The Tower Colliery in Hirwaun had been bought and operated successfully by a workers' collective since the National Coal Board had deemed it uneconomic in 1994.

2011

A further referendum is held asking whether the Welsh Assembly should be able to make laws without the approval of the UK Parliament; 64% of the population vote 'yes'.

Culture

Cultural debate in Wales coalesces on one theme: identity. What is the identity of Wales in the 21st century? What are the defining elements of Welsh culture? Historically Wales struggled to overcome negative stereotypes about its lack of sophistication. But Welsh pride has been buoyed by the success of its pop and rock stars, actors and film-makers, writers and thinkers. To be Welsh today is a complex blend of historical association, ingrained defiance and Celtic spirit.

Myths & Legends

Considering Wales' lyrical language, complex history, fairy-tale landscape and wealth of mysterious ancient sites, it's hardly surprising that Welsh culture is rich in legend and mythology. Embellished by generations of storytellers, musicians and poets, these tales of supernatural strength, magic, grotesque beasts and heroic adventurers offer an insight into the pagan Celtic world.

Few of Wales' ancient myths and legends were written down and consequently many were lost. *The Mabinogion* (Tales of Hero's Youth), a translation of two remarkable 14th-century folk-tale compendiums, remains the key source of Welsh legends.

The Red Dragon

One of the first mythical beasts in British heraldry, the red dragon is a powerful symbol in ancient legends. It was apparently used on the banners of British soldiers on their way to Rome in the 4th century, and was then adopted by Welsh kings in the 5th century to demonstrate their authority after the Roman withdrawal. The Anglo-Saxon King Harold and Cadwaladr, the 7th-century king of Gwynedd, liked it so much they used it for their standards in battle, forever associating the symbol with Wales. In the 14th century Welsh archers used the red dragon as their emblem, and Owain Glyndŵr used it as a standard in his revolt against the English crown. A century later, Henry Tudor (later King Henry VII) made the dragon part of the Welsh flag, though it was only in 1959 that Queen Elizabeth II commanded that the red dragon, on a green-and-white field, be recognised as the official flag of Wales.

King Arthur

King Arthur has inspired more legends and folk tales, and given his name to more features of the landscape in Wales, than any other figure. He is mentioned in the oldest surviving Welsh manuscripts but his true identity remains unknown. Depicted as a giant with superhuman strength, a dwarf king who rode a goat and a Celtic god, it is most likely he was a 5th- or 6th-century cavalry leader who led early Britons against Saxon invaders. By the 9th century, Arthur was famous as a fighter throughout the British Isles and in the centuries that followed, other writers – most recently and perhaps most famously the Victorian poet Alfred Lord Tennyson – climbed on the bandwagon, weaving in love stories, Christian symbolism and medieval pageantry to create the romance that surrounds Arthur today.

Merlin the Magician

This great Welsh wizard is probably modelled upon Myrddin Emrys (Ambrosius), a 6th-century holy man who became famous for his prophecies. It was probably Geoffrey of Monmouth who changed Myrddin's name to Merlin and presented him as the wise, wizardly advisor to Arthur's father King Uther Pendragon. One of Merlin's seminal acts was to disguise Uther as Duke Gorlois, allowing him to spend the night with the duke's wife, Ygerna, who duly conceived Arthur. Merlin also predicted that Uther's true heir would draw a sword from a stone and acquired the sword Excalibur from a Lady of the Lake. Merlin's own end appears to have come courtesy of this same lady when she trapped the wizard in a cave on Bryn Myrddin (Merlin's Hill), east of Carmarthenshire, where wind-carried groans and clanking chains are part of local lore even today.

Literature

Dylan Thomas' reputation for hard drinking almost overshadows the impact of his literary works, but he is acclaimed for writing half a dozen of the greatest poems in the English language, including such timeless works as *Fern Hill* and *Do Not Go Gentle into That Good Night*.

Wales has an incredibly rich literary history, with storytelling firmly embedded in the national psyche. The Welsh language is also a defining characteristic, its lyrical nature and descriptive quality heavily influencing the style of Welsh writers. Caradoc Evans' (1883–1945) controversial collection of short stories, *My People,* was one of the first works of fiction to bring Welsh literature to a worldwide audience. Its publication in 1915 saw a move away from established nostalgic themes and instead exposed a darker side of Welsh life.

In an international sense, however, it was the bad-boy genius of Welsh literature, Dylan Thomas (1914–53), who was Wales' most notable export. He is probably best known for his comic play for voices, *Under Milk Wood,* describing a day in the life of an insular Welsh community. You can visit his boathouse home in Laugharne.

Welsh literature also matured with home-grown heroes taking on the clichés of valley life and developing more realistic, socially rooted works. Among the leading figures, poet and painter David Jones (1895–1974) began the trend with his epic of war, *In Parenthesis,* published in 1937. Kate Roberts (1891–1985) explored the experiences of working men and women in rural Wales, often evoking qualities of a time since past with *Feet in Chains*. The elegant *On the Black Hill,* by Bruce Chatwin (1940–89),

THE EISTEDDFOD

Nothing encapsulates Welsh culture like the eisteddfod (ey-steth-vot; literally a gathering or session). Infused with a sense of Celtic history and drawing heavily on the Bardic tradition of verbal storytelling, this uniquely Welsh celebration is the descendant of ancient tournaments in which poets and musicians competed for a seat of honour in the households of noblemen.

The first recorded tournament dates from 1176 but the tradition slowly waned following the Tudor Acts of Union in the mid-16th century. In the late 18th century Edward Williams (better known by his bardic name of Iolo Morganwg) reinvented the eisteddfod as a modern Welsh festival. Today the National Eisteddfod (www.eisteddfod.cymru) of Wales is one of Europe's largest cultural events and a barometer of contemporary Welsh culture, with aspiring bands and emerging artists often making their debut there. The whole event takes place in Welsh, but there's loads of help on hand for non-Welsh speakers. The festival is held during the first week of August, alternately in North and South Wales.

Another event to watch out for is the International Musical Eisteddfod, which is held in Llangollen each July. Acts from over 40 countries compete with folk tunes, choral harmony and recitals. Competitions take place daily and famous names take to the stage for gala concerts every night.

WALES IN WORDS

How Green Was My Valley (Richard Llewellyn; 1939) Spellbinding account of life in a South Wales coal-mining community.

Portrait of the Artist as a Young Dog (Dylan Thomas; 1940) Short-story collection capturing lovely-ugly Swansea and evoking the stoic spirit of early-20th-century South Wales.

The Mabinogion (Penguin Classics; 1976) Classic collection of folk tales.

On the Black Hill (Bruce Chatwin; 1982) An engrossing look at 20th-century rural life in the borderlands, as experienced by an eccentric pair of twin brothers.

Wales: Epic Views of a Small Country (Jan Morris; 1998) A love letter to Wales celebrating the origins of its culture.

Neighbours from Hell (Mike Parker; 2007) Informed look at Anglo-Welsh rivalry.

also evokes the joys and hardships of small-town life, exploring Welsh spirit and cross-border antipathy through the lives of torpid twin-brother farmers.

Poetry

The loss of the referendum for devolution in March 1979 was a cathartic moment for modern Welsh literature. It sparked a flood of political and engaged writing and poetry, most notably the left-wing historian Gwyn Alf Williams' re-evaluation of Welsh history in his masterpiece *When Was Wales?*

This renaissance of Welsh poetry among a younger generation of poets, such as Menna Elfyn, Myrddin ap Dafydd, Ifor ap Glyn and Iwan Llwyd, took poetry out of the chapel, study and lecture room to be performed in pubs, clubs and cloisters. This led to a series of poetry tours, making Welsh-language poetry once again a popular medium of protest and performance. Recent years have also seen an increasing crossover between Welsh and English poetry and literature with poets and musicians, such as Twm Morys and Gwyneth Glyn, establishing new audiences with their blend of words and music.

Literary Events

Laugharne Weekend, April

Hay Festival, late May

National Eisteddfod, August

Dylan Thomas Festival, late October

Music

According to a Welsh proverb, 'to be born Welsh is to be born with music in your blood and poetry in your soul'. Hence, Wales is officially known as the land of song. But where does this close association between Wales and music actually originate?

There are references to the Celts as a musical race as early as the 1st century BC when ancient scholars wrote of bards (poets who sing songs of eulogy and satire) and Druids (philosophers or theologians who are held in extreme honour). There are traditional Welsh songs with harp accompaniment from the early 19th century and unaccompanied folks songs that tell a story in the form of verse.

Today the diversity of music in Wales is huge, yet united by a common factor – music remains at the heart of this nation. The Cory Band from the Rhondda Valley has won the European Brass Band Championships five out of the last eight years. Child star Charlotte Church swapped her classical beginnings for perky pop before evolving into a more mature experimental sound. And the Welsh National Opera has continued to grow in stature since launching the career of opera singer Bryn Terfel, plucked from a North Wales sheep farm to become a national champion for the Welsh voice.

THE POETRY OF RS THOMAS

One of Wales' most passionate and most reclusive modern writers, the priest-turned-poet RS Thomas (1913–2000), was an outspoken critic of the so-called Welsh 'cultural suicide' and a staunch supporter of unpopular causes. Nominated for the Nobel Prize in Literature in 1996, his uncompromising work has a pure, sparse style, which he used to explore his profound spirituality and the natural world.

RS Thomas was also more politically controversial than any other Welsh writer, becoming the Welsh conscience and campaigning fervently on behalf of indigenous language and culture. In the late 1980s and early 1990s he was at the centre of a highly public row when he publicly praised the arsonists who firebombed English-owned holiday homes in Wales.

You can follow sites closely associated with Thomas around the Llŷn Peninsula, including the Aberdaron church where he was the local vicar from 1967 to 1978.

Folk

The flame of traditional Welsh music is kept alight by both orthodox folk bands and emerging nu-folk artists. Catch a live session at local pubs, folk clubs or smaller festivals, and look out for bands such as 9Bach and Calan, which blend traditional and contemporary Welsh sounds with international influences. Welsh folk music even has a permanent home at Tŷ Siamas (p232; National Centre for Welsh Folk Music) in Dolgellau. Events at the centre are an ideal way to keep abreast of new acts and influences.

Contemporary

The late 1990s marked the high tide of the Cool Cymru movement and it was rock music that really put Wales on the map. A series of Welsh groups, including Manic Street Preachers, Catatonia, Stereophonics and Super Furry Animals, made headlines with their innovative sounds, clever lyrics, rabble-rousing rock sound and poignant ballads packed with pathos. They changed the staid image of Wales as a nation of melodious harpists and male voice choirs forever.

Wales' biggest music festival, the Green Man Festival, features over 400 acts on 10 stages, as well as a fringe event featuring holistic therapies, talks, comedy, workshops and youth events.

Today the Welsh music scene may not be as hyped as it once was, but its true substance has come to the fore with an important network of artists, labels and agencies. The Manics are still going strong, while their contemporary Gruff Rhys, lead singer with the Super Furry Animals, has pursued an acclaimed solo career.

Multi-award-winning singer Duffy, who released the album *Rockferry* to global and critical acclaim and won a Grammy award in 2009, has all but retired from the music scene, while a host of new names is gaining ground. Look out for Gwenno, who won the Welsh Music Prize in 2015 for her album *Y Dydd Olaf*, alternative rockers Future of the Left and The Joy Formidable, singer-songwriters Georgia Ruth and Cate le Bon, and indie popsters Joanna Gruesome and Los Campesinos!.

The Welsh metal scene has Bullet for My Valentine, while comic rappers Goldie Lookin Chain from Newport fly the flag for Welsh hip-hop.

Theatre & Dance

Theatre is thriving in Wales. The leading English-language professional company is the Clwyd Theatr Cymru (p223), based in northeast Wales and attracting top-name performers such as Sir Anthony Hopkins. Cardiff's acclaimed theatrical organisation, Sherman Cymru (p67), produces a wide range of productions each year, including theatre for young people and inventive adaptations of classic dramas. The highly acclaimed Music Theatre Wales, a pioneering force in contemporary opera, has a growing international reputation. Dance lovers should look out for Earthfall, Wales' leading dance-theatre company and one of the most sought-after companies across Europe.

The most ambitious theatre event in Wales in recent years was a 72-hour live production by the National Theatre Wales and Michael Sheen. The *Passion in Port Talbot* was a hard-hitting retelling of *The Passion of the Christ*, which included a 'last supper' of beer and sandwiches at a local social club.

For more, visit the website of the Arts Council of Wales (www.arts.wales).

Various Hollywood stars, including Charlie Chaplin, Christian Bale and Catherine Zeta-Jones, first trod the boards at regional theatres in Wales. The highest-profile performances are found at the Wales Millennium Centre in Cardiff Bay, while the city's Chapter arts centre is an important venue for fringe events.

Cinema

The first genuinely Welsh film was Karl Francis' *Above Us the Earth* in 1977. Based on the true story of a colliery closure, it featured an amateur cast in real valley locations. More recently, the Welsh film industry has matured considerably with a growth in high-quality independent productions.

One of the most successful recent releases is *The Edge of Love* (2008), the biopic about the life and loves of Dylan Thomas, which starred Keira Knightley, Sienna Miller and Matthew Rhys in the role of Thomas. Another cult success was a low-budget documentary about life in a Mid-Wales village, *Sleep Furiously* (2008), described as an elegy for the landscape and population of Trefeurig, Ceredigion. The film was directed by Gideon Koppel, who himself was brought up in Trefeurig – where his family sought refuge from Nazi Germany. Welsh director Justin Kerrigan has enjoyed considerable commercial success with a series of films including Cardiff-based *Human Traffic* (1999), the story of drug-fuelled hedonistic youth that captured the late-'90s zeitgeist. Another exploration of urban decline, *Twin Town* (1997), set in Swansea, was a funny but clichéd comedy that launched the career of Rhys Ifans.

More recently the Bafta-nominated comedy-drama *Submarine* (2010) was critically acclaimed and enjoyed a highly successful global release. Based in Swansea, it was an incredible debut performance by director Richard Ayoade. Even more successful was *Pride* (2014), an uplifting true story about an unlikely alliance between gay rights activists and striking South Wales miners in the 1980s.

For more information about Welsh film, visit the website of the Film Agency for Wales (www.filmagencywales.com).

Television

The Welsh-language TV channel S4C has been instrumental in supporting emerging talent and promoting Welsh culture to the outside world. A fantastic success story for S4C was the Welsh-language docudrama

MALE VOICE CHOIRS

Born out of the Temperance Movement in the mid-19th century, the male voice choir *(cor meibion)* became an institution in the coal-mining towns of the southern valleys. With the collapse of the former mining communities, the choirs struggled to keep numbers up and some even allowed women to join their ranks.

They have enjoyed a renaissance of late, with younger people signing up to their local choir to flex their vocal chords. In 2008, Only Men Aloud!, an 18-strong Cardiff-based choir of part-timers, beat off stiff competition to win BBC TV reality show *Last Choir Standing*.

Local choirs still practise in the back rooms of pubs and church halls each week. Most are happy to have visitors sit in on rehearsals.

Rugby star Dan Biggar about to kick a goal at Principality Stadium (p51)

Solomon a Gaenor, nominated for an Oscar for Best Foreign Language Film in 1999. Another S4C production *Eldra*, a coming-of-age tale about a young Romany girl growing up in a slate-quarrying community in North Wales, won the 2003 Spirit of Moondance award at the Sundance Film Festival.

S4C and BBC Wales have also provided a springboard for small-screen success, challenging preconceptions and fuelling independent production, while the Bafta Cymru awards are promoting the work of Welsh actors, directors and camera crews to a far wider audience.

Visual Arts

Wales was first recognised by the arts world as a fashionable place for landscape painters, particularly at the end of the 18th century, when the French Revolution effectively closed Europe to British artists. The rugged mountains and undulating valleys around Dolgellau made it a popular retreat, while rolling hills inspired artists such as Richard Wilson and, later, JMW Turner, who painted both the Wye Valley and Valle Crucis.

Ceri Richards (1903–71), heavily influenced by Matisse, is one of the leading lights of the 20th-century art movement. His work is on permanent view at the Glynn Vivian Art Gallery (p121) in Swansea. But best known of all contemporary artists is Sir Kyffin Williams (1918–2006), whose trademark is thickly layered oil on canvas. Williams returned to the Welsh landscape for his inspiration and his starkly striking portraits capture perfectly the essence of Welsh life. His work is collected at the Oriel Ynys Môn (p287) in Llangefni, Anglesey.

Wales' leading international art prize is the Artes Mundi (Arts of the World) award. The prize brings together outstanding artists from around the world who stimulate thinking about the human condition and humanity. Its aim is to give a platform to contemporary artists who are established in their own countries but have received little critical recognition in the UK. The £40,000 award, one of the UK's biggest arts prizes, is awarded on a biannual basis. The shortlisted entrants are displayed at the National Museum Cardiff (p45).

For more information on art in Wales, visit the website of the Arts Council of Wales (www.arts.wales).

Castles & Architecture

Castles are Wales' most famous historical and architectural attraction and the country is covered with them – the 'magnificent badge of our subjection', as the writer Thomas Pennant put it. They are a living-history statement on Wales' past and a symbol of its complex social heritage. The most impressive castles are those built by Edward I in North Wales. Among them, Caernarfon Castle (p268), built between 1283 and 1330, has retained all of its original strength and beauty, and Harlech Castle (p239) is a great example of a perfectly concentric castle, whereby one line of defence is enclosed by another. Conwy Castle (p276) is considered to be one of the greatest fortresses of medieval Europe, and the medieval city walls are among the most complete in the world.

Apart from castles, Welsh architecture is most commonly associated with the country's industrial heritage and its contemporary, post-millennium transformation. Among the former, Blaenavon's ironworks, quarries and workers' houses received Unesco World Heritage status at the turn of the millennium. The town was recently joined on the Unesco World Heritage list by the Pontcysyllte Aqueduct (p224) in Llangollen.

For a taste of modern architecture, Richard Rogers' Senedd (p53), the National Assembly debating chamber in Cardiff Bay, is an elegant mix of slate and Welsh oak, while its neighbour, the Wales Millennium Centre (p53), has a striking design of stacked Welsh slate topped with a bronzed-steel shell. Also worth a look in Cardiff is the award-winning, purpose-built facility for the Royal Welsh College of Music & Drama (p67) on the edge of Bute Park.

Film Locations

Freshwater West (Harry Potter & the Deathly Hallows, Robin Hood)

Snowdonia (Tomb Raider II, Quantum of Solace)

Tenby (Edge of Love)

Caerwent (Captain America)

Rugby

The Kiwis come close, but we'd argue that there's nowhere more passionate about the game of rugby union than Wales. The national team punches well above its weight and has proved to be a giant killer at various international tournaments over the years.

The big annual tournament is the Six Nations (p57) held in February and March between Wales, England, Scotland, Ireland, Italy and France. Wales has won three out of the last nine championships. Tickets for international matches are guaranteed to sell out, while success on the pitch has turned the team's star players, such as Alun Wyn Jones, Sam Warburton and Gethin Jenkins, into national sporting heroes.

Rugby union is equally well supported at club level, with four teams (Cardiff Blues, Swansea Ospreys, Newport Gwent Dragons and Llanelli Scarlets) representing Wales in the Pro12 competition.

The rugby season takes place between September and Easter; for more information, check the Welsh Rugby Union website (www.wru.co.uk).

For more on Welsh sport, see www.walesonline.co.uk/sports.

FANFO / SHUTTERSTOCK ©

Food & Drink

A quiet revolution has been taking place across the kitchens of Wales. Boosted by the abundance of fresh, local produce and a new generation of young chefs with an innovative, modern take on traditional Welsh recipes, the food scene is buzzing.

Welsh Specialities

Historically, Welsh cuisine was based on what could be grown locally and cheaply. Food was functional and needed to satisfy the needs of labourers on the farm or workers down the mine. It was hearty and wholesome but not exactly haute cuisine.

Above A bowl of traditional *cawl*

The most traditional Welsh dish remains *cawl*, the hearty, one-pot soupy stew of bacon, lamb, cabbage, swede and potato. It's one of those warm, cosy dishes that you long for when you're walking in the hills. Another famous favourite is Welsh rarebit, a kind of cheese on toast, generously drizzled with a secret ingredient tasting suspiciously like beer. For breakfast, there's nothing more Welsh than laverbread. It's not actually bread at all, but a surprisingly delicious concoction of boiled seaweed mixed with oatmeal and served with bacon or cockles.

Traditional staples feature prominently in contemporary Welsh cooking. Fancy versions of *cawl*, rarebit and laverbread abound, and menus showcase Welsh lamb (particularly the strongly flavoured meat originating from the Gower salt marshes) and Welsh black beef. On the coast, look out for *sewin* (wild sea trout), Penclawdd cockles and Conwy mussels.

Local cheeses also feature prominently, either added to dishes or served on their own. The most famous three are the hard, crumbly Caerphilly, the brie-like Perl Wen and the creamy blue Perl Las. Two notable, award-winning producers include Carmarthenshire's organic cheesery, Caws Cenarth (p146), and the Blaenavon Cheddar Company (p118), located in the industrial town of Blaenavon, where handmade cheeses are matured down the mineshaft of the National Coal Museum.

For something sweet try Welsh cakes, small scone-like sweets laced with sugar and raisins and cooked on the griddle, or *bara brith*, a traditional heavy fruit loaf served with tea.

Local Treats

- *Bara brith*
- *Cawl*
- *Faggots*
- *Laverbread*
- *Perl Las*
- *Sewin*
- *Welsh cakes*

Regional Treats

Our pick of the specialist food outlets in Wales:

Carmarthen Ham (www.carmarthenham.co.uk; Carmarthen Market) Delicious ham produced the farmhouse way.

Caws Cenarth (p146) Organic cheesemakers.

E Ashton's (www.ashtonfishmongers.co.uk; Cardiff Market, btwn St Mary & Trinity Sts) Fantastically fresh sea trout.

Penarth Vineyard (www.penarthwines.co.uk; Pool Rd, Newtown) Fruity Welsh wines – try the Pinot noir.

Rhug Estate Farm Shop (www.rhug.co.uk; Corwen;) Slow-grown and grass-fed Welsh beef.

Cooking Classes

Cooking with Angela Gray (☎01443-222716; www.angelagray.co.uk; Llanerch Vineyard, Hensol) Tailored courses from the Welsh TV chef.

Culinary Cottage (☎01873-890125; www.theculinarycottage.co.uk; Rose Cottage, Pandy; courses £55-900) Half-day to five-day themed courses, plus the option to stay on site near Abergavenny.

Drovers Rest (☎01591-610264; www.food-food-food.co.uk/courses.htm; Y Sgwar; day-long courses from £165) Private and group classes from dinner parties to Welsh game held at a charming Mid-Wales restaurant.

Dryad Bushcraft (☎01792-547213; www.dryadbushcraft.co.uk; adult/child £90/60) One-day Wilderness Gourmet course combines bushcraft with wild camping.

Fungi Forays (☎01597-811168; www.fungiforays.co.uk; Tan-y-cefn) Mushroom hunting, preparation and cooking in Mid-Wales as part of weekend breaks in October.

First Catch Your Peacock by Bobby Freeman is a classic guide to Welsh food, combining proven recipes with cultural and social history.

PRICE RANGES

The following price ranges refer to a main course.

£ less than £10

££ £10–20

£££ more than £20

DON'T MISS EXPERIENCES

Farmers markets Sniff out a local market such as Cardiff's Riverside Market (p64) for the pick of organic produce and tasty snacks.

Distillery tours The return of Welsh whisky is celebrated with tours and tastings at the Penderyn Distillery (p112).

Real ale Stock up on Snowdonia Ale at the Purple Moose (p257) brewery, one of Wales' growing band of microbreweries.

Cafe culture Sniff out some good espresso in one of Cardiff's historic shopping arcades.

Culinary stars Wales now boasts five Michelin-starred eateries; book ahead for world-class fine dining with a Welsh slant.

Where to Eat

Pub grub remains the most convenient and affordable option with most pubs serving food between noon and 2pm, and 5pm and 9pm. It can be hit-and-miss, but mostly you get a perfectly reasonable lunch or dinner. An increasing number of places are championing local produce and bringing the concept of the gastropub to Wales. The trend for talented chefs to abandon their urban stomping grounds, wind down a peg or two and get closer to their ingredients is making waves in rural Wales and could turn your quick pit-stop lunch into a long, lingering affair.

In larger towns and cities you'll find switched-on bistros and restaurants serving anything from decent to superbly inspired food. An increasingly popular extension of the restaurant business is the concept of the restaurant with rooms, whereby fine dining and a cosy bed are generally only a staircase apart. Most of these places combine gourmet food with a small number of lovingly decorated rooms.

For most restaurants you'll need to book ahead, particularly on weekends, and a 10% tip is customary for good service but not obligatory. In smaller towns, the only food available on Sunday may be the popular roast dinner served at pubs and hotel restaurants.

There are plenty of cafes in Wales but very few to satisfy serious coffee lovers – although this is slowly changing and there are now some great places scattered about. Most can be relied upon for at least a decent cup of tea and an old-fashioned bacon sandwich, dripping in brown sauce. Practically every eating place, including pubs, has at least one token vegetarian dish, though don't expect it to always be inspired.

Local Brews & Drams

A new generation of local microbreweries is crafting tasty real ales, lagers and ciders, supplying local bars and selling to specialist stores. One name to look out for is Newport's Tiny Rebel brewery, which took out Camra's Champion Beer of Britain award in 2015 for Cwtch, its Welsh red ale.

Cardiff's Zerodegrees (p63) is a microbrewery with a great selection of artisan beers with a flavoursome twist. In Brecon, the chaps behind Brecon Brewing have just crowd-funded their own beer-and-pie bar, the Brecon Tap (p107). The North Wales town of Porthmadog, located on the fringes of the Snowdonia National Park, is home to the Purple Moose (p257) brewery, one of Wales' most successful microbreweries, supplying pubs from Anglesey to Harlech. Its Snowdonia Ale and Dark Side of the Moose have both been award winners. Similarly, the Gower Brewery is now well represented in pubs throughout the peninsula.

Welsh whisky is also enjoying a renaissance with the Penderyn Distillery (p112), located in the southern reaches of the Brecon Beacons National Park, boasting an impressive visitors' centre.

The Welsh Table by Christine Smeeth contains simple, traditional Welsh dishes, kitchen anecdotes and words of wisdom.

The Natural Environment

No other country in Europe is as densely packed with conservation sites as Wales, and the natural environment here is protected with a near visionary zeal. The craggy peaks, rugged coastlines and patchwork fields harbour numerous historic, cultural and economic treasures and the Welsh people are fiercely proud of them. Thankfully, the National Assembly is now equally passionate about Wales' diverse landscapes, enshrining sustainable development into the statute books.

Geology

Wales can claim one of the richest and most diverse geological heritages in the world; and it is geology, more than anything else, that has helped shape the destiny of Wales in modern times. Since the 17th century, geologists have pondered the mysteries of Wales' rippled rocks, puzzling

Above Brecon Beacons National Park (p95)

fossils and ice-moulded valleys. In contrast with Wales' relatively young evolutionary age of just 200 million years, some of the oldest rocks in the world lie exposed at St Davids Head on the Pembrokeshire coast.

The flat-topped Brecon Beacons in South Wales are the product of extreme, rock-shattering temperatures. The mountains were eroded to form the red-sandstone moorland and the porous limestone cliffs were perforated with waterfalls, creating massive cave systems. Rich deposits of coal south of the Brecon Beacons and the slate mountains of Snowdonia altered the face of Wales, sparking an industrial revolution that attracted hordes of fortune-hungry workers.

Two of Unesco's Global Geoparks, protected sites of international geological significance, are found in Wales: Fforest Fawr, in the western half of the Brecon Beacons National Park, and GeoMôn, in Anglesey.

Fossilised marine life on Snowdon's summit reveals that Snowdonia's peaks and valleys are remnants of a continental collision that occurred 520 million years ago, swallowing the ancient Iapetus Ocean that divided Britain.

Fauna

Offering opportunities for unexpected encounters, Wales is less of a wonderland and more of a wild card when it comes to wildlife. Atlantic grey seals headline the fascinating coastal wildlife, delivering around 1000 fluffy white pups on Pembrokeshire's shores in late September and early October.

Twitchers, meanwhile, head for Pembrokeshire's offshore islands, a haven for seabirds from April to mid-August. Grassholm Island, in particular, has one of the world's largest gannet colonies, with 39,000 pairs nesting there during breeding season (April to September). Colonies of guillemots, razorbills, storm petrels, kittiwakes and puffins crowd the rock faces of Skomer and Skokholm Islands and together with nearby Ramsey Island they play host to 50% of the world's Manx shearwater population. Rare red-billed choughs can be seen on Ramsey, at South Stack on Anglesey and on deserted parts of the mainland coast, particularly around Pembrokeshire.

In North Wales numbers of hen harriers and Welsh black grouse are increasing, and otters are re-establishing themselves along the River Teifi and in the border area of northern Powys. Pine martens and polecats – staples of Welsh wildlife – are found almost everywhere.

For an impression of how the oak forests of the Welsh landscape once looked, visit one of the sites managed by Natural Resources Wales, such as the Coed y Brenin Forest Park Visitor Centre (p232) near Dolgellau.

Flora

Following years of industrialisation, just 14% of the Welsh countryside remains covered by woodland, characterised mostly by non-native Sitka spruce, a fast-growing crop shirked by most wildlife. In many areas erosion caused by cultivation and overgrazing has prevented native species from rooting and reseeding, although native ash is thriving on the Gower

RED KITE COUNTRY

Doggedly fighting its way back from the verge of extinction, the majestic red kite *(Milvus milvus)* is now a common sight in Mid-Wales. This aerobatic bird with its 2m-long wingspan was once common across the UK and was even afforded royal protection in the Middle Ages. However, in the 16th century it was declared vermin and mercilessly hunted until only a few pairs remained.

The red kites owe their reprieve in part to a 100-year-long campaign in the Tywi and Cothi Valleys of Mid-Wales, the longest-running protection scheme for any bird in the world. Despite persistent threats from egg-hunters and poison intended for crows and foxes, more than 400 pairs of red kites navigate the Welsh sky.

If you want to see these magnificent creatures up close, head to one of the feeding stations such as Gigrin Farm (p203), near Rhayader, or Llanddeusant (p113) in Brecon Beacons National Park.

ALTERNATIVE ENERGY

Innocuous though they may seem, land-based wind turbines have become one of the most contentious and divisive issues in rural Wales. Nobody disputes the need for sustainable energy and few object to community-based schemes that bring much-needed income to small towns and villages. However, the huge visual impact of commercial schemes and their irregular output has brought both locals and campaigners out in droves. It's an emotive issue, pitting one environmental campaign group against another. Although the focus has turned to offshore wind farms and tidal power as viable alternatives, the battle continues with every new planning application.

More recently, controversy has surrounded the proposal to open a new nuclear power plant on Anglesey by the mid 2020s. The previous nuclear plant, Wylfa, ceased operation in 2015, but Wylfa 'B' could become one of the first of the new generation of nuclear power stations planned across the UK. The island's council estimates that the development could bring £8 billion into the local economy but local people are fiercely opposed.

Peninsula and in the Brecon Beacons. Several types of orchid flower grow in its shade, together with common dog violets, from March to May.

Away from grazing animals, alpine-arctic plants breed in mountainous regions, although hikers and climbers can cause irreparable damage to purple saxifrage and moss campion nestling between the rocks on higher slopes. Rare cotton grass sprouts from inland bogs and soggy peat lands in midsummer, among bog pimpernel and thriving myrtle. Butterwort, one of Britain's few insectivorous plants, traps insects in wet grassland at Cwm Cadlan near Penderyn, in southwest Wales. Evening primrose, sea bindweed and marram grass may be spotted on the coast between the sand dunes, while thrift and samphire grace the Gower Peninsula.

Protected Species

Animals once on the endangered list, such as bottlenose dolphins, Risso's dolphins, minke whales and lesser horseshoe bats are no longer officially endangered per se, but they are each subject to a National Biodiversity Action Plan.

A vestige of the last ice age, the Snowdon lily has survived on the slopes of Snowdon for over 10,000 years, yet warmer climates and overgrazing have drastically reduced its numbers. It could be mistaken for a grass before its white flowers emerge between May and mid-June. Also on the critical list is the distinctive shrub Ley's whitebeam, which flowers in late May and early June in the Taff Valley. The fen orchid, rare throughout Europe, is protected in the Kenfig National Nature Reserve near Port Talbot.

One of only two semiresident bottlenose dolphin populations in the UK can be found in Cardigan Bay. Sightings occur year-round, although numbers increase in summer, peaking in late September and October. Common and Risso's dolphins are found further out to sea, along with minke whales.

New Environmental Challenges

When it comes to environmental issues, Wales is hugely ambitious. In part the environmental focus is sharper in Wales because the crucial tourism industry is so closely associated with the country's natural environment. Dogged in this endeavour, the National Assembly sought and received independence from the rest of the UK on environmental legislation.

The 'One Wales: One Planet' manifesto lays down challenges to be achieved by 2025, among them a minimum 80% reduction in carbon-based energy reliance and an electricity supply derived entirely from renewable sources. Bolstering its ambition to eliminate waste production by 2050, Wales already recycles and composts more than 45% of its rubbish.

Atlantic Puffin, Skomer Island (p167)

The enthusiasm for sustainable lifestyles in Wales can be traced back to St David himself who taught his followers the importance of living in harmony with nature. He was a committed vegetarian, as were his successors for the next 400 years.

Although agri-environment schemes such as 'Glastir' remunerate farmers who adopt environmentally sensitive practices and incorporate tree-planting programs aimed at dramatically expanding woodland, the comprehensive 2013 State of Nature study warned that wildlife in Wales was at a crisis point with one in 10 species facing extinction. Farming practices were blamed for loss of habitat, and woodland management policies were under fire for not placing enough emphasis on biodiversity. Upland wading birds, such as curlews, lapwings and golden plovers, and wildflowers, butterflies and woodland plants are particularly affected and conservation groups believe the next decade will be crucial to their survival.

Critics also maintain that government policies are not always in line with sustainable development indicators. In 2012 test drilling for shale gas was approved, a decision that could have major implications for the Welsh environment. Campaigners warn of catastrophic consequences if companies are allowed to use fracking (a controversial extraction technique that blasts water, sand and chemicals through rock at extreme pressures) to release gas in the abandoned mines of South Wales. The UK government maintains that if fracking is approved, high standards of safety and environmental protection will be ensured. Regardless, in 2015 the Welsh Assembly imposed a moratorium on the practice.

Survival Guide

Directory A–Z

Accommodation

Wales has been attracting tourists in the modern sense for 350 years, so it's fair to say that the country is well prepared for visitors. Visit Wales (www.visitwales.com), the national tourist board, operates a grading system based on facilities and quality of service. Participating establishments usually display their star rating (from one to five), although some excellent places don't join the scheme as it costs to do so. Tourist offices rarely mention good nonparticipating places or may simply dismiss them as 'not approved'. In practice there's variability within each classification, and a one-star guesthouse might be better than the three-star hotel around the block.

Bed-and-breakfast (B&B) accommodation in private homes is plentiful and often the only option in smaller towns and villages. Some of the best and most family-friendly B&Bs are in rural farmhouses (used to the muddy boots and large appetites of walkers, cyclists and climbers). Guesthouses, often just large converted houses with half a dozen rooms, are an extension of the B&B idea. In general they're less personal and more like small hotels, but without the same level of service.

B&Bs and guesthouses usually have, as a minimum, central heating, TV, tea-and-coffee-making facilities and a washbasin in the bedrooms. They range from boutique establishments with chic decor, en suites and every gadget imaginable to basic places with shared-bathroom facilities. Likewise, the standard of breakfast varies enormously, although the norm is a full Welsh fry-up – bacon and eggs (and often mushrooms, tomatoes, black pudding and baked beans) on toast – with cereal, yoghurt and fruit also provided.

The term 'hotel' is used with abandon in Wales and may refer to anything from a pub to a castle. In general, hotels tend to have a reception desk, room service and other extras such as a licensed bar. The very best hotels are magnificent places, often with restaurants to match. In rural areas you'll find country-house hotels set in vast grounds, and castles complete with crenellated battlements, grand staircases, oak panelling and the obligatory rows of stags' heads. A new breed of boutique hotel has emerged, offering individually styled designer rooms, club-like bars, quality restaurants and a range of spa treatments.

A variation is the restaurant with rooms, where the main focus is on gourmet cuisine; the attached rooms sometimes come comparatively cheaply. Such places usually offer dinner, bed and breakfast (DB&B) rates.

Many pubs offer accommodation, though they vary widely in quality. Staying in a pub or inn can be good fun as it places you at the hub of the community, but they can be noisy and aren't always ideal for solo women travellers. Many of the better pubs are former coaching inns (places where horse and coach passengers would stop on long journeys).

For longer stays, self-contained weekly rentals are popular. Options include traditional stone farmhouses, tiny quaint cottages, gracious manor houses and seaside hideaways. For something special, the National Trust Cottages (www.nationaltrustcottages.co.uk) has rural properties that are let as holiday cottages.

SLEEPING PRICE RANGES

The following price ranges refer to the cheapest double on offer in high (but not necessarily peak) season. Unless otherwise stated, prices include private bathrooms.

£ less than £65

££ £65–130

£££ more than £130

Similarly splendid rentals are offered by the **Landmark Trust** (☎01628-825925; www.landmarktrust.org.uk), an architectural charity that rescues unique old buildings and supports the work by renting them out.

Hostels in Wales are often spectacularly located, very handy for long-distance walkers and can be a great place to meet fellow travellers.

Free camping is rarely possible in Wales but there are plenty of campgrounds around the country, concentrated in the national parks and along the coast. Most campgrounds have reasonable facilities, though quality can vary widely and some can be tricky to reach without your own transport. Price structures vary widely but will often include a per-person charge, an additional charge for a vehicle or a powered site, and sometimes a minimum site charge at busy times regardless of how many people are staying.

Seasons & Booking

Wales is a popular 'weekender' destination for people throughout Britain. Consequently, prices shoot up and availability plummets on Friday and Saturday nights, regardless of the season, especially in popular beauty spots such as Pembrokeshire and Snowdonia. In business-orientated establishments in Cardiff, prices sometimes drop over the weekend, depending on what's on in the city. If there's a big rugby game scheduled, you won't get a room in the city or its surrounds for love or money.

It's essential to book ahead for Easter and Christmas. Otherwise, the high season runs from mid-May to mid-September, with the absolute peak (especially in seaside towns) between July and August. Prices are generally cheaper for longer stays and advance bookings.

Outside the high season, room rates are often reduced and special offers may be available – it's always worth asking. Some establishments, especially hostels and camping grounds, shut up shop completely from November until Easter.

Most tourist offices will book accommodation for you for a small fee.

Climate

Llandudno

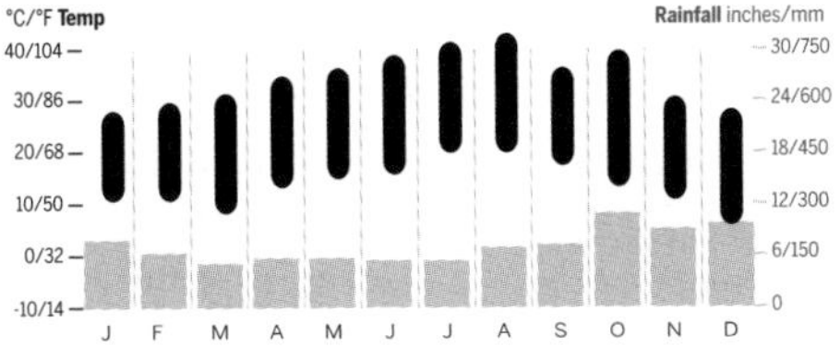

Aberstwyth

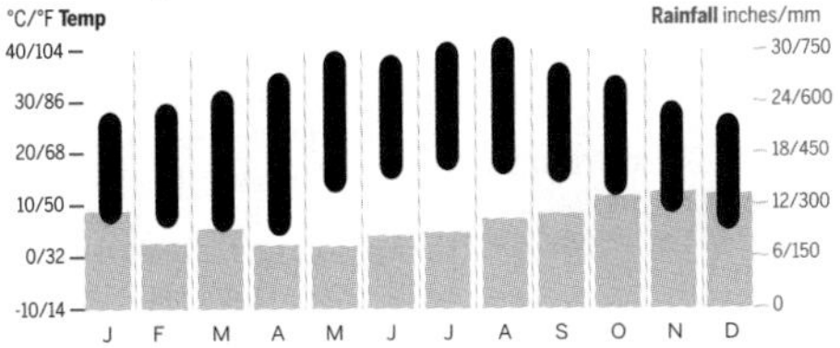

Cardiff

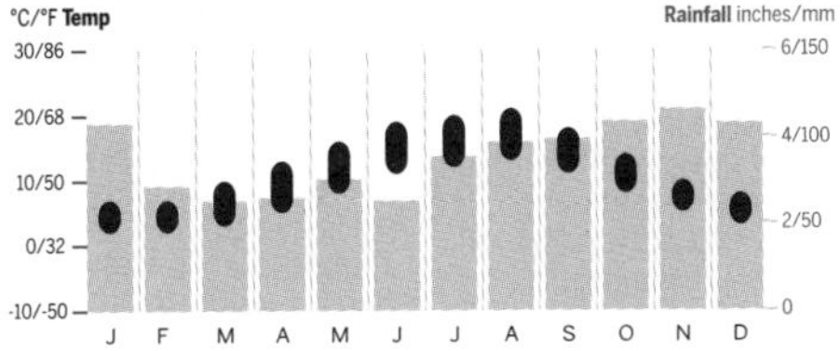

Hostels

The concept of flashpacking has only recently been introduced to Wales and many hostels and bunkhouses still run the risk of triggering repressed memories of school camps and scout dens. On the upside, many of them are spectacularly located and well set up for walkers, with drying rooms and places for muddy boots.

Britain's **Youth Hostel Association** (YHA; ☎01629-592700; www.yha.org.uk) has recently upgraded most of its Welsh hostels, making them a comfortable option for filling overnight gaps in your walking or cycling itinerary. The more remote ones close or are only available for groups from November to Easter.

BOOK YOUR STAY ONLINE

For more accommodation reviews by Lonely Planet authors, check out http://lonelyplanet.com/hotels/. You'll find independent reviews, as well as recommendations on the best places to stay. Best of all, you can book online.

Customs Regulations

➡ Goods brought in and out of countries within the EU incur no additional taxes provided duty has been paid somewhere within the EU and the goods are strictly for personal consumption only. Duty-free shopping is available only if you're leaving the EU.

➡ Travellers arriving in the UK from other EU countries can bring in up to 800 cigarettes, 400 cigarillos, 200 cigars, 1kg of tobacco, 10L of spirits, 20L of fortified wine, 90L of wine and 110L of beer, provided the goods are for personal use only.

➡ For travellers arriving from outside the EU, the duty-free allowance for adults is a maximum of 200 cigarettes *or* 100 cigarillos *or* 50 cigars *or* 250g of tobacco; 4L of still table wine; 16L of beer; 1L of spirits *or* 2L of fortified/sparkling wine; and £390 worth of all other goods (including gifts and souvenirs). Anything over this limit must be declared to customs officers. People under 17 do not get the alcohol and tobacco allowances.

➡ For details of prohibited and restricted goods (such as meat, milk and other animal products), and quarantine regulations, refer to the HM Revenue & Customs section of www.gov.uk.

Discount Cards

There are several passes available to travellers that offer good value for people keen on castles, stately homes, ruined abbeys and other properties owned by Wales' two heritage trusts, Cadw (*ka*-doo; Welsh for 'to keep') and the Welsh arm of the UK-wide National Trust (NT).

A one-year **Cadw** (☎01443-336000; www.cadw.gov.wales) membership costs £41 for individuals, £61 for couples and £66 for a family (two adults plus all children under 16 years). Visitors with disabilities, together with assisting companions, are admitted free to all Cadw monuments.

A one-year **National Trust** (NT; ☎0344 800 1895; www.nationaltrust.org.uk) membership costs £63 for individuals, £105 for a couple and £111 for a family (two adults plus up to five children under 18). As well as entry into NT properties, membership allows free parking at the many trust-owned car parks, particularly those dotted around the Pembrokeshire and Gower coast.

Membership of one, or both, of the trusts is well worth considering, especially if you're going to be in Wales for a couple of weeks or more. Both organisations care for hundreds of spectacular sites and membership allows you to visit them for free. You can join at any staffed Cadw or NT site, by post or phone, or online.

It's also worth noting that students carrying valid National Union of Students (NUS) cards and people carrying a valid 16–25 Railcard (www.16-25railcard.co.uk) can get discounted entrance to many attractions across Wales.

Travellers aged 60 and over can get 30% off standard National Express bus fares with a Senior Coachcard (www.nationalexpress.com; annual fee £10) and 30% off most rail fares with a Senior Railcard (www.senior-railcard.co.uk; annual fee £30). Many attractions have lower admission prices for those aged over 60 or 65; it's always worth asking even if it's not posted.

If you plan to do a lot of travelling by bus or train, there are some good-value travel passes. Most local bus operators also offer day and family passes.

Electricity

Health

Visiting Wales doesn't pose any particular health concerns for the international traveller, and no specific vaccinations are required. Tap water is safe to drink in Wales.

Availability & Cost of Health Care

The National Health Service (NHS) provides free treatment for residents across the UK, including Wales, and foreign nationals are entitled to register with a local doctor if staying in the UK for an extended period.

EU nationals are required to present their European Health Insurance Card (EHIC) in order to receive free NHS treatment. If overseas visitors are not able to do this, they will be liable for NHS charges. Any prescriptions issued will still be chargeable unless the patient is covered by one of the NHS exemptions. For more details of the scheme and how to apply for an EHIC card, visit www.nhs.uk/NHSEngland/Healthcareabroad/EHIC.

Citizens from non-EU countries should find out if

there is a reciprocal arrangement for free emergency medical care between their country and the UK.

Insurance

However you're travelling, make sure you take out a comprehensive travel insurance policy that covers you for medical expenses, luggage theft or loss, and cancellation of (or delays in) your travel arrangements. When choosing a policy, check whether the insurance company will make payments directly to providers or reimburse you later for overseas health expenditures.

Paying for your flight tickets with a credit card often provides limited travel-accident insurance (ie it covers accidental death, loss of limbs or permanent total disablement). You may be able to reclaim the payment if the operator doesn't deliver the service, but this should not be relied upon instead of a full travel insurance policy.

It's a good idea to photocopy all of your important documents (including your travel insurance policy) before you leave home. Leave one copy with someone at home and keep another with you, separate from the originals.

Worldwide travel insurance is available at www.lonelyplanet.com/travel-insurance. You can buy, extend and claim online anytime – even if you're already on the road.

Internet Access

If you're travelling in Wales with a digital device, getting online has never been easier. Most accommodation providers now offer free wi-fi internet access to guests – with the exception of some top hotels, budget chain hotels and hostels. Plenty of cafes, bars and tourist attractions also offer free wi-fi, as do some train and coach services.

With the widespread availability of free wi-fi, internet cafes are few and far between these days. If you don't have your own device, the best places to check email and surf the internet are public libraries – almost every town and village in Wales has at least a couple of computer terminals devoted to the internet, and they are mostly free to use. Many of the larger tourist offices across the country have internet access as well.

Legal Matters

If you are a victim of petty crime, head to the nearest police station to file a crime report; you will need this for your insurance claim. It's a good idea to take some identification with you, such as a passport.

Police have the power to detain anyone suspected of having committed an offence punishable by imprisonment (including drug offences) for up to six hours. They can search you, take photographs and fingerprints, and question you. You are legally required to provide your correct name and address – not doing so, or giving false details, is an offence – but you are not obliged to answer any other questions.

After six hours, the police must either formally charge you or let you go. If you are detained and/or arrested, you have the right to inform a lawyer and one other person, though you have no right to actually see the lawyer or make a telephone call. If you don't know a lawyer, the police will inform the duty solicitor for you.

Possession of a small amount of cannabis is an offence punishable by a fine, but possession of a larger amount of cannabis, or any amount of harder drugs, is much more serious, with a sentence of up to 14 years in prison. Police have the right to search anyone they suspect of possessing drugs.

Drivers may not exceed a blood alcohol level of 80mg/100mL (35mg on the breath). Traffic offences (illegal parking, speeding etc) often incur a fine, which you're usually given 30 to 60 days to pay. Speeding incurs a minimum £100 fine and three penalty points if you hold a UK driving licence.

PRACTICALITIES

DVDs Wales, the UK and most of the rest of Europe uses the Region 2 DVD format, which is also used in the Middle East and South Africa.

Newspapers The *Western Mail* is Wales' only national English-language daily newspaper.

Magazines For the low-down on what's happening around the country, try the magazines *Cambria*, *Planet* or *Golwg* (Vision), the latter only available in Welsh.

Radio Tune in to BBC Radio Wales for English-language news and features or BBC Radio Cymru for the Welsh-language version; both are broadcast on a range of frequencies.

TV The national Welsh-language television broadcaster is S4C (Sianel Pedwar Cymru), while BBC Wales services broadcast mainly in English.

Smoking Forbidden in all enclosed public places. Many pubs now have an outdoor smoking area.

Weights & Measures Wales uses the metric system for weights and measures. However, speed and distance are measured in miles and pubs still pull pints.

LGBT Travellers

In general, Wales is tolerant of homosexuality but the macho image of the rugby-playing Welshmen still prevails in some smaller communities – although the public 'coming out' of Welsh rugby hardman Gareth Thomas has challenged even that bastion of blokedom.

Cardiff, Swansea and Newport have at least some gay venues, with Cardiff's being by far the best, however, even the Cardiff scene is rather sluggish. Wales' biggest LGBT bash is **Pride Cymru** (www.pridecymru.co.uk; ⏲mid-Aug), held in Cardiff.

Diva (www.divamag.co.uk) British lesbian magazine.

Gay Times (www.gaytimes.co.uk) A longstanding gay magazine.

Gay Wales (www.gaywales.co.uk) Wales-specific site, with news, events, listings and helplines.

Pink UK (www.pinkuk.com) UK-wide gay and lesbian resource.

Switchboard (☎0300 330 0630; www.switchboard.lgbt; ⏲10am-11pm) London-based LGBT helpline.

Maps

For motorists, there is a huge array of maps available. You can pick up a decent detailed road map, such as the *Philip's Navigator Wales Cymru* or the *AA Road Atlas Great Britain and Ireland*, at just about any motorway service station you stop at on the way through Wales.

For walkers and cyclists, it's essential to have a good map before setting off on any trip. Most tourist offices and local bookshops stock maps produced by the UK's national mapping agency, the Ordnance Survey (www.ordnancesurvey.co.uk), which cover its regions, including the useful 1:50,000 Landranger series and the extremely detailed 1:25,000 Explorer series. The Pathfinder Walking Guides cover short walks in popular areas at 1:25,000. Maps can be ordered online at the OS website or purchased from tourist offices, national park offices, outdoors stockists and bookshops.

Money

ATMs & Eftpos

Nearly all banks in Wales have ATMs linked to international systems such as Cirrus, Maestro or Plus. However, an increasing number of ATMs, especially the ones you find in small shops and at service stations, will charge for withdrawal (at least £1.50). It's best to avoid these and simply seek out a regular ATM that offers free withdrawals.

Credit & Debit Cards

Visa and MasterCard are widely accepted in Wales (American Express and Diners Club less so), although some smaller businesses and B&Bs may prefer payment in cash. If your credit card is lost or stolen, contact the relevant provider.

Currency

The currency in Wales is the pound sterling (£) and Wales has the same major banks as the rest of the UK. There are 1p, 2p, 5p, 10p, 20p, 50p, £1 and £2 coins and £5, £10, £20 and £50 notes.

Money Changers

Most banks and larger post offices can change foreign currency; US dollars and euros are the easiest currencies to change.

Taxes & Refunds

Value-added tax (VAT) is a 20% sales tax levied on most goods and services and is included in advertised prices. Travellers living outside the EU can claim the tax back by presenting the (unused) goods and a completed VAT 407 form (obtained from the retailer) as they leave the country. Note, only some 'tax-free' retailers can issue the VAT 407 forms.

Tipping

There is absolutely no obligation to tip in Wales, even if a 'service charge' has been automatically added to your bill (although this is still uncommon in Wales). Tips are only left if the service is particularly good or at least satisfactory.

Restaurants, cafes and bars with table service Up to 10% for good service. If you order at the bar or counter, you're not expected to tip.

Taxis Fares are often rounded up.

Opening Hours

Wales follows the general UK conventions when it comes to opening hours, but as Great Britain moves closer to a 24-hour society, hours are extending and Sundays are no longer a day of rest.

Business hours are generally 9am to 5.30pm Monday to Friday. Banks are open from 9.30am to 5pm Monday to Friday and 9.30am to 1pm Saturday (main branches). Single-function post offices open from 9am to 5pm Monday to Friday and 9am to 12.30pm Saturday, although many of Wales' postal services are now handled by retail stores and offer greatly expanded hours.

Shops generally open from 9am to 5.30pm or 6pm Monday to Saturday, with an increasing number of shops also opening on Sunday from 11am to 4pm. Late-night shopping (to 8pm) is usually on Thursday or Friday nights.

Cafes tend to open from 9am to 5pm Monday to Saturday and from 11am to 4pm Sunday, while restaurants generally open from noon to 2pm and also 6pm to 10pm. Many restaurants close on Sunday evenings and all day Monday. Pubs and bars usually open at around 11am and close at 11pm (10.30pm on Sunday). Many bars in larger towns have a late licence and stay open until 2am from Thursday to Saturday.

Some businesses in small country towns still have a

weekly early closing day – it's different in each region, but is usually Tuesday, Wednesday or Thursday. However, not all shops honour it. Early closing is more common in winter. From November to Easter many tourist sights and associated businesses close entirely.

If someone tells you a place (eg a shop, cafe or restaurant) opens daily, they may mean 'daily except Sunday'.

Post

The Royal Mail service (www.royalmail.com) is generally very reliable. There's a handy branch finder on www.postoffice.co.uk.

Mail sent within the UK can go either 1st or 2nd class. First-class mail is faster (normally next-day delivery) and more expensive (64p for a letter up to 100g) than 2nd-class mail (55p); rates depend on the size and weight of the letter or package.

International services start at £1.05 for a postcard to anywhere in the world.

Public Holidays

If New Year's Day, Christmas Day or Boxing Day falls on a weekend, the following Monday is usually treated as a public holiday instead.

Most businesses and banks close on official public holidays (hence the quaint term 'bank holiday') but most larger attractions stay open for all but Christmas Day. However, if a smaller museum or other attraction usually closes on a Sunday, it will probably be shut on bank holidays as well.

Virtually everything – attractions, shops, banks, offices – closes on Christmas Day, although pubs are often open at lunchtime. There's usually no public transport on Christmas Day and a very minimal service on Boxing Day.

New Year's Day 1 January

Good Friday March/April

Easter Monday March/April

May Day First Monday in May

Spring Bank Holiday Last Monday in May

Summer Bank Holiday Last Monday in August

Christmas Day 25 December

Boxing Day 26 December

Safe Travel

Wales is a pretty safe place to travel, but use your common sense.

Never assume that it will be warm and dry, even in summer, and especially in the mountainous parts of Brecon Beacons and Snowdonia national parks. Mist can drop suddenly, leaving you dangerously chilled and disoriented. Never venture onto the heights without checking the Met Office (www.metoffice.gov.uk) mountain forecast and without being sensibly clad and equipped with good waterproof gear and a compass. Always make sure someone knows where you're heading.

High winds can be treacherous for coastal walkers, particularly if you're carrying a large backpack.

Telephone

The UK uses the GSM 900/1800 mobile phone network, which is the standard for most of the world but isn't compatible with the GSM 1900 network commonly used in the Americas. Most modern mobile devices can function on both networks; check before you leave home, just in case.

The EU has largely gotten rid of roaming charges for member states, but for all others international roaming rates can be prohibitively high and you'll probably find it cheaper to get a UK number. This is easily done by buying a SIM card (around £10, including credit) and sticking it in your phone. Your phone may be 'locked' by your home network, however, in which case you'll have to either get it unlocked or purchase a pay-as-you-go phone along with your SIM card (around £50).

Pay-as-you-go credit can be recharged by buying vouchers from a large variety of shops or online.

To dial a UK number from overseas, dial your country's international access code, then 44 (the country code for the UK), then the local number *without* the initial 0. To call internationally from the UK, dial 00 and then the country code.

Toilets

UK toilets are almost always of the plain, sit-down variety.

Public toilets can be a hit-and-miss affair, depending on how much the local council spends on their upkeep, but they are almost always equipped with toilet paper and hand soap. In major towns and cities, public toilets are generally clean but there may be a small fee to use them. Toilets at train stations and motorway service stations are regularly maintained and fine on the whole.

For a more luxurious loo off the beaten track, you can always stop off at a local cafe, a village pub or a rural coffee shop to use the facilities. You will be expected to buy a drink while you're there, but it's a chance to sit down and plan your route at the same time.

Tourist Information

Austerity measures have forced the closure of many local tourist offices in recent years, but where they're open, you'll find them excellent. They're usually well stocked with free maps and brochures and often also sell books on Welsh culture and local sights, Ordnance Survey maps for walkers and even local art. Staff speak English, often

Welsh, and sometimes have a basic grasp of other major European languages. The national parks also have their own tourist offices, which are well worth visiting for advice and details of track and weather conditions.

Many tourist offices make local hotel and B&B reservations, sometimes for a small fee. Some tourist offices also have internet access.

Visit Wales (☎0333 006 3001; www.visitwales.co.uk; ⏰9am-5pm Mon-Fri) The department for tourism within the Welsh Assembly.Your first port of call for information on holidays and short breaks in Wales.

Visit Britain (www.visitbritain.com) Run by the UK's official tourist board and has in-depth coverage of the entire island.

Travellers with Disabilities

For many travellers with a disability, Wales is a strange mix of user-friendliness and unfriendliness. Most new buildings are wheelchair accessible, so large new hotels and modern tourist attractions are usually fine. However, most B&Bs and guesthouses have been converted from hard-to-adapt older buildings. This means that travellers with mobility problems may pay more for accommodation than their able-bodied fellows.

It's a similar story with public transport. Newer buses sometimes have steps that lower for easier access, as do trains, but it's always wise to check before setting out. Most tourist offices, tourist attractions and public buildings reserve parking spaces for people with disabilities near the entrance. Most tourist offices in Wales are wheelchair accessible, have counter sections at wheelchair height and provide information on accessibility in their particular area.

Many ticket offices and banks are fitted with hearing loops to assist the hearing impaired; look for the ear logo.

Visit Wales (www.visitwales.co.uk/explore/accessible-wales) Publishes useful information on accessibility on its website.

National Trust (www.nationaltrust.org.uk/features/visitors-with-disabilities) Has information for visitors with disabilities on its website and offers free admission to all sites for companions of people with disabilities.

Cadw (☎01443-336000; www.cadw.gov.wales) Allows wheelchair users and the visually impaired (and their companions) free entry to all monuments under its auspices.

Disability Rights UK (☎020-7250 8181; http://disabilityrightsuk.org) Publishes *Holidays in the British Isles*, an annually updated guide to accessible accommodation in the UK and Ireland.

Disability Wales (☎029-2088 7352; www.disabilitywales.org) The national association of disability groups in Wales; a good source of information.

Royal National Institute for the Blind (RNIB; ☎0303 123 9999; www.rnib.org.uk) Offers support for people affected by sight loss.

Shopmobility (☎01933-229644; www.nfsuk.org) A UK-wide scheme under which wheelchairs and electric scooters are available in some towns at central points for access to shopping areas.

Tourism for All (☎0845-124 9971; www.tourismforall.org.uk) AUK-based group that provides tips and information for travellers with disabilities.

Lonely Planet's Accessible Travel guide (http://lptravel.to/AccessibleTravel) Download for free.

Visas

- If you're a citizen of one of the European Economic Area nations or of Switzerland, you don't need a visa to enter Britain.
- Citizens of Australia, Canada, New Zealand, Malaysia, Japan, Israel, Brazil, Argentina, the USA and several other countries do not require a visa to stay for up to six months as a tourist, but are prohibited from working.
- Visitors from most other countries will need to apply for a Standard Visitor visa (£87).
- Visa regulations are always subject to change, so check with your local British embassy, high commission or consulate before leaving home. For more information, visit www.gov.uk.

Volunteering

For volunteering opportunities within Wales, refer to the websites of Volunteering Wales (www.volunteering-wales.net) and the Wales Council for Voluntary Action (www.wcva.org.uk).

Women Travellers

Women travellers shouldn't encounter any particular problems in Wales, though it's worth keeping your wits about you and taking the usual precautions for your safety in larger cities, especially at night.

Work

- Although regulations could potentially change, at present most citizens of the European Economic Area can work in the UK.
- Commonwealth citizens with a UK-born parent may have a 'right of abode' (including to work) in the UK.
- Commonwealth citizens with a UK-born grandparent could qualify for a UK Ancestry visa, allowing them to work full-time for up to five years in the UK.
- The Tier 5 (Youth Mobility Scheme) visa allows citizens of certain countries (Australia, Canada, Japan, Monaco, New Zealand, Hong Kong, South Korea, Taiwan), aged 18 to 30 and with £1890 in savings, to work for up to two years in the UK.

Transport

GETTING THERE & AWAY

Aside from ferries from Ireland and a small range of international flights to Cardiff airport, the bulk of visitors to Wales arrive by train, car or coach from neighbouring England. Flights, cars and tours can be booked online at lonelyplanet.com/bookings.

Entering the Country

The UK strictly controls its borders and will not hesitate to deny entry to travellers who are lacking the correct visas or other appropriate documentation.

Air

Although Cardiff has an international airport, most overseas visitors fly into London. Five international airports service the UK's capital but Heathrow is by far the biggest, serving most of the world's major airlines. It is also the closest to Wales. Other options include Manchester, which is handy for North Wales, and Bristol and Birmingham, both close to the Welsh border.

Many of the airlines directly servicing Wales are budget operators, which means you might get a good deal if you're coming from one of the handful of destinations that they fly from.

Airports & Airlines

Cardiff Airport (☎01446-711111; www.cardiff-airport.com) is 12 miles southwest of Cardiff, past Barry. Aside from summer-only services and charters, these are the airlines flying into Cardiff and the destinations they serve:

Aer Lingus (www.aerlingus.com) Dublin.

Citywing (www.citywing.com) Anglesey.

Eastern Airways (www.easternairways.com) Aberdeen and Newcastle.

Flybe (www.flybe.com) London City, Glasgow, Edinburgh, Belfast, Cork, Dublin, Jersey, Paris, Berlin, Munich, Milan and Faro.

KLM (www.klm.com) Amsterdam.

Ryanair (www.ryanair.com) Tenerife-South.

Thomson Airways (www.thomson.co.uk) Málaga, Alicante, Gran Canaria, Tenerife-South and Lanzarote.

Vueling (www.vueling.com) Málaga and Alicante.

Land

The entire eastern edge of Wales shares a land border with England and aside from the odd 'Welcome to...' sign, you'd barely notice you were crossing between the two.

Bus

Buses between England and Wales are generally slower,

CLIMATE CHANGE & TRAVEL

Every form of transport that relies on carbon-based fuel generates CO_2, the main cause of human-induced climate change. Modern travel is dependent on aeroplanes, which might use less fuel per kilometre per person than most cars but travel much greater distances. The altitude at which aircraft emit gases (including CO_2) and particles also contributes to their climate change impact. Many websites offer 'carbon calculators' that allow people to estimate the carbon emissions generated by their journey and, for those who wish to do so, to offset the impact of the greenhouse gases emitted with contributions to portfolios of climate-friendly initiatives throughout the world. Lonely Planet offsets the carbon footprint of all staff and author travel.

cheaper and more flexible than trains. Local buses zip across the border from Gloucester, Hereford and Ludlow.

National Express (☎0871 781 8181; www.nationalexpress.com) operates services to Wales' major cities and tourist towns from some major English cities.

Megabus (☎01413-524444; http://uk.megabus.com) offers one-way fares from London to Cardiff (via Newport) from as little as £5.

Car & Motorcycle

From London, getting to Wales is a simple matter of heading west on the M4 motorway (which passes Heathrow airport) and sitting on it until you cross the impressive bridge over the River Severn.

There's a toll for cars passing into Wales of £6.60; motorcycles are free. There's a second bridge a little further north on the M48 leading to Chepstow, which has the same toll. There's no charge for crossing in the other direction, from Wales into England.

Train

Trains in the UK are privatised and expensive, and the fare structure is bewildering. In general, the cheapest tickets are those bought well in advance. Timetables and fares are available from http://thetrainline.com.

All rail connections from Continental Europe to Wales pass through the Channel Tunnel to London. The high-speed passenger service **Eurostar** (☎01233-617575; www.eurostar.com) links London St Pancras International with Paris or Brussels. Book early to secure the best fares. Cheaper rail connections can be had by crossing the Channel by ferry.

Fast train services run to Cardiff from Bristol, Birmingham and London Paddington. Direct trains from London Paddington also stop in Newport and Swansea. Trains from London Euston head all the way to Llandudno Junction, Bangor and Holyhead in the far north.

From Manchester, there are trains to Llandudno Junction, Fishguard Harbour and Abergavenny. Frequent services shunt across the border between Gloucester and Chepstow.

Main lines heading through the centre of Wales:

Cambrian Line (www.thecambrianline.co.uk) Birmingham to Aberystwyth through Shrewsbury, Welshpool, Newtown and Machynlleth.

Heart of Wales Line (www.heart-of-wales.co.uk) A scenic route through the heart of Mid-Wales from Shrewsbury to Swansea via Knighton, Llandrindod Wells, Llanwrtyd Wells, Llandovery and Llandeilo.

Sea

Ferries from Ireland operate from Dublin to Holyhead (1¾ to 3½ hours) and from Rosslare to Pembroke Dock (four hours) and Fishguard (3½ hours). The main ferry companies are **Irish Ferries** (☎08717 300 400; www.irishferries.com) and **Stena Line** (☎08447 70 70 70; www.stenaline.co.uk).

Fares vary considerably depending on the season, day, time and length of stay. Typical one-way fares start at £31 for a foot passenger and £79 for a car and driver. Bikes can be transported for £10. It's worth keeping an eye out for promotional fares that can reduce the cost considerably.

Ferries to England

There's a wide array of ferry services to England from Continental Europe, including services from Denmark to Harwich; from the Netherlands to Hull and Harwich; from Belgium to Hull; from Spain to Portsmouth; and from France to Dover, Newhaven, Portsmouth, Poole and Plymouth. For details check out www.directferries.co.uk or www.ferrybooker.com.

All of these port towns are linked into the train network, allowing you to get to Wales with two or three connecting trains.

MAJOR BUS CONNECTIONS

FROM	TO	COST (£)	TIME (HR)
London	Cardiff	from 5	3½
London	Chepstow	from 12	3
London	Swansea	from 7	5
London	Tenby	from 18	6¾
London	Aberystwyth	38	7
London	Caernarfon	40	10¼
London	Bangor	39	9½
Birmingham	Monmouth	20	1¾

MAJOR TRAIN CONNECTIONS

FROM	TO	COST (£)	TIME (HR)
London Paddington	Cardiff	from 40	2
London Paddington	Swansea	47	3
London Euston	Bangor	91	3¾
London Euston	Holyhead	95	5
Gloucester	Chepstow	10	½
Birmingham	Machynlleth	21	2¼
Birmingham	Aberystwyth	30	3
Manchester	Abergavenny	from 25	3
Manchester	Fishguard Harbour	30	6½

GETTING AROUND

When people talk of the north–south divide in Wales, it's not just about language – part of it is physical. The barrier created by the Cambrian Mountains, Brecon Beacons and Snowdonia means that it's often quicker to duck in and out of England to get between north and south Wales. The same is true by train: there's a network of lines that slowly zigzag their way through the country but the faster trains head through Bristol and Birmingham. That said, both roads and rail lines are extremely scenic. In Wales that old adage about the journey outweighing the destination is aptly demonstrated.

Wales is one of those places where Brits come to get back to nature, so it's extremely well set up for walkers and cyclists. With a flexible schedule and a modicum of patience, it's quite possible to explore the country by public transport. However, it's worth considering hiring a car for at least part of your trip, especially if you're on a limited time frame and you're not averse to losing yourself in the sort of narrow country lanes that require pulling over when a car approaches from the other direction.

Buses are nearly always the cheapest way to get around but you'll generally get to places quicker by train. For information on services, your best bet is the local tourist office where you'll be able to pick up maps and timetables. For up-to-date information and a journey planner covering public transport throughout Wales, visit **Traveline Cymru** (☎0300 200 22 33; www.traveline-cymru.org.uk).

Air

The only useful internal flights are the Citywing (www.citywing.com) services between Cardiff and Anglesey.

Bicycle

Rural Wales is a great place for cycling: traffic on back roads is limited, and there are loads of multi-use trails and three long-distance cycling routes as part of Sustrans' National Cycle Network (www.sustrans.org.uk). For long-distance travel around Wales, though, the hilly and often mountainous terrain is mostly for experienced tourers.

SAILRAIL

A little-known option for travelling between the UK and Ireland, SailRail is an absolute bargain. The combined train and ferry service connects all UK and Irish train stations, and by comparison to airlines' restrictive fare rules, it's incredibly flexible. You can make changes to your booking, get a partial refund for some types of unused tickets and you can even rock up to a train station and buy your ticket on the day. And the best bit? Tickets cost from just £33 one way, children aged five to 15 pay half-price and under fives go free (but must have a reservation for the ferry). It's worth checking the main rail routes before booking to avoid unnecessary connections.

Check the following websites for details:

- Arriva Trains Wales (www.arrivatrainswales.co.uk/sailrail)
- Irish Ferries (www.irishferries.com/uk-en/offers/sail-rail)
- Stena Lina (www.stenaline.ie/ferries-to-britain/rail-sail)

TRAVEL PASSES

If you're planning a whirlwind tour of Wales by public transport, you might like to consider an Explore Wales pass (www.arrivatrainswales.co.uk/ExploreWales/; adult/child £99/50). It allows free travel in Wales and adjacent areas of England on all rail routes and nearly all bus routes. The passes allow unlimited bus travel plus four days of train travel within an eight-day period. Cheaper passes (£69/35) are available if you're only wanting to visit South Wales or North and Mid-Wales. The passes can be bought at most staffed train stations and rail-accredited travel agencies in Wales.

In the larger towns and cities, there are few bike lanes and the usual problems with inconsiderate motorists. Bike theft can also be a major problem in urban areas.

Bikes can be taken on most trains, although there is limited space for them. On most services it's worth making a reservation for your bike at least 24 hours in advance; there is a small charge for this on some routes.

Arriva Trains Wales (☎03333 211 202; www.arrivatrainswales.co.uk), which operates most rail services in Wales, publishes an annual guide called *Cycling by Train*. It's also available for download from the website.

Hire

Most sizeable or tourist towns in Wales have at least one shop where you can hire bikes from £14 to £28 per day for a tourer and £25 to £50 for a full-suspension mountain bike. Many hire outfits will require you to make a deposit of about £50 for a tourer and up to £100 for a top-of-the-line mean machine.

Boat

Aside from tourist boats to some of the offshore islands, there are no ferry services between ports in Wales.

Bus

Wales' bus services are operated by dozens of private companies but you'll find centralised information on routes and timetables with **Traveline Cymru** (☎0300 200 22 33; www.traveline-cymru.org.uk). Buses are mostly reasonably priced and efficient, although some have limited weekend services (many routes don't run at all on Sundays). Generally you'll need to hail the bus with an outstretched arm and pay the driver on board. Some buses, particularly in the cities, don't give change, so it pays to carry coins.

Coaches are mainly run by **National Express** (☎0871 781 8181; www.nationalexpress.com), and for these you'll need to book and pay in advance.

Long-distance bus services are thin on the ground. Following are the principal cross-regional routes, most of which operate daily:

701 Cardiff, Swansea, Carmarthen, Aberaeron, Aberystwyth

T2 Aberystwyth, Machynlleth, Dolgellau, Caernarfon, Bangor

T3 Wrexham, Llangollen, Bala, Dolgellau, Barmouth

T4 Cardiff, Merthyr Tydfil, Brecon, Llandrindod Wells, Newtown

T5 Haverfordwest, Fishguard, Cardigan, Aberaeron, Aberystwyth

Bus Passes

Apart from the combined bus-and-rail Explore Wales passes, there are lots of regional and local one-day and one-week passes, but many are only worthwhile if you're planning to do a lot of travelling. You can usually buy tickets from the bus driver.

First Week South & West Wales Pass Unlimited travel on all First bus services in South and West Wales for seven days (adult/child £25/14).

First Day Swansea Bay Pass Unlimited travel on First and Pullman buses in Swansea and the Gower Peninsula for the day of purchase (adult/child £5/3.50). You can buy these passes at Swansea bus station, or from the driver on any First bus.

Red Rover Valid for one day on buses 1 to 99 in Gwynedd and the Isle of Anglesey in northwest Wales (adult/child £6.80/3.40). You can buy these tickets from the driver; for full details ask at a tourist office.

If you are planning to travel throughout the UK, National Express has a variety of passes and discount cards, including options for senior travellers. More information is available online at www.nationalexpress.com.

Car & Motorcycle

If you want to see the more remote regions of Wales or to cram in as much as possible in a short time, travelling by car or motorcycle is the easiest way to go.

Getting around North or South Wales is easy, but elsewhere roads are considerably slower, especially in the mountains and through Mid-Wales. To get from the northeast to the southeast, it's quickest to go via England. Rural roads are often single-track affairs with pass-

SPEED LIMITS

➡ 30mph (48km/h) in built-up areas

➡ 60mph (97km/h) on main roads

➡ 70mph (113km/h) on motorways and dual carriageways

ing places only at intervals, and they can be treacherous in winter. In built-up areas be sure to check the parking restrictions as traffic wardens and wheel clampers can be merciless.

Wales can be a dream for motorcyclists, with good-quality winding roads and beautiful scenery. Just make sure your wet-weather gear is up to scratch.

If you're bringing your own vehicle from abroad, make sure you check that your insurance will cover you in the UK; third-party insurance is a minimum requirement. If you're renting a car, check the fine print – policies can vary widely and the cheapest hire rates often include a hefty excess (for which you are liable in the event of an accident).

Automobile Associations

The main motoring organisations – such as the **Automobile Association** (AA; ☎0344 209 0754; www.theaa.com), **Royal Automobile Club** (RAC; ☎0330 159 1111; www.rac.co.uk) and the **Environmental Transport Association** (ETA; ☎0333 000 1234; www.eta.co.uk) – provide services such as 24-hour breakdown assistance, maps and touring information. Others, such as the **Auto-Cycle Union** (☎01788-566400; www.acu.org.uk) and **British Motorcyclists Federation** (☎01162-795112; www.bmf.co.uk), are more like clubs.

Hire

Hire cars can be expensive in the UK but you'll usually get a better rate by booking online in advance. To hire a car, drivers must usually be between 23 and 65 years of age – outside these limits special conditions or insurance requirements may apply. You will also need a credit card to make an advance booking and act as a deposit.

For a compact car, expect to pay in the region of £110 a week (including insurance etc). Most cars are manual; automatic cars are available but they're generally more expensive to hire. If you need a baby chair or booster seat, specify this at the time of booking.

Hire-car companies include the following:

Alamo (☎0800 028 2390; www.alamo.co.uk)

Avis (☎01753-849004; www.avis.co.uk)

Budget (☎0808 284 4444; www.budget.co.uk)

Europcar (☎0871 384 1087; www.europcar.co.uk)

Hertz (☎029-2022 4548; www.hertz.co.uk)

Holiday Autos (☎020-3740 9859; www.holidayautos.co.uk)

Road Rules

A copy of the Highway Code can be bought in most bookshops or read online at www.gov.uk/highway-code.

The most basic rules:

➡ Drive on the left, overtake to the right.

➡ When entering a roundabout, give way to the right.

HERITAGE RAILWAYS

To a large extent, trains along Wales' north and south coasts were built to link the English rail network with seaports at Swansea, Pembroke Dock, Fishguard and Holyhead. But there are some fine rail journeys across the middle of the country and a staggering number of 'heritage' railways (mainly steam and narrow-gauge), survivors of an earlier era, worth seeking out for their spectacular scenery and hypnotic, clickety-clack pace.

Ffestiniog & Welsh Highland Railways (www.festrail.co.uk) An integral, but incredibly scenic, part of the network heading from Porthmadog (on the Cambrian Coast Line) to Blaenau Ffestiniog and Caernarfon.

Heart of Wales Line (www.heart-of-wales.co.uk) One of Wales' most beautiful railway journeys heading from Shrewsbury to Swansea through southern Mid-Wales.

Cambrian Lines (www.thecambrianline.co.uk) The Cambrian Main Line crosses northern Mid-Wales from Shrewsbury to Aberystwyth, and its spectacular branch line heads up the coast from Machynlleth to Pwllheli and the Llŷn.

Conwy Valley Line (www.conwy.gov.uk/cvr) A little gem heading down through Snowdonia from Llandudno to Blaenau Ffestiniog.

➡ Safety belts must be worn by the driver and all passengers.

➡ Motorcyclists and their passengers must wear helmets.

➡ The legal alcohol limit is 80mg of alcohol per 100ml of blood or 35mg on the breath.

➡ It is illegal to use a mobile phone while driving a car unless you have a hands-free kit installed.

Taxi

You'll usually find a taxi rank outside the train station in bigger towns. In smaller places, the best place to find the local taxi phone number is in the local pub.

Train

Like in the rest of the UK, the Welsh rail network has been privatised. **National Rail** (☎03457 48 49 50; www.nationalrail.co.uk) provides centralised timetable information for all train operators in the UK, and allows you to buy tickets online using a credit card. You can also buy tickets online through http://thetrainline.com.

In Wales, most of the services are operated by **Arriva Trains Wales** (☎03333 211 202; www.arrivatrainswales.co.uk), although the **Great**

Train Routes

Western Railway (☎0345 700 0125; www.gwr.com) operates the London Paddington–Newport–Cardiff–Swansea route and **Virgin Trains** (☎0871 977 4222; www.virgintrains.co.uk) has the London Euston–Chester–Llandudno Junction–Bangor–Holyhead route.

Classes & Costs

There are two classes of rail travel in the UK: 1st class and 'standard' class. First class costs about 50% more than standard and simply isn't worth the extra money.

You can roll up to a station and buy a standard single (one-way) or return ticket, but this is often the most expensive way to go. Each train company sets its own fares and has its own discounts, and passengers can only use tickets on services operated by the company that issued the ticket.

You might find that the same journey will have a different fare depending on whether you buy it at the station, over the phone or online. The fare system is so bizarre that in some cases two singles are cheaper than a return ticket, and even a one-way journey can be cheaper if you split it into two (ie if you're going from A to C, it can be cheaper to buy a single from A to B, and another single from B to C; go figure). You can check your options at www.splityourticket.co.uk.

The least expensive fares have advance-purchase and minimum-stay requirements, as well as limited availability. Children under five years travel free; those aged between five and 15 pay half-price for most tickets. When travelling with children, it is almost always worth buying a Family & Friends Railcard.

Main fare classifications:

- **Advance** Has limited availability so must be booked well in advance; can only be used on the specific trains booked.
- **Anytime** Buy any time, travel any time.
- **Off-peak** Buy any time, travel outside peak hours.

Railcards

Railcards are valid for one year and entitle the holder to discounts of up to 30% on most rail (and some ferry) fares in the UK. You can buy a railcard at most train stations or at www.railcard.co.uk, but it must be delivered to a UK address. Railcards are accepted by all train companies.

- **16–25 Railcard** (£30) For those aged 16 to 25 years, or a full-time UK student of any age.
- **Two Together Railcard** (£30) For two people travelling together, aged 16 or over.
- **Disabled Persons Railcard** (£20) Applies to its holder and one person accompanying them.
- **Family & Friends Railcard** (£30) Allows discounts for up to four adults travelling together (only one needs to hold a card and you'll need one child in tow), and a 60% discount on children's fares.
- **Senior Railcard** (£30) For anyone aged 60 or over.

Train Passes

BritRail passes (available only to non-Brits and bought overseas) are not cost effective for a holiday in Wales. More useful are the Rover and Ranger day passes (adult/child £12/6) offered by **Arriva Trains Wales** (☎03333 211 202; www.arrivatrainswales.co.uk), covering its Cambrian Coast, Cardiff and Valleys, West Wales and North Wales networks. Other passes include the Ffestiniog Round Robin (£36/17) and Heart of Wales Circular (£39/20).

Language

You can get by almost anywhere in Wales these days without speaking Welsh. Nevertheless, anyone who's serious about getting to grips with Welsh culture will find it fun trying to speak basic Welsh.

The Welsh language belongs to the Celtic branch of the Indo-European language family. It's closely related to Breton and Cornish, and more distantly to Irish, Scottish and Manx. It's estimated there are over 700,000 Welsh speakers in Wales.

Pronunciation

All letters in Welsh are pronounced and the stress is usually on the second-last syllable. Letters are pronounced as in English, except for those listed below. If you read our coloured pronunciation guides as if they were English, you will be understood.

Note that vowels can be long or short. Those marked with a circumflex (eg ê) are long; those with a grave accent (eg è) short.

a	short as in 'map'; long as in 'farm'
e	short as in 'pen'; long as in 'there'
i	short as in 'bit'; long as in 'sleep'
o	short as in 'box'; long as in 'bore'
u	as i (short and long)
w	short as the 'oo' in 'book'; long as the 'oo' in 'spook'
y	as i (short or long); sometimes as the 'a' in 'about', especially in one-syllable words such as *y, yr, fy, dy* and *yn*

WANT MORE?

For in-depth language information and handy phrases, check out Lonely Planet's *British Language & Culture*. You'll find it at **shop.lonelyplanet.com**, or you can buy Lonely Planet's iPhone phrasebooks at the Apple App Store.

In words of one syllable, vowels followed by two consonants are short – eg *corff* (body). If a one-syllable word ends in *p, t, c, m* or *ng,* the vowel is short – eg *llong* (ship). If it ends in *b, d, g, f, dd, ff, th, ch* or *s,* the vowel is long – eg *bad* (boat) – as is any vowel at the end of a one-syllable word, eg *pla* (plague). In words of more than one syllable, all unstressed vowels are short, eg *cariadon* (lovers). Stressed vowels can be long or short and in general follow the rules for one-syllable words. Welsh also has several vowel sound combinations:

ae/ai/au	as the 'y' in 'my'
aw	as the 'ow' in 'cow'
ei/eu/ey	as the 'ay' in 'day'
ew	as a short 'e' followed by 'oo'
iw/uw/yw	as the 'ew' in 'few'
oe/oi	as 'oy' in 'boy'
ow	as the 'ow' in 'tow'
wy	as 'uey' (as in 'chop suey') or as the 'wi' in 'wing' (especially after g)

The combinations *ch, dd, ff, ng, ll, ph, rh* and *th* count as single consonants.

c	always as 'k'
ch	as the 'ch' in the Scottish *loch*
dd	as the 'th' in 'this'
ff	as the 'f' in 'fork'
g	always as the 'g' in 'garden'
ng	as the 'ng' in 'sing'
ll	as 'hl' (put the tongue in the position for 'l' and breathe out)
ph	as 'f'
r	rolled
rh	pronounced as 'hr'
s	always as in 'so'
si	as the 'sh' in 'shop'
th	always as the 'th' in 'thin'

BASICS

Hello.	
Sut mae.	sit mai
Good morning.	
Bore da.	*bo*·re dah
Good afternoon.	
Prynhawn da.	*pruhn*·hown dah
Good evening.	
Noswaith dda.	*nos*·waith thah
Good night.	
Nos da.	nohs dah
See you (later).	
Wela i chi (wedyn).	*we*·lah ee khee (*we*·din)
Goodbye.	
Hwyl fawr.	hueyl vowr
Please.	
Os gwelwch in dda.	os *gwe*·lookh uhn thah
Thank you (very much).	
Diolch (in fawr iawn).	dee·*olkh* (uhn vowr yown)
You're welcome.	
Croeso.	*kroy*·soh
Excuse me.	
Esgusodwch fi.	*es*·*gi*·*so*·dookh vee
Sorry./Forgive me.	
Mae'n ddrwg gyda fi.	main throog *guh*·da vee
Don't mention it.	
Peidiwch â sôn.	*pay*·dyookh ah sohn
May I?	
Ga i?	gah ee
Do you mind?	
Oes ots gyda chi?	oys ots *gi*·da khee
How are you?	
Sut ydych chi?	sit *uh*·deekh khee
(Very) well.	
(Da) iawn.	(dah) yown
What's your name?	
Beth yw eich enw chi?	beth yu uhkh *e*·noo khee
My name is ...	
Fy enw i yw ...	vuh *e*·noo ee yu ...
Where are you from?	
O ble ydych chi'n dod?	oh ble *uh*·deekh kheen dohd
I'm from ...	
Dw i'n dod o ...	doo een dohd oh ...
I don't understand.	
Dw i ddim in deall.	doo ee thim uhn *deh*·ahl
How do you say ...?	
Sut mae dweud ...?	sit mai dwayd ...
What's this called in Welsh?	
Beth yw hwn yn Gymraeg?	beth yu hoon uhn *guhm*·raig
I don't know.	
Wn i ddim.	oon ee dhim

Yes & No

How you say 'yes' and 'no' in Welsh depends on the verb used in the question. So, rather than simply 'yes', you might answer 'I do' *(Ydw)* or 'It is' *(Ydy)*. Here are just a few examples:

Yes./No.	*Ie./Nage.*	yeh/*nah*·geh
(general use when the question doesn't start with a verb)		
I do./I am.	*Ydw.*	uh·*doo*
I don't./ I'm not.	*Nac ydw.*	nak uh·*doo*
It is.	*Ydy.*	uh·*dee*
It isn't.	*Nac ydy.*	nak uh·*dee*
There is.	*Oes.*	oys
There isn't.	*Nac oes.*	nak oys

EATING & DRINKING

Are you serving food?	
Ydych chi'n gweini bwyd?	*uh*·deekh kheen *gway*·nee bweed
A table for ..., please.	
Bwrdd i ... os gwelwch yn dda.	boordh ee ... os *gwe*·lookh uhn thah
Can I see the menu, please?	
Ga i weld y fwydlen, os gwelwch yn dda?	gah ee weld uh *voo*·eed·len os *gwe*·lookh uhn thah
What's the special of the day?	
Beth yw pryd arbennig y dydd?	beth yu preed ar·*be*·nig uh deeth
Can I have ...?	
Ga i ...?	gah ee ...
The bill, please.	
Y bil, os gwelwch yn dda.	uh bil os *gwe*·lookh uhn thah
Cheers!	
Iechyd Da!	*ye*·khid dah

I'd like a (half) pint of ...	*Ga i (hanner o) beint o ...*	gah ee (*ha*·ner oh) baynt oh ...
bitter	*chwerw*	*khwe*·roo
cider	*seidr*	*say*·duhr
lager	*lager*	*lah*·guhr

TIME, DATES & NUMBERS

minute	*munud*	*mi*·nid
hour	*awr*	owr
week	*wythnos*	oo·*ith*·nos
month	*mis*	mees
today	*heddiw*	*hedh*·yoo
tomorrow	*yfory*	uh·*voh*·ree

PLACE NAMES

Welsh place names are often based on words that describe a landmark or a feature of the countryside.

bach	bahkh	small
bro	broh	vale
bryn	brin	hill
caer	kair	fort
capel	ka·pl	chapel
carreg	kar·eg	stone
clwn	kloon	meadow
coed	koyd	wood/forest
cwm	koom	valley
dinas	dee·nas	hill fortress
eglwys	eglueys	church
fach	vahkh	small
fawr	vowr	big
ffordd	forth	road
glan	glahn	shore
glyn	glin	valley
isa	issa	lower
llan	hlan	church/enclosure
llyn	hlin	lake
maes	mais	field
mawr	mowr	big
mynydd	muhneeth	mountain
nant	nahnt	valley/stream
ogof	o·gov	cave
pen	pen	head/top/end
plas	plahs	hall/mansion
pont	pont	bridge
rhos	hros	moor/marsh
twr	toor	tower
tŷ	tee	house
uchaf	ikhav	upper
ynys	uh·nis	island/holm

Monday	*Dydd Llun*	deeth hleen
Tuesday	*Dydd Mawrth*	deeth mowrrth
Wednesday	*Dydd Mercher*	deeth merr·kherr
Thursday	*Dydd Iau*	deeth yigh
Friday	*Dydd Gwener*	deeth *gwe*·ner
Saturday	*Dydd Sadwrn*	deeth *sa*·doorn
Sunday	*Dydd Sul*	deeth seel

January	*Ionawr*	yo·nowr
February	*Chwefror*	*khwev*·rohr
March	*Mawrth*	mowrth
April	*Ebrill*	*ehb*·rihl
May	*Mai*	mai
June	*Mehefin*	me·*he*·vin
July	*Gorffennaf*	gor·*fe*·nahv
August	*Awst*	owst
September	*Medi*	*me*·dee
October	*Hydref*	*huhd*·rev
November	*Tachwedd*	tahkh·weth
December	*Rhagfyr*	*hrag*·vir

0	*dim*	dim
1	*un*	een
2	*dau* (m)	dy
	dwy (f)	duey
3	*tri* (m)	tree
	tair (f)	tair
4	*pedwar* (m)	*ped*·wahr
	pedair (f)	*ped*·air
5	*pump*	pimp
6	*chwech*	khwekh
7	*saith*	saith
8	*wyth*	ueyth
9	*naw*	now
10	*deg*	dehg

GLOSSARY

AONB – Area of Outstanding Natural Beauty

aber – confluence of water bodies; river mouth

ap – prefix in a Welsh name meaning 'son of' (Welsh)

bridleway – path that can be used by walkers, horse riders and cyclists

byway – secondary or side road

Cadw – Welsh historic monuments agency (Welsh)

castell – castle (Welsh)

coasteering – making your way around the coastline by rock climbing, gully scrambling, caving, wave riding and cliff jumping

Cool Cymru – rise of Welsh bands during the mid- to late 1990s

cromlech – burial chamber (Welsh)

Cymraeg – Welsh language (Welsh)

Cymru – Wales (Welsh)

dolmen – chambered tomb

eisteddfod – literally a gathering or session; festival in which competitions are held in music, poetry, drama and the fine arts; plural eisteddfodau (Welsh)

Gymraeg – Welsh language (Welsh)

hiraeth – sense of longing for the green, green grass of home (Welsh)

Landsker Line – boundary between Welsh-speaking and English-speaking areas in south-west Wales

Mabinogion – key source of Welsh folk legends

menhir – standing stone

merthyr – martyr (Welsh)

mynydd – mountain (Welsh)

National Assembly – National (Welsh) Assembly; devolved regional government of Wales, in power since 1999

newydd – new (Welsh)

NT – National Trust

ogham – ancient Celtic script

oriel – gallery (Welsh)

OS – Ordnance Survey

Plaid Cymru – Party of Wales; originally Plaid Cenedlaethol Cymru (Welsh Nationalist Party)

RSPB – Royal Society for the Protection of Birds

S4C – Sianel Pedwar Cymru; national Welsh-language TV broadcaster

SSSI – Site of Special Scientific Interest

Sustrans – sustainable transport charity encouraging people to walk, cycle and use public transport

towpath – path running beside a river or canal

tre – town (Welsh)

urdd – youth (Welsh)

way – long-distance trail

y, yr – the, of the (Welsh)

YHA – Youth Hostel Association

Behind the Scenes

SEND US YOUR FEEDBACK

We love to hear from travellers – your comments keep us on our toes and help make our books better. Our well-travelled team reads every word on what you loved or loathed about this book. Although we cannot reply individually to your submissions, we always guarantee that your feedback goes straight to the appropriate authors, in time for the next edition. Each person who sends us information is thanked in the next edition – the most useful submissions are rewarded with a selection of digital PDF chapters.

Visit **lonelyplanet.com/contact** to submit your updates and suggestions or to ask for help. Our award-winning website also features inspirational travel stories, news and discussions.

Note: We may edit, reproduce and incorporate your comments in Lonely Planet products such as guidebooks, websites and digital products, so let us know if you don't want your comments reproduced or your name acknowledged. For a copy of our privacy policy visit lonelyplanet.com/privacy.

OUR READERS

Many thanks to the travellers who used the last edition and wrote to us with helpful hints, useful advice and interesting anecdotes:

Alan Houston, Andy Newham, Corry Waasdorp, Don Godfrey, Fiona Grahame, Joana Ferrer, Karen Eldridge, Michael Hughes, Richard Lysons, Sheila Payne, Vivien Palcic.

WRITER THANKS

Peter Dragicevich

It's always a joy to meet up with friends on the road, so many thanks to Tim Benzie, Rob Carpenter Catherine Cole, Matt Swaine, and Kerri and Finn Tyler for your company and good cheer.

Hugh McNaughtan

All possible thanks to Peter Dragicevich for his guidance on this project, to my editor James Smart, to the kind people I met in Wales, and most importantly, to Tasmin, Maise and Willa.

ACKNOWLEDGEMENTS

Climate map data adapted from Peel MC, Finlayson BL & McMahon TA (2007) 'Updated World Map of the Köppen-Geiger Climate Classification', Hydrology and Earth System Sciences, 11, 163344.

Cover photograph: Broad Haven, Pembrokeshire, Billy Stock/4Corners ©

THIS BOOK

This 6th edition of Lonely Planet's *Wales* guidebook was researched and written by Peter Dragicevich and Hugh McNaughtan. The previous edition was written by Peter Dragicevich, Etain O'Carroll and Helena Smith. This guidebook was produced by the following:

Destination Editor James Smart

Product Editors Kate James, Kate Mathews

Senior Cartographer Mark Griffiths

Book Designers Fergal Condon, Mazzy Prinsep, Wendy Wright

Assisting Editors Michelle Bennett, Nigel Chin, Melanie Dankel, Kellie Langdon, Rosie Nicholson

Cartographer Rachel Imeson

Cover Researcher Naomi Parker

Thanks to Jennifer Carey, Neill Coen, Andi Jones, Claire Naylor, Karyn Noble, Lauren Wellicome, Tony Wheeler, Dora Whitaker

Index

D

E

Map Pages **000**
Photo Pages **000**

S

T

V

W

Z

Map Pages **000**
Photo Pages **000**

Map Legend

Sights

- Beach
- Bird Sanctuary
- Buddhist
- Castle/Palace
- Christian
- Confucian
- Hindu
- Islamic
- Jain
- Jewish
- Monument
- Museum/Gallery/Historic Building
- Ruin
- Shinto
- Sikh
- Taoist
- Winery/Vineyard
- Zoo/Wildlife Sanctuary
- Other Sight

Activities, Courses & Tours

- Bodysurfing
- Diving
- Canoeing/Kayaking
- Course/Tour
- Sento Hot Baths/Onsen
- Skiing
- Snorkelling
- Surfing
- Swimming/Pool
- Walking
- Windsurfing
- Other Activity

Sleeping

- Sleeping
- Camping

Eating

- Eating

Drinking & Nightlife

- Drinking & Nightlife
- Cafe

Entertainment

- Entertainment

Shopping

- Shopping

Information

- Bank
- Embassy/Consulate
- Hospital/Medical
- Internet
- Police
- Post Office
- Telephone
- Toilet
- Tourist Information
- Other Information

Geographic

- Beach
- Gate
- Hut/Shelter
- Lighthouse
- Lookout
- Mountain/Volcano
- Oasis
- Park
- Pass
- Picnic Area
- Waterfall

Population

- Capital (National)
- Capital (State/Province)
- City/Large Town
- Town/Village

Transport

- Airport
- Border crossing
- Bus
- Cable car/Funicular
- Cycling
- Ferry
- Metro station
- Monorail
- Parking
- Petrol station
- S-Bahn/Subway station
- Taxi
- T-bane/Tunnelbana station
- Train station/Railway
- Tram
- Tube station
- U-Bahn/Underground station
- Other Transport

Note: Not all symbols displayed above appear on the maps in this book

Routes

- Tollway
- Freeway
- Primary
- Secondary
- Tertiary
- Lane
- Unsealed road
- Road under construction
- Plaza/Mall
- Steps
- Tunnel
- Pedestrian overpass
- Walking Tour
- Walking Tour detour
- Path/Walking Trail

Boundaries

- International
- State/Province
- Disputed
- Regional/Suburb
- Marine Park
- Cliff
- Wall

Hydrography

- River, Creek
- Intermittent River
- Canal
- Water
- Dry/Salt/Intermittent Lake
- Reef

Areas

- Airport/Runway
- Beach/Desert
- Cemetery (Christian)
- Cemetery (Other)
- Glacier
- Mudflat
- Park/Forest
- Sight (Building)
- Sportsground
- Swamp/Mangrove

OUR STORY

A beat-up old car, a few dollars in the pocket and a sense of adventure. In 1972 that's all Tony and Maureen Wheeler needed for the trip of a lifetime – across Europe and Asia overland to Australia. It took several months, and at the end – broke but inspired – they sat at their kitchen table writing and stapling together their first travel guide, *Across Asia on the Cheap*. Within a week they'd sold 1500 copies. Lonely Planet was born.

Today, Lonely Planet has offices in Franklin, London, Melbourne, Oakland, Dublin, Beijing and Delhi, with more than 600 staff and writers. We share Tony's belief that 'a great guidebook should do three things: inform, educate and amuse'.

OUR WRITERS

Peter Dragicevich

Cardiff; Brecon Beacons & Southeast Wales; Swansea, the Gower & Carmarthenshire; St Davids & Pembrokeshire; Plan Your Trip; Understand Wales; Survival Guide After a successful career in niche newspaper and magazine publishing, both in his native New Zealand and in Australia, Peter finally gave into Kiwi wanderlust, giving up staff jobs to chase his diverse roots around much of Europe. Over the last decade he's written literally dozens of guidebooks for Lonely Planet on an oddly disparate collection of countries, all of which he's come to love. He once again calls Auckland, New Zealand his home – although his current nomadic existence means he's hardly ever there.

Hugh McNaughtan

Aberystwyth & mid-Wales; Snowdonia & the Llŷn; Angelsey & the North Coast A former English lecturer, Hugh swapped grant applications for visa applications, and turned his love of travel into a full-time thing. A long-time castle tragic with an abiding love of Britain's Celtic extremities, he jumped at the chance to explore Wales, from the Cambrian Mountains to the tip of Anglesey. He's never happier than when he's on the road with his two daughters. Except perhaps on the cricket field...

Published by Lonely Planet Global Limited
CRN 554153
6th edition – Apr 2017
ISBN 978 1 78657 330 8
© Lonely Planet 2017 Photographs © as indicated 2017
10 9 8 7 6 5 4 3 2 1
Printed in China

Although the authors and Lonely Planet have taken all reasonable care in preparing this book, we make no warranty about the accuracy or completeness of its content and, to the maximum extent permitted, disclaim all liability arising from its use.

All rights reserved. No part of this publication may be copied, stored in a retrieval system, or transmitted in any form by any means, electronic, mechanical, recording or otherwise, except brief extracts for the purpose of review, and no part of this publication may be sold or hired, without the written permission of the publisher. Lonely Planet and the Lonely Planet logo are trademarks of Lonely Planet and are registered in the US Patent and Trademark Office and in other countries. Lonely Planet does not allow its name or logo to be appropriated by commercial establishments, such as retailers, restaurants or hotels. Please let us know of any misuses: lonelyplanet.com/ip.